Dynamic Use of Option Strategies

in Fund Management, Basic Analysis and Technical Analysis

Ömer Evren Tanyaş

Entropy Publishing

Name of Book: **Dynamic Use of Option Strategies in Fund Management, Basic Analysis and Technical Analysis**

Author: **Ömer Evren Tanyaş**

Redactor: **Dilek İnci Tanyaş**

ISBN: **978-605-71861-2-6**

1st Edition

Technical Preparation: Book InDesign

The investment, information, comments and recommendations contained in this book are not within the scope of investment advice. Your financial position may not have the appropriate consequences for your expectations of investment decisions based solely on the information contained in the book, without regard to your risk and return preferences. The liability of any consequences arising from the use of the information belongs solely to the investor, and the author does not accept any responsibility.

Entropy Publishing

To my cousin;
Ozlem Soran

ÖMER EVREN TANYAŞ

He was borned in 1968.

He received his bachelor and master degrees on economics, sociology and social psychology.

He has academic studies, articles and books on these subjects. He also studies and books on logic and theology.

Since 1990 he has been active in various sectors; on stocks, international commodity trading and finance. He directed funds in international derivative markets.

Books:

— Weber'de Kapitalizmin Ruhu ve İslam Üzerine Sosyo-psikolojik Bir Deneme.

(A Socio-psychological essay on the Spirit of Capitalism and Islam in Weber, Kaknus Publications, 2007)

— Ayna İçinde Ayna; Aklın ve Kalbin Sezgisine Bakış.

(The Mirror in the Mirror; A Look at The Perception of Reason and The Heart, Kaknus Publications, 2009)

— Teknik Analizde Gann, Andrew ve Elliott

(In Technical Analysis Gann, Andrew and Elliott, 2016, 2nd Edition)

— Teknik Analizde Trend ve Benzeri Metotları: Konular; Güçlükleri ve Örnekleri.

(Trend and Similar Methods in Technical Analysis; topics, difficulties and examples, 2016)

— Sosyal Ekonomi Yazıları.

(Social Economy Articles, 2016)

— Opsiyon Stratejilerine Giriş

(Introduction to Option Strategies, 2016)

— İleri Opsiyon Stratejileri

(Advanced Option Strategies, 2017)

— Fon Yönetiminde Opsiyon Stratejilerinin Dinamik Kullanımı: Temel Analiz ve Teknik Analizle

(Dynamic Use of Option Strategies in Fund Management; with Macro Analysis and Technical Analysis, 2017)

— Rewritten in English; Dynamic Use of Option Strategies in Fund Management; with Macro Analysis and Technical Analysis, 2018

L 'imagination est l'hôte de l'inconnaissable
Ayant plongé au fond de l'inconnu
Elle en revient en poèmes chez les humains
Leur dit avec les images
C'est inimaginable mais c'est comme ça

Michel Deguy

Imagining is the host of unknowable
Having plunged at deep of unknown
Invading by poems, at human
Tells them   with the images
It's unimaginable although it's like that

I would like to thank to my dear wife Inci;

for the sophisticated assistance and support in preparing the book.

INTRODUCTION

It is known that the option written on a real entity was first used in ancient Egypt 18th century B.C. These options were valid for 7 production years / period, with the purchase right for cereals as same call options. Again in the ancient city of Mari in Iraq, records of various derivative products for cereals and metals were found in the tablets of the period between the 19th and 16th centuries B.C. According to Aristotle's transmission, the most famous example of the use of options in antiquity; philosopher, astronomer, mathematician Thales (620-546 B.C., Miletus / Aydin) was to make a great profit by taking the "call" option on olive oil.

I came across in many sources were shown as an example of option contracts also in Bible that prophet Jacob made the agreements with his uncle for to receive his first and second wives. In Koran, similar case was mentioned for Moses. In all these cases (The Koran, The Bible etc.) as in ancient Egypt, there is mentioned a period of 7 years/ seasons.

At the New Age, it is known that the option was used in the Antwerp Stock Exchange in the 16th century. In Japan, the call contracts were received over rice in the 17th century. During the same period in the Netherlands, the Amsterdam Stock Exchange options were used that was described by in Jose Penso de la Vega's famous work Confusion of Confusions (1688). In this book La Vega had explained derivative transactions and products in detail. During the Tulipmania, the options were used both in the Netherlands and in the U.K.

Although it is controversial when and where the options have used as a common and organized, increasing use of options have been seen in the London and Paris stock exchanges in the 18th and 19th centuries. The use of options in the Americas began in the Chicago stock market towards the end of the 19th century. In the following periods, options are subject to various restrictions by court and authoritarian decisions. These obstacles have increased during the Great Depression. In the past, call options have begun to be used more common than put options. Put options are considered risky even in recent times (puts for shares are processed by the CBOE in 1977).

We had to wait for the CBOE in 1973 to start listing options and common options transactions. At this date, three factors play a role in the start of options:

1) the emergence of microprocessors in 1971,

2) the widespread, easily accessible and low-commission exchanges that will operate to protect the reserve currency capability of the Dollar when the US abandons the Gold standard [this is most important political-social influence],

3) the development and maturation of option models. Option models (the most common Black-Scholes) have partly stabilized the manual pricing and thus risk calculations which was used through the history.

We will try to give the brief information on the Markov chain and the Brownian movement, which form the basis of the option models. Thus, we want to draw attention to the main notions and historical formation background of the option.

The movement of particles like pollen, coal and dust in water and alcohol-like fluids was observed and investigated by two botanists at the end of the 18th and the beginning of the 19th century: Jan Ingenhousz (1730-1799), Robert Brown (1773-1858). But these botanists have not developed any explanation or model. Later, referring to Robert Brown, multiple scientists will struggle to define and mathematically explain the random movement, which is generally known as Brownian motion.

In 1896, Ludwig Boltzman, who studied the kinetics of gases, is regarded as the person who finds the relationship between kinetic energy and fast movements under heat. These statistical studies will be used in the modeling of the Brownian movement. Danish astronomer, mathematician, actuary Thorvald Nicolai Thiele who was adopted as the first to identify the Brownian movement by statistically with the least square method (1880). Again in 1900, Louis Bachelier (1872-1946), with his doctoral thesis on the prediction of stock market price movements (Theorie de la speculation); sets out the mathematical formula of financial options. This thesis is also the source for the first model ofthe stochastic (etymological meaning in ancient Greek guessing, aim at a target) process of explaining the Brownian movement. Bachelier's work will then be used by Einstein to explain the movements of atoms and molecules.

The Leningrad mathematician Andrej Markov (1856-1922) describes the stochastic process which was called with his name; "Markov chain". In the sense that there is no memory of the system in discrete times or discrete times and spaces; while the future situation is covered in the present case, it is independent from the past. The future situation is reached through the probabilistic process. Markov's concepts were developed by Norbert Wiener (1894-1964). The stochastic process called

'Brownian movement'; after Wiener's contribution, is beginning to be remembered in his name also.

Developed with the contribution of a large number of scientists, this stochastic modeling is the basis for Black-Scholes and Black models in the commonly accepted (we do not mention premise option models or other option models here).

Stock exchanges are influenced by financial, economic, social, political, geopolitical and even historical factors. On the stock exchanges prices are constantly swinging up or down. The horizontal market is regarded as a temporary situation that occurs only in short periods. The deterministic methods of the sciences about the physical space do not give efficient results many times in order to find answers to questions such as what the price will be? when the price movement will be? and the duration of the price movement. Even multidisciplinary methods of social sciences are insufficient to explain price formation. It is obvious that the methods that are inadequate in explaining also will be weak for prediction. As a result, a perspective consisting only upward, downward or horizontal choise is insufficient to explain the price movements. This point of view is difficult for prediction. Also taking position (for trade) with this prediction is like going through the fog.

By means of technical analysis, it is attempted to predetermine the up and down movements primarily in size of price (price distance) and sometimes when and where they will start. The price movement for the market actor (analyst and trader) as an observer is almost ' the universe of uncertainty '. The reality that will be encountered in the future, is a bundle of possibility for today's observer.

The reality that in accordance with nature of the things behind the observer's view point; is it completely deterministic? Although reality carries deterministic character (obligations), it develops and transforms with possibilities rather than these obligations. Based on this acceptance; in the spot or future market, we can move / take positions in the "universe of possibilities" through options, beyond up / down or buy/ sell behavior. While trying to predict the reality to be encountered in the future, we may have multiple "verdicts" about what will not happen even if we can not find what will happen. For example; X event, we can not identify "when" the X event will occured but we can identify "the period and / or the periods" that are not likely to occur. If there is one thing to ocur; there are more things that will not occur. Based on these, more choise to take positions becomes a possibility in the future.

With options, we can keep the position for the price movement to go up or down or we can keep position for the time we have set as the period. Moreover, if one of the other direction occurs, we can restrict the negativity from the previously or we can take position even for the price range that will not be possible or for the impossible period.

At the time of the market, at least the capital which is decreased due to the cost of carry, you can earn money directly through options. Thus, thanks to the options, it is possible for us to take position in "the lord of time" which is the main determinant of the stock markets. Let's not forget that the price is one of the reflections of value. During the period of fluctuation; when the systems of basis as same paper currency, previous metal were shocked; as values become obscured, traders feel more of time power importance and which is the actual master of the stock exchanges.

While learning the structure of option strategies; it is essential to learn how they connect with each other, how they are transformed, what strategies are incorporated, what strategies are different from other strategies, and which strategies can be transformed into what kind of strategies. However, in this case with universe of possibilities which is the main objective of the options is to respond to the market and at the same time we get in harmony with the real nature of the market. "Fire and forget" is a strategy also (a military term like forgetting with fire), but at the same time by this approach most advantages that the options offered are neglected.

If we understand that the financial, economic or social analysis of the market is often only based on possibilities, we also find out what strategy we should use and under what conditions we should change this strategy. Even if we can not do economic-social analyzes in this context but to transform and change into strategies as dynamic processes, we still have to conceptualize strategies to adapt to the "universe of possibilities" which is the beyond of the market reality. Sometimes, gaining the ability is a necessity to pass completely opposite and chain strategies which need to be learned from their connections. If we learn these things, we will gain the ability and understand the nature of the market.

The links, relationships, conversions, modification that we talk, can be difficult for the general reader.

Since 1990, as a person operating at high levels in international trade, commodity speculation, fund management, I have personally witnessed in recent years that "quality" has fallen all over the world. I see that business ethics and norms are being erased as knowledge, experience and even curiosity.

I have repeatedly witnessed from first-hand the ignorance and irresponsibility of fund managers (even some of who were selected as "Market Wizards") based in New York or Switzerland. In every great crisis, harmful fungus individuals, who are not embarrassed to g oto rack and ruin that was saved by causing the deterioration of economic-social structure beyond the financial system with the help of central banks, have boasted their ignorance: "if crisis is going to come out, no one can know", "macro analysis will not predict", "Technical analysis does not work". In conversations I watched with regret that same of these types, boasted with their big but empty libraries.

I write three set of books about option strategies and trade of the option strategies:

Book 1; Introduction to Option Strategies,

Book 2; Advanced Option Strategies,

Book 3; Dynamic Use of Option Strategies in Fund Management; with Macro Analysis and Technical Analysis.

In the first book it is presented; basic strategies, income strategies, vertical spreading strategies. Greeks and price fluctuation on the end of maturity/ option pain have been processed as separate sections in these books. American type options have been addressed, specially exemplified in CME. Strategies have been introduced with texts and examples.

In the second book; Advanced Option Strategies: Horizontal strategies, directional strategies, synthetic strategies, leveraged/ unbalanced strategies have been processed. Strategies have been examined with examples. Again, Greeks and and price fluctuation on the end of maturity/ option pain are added as separate sections.

Our first and second books on option strategies are the most comprehensive among its similars in all languages. Differences from similar books are that given in detail with the requirements for "entry phase" to option strategies and supported by examples from technical analysis. Strategies were tried not to be presented in separate patterns; it was explained the relations with other strategies, the transformations, which strategies were added, and which strategies are opposite (in the sense of reflection). Thus, it is aimed to establish the relationship and continuous knowledge accumulation, in the reader's imagination. Like the options, there is an active and multi-dimensional area, trying to overcome the deadlock of thinking with patterns. Also, during "the exit phase" from the option strategies are discussed in detail. It was given to readers first step information in order to learn how to transform the option strategies and use the chain strategies.

These books can be used as a reference guide to learn about topics, to check different positions while the first establishment phase or adjustment/ readjustment phases or to reach different solutions at exit phase. That is to say, they are not only for teaching and learning, they are the answer to the dynamic structure which is primarily "trader" use.

If we return to our book; let's briefly discuss the contents of the book and how it will benefit by readers: 3rd book; how to use option strategies in trade with technical analysis and macro analysis; It is about chained and transformed of strategies.

I would like to point out some concepts and methods used in the book. Let's briefly discuss; the intersection, covering and inclusion, relations of the strategies. The expression intersection; in the sense that one strike is common, the expresssion covering; in the sense that the two strategies are partly common to strike distances or term/ maturity, the term inclusion; a strategy implies that the other strategy contains the strike distance and/or term (maturity).

Various strategies can be used in relation to covering and inclusion from two perspectives:

A) Strike

B) Maturity/term

Generally, the medium-long term strategy can include shorter term and different types of strategies. Contrary is also possible. Longer-term strategy can also be include by a short-term strategy before a significant macro-data disclosure, news anticipation or short-lived technical breakout.

Dimensions of covering and inclusion relationship:

A) Full containment; inclusion.

B) Partial containment (we can include this choise for "the intersection" relationship).

If we describe the aspects and dimensions of the covering and inclusion relation we mentioned in the above paragraphs and define them in the methodical sense in the chapters:

A) Inclusion as both term (maturity) and strike.

B) Inclusion only at term, partial covering as strike.

C) Partial covering at term, inclusion at strike.

D) Partial covering as term and strike.

Overlapping strategies;

While a mid-long term strategy continues, it may be able to hedge, short or short term strategies against the objective of this strategy (mid-long term). This hedging can be full or partial.

In inclusion, the short-term strike and term of the strategy are fully covered by the medium-long term strategy.

At the partially covered (covering) strategy is partially covered by the strike distance and / or by the term.

Consider this title in more detail;

a) partially covered strike distance and inclusion term

b) partly covered strike distance and partially covering term (the most risky situation),

c) inclusion strike distance and partially covering term (high risk)

The medium-long term strategy is mostly aimed participate in the price movement (giving premium); a short-term strategy is mostly aimed at received premium income.

For example; in long - term call bull spread, establish another call bear spread. New call bear spread:

a) weekly maturity (short term)

b) at the narrow strike distance (full covering/ inclusion strikes distance)

The new call bear spread will try to take advantage of the horizontal price movement.

Strategies beyond covering and inclusion relationships can be transformed:

A) Full transformation.

B) Partial transformation.

C) Repeated partial transformation.

Choice "A" describes; the transformation of a strategy or complex strategy group to a totally different strategy or complex strategy group.

Trade cases are repeated in choice band; B and C especially in the form of opening or closing the leg or wing for premium income.

Strategies that give premiums can also be transformed. In these strategies for participating in the underlying asset price movement, the strike of the short leg may be increased or the strike may be reduced to obtain premium income (the description is based on the call option, for the put option must be opposite side) to modify and expand the target of price movement participation.

Take bear call spread as an example of both intersecting and transforming strategies. The bear call spread strategy, which is aimed at obtaining premium income with a horizontal and downward price movement at the end of maturity; is hedged with the long future, because of the expectation of the increase in the price movements for not to write down the loss. So, future long and call short turn to the covered call startegy. The idle call long leg (again from the example), may continue to be held with the expectation of a significant breakout price movement.

Thus, two different strategies appear that the middle legs are the same; bear call spread and covered call intersect at the same strike and same term at call short leg.

Call long

Call short

Future long

A single call short can only be implemented with one of the future long or call long.

In the example scenario, if the end of maturity price remains in the call short strike:

a) Premium income from the call short,

b) getting profit from the distance between call short strike and future long price level.

In the other scenario, if the price movement results in a call long strike that, in-the-money at the end of the maturity;

Beyond of call long strike + Premium cost make a profit, from three sources by using price movement. Let's make it clear that we are dealing with the most optimistic scenario here.

Let me explain the balancing method in option strategies; if the underlying asset price is moving partly in one direction and our strategy for collecting premiums in-the-money situation remains; on the other direction short-term or very short-term near out-of-money or at-the-money rarely in-the-money, options can be sold without hedging to make premium income. Thus, in one direction of a price advance and loss of premiums for balancing is taken positions in the other direction. During the balancing activity, besides selling naked (without hedging) options, spreads can also be used to obtain premium income.

If we define balancing with the help of technical analysis; we can say that in the partial progression of one direction in the horizontal market, in the partial and temporary breach of a side/ edge of the horizontal band; at the other side/ edge new option strategy established for receiving premium income.

Beyond expectation, in the case of deep progress in one direction, balancing strategies can only provide partial benefits. Moreover, in the corrections of this deep progress, the risk of in-the-money or even deep in-the-money at end of maturity may arise.

Now, let's briefly consider the strategies for premium income that are generated during the price movements fluctuation and make premium income as much as the strike distance: if the position is taken in the at-the-money or partial in-the-money strike with short legs in the fluctuating market (horizontal or in the one direction channel) and the purchase (buying) of long leg that at the opposite direction to the fluctuation, is also implemented before or after the short leg position; premium income can be obtained as much as strike distance of spread or even beyond of the distance. Through this premium income, even if the two legs of the spread at end of maturity are in- the- money, can not harmed in total and even profit can be obtained.

If the spread for participating in the price movement becomes in-the-money with two legs at the end of maturity; the spread size can be used as a distance profit buffer and naked option or spread strategy can be sold. In this approach, the premium income aimed strategy starting from the same strike with the short leg of the spread targeting to participate the price movement, can also be used as the other choise.

For example:

(A strike put long - B strike put short) + (B strike put short - C strike put long)

AB = BC equal distances.

Or:

(A strike put long - B strike put short) + C strike put short

AB = BC

C strike is naked short.

Or:

B and C are different strikes;

(A strike put long - B strike put short) + (C strike put short - D strike long)

AB = CD

Repeated partial conversion method: The short option leg, which benefits from market price fluctuations, can be opened and closed more than once on the maturity period. Thus, against the long leg given a single premium, from the other leg premium income sequent can be obtained. The horizontal and floating market allows for the use of this type of dynamic strategy.

In complex strategies, it is also possible to replace the short wing (or wing for premium collection) more than once.

Let's take a sample scenario:

In the Guts strategy in both directions, positions are taken to participate in the price range.

When the movement develops in the single direction, for example, in the maturity period, the long leg is closed when the two legs of the call bull spread are in-the-money. It is tried to keep the other short (leg) and convert to call bear spread for premium income. The size of the new call bear spread shall be established at a distance (with strike distance) to be met by the total profit from the Guts to avoid damage;

(call bull spread profit – put bear spread damage) - (call bear spread profit) ≥ 0.

In the maturity period if the price movement evolve downward, the profit is also written in the call bear spread that we created in the second phase. During the price fluctuation in maturity, the call short leg can be sold and buy more than once.

In the first phase, the put bull spread can also be established based on the put long leg of the put bear spread, which was inoperable during the upward price movement. Later, due to the price of the underlying asset which move horizontal, all options will be out-of-money at the end of the maturity.

In this optimistic scenario, from call bull spread, call bear spread, and put bull spread profit is written from while put bear spread is written in premium damage. In total, the profit is very likely.

After the concepts and methods we used in option strategies, let's take a look at the methods and approaches we use in macro and news analysis. Although it is possible to estimate in short and medium period with macroeconomic models some macro datas, it should not be forgotten that this is not the main purpose of a trader. The trader observe the price to be made in the market, can estimate the price for the future and tries to take position in that direction. In line with the expectations of market actors, it is possible to predict the macro data near to the truth. Often, these estimates can only be successfully performed with some deviations. A trader can also make certain / limited profits using these estimates. However, serious medium deviations from macroeconomic expectations of the market (and the anticipated trader expectation) can lead to significant losses. These deviations can lead to large price ratios, even if they are small in number.

Take this last determination in reverse, it can provide significant profits, if the estimates made right and that is outside of the exceptions in market participant. Even under this condition, it is necessary to realize the trader's profit within hours or even minutes. It is difficult to transform the success of forecasting into profit if the process of price forecasting is not in the direction of expectations, or if macrodata outside expectations are within a certain trend (or consolidation pattern within repeated levels). It is the ideal of every trader to make profit on the market that is moving in the direction of the trend with news flow.

News Market Impact: News market impact is not just about content. It is important that at which phase in the market, news has come. Here we use the term phase to mean accumulation and distribution stages.

The effect of the news differs in the directional / trend market or in the consolidation 'phase' or in the market that has reached saturation (overbought).

Sometimes there is an upward movement despite bad news. Bad news does not change the trend except for intermittent selling. Sometimes, despite good news, there is not a tendency to go out of consolidation, even downward movement occure. As an example, with the good news coming to; a long and end of the saturated trend or in the prolonged decline and the subsequent follow-up of the consolidation movement, have an entirely different impact.

Whether macro data is within expectations or outside expectations; if the forecast not reflects a certain trend (or the consolidation pattern between the repeated levels), it is difficult to convert the forecast success to profit. For example, it's like changing direction some bad news after long-term good news flow. If the bad news strews in the between of the good news flow, maybe it will not happen at all.

That is to say, the news should be considered together with the factors such as the place in the flow of the other news + the general macro situation (the meaning of the news content depends on the enviroment) + the technic movement in which phase. In short, the news should be evaluated together with other similar news and the stage in which the market is located.

The market is not just news, it even influences expectations. Whether the expectation is on a long-term agenda or the "surprise effect", there are different reflections on the market.

Even "uncertainty", which can be regarded as a risk, can have an important effect, apart from news and expectation. For example, a prone direction market (up or downward) in a news anticipation, may move horizontally in narrow band when it is influenced by another news anticipation. However, if the so-called third risk comes to the agenda/ foreground, the "three uncertainty principle" is likely to enter the market and the market is likely to turn into sales.

I do not think number three (3) is a special value. But I prefer this number (3), because it is difficult for the human mind (here sociological term; market actors mind) to follow more than two variables at the same time and to form combinations between them, it's a necessity to have prediction in the future.

To understand the short-medium term macroeconomic outlook and to make predictions, it is necessary to monitor macro data. So, it is known the way in which economies developed or handled with the handicaps. Relations between different economies can also be determined. For example, it is related to Chinese industry and German foreign industry orders. Even if the economic outlook is not foreseeable, only it can be monitored and understood.

The economic outlook is closely linked to the market pricing, though not individually. The short-medium-term macro outlook is understandable and predictable, which means that the market position can be taken in the market. What should be noted here is that the market's view or prospect has not been fully priced or even taken into the agenda. It is the most preferable situation that the judges have started to enter the agenda.

In macroeconomic and / or data estimation, when there is no strong opinion; it should be left to one side to try to predict the macro data and it is necessary to try to predict which estimate that the market will "buy". Thus, foreseeing market psychology, position can be taken for 5-10 days before macro data news arrives.

So;

A) Once the macro data is declared, to take the position for this effect that, it takes many times only hours or even minutes. But the position is taken as 5-10 days, in other words; a longer period was preferable.

B) as the period in which the volatility is lower can be found, it can be removed from the position with a narrower stop loss interval.

There is very little time for exit to get the position that directly according to the macro data news. However, there is a longer period of time for exit from the "market forecast position". Thus, lower volatility is possible. In this case, for exit, it is best at the last 1 or 2 days left that the description of the macro data.

Let's now consider the approaches to be used when addressing macroeconomic datas and Central Bank disclosures:

The Central Banks even decided according to macro datas;

a) The datas are evaluated by means of models. If the trader / fund manager decides for position, he must know which of these models or model are used. For this to happen, the members' opinions should be tried to be learned, especially the president's and the vice chairman's (e.g. FED, especially the New York FED regional president). You should also be informed about the members studies, doctoral or their post-doctoral studies etc. With this information, it can even be predicted which models will come into existence.

b) Central banks and members' languages should be monitored like diplomatic language. Beyond that, the rhetoric written "Fed speak" must be read carefully.

c) The macroeconomic imperatives of countries (Japan and Switzerland's dependency on exports, etc.) should be kept in mind. The recurring patterns of behavior of loyal central banks should be kept in mind also (meaning macroeconomic policy, commitment to decision methods and reactions of MBs).

d) Besides the economic data and orientations of the central banks, the actions to be taken due to their systematic duties and concerns about the security of the system should also be tried to be foreseen. We can give that example; the negative effects of low interest rates and even negative interest rates on German banks were coming like a reminder to the German authorities as of the conditions that destroyed the Weimar Republic in the 1930s. On the contrary; relatively similar environment for Italy suggests a period of strong growth in the 1960s and beyond.

e) The definitions of the central banks' job descriptions according to the countries should be known. For example; like the relationship between BOJ and MOF in Japan. Coordinated movements should be carefully monitored between central banks. Again, if the appointed members and the presidents have common backgrounds, it should be tried to predict how this will be reflected in the policy. The example is the rise of Goldman Sachs employee in the last 10 years as president and members of the Central Banks. Some of these people, even the Prime Minister assigned to the troubled country.

f) Decisions of central banks, which play a role locally in the global economy or are successful in macroeconomic policies, may be the leading signals. For the decisions of other central banks, the axioms of these MBs should be watched as signposts.

g) The successes and failures of central banks implementing pioneer model policies stimulating by IMF or for testing the trendy economic models, should be monitored. If the model is successful, it is expected to be implemented in other central banks as well. For example; the role of Ben Bernanke in monetary expansion in Japan in the 1990s was later inspired to the QEs in USA and etc.

We have included some of these methods in our article. For example, during the fund management studies in 2013, strategies established in different contracts by macro economy and politics analysis that according to the game theory. These strategies which were established in different contracts, attempted to foresee the most probable scenarios expected and in contract choise; that would arise in the event of their failure. In the last phase, all these strategies were put together. Again, with the possibilities of dilemma in the setup of the strategies these are primarily preferred. In this book, only a few of these strategies have been handled separately.

These three books complement each other. In the first two; knowledge transfer on strategies, and the transformation of strategies into one another are explained in details. In last book; practical use of strategies and market evaluation examined together in the context of risk management. These strategies have to be established in characters; alternating or even opposite directions and/or continuous, sequential (chaining). The pioneering of technical analysis or macro analysis has been considered as the first step of strategy setup.

In organized markets, the common use of options began in 1973. Although there are few books available that utilize technical analysis in the process of setting up and trading option strategies, especially in the last 10 years, with weekly options becoming common, the situations where options generate signal before technical analysis have come to the forefront. For this reason, the buy-sell / trade plan; based on macro or technical analysis (or other quantitative methods, etc.), even if fictionalised on one or more of them; should be inspected and supported in priority of the options same as the indicator.

In only one book of this trilemma, the title “ introduction “ is used. In fact as a whole this trilemma is written to be an “ entrance “ for the preparation of a book intended for further writing. This work will use modal logic proposals that best explain the provisions of the universe of possibilities. It will also show how to make feedback by taking leading signals with option indicators which is in pricing and time analysis, that for based on macro and technical analysis pioneering. It will aim to convey to the reader, the original methods used by the author in de facto managed funds, as a work supported by Greek and mathematical representation as well as three dimensional (3D) visual analysis.

We used English and French literature as a source. I have followed the literature for twenty years, the development in French is weak. “Stochastic Process” which was described in the History section, we tell the development of a large number of scientific methods as based for option modeling efforts (versus option strategies). Understanding these methods and basics in the background can find a place in the imagination of readers to understand modeling options (partial understanding of knowledge or only knowledge of information is useful even). Otherwise, memorization and repetition of insignificant forms will lead to problems, failures and at least inefficiency. For this reason; follow the literature from different languages (here again emphasize that attention is drawn to the difference of the schools, not the language difference). English, German may be French etc. resources should be reviewed periodically.

Finally; I advise readers to think complex for success. Understanding, learning, analyzing there must be, complex processes. When the trade plan is established, complex effort is required again. On the contrary; entry, target, especially exit choices in a clear and simple structure should be the reason for preference. While watching the position and strategy, look complex and look to new horizons for learning and analysis. However, apply exact and simple rules with strictly discipline for risk management.

Simple essences are only for the gods stage (Mele-i Ala) or for the great philosophers, mathematicians, physicists. There is no other way of reaching the secrets of essences for mortals, numerous steps of steep staircases. In this effort, we need to move forward without fear.

It can be benefited or not at all from almost every work, according to the level of the reader; very few people can overcome a work/book while learning. Besides, some texts are written in multiple planes and are available for reading. To take advantage of such works (based on the book in your hand); stoic logic and modal logic in Western or near-centuries of Turkish-Islamic sources will help you to form the basis.

As a rule, including the subject of options, as well as dynamic topics, containing simultaneous uncertainties and a multitude of possibilities;

a) you read basic works,

b) you read parallel books (similar to the book intended to be read),

c) if you think that there are some "touchstone" in the text, I recommend you to read cross read from other sources.

I hope this book will help you to learn, understand and be with you throughout the years, especially if you use it in practice.

The effort is ours, the success is from Lord/Allah.

Autumn 2018

Pasabahce, Beykoz

Contents

INTRODUCTION **7**
2013 Gold Silver **23**
Gold 23
Strategy: 27
10 Year US Bond Analysis 30
US Bonds 2013 - 2014 Technical Analysis 31
US Bond Future Trading 34
German 10 Years 35
German 10 Years in the Weekly Period with Action-Reaction Method 37
Transactions in German Bills 38
MIBTEL 40
Mibtel Analysis by Action-Reaction Method 42
Italian Political Situation and Positions in MIBTEL 43
Gold 2016 46
Strategy: 48
Yen 50
2016-2017 Reports by Date **53**
12/12/2016 53
December 18, 2016 56
December 26, 2016 59
January 1, 2017 61
January 9, 2017 62
January 16,2017 64
January 22, 2017 66
January 1, 2017 68
February 4, 2017 70
Strategy: 72
February 12, 2017 74
February 19, 2017 77
March 6, 2017 82
March 10 84
March 27, 2017 86
Strategy: 88
Euro 92
Strategy: 93
April 12, 2017 96
April 20, 2017 97
Strategy: 99
April 24, 2017 102
Strategy: 104

June 1, 2017 108
September Maturity Euro Bund 108
Strategy: 109
June 3, 2017 114
June 9, 2017 116
Momentum: 117
Key reversals: 119
Strategy: 120
Bank Rescue Operations in Italy and Spain in 2017 121
Strategy: 129
Strategy: 132
Notes On The Sintra Meeting and Draghi Talk 133
Strategy: 134
Strategy: 135
ECB Decision and Draghi Speech 137
July 20, 2017 138
Strategy: 140
Closing last Bund positions 141
Option Pain: Upcoming End Of Maturity and Price Fluctuation 143

APPENDIX 145
Z H M U MONTHS TERMS CONTRACTS: DAILY and 60 MINUTES GRAPHICS 147
DECEMBER and MARCH TERMS GERMAN CONTRACTS:
DAILY and 60 MINUTES GRAPHICS 181
VARIOUS GRAPHICS 189
OPTIONS GRAPHICS 213
GBL MARCH OPTIONS GRAPHICS 215
4EU 28 APRIL GRAPHICS 233
EUU 28 APRIL GRAPHICS 247
28 APRIL OGB4 GRAPHICS 261
GBL MAY OPTIONS GRAPHICS 271
OGB1 2 JUNE GRAPHICS 283
9 JUNE OGBL2 GRAPHICS 293
16 JUNE OGBL3 OPTION GRAPHICS 301
GBL JUNE OPTION GRAPHICS 311
OGBL5 30 JUNE GRAPHICS 329
OGBL JULY GRAPHICS 341
GBL SEPTEMBER GRAPHICS 359
ZN SEPTEMBER GRAPHICS 379

2013 Gold Silver

Gold

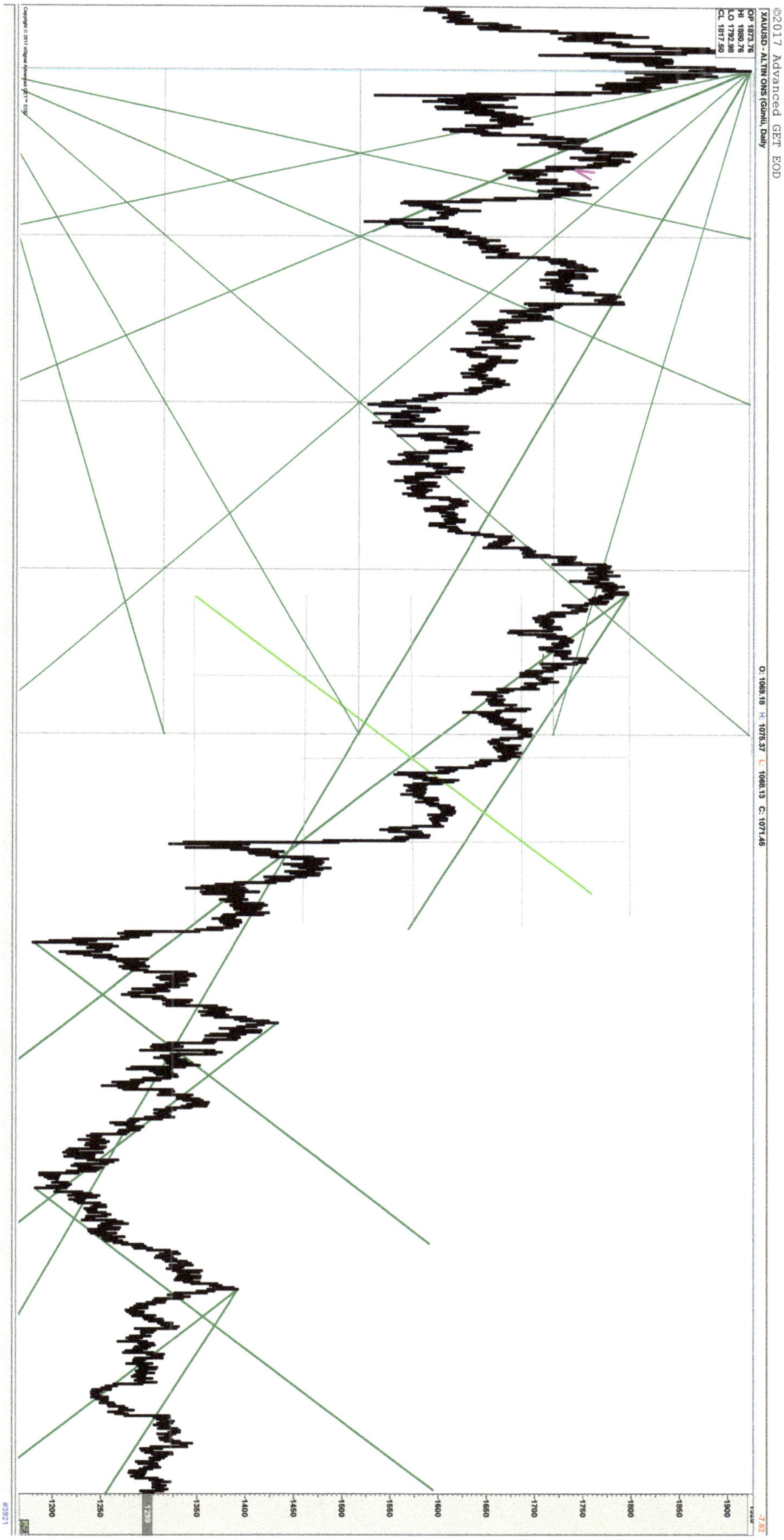

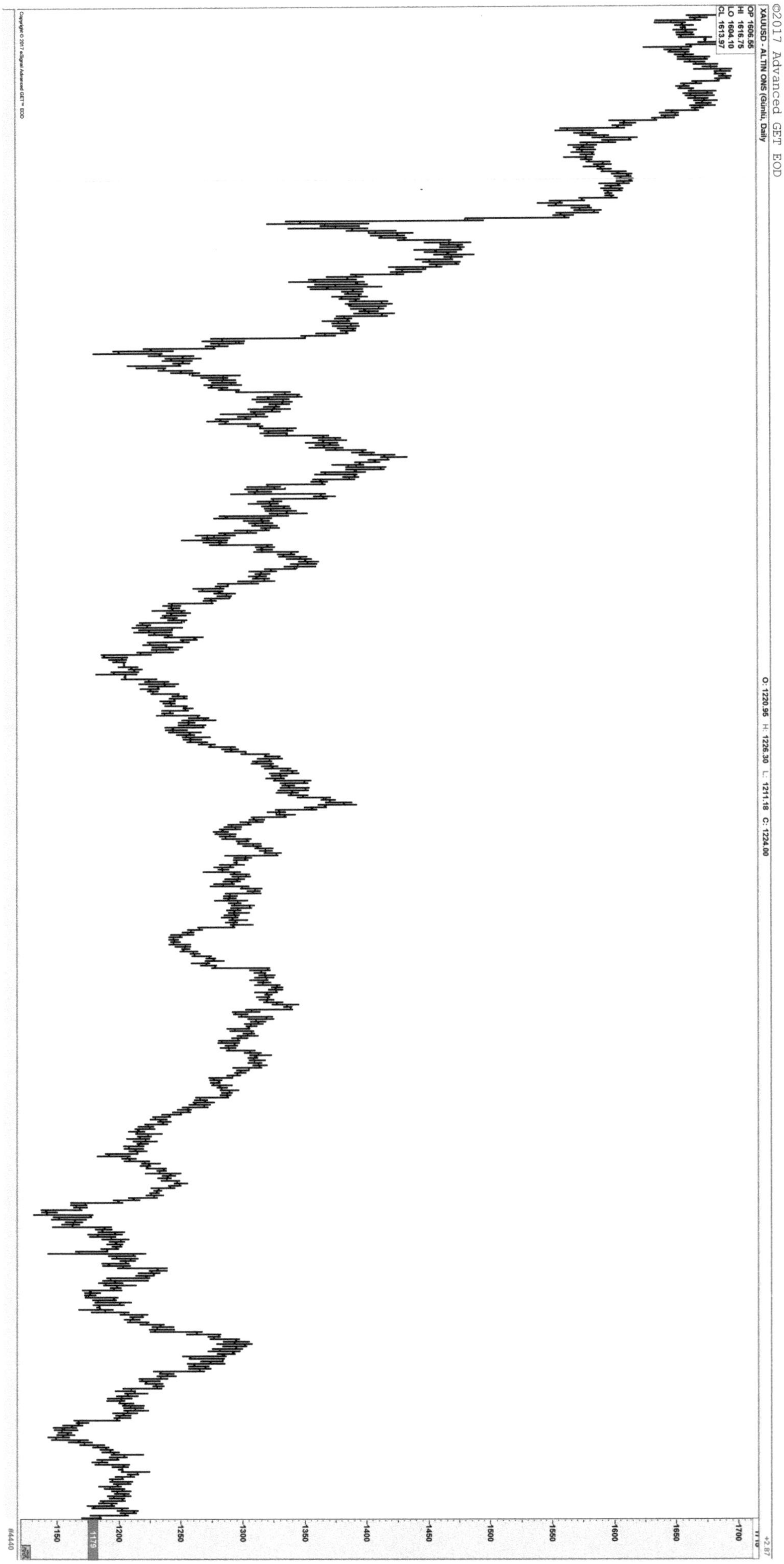
©2017 Advanced GET EOD
XAUUSD - ALTIN ONS (Günlü, Daily
OP 1606.55
HI 1616.75
LO 1604.10
CL 1613.97
O: 1220.96 H: 1226.30 L: 1211.18 C: 1224.00
1150
1200
1250
1300
1350
1400
1450
1500
1550
1600
1650
1700

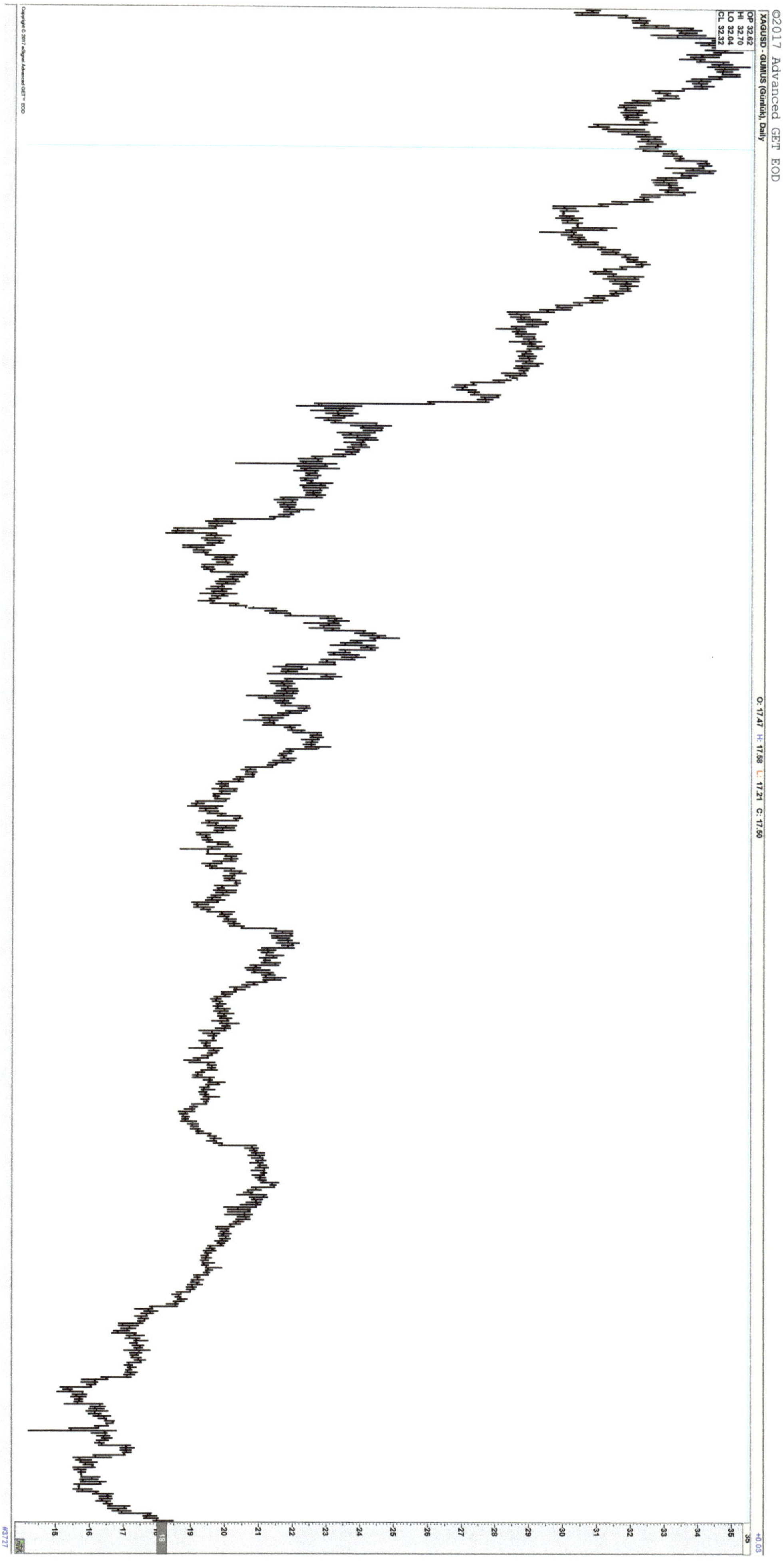
©2017 Advanced GET EOD
XAGUSD - GUMUS (Günlük), Daily

Between July 2011 and July 2014, we will analyze the daily chart of the Golden Cash chart with Gann boxes and Gann angles.

All Gann angles in this analysis are at the same price / time ratio, or the small Gann box derived from the large Gann box.

The same rates have been used for three years. In this book, we have shown, in detail, the successful trade we made in the course of time, only in 2013 and beyond.

We will consider the corresponding technical analysis from the establishment of the major Gann box. On September 5, 2011, the pivot at the price level of 1920, with the 1911 price-level pivot on August 22, made a near-term double peak, when breaking the 1850 price level we confirmed.

So we drawed the Gann box on September 5, 2011 pivot. The Gann box was found by calculating the wave height [high-low pivots] in the previous price movements of Gold.

The rates at which any contract is repeated as price interval and time interval; according to the same (1X1) or short interval to be foreseen; multiplied / divided by ; ½, 1/3 or so, 2X on for the long-term forecast. Thus, they form the basis for the establishment of the Gann box.

In the Gann box;

1) angles; they appear in the price / time ratio

2) by means of horizontal and vertical lines (again part of the specific time/expiry and part of the price difference); support for prices, resistance zones are foreseen. Vertical lines are also expected to inform possible break times.

The downward trend, which began on September 5, turned into a sudden fall after the squeeze/jam area of 1800-1760.

The decline up to level 1535 corresponds to the horizontal Gann box line. When this horizontal line is approached too much, it is reacting upwards. The reaction was up to 1X4 Gann. This angle confirmed itself at the beginning of the downturn in the 1950-1800 range.

The reaction, starting from 1530, stopped at 1X4 and then moved downward with this angle for a while.

The rise on the week of October 24 ended at the 1X1 angle after having fluctuated at 1X2.

The decline starting from the 1803 level on November 7 will continue until the end of the year. During this decline, the fluctuation between the 1X1 and 1X2 angles is driven.

As the upward trend started with the new year, at the end of February 2012, faced with the 1X2 angle (angle to the other side), the face was reversed and turned down again. The downward movement continued until May 14, slightly above the

1X1 angle. On May 14, the downward movement ended at exactly 1X1 angle and at the point where Gann box met with the middle time line. For a while, the price movement released here, the energy-coil like formation, the power for the new movement to collect.

May 14 pivot, 1X1 Gann angle and vertical time line, as well as Gann box horizontally the price line is formed. This pivoted start movement will take up to the beginning of August.

The rise between May 14 and early October continued around the other 1X1 angle, a reflection of the 1X1 angle.

On October 1, a peak was formed around the 4th Vertical time at line of Gann box and 1X4 Gann angle (the other side angle). This pivotal decline accelerated by passing below the 1X1 reflection angle, and the decline continued under the 1X4 angle.

November 7, 2011, February 27,2012 and October 1, 2012 the tops; formed in the same level as the triple peaks/tops. Even if the time between them is different, another resemblance gives the trigger line of sale from these tops. The second horizontal line from the top of the box is around 1720. These three peaks/tops are formed just above this line. As soon as the line has passed, the sale have accelerated.

From October 1, 2012, we are drawing a new Gann box. This Gann box; It was created from ¼ of our big Gann box.

During the ongoing decline between the 1X2 angle and the 1X1 angle of this new Gann box, the horizontal and vertical lines (light gray) again gave support ,resistance tasks and break times with near exact accuracy.

The decline from the 1920 levels will end at 1180 on June 24, 2013.

During the fall, the oscillation continued around the new 1X1 angle.

The rise after June 24 can be defined by the same rate of 1X1.

The decline that began on the August 26 pivot continued just below the same 1X1 angle. The upward movement, which started after the decline until the end of 2013, will continue until 2014, on the same Gann angle.

Gann boxes is the underlying of Gann angles with the same price / time ratio, which explain all these price movements. These angles and time/price horizontal, vertical lines (divisions) both share the anticipation of the harmonic motion of Gold.

Strategy:

Silver prices, approaching 18 at the end of June 2013, were squeezed upward in the middle of July, above the 19th level.

In the beginning of July 2013, 20 contracts long positions were taken in silver future. Puts were sold at different expirations and strikes; 19 and 19.5 strikes in that ended on July 25(expiration date of contract), 17 strike in that ended on August 27 and 16 strike in that ended on September 25.

In gold, in mid-July, on the contract with expiration date on July 25, from 1250 strike; On the contract with expiration date on October 28, 1100 and 1150 strikes were sold in large quantities.

At the end of June 2013, gold prices fall below 1200. But at the beginning of July Gold prices rose above 1200.

Also at the beginning of July, we started to take long positions at gold mining companies such as Yamana Gold Inc., Freeport Mc Moran, Kinross Gold Corp. and Newmont Mining.

In the middle of August 2013, the positions puts of Gold and Silver (Gold rose to the level 1440 and Silver rose to the level of 25) were closed with premium profit (or with all premium income at expirations dates). Mining shares and future longs were also closed with profit.

In early October, future long positions were reopened in Gold and Silver. In response to these longs, on the contract which is expiration date October 28, the amount of calls from 1370, 1375, 1400, 1420 in Gold was sold and premium was received. Short calls were bought from 1440 in the same expiration for the part that could not be met with futures longs. Thus, covered call and call bear spreads were established.

Again in Gold, on October 28 expiration date contract and at 1250 strike puts were sold and premiums were taken. Gold prices fluctuated between 1270 and 1360 in October.

In Silver, the longs were countered by a strike of 22 strike calls on October 28 (covered call). 20 and 21 strikes on the expiration on October 28; 19,5 and 18,5 strikes on November 25 puts were sold. Silver has remained in the range of 20,750-23 in October 2013.

In November 2013, the longs were countered at 1325 and 1350 strikes calls on the November 25 expiration contract (covered call strategy). In the same expiration contract, 1225 strike puts were sold. Thus, at the end of December 2013, during the Gold prices withdrawn up to 1200, the long positions were increased (returning from the put shorts) while premiums were received with futures longs on hand and the same period, we sold calls which were hedging with future long. We have taken premium from call short (covered call strategy).

In Silver, the longs were countered by 21, 22 and 23 strikes calls which were sold on the November 25 expiration (future long + call short); covered call hedge strategy.

At the beginning of December, 1150, 1170, 1175, 1200, 1225 strikes puts were sold intensively and premiums were collected on the December 26 expiration Gold. Also at the beginning of December, in Silver on December 26 expiration contract, 18,5 and 19 strikes contracts were sold and the premium was collected.

At the end of December 2013, 1175 and 1200 strikes were puts were sold and was taken premiums on expiration contract on January 28, 2014.

At the end of December, Gold down to around 1200 and Silver down to around 19. Also at the end of December, shares were obtained from companies that made various Gold and Silver mining operations.

Along with the year 2014, the prices of Gold and then Silver went upwards. At the end of February, Silver approached the level of 22, and Gold approached the 1400 levels. In this ascension, puts were closed with premium profits. Also future longs and mining stocks were gradually closed with profit.

10 Year US Bond Analysis

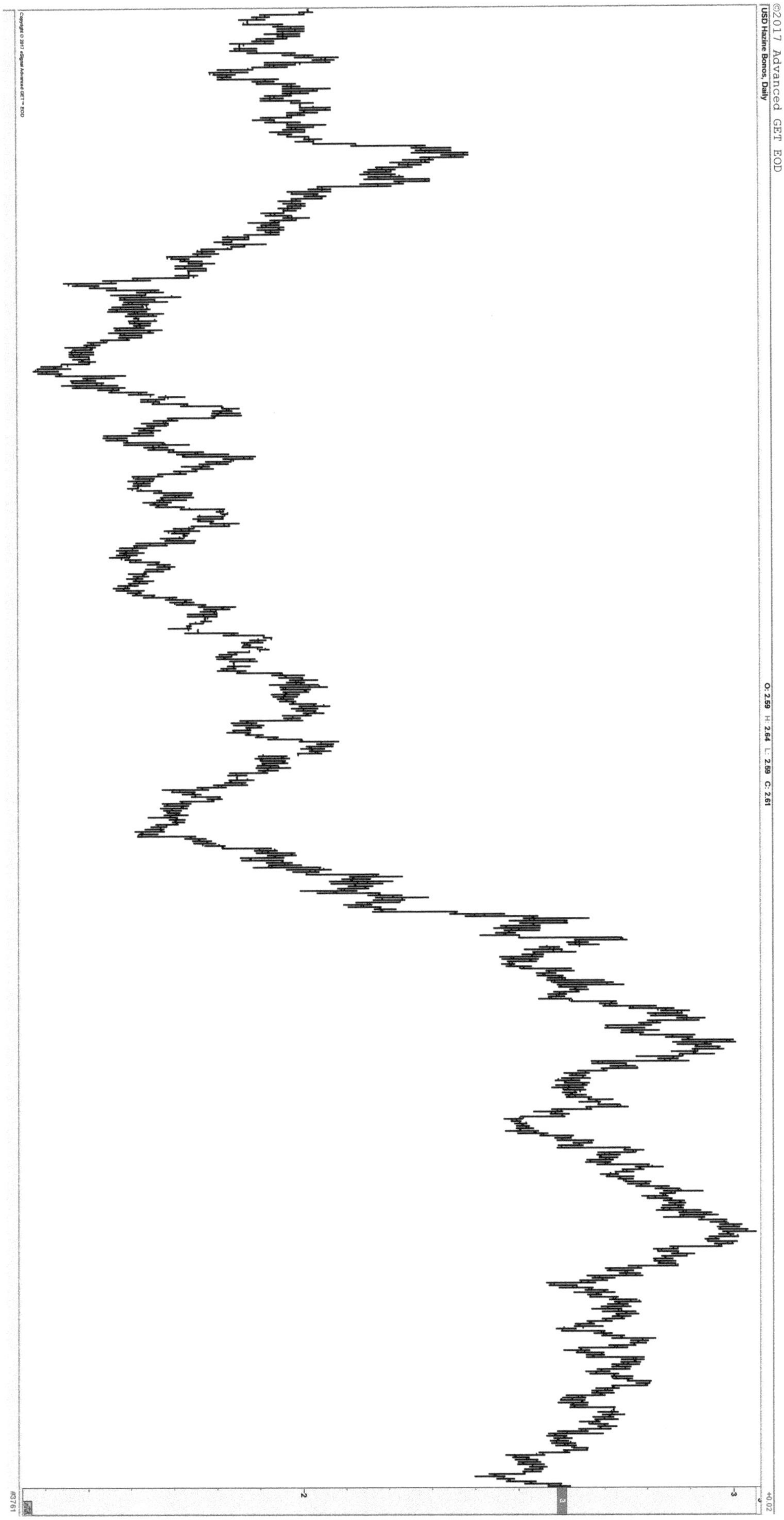

US Bonds 2013 - 2014 Technical Analysis

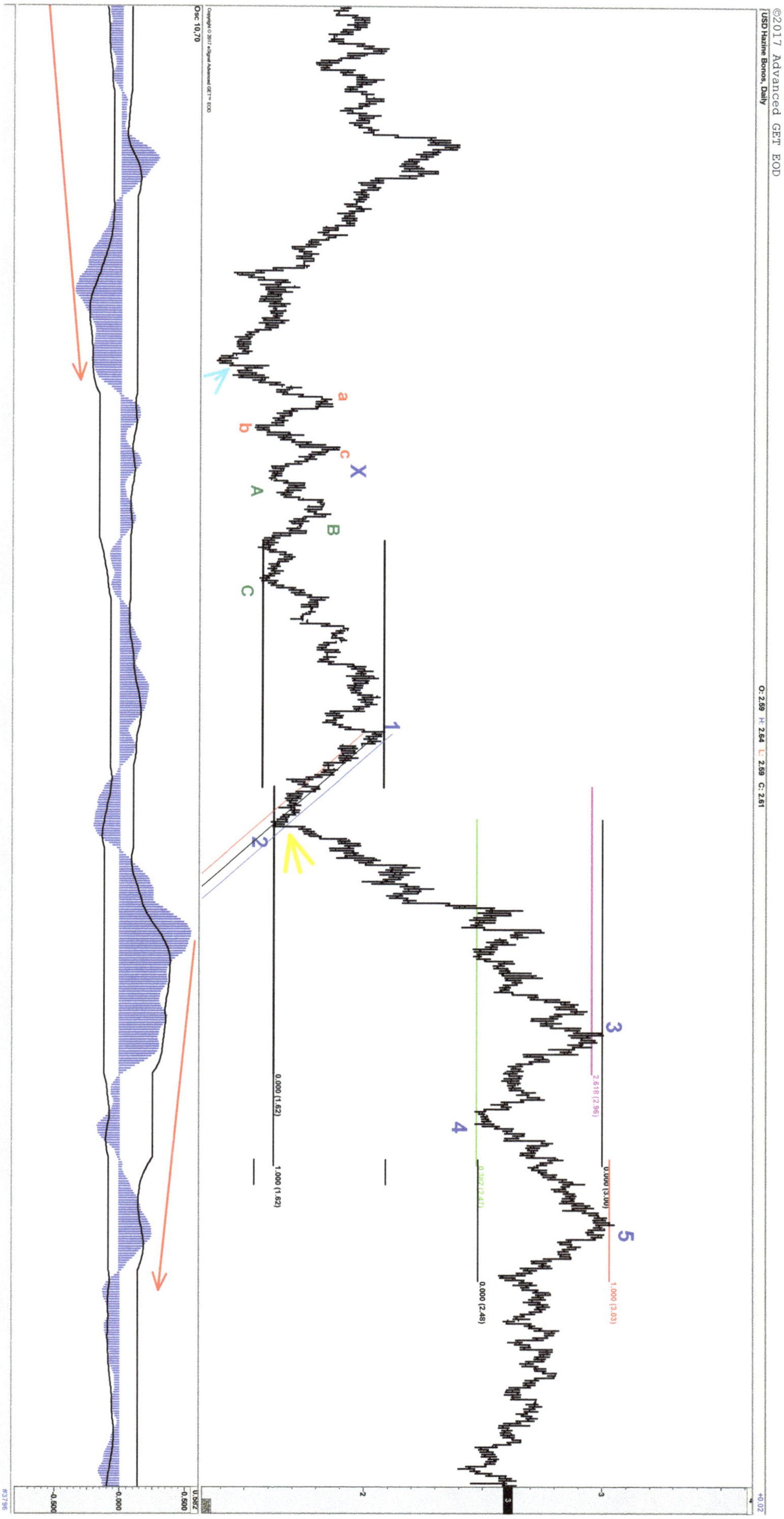

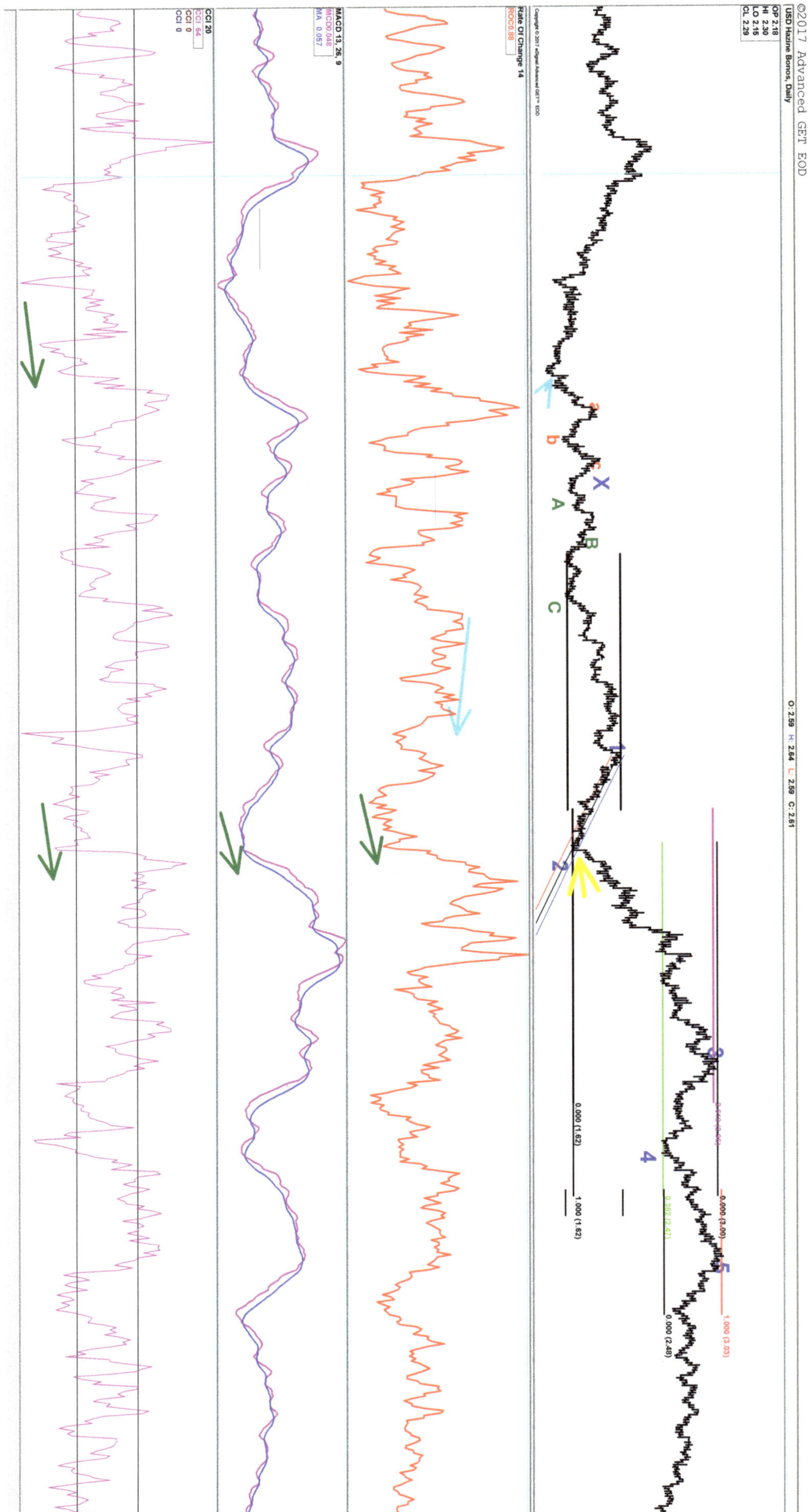
©2017 Advanced GET EOD
USD Hazine Bonos, Daily

In the technical analysis of 10-year US bond yields; we will use the Elliott wave count, Fibonacci rates and the 10/70 period oscillator together with the regression channel. The ongoing downward trend since 2007 has come to an end between June and August of 2012. The divergence of the peak of the oscillator (red arrow) which is outside left of chart and the price incompatibility signify this.

Another delineation of the ascension starting from the bottom level shown by the blue arrow is the divergence of the CCI indicator (another technical drawing) calculated over the momentum. In this incoherence and divergence, prices are moving downward, but they have bottomed at a higher level.

If we continue over the price chart; after the bottom indicated by the blue arrow, X wave correction was made. Correcting with X wave after a long decline is the usual situation. In the under wave count of the X wave, the wave "c" remains short and has the same size as the wave "b". This information shows us that the post-decline consolidation can take a long time.

The "Rate of change" indicator confirms that the consolidation is continuing by providing strong oscillations in the "a" wave and a relatively long length (short time interval) in the subsequent waves.

After the green A, B, C correction, the 1st wave starts to rise. During the «1st.wave" movement, the rate of change (blue arrow) loss power and make divergence, along with the rise, tells you that 1st. wave would be limited. It was confirmed by the divergence of all the signs, on the last top of the 1st wave.

The second wave correction was made at a deep price. It is normal for the second wave to take place deeply due to the size and power of the declining motion since 2007.

The 2nd wave motion followed by the regression channel was broken with a hard motion at the point indicated by the yellow arrow (2nd quarter of 2013).

The importance of this breakdown;

a) divergence at the CCI indicator

b) divergence in the rate of change (before the green arrow, notice of the end of wave 1 of the blue arrow increases the significance of this indicator).

c) We can confirm with the "dead kiss" formation in the MACD demonstration. The kiss of death means that the diversion suddenly turns upward (or vice versa) while breaking down. Here is the MACD indicator; divergence + upward direction of lagging curve + gave strong signal with dead kiss.

d) Finally, the oscillator (although delayed) informs that the 2nd wave is over.

The uptrend will take place until August and September of 2013. The 3rd wave target was approximately fully realized with a fibonacci number of 2.618. When this goal is achieved, the oscillator's power loss has also signaled the end of the wave.

The 4th wave was ending just above the 0.382 retreat rate. The 5th wave formed by the upward movement during the winter of 2013, the double peak with the 3rd wave and the "1" ratio length with the 1st wave.

The oscillator's divergence (with the same price level, the oscillator on the downside, the weaker 2th peak) with a double top return signaled the end of the 5-wave ascension.

The decline that started here continued until the beginning of 2015 and stopped at only 1.7 levels.

US Bond Future Trading

On January 3, 2013, futures were sold on US 10-year note.

— At the beginning of May, we took position on US 10-year and 30-year t notes, positions in the direction of rising interest rates. Positions increased during May.

Between August 15 and August 27, futures short positions in US t-note were closed with profit.

— 10-year US bond yields, which were 1.65 at the beginning of the May, rose to 2.9 at the beginning of September.

German 10 Years

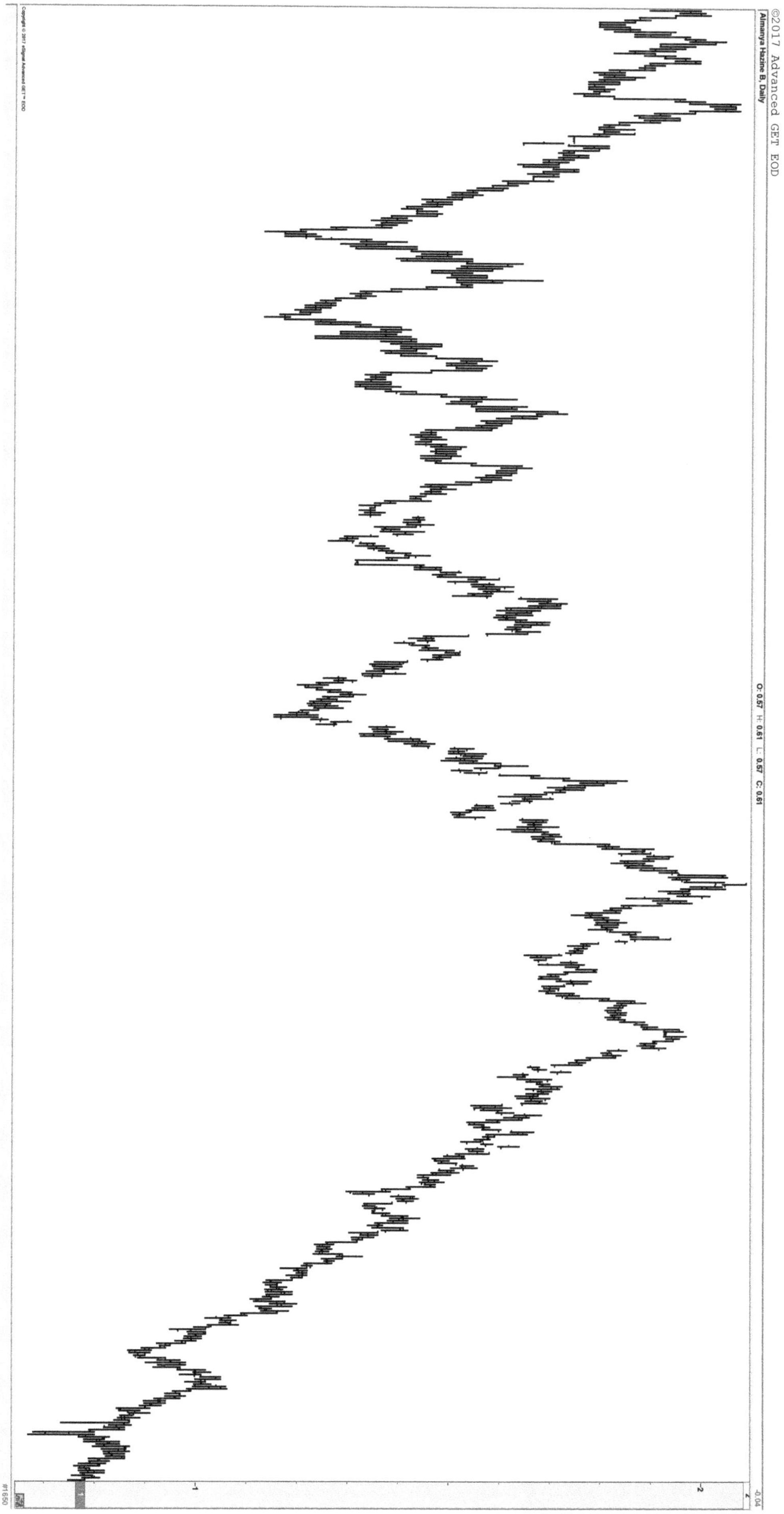

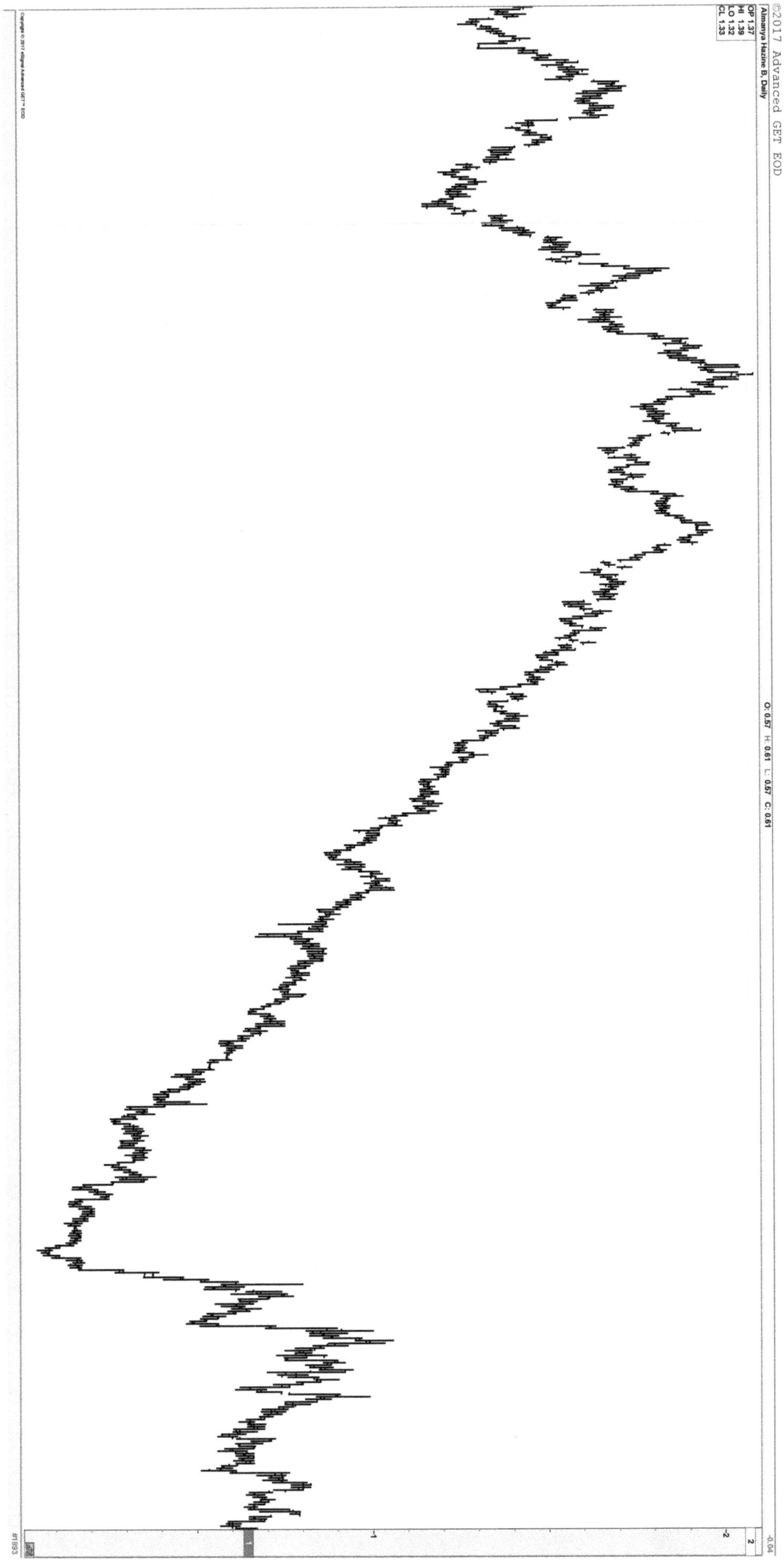
©2017 Advanced GET EOD
Almanya Hazine B. Daily
OP 1.37
HI 1.39
LO 1.32
CL 1.33
O: 0.57 H: 0.61 L: 0.57 C: 0.61

German 10 Years in the Weekly Period with Action-Reaction Method

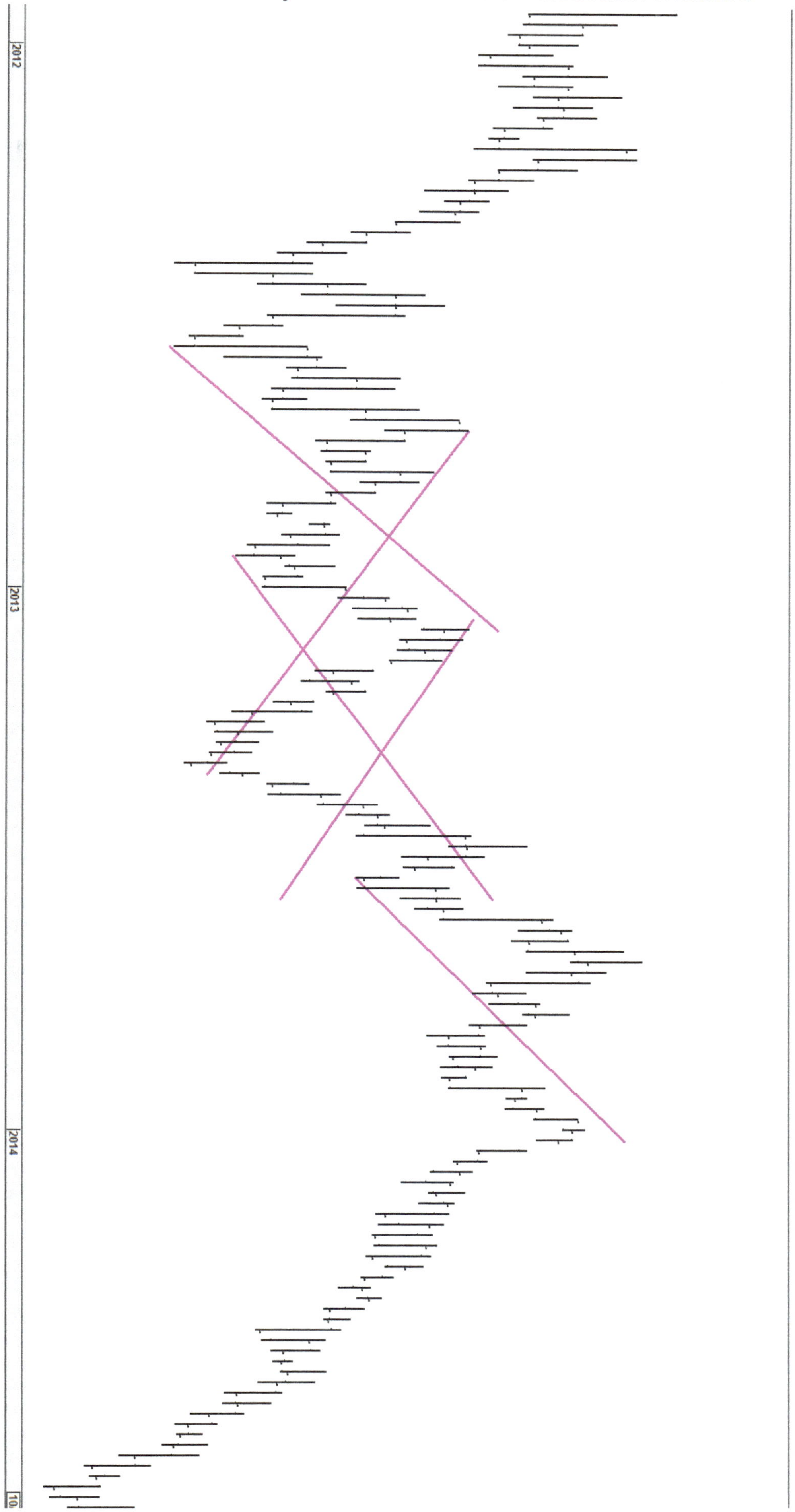

In this graph of Germany's 10-year bond yields we used between 2012 and 2014 in the weekly period, we used the action-reaction method analysis. We examined the horizontal and volatile consolidation period between July 2012 and July 2013 with consecutive action-reaction methods.

The pivot of the week of July 27, 2012, together with the first week of June, formed the double bottom. The upward trend started on July27, peaking on September 21. The fall that started on the same day will be completed on December 14. On first week of January, we will draw the median, which runs through the middle of the price level between September 21 and December 14, starting from the July 27 pivot, and we will make the necessary drawing to anticipate the end of the reaction if we extend it to the right side. At the beginning of February 2013 the approaching price movement of the median, that is paused at a little distance to the contact. Towards the end of February, we understand that the reaction is over by turning down.

This time, with September 21 pivot, we are drawing the median from the middle of the price movement from December 14 to February 1. The price movement and this median will intersect at the end of March. Fluctuation above the median, results in energy coil. Strong price movement going through the gap with the discharge of this energy coil on the week of May 10, will continue in the upward direction.

If we extend the drawing to the right on December 14 pivot from the center of the pivotal range at the beginning of February with the beginning of May's pivot, we will see that the price movement has touched the median and it turned to the reverse at the end of June. On July 26, the price movement will give an end attempting to approach the median which passed through in the middle of May 3 to June 28 pivots and which started from an initial pivot on February 1. The upward direction will begin. As the upward movement became stronger in the middle of August, it became clear that the reaction to reach the median passing through the middle of May 3 - June 28 could not reach the result.

Transactions in German Bills

German bonds were placed in the direction of interest rate cuts. At the beginning of February the call bull spread was gradually established. Euro Bund April 2013 (expiration/maturity is March 30) contract received 143 strike call long. As the other legs, the call was sold from the strikes of 144.5 and 144 in April term and the premium was taken.

According to the yields moving in the opposite direction of the futures, these positions were opened with a 10-year bond yield around 1,644 and closed at around 1,118 at the end of March with profit.

In the Euro Bund (10-year German bond futures), the Central Bank took a position in the middle of July to raise interest rates. Put bear spreads were established. These spreads, which were established on September expiration contract (with the August 23 expiration/maturity date), were closed with profit at maturity. In German 10-year bond, interest at 1.52 in mid-July rose to 1.95 at the beginning of September.

MIBTEL

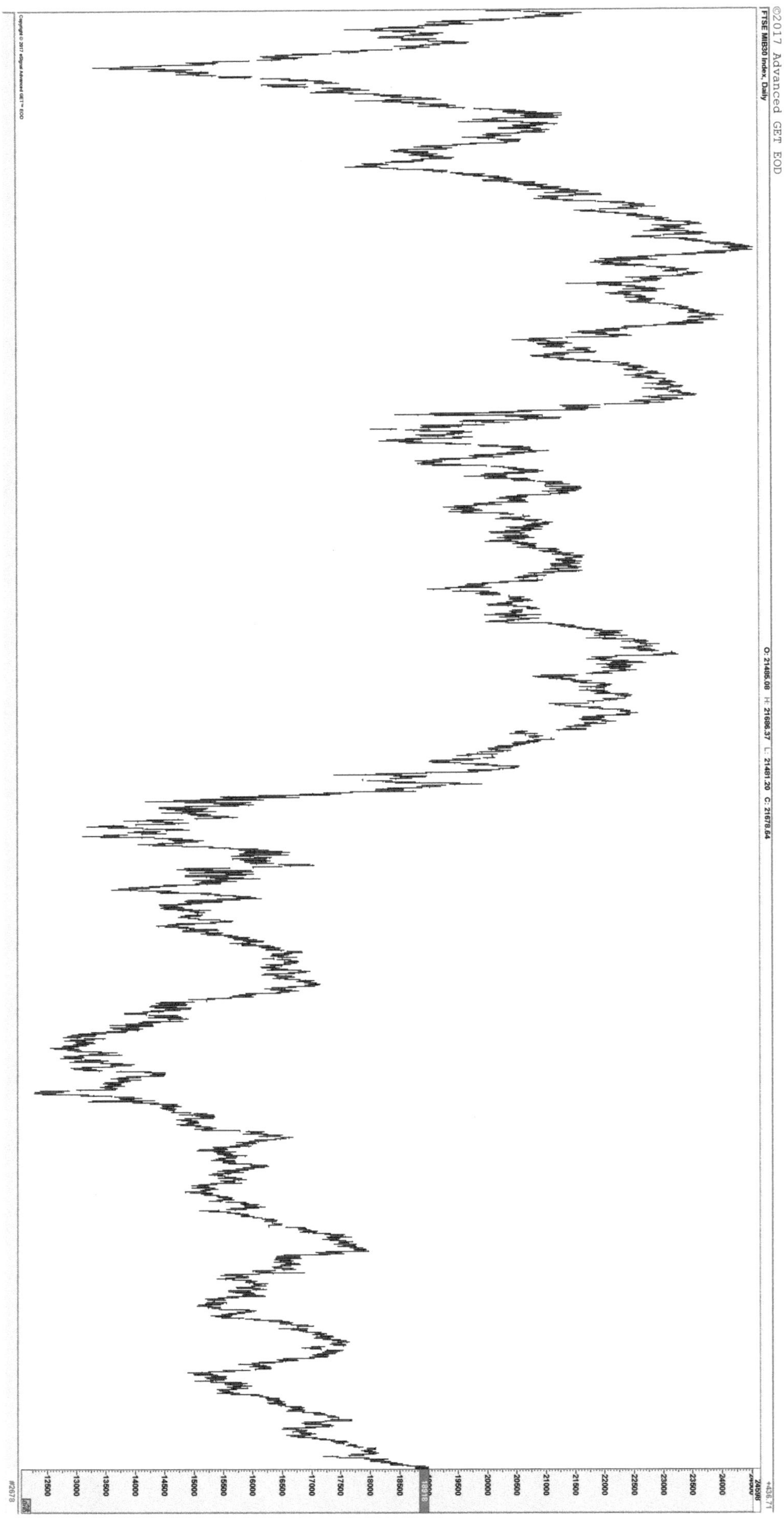

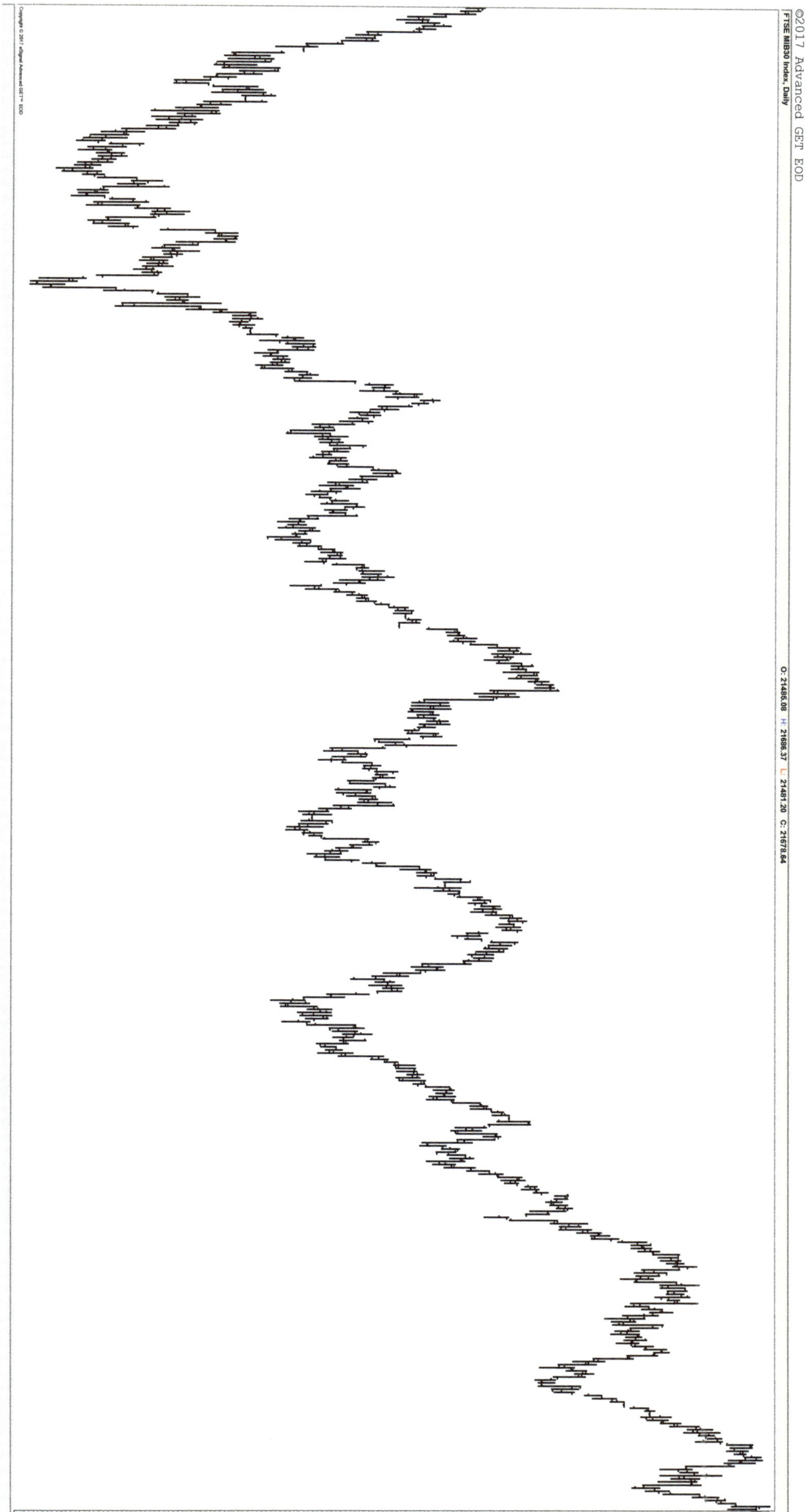
©2017 Advanced GET EOD
FTSE MIB30 Index, Daily
O: 21485.08 H: 21686.37 L: 21481.20 C: 21678.64
12500
13000
13500
14000
14500
15000
15500
16000
16500
17000
17500
18000
18500
19000
19500
20000

Mibtel Analysis by Action-Reaction Method

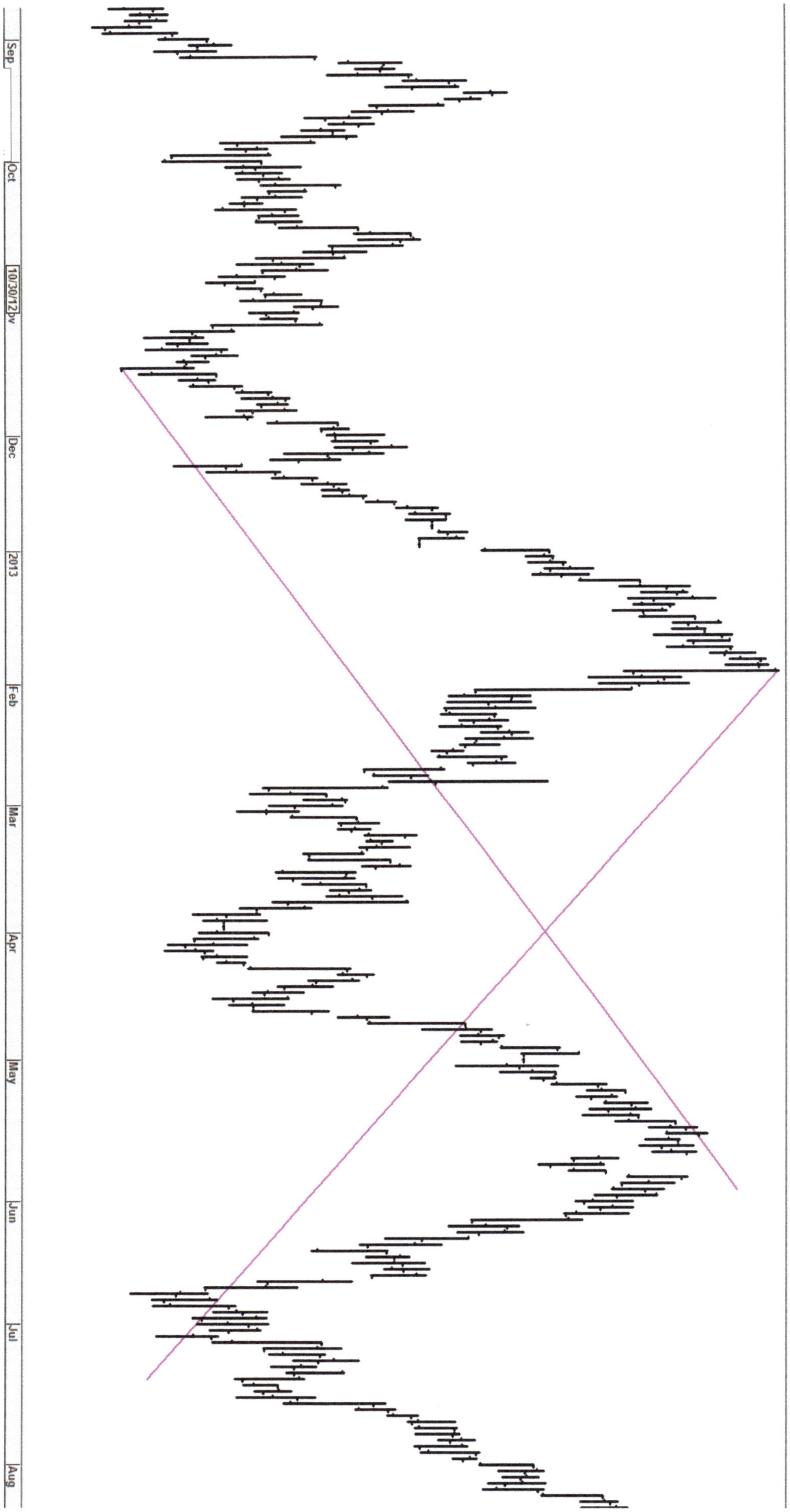

This chart is the continuation of Mibtel index's other consecutive Mibtel samples, from which we examined the price movements between August 2012 and August 2013. This time, we will do our analysis by Andrew's action-reaction method.

November 16 pivot's, let's assume the start of the action-reaction median. In the middle of the distance between January 30 and April 5, 2013, let's draw the media starting from the November 16 pivot. The price move connect with this median is on May 17. The reaction will end on this date. May 17, at the same time, the peak of the rise of April was over. The downward movement starting from this top will take back all of your ascension.

With the same method, let's start with the January 30 date and draw the median from the middle of April 5-May 17 price movement. The price action cut the media on June 21 and was released around the median for 7 days after one day of further decline. This energy coin ending price movement has started to reverse the trend after July 3. The reaction has come to an end on this date. Continued direction has turned upward. The entire downward will be recovered within a month.

Italian Political Situation and Positions in MIBTEL

First of all, let's look at the analysis of the Italian political situation:

On Monday, February 25, 2013, at 10:00 am, there is a movement of 50 points in 1 minute, with no news; close to 1% !!! These are abnormal situations: The crumbs in Italy close at 16:00. For this reason, at 10:00 am the result was unknown. DAX was up 1%, while Milano was up 0.3%. If it was known, Milano would be ahead! The question is to stop shorts! ..

As for the purchase of bond in the evening of February 27, 2013, Italy fell. We also increased the position in the bond and we also increased the position in the Italy index (in the direction of purchase). We also sold the Yen in plenty.

At the beginning of 2013, the political situation in Italy is as follows: The lower council (cabin) has provided a majority of the center-left (Bersani-Monti), the upper parliament (Senate) has not achieved the majority (5 votes are missing). There are two options for the establishment of government; either a broad-based national reconciliation rule extending from the center left to the center right will be established or the elections will be renewed. Presumably, president Napolitano will likely prefer the first and will force the formulations of government. At the game theory suit, the comedian Grillo or Berlusconi can support a weak center - the leftist government whose cords are entirely in their possession. This may allow the market to drop the tension for the time being. Comedian Grillo is on the forefront when I think who would go for a second election pick. That is why Berlusconi may be a little closer to supporting the establishment of government.

Berlusconi's statement 'a left-right coalition that left Monti out of the way could be considered' was bought by exchange. This is a serious political possibility. I think Berlusconi does not want a new selection. On either side, there are competitors close to the party's views. Comedian against EU, Monti + Bersani supporter EU. Berlusconi may lose votes in these two side.

Berlusconi's point is Monti and Merkel. Berlusconi hate them for dropping himself from power (he had statements saying he wanted revenge for great powers because of Gaddafi).

In the worst and distant scenario, if Italy breaks the EU, it will emerge from the German axis. With its increasing exports, it quickly recovers itself. When I was writing about them; Berlusconi said "Going back to the election is not a practical way". Result; After a while, the government is established. The great coalition already exists in Italy: the example of Aldo Moro ...

Now let's go through the strategies and operations:

(Index values are written over the spot, options and futures are written on futures values).

Mibtel Option Transactions, Futures and Share Purchases:

When these operations are being performed;

— On February 27, puts were sold on 14,000 strike, on April expiration. When this was done, the spot index was around 15,600.

On March 7 and 8, FIAT and INTESA shares were bought intensively.

—Mibtel index in March expiration, while the spot index was around 16,000 on March 18; From 14,500, puts were sold on March 15.

In Mibtel, while the spot index was around 15,500, puts were sold from 13,500 on May 2013 contract (expiration May 2013).

At the beginning of April, the spot index fell to 15,250. In the middle of April 15,750 attacked.

— Transactions between April 9-29:

On April 9, April 2013 futures contract; 15,600 strike calls were purchased.

On April 9, the spot index was around 15,700 and turned upward; first options, puts were sold and calls were bought. Subsequent futures were bought.

On May 10, at May 17 expiration contract, puts were closed. These puts sold in the previous month with high premium. For these operations, 13,500 strike heavily loaded. In the following hours, at the contracts which is June 21 is the last maturity/ expiration date; the puts previously sold from 13.000-13.500-14.000 strikes, were also covered with profit.

On April 10, April expiration contract, (on the contract to be completed on April 19), from 15,800 strike to 15,250 strike put were sold gradually. Thus, puts with deep out-of-money in the long-term (May, June) contracts were closed with high profits. Subsequent the premium was tried to be collected by selling puts at-the-money and near-out-money strikes. If these contracts cover the valuation in-the-money; we are also shown that we are willing to open a long position from the relevant strike (here I will note that the option is usually written on the futures to return directly to the long position. If option is written at spot and at expiration return cash; it may buy futures contract same date. The same objective will be achieved).

— On April 10, while the spot was at 15,500; it was bought intensive at futures contracts.

— As soon as we go up the market, call short positions are started to open (once we bought call long). In other words, gradual call bull spreads have been established. As counter against previous call purchases, 16,100 strike calls were sold in the same expiration contract. Thus, by taking advantage of the upward prices, premiums were sold in increasing call contracts and the premiums of previously purchased call longs were tried to be withdrawn.

On April 11, while the spot index was around 15,700; on the June contract, as the index went up, the pyramid-like amount decreased in the futures longs.

The Mibtel index continued up until the end of May. Thus, call buying were turned into call bull spreads with call sales and these were closed with profit. As the index went up, May-June expiration/maturity puts, which were sold in mid-March, were closed with profit. The futures (long positions) received on April 10 were also gradually phased out from mid-May.

In mid-May, the spot index gained close to 17,700 and reached the top. It was in the consolidation at mid-May to mid-June. From the beginning of June, it started to head down.

July 4, 2016

Gold 2016

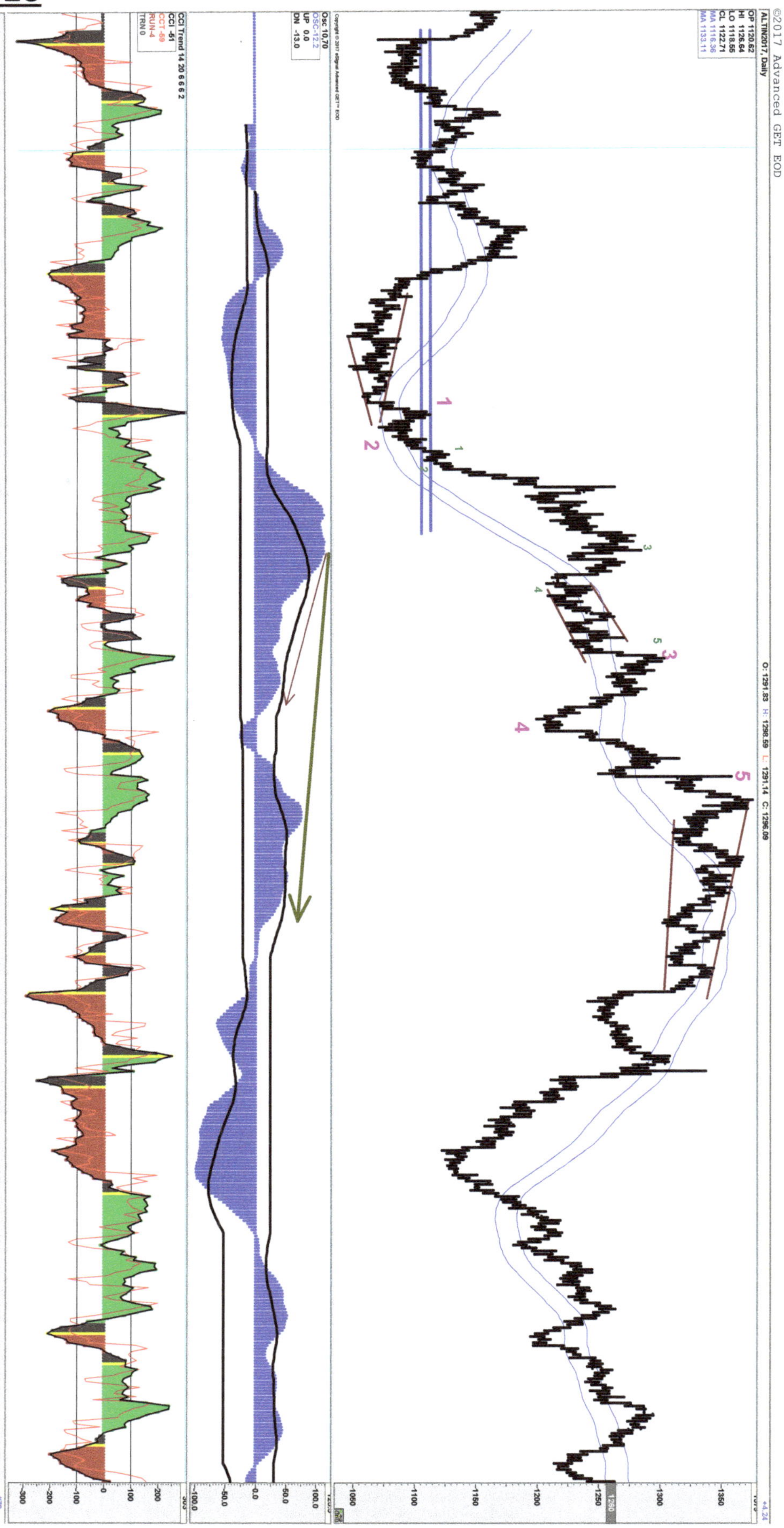

The last phase of the fall in Gold, which began in August 2012, was finalized by triangle formation between November 2015 and early 2015. The shortness of this triangular exit ("1st" wave) motion can be explained by calming of the market, with the sequential consolidation movements observed over the previous months coming one after another.

The 2nd wave after the short wave is formed in a simple structure. After the quick ending consolidation, the 2nd wave has exceeded the first wave's high. This was the signal of that the 3rd wave would be stronger than the 1st wave.

The largest size of the consolidation triangle on the chart is about 50 dollars. The figure of this level added to the break point of the triangle is approximately 1125. The first wave peak also approaches this level (1110).

The channel formed by two horizontal blue lines drawn from July 2015 shows the 6-month resistance line of Gold. This channel is about 1100 level. As a result; By passing level 1110-1125 (canal), it is expected that the strong 3rd wave begins.

After the end of the first month of the 2016 season, the third wave began, expected after a two-day small pullback,

After rising until March 14, Gold rallied after a month's consolidation too. After reaching peak in May, Gold entered a correction.

The March 14 peak is marked with a green "3" and the May 2 top with a green "5". The green waves are the sub wave count of 3 waves.

In this blue oscillator (below), the red arrow shows the divergence with the 3rd sub wave count is confirmed.

Again, the red "4th" wave at the bottom of May 31 and the red "3rd" wave at the top of May 2; the red "1st and 2nd" waves; it shows the count of the greatest wave count.

On July 7, with the red 5th wave (the minor double peak) at the 1369 price level, we confirm with the yellow arrow that the red 3rd wave's divergence in the oscillator.

The price level of July 7, even if it appears to be the 5th wave top; the structure of movement up to this level in the follow up emerging the horizontal triangle + the sign given by oscillator for the 5th wave; I prefer to assume that the fifth wave completes right at the end of September.

After the 5th wave, A wave of the beginning of October, the correction of the B wave in the first days of November, reached the goal with C wave at the end of the year.

There are two outliers in the wave count of this graph using the Elliott method: the waves 2 and 4 are of a similar nature and the result of the 5th wave which is a horizontal triangle that is rarely seen.

We can fulfill the requirement that the 2nd and 4th wave counts be alternatives: We accept that the consolidation continues with the horizontal triangle opened after the 4th green wave. Thus, the above-mentioned outliers are lifted.

We can also support wave counting with the second lower horizontal window's momentum (cci) indicator seen in our graph and the blue moving average envelope above the graph. Now let's take a look at our analysis with these two indicators instead of the oscillator. We consider the price movement as the wave of the impulse (1,3,5, A, C) above the envelope and the place of consolidation (2,4, B) below the envelope. This definition is for the upward wave motion expectation. Downward movement changes the envelope above and below the envelope.

On the CCI indicator, we refer to the green colored areas as impulse wave and the red colored areas as consolidation / correction wave.

We can confirm the wave count by selecting the sections where the envelope and CCI section signal in the same direction.

— 1st wave green and above envelope

— 2nd wave envelope in the intermediate zone

— 3rd wave green and above envelope

— Again, the consolidation sections of the 3rd wave are below the envelope or around the envelope while the CCI indicator is in the red or gray zone.

While the 5th wave is usually above the envelope, it has suffered power loss by time and has passed its last period under the envelope. In the same process, the CCI indicator also crossed the red downward direction from the green descending tops.

Strategy:

While testing Gold 1100 in the second week of January 2016, premiums were received by selling puts from 850 and 900 strikes in December.

a) The contract, which will be transformed to the future, is intended to be transported in medium term.

b) It is desired to earn premiums revenue to use in the call bull spread purchase which will be established to participate in the upward movement when the Gold goes up from the level of 1100.

On the last week of January, when the Gold went up, call was bought from 1250 strike in December, and a call bull spread was established (5 call contracts; 5 call long, 5 call short) by selling 1400 strike calls in the same term/expiration.

To take back the premium which was given to this call bull spread;

1) The call was sold from 1350 strike in April. This call sale is a partial hedge with a call bull spread established between 1250-1400 strike.

A kind of calendar spread has been established covering up to 1400 strikes.

2) In May expiration, puts were sold at 1175 and 1180 strikes. Thus, three strategies were utilized to recover the premium given to December 1250-1400 call bull spread:

a) April (April) Expiration/maturity 1350 call short

b) May term 1175,1180 put short

c) December maturity 850, 900 strike put shorts.

Upward trend in April, December term 850, 900 strikes puts shorts were closed with high premium income.

Also at the beginning of May, 1175 and 1180 strikes puts shorts of May term were closed with high premium income. April term/maturity of 1350 strike calls was completed as out-of-money. All the premiums are written as profit.

At the beginning of May, at the level of 1305, Gold was going down; at May term, at 1350 and 1375 strikes calls was sold. To hedge these feet, calls were purchased from 1425 and 1450 strike in the same term. The contract is due on May 25.

These call bear spreads are hedged partly by December maturity call bull spreads which were established between 1250-1400 strikes. In other words, a kind of calendar spread strategy has been established between December call bull spreads and May call bear spreads.

Again, 1240 strike puts were sold in the May term/expiration. 1240 strike put shorts were hedged by taking puts from 1200 strikes.

It was aimed to obtain premium income with put bull spreads established between 1240 and 1200. In the term, the prices that went below 1240 strike went back to 1245 at the end of the month.

In May, during the withdrawal to 1205, new put bull spreads were established in the same expiration with put shorts from 1195 and put longs from 1160. All these strategies were closed with profit.

A new wave rises along with June at Gold which prices have reached the level of 1375 at the beginning of July. December term call bull spreads (1250-1400) were closed pre-expiration with profit when the second peak (top) fell below this level (1375) at the beginning of August and under the previous peak at the beginning of September.

June 2016

Yen

During the June-November 2016 period, the Yen / Dollar parity fluctuated between the levels of 1 - 0.93. The supportive interventions (aimed at depreciation of the Yen) that the BOJ made when approaching the level of 100 (the future 1) are to protect the export power of the Japanese economy (BOJ interventions by means of Ministry of Finance / MOF). After the macro-economic analysis reaching the argument that the BOJ would not want to overcome level 1, we sold calls for months at a level near the 1 level (call bear spreads with hedge) for the first time in the testing level. 1 level testing , and in the case of partial overruns, the amount of call sales is increased.

Strategies were established at near-weekly weekends contracts (risk mitigation + combined weekly premiums due to significant monthly premium overruns).

While 1 level is being tested, longer term call bear spreads are also established.

In the case of approaching levels of 96, put bull spreads were established and premiums were tried to be taken from the other side. At July- August and beginning of September, in downward attacks if the put short strike level is exceeded immediately after the position is opened and the put short strike is in-the-money for balacing; the at-the-money or near-out-money Call bear spreads are established by selling call. In these spreads, the call short strike and put short strike legs often overlap or nest.

So; a) try to balance in-the-money put short, we sold call short with premium.

b) Both call short and put short strike feet are intended to reset / neutralize each other if they complete the in-the-money valuation (future long + future short = 0).

c) With put long and call longs, the risk of attacks is limited. No sale of puts after September.

At the beginning of November, with the BOJ's support and the technical outlook turning in favor of the Dollar, the Yen's depreciation began with a sharp move in line with the breakout model.

Now let's look at price levels and just a few of the strategies we have set up:

The Yen futures, which saw the lowest level at 0.967 in the week of June 27, rose to 1 level (0.09972) on July 4.

In the last week of June, the call bear spread was established on the same day (June 30) by call short position from 0.1025 and strike call long to 0.1 strike (equivalent to 100). The objective of this spread is to collect the premium.

On July 4, the Yen (the future) was at the highest level of 1, followed by the lowest level of 0.94 during the following week of July 11. Call from 1.01 strike was sold and call from 1.04 strike was taken. Thus, a call bear spread is established between 1.04 and 1.01, and it is objective to receive a premium.

In the same expiration, 1.01 strike calls were sold and 1.02 strike calls were taken. With the second step (1.02 call long) made 2 days after the first step, the call bear spread was established with a lower premium (the call length was paid less).

When the trend pivot of the price movement becomes clear, the call bear spreads are started to be established in for expirations the weekly or monthly terms instead of the nearest weekly. Strategies have been implemented in the nearer week or so, if the price movement is mature, but the pivot is not clear.

2016-2017 Reports by Date

12/12/2016

First, I want to write a few lines on methodology. Fund management / trading; I'm of the opinion that it is not just up or down direction of the signals given by macro analysis, technical analysis or similar methods. Also it is not the right approach to make virtual management on a capital that has no risk / return demand, maturity and quantities.

a) Capital's risk perception and its risk,

b) search (expected) and level of return,

c) agreement between a and b,

d) capital size,

e) the capital maturity (associated with a and b).

These are internal factors. The external factor is that once the internal factors have been adjusted, the market is able to offer these profile and the style and capacity of the fund manager / trader can meet expectations.

Even the optimum balance is achieved between the internal factors but one of the internal factors is missing;

a) the project should be abandoned if there is a problem with the fund manager / trader.

b) If the market realization is incompatible with the internal factors, revision should be sought at the appropriate time (for position acquisition or fund management activation) or at the risk / return and maturity balance we mentioned at the beginning.

As I have described in the lines of methodology briefly, it is not possible to envisage a fund management that has a risk perception of *Y*, maturity of *T*, amount of capital *X* and in the search for return of *Z* or in other words, it's not possible to envisage a fund management if its value is not determined.

What is the macro analysis axiom? Let's go to this question; the macro analysis axioms is the "opinion", which will create "the agenda of the market" (opinion) in 6-12 months.

In other words, the "opinion" is not only the social-psychological thought, perception, evaluation that dominates the market actors with macroeconomic analysis by the fund manager / trader, should be a judgment that is substantiated by objective economic and financial criteria. Only traders' fashionable or unfavorable views can not be targeted.

In other cases;

a) a judiciary established solely on the perception of the other actors (right or wrong)

or

b) if the judgment is not reflected in the market (and not reflected at time 'x') with only the fund manager / trader's analysis methods (wholly consistent analysis and correct result), fund's position can not reach to the target.

Briefly; 1) economic social reality,

2) analysis of this,

3) willingness for purchase of the market analysis

and all these factors should intersect in the near future.

When we consider these factors together, we expect global economic growth and inflation pricing to come into question for the next 6-12 months (we emphasize we are talking about pricing of anticipation, not realization).

We therefore expect an increase in bond yields.

As December 2016 is our starting date, we are not waiting for technical opportunities in US treasury purchasing this scenario.

In Europe, we are expecting a rise in government bonds, which is the result of the QE exit anticipation in the EU economy.

The ECB's buying schedule will probably end after 9 months:

a) This date includes election date of Germany, France, and so on.

b) The difference in the bond interest between the EU and the US can not remain open for a long time (we consider Japan as an exception for reasons such as the borrowing market being domestically owned).

In spring, the rise of German ten years (south direction in the future contract) may begin. For this act;

1) call buying for possible hedging call longs and future short position + put short for premium revenue,

2) in accordance with the main scenario; premium purchase by option,

3) option strategies for obtaining premium income because there is more time for the main scenario (spring and summer months)

4) use of the 3rd option to take back the premium given in the 2nd option (2nd and 3rd combined use),

5) the timing of all these options together.

When the option position is taken, when we accept the use of Eurex as an axiom, we will take advantage of the time decay with weekly options and trade positions.

If we take longer term positions (1st and 2nd options); it is possible to use these positions as a basis, to take positions in weekly options where we can reduce the risk and collect premiums. For example; medium-term in-the-money put long, such as weekly call sales that will remain in the strategy ... (here, breaking times of the market should be noted).

Strategic Basis and Criteria for Positions:

German bonds (Euro Bund) will be used to the position. Italy and Spain will be triggers of the financial risk.

In the German bonds, short-term 2-and 5-year treasury turnover and over-trading indicators again trigger our position.

French and US bond movements are used for parallel movement and correlation analysis.

We will look at what macro indicators are for this position and I will write down other strategic basis and criteria that we will use according to political reinforcement.

December 18, 2016

Last week Italian bonds were bought. It was within my expectation that the capitalization process of the Italian banks after Renzi's resignation would work in spite of the EU commission.

The chartists, who commented on the continious contract, were in the wrong corner of the forecast for Italian and French bonds. Always pay attention to maturity pricing on charts traded (traders must dealt with expiration dates separately). Near-medium term analyzes should be made on the futures contract chart. There is not much time difference on the continious charts. The continious charts are only suitable for medium to long term analysis.

In the end and initial periods, such as the end of December - March, the two contracts must be examined together. Volume and open interest should be tracked in which contracts and when the market passes (Eurex and CME future bond contracts).

Technical and macro analysis should be compatible. The effects of the macro factors we have discussed above and discussed in the rest of the report should be confirmed on the charts. If no verification can be made;

a) question mark should be put in,

b) the macro analysis should be returned,

c) the factors that may be news influences should be recalled,

d) if no harmonized result can be obtained on the chart (if verification can not be achieved). The question mark should be accompanied by an " achtung" next to be alarmed.

We did not find any inconsistency between the charts due to the fact that we detected in the German, French, Italian bonds that which expirations (December → March) would come to the forefront from the pivot in the previous week. When the scenarios that we expected were going on, the movements that we detected in the charts were realized.

Now respectively let' have a look to;

A) relationship of the German bond and other EU bonds,

B) some of the relations between Euro and macro data with 2, 5, 10, 30 year German bonds.

(I do not get into the details of our macro analysis details and technical analysis, as we use these reports for correlation analysis, ratio / spread etc.).

Let's examine A first, then B's (third choice)

1) German bonds; (in broad sense) followed the Italian, Spanish and even French bonds

and responded (in the north). German bonds have still survived the safe haven function. They are slow to participate in global bond sales.

2) German bond did not follow sales in US bonds (even in the case of minor sales to Japanese bonds). This is us; a) a short duration of the sale of US bonds after the Fed, or b) a sign that German bonds are under a separate factor effect from other bonds.

In these two cases (a and b);

a) is exogen (external), the second; b) is endogen (internal) factor.

3) I] The two-year German bonds passed strongly the top before the referendum, wiping out the summit down the road before the referendum in Italy. Possible reasons for this movement can be explained with a)the possible effect of new criteria for ECB purchase,

b) hedging against Euro short market,

c) use as a shelter against possible crisis in the euro area

We are eliminating 'c', 'a' choices: Although the ECB statement is theoretically open for German bonds, the ECB's target is the troubled southern EU countries. We got 'b' as option.

II] The 30-year-old German bond may have put an end to a strong trend (downward direction) starting from the September pivot. We take close monitoring with technical and correlation analyzes.

III] The 5-year German bond were rejected downward movement from the top before the Italian referendum. They act like two years. They stopped on the top before the referendum.

As a reslut of all the data and factors we have mentioned above, we established the strategy of this week as follows:

We will not be able to use these bonds for a week because December 30 Euro Bund options have been cancelled by Eurex (confirmed).

a) Our call short (call bear spread) closed out of money (expiration December 16, weekly options). Premium income is written.

b) Our December 23 call shorts are waiting out of money and near out of money (it is call bear spread, insured upwards),

c) On January 5 expiration date contract (because there is no 30 December), we sold out of money call (call bear spread)

d) We started call bear spreads in February (few)

e) 10 year positions, although hedged; 1) They receive calls in 5 years of German bonds and are taken into protection against upward attack by 2/5.

Summary; call short for 10 year bund (insured), call long for 5 year. These positions are edited in 2/5 ratio. A put bear spread was set up in the end of February, in response to the 5-year-old German bond moving down in the case of not reaching the top before the Italian referendum. The basics of all these processes are:

I) 10 years can rise gradually, which will be a sales (short) opportunity. The call for this preparation has been sold (I pass the answer to the question 'Why is it in different dates?' I'm going to answer it later). The technical levels are ours.

II)5 years was used in a row to move upwards and downwards (give premiums, join price movements) because they move faster and have a momentum of 2 years.

Separate expiration (options) for up and down directions were used in the 5-year position taking. The downward expiration contract (time, maturity) is more prolonged. This is because; a) the direction in our macro expectation is down,

b) Potential acceleration of the 5-year upward direction is only the potential for short-term emergence (macro + technical analysis result).

All positions were opened considering premium costs (premium loss / grant) during price fluctuations.

We would like to touch on our views on the relationship between German bills and macroeconomics and on the effect of our positions later.

December 26, 2016

This week, France, Italy 10 years (bonds) stay horizontally; partial purchases were observed in Germany and Spain 10 years (remember that we always mention about futures contracts). Switzerland and the British 10-year near the EU region also received minor purchases.

While German 30 years and 10 years move in parallel, 5 years are up and 2 years are down.

I have mentioned in the previous report that we expect upward technical action in the 5 years. In line with this expectation, we have taken a call long position (with a 10-year ratio, see our previous report for our 2/5 position).

Along with this movement, we completed the call bull spread by selling calls from the upper strike (with call long + call short). Thus, while maintaining an upward position, we partially repaid the premium we gave. In 5 years, call shorts and longs are opened at the same quantity.

Week of 10-year Bonds with monthly options expiration date (December 23, Friday); the next day after Monday's upward movement and downward trend was limited, we aimed to take advantage of the decreasing put premiums during the up-movement, sell at-the-money and near-out-money puts to balance our call short at-the-money positions and close in-the-money positions (calls).

Put positions opened at 3:5 call count. All put shorts were hedged in the same expiration by put longs (put bull spreads were established).

Since our call shorts mostly 163 to 163.5 strikes which were waiting since last week. On Thursday with the attacks under 163 we closed the call shorts partially by time decay. We get partial succes.

On Thursday and Friday, positions were closed (put and call options) based on the decay premiums (70% or more of the premium yield) (Friday is the time before the option end time).

10-year Bund (Euro-bund) closed at 163.66 (Friday), put shorts were successfully concluded at the 163.50 level we were targeting (they were sold out-the-money close on Tuesday).

On Thursday and especially Friday, new calls were sold on a 2 week wedge (as there was no weekly option on December 30). We are hedged with call-longs from the beginning of the week (before the possible upward movement before the price movement wasn't taken from the full reflection on the premiums).

We expect a flat / partial uptrend in the 10-year German bond, mainly in the 30-year bond (Buxl). For the next month, stagnation between 175 and 177 on a 30-year bond (March maturity contract) is the baseline scenario.

If we go above 180, our alternative reaction scenarios will come into play.

In the first week we mentioned briefly the macro data:

The rise observed in German inflation (consumer inflation) since April 2016 has settled in the last two or three months. Over the past few months, anticipations for new year headlines for inflation exceed expectations, even if they are minor, on top of this plateau.

Similar to France but with a lower inflation outlook (realization + anticipation).

While Italy's inflation is minus on zero axis, Dutch inflation is the image following Germany's inflation. Spanish inflation has made a partial jump in the last two months from zero levels and expectations are on the rise.

Finally; Sweden inflation, which we think may be a pioneer for the region but out of the region, has exceeded level 1 since the beginning of 2016 and is around 1.5. The expectation is that this high rate is to be protected.

If we touch briefly on the relations between the inflation of countries; Germany, the Netherlands are evaluated close. Sweden is a pioneer and a control. If France is close and parallel, buying bonds in the future will be at the forefront. We will also look at other countries and correlations we have seen for German inflation next year. We will touch on the inflation of large non-EU countries next week.

I would like to mention two news: This week, warning that the president of Bundesbank is approaching low interest rate and we should pay attention to the rhetoric of the ECB not to be late for interest rate hikes.

In Italy, we anticipate that the Italian government will be inaugurated in order to rescue the Monte Paschi bank. This approach, which is accepted by the EU as an implicit, we expect for the long term that it will open the way for bank risks to turn into public burden, which is the price of state bonds. In short and in medium term, it will be evaluated in positive direction.

In short, macro analysis and news flow confirm our expectation for now.

January 1, 2017

In the week before the beginning of the year, the German 10 year Bunds (Euro-Bund) were relatively active.

On Tuesday, December 27, it crossed the 164 level and crossed the pivot of the end of November. Thus, the effect of the movement that started at the end of October was removed. The way to the next target, 165-165.5 was opened. Unless otherwise stated, the mentioned strike shows the Euro Bund. For Euro Buxl, Bobl etc. we also write down the name of the bonds.

The 165-165.5 line is the bottom of two wave movements from September to October. On December 27 up moving we waited for Thursday, December 29, for call sales (call shorts).

When Euro-Bund was approaching 164.5, we sold the call from 164.5 and 165 strikes and on the other hand we sold at-the-money or close out-of-money puts from 163.5, 164 strikes.

Both put and call shorts were insured with put and call longs. We did all of these on weekly options, which will end on January 5. ¼ of the put shorts are also close out-of-money ones; covered with close in-the-money call shorts (strike covers each other).

We keep the call bull spread for 5 years Bobl. The correction, which came just above the 165.5 level on Friday, December 30, was volumeless.

In this short week in Italy and French 10 year bonds (we always talk about future) the horizontal upward trend continues.

Spain 10 years are moving closer to the German 10 years. German 30-year bonds stay horizontal Tuesday, December 27 and Thursday, December 29 at minor two top. They returned to the below of level 175 at Friday. It does not make much sense of a single day's non voluminous motion and we continue to monitor the 175 level as we did in the previous report.

January 9, 2017

On Monday, January 2, Eurex German bonds; Euro bund was traded. Seeing the level of 164.94 in the first half of the January 2 session, the Euro Bunds confirmed our January 2 report. In the second and third paragraphs of the report; "At 165 - 165.5, the front of the attack was opened, and this line is like bottom of two wave movements from September to October."

Again the same report; "When we were approaching 164.5, we sold calls from 164.5 and 165, and on the other hand we sold ATMs and nearby OTMs from 163.5, 164 strikes."

The price movement returned to 164.5 as of January 2 mid time and on the following day, January 3, after the first 2 hours, it broke 164.5 level (January 29, 30 peak level at the same time), it proceeded to south with a massive volume.

With the inflation rate higher than the expectations, we joined this downward movement with futures shorts (more than the put shorts in hand). 165-164.5 call shorts were closed with profit with a premium decay.

Again on January 3, during the attack on level 163, 162.5 strike put shorts was sold in options during the following week, corresponding the future shorts (covered put). We have again, the put option was sold (Monthly option expiration date on January 27) at 162 strike; put shorts (futures short covering covered put).

All futures shorts are hedged with call longs in same maturity (put short). In the same maturity, more far out-of-money calls have been bought for unexpected upwards prepared.

On the evening of January 3, 163.5 calls from the at-the-money were sold (with previous call longs hedged). Thus, 164 call shorts at hand and 163.5 and 164 strikes new call shorts (near term end on Friday, January 6) were targeted to receive premiums by decay time (decrease premium by time).

On January 4, 164 call shorts were closed with profit. On the same day, puts from near out-of-money in 5-year German bond were bought (put long). The puts taken in the next two months are intended to prepare for possible downward action.

Reasons for making preparations for a possible downward movement in five-year bond (Euro Bobl);

1) Failure of January 2 upwards

2) With the downward movement of January 3, the appearing of the pivot December 27 - January 2 and finally;

3) Approving the January 3 downward move with 'inside day' on January 4th.

On January 4 and 5, the remaining 163.5 and 164 put shorts from the previous week were closed: At-the-money and near in-the-money puts were closed; in return on January 13- January 20 and January 27, 162-162.5 strike puts were sold.

These transactions were made during daytime fluctuations (long-term and near-term premium increases, decreases was evaluated).

On January 5, 163.5 call shorts (expiration/maturity on January 6, weekly options) were closed with a profit on downward movement to 162.8 in the morning.

Also on January 5, the 5-year (Euro bobl) call bull spread we had set up was closed with a minor profit (not to lose a premium over time because of the downward pivot).

On January 6, two year bond, put longs were received (2 months ahead of contracts).

164 call longs held for insurance purposes and disabled by closing 163.5 calls were closed back at upward attack.

Friday evening at 163 level weekly closing justifies our downward position.

January 16,2017

This time we will begin the report with a weekly technical assessment:

At January 9, the Euro Bund were sold in on the first hour of Monday, showing a level of 162.5, but in the following hours the fast and steady upward movement lasted up to 163.5. The closing at the end of the day was above 163.20 despite the sales coming towards the 163 level. The following day, it was understood that when the level above 163 was maintained, the rest of the week would be upward intented.

The downward movement started on January 2 at the 165 pivot and ended with the closing on January 9. On January 12, first 3 hours 164.20 level has been touched. This attack was met at the level of 163.50 on January 12 and January 13 (04.30 PM to US retail sales figures).

At January 13, despite the strong and volatile sales following US retail data: Euro bund, in parallel to American bonds, it turned upward and closed just above the week 163.50. In the above paragraph, we indicate the level of 163.20 as support for January 9-10 the first half of January 11. From the short review of week we get:

1) The Euro Bund movement respects the technical level, but is highly volatile.

2) Germany 10 year – Us 10 year bonds correlation is strong.

If we evaluate with the movements in the previous weeks; while sales to the Euro Bund are sudden and voluminous, purchases are stable and relatively low volume.

Macro data we think will affect the Euro Bund in the coming week came in line with our positions and in excess of the general expectations. As an example, Germany full year GDP had higher than expected and wholesale were well above expectations. Spain, France, Italy, the Netherlands, Sweden and Denmark's industrial production were higher than expectations.

Sweden, Czech Republic, Norwegian inflation, higher than expectations (also Czech retail sales). We consider Czech datas to be a pioneer for Germany. We use Swedish data, mainly the Netherlands and Denmark, for control purposes in upward and downward deviation in German data. Expectations in datas showing upwards economic activity in the past weeks are upwards in the direction of our position (also our macro expectancies) and general expectations are higher, but we may have increased risk of normalization this week. This week the inflation data will be on the foreground.

If we take our positions; 162.5 put shorts; on the weekly January 13 (expiration), with upward trend towards the week earlier, are closed with high premium income. In January 20 (3rd week option) and January 27 (monthly) option contract corresponding to these closing positions, we sold 162 puts (covered puts, covered futures shorts).

On January 11 and January 12:

1) With the upward movement, January 20 (put on the 3rd week option), we got 162 strike put short premiums and were closed early.

2) Some of the 162 puts, dated January 27 expiration, were closed with premium profits.

3) In the June option (on the monthly), bear put spread was established. The bear call spread was set up at the same maturity to get the premium back.

In the downward direction, we started taking positions for April (we expect the actual downward movement from late March to early May) to wait for the actual movement.

In Euro Bobles, short future with hedge opened with call long. In addition to the call long hedges that we have taken against the upcoming attack on January 12-13, the call bull spreads in the 2nd maturity have been hedged in addition to futures shorts for possible upward movement (with forward maturity and close strike).

On February 24, 161 and 161.5 strike put shorts were sold and premiums were received instead January 13 contract on of 162-162.5 strikes put shorts (reminded that they were covered puts) closed with weekly profits.

Taking put longs for the lower level of 160.5; during the possible deep downward movement, the covered puts were prevented from covering/restricting the futures short profit.

This week, January 12 and January 9, pivots will be followed in the technical sense. For the macro economy, German inflation and the January 19 ECB meeting will be followed.

January 22, 2017

In the last paragraph of the last report, technically; We mentioned that the pivots of January 12 and January 9 will be followed. In terms of macroeconomics, we said that Germany's inflation and the January 19 ECB meeting will be followed. Again, we noted in the report macro economic datas that in the past weeks which they have exceeded expectations in the positive direction.

Datas in the EU countries came in the direction of expectations, with a few exceptions. German inflation also rose as expected.

After the ECB meeting, the response to Draghi's questions about strong economic data and in particular the question of inflation whether could open or not open the door to tapering, was negative. In the meeting, he said that this issue did not come to the agenda, and the expectations were already in this direction. After emphasizing that the inflation is weighted heavily with energy, it does not see the desired increase in the core, then it sets the threshold for the perception of the inflation increase as a signal for tapering: medium-term stability, limited return, regionwide prevalence, continuity on its own.

Despite the comments of Draghi, the Euro-Bunds broke the bottom on January 19 after half a session. Moreover, they realized this, with accelerating beyond correlations with US bills. From here we draw the conclusion that the Euro-Bunds are willing to downward.

If we go back to macro perspective; we continue to think that there is time for the actual downward movement (in the previous reports, we gave the interval we expected for the start time of the downward movement).

Technically, if we consider last week; the January 12 pivot, which we mentioned, was tested on January 17. When the level was rejected in the morning session, the closing was done due to the day's fall. During the next 3 days experienced a strong turn-down by down the pivot. This downward movement justified us to draw attention to the January 12 pivot.

Pivot 2, the pivot on January 9, was attempted by downward on the close of the option market on Friday. But January 20, the close of the week was on the exact pivot (162.5 level).

Correlation with US bonds could be strengthened this week because of Trump's speech and first week of presidential.

Now let's take a look at the transactions we made last week: On January 13, February 24 expiration contract, we sold 2 puts from 162.5 strike (covered with future short). We also got 3 puts from 160.5 in the same expiration/term.

So when putting premiums on put shorts, if 160 strike technical level breaks, we were in the down position as well. We left the put longs back empty, so we can take back the premium in whole or in part by selling put shorts (3 put short + 3 put long) with increasing premiums during possible down movement.

We also got calls from the near OTM strike the 3 contract in the same maturity/term (with the other call short leg). We received, set up a bull spread, and protected the futures shorts (the guard calls we received in the beginning are forward looking, but these calls are left on the OTM strike with downward movement) .

Again on January 13; in January 27 expiration contract are closed 162.5 puts and 161.5 puts we had previously sold with premium profit. We have covered the futures shorts, which have been borned with them, with the February 24 maturity put shorts we mentioned in the previous paragraphs. We took care to do this in a way that would be advantageous during daytime fluctuations.

On January 18 and January 19 we closed 164 and 164.5 strikes call shorts, which we previously sold in the January 27 (expiration date contract) with high premium profits.

I set up a bull call spread with the near OTM calls January 27 (expiration date contract) in order to hedge the profit of the future short (call long, call short). So we took a profit to protect against turning up from January 9 162.5 pivot.

Again on January 19, 2 put long (161.5 strike) with increase in premiums, which we bought earlier, with a maturity of January 27 was closed.

On February 27 expiration contract, we sold 3 puts from 159 strike (put bear spread was established). A premium income of 159 strike put shorts meets same expiration contract which were bought 160.5 strike puts (puts long + put short= put bear spread).

On January 19 put sold at 160 strike. 160 strike put short was covered at on February 24 by the futures short that had been idle from the previous week.

Our principle in all these transactions is; we have been positioned for January 9 162.5 level pivot in case of exceeding, in two directions.

On January 20, two put shorts, previously sold on 161.5 strike (on February 24 maturity), have been moved to 160 strike levels. Next week, EU territory PMI and consumer confidence and Germany IFO data will be followed. As we noted on previous pages, the first week of Trump may be correlated with US bonds. However, in the past week, the Euro Bunds should not forget that their internal dynamics show their power by moving beyond US bonds.

January 1, 2017

We have stated that the Euro-Bunds are in a strong downward trend anda re moving the past week are moving momentum beyond their correlations with US bonds. The strong downward trend that began on morning Tuesday January 24, (161.33 was seen twice), came close to 161 level,this level is multi-bottoms at the end of November – begining of December. The higher than US bonds momentum movement by Euro Bund, evolved into a close/near correlation with US bonds towards the end of Thursday's session. The week closed to 162 level with some reaction up. We mentioned last week's report in the 8th and last paragraph of the report that it could draw attention to the strong internal dynamics of the Euro-Bunds and strengthen the correlation with US bonds. As a result; The Euro-Bunds made the move we had expected.

From a macro point of view, European PMI data is strong. Germany's inflation has risen far above expectations. Although Euro region datas have come at rates that exceed anticipated inflation expectations, IFO and consumer, business confidence datas have come storong while some has come weak; Italy's same macro datas came weaker than expected.

In contrast to the Draghi discourse of the previous week, some of the members emphasize that"enough macro environment appeared to begin tapering".

Let's take a brief look at what we did last week:

On the morning of January 24; a call was sold short from 163.5 answer to strike for 163 call longs (to hedge futures shorts) bought from the previous week and a call long from 164 strike with falling premiums;

A) a portion of premiums for 163 call longs, were taken by 163.5 call shorts.

B) The call long was made with a low premium payment from 164, and insurance was purchased for possible upward movement. The previous week, preparations were made for both directions, arguing that two-way action is possible because the monthly options (January 27) will be finalized. The amount of premiums paid for the preparations made with the premium costs before the attacks of option pain was taken back.

Our main anticipation was that while the main position we took for the downside was maintained, the futures short, which was transformed from the previous week's puts, was sold to the nearby OTM strike and have premiums. For this futures short, for the other side (for insurance), the position was taken with the nearest OTM strike call bull spread + OTM call long. This combined position successfully closed the week (January 27) with a profit of the week (future short + put short + bull call spread + call long).

In the previous weeks, 165 strike call longs (for hedging futures shorts) were closed (on February 24 expiration contract). Thus, it was tried to withdraw the premiums before the downward trend, that started on January 24. On the same day, in the 24th of February expiration contract the call bull spread was established with 164 call longs and 166 call shorts (as futures shorts). Before this possible downward movement:

a) 165 call long premiums were retrieved,

b) upwards direction which is little possibility, insured (in terms of time and price) with bull call spread (paying lower premium).

In the Euro Bobl February 24 expiration contract, which was bought put longs in previous weeks, put shorts were sold in the first half of Thursday, January 26th. Thus, by establishing bear put spreads:

a) The premiums of previous put longs have been partially or completely recovered.

b) Since puts received nearby OTM to previous weeks are in-the-money, new put shorts have allowed higher prime. Thus, the total cost is reduced by spread.

As a result; our position and predictions for the previous week were realized last week, so we watched calmly the profits our positions.

Let's share our technical anticipation earlier this week: As we have seen from the Euro-Bund and Euro Buxl, consolidation is possible for a period of repetitive November-December price levels.

Downward-sloping consolidation expectation to be more likely, following the partial option pain-like move that took place on the last two days of January 27 (with increasing correlation with US bonds) although we expect upward trend.

We can build bull bear spreads in possible upward reactions. We can close put shorts that we have traded in the previous weeks (future shorts) with profits with falling premiums.

This week has a loaded agenda in terms of macroeconomic data. We will pay attention to the core inflation when the FOMC meeting, the European region's inflations datas are followed. Again PMI data will be monitored. On the last day of the week, hourly wages will be watched with the euro retail sales and US employment data.

Trump's taxation speech to Mexico should be watched carefully for the possibility of spreading to other countries for the coming period. Such a possibility leads to turbulence.

February 4, 2017

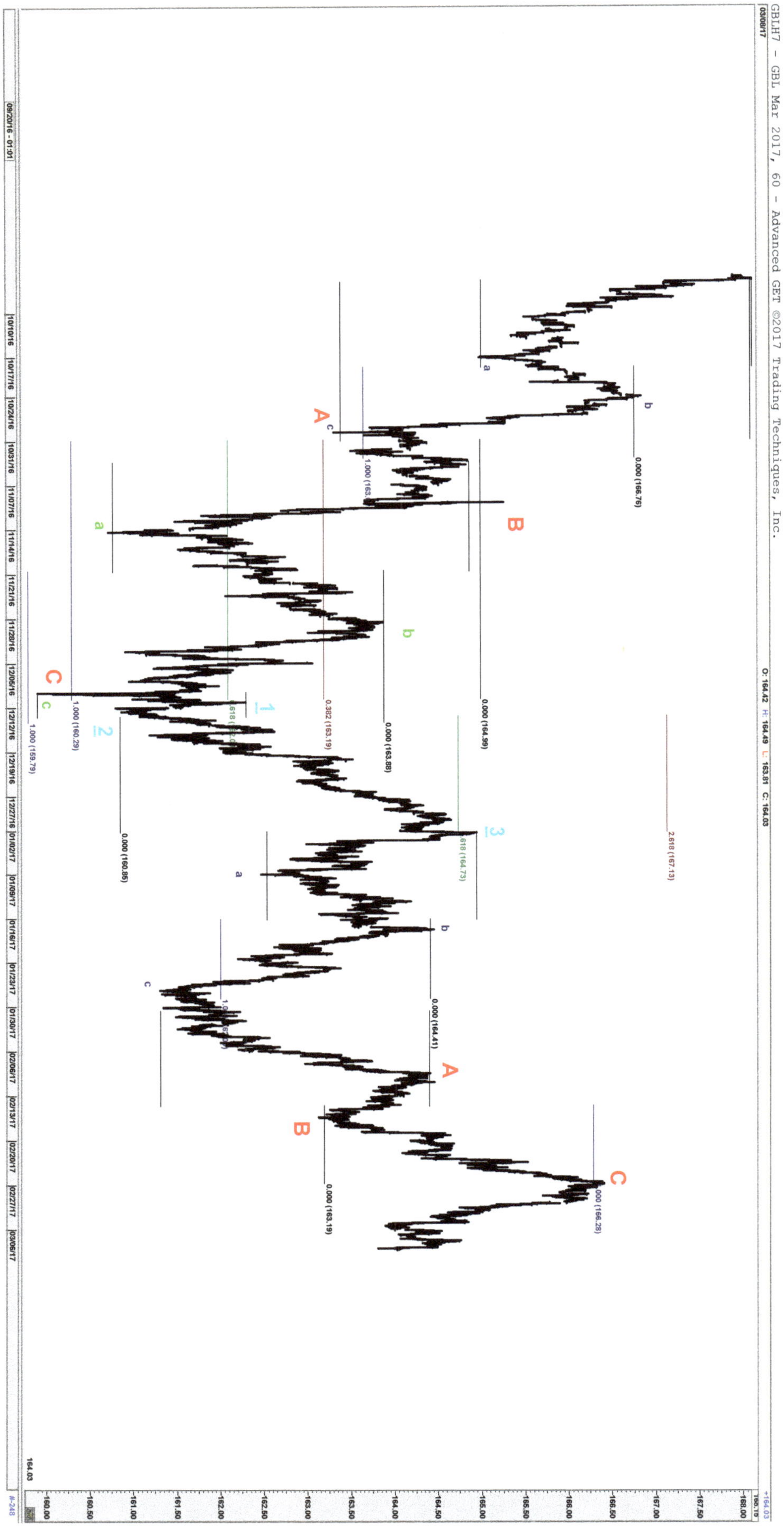

In the 60-minute period of the chart, the future contract of 10-year German bond is seen.

Technical analysis was performed with Elliott wave count and Fibonacci ratios.

The downward movement, starting at level 168, was found at the bottom of 165 level in the middle of November (small a). The reaction from here is ending at 166.76 (small b). When the "a" wave length is subtracted from the price level "b", the c wave target is set at around 163.90.

At the end of October, this level was reacted upwards. On the first top that formed from this reaction, the price level was tried twice and step by step was turning towards downward trend. The second upward movement (beginning of November) is a single bar movement with a gap. For this reason we chose the first peak (top) as a stronger point for the B wave (red big B).

The price of 160.29 is determined as the C target (red big C) when the movement with red big A is removed from that level. This target will be approached in mid-November first and then in early December.

In the middle of November, the green color "a" wave height will be subtracted from when the wave of "b" in the end of November. We find "c" (green color) wave at 159.79 level. This level will be reached at the beginning of December.

Thus, from the end of September, the downward movement has been defined by three waves intertwined.

- Big red ABC
- Small abc
- Small green abc

In all of these waves, 1X1 size movements have occurred.

In the ABC motion, AB = BC, and counting from 3 waves of C wave is irregular. This happens in instruments that move at short intervals, such as bonds.

The rise starting from the beginning of December is shown in blue color and with 1,2,3. 3 waves long lasted and continued as the 1.618 of the first wave (approaching the 165 level).

At the end of December, the downward correction (small gray a, b, c) occurred just below the level (wave target) found by subtracting wave "a" from wave "b", c wave ended.

At the end of January (big red A, B, C) an upward direction begins, the A wave adding to the B wave reaches to C wave will end at 166.28.

In the analysis carried out over this entire period, the 1X1 wave length gave the price targets exactly except for the one exception (1,618).

Strategy:

In my last report, we stated that "In the Euro-Bund and Euro-Buxl, there may be consolidation for some time at the end of November - early December" and "We see consolidation with upward tendency more likely".

After the horizontal consolidation from Monday January 30 to February 1 Wednesday, the two-day consolidation period was spent on upward-direction consolidation.

The past week's macro data was mixed. While non-German EU data is relatively strong, Friday's data on US wages did not meet expectations.

The Euro-Bunds followed in part Euro-Bobl and Euro-Schatz, drawing closer to upward-sloping consolidation, while Italy and France were eagerly down in the Euro-Buxl for 10 years.

Before the presidential election in France, claim of corruption about Fillon's wife, Le Pen came to the forefront in recent polls, creating a partial uneasiness.

On the US side, 10-year bonds entered a slightly upward-sloping consolidation. The FED's comments interpreted "the pigeon", markets were influenced by Trump's and his team's unusual style in the middle of the week. Friday's lower-than-expected wage rates led the market.

Spent on expectations of infrastructure expenditures and tax deductions were delayed:

a) The Congress has announced the earliest of the tax cuts will be in the spring.

b) It is expected that the first explanations for infrastructure expenditures will be made at Abe - Trump meeting in mid - February.

However, there are also political observers pointing out that Trump's extraordinary management approach could, lead some tax cuts by the "presidential decree".

What have we done this week?

Taking into consideration the possibility of an upwards movement in the morning session on January 31; 3/5 of call short's leg of the bear call spreads, which were established about 1 month ago in order to cover the premium cost of the June contract (same expiration date) bear put spread; it is closed with profit.

Again the same number of calls were sold from the upper strike (with the old call longs hedged). Thus, when significant premium income is obtained from call bear spread, the margin that can be encountered in case of possible loss is reduced (distance between the strikes). In a short expression; more narrow spread was established.

On Friday, February 3, after the US employment data, Euro-Bund and Euro-Bobl futures shorts were closed with profit.

I also remind you that we established a bull call spread to hedge futures shorts in previous weeks when futures shorts are closed;

a) The call's short wing of the spread was also closed with premium profit.

b) So that nearbly OTM strike calls were sold referring to call longs wich was previously taken (in March maturity).

With these operations, our call bull spread has been returned to the call bear spread for getting premium.

In the new call bear spread we sold the call from the difference strike. We determined the sales levels corresponding to the strike by technical analysis (price and time analysis).

We also set up a bear call spread by selling calls from the ATM strike in the near expiration contract (1 week remaining) and taking calls from nearby OTM.

Based on previously covered put shorts and bear put spreads, we established new advanced option strategies.

When futures shorts are closed;

a) The put short foot of the bear put spread was closed with premiums falling by the rising price and time, and the profit was written.

b) The puts were sold on and under this strike, with the long puts of the bear put spread being the middle wing. Thus premium income was aimed. Since this strategy is a modified leveraged short put butterfly, it will be partly profound the downside and the profit will increase.

Since all call and put spreads prices distance are short and the potential loss is small.

As a result; On the March futures contract, which will end on February 24 (maturity/term), we have revised our position based on a large horizontal consolidation (expectation) area in Euro-Bund. In the last weeks when time decay has accelerated we have turned to premium income (remember that future shorts are already closed with profit).

The put bear spreads in Euro-Bobl, gradually established (in terms of time and price) in previous weeks, were closed with very little loss. As noted at the beginning of the report, I will also point out that the future short Euro-Bobl has been closed with profit.

This week is relatively light in terms of economy. In the US, we will carefully monitor Trump and his team's unconventional management mentality to disturb the market. Normally the markets reflect the reactions to the political styles in the medium term. If this reaction is carried to the near term, it means a real discomfort.

February 12, 2017

Last week was weak in terms of economic data. Economic data with relatively few importance came mixed; A little weaker than anticipated in Germany and France, stronger than anticipated in Italy ...

On the political side, it was clear that Fillon's increasing scandals would leave Macron and Le Pen alone in the second round. If Fillon resist withdrawing his nomination, the prospects of Le Pen's victory, which could get a vote beyond the polls in Macron-Le Pen competition, are partly a worry for the markets.

The comments of Trump who meets with the Japanese prime minister, who spoke on the telephone with the Chinese president, and the comments of the Chinese president after the phone interview, dropped his trade wars' rhetoric on the market agenda for the time being.

When we examine the news flow in terms of market psychology; We noted that on February 9, the CAC40 index had almost no response downward to the nuclear power plant explosion in France. As there was no downward movement for an hour after the news, the probability of closing upward was much higher. The market, which did not respond to bad news, closed up with the day as we expected. I came across a similar incident and market reaction after September 11, 2001. After the attack on the airport in France, the CAC 40 turned upside.

The US reversed the rise in the US 10 year bond (we always talk about the future), the same day but later in the day, after the meeting with officials of Trump's aviation companies, "we can bring tax adjustments that will sound after 2-3 weeks".

What did we do last week?

Once we closed the futures shorts in Bund in the previous week with profit, we said we were selling two-way (up and down) options in the wake of a broad band spreads. Again, in the previous week's report, we stated that these spreads were set in very narrow ranges (chained and transformed option strategies).

Euro Bunds, which were on the trend line at 162.5 levels last week, turned upwards. We finished the week; with 163.5 strike the majority call shorts and 164 strike call longs, in-the-money position.

During this ascension, our put bull spreads on the other side and our "leveraged short put Butterfly" positions were closed with profit.

Now let's write the operations in day order:

1) On February 6 OGB2 maturity options (weekly), with 164 call long, 163 call short, 163 put short, 162 long; a long iron butterfly was established.

2) The short put butterfly that was set up the previous week was changed with the rising prices:

a) 160 strike put shorts were closed with profit, and 161.5 put shorts were sold to their places.

b) Thus the put bull spread was established, keeping the mid feet of the short put butterfly.

3) On February 7, the OGB3 expiration contract (13 days remaining weekly option)

164.5 call long, 163.5 call short

With 163.5 put short, 162.5 put long iron condor was esthablished.

4) On February 7, 162.5 put in OGB2 were closed with profits, and 163 put were sold in place. Thus, rising prices were monitored and decay premiums were utilized.

5) Again, based on the 164.5 call long position, taken on February 6; took advantage of the rising prices and sold the call from 163.5(at the OGB2 contract).

6) On February 8, the 161.5 strike put shorts and 161 strike put shorts at the monthly maturity contract, were closed with a profit with high premium income.

Thus, within 4 to 5 business days with rising prices, 4 chained strategies were established and they were renewed with profit.

161 strike put longs are still protected. We intend to use them with option pain, which is expected to begin until February 15-16.

7) Going daownward OGB3 in the maturity contract (weekly 3) with 165 call long, 164 call short and

164 put short, 163 put long; long iron condor was established.

8) The long iron condor 's put short in the previously established OGB2 was closed with high premium profit. Put long was held against the possibility of a down attack (OTM was completed, since Thursday's afternoon after the US 10 year bond downgrade did not reflect on the Bunds).

As a general principle, we often hold the long option, which has a very low premium. The reasons for this are:

A) Since the resale does not generate excess premium income,

B) To use for the possible attack in the relevant direction, as a long (as future) or spread etc. to use for.

9) Covered 162 strike short put (monthly maturity) were closed with high premium profit.

The same strike put sold at the end of the maturity (February 24, monthly) when the insured call long position (which has insured covered short put's future short) strike is

ATM. Thus, a new flat covered put strategy (horizontal) was created. Against the future short we used in this strategy, the 4th put short was opened in the last 1 month.

Let's formulate this final strategy: (put short + future short) + call long

Put short and call long are on the same strike and are currently ATM.

10) On February 10, a wing of long iron condor in OGB2 was moved to OGB3:

164 call short, 165 call long; 164 call short when ATM strike, 165 call long is nearby OTM.

Again in the OGB3 expiration date, 164.5, the downward hedged position was taken with call long + future short.

On February 7 last week, BOE's announcement of 'we can increase interest' has not been priced even during the day. Bundesbank, between Weidmann's line of speech; the message that "inflation is under the target in a sustainable way was noteworthy for the fact that this comment overlapped the ECB rhetoric, although it did not find much in market commentary.

For next week, Italy, Netherlands, Germany GDP, Germany-UK inflation figures, Germany ZEW index will be followed on Tuesday.

Spanish inflation, UK unemployment, US retail sales, industrial production and inflation figures will be followed on Wednesday, February 15.

In 10 year Bonds; the participation of the Bunds has been weak as of Friday closing for the formation of a downward pivot in BTP; US bond, Gilt's and even Minor OAT . 164.80-165 is the important line in the upward direction. Rising on this line may indicate a significant change in the market.

According to Option Pain, it is possible to begin partial downwarding until February 15-16.

The intraday Bund movements for Thursday, Friday are not harmonic. This has also manifested itself with ineffective price movements and formations. According to the daily chart generated from the Intraday data (end of the day's chart is different so we emphasize the difference), the price movement is unstable and uncertain for downward attacks.

February 19, 2017

Last week, Germany's GDP inflation and ZEW indices came low or expected level. European data are mixed, on the US side, strong sales figures and inflation, even the Philadelphia Fed index has reached record highs in the last 33 years. Despite the strengthening of hard and soft data on the US side in 10 year bond; after Abe-Trump interview, the direction turned upside (aside downward direction with breaking of the bottom).

The following week, on February 28, Trump's anticipation of bringing the tax package and infrastructure program to the public during the speech in front of the congress, and the anticipation that this program and package will try to pass customs tax proposal in the income statement to receive congressional support will create anxiety. Trump's management style has not made content and not planning the legal for the promised reforms causing turmoil in the market.

On the latest third paragraph of our report last week, we mentioned that the Euro Bund is weaker for downward direction than other countries' treasuries. Same report, latest second paragraph; " start of a partial downward direction until February 15-16," we also said.

As we said, on the evening of February 14, the downward movement started and this movement was partial.

On the evening of February 14, the level was down to 163.70 (± 5, 10 points). This level has been tried 2 times on February 10, 2 times on February 13, 2 times on February 14 and not break. Again, on February 7 , it was also on the top (see the additional green horizontal line and the roundabout).

After the descent of 163.70, there was 163.20 (± 5, 10 points) level. On February 14 and February 15 three attacks were made. The first two of these attacks consisted of breaking the 163.70 level and the second try of level (163.20); The attack on February 15 occurred with the effect of news / data (see additional first red down arrow). Despite technical and even news / data influences, the first nail bottom ended in 30 minutes, (breaks 163.70), the second nail bottom ended in 10 minutes. The third attack break lasted only 10 minutes, resulting in a double bottom. So the down waves are not strong and they are getting weaker.

The market has recovered immediately from this level each time, with 50% of the first wave decline, 61.8% of the second, and the 100% of 3rd wave decline recovered in a short time.

a) Lower attacks are short-lived and relatively simple.

b) Not much time has passed in the bottoms.

c) Upward recovery is getting stronger.

d) The attacks made by technique and basic reasons did not give a different result.

We started to observe the rising bottoms from February 15.

On February 16, the single-bar downstroke, which came with strong US data, was quickly recaptured (see, down red 2nd. arrow).

In the following hours, the complex downward attack towards the bottom, which was formed by US data, upward trend probability increases as a result of the second bottom.

As you might remember; in the last paragraph of my previous week report, "Intraday Bund movements for Thursday, Friday are not harmonic. This has also manifested itself with ineffective price movements and formations ... the price movement is indeterminate for undecided and downward attacks ".

The fuzzy, failed attacks that occurred in the middle of the week were the result, the possibility for the upward direction was strengthened after the session on February 16.

In the morning session on Friday, February 17, the last withdrawal lasted until 163.60, only in the first hour. The movement starting from here (see technical graph, up turquoise coloured arrow) quickly overturned pass the level of 163.70, confirming the upward direction.

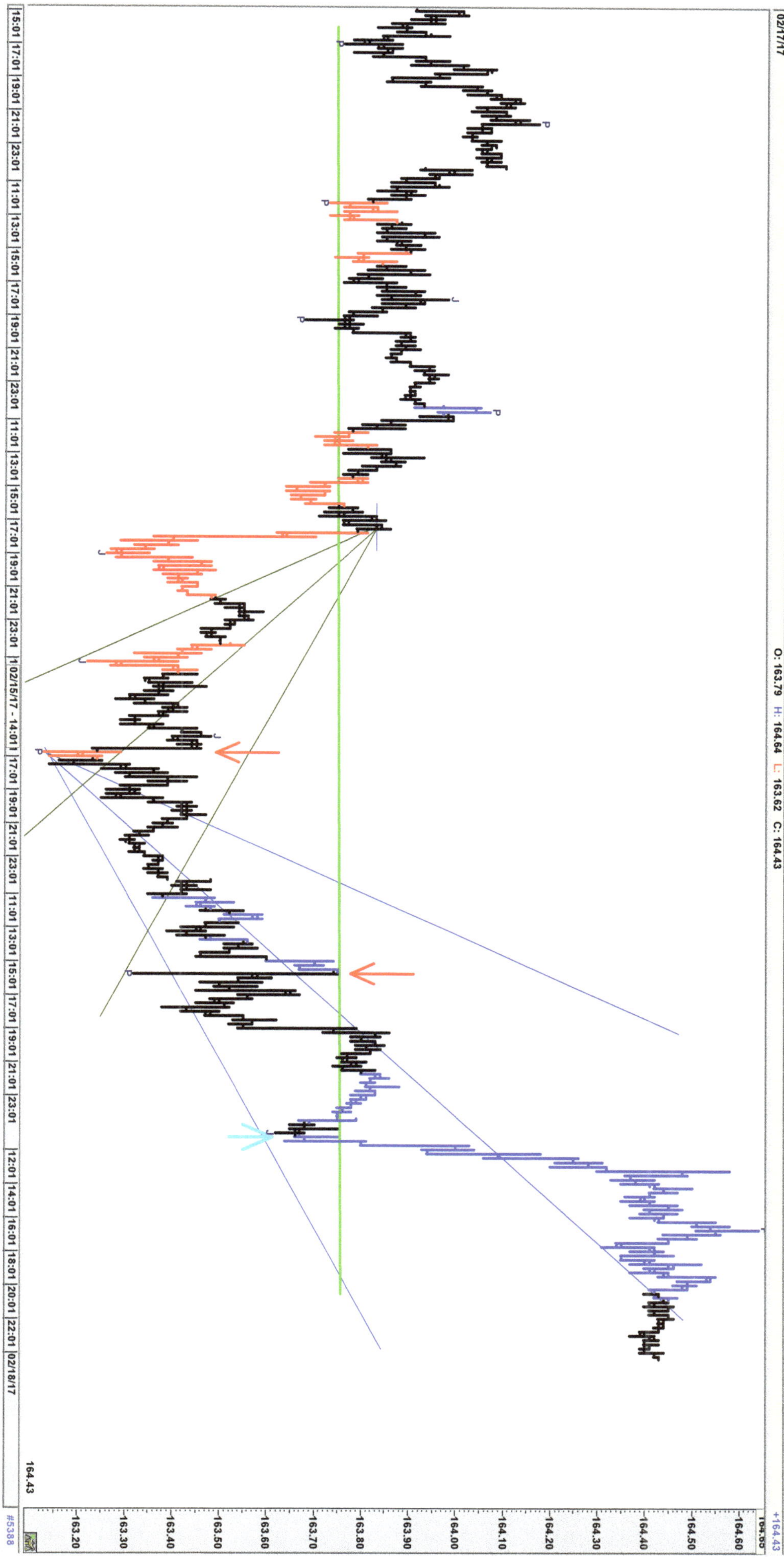
GBLH7 - GBL Mar 2017, 15 - Advanced GET ©2017 Trading Techniques, Inc.
O: 163.79 H: 164.64 L: 163.62 C: 164.43

In the previous page, technical analysis study (15 minutes bar), we examine the price movements, with Gann angles; down yellow angles show downward direction, blue angles Show up direction and all drawn at the same ratio/proportion (time/price).

1x1 angle which was drawn from the intraday pivot on February 14 for the downward direction and 1x2 angle on the two sides describe the important part of the movements; the last part of February 14 session and the February 15 session.

At February 15, in attack of level 163.13 (P pivot), the 1x1 angle was passed, but soon afterwards it turned over. At the end of the session, the right 1x2 angle was reached, signifying that the downward direction power lost.

The closing on the 1x2 at the end of February 15 session and the support of this angle at opening on February 16, the next day, the upward direction became clear at the end of the first hour.

Now consider the angle drawing at 163.13 (P) pivot: During the ascension between the 1x1 and 1x2 blue angles starting from the February 15 pivot (163.13), the downward trend pointing with the red down arrow, overturning from yellow downward trend 1x2 angle is proof of completely rejection.

The rise movement from February 15 pivot, continued between 1x1, 1x2 blue ascending Gann angles until the end of the first hour of February 17. On February 17, with the pivot pointed by the open turquoise-colored up arrow, the price movement touch the 1x2 angle, accelerated upwards like an expanding triangle and rose to almost 90 degrees.

As a result; by taking advantage of Gann's angles, we can say that after the first hour of February 16, the rise movement began. After the first hour of February 17, the rise was confirmed with Gann's angle or classical technical analysis.

As we recall what we did:

We closed all short futures at 162.5 level in the previous week. As a statistic in Euro-Bund; it is observed that the approaching option contract expiration date, strengthens the upward tendency together with the approaching futures contract expiration date. We had 163.5 strike majority call shorts and 163.5, 163 strike put shorts (we had iron condors consisting of bull put spreads and bear call spreads), with 164 strike call long limited. This strategy detailed in previous reports.

We still had 164 and 163.5 strike, mid-leg condors in the OGB3 contract (at the end of Friday, February 17).

During the down attack on Wednesday, February 15, we closed 164 and 163.5 call shorts at the OGB3. When the wings were closed with a decreasing premium, the call longs (164.5 strike) were kept. Put wings (short and long feet) were kept on hand.

Based on the future short, which was opened for the OGB3 maturity (we anticipate a possible partial downgrade until February 15-16, we wrote the report in last week), we sold put at 163 strike, near 163 level. Covered put short strategy was established. On February 16, 163 put shorts were closed. The covered put short strategy was revised by selling put at 163.5 strikes.

When the retraction of 163.60 in the morning of February 17 failed in the first hour, all positions not restricted to 164 strike call longs were closed. These are the June maturity/ term, bear put spreads and call bear spreads that were opened in previous weeks.

The Friday term weekly contract OGB3s, condors, ended on February 17 (in the previous paragraph, I mentioned call wings).

Condors with February 24 maturity are limited to 164 strike call longs. The put and call wings of these narrow / short condors will end on February 24. While the optimum equilibrium points are 163.5, the upward direction limit values are established to 164 strike calls. These strategies are equal wings lenght and wings lenght in two directions same with premium incomes value (premium incomes is equal lenght wing) .

As a result; exceeding in the up or down direction does not cause damage, or even profit. However, the departure from the optimal balance strike causes the highest profit to decrease.

Again, on February 24, 164 call long + 164 put short + 1 future short, the modified short put strategy will also end with profit (this strategy is profitable in every case since it is chained. We wrote detail in previous reports).

March 6, 2017

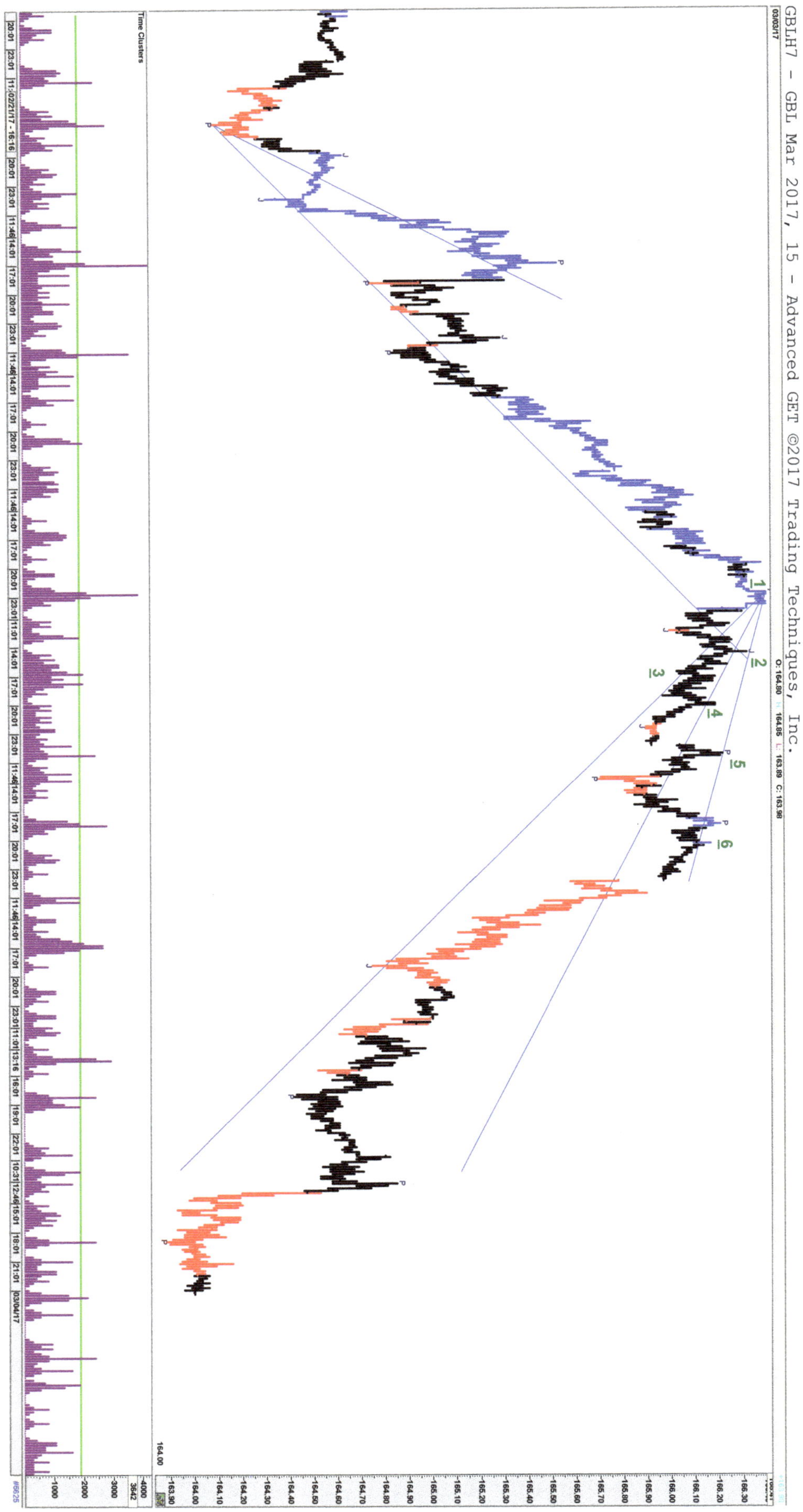
GBLH7 - GBL Mar 2017, 15 - Advanced GET ©2017 Trading Techniques, Inc.
Time Clusters

Euro Bund March maturity analysis on 15-minute chart, Gann angle from P pivot on February 21, pass through down direction; on the morning of February 27 with sales coming from the pivot 1. Again, Gann angle which broke the same day, tried to return with two pull backs, but pivot 2 was the last attempt.

The Gann angles drawn from the 1 pivot, are subject to the same parameters as those drawn from the P pivot. 1 pivot on February 27 and the pivot points 2, 3, and 4 were tried on the same day and their verifications were verified with the Gann angles.

The next day, on the morning of February 28, the attack on the 5th pivot (P) was unsuccessful. Downward positions were taken after the afternoon of the February 28 (with local time of Turkey): Although acceleration was cut in the downward direction, in mid time, but later on as the effort to remain under the angle (1x1 angle, passing through 1 and 4) and acceleration of downward mouvement.

On March 3, 162.5 put longs were purchased. On March 10, 162.5 put long -161.5 put short and put bear spread were established. The underlying asset of such options is the Euro-Bund contract with a maturity of June.

We made the technical analysis through the regular / uninterrupted March maturity contract which is active and historical data. On February 28, the difference between these two contracts was around -3.5. The June maturity was 162.5, while the March futures contract was at 166. On the same day (Feb. 28, 2017), the two attacks that were made in the upward direction at the end of the option process and at the time of the US session also returned from the Gann angle (P and 6).

The next morning; the morning session on March 1, was opened with a downward gap.

March 10

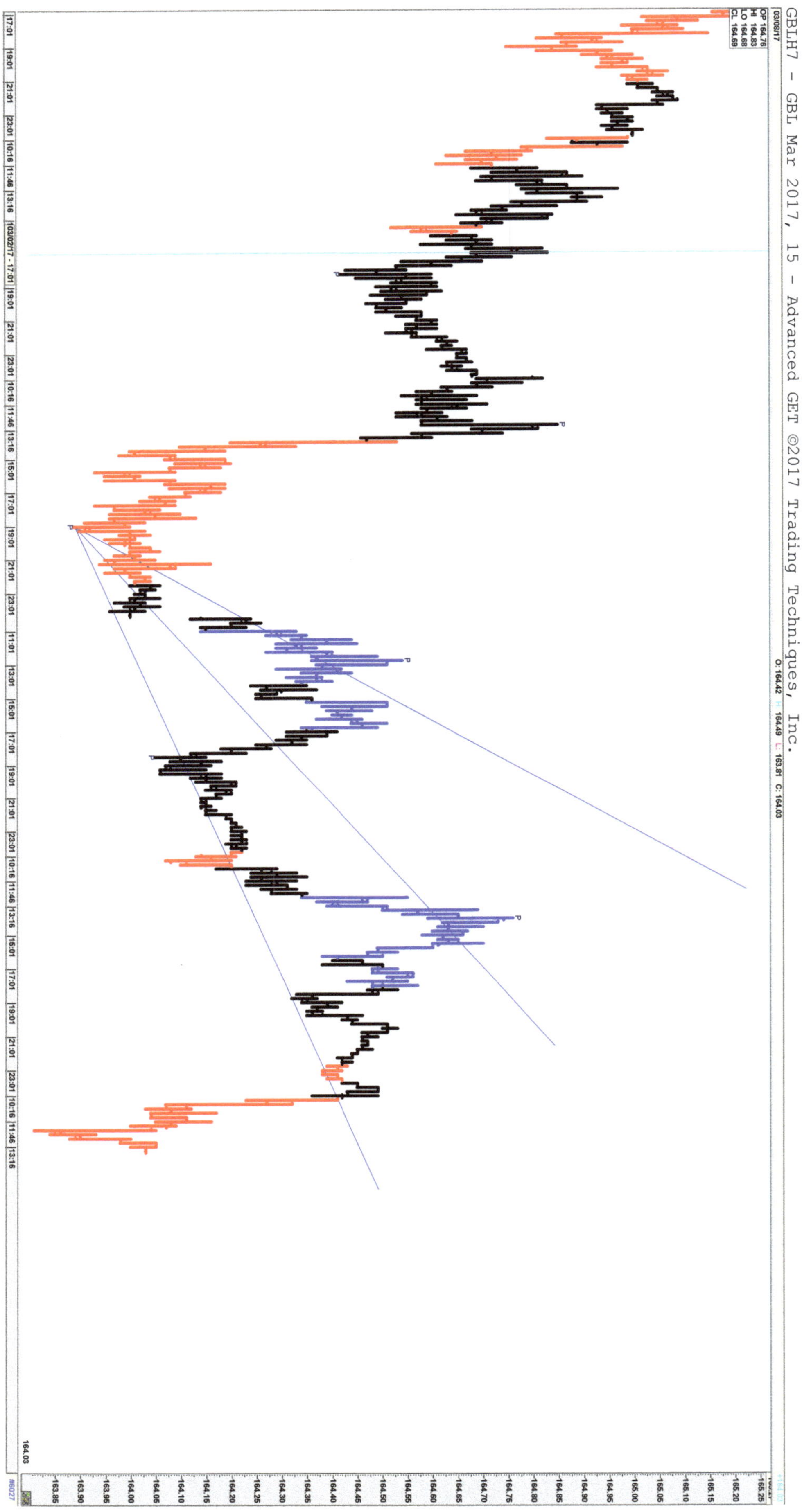
GBLH7 - GBL Mar 2017, 15 - Advanced GET ©2017 Trading Techniques, Inc.

On 3 March maturity/term the long put option was closed with profit. In the morning session on March 7, put bear spread was closed on March 10 maturity.

In the same maturity, it was aimed to receive premiums by establishing a bear call spread with 162 call shorts and 163 call longs. A higher call sales at 162 strikes were also recorded with anticipation of an upcoming attack. The intraday upward attack closed on the 1x1 Gann's angle with one bar. The following bars oscillated around the angle. Continued movement returned to 1x2 angle. 1x2 angle continued to support, but on March 8 this angle was broken.

On March 10, our bear call spread was completed with profit.

March 27, 2017

Euro Bund June Maturity, 15 Minutes

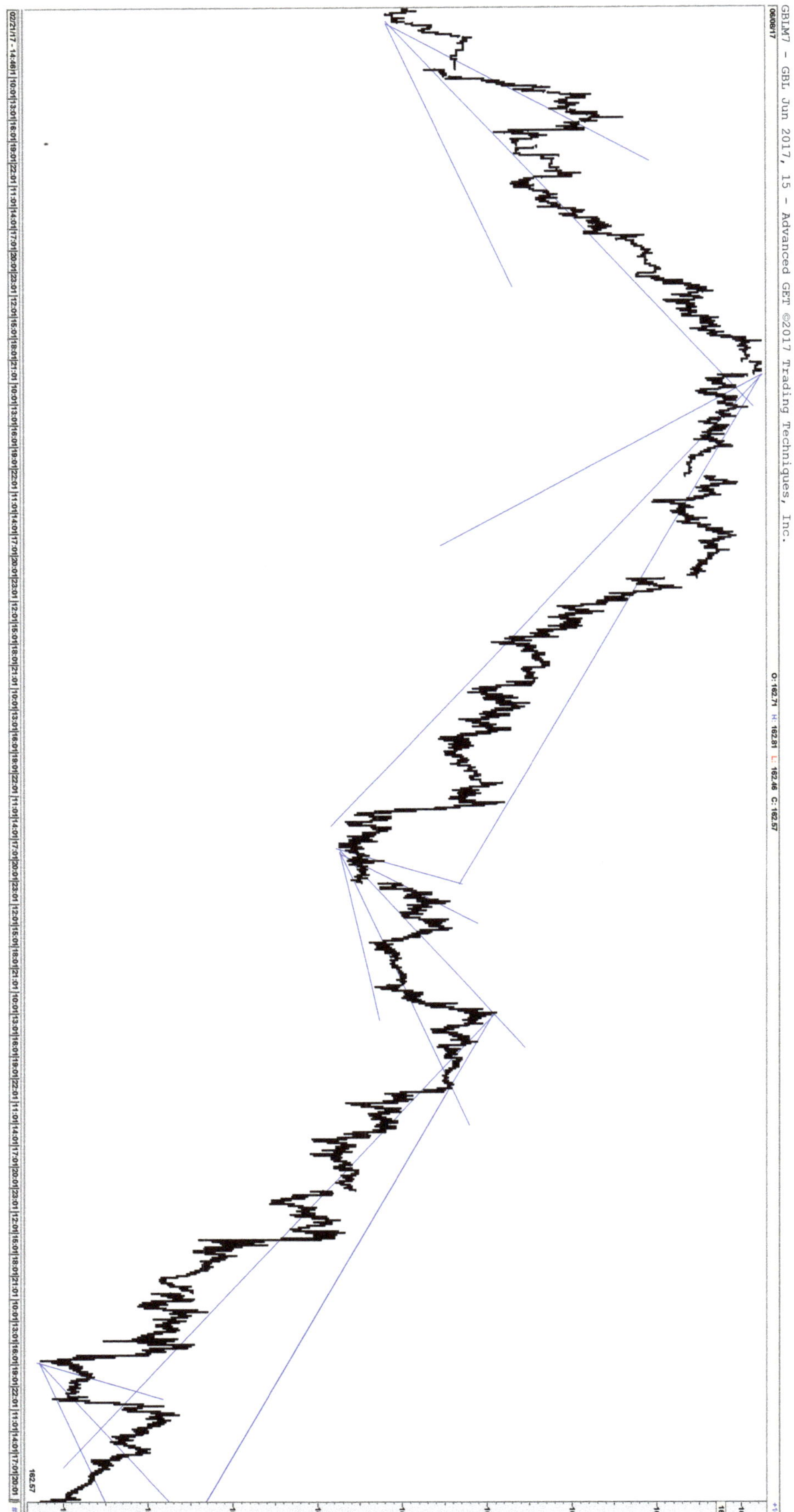

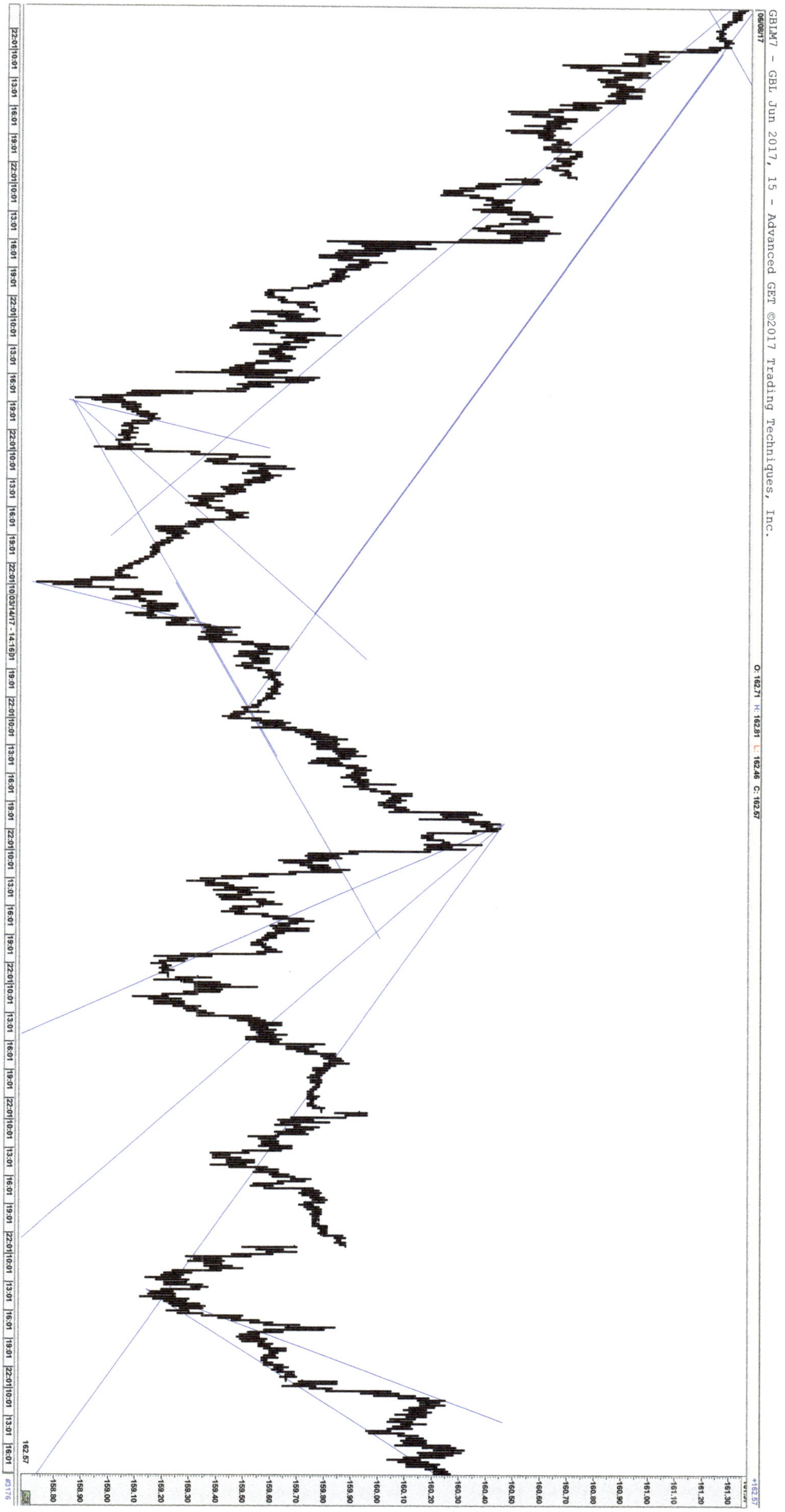
GBLM7 - GBL Jun 2017, 15 - Advanced GET ©2017 Trading Techniques, Inc.

We show the technical analysis of the Euro Bund (June term/ maturity) with 2 charts starting from February 21, at 15 minute intervals.

In these charts, which lasted until May, we used only Gann's angles. 1x1, 1x2, 1x4, and very rarely 1x8 (two-way) angles.

With 15 minute analysis, it is suitable to trade in 3 to 5 day periods under the name of intraday or swing trade. However, experienced traders can benefit from this periodic analysis for trade over a much longer period of time, with multiple angles on hand.

All charts have the same price / time ratio. I used the same price / time based angles in all 15 minute analyzes I made in 2016, 2017. Although the trend line can be identified and used after two or even three points, the greatest advantage of the predefined Gann angle is that it is possible to place a single pivot from the beginning with the possible angle carrying price movement. With this advantage, the late drawing problem of trend setting is eliminated. How can we anticipate the price movement without knowing the answer of the question, "At which point will the price movement continue?" Is it 1x4? , 1x2? or should we follow the 1x1 angle?

We can answer these types of questions with a general category: 1x1 and maybe 1x2 angles are more likely vehicles for long price movements.

1x4 especially 1x8 angles can only be used at very fast and stiff price movements. It is also generally accepted that such price movements will not last long.

Fluctuations between Gann's angles are also intense in after long-running declining or rising periods, reaction-based horizontal motion fields/spaces, or partial response movements (up or down). Only very fast trade can be done during these periods. The other method is to wait for the end of this consolidation movement and not to trade. If options are used, it is a method to obtain premium income by making use of time decay to make calls and puts (with other wings or legs being hedged) out of certain bands during these periods.

Again, while trading in a period of time such as 15 minutes, a Gann angle that is exceeded due to high volatility; it is probable that the account will be able to function again in the future if it is confirmed that it is carrying the price movement before.

In the graphs, the period analysis between February 21 and March was made by Gann. June term during the 15 minute periodic analysis of the Euro Bunds, generally 1X1, 1X2 (two direction) angles were used. Sometimes the 1X4 angle is used.

The angles placed in the pivots have the same price and rate in all contracts in 2016 and 2017 (same period in Euro Bund, same period in Euro etc.).

Strategy:

On March 10; On March 17 maturity contract, the OGB3 (3-week Euro Bund option), 160 strike calls were sold. Counter leg was call taken from 161.5 strike. Thus, by establishing a bear call spread, it was tried to collect premiums on a partial downward-sloping or horizontal market.

On the same day, the monthly Euro Bund option with March 24 maturity was sold from 161 strike calls. As a counter leg, 162.5 strike calls were received (call long). With bear call spreads established, it was aimed to receive a premium profit in horizontal or downward market. In the same term/ maturity, 160.5 strike calls were taken and other bear call spreads were established.

Thus, two call spreads;

a) Starting with separate strikes,

b) maintaining the same distance between the legs,

c) are terminated in separate strikes.

161 call short, 162.5 call long

160.5 call short, 162 call long

These two spreads were built during daytime price fluctuations. The total premium (call long = premium given) is the same in both strategies.

Due to call shorts in the near-out of money location, premium incomes are low, and according to corresponding macro and technical analysis, spreads are also less likely to happen in-the-money.

Again according to macro and technical analysis, spreads are closed in the money and return to the future position; it is more likely that the downward direction (shown by the futures short) is visible in the mid-range on apparent conditions.

On the same date, another bear call spread was established with 160.5 call shorts and 162 call longs in OGB3 weekly options with March 17 maturity.

In this spread, the premium received, the call short premium, is less than ½ of the OGB / monthly spread (there is only one week difference between them). The difference between call-long premiums is less with the effect of out-of-money.

As a result, possible risks (in-the-money conversion of the call short leg to futures) were distributed with spreads in different strikes and trades, against the price realization (March 17 and March 24).

On March 13, by taking advantage of the price movement a call spread was established by taking a call from the counterpart spouse of 161.5 by selling 1 call from 160.5 strike on March 24 maturity contract.

The long-leg strike was pulled down due to the upcoming maturity while using the increased premium (160.5 strike). A distance of 150 points in the previous positions has been reduced to 100 points (160.5 - 161.5 = 100 pips with other display 1).

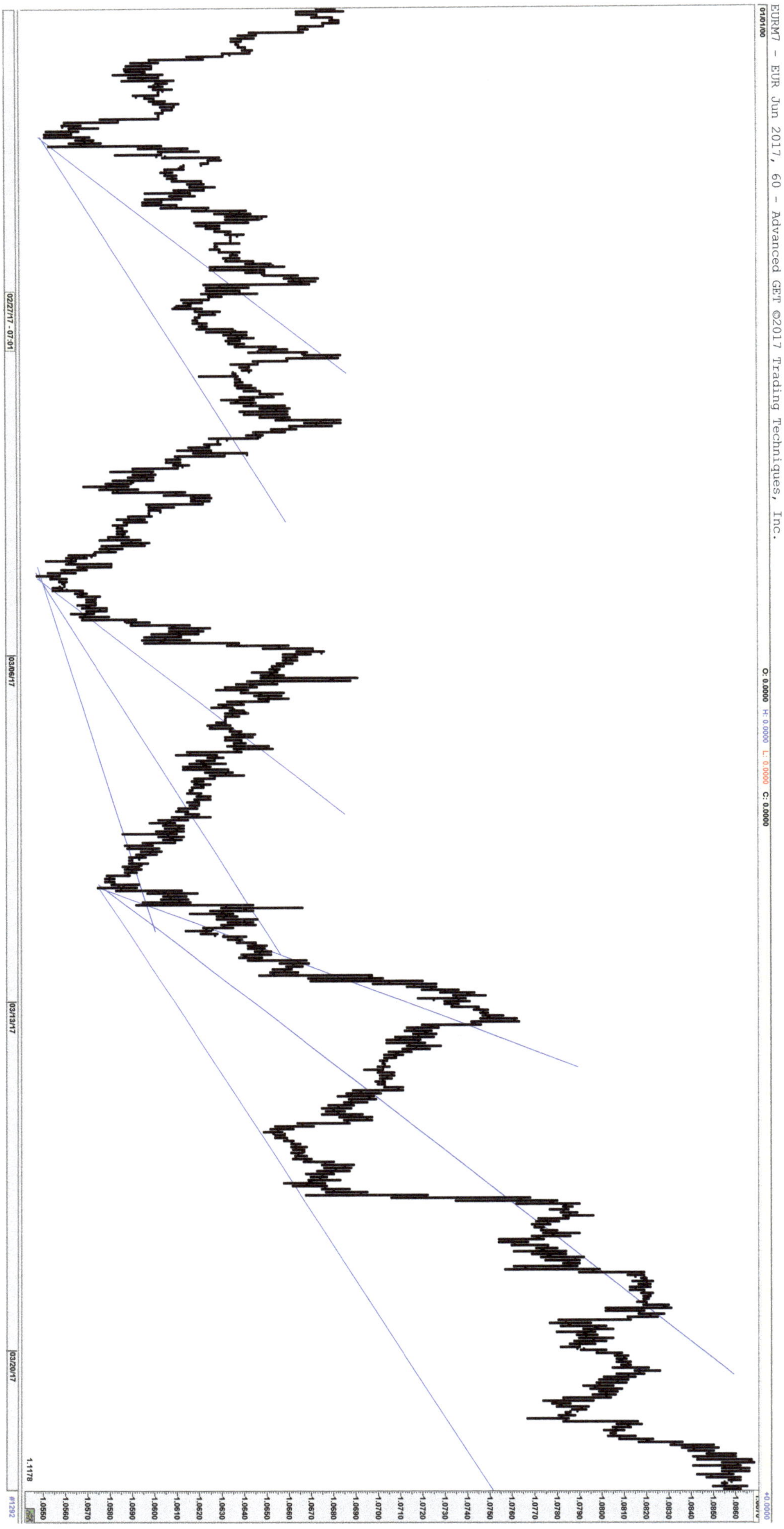
EURM7 - EUR Jun 2017, 60 - Advanced GET ©2017 Trading Techniques, Inc.
02/27/17 - 07:01
03/06/17
03/13/17
03/20/17

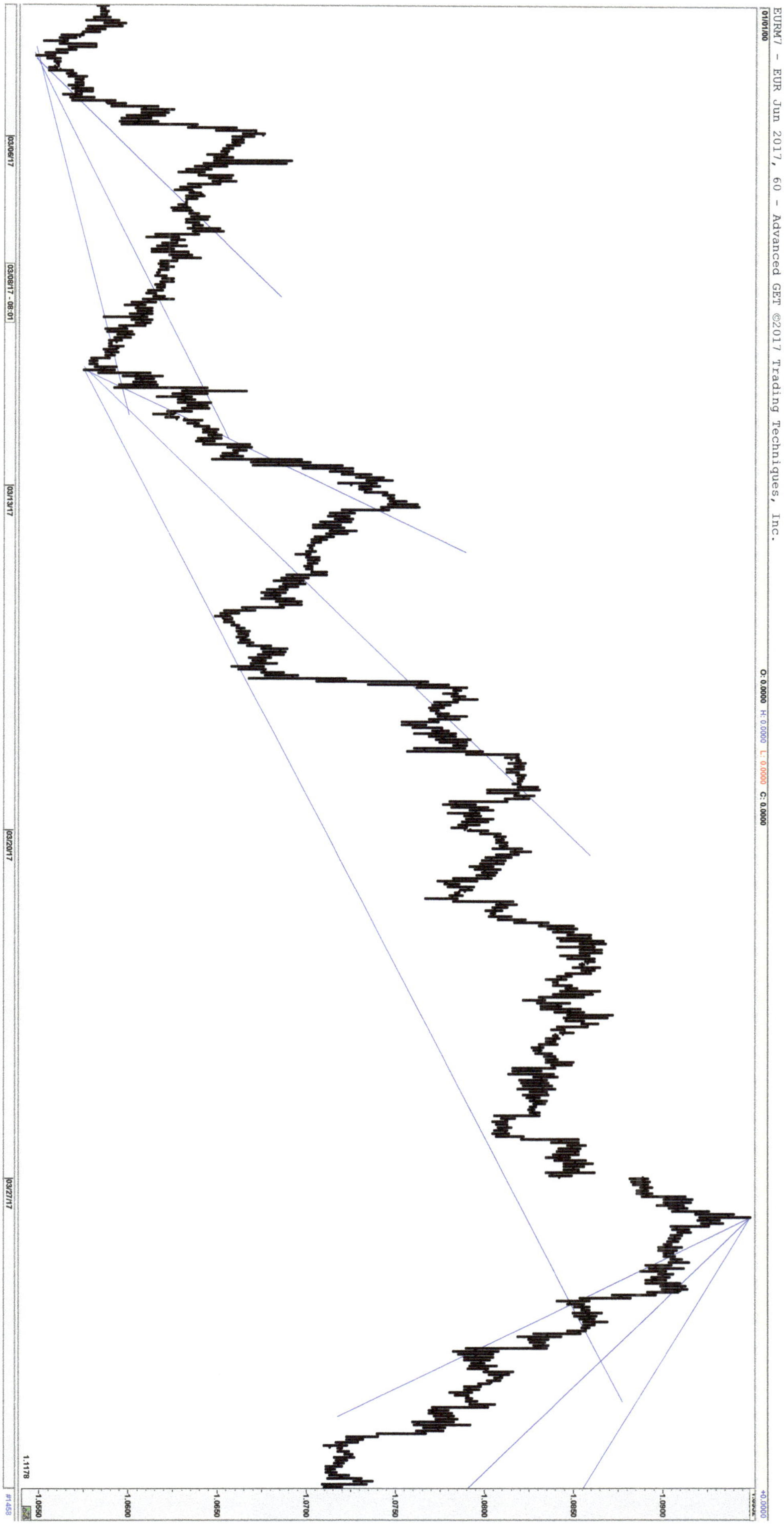
EURM7 - EUR Jun 2017, 60 - Advanced GET ©2017 Trading Techniques, Inc.
O: 0.0000 H: 0.0000 L: 0.0000 C: 0.0000
01/01/00
03/06/17
03/08/17 - 08:01
03/13/17
03/20/17
03/27/17
1.0900
1.0850
1.0800
1.0750
1.0700
1.0650
1.0600
1.0550

Euro

We take a 60-minute periodical technical analysis of the Euro Dolar Fx June term contract with a graph showing Gann angles.

On February 22, the Euro, which hit the bottom with a double dip, advanced with attacks until February 28.

The Gann angles, which rises with price movement after February 22 (this angle conveyed upward movement), broke on February 24. The price movement touched same angle on February 27, was suddenly reversed. The next day, February 28, when the attack on the nearest price level was suddenly reversed, the resulting 3-point top formation the other Gann angle was broken with the resulting sales.

So when the Gann angle, which carried the price fluctuation from February 26 to February 28, broke down and began to decline, the pullback failed. The decline after this failure will last until March 2.

Beyond the Gann angle drawn on the next day of March 2 pivot, I would like to state that all of the Gann angle we have discussed here are at the same price / time ratio on other maturity contracts (Euro contracts).

Since the Gann angles are of the same proportions when the pivot appeared, Gann angle can be positioned. In trend and similar methods, lines can only be drawn in the progressive and multiple confirmation ends (pivot etc.), but this process is completed after pivot determination with certain Gann proportional.

If we return to our analysis; The Gann angle, drawn on the March 2 pivot and fully functioning on March 3, continued to decline until March 9 when it was broken on March 6.

On March 6, when the angle was broken, the pull back confirmed the angle. The confirmation of the power of the angle also indicates that the decline after the break will continue.

It is noteworthy that the March 9 pivot (which will be followed by a major upward movement) on the other Gann's angle, although the Gann angle passed on March 8 has no reaction.

The February 22 and March 2 pivots are at the same level and give a double bottom view. The run-up of uptrend after March 2 shows that this double bottom is approved by the market. On March 9 bottom, it was formed just above the double bottom level. The upward movement (similar 90°), which started after the ascending bottoms, informs the bull market.

The steepest Gann's angle drawn from the March 9 pivot, shows a upward, up to March 13. Since there may be a lot of volatility in upright movements, some violation of the angle of this movement should be tolerated.

Although no reaction was given to the first angle in the decline that started after March 13. On March 15, the double bottom which rises just above the other angle was made. The rise starting here was limited by fluctuations on the previous angle until March 17.

On March 21, the angle which support the rise on March 15 was retried, and the upsurge was accelerated once more by the reaction from here. On March 29 and March 30, it was returned to this angle. The decline that begins after horizontal movement on the angle (continue 12 hours) will last until April 10. With this decline, the whole bullish rally, which began on March 2, was almost reversed.

Strategy:

In March 13, the 3 Eu weekly March 17 (maturity contract) was sold at 1,065 strike put, the opposite leg was taken from 1.05 strike put long; the bull put spread was established.

Again in the 4 Eu weekly options with March 24 (maturity contract), the second bull put spread was established with put short 1.045 strike, put long from 1.06 strike.

By taking positions in such different strikes and term/maturity; It is aimed to benefit from the horizontal, upwards possible price movement in the euro, with premium collection strategies.

Due to the difference in maturity between the 3rd and 4th week options, the premium for the far option is higher.

In the Euro Bund, on March 15, the OGB3 (maturity contract) was sold at a 160 strike calls during the partial upturn, while 161 strike calls were received (call long). Due to the near-term end date of the bear call spread, a high premium was obtained from the at-the-money call short leg, while a low premium was given to the call long leg with time decay.

On March 16, the call short leg of the bear call spread that was established the previous day was closed with a premium income of 85%. At-the-money strike has benefited from the price movement at the end of the maturity. At the same time, the potential risk has been reduced, with a large number of positions taken in the same direction (meaning bear calls spreads, even in separate strikes and terms).

The other foot call was not closed, because the lower premium was further reduced (near zero). It is held for unexpected price shocks called "possible black swan movement". During unexpectedly large price shocks, which are even fewer in a row, very low premium long positions can make significant profits. Instead of closing positions with a value close to zero prime, holding it until the end of the expiration date/end of maturity in a few years, can bring success as a separate strategy.

On March 16, weekly Euro options of 4 Eu with March 24 maturity contract, were established bull put spreads with put short from 1.07 strike and with put longs from 1.055 strike.

In the Euro Bund; On March 17, on March 24 maturity contract; 161 strike call short was closed with high premiums. On the other hand, 160 strike calls were sold in the same maturity. Thus, besides benefiting from time erosion, which accelerated due to the approaching maturity, it was aimed to purchase high premium by selling nearby strike option.

As the potential risk is reduced due to reduced working days due to shortening of the valuation, we can move the option strike to be sold to the underlying asset price.

Again on March 17, the put option was sold at 1,075 strike on the Euro option contract of the 4 Eu of the 4th week with March 24 term. The bull put spread was established by taking put from 1.06 strike.

Thus, as the possibility of an upward movement in the Euro-dollar parity appears, we are bringing the short strike of the spreads closer to the prices (strategies for collecting premiums).

However, we keep the spread inside distance the same and even make it narrow. In this way we reduce the potential risk.

On March 21, March 31 maturity 5 Eu, the euro weekly option, the bull put spread was established: put short on 1.08 strike, put long on 1,065 strike.

The 4 Eu, March 24 maturity was set up in the weekly contract; while another spread was set up between 1.08 put shorts and 1.07 put long strike.

Strategies established up have on the occasions where in-the-money has not been made at the end of the maturity, in other words, spreads that have been successfully completed; not been rewritten. We will continue this approach. We chose not to distract the reader from the list of successful ones. We explain which were closed before the maturity:

On March 23, 1,075 put shorts in 4 Eu term contract (a leg of spreads) were closed pre-maturity with profits.

On March 21, the Euro Bund with 160 strike call shorts and 161 strike call long, were esthablished spreads on the [March 31 (Euro Bund 5) maturity contract].

On March 24, the OGB1 weekly Euro Bund option with a maturity of April 7;

161 strike call short,

162 strike call long:

call bear spread was established (the future at 160.22 level).

The 5 Eu, March 31 maturity, was sold put short at 1.075 strike (on the weekly Euro option contract).

The spread was completed with 1.06 strike put longs, which was used during the previous put bull spread and opponent leg were closed with profit.

At EuroBund, at OGBL 5 weekly option with March 31 maturity, call was sold from 160 strike (call short), and 161 strike call bought (call long).

OGB1 Euro Bund contract with April 7 maturity; call sold at 160.5 strike, call bought from 161.5 strike.

On March 24, the call shorts of the bear call spreads were closed with profit during the daytime fluctuation.

On March 27, Euro Bund call was bought from 162 strike on March 31 term at weekly options. On April 7, maturity contract call was sold at 161 strikes. Thus, a calendar bear call spread was established with different expiration dates. The basic idea is based on the argument that the effects of the political and economic developments affecting the US bills (the effect of which was the withdrawal after the morning opening of the Euro Bund in the gap) might even be partly or positive for Euro Bund due to the removal of BAT taxes from the agenda.

The Euro Bunds opened with a gap on the morning of March 27, and on April 7 maturity contract calls were sold at 161.5 strike.

By using the Euro Bund prices, which is regressing towards the middle of the day, 162.5 strike calls are taken at the same maturity with decreasing premium and bear call spread was set up.

On March 27, 1,075 strike put short positions in the Euro Dollar parity (weekly options of 5 Eu, with a maturity of March 31) were closed with high premium profit. Thus, from parity move upward with gap, beginning of the week, was utilized. Spread's call long leg was held. Possible profits during the week will also be used as the other leg in call sales.

April 12, 2017

May 5 term Euro Dollar Fx option, [(EUU) June term future underlying asset]:

1.065 call long,

Call bull spread was established with 1.08 call short. A total of 770 pips premiums were awarded. To partially redeem premium:

1.035 strike put and 1.02 strike put (same maturity) were sold. In the other leg, 2 puts from 1 strike were taken and a total of 2 put bull spreads were established. The total premium is 450 pips. Thus, in the sum of all strategies, a maximum return of 1500 pips is aimed by giving 770 - 450 = 320 pips.

Euro Bund on April 13, based on big A, B, C (wave count); 164 - 163.5 with a return expectation [AB = BC], from 163.5 strike 2 put were purchased. 370 X 2 = 740 Euro premium has been paid for this position taken on April 21 maturity (May Euro Bund) options contract.

On April 21, 2017, the underlying asset was trading at around 162.60 during the close of the option session. Thus, a profit of 163.5 - 162.6 = 90 pips (900 euros) was received.

While the profit on one contract was 900 - 370 = 530, a total of 530 x 2 = 1060 euros was written as two contracts were received.

On April 12, 10-year US note with weekly contract of May 5 maturity with ZN1 code

128.5 call long,

Call bear spread was established with 127call short.

Weekly contract of ZN4 with April 28 maturity at 126.75 call short with

128 call long'la

and

127 call short

With 128.25 call long

Two call bear spread were established. Thus, a total of 3 call spreads were established.

In the euro dollar Fx, a call bull spread was established on April 18 at the end of the weekly contract of April 28 with the code 4Eu, between 1065 call long and 1085 call short. 1490 - 410 = 1080 pips Premium was given, 2000 pips premium targeted.

April 20, 2017

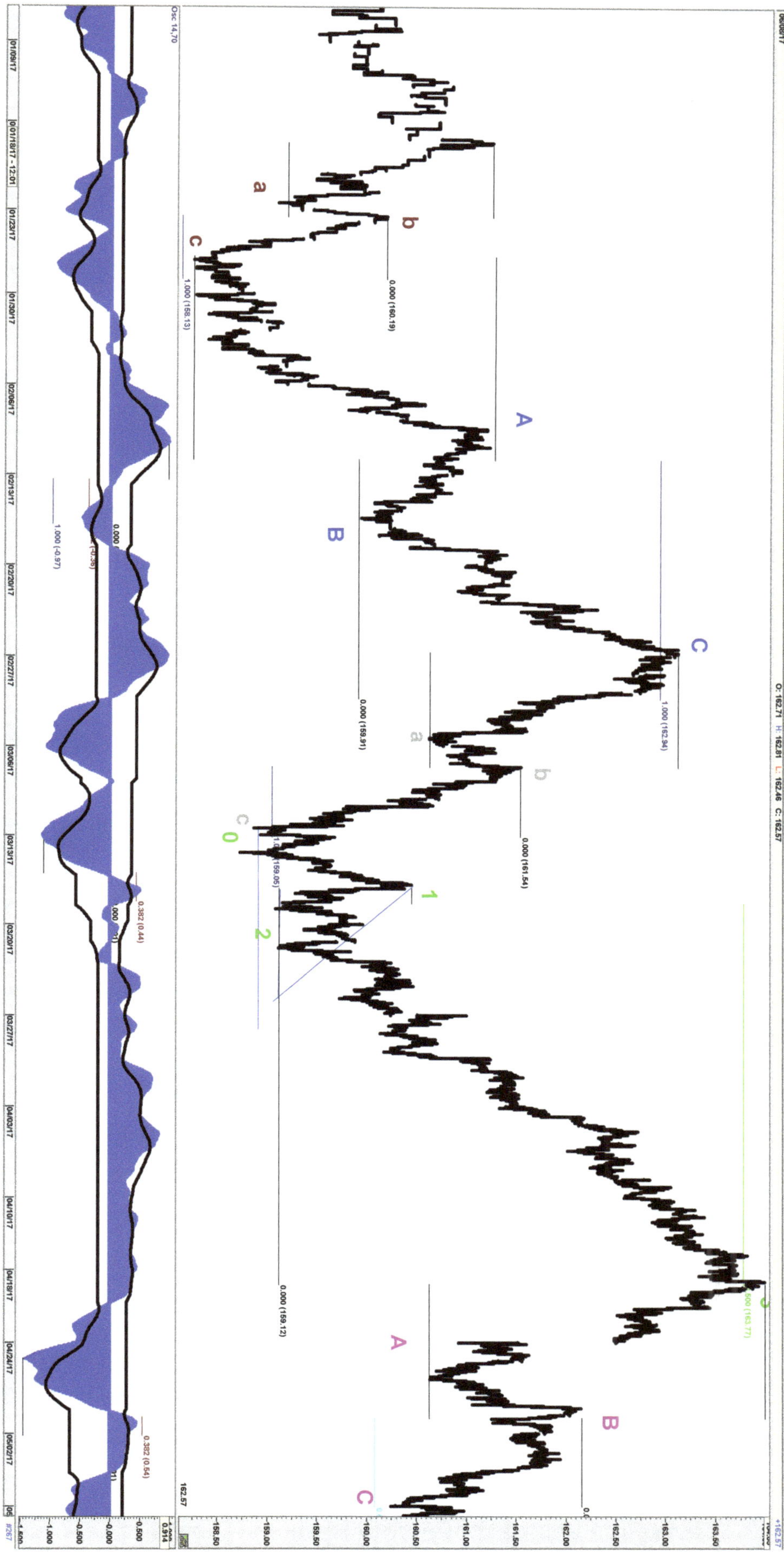

We will look to June maturity German 10-year futures (Euro Bund, June 2017) price graph by technical analysis with Elliott wave count, fibonacci rates, and oscillator.

From January 17, 2017, the "a" wave (red color) developed until January 20. The top on January 24 show the end of the wave "b". The bottom level on January 26 was predicted with subtraction a wave lenght from the top of the wave b. In other words, the a and c waves have the same lenght. The rise, which started from the bottom of January 26, peaked on February 8. This peak is indicated by the big green "A". On the other hand, the return from "A", ended was on February 15. This point in the level of 159.91 is "B" bottom. At point "B" we find 162.94 by adding the "A" wave.

The "C" top will take place on February 26 on 162.88 level. Thus, the return point is predicted with a difference of 162.96 - 162.88 = 0.08 !

We observe the lower window (blue oscillator oscillations) that the oscillator during the "B" wave motion are pulled back only 0.382 of "A" wave oscillator peak a ratio of 0.382 is indicative that the wave B is intermediate/recessional wave and that a new wave guide like A begin.

The decline that began on February 24 reached the lowest level on March 3. This bottom was showed with a light gray "a".

"b" is a retraction minor movement at 161.54 on March 7. Passing over this level "a", fast and steep c movement is expected. The wave "c" after "b" will repeat the lenght of wave "a" again, and will end on March 10 at 159.05. The ongoing consolidation movement throughout March; appeared triangle formation and it caused motion in the oscillator window only in the 0.382 retraction band. Based on the oscillator movement, we will consider the March squeeze like 1st. wave elevation and a 2nd. wave consolidation. Long-term gradual rise after consolidation ending in March; on April 18, the peak was at 163.99. This level is close to 3.5 times/ratio of the first wave. Since 3.5 times does not show any particular value, the level does not make much sense in terms of forecasting.

What we saw in the H maturity contracts A, B, C wave motion, we also see in M (June) maturity contract. Such movements are seen in contracts released in a relatively narrow range such as bonds. In such contracts/issues, 3-wave motion is more probable than 5-wave motion, this can be seen explained on the basis of short-term periods. Based on this axiom, it is important to note that with the turn at level 164, the end of the upward movement is most likely to end.

Analysts who are able to make these assessments will be able to participate in the next down movements (author implemented this with intensive future and option strategies, combining the technical forecast with economic and political analysis).

After April 18, the decline will continue until April 26. The reaction from this level created a wave of B (red) with a sudden rise until the peak on April 27. In the following days, the price movement, which is consolidated and depressed, is a typical "B" wave. It is also noted that during the B wave, which suddenly ended on May 3, the oscillator in the lower window returned from the 0.382 rate.

The fall will end on May 11. The C wave (red) is formed around 0.618 of A wave lenght (right outside your graph).

Strategy:

On April 20, weekly contract with 4 Eu codes, expiration date April 28;
Call bought from 1.065 (call long) {Bull call spread}
1.095 call sold
1.410 pip was given, 3000 pips were targeted.

4 Eu-coded, weekly contract expiration date April 28:
1.06 put long {put bear spread}
1.04 put short
400 pips were given and 2000 pips were targeted.

These two strategies are;
a) total for upward movement 1410 + 400 = 1810 given and 3000 targeted
Net profit: 3000 - 1810 = 1190 pips
b) downward motion
2000 - 1810 = 190 pips total profit.

However, after the orientation to occur, other strategies may be developed and profitable, based on at least one leg of the wings.

In Euro Bunds all trade was done at OGB4, April 20 maturity contract, while the underlying asset was traded at June future 162.80:

(we did not write strike words every time not to get tired the readers).

Put long from 162.5

From 161 put short 89 - 25 = 64 pips given, 150 pips targeted.

A put bear spread was established with 5 contracts. A maximum profit of ratio; 150/64 = 2.34 was targeted.

163 call long

165 call short 98 - 35 = 63 pips given,

Call bull spread was established. Based on this call bull spread, the number of equal strategies, the future short opened in the underlying asset. Thus, the underlying asset shorts were partly protected in upside.

From 165.5 strike call long

From 167 strike call short position was taken: 31 - 12 = 19 pips given.

If we subtract 19 + 63 = 82 pips cost from future short, there is unlimited profit under 161.98 (put bear spread profit and therefore the possibility of decrease in total future cost is excluded).

On April 20, the aim is to hedge the June maturity futures;

A bull call spread was established with

163 call long

165.5 call shorts.

5 x 163 call long

5 x 165.5 call short

710 pips Premium was given. 2500 pips premium targeted. 1 → 3.5 is a rare coefficient.

On the other direction; at the same maturity

5 x 163 put long

5 x 163.5 put long

And put bear bear spread esthablished with 10 x 161 put short. When all these transactions were done, the underlying asset futures were around 162.9.

An average of 1015 pips was given for put bear spreads and an average of 2250 pips were targeted to take back.

Since there is a ½ position ratio between the Bull call spread and the put bear spread, the maximum possible net profit in the downward direction is 880 pips at the position.

(2250 - 1015) - (710/2) = 880

Thus, we have implemented a complex strategy, some with straddle, some with strangle, but different positons number at wings according to directions, but with different wing lenghts according to directions at the same time. This strategy was put in practice; with the anticipation of the first round of the selection of France, we find that, as the favorable expectation for the puts are more homogeneous and in the negative results (in the opposite direction to the market expectation) at the calls; the deeper pricing is done, call premiums are higher with the call strike (relative to normal times).

On April 20, on the other side of the previous bull spreads; for hedging put bull spreads (Premium purpose) with 1.04 put short and 1.06 put long, bear put spread was established (they may be targeted directly for profit if the possible downward movement does not get deep).

650 - 310 = 340 pips was given

2000 pips were targeted.

1 → 5.9 times is rarely seen. Because of the occasion of 1.st tour of France election a high premium is given in the downward direction. The opposite of the situation in the call in the Euro Bund emerges here in the puts.

[Call bull spread]:

1 x 1.085 {call short}

1 x 1.08 {call long}

2 x 1,065 {call long}

[put bear spread]:

1.06 put long

1.04 put short

[put bull spread]:

1 x 1,035 put short

1 x 1.02 put short

2 x 1.00 put long

1.065 call long, upside profit with 1.085 call short,

1.06 put long, downward profit with 1.04 put short,

With 1.035 and 1.02 put short and 1 put long premium profit in the upward or horizontal movement was targeted.

April 24, 2017

Euro Bund June Term 60 Minutes

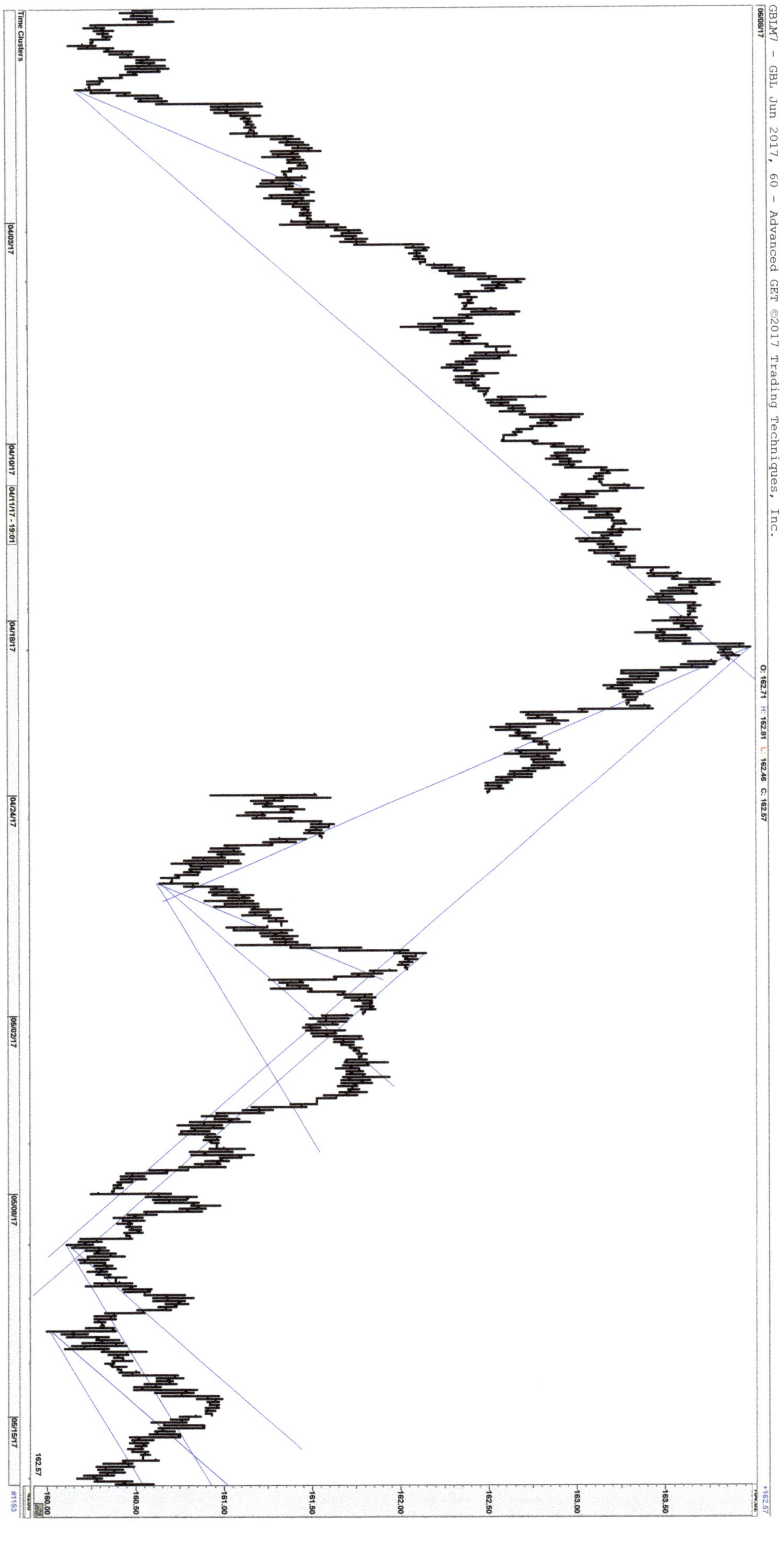

At left of graph; after the double bottom on March 10 and March 14, on March 17, March 21 and the double bottom was formed just above the price level.

Thus, bottoms were rising from March 24, March 28 and March 29 after the bottom search was completed between March 10 and March 22; this is the preparation for the upward movement. The strong upwards movement that begins with the ascension from the bottom March 28 and 29, which we have seen on the left of the chart, will last until April 18.

The Gann's angle we draw from the pivots on March 29, at the same time was used in this chart and all other charts at the same price / time ratio. Generally 1x1, 1x2 (up and down) angles are shown, but sometimes 1x4 angles are also used.

The 1x2 angle drawn from the March 29 pivot completed its function on March 31, while the 1x1 angle was accompanied by the upward trend until the April 18 peak. The 1x1 angle was tested on April 12, three times in a day.

Although on April 18 it was obviously hanging down in the morning session, the closing in the last hours with the attack towards the closing was in a cramped appearance and on the angle. However, on April 19, (the angle) was broken with the gap at opening session. Sales are accelerated in the following hours. With this sale, it is confirmed that the angle bearing the ascension near to 20 days is broken; it is necessary to participate in sales. The next day (March 20), sales will accelerate again after a very small reaction at the opening.

The price movement, which completed April 21, with a "B" wave-like, opened with gap on April 24 with the results of the French elections. Thus, we have shown that we could foreseen the April 24 election results were began to be bought starting from April 19 can be foreseen by the 1x1 angle.

The angle drawn from the April 18 pivot predicted the April 26 pivot: the rise that began with the passing of this angle, which accompanied the decline until April 26, continued until the 2.nd angle drawn from the April 18 pivot. The decline that started with the pivot, which was slightly over the angle opening on April 27, continued until May 9. This downtrend continued throughout the 2nd. angle drawn from the April 18 pivot. With the rise starting on May 9, the angle has been abandoned. In this case;

We can foresee that a) the decline is over, b) the bottom effort or the uprising will begin.

In the following days in the bottom effort, even if the pivot is slightly below May 11, the new ascension will begin with May 16, after the bottoms that occurred on multiple and almost same level.

Strategy:

In the Euro Bund; all transactions were carried out on a weekly option contract with OGB4 code, April 28 expiration date: Calls sold at 165 on April 20 were taken back at '0.02' and closed on the morning of April 24. 163 call longs, 165 call shorts; for the call bull spread was sold from 162.5 calls, based on the free/unattached long leg (163 strike call longs). Thus, 163 call long and 162.5 call short legs with a bear call spread was established targeting to get premiums. When these transactions were made, the underlying asset price was around 161.40.

Puts was sold from 161.5 and 161 strikes based on the underlying asset future shorts (positions opened on April 20). Future short + put short with the position of covered put strategy position was taken. While targeting downwards with futures shorts, it is aimed to taken premiums with hedges as well, with short puts (all premiums can be written with time decay as futures covered).

Weekly options based on 10-year US note with maturities of April 28 and maturities of May 5 (June maturity contract, underlying asset, ZN4 and ZN1 coded) include call bear spread's call short legs which established on April 12(call short from 126.75 and 127 strikes, call longs from 128 and 128.25 strikes; ZN4 / April 28 maturity time) were closed with maximum profit (1/64 price) on April 25.

In Euro Bund; on April 24, call bull spread between 165.5 call shorts and 165.5 strike call shorts, which were established on April 20; call short leg were closed (165.5 call shorts) with 90% premium income. Based on the 163 call long, which is a long leg, call was sold from 162.5 and a call bear spread with a maturity of April 28, was established.

Based on the profit potential of put bear spreads 163 and 163.5 strike put longs and 161 strike put shorts which was established on April 20, from 160.5 strike puts were sold. Thus, it was aimed to earn premium income by selling puts from 160.5, using a 163.25 average - 161 = 2.25 spread length, but with premium payment/expense 1.5 pips (150 pips) profit /length was used as loss buffer.

The technical analysis + profit margin buffer giving the level of 160.5 is the basis of this strategy. 160.5 Puts were taken from 159.5 and 159 strikes to hedge put shorts, and strong strategies were established as put bull spread (targeting hedged premium income).

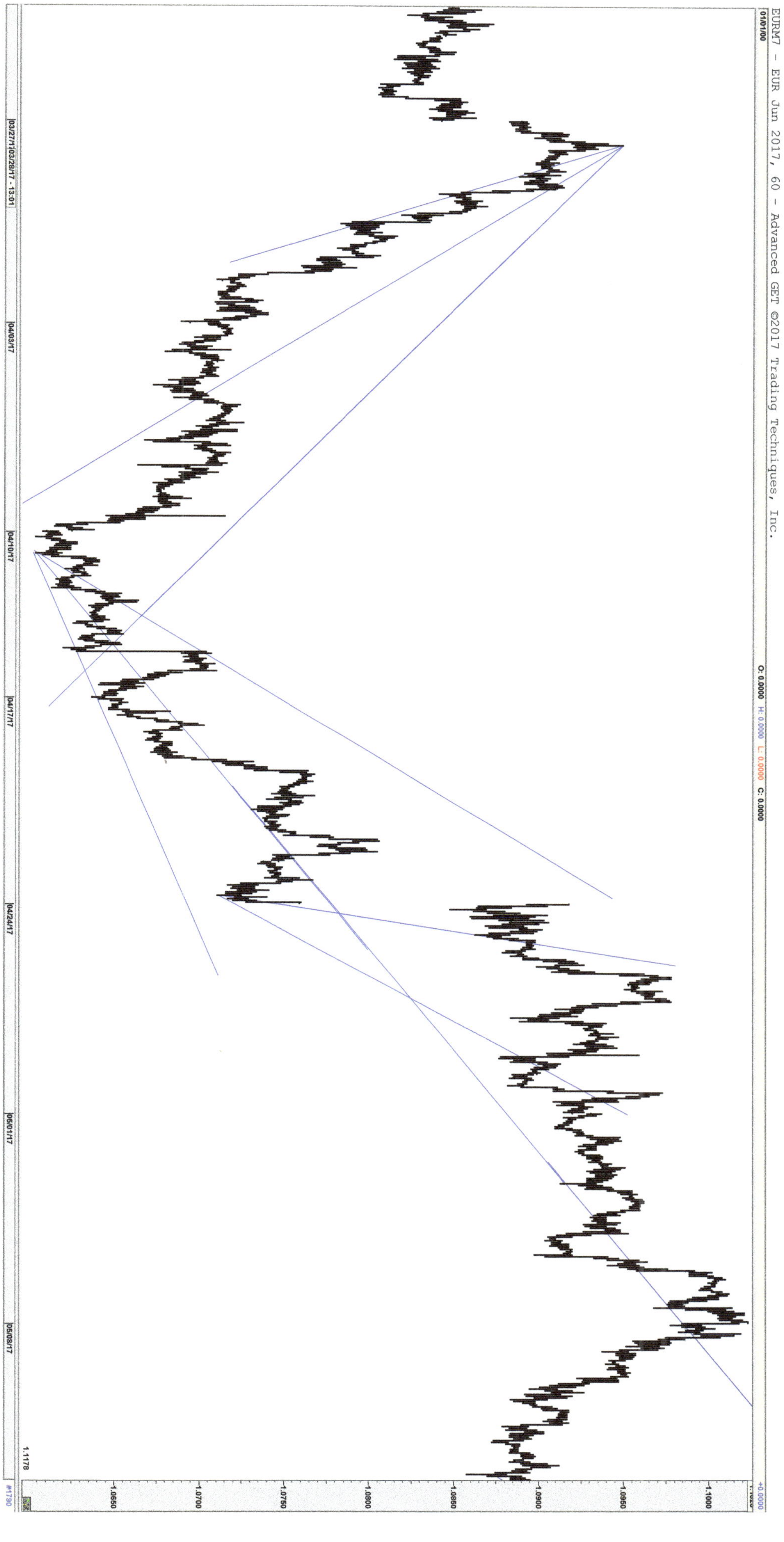
EURM7 - EUR Jun 2017, 60 - Advanced GET ©2017 Trading Techniques, Inc.
O: 0.0000 H: 0.0000 L: 0.0000 C: 0.0000
04/03/17
04/10/17
04/17/17
04/24/17
05/01/17
05/08/17
1.0650
1.0700
1.0750
1.0800
1.0850
1.0900
1.0950
1.1000

On April 24, put shorts (4 Eu for April 28 expiration date and EUU options for May 5 expiration date), previously sold at 1.02, 1.035, 1.04 strikes, were closed with a high profit. These strikes (which are the other legs of the bear put spread and bull put spread) were used previously with 1.06 put long leg. Now, using these unattached 1.06 put long; 1.07 and 1.08 strikes put shorts, were sold for established new bull put spreads. Thus, strategies were set up to achieve premium income with hedging. On 1.08 strike was established for the week of May 5 (expiration date); 1.07 strike was established for the week of April 28 (expiration date).

The week of April 28, for upward direction, 1.095 strike call were sold and 1.11 strike call were bought for established call bear spread.

Thus, positions based on the assumption that the Euro Dolar Fx will be between 1.08 and 1.095 on April 28, were taken.

a) 1.06 put long → 1.07 put short; put bull spread

b) 1.095 call short → 1.11 call long; call bear spread

c) 1.065 call longs → 1.08 and 1.085 call shorts; call bull spread

In the Euro Bund; on April 24 after lunch, in the OGB4 weekly option contract,

a) based on futures short + put short and

b) based on the profit / distance of bear put spread strategies, puts from 160.5 strike were sold. From 159.5 strike put was bought: Bull put spreads were established.

So; beyond the strategies ending with 161 strike put shorts in the a and b choices; puts were sold in 160.5 and the aim was to receive a premium. It is predicted that the level of 160.5 will be the limit in the technical analysis at this week (April 28 maturity) contract.

After lunch on April 25, all positions in the Euro Dolar Fx option were closed. While the June maturity (E6M17) future contract was around 1.0955-1.096, EUU and EU4 options positions (short or long) were closed. The reason we get this decision before maturity is;

a) The possibility of the volatility increase by the Thursday ECB meeting and the Draghi press conference following it,

b) In the US, increased uncertainty about Obamacare, tax regulations and financial holidays.

Euro Dolars the Fx made the decision to close positions early when it came to the 1.095 border (were waiting for on April 28 maturity). The call-bull spreads, which are in-the-money and have a short time for maturity, have maximized profits. In the case of bear put spreads, the premium income was nearing completion. Only a small number of call bear spreads were closed slightly above the cost (at the close of the call bear spread, the relatively low premium was paid for the net total, as the call premium for the other leg's call long 1.11 strike increased).

In Euro Bund; on the evening of April 25, when the future contract reached 160.8 level, in the OGB4 contract; from 160 strike put sold and premium was received.

On the morning of April 26, GTC orders for closing 162.5 strike call short positions were realized (90% premium profit) on the OGB4 contract with the first transactions.

On the afternoon of April 26, all positions in OGB4 contract (option long and short + futures short) were closed.

Reasons for not waiting for the completion of the April 28 maturity contract;

I) Technical reasons:

a) The beginning of the upturn after approaching the level of 160.5 on the evening of April 25,

b) A forecast of in US bond, showing the bottom of week.

II) In the news flow and macro analysis factors: a) The ECB meeting on April 27, followed by the Draghi press conference,

b) In the US, Obamacare, tax regulations, the purchase of expectations for fiscal holidays (Trump press statement to be made on the evening of April 26), and the uncertainties in these matters, were not expected to ending of maturity/ expiration date.

When the GGM17 / GBLM17 coded future contract was around 160.80, all positions were closed, starting with the future shorts, then the put longs.

Excepts 161 and 160.5 put shorts, were written in large profits from futures shorts and put-longs (161 and 160.5 put shorts were ATM or near ITM strikes but due to reduced volatility , they are asking for a low premium to close).

On April 28, underlying asset prices during the closing hours of the respective options;

1) For Bund the GBLM17 is around 161.8,

2) For the Euro Dolar Fx June 2017 contract is at around 1.0923.

The lowest level of the Euro Bund is seen during the week is around 160.60 at night of April 25.

Here; a) the technical level of our predictions were realized and

b) it has been observed that our predictions of time-based movement have been successful.

June 1, 2017

September Maturity Euro Bund

Euro Bund September Maturity, 60 Minutes

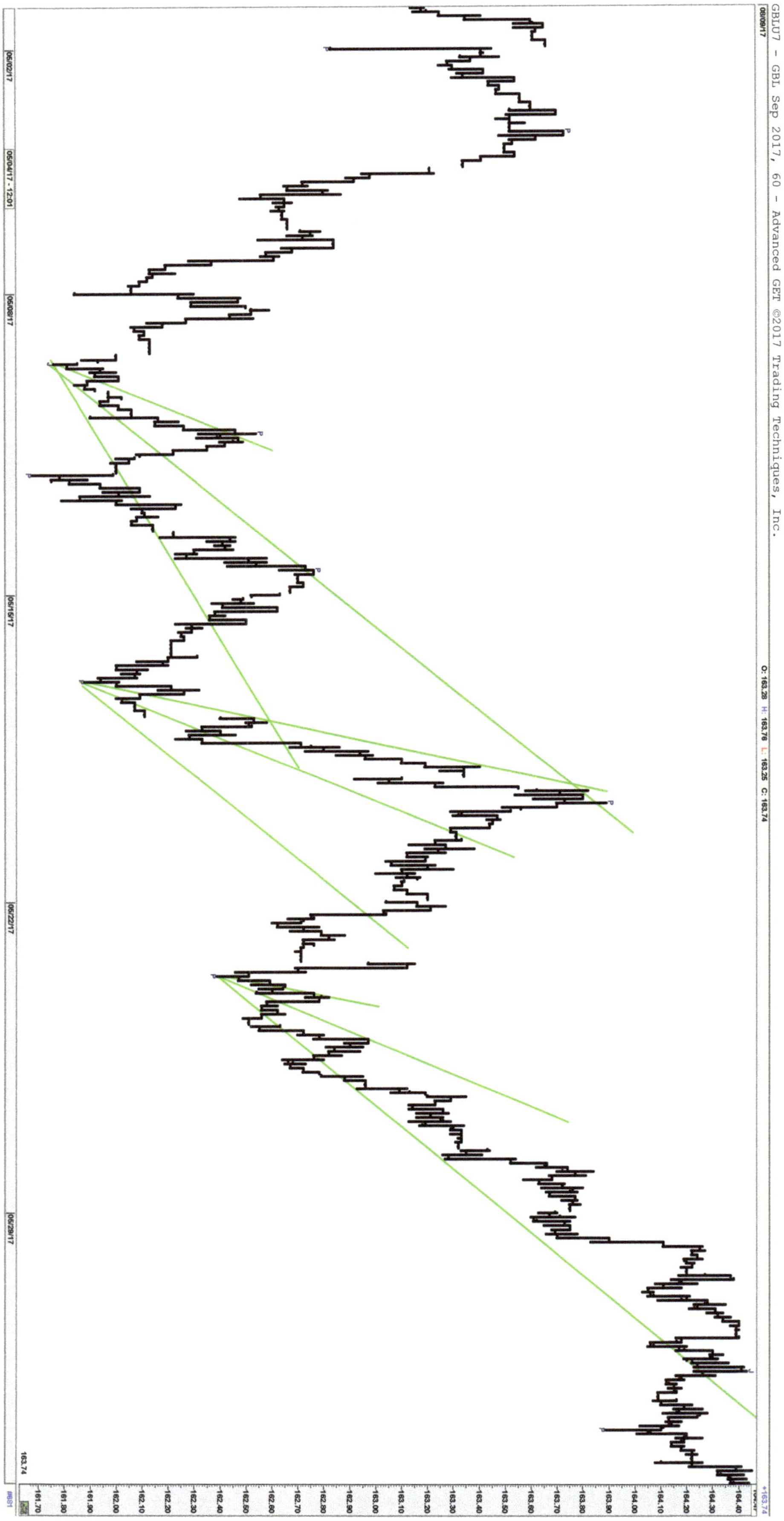

In the graph, a 60-minute period analysis of the September Euro-Bund contract, between May 2 and June is presented.

The contract has gained volume by the middle of May. The June maturity, which ends in mid-June, will be replaced by the September maturity contract, the volume step by step increased before the maturity date.

The 1x1 and 1x2 angles drawn from the May 9 pivot. The 1x2 angle to the left, has functioned like a resistance line on sudden upward movement.

The downward movement which has strarted on May 10, at 1X1 angle not functioning. The reasons for the 1x1 angle not functioning at all is that:

a) occurence of pivot is new and for this reason volatility is high and

b) the rapid decline from the May 3 pivot has yet to be absorbed in the consolidation area.

On May 9, May 11 morning and evening session (apart from the one-hour sag on May 11) will be at the same price level, and later on May 16 will be at the same price level.

The market, which rises up again on May 11, on May 12 upward movement first touched at 1X1 angle (from drawing May 9 pivot), with this touch upward movement reversed sudden.

On May 18, second touch at same angle(1X1), the second decline came after the third hour, and this sale lasted until May 23.

The Euro Bund, which rose with fluctuation between the two angles drawing from the May 16 pivot, after returning from the May 18 pivot point indicated in the above paragraph, headed down until the May 23 pivot.

The upward movement beginning from the double bottom of May 23 and May 24 lasted until June.

The upward movement which drawn between May 23 pivot's angles rose with fluctuation. At May 31, angle was broken and correction phase started.

Which is right outside your graph, during June, a long horizontal consolidation period, after a slight step upwards, will end with a deep decline at the end of June. It is striking that the deep and rapid decline at the end of June will accelerate with the breaking of the May 31 pivot level.

Strategy:

In Euro Bund, the September futures contracts substituted by June contract, I decided to set a position for the downward mainstream movement. The main pillars of this decision are:

1) If the ECB program is to be revised at the end of the year, the first signal will come in the September term. Until the September meeting, the market anticipates ahead with possible preliminary signals.

2) Due to the ending maturity of June futures and options contracts, it is expected to move upwards.

It is possible that the option contract on the underlying the September futures will begin to move downward as soon as it becomes the maturity of the 1 st near term/maturity. Due to the upward movement occured on almost every ending term/maturity (after some time of the new term becomes active and downward movement become).

As of May 22, we started to take positions by selling calls (call short) after that put bear spreads were established.

The future contract, which saw the highest level of 163.89 on May 18, on May 22 when May 18 was occured as the pivot and downward movement started, calls were sold from 164 strike (July Euro Bund option contract, Interactive Brokers code OGBL) and 165.5 strike calls were bought. So the bear call spread was established.

For 164 call shorts, 52 pips premium were received. For 165.5 call longs, 16 pips premium were given: thus the probability of a loss of 150 pips was taken when the premium was taken at 36 pips. The logic for this strategy is to sell the call, for taking the future short position in June or in the later maturity/term (underlying asset as future short in September term). So it will participate in downward movement. Remember that, ending maturity, if call option remain in-the-money, it will return to the future short. Selling calls at 163 levels and above, buying calls arround 165 level for a hedging;

a) premium collection by maturity

b) as well as the future short position for the downward trend in June or after were aimed.

Decision not to participate the attacks at 163 arround or down this level. It is anticipated that possible attack on episode late May - early June; will be premature and there will be a unsuccessful flow of ECB signals.

On May 22, June 9 maturity OGB2 weekly options: calls were sold at 164 and received a premium of 67 pips. With this strategy, it is aimed to have a future short position from 164.67 pips (calculated by neglecting the commission) at maturity.

Also on May 22, June 2 term/ maturity OGB1 weekly options; 163.5 strike calls were sold, 36 pips premium received,

164 strike calls were sold and 20 pips premiums were received.

These two positions were hedged with calls at a cost of 5 pips from 165.5 strike.

Thus two call bear spreads were established.

If the commission is neglected at the end of the maturity, it is intended to get futures shorts from 163.81 and 164.15.

On May 23, 10-year US bond yield dropped below 2.20, opening positions for participate possible upward movement. Forecasts that the pricing of 2.20 and below will be temporary; The weekly options with June 2 maturity (ZN1) were sold from 125.75 and 126 strike call (19/64, 29/64 premium received). In the same term/ maturity, call longs were bought from 126.5 and 127 strike (7/64, 3/64 premium was given). Thus, by establishing 2 call bear spreads;

a) premium was received,

b) with the pricing between the spreads at the end of the maturity, aimed to have a future short position.

On May 24 at the Euro Bund, OGB2 maturity is available on weekly options;

1) From 163 strike call was sold. From 164.5 strike call was taken to hedge this leg. 33 pips premium was received. 5 pips premium was given.

2) Call from 163.5 strike was sold. Bought call from 165 strike to aim hedging. 35 pips premiums were received and 9 pips premiums were given.

3) At OGBL contract, July maturity at 164 strike call was sold; 53 pips premium was received. In the other leg, 16.5 pips were given for 165.5 call were bought.

Thus 3 call bear spreads were established.

a) the first purpose is taking premium,

b) the second purpose; the futures short position, which is cost reduced by premiums received between 163 and 165 strike, is to accumulate for June and later period.

Again on May 24, the call was sold with a premium of 37 pips from 163 strike in the near-term (OGB1) weekly option and a call was bought with 10 pips premium was given from 164 strike.

July maturity in OGB; two calls were sold from 163 strike. 79 pips premium was received from per option. To hedge these two options, calls were bought with a cost of 39 pips from 164 strike and 25 pips from 164.5 strike.

With these operations, 3 call spreads were established. In all call spreads that are established, there are near strikes, but the spread ranges/ lenghts and term are different. The aim is; the desire to determine with distribution the number of positions and their costs, due to the underlying asset price (future short) to ending of maturity. Concentration at the same or similar term and strike; it is desirable to avoid this, since it may prevent the optimum benefit because of the fluctuation of the underlying asset in prices.

The reserve margin is maintained for the possibility of adding new positions at a possible price increase (future Euro Bund), and thus it is not desirable in this phase to reach above 164 strike levels.

Future Euro Bund prices, which saw the lowest level at 162.52 on May 24. Closed at 163.74, with the highest level of 163.84 on May 26. With the May 18 pivot being closed to offset the near-term call bear spreads, the weekly contract of June 2 term, was sold 163.5strike put and received 34 pips premiums. For hedging this position was taken put (put long) from 163 strike and put bull spread was estabished.

In this respect, during the upward attack, it is desired to obtain premium income by selling put which was hedged.

On May 29, at a underlying asset close to the day high (164.31), 164.5 strike calls were sold at the July term (June 23 expiration date) and 53 pips premiums were received. A call from 165.5 strike was bought to hedge this leg (22 pips premium was given).

Again on May 29, call bear spreads, 2 x 166 strike call shorts and 2 x 167.5 strike call longs were established in the OGBL monthly option of August 26 maturity ending September.

Call shorts received premiums of 65 pips per leg, with a premium of 29 pips given per call long. A total of 36 pips premiums were received.

In addition to these strategies, put bear spread was established. Two put longs of the 164 strikes were bought in the same term. A premium of 134 pips per leg was given. The other leg of the put bear spread 2 puts were sold from 162 strike and 66 pips premium received. A total premium of 68 pips was given.

With call bear spread;

a) premium was taken and the cost of put bear spread was tried to be reduced.

b) it is aimed to obtain a future short position if it remains above 164 or even 166 at the end of the maturity.

Let's show the cost of the downward (aimed) position with the two-winged strategy of call bear spread and put bear spread:

164 → 162 = 200 pips (or 2 full points) is the maximum possible profit.

Put bear wing given 68 pips premium (per strategy / two legs), call bear spread received 36 pips premium.

The sum of the premiums of the two strategies:

68 - 36 = 32.

Thus, a premium of 200 pips was obtained by giving a premium of 32 pips.

The probability of "1 given, about 7 take" was purchased. This ratio (1/7), as profit / cost, is rare.

On May 31; in the OGB2, between 164 and 163 strikes; a put bear spread was established with 4 puts long + 4 puts shorts.

For 164 strikes 38 pips were given, and 163 strikes 11 pips were taken. A total of 27 pips given for aimed with 100 pips (1 full score). Thus, premiums were given to participate in the downward correction move.

On the same date, 4 calls were bought from 164.5 strike in the near-weekly term (OGB1). 19 pips were given for per call.

In OGB1, 4 puts from 164 strike were bought and for each option was given 14 pips. Sum of premiums given in two directions; 19 + 14 = 33 pips. In order to make a profit, there must exceed beyond 33 pips in one direction.

The short-term movement expected downward after May 31, (OGB1 and OGB2 downward, OGB1 upwards), turned upward in the following day, although the lowest level of 163.89 was seen during the day on June 1. With the gradual upturn, the prices stepped up until mid-June (the highest, June 14, 165.55, closing at 165.46).

The premiums given to the downward strategies targeting the short term have been wasted and partly participated in the upward movement.

June 3, 2017

On the evening of June 2, the 3 call shorts, previously sold in the OGB1 weekly options, were turned into 3 future shorts when it became apparent that the in-the-money would close at expiration date/ ending of maturity (the 3 future shorts to be delivered by the exchange on June 5, OGB1 3 call short were unexpectedly closed and 3 future short positions were opened).

The contract was concluded on June 26th (July term) 3 futures short contracts were hedging by 3 calls which were bought from 165 strike (38 pips premium was given).

a) To take back the premium given in July,

b) In order to obtain premium income on the possible horizontal market during the month of June,

On August 25, the end of September maturity contract; were sold 3 puts from 164 strikes. 160 pips premium was received. So;

A 3 legs strategy was set up with; 3 call longs (July maturity) + 3 future shorts + 3 put shorts (September maturity):

a) With 3 future short + 3 call longs, synthetic put strategy was established

b) 3 future shorts + 3 put shorts were used to form a covered put strategy.

Because we generally look downward movement, we can be named this strategy a limited synthetic put.

Since the strategy took 160 pips and gave 38 pips,

Target is 160 - 38 = 122 pips premium revenue .

The closing on June 2 was from 164.66 (future contract price). The maximum profit of the strategy;

164.66 - 164 = 0.66 (3 futures short's price level - 3 put short strike), 66 + 122 = 188 pips is the maximum profit per of each strategy. 3 (3 long calls, 3 futures short, 3 put short);

188 x 3 = 564 pips total possible maximum profit.

The lowest profit (at maturity of 165 strike or higher at closing);

165 - 164.66 = 0.34, in other words 34 pips

122 - 34 = 88 pips profit.

However, should not be forgotten that 3 put short are in September term and 3 call longs are in July term.

When we analyze the Euro Bunds, our main argument is: Recalling that the bullish rally around the 165 price level is to accumulate futures shorts and participate in possible downward movements in June and the following months, we also know that should be to keep the futures shorts in upwards movement (for later months).

3 call long costs 38 pips guard us;

a) protect from the market's unexpected shocks,

b) allows opening a new position by relaxing the account in terms of margins.

We expect the downward movement in July to begin with the main move;

1) 164 September puts can be closed or

2) these 3 puts can be closed and the downward price development can be reopened from the lower strike very soon (for example; 163 or 162 strikes). Thus, the price movement in the downward direction is joined with futures shorts or reapplied by put shorts, resulting in approximately the same premium income (considering the time diminishing between opening and closing the position).

Before the closing on the evening of June 2, 3 positions were added to this type of strategy, which was formed with a 3 at a timr contract, (strategies before added; 3 call longs, 3 futures shorts, 3put shorts). Thus, a total of 6 strategies were created in total of 6 at a time contracts.

On June 2, call bull spreads were established on the US 10-year note at ZN2, with 126.5 call long (15/64 pips premium) and 127 call short (6/64 pips premium) for short term upwards.

In Zn3 maturity, expecting medium-term downward direction, 126 strike put was sold for covered put that covered put strategy. 13 / 64 pips premium was received. To convert this position to covered put in underlying asset future was sold (future short).

Again in the Euro Bund, on June 2, the OGBL2 weekly contract was sold call at 164.5 strike (June 9 maturity). Call was bought from 166 strike. With short-term upwards direction; 164.5 strike put was sold (on the same term) and the other leg has bought put, from 163.5 strike.

With 166 call long and 164.5 call short, a call bear spread was established and with 164.5 put short and 163.5 put long a put bull spread was established. Another definition; these two wings are considered together to form the long iron butterfly strategy. The main idea here is to get a futures short which is cost reduced by premium income at end of maturity. The closing at the end of June 9 maturity was at 164.87 (future price). A total premium of 48 pips was obtained and added with 164.5 strike; 164.5 + 0.48 = 164.98 cost futures short. After one week this strategy will end successfully.

June 9, 2017

Some of the positions from previous call shorts that returned in-the-money, were turned into new call bear spreads. OGB July 1, 163.5 strike call short, in-the-money and 165 strike call long, near out-of-money, positions have established call bear spread. Thus, if the end of term is below 163.5 level, the maximum profit has realized. In this strategy for 165 call long 40 pips premium was given. A premium of 139 pips was received with 163.5 strike call shorts. 139 - 40 = 99 pips

A total of a maximum of 99 pips premium was targeted (under 163.5 strike). If the end of maturity remain at 165 strike and above, it is possible a loss of 150 - 99 = 51 pips. The level of 164.49 is at par. In other words, under 165 strike, we received future short that cost is 164.49.

On June 9, call bear spreads were established between the 164 strike call short and 165 strike call long in OGB3 maturity weekly options. 87 pips premium received from 164 strike short. For 165 strike call long 28 pips premium was given. A maximum of 59 pips profit was targeted under 164 strike. 41 pips damage will be occur above 165 strike. Just below 165 strike, we can get future short with cost of 164.59. We are looking forward to the downside movement and in any case we aim to pass the futures short at end of maturity. Call shorts are sold a consecutive; in terms; in-the-money situation, the positions will return as a future short, the total cost will also decrease.

On June 9, the Euro Bund was sold a call at 164.5 strike (in-the-money) in the OGB3 (June 16 maturity) weekly option contract, resulting in a premium of 51 pips. In the same maturity contract, a call from 165.5 strike was bought and a premium of 12 pips was given. With total of 39 pips, call bear spreads were established and it is intended to have a future cost of 164.89 at the end of the maturity.

Momentum:

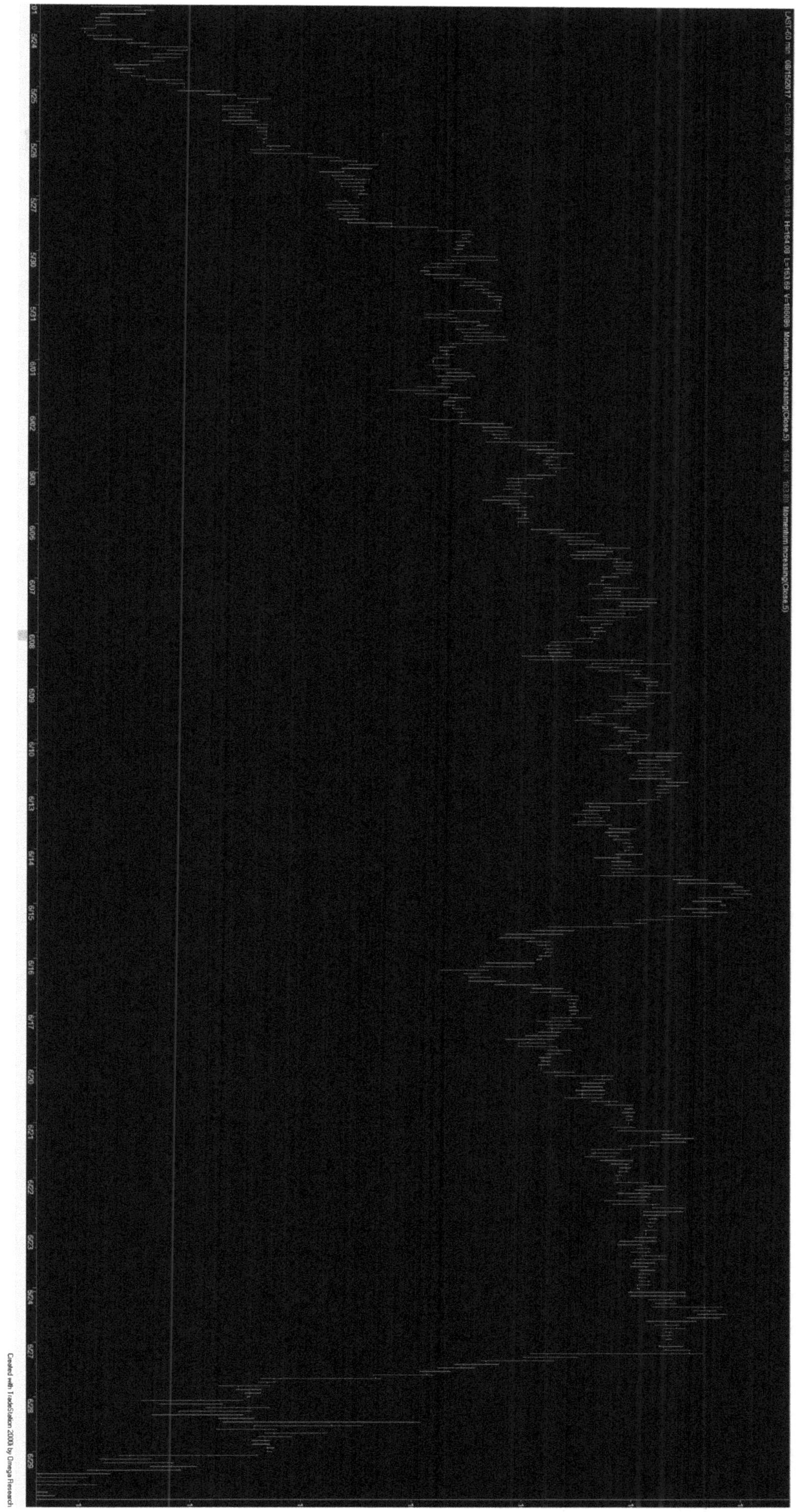

In this section, robot mechanical trade methods are used.

In September term; those that their momentum increases and decreases in the 60-minute period are examined:

On the upward movement between May 26 and May 28, the increasing momentum with blue color; partly in line with rising bullish. Consolidation periods, red is marked for down movement and momentum.

From May 28 to June 1, horizontal movement and continuation; in the horizontal zone from June 3 to June 14, the ones shown in red are moments that are diminished. They are increasing momentums which are shown in blue. These colorful momentums are repeated at a later stage.

By examining closer; except for the horizontal movements of June 1, 13, and 14, the decreasing or diminishing momentums progressed in same direction with price movements (blues follow blues, reds follow reds).

Momentum indicators followed the declining movement from June 15 to June 17 and followed the consolidation movement (with blue in red first). Between June 20 and June 27, however, some momentum movements were visible, but price movements remained mostly flat. Transitions between ascending and descending momentum have been seen in succession. The blue and red signs are in succession. Their graphical appearances are blue to red, red to blue.

The decline that began on June 27 will clarify the assessment of the increasing and decreasing momentum. The decline shown in red between June 27 and June 28 will leave its place upside down on June 28. The blue colors are marked in a row. When this up-reacting flow is over, the downward momentum process, shown in red in color, will re-engage and the great decline will continue.

Key reversals:

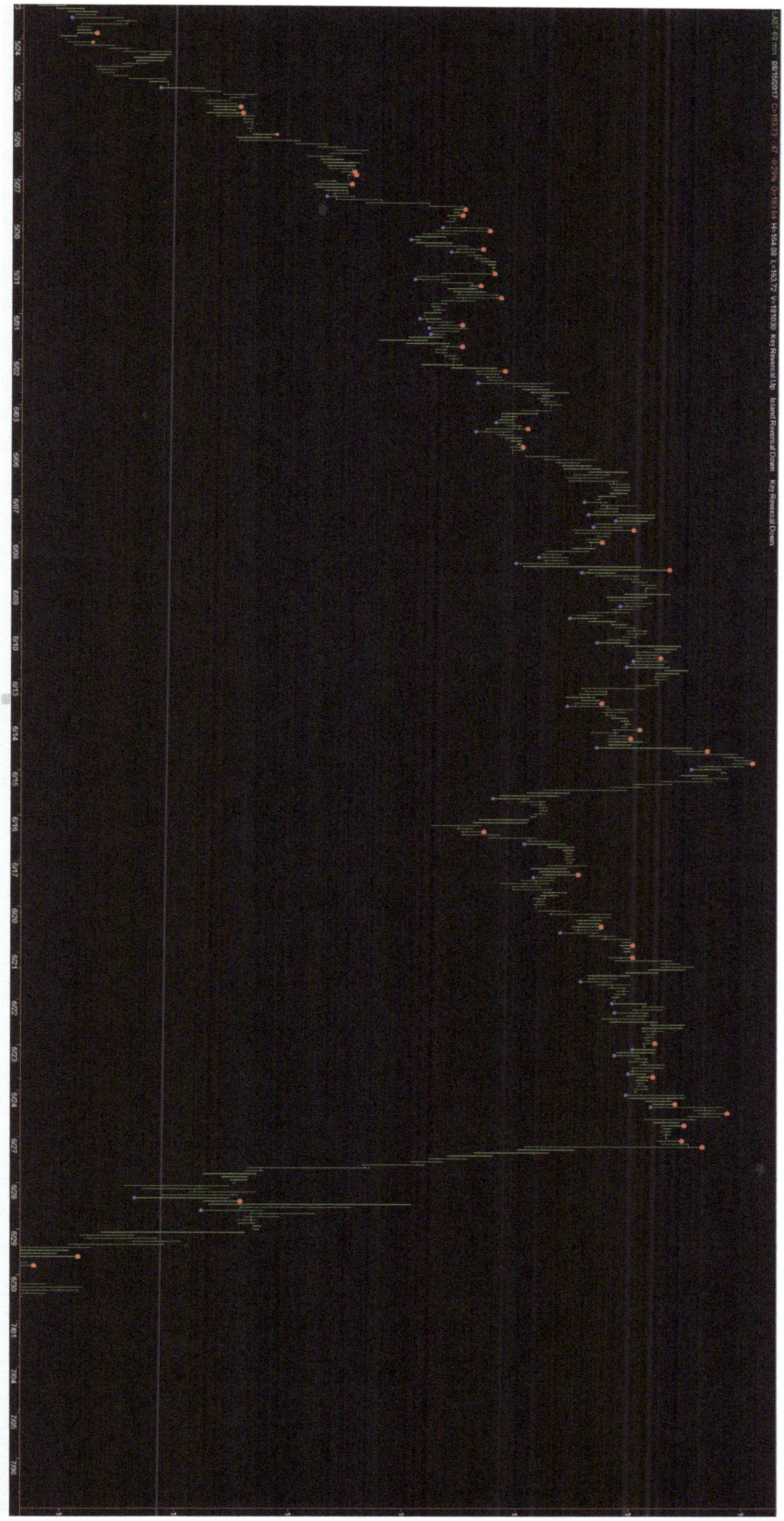

On June 26 and on the morning of June 27, the signs of probability downward, shown by a total of four red dots, are noticeable intensity as a stack.

The similar intensity is shown in red in the downward direction, between May 29 and June 1. However, there are also a number of blue points pointing upwards as a red downward counter-sight. Briefly, blue and red points are balanced. In reponse, counter – sight of red dots on June 26 and 27 are empty (red dots shown probability downward movement). In other words, the downward direction is concentrated solely (red).

As a result, the decline that began later in the morning session on June 27 will justify this last red stack pointing downwards.

Strategy:

On June 16, the call was sold in OGB5 weekly options at 163.5 strike with 122 pips premiums received. In order to hedge this leg, call was bought from 165 strike by giving 32 premiums in the same maturity. With the call bear spread thus created, the closing strategy in previous trades was repeated (the method in the paragraph above was applied) .To the maximum profit potential is 122 - 32 = 90 pips below 163.5 strike.

Again on June 16, July term OGBL monthly option contract 1 call was sold at 164 strike, 67 pips premium received. One call was bought from 165 strike and 14 pips premium was given. The maximum profit of this call bear spread is 67 - 14 = 53 pips. At end of maturity, maximum profit is reached under 164 strike. The maximum damage is fixed at 165 strike and above: 165 - 164 = 1 (100 pips).

100 pips - 53 pips = 47 pips (total premium revenue).

In other words; the maximum damage at the end of the maturity transform can be futures short position with 164 + 0.53 = 164.53 cost (above 165 strike, call short and call long neutralize each other and becomes "0" position). But our main strategy is; (or put long) participate in the downward movement. If action is until the beginning of the movement, our main targets are:

1) Benefit time decay with premium income (call shorts),

2) In-the-money situation, it should have obtained low cost futures shorts (transformed call shorts). Once the decline phase become, let me remind you that it is the mean idea; to open future shorts or puts. Future shorts that return in the -money options case will be the ideal situation if they are stocked (at reduced prices with premium incomes).

On June 16, the underlying asset was 10-year US note; August maturity options contract; call were bought from 128 strike. The calls from 127 strike were sold. While paying 12/64 premiums for 128 strike calls, 30/64 premiums were received from 127 strike shorts. With this call bear spread, it is aimed to obtain a futures short (at maturity finishes exceeding 127 strikes) which is cost reduced (through premiums); primarily at premiums received.

On June 16, strategies were implemented options that using the US 10-year note futures (ZNU17) as underlying assets and also using underlying asset futures.

The puts from the 126.5 strike were sold, so that hedging by futures short previously sold. Covered Put strategy was applied. Again for put shorts sold at 126.5 strike, put longs from 125.75 strike were bought. Thus, put bull spreads were established. These two strategies can be called synthetic iron butterfly appropriate to the futures short leg.

While put shorts are sold for profit, future shorts and put longs are for hedging purposes. At the same time, it was aimed to make profits from the price decrease by futures short until put short strike.

Euro Bund is under contract on September maturity; with 163.5 call shorts (received 2.13 premium) and 165 call longs (given 1.17 premium) were established in-the-money strikes call bear spreads. If the maturity ends at 163.5 strike and below it is aimed maximum profit: 2.13 - 1.17 = 0.96 pips.

Bank Rescue Operations in Italy and Spain in 2017

The ECB announced that it halted funding of two large Italian banks (Veneto Banca, Banca Popolare di Vicenza), while almost all futures markets closed at around 23:00 EET on Friday, June 23. In the same statement, these banks were single-handedly subject to Italian bankruptcy proceedings. In terms of ECB in practice, it means that the acceptance of the bankruptcy of two banks and the subsequent fate of the banks are under the Italian state's responsibility. It is clear that the decision must not be taken separately from the Banco Popular Espanol operation, which was bankrupt on June 6 when Spain's sixth largest bank, and which had been transferred to Santander Bank for 1 euro. Banco Popular Espanol remained under the real estate portfolio as a result of the 2008 crisis, and in the following years it tried to recapitalize and help with ECB liquidity operations. However, it was clear that the share price, which had been depreciating nearly 50% in the week before June 6, (after which large shareholders such as Blackrock had reduced their share nearly %50 in this period) it is evident that it is moving recapitalization or take over. In this process, it was understood from the market indicators that the statements of the Spanish government "calmly watching the event" were to be interpreted as the helplessness during the 2008 crisis, but pointed to a controlled rush (take over or recapitalization) in the conjuncture of 2017. At the night of June 6, after the symbolic price 1 euro take over, especially in Spanish bank shares, such as Santander, the shares rise in the following days will justify the behavior of the market.

If we go back to June 23; we must admit that the Italian banking operation was coordinated with the Spanish banking operation. Spain and Italy banks, two major countries representing the troubled banking of Europe, have been supported by the ECB QE program, and some have returned to life. Others are moving out of the system in June 2017. So; a period is closing, at least the ECB and the competent authorities of the country concerned are preparing for a new turnaround. Why is this decision taken in the middle of 2017? Before looking for an answer to this question, let's look at the market reaction on June 23: Euro Fx gave almost no response. The Euro Bunds are closing at 23:00 GMT and although their volume is very low at this time, it is noteworthy that they do not react at all. US note are open to processing until EET 24:00 and are relatively voluminous. Despite this, they did not show any significant reaction.

If we take the ECB's decision; there is a high possibility that the ECB's disengagement and the transfer to the Italian authorities are coordinated. On the other hand, systematic risk arises that neither ECB nor Italy wants. If we consider the recent history of the two banks in question in particular, these banks benefited from special funds (Atlante 1 and 2) that were set up to save Italian banking after the 2008 crisis. These funds were aimed to support the problematic banks, led by Italy's large and relatively solid banks. Veneto Banca and Banca Popolare di Vicenza are also supported by this fund. A giant like Monte Paschi Bank has contributed to this funds, despite its problems and has been given a sign that it will remain in the system of the market. The problems of Veneto Banca and Banca Popolare di Vicenza were known by markets participants. During the past few months, there have been long discussions and conflicts in Italy and European authorities, which are reflected in the public about the situation of the Italian banks. Briefly, the banks and their problems were the "subject matter" for the markets.

Are Italian authorities ready to meet this step from the ECB? We can strongly predict that they are ready for this problem that is long on the agenda. The implication of the ECB at the end of the declaration is that they will be subject to the Italian bankruptcy proceeding, indicating that the Italian authorities have received approval and made the prepares. At the same time, the debate on bank rescue between the European Union authorities and the Italian authorities is at least convincing that this issue has been resolved.

Let's get back to our question; why is this decision taken in the middle of 2017? Before the answer to this question, let us also remember the bankruptcy of the Spanish bank Banco Popular again in June. The ECB QE program, has been launched to stimulate the economy openly, in particular to bring back the troubled banking of southern European countries. While the revival in the eurozone is clearly visible, it is highly probable that banks failing to solve problems can be taken out of the system and prepared for end of ECB program. So; In mid-2017, the ECB decided to "normalize".

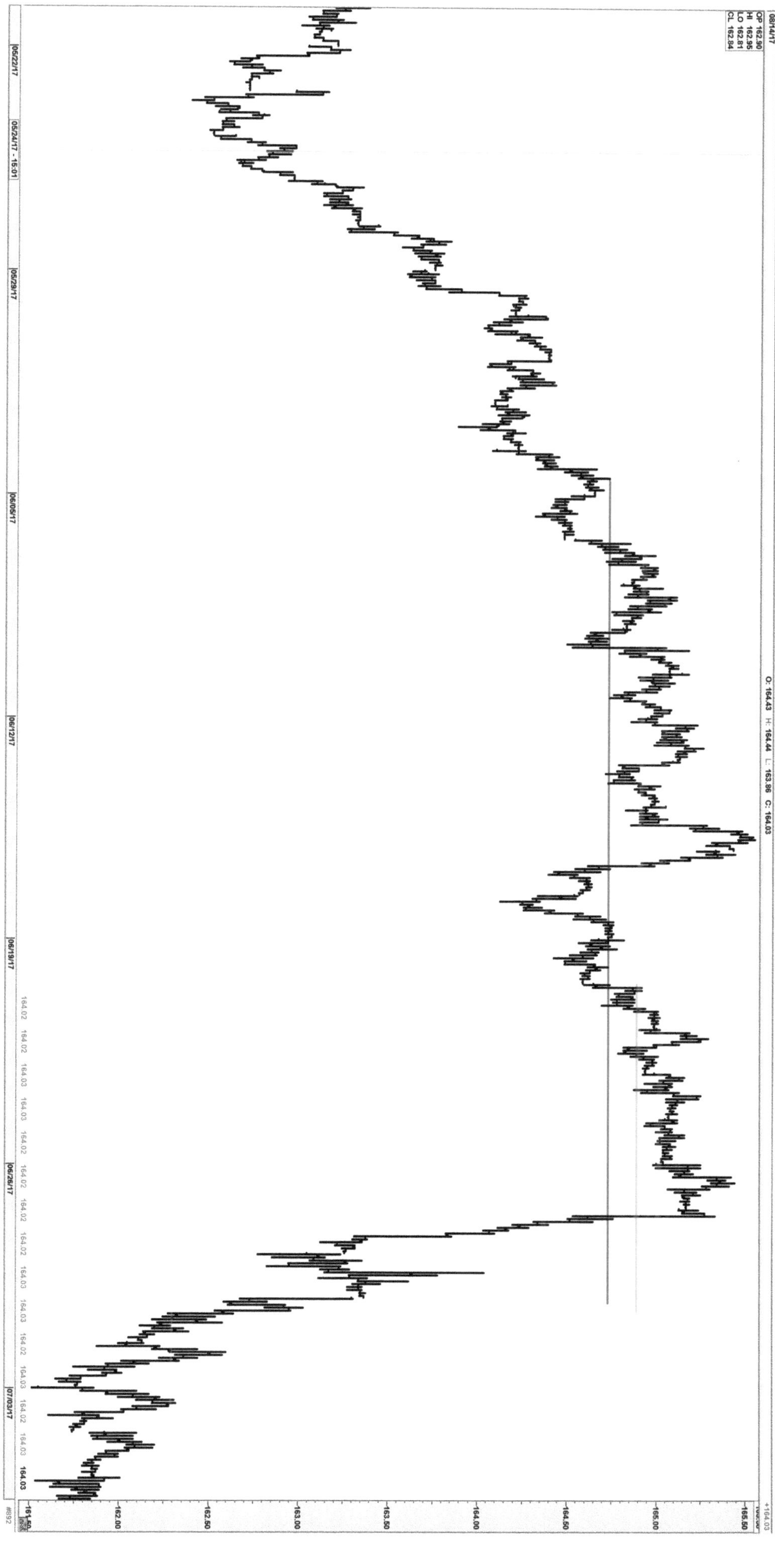
GBLU7 - GBL Sep 2017, 60 - Advanced GET ©2017 Trading Techniques, Inc.

It is expected that the market reaction on Monday and the next few days trend will bring this issue to light. If the market is positive, our scheme is confirmed.

Euro Bund; in a total of three days before June 23; and same day, with two inside day bars, bund price has narrowed like nearly symmetrical triangle. The exit from this formation is expected to give us the direction of the future. Top/peak developed between June 12, 14(June 14 is the highest), if it is completed on the right hand side, it will be possible for a significant movement downward. Towards the upside, a new upturn is expected to begin, with the mass area around 165.44 (opening 165.33) on June 15 and 165.55 (closing 165.46) on June 14, exceeding it with closing / close data. In the direction of downturn is a positive evaluation of the market and the movement in the direction of ascending is a negative evaluation.

Our trigger line for the downward direction should be selected from around 165 level which has the open and close price on June 21 and around 164.90 that has next two day's bottoms. We expand this range by 10 pips and draw up to the level of 164.80, which is the widest lenght of the symmetrical triangle, (June 21). When the technical levels are determined, the price and time levels should be investigated not only according to one method but also considering the others.

On June 26, the Intesa San Paolo Bank emerged by taking over the good assets while the Italian authorities that setting up a 'bad bank' took over the bad loans of the two banks in question. Initially, Intesa Bank and Italian banks shares moved upwards, while Italian bonds reacted in part.

Euro Bund rose to 165.44 during day. The closing was 165.33, that is near to day low 165.31 level.

The following morning, at the opening, the first level of 165.33 was seen as the highest level, followed by the 90 degree angle downward movement and it reached 164.5 level in the first stage. Although the reaction from here rose 164.76 next hour, the downward movement accelerated again throughout the day. Approached to level 163 at closing. The downward movement that we had anticipated began with breaking the band of 164.90 - 164.80, which we previously set as the trigger line (remember that the pull back is limited to 164.76).

Through this text, we explained how we found this movement together with macroeconomic analysis + news evaluation + technical analysis.

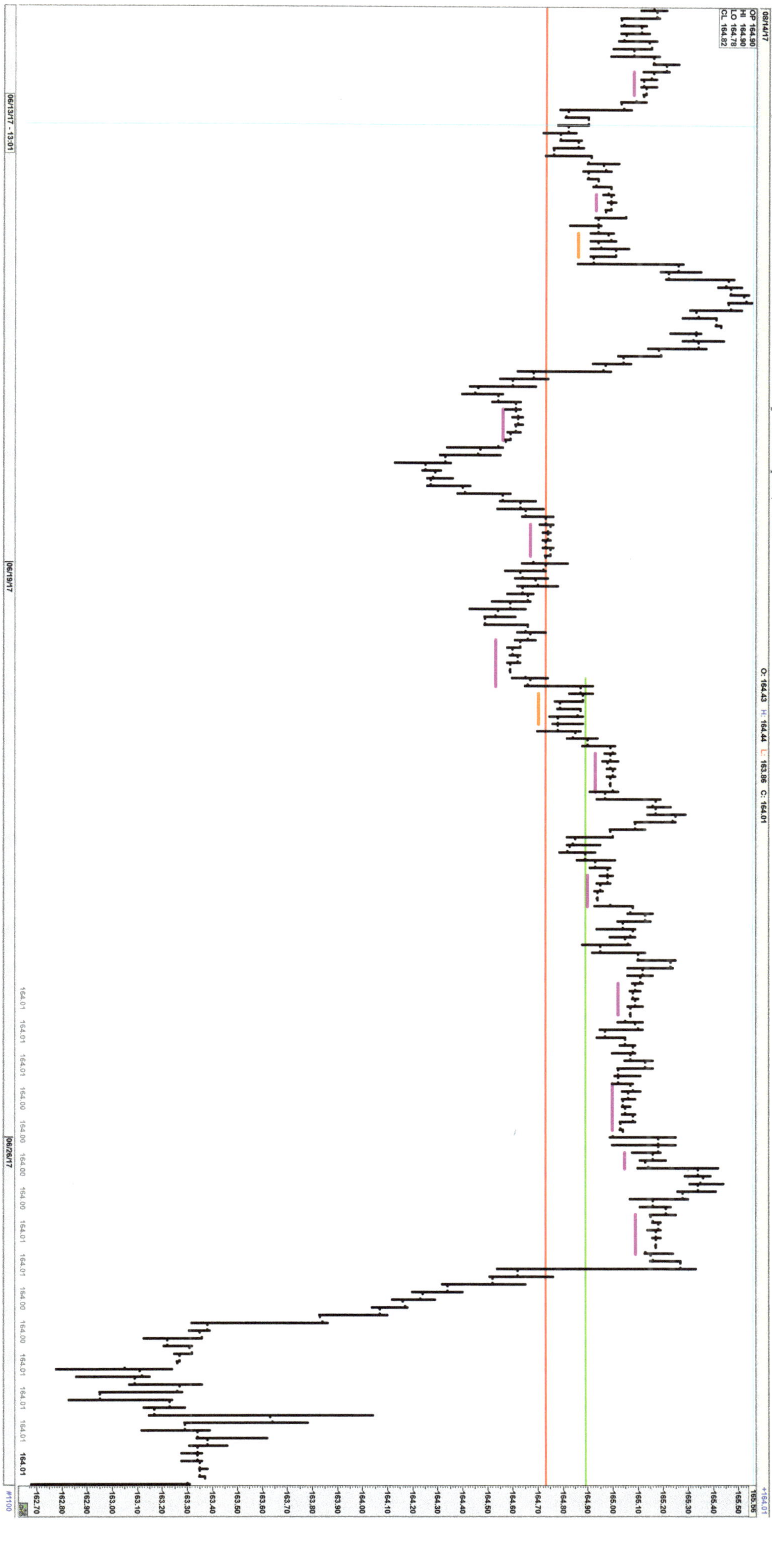
GBLU7 - GBL Sep 2017, 60 - Advanced GET ©2017 Trading Techniques, Inc.

We will consider a 60-minute analysis of the Euro Bund contract at September maturity.

The horizontal red line drawn on the top of June 2, appeared after the June 14 top and June 16 pull back.

After the tops of June 7, 9, 13; June 14 top appeared. With this last top, the first half of heads and shoulder like formation began to appear. After the June 16 pullback was overrun on June 20, the two over-the-counter trials increased the likelihood of being evaluated as a neckline on the red horizontal line.

The horizontal green line drawn between June 20 and June 26 is the right shoulder support level.

The area between the green and red line (164.90 - 164.75) can be considered as the trigger line area. After violation of a single bar on June 27, the decline began. This decline began after pull back on the red horizontal line, which was prevailed only one hour, will drop at 90° like the wall.

The writer of these lines identifies this trigger line / field before breaking occurs.

In the other chart, the post- June 12 price bars were examined with the inside bars and breaks.

Red cut lines show inside bars. These bar stacks usually consist of 4 and 6 bars.

The June 14 morning stack, and especially the June 20 stack, is the energy coil (bar-code-like) view of the algo traders.

Other stacks are; saturated price movements, overpriced expectations, and over-the-top selling of confidential news (or purchases) in big hands (by speculator etc.).

When confidential news were matured, the big hands (the players) distribute the goods / contracts in the saturated market. It is a fact that these stack areas are broken up in various ways, resulting in very small movements.

The up attacks that started as a breakdown remain because of distribution.

We can see from inside bars / energy coils clustering along the green horizontal line as the start time of the downward direction approaches.

During such occurrences to find the breaking moment, it is necessary to examine the news flow and the expectation which was bought/ started or ended. In Euro Bund contract; although the ECB's attempt to end the Italian banking crisis (cutting funding and transferring to Italian authorities) was intended to be used to launch an upward movement on Monday following the news on Friday evening, June 23, the move was only effective in the Monday morning session. The up attack has limited below June 14 top. Moreover, the second session was stagnant and the price movement ended in the evening with coil.

After the last upstep on Tuesday morning (June 27), the anticipated big decline began, with previously determined green and red lines crossing down.

The market saturated with the big hands/ players who previously sold the news of the ECB, the failure to upturn and the deepening of the decline with new news (Sintra meeting) continued until July 7.

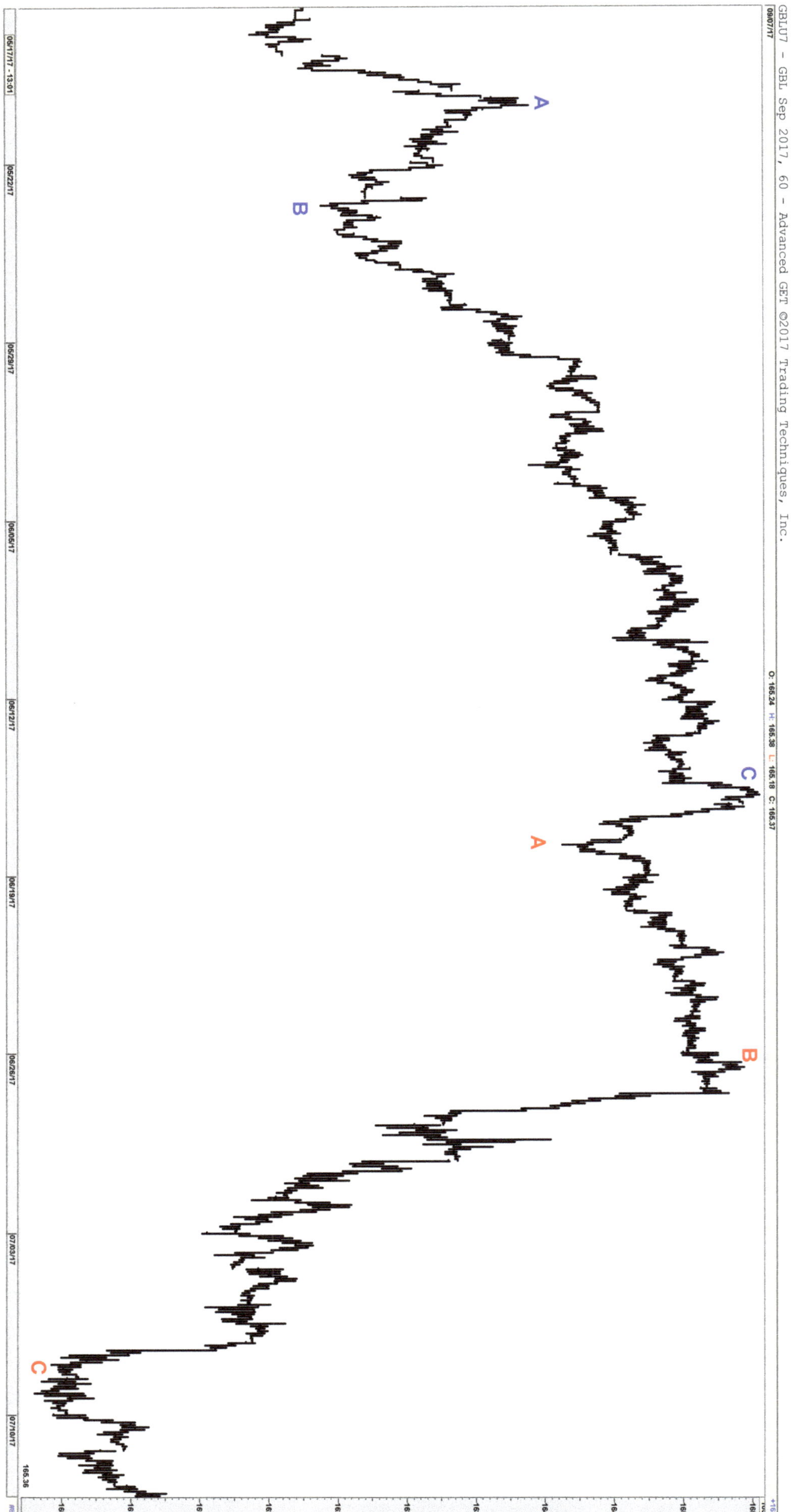
GBLU7 - GBL Sep 2017, 60 - Advanced GET ©2017 Trading Techniques, Inc.
A
B
C
A
B
C

The period can be analyzed by the Elliott wave count as well as the shoulder head shoulder and neck line.

June 14 top at same time, has the top of 3rd wave (or blue C wave). June 16 is the bottom wave (red color). June 26 is the top of the B wave.

The narrow and dull character of the June 20-26 formation is very suitable for the B wave.

The great decline of C wave will begin with June 27.

Strategy:

On June 23, 2 puts were taken from 162 strike, which were due on July 21 contract. 8 pips has given.

In September maturity contract that end of term is August 25, 2 calls were bought from 165 strike. From 167 strike, 2 calls were sold. This call bull spread was paid 120 - 36 = 84 pips premium (per strategy). Based on the hedge of this call bull spread, the futures contract of September opened 2 future shorts. Again in August 25 term option contract, 2 were sold from 163.5 strike and 56 pips premium received.

Thus, through the futures shorts protected by call bull spreads, the position was taken for possible movement downward. A total of 84 - 56 = 28 pips premiums paid. Whereas, futures short profit was targeted at 165.10 (futures short price) - 163.5 = 160 pips. Total maximum profit is below 163 strike; 160 - 28 = 132 pips (per strategy). In this combined strategy; [Future short + put short = covered put] and [call bull spread + Future short bounded synthetic put] strategies together.

On June 23, 165 strike put was bought in the July term option contract (68 pips premium was given). From 163.5 strikes put was sold (23 pips premium was received). Thus, 68-23 = 45 pips premium was given (165 - 163.5) - 0.45 = 1.05 (105) pips maximum profit was targeted. At the end of the July 21 maturity, the maximum profit is reached if it stays 163,5 strikes and below this level.

Again on June 23, in the evening hours, the strategy; with 167 strike call short, 165 strike call long (call bull spread)+ future short + 163.5 strike put short was repeated in the September maturity contract which we wrote earlier and 3 more positions were added.

June 27, on Tuesday, in Sintra; at the meeting of the presidents and members of the Central Bank of the developed countries, Draghi said that the deflationary factors in the euro area were replaced by inflationary factors. Again, Draghi stated that the withdrawal of the inflation is temporary. This talk came after the Italian bank rescue operation and the perception has brought that ECB is beginning to normalize. Significant price movements were observed in various instruments, particularly in the bond market and the euro. On june 28, when the downward trend in the bonds continues, an uncertain ECB source did an explanation; "Draghi did not say anything other than ECB decisions" and simultaneously price movement occurred. Euro Bund interest rates fell, the euro depreciated. The content of this explanation is; "Draghi can not explain a new decision prior to the ECB meeting, it can not dictate to the ECB board alone" it is nothing more than than a known.

Beyond this, however, declarations on unofficial platforms such as Sintra, continue to carry a possible signal identity.

The market participants have realized /apperceived this fine detail and the Euro rose again as interest rates were rising. While BOE chairman Carney said that "BOE is likely to start raising interest rates and that it will be discussed in the coming months". At the same upward movement has become strong, Bond interest rate hikes (down direction for the Euro Bund futures) and the Euro increase have begun to turn a trend with these main news effect.

These statements prevailed in the sense that developed Central Banks were preparing for monetary tightening (or reducing monetary expansion for the ECB in the same sense).

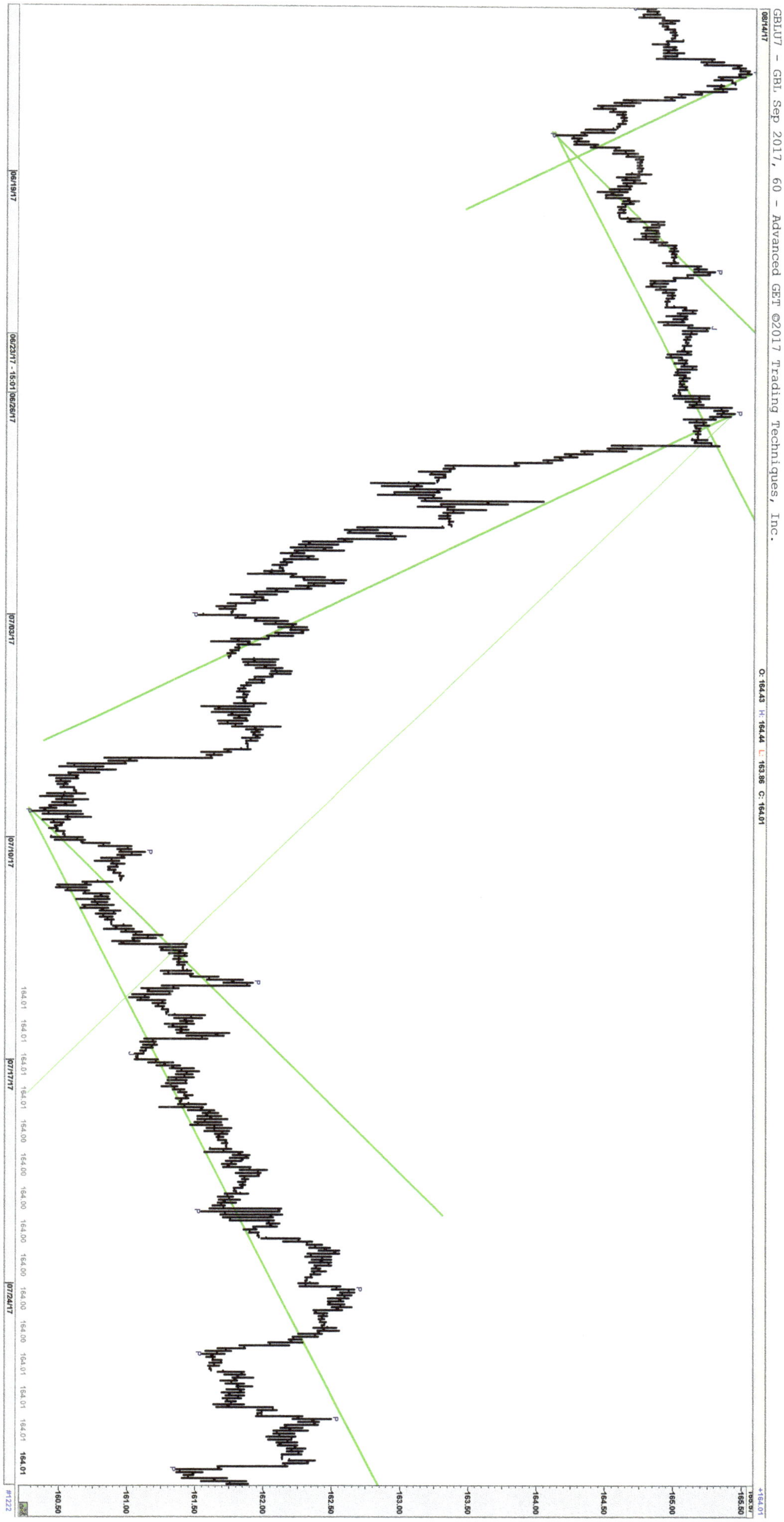
GBLU7 - GBL Sep 2017, 60 - Advanced GET ©2017 Trading Techniques, Inc.
O: 164.43 H: 164.44 L: 163.86 C: 164.01

We used Gann angle in the technical analysis of the Euro Bund September term contract, a 60-minute period. In particular, Gann's angles have not been determined with this chart's price/ time ratio. Throughout this book the same rate (per period) was used.

The 1X1 angle drawn from the top of the June 14 top showed exactly the decline continuing two days.

June 14th top will be the highest price level for nearly 3 months.

The price movement between the two angles during the ascension, which started from the bottom of June 16, closed below the angle on the evening of June 26. The next day, the morning session started with the fall that began after the failure of the experiment to go up to the same angle and the downward movement that will continue until July 7th. During this decline, the 28th of June pull back was overturned just above the downward angle.

The consolidation period, which began after the July 3 at bottom and crossed up angle, continued until the last downfall on 6 July. It is remarkable that this latest down-wave bottom, is also supported by the crossed up angle has ended on July 7th.

Drawing from the top on June 26th, the 2. Angle crossed up and a new upward movement started on July 12th. It is striking that during this upward movement the price swing remains between the two angles drawn from the July 7 bottom. On July 25th, after the angle of grafting downwards, the pull back at 27th of July, was finally over when we reached the same angle.

Strategy:

On June 27 at around 10:00 am (EET/ EasternEuropean Time), at OGB5 maturity weekly options contract was sold 165 strike calls. 37 pips premium was received per contact. In order to hedge these call shorts; calls were bought to 2 pips from 166 strikes in the same term at a later time.

With these call bear spreads established, the maximum profit of 37 - 2 = 35 pips was targeted with closing below 165 strike.

On June 27, at around 11:00 (EET), when the September future price was slightly above 164.50:

In OGB5 weekly futures options, 164.5 strike calls were sold based on the hedge of 166 strike call longs. The OGB1, which is the next weekly maturity from the same strike, also sells calls with a premium of 38 pips (also from 164.5 strike).

On the same day, sell stops were written at 163.54 level in order to open future short positions. These positions have been realized during the evening of the EET.

On June 27, September term contract, when the future pass down level 164.90, the puts previously sold from 164 strike(leg of covered put strategy) were closed and reopened from the strike at 163.5, 163 and 162.5 in the same term. With some loss of premiums, it was aimed to participate in price movements over a longer period.

Also in the evening hours, when September futures moved to 163.5 level; the puts were closed that previously sold from 163.5 strike (covered put strategy leg) and reopened from the strike 163, 162.5 and 162 strikes in same term.

When we sold new puts on low strikes, these out of money strikes puts premiums increased (example here is; 162,5 strike). At the money or near out of money are closed (example here is; 164 strike). The out of money puts short were opened instead of being closed ones. Thus;

a) possible future short profit is increased,

b) With a few total loss of premiums; compare to premiums given for puts closed that received premiums increased by out of money strikes puts which were sold (reopened).

Let us also remember that; the puts we had previously sold from 164 strike, wrote a partial profit over time.

Notes On The Sintra Meeting and Draghi Talk

Let's take a closer look at the fluctuations in the Sintra meeting. With Draghi's comments, the German bond interest rates have increased with the market view, which suggests that the ECB is going to exit from the QE program. The next day in the market movement with Draghi's explanations; the explanation of "the Draghi did not say anything new, did not express a different opinion from the ECB's current judgment" came from an anonymous ECB source, causing a withdrawal which only affected in the session. The price movement continued in the following days, strengthening in the previous direction.

We need to pay attention to two things in order to understand Draghi's description and the least effect of explaining it is to deny it:

A) Commenting on the interest rate hike in the speech of Sintra on behalf of the Bank of England after the unnamed ECB statement, it confirmed that the possible exit from the monetary loosening at the world's leading central banks meeting was assessed.

B) Draghi evaluates possible exit from the other developed Central Bank members in Sintra; will not allow this change to be announced before the ECB meeting, even if the current ECB board can change the decision on its own or take a decision before the board meeting. Even if there is an opinion (or even a changing view of the board / management board) in this direction, Draghi is unlikely to be in a position to diminish the effect of QE program. The fact that the exit of the ECB's program is already dependent on datas (priority inflation) is main rule.

As a result; at the Sintra meeting speeches, there were messages prepared to exit for the market, and the unnamed ECB source tried to stabilize the explanation so that the market reaction did not go too far and did not reduce the benefit of effect of QE program. If the market reaction goes further than the ECB, try to be balanced with the comments from the other members first, and if necessary, a hawkish explanation is made at the next meeting.

Strategy:

On June 30, options on 10-year US note; the ZN1 code weekly contract; call was sold from 126 strike. 13/64 pips premium was received. To hedge this leg, 127.75 strike call was bought in the same term, 1/64 premium was given. With this call bear spread, which was established in July 7 term options, a maximum profit of 12/64 pips in total was targeted. In the weekly contract of July 14 with ZN2 code, a call bear spread was established with the calls longs/shorts from the same strikes. On the OZN coded August maturity contract; call was sold at 126.5 strike. Call was bought from 127 strike. In the same term, from 125.5 strike put was sold and from 124.5 strike put was bought.

Thus, in the OZN-coded contract options, call bear spread and put bull spread were set up to receive the premium income from two direction. A modified long iron butterfly strategy was set up in different strikes in the middle legs in the form of unequal wing lenghts.

In such strategies, the aim is not only to wait for the end of the maturity and to obtain premium income, but to close and reopen the short legs or the legs one by one in the same or different strike which increases the premium with fluctuating underlying asset prices. Thus, once a premium is given to long legs but premiums are earned multiple times from short legs (close and open, or reopen).

Based on the short futures available on June 30, in the August maturity OZN contract, put was sold from 125.5 strike. With this covered put strategy, it was aimed to partly participate in possible downward action via future short + premium revenue. 125.5 strike put sales with 28/64 pips premium was received.

On July 3, in USA the ISM data was higher and this reported that the economy revival had strengthened one more level. The stronger signals that the BOE, the ECB and perhaps the BOJ are able to withdraw from excessively loose monetary policies, it need to be taken into account in a meeting held in Sintra where the chairman and members of the developed country's Central Bank can generate more free ideas. Although there are strong signals from the economies in the countries concerned;

a) the increase in wages is limited despite falling unemployment.

b) inflation is still far from its expected higher level.

For this reason it is necessary to approach the Sintra meeting signals or the announcements that correspond to the same period and the official source of the central bank is uncertain.

Bond interest rates as a pioneer in wage increases and / or recovery up to inflation; not only the Central Bank signals and economic data, but also North Korean geopolitical tension, Trump-Congress tax planners' wars, and Trump-related inquiries. The most obvious price impressive factor that is currently visible is expecting FED's withdrawal program to begin in September.

Strategy:

On July 6, 163.5 call shorts, previously sold in the Euro Bund options, were closed with high premium income. The future price of the underlying asset is reduced to 160.50 same day; 167 strike call short legs, which were legs of call bull spread that aimed hedging of futures short and were previously out-of-money, were closed with profits as a result of a very large premium income.

On July 6, OZN and OZN2 (weekly) futures contracts that used US 10-year note futures as underlying assests's call shorts previously sold, were closed. Call long legs were held for the purpose of being used for the possibility of a new call bear spread because the maturity did not end.

On July 6 again, in the Euro Bund September term, the deep in-the-money 163.5 strike put shorts and futures shorts which were hedged by them, were closed successfully. As the 163.5 strike become deep in-the-money, the price remaining below this strike is almost entirely covered by the future short. In other words; at deep in-the-money, time premium is reduced too. In our practice, we received a decision to terminate the strategy when it was close to the end of the targeted premium income, as the time premium has been eroded by time. During the upcoming period (close to 2 months), we have increased our ability to open a new position with upward movement possibility.

In Euro Bund, in the early morning session on July 12, 162.5 put shorts in the August term (July 21 maturity) and September term futures shorts which have made hedged, were closed with premium income and future short earning.

Put shorts;

a) when it becomes deep in-the-money and

b) As the time is eroded, the strategy is closed successfully before the maturity, when the immediate full amount of the premium income is obtained.

Thus, in the remaining of the maturity avoiding from the fluctuations was possible that because of these causes:

1) Option pain influence and

2) Possible macro news flow effects.

On July 12, call shorts were sold in July 14 term options contract and July 21 term options contract, based on previously held call longs, which used US bond futures as underlying assets. September maturity (ZNU17) bond futures, which saw the lowest level at 124.255 in the July 6 pivot, saw the highest level at 125.235 on July 12.

On this rise, 126 strike call short was sold on July 14 term options contract, which was hedging by 127.25 strike call long.

As a result of the news about Trump's son on the Russian scandal, it is expected that his authority, which is low on the party, will be shaken thoroughly. In this case, some senators may object to the senate in which wants to change Obamacare. Senators by objections may show that they do not approve of Trump over Obamacare. The centuries-long nature of the political era has been built with such power shows.

As for July 14, when US inflation was low, we closed the covered put positions on the Euro bund September term, which were formed from the futures short + put short, on July 17. On the same day we built call bear spreads based on the call longs available (165 call longs from the previous strategies) and selling calls from 163.5 strike (September maturity). Again on July 17; put bear spreads, which were established in September term (164 strike put long and 162 strike put short), were closed with premium income approaching 80%. Despite the 20% profit to be made if it was held until the end of the maturity, it was aimed to avoid possible upward movement. Also on the same day in the August term contract, with futures short and 162.5 strike put short; covered put strategies was also closed with high premium profits. All of these strategies are aimed at profit before the end of the term;

a) It is an effort to maintain profits near to full prime (75% and higher yield) despite the remaining time of the maturity,

b) Preservation of profits due to upward price movement expectation for basic and technical reasons.

Based on 165 call longs on July 18 at the Euro Bund, we sold from 163 strike calls and 163.5 strike calls in September. It is aimed to obtain premium income with these call bear spreads.

While with EET on July 17 night, two US Republican senators announced that they were against health insurance/Obamacare (in parallel with our previous analysis)stress began to increase in US bond. With this political news after the US inflation data, we are more likely to see closed our position in the Euro Bund to be justified.

If there is no signal of reduction in the BOJ and ECB meetings on July 17 - July 21, interest rates may decline.

ECB Decision and Draghi Speech

On Thursday July 20, no changes were made as expected in the ECB decision text. In the ECB June meeting notes, we came across discussions that members could withdraw their commitment to QE increases if necessary. However, at the July meeting it seems that no decision has been taken in this direction. The market will have a exception of the September meeting for this decision.

Explain of Draghi on Thursday after the decision text, he has been seen as 'pigeon'. Besides, Draghi's talk; "for inflation target is in favor of financial conditions; stable, sustainable rise", it was a signal to the hawk / hawkish for the future (Draghi with the corresponding assessment in July, changed his views slightly observed that during the relatively high inflation in the spring; "The needed conditions are stabilized for inflation"). Even if the Euro reacted to this with rising bond markets made unstable oscillations. Up and down swings in the Euro Bund over a certain interval (bar code-like price bars); it marks the period of instability of the algo's. It is highly probable that the output from this energy coil will result in an attack on one direction.

On July 20, the Euro Bund, which move up and down in equal proportions in barcode appearence; after the ECB decision, the comments given to the economy press by the "anonymous ECB sources" showed that no signal will be given prior to the October meeting + as the Trump inquiry spread to Trump companies, Euro Bund move upward direction as US note. At the end of August, Draghi will to speak at the Jackson Hole meeting; this period does not seem to be factor to move interes rates upward (except for the possibility of a sharp change in macro data).

For this reason, there is a downward trend in bond interest rates from late July to mid-August.

Based on the above deduction, we have closed almost all of the 163, 163.5 and 164 strike call shorts in the Bund with the same price or little damage (one leg of the bear call spreads).

We assume that we will be able to rebuild these strategies at a better price in the possible interest rate decline till mid-August.

July 20, 2017

Assessment on Central Banks Statement and the Political Struggle between Trump and the Senate:

As BOJ did not make any changes, Kuroda explained that even the slightest hawkish message was not given, saying ETF purchases did not cause imbalance.

Draghi, along with other Central Banks (apart from the BOJ), signaled the first tightening signal through closed communication in Sintra, and the markets showed reaction to it particularly in the bond market. At the first ECB meeting (July) + Draghi's press conference at a hawkish message could lead to a second upward reaction at the market and the rise in bond interest rates could almost turn into a trend. In such a case, strong market orientation (increase in bond rates, excessive strengthening of the euro) would neutralize the impact of the ECB's ongoing buying program.

In Draghi's press conference; strong emphasis on inflation expectations and statements that can be commented as negative interest will continue after the reduction in purchases; coupled with the absence of any exit signs, strengthened the likelihood that market interest bond yields would not be on the rise.

In the United States, Trump began to struggle to get over the proposal that would lift Obamacare. The Euro Bund covered put closed prematurely once the possibility of a fall in US bond interest rates due to leaked news about Trump inquiries. Thus, the possibility of damage from the future short was avoided in the possible rise.

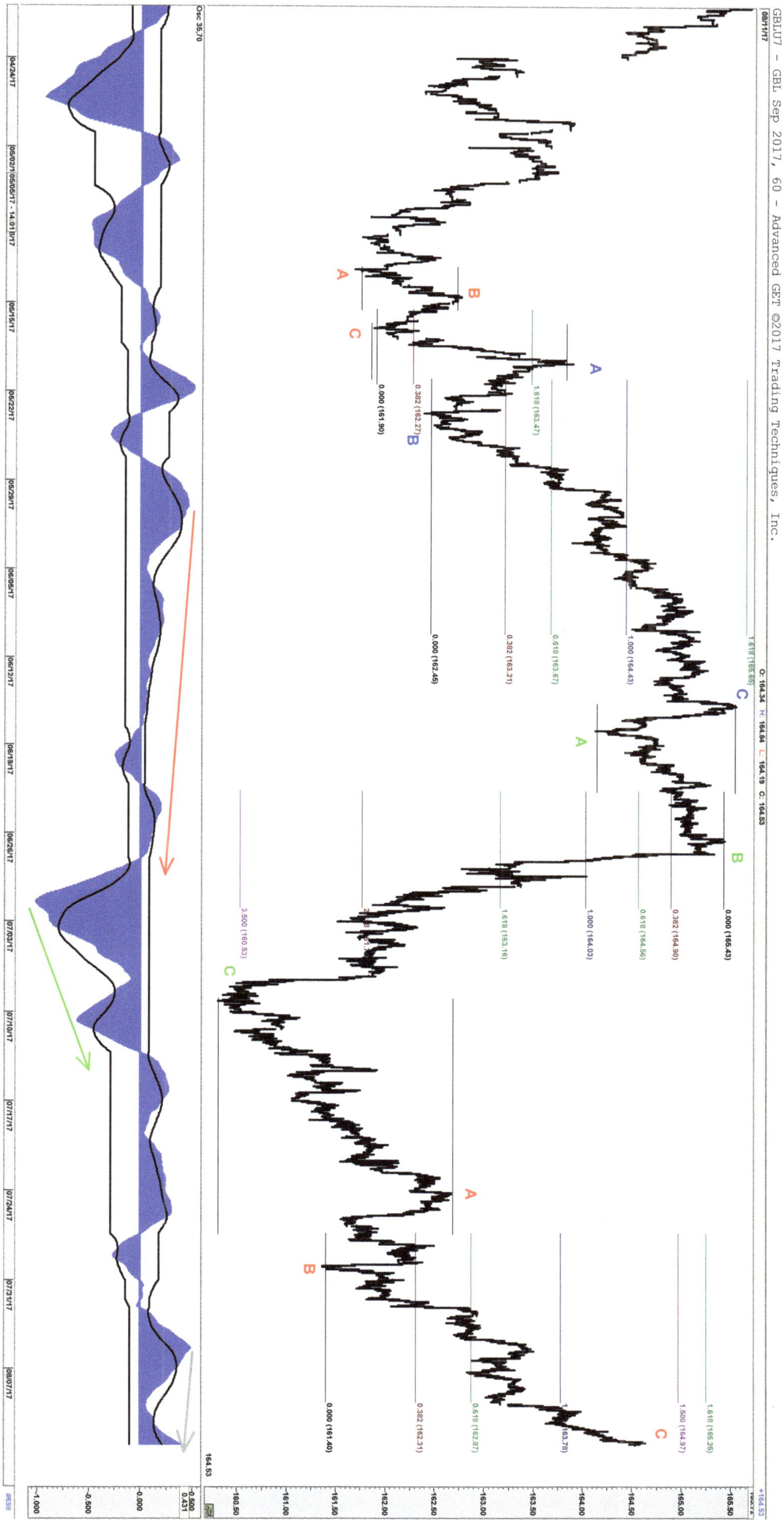
GBLU7 - GBL Sep 2017, 60 - Advanced GET ©2017 Trading Techniques, Inc.

We are going to deal with Euro Bund, U (September) maturity contract, 60-minute periodic chart technical analysis made with Elliott wave count, fibonacci rates and oscillator.

The rise starting from the end of the red C wave (May 16) ended at 163.80 on May 18. We show this movement with a green "A" wave.

The downward movement starting from the "A" wave will end on May 23 at the 162.45 level. The upward movement, which starts after the typical "B" wave with stagnating motion, will end on June 14 at 165.48.

This top is indicated by "C". The "C" wave was formed in the size of almost 1.618 of "A" waves. In the movement up to the rate of 1.618; 1, 0.618, 0.382 levels are also shown in the graph. Note that support / resistance zones are formed around these levels. These occurrences indicate that the price action follows the fibonacci rates (and 1 coefficient).

The downward movement, which started with the blue color "C", paused on June 16, approaching level 164. The upward movement, starting here, ended on June 26 just above the 165 level (green B).

The declining motion after wave B was sudden and very steep. I would also like to draw attention to the fact that I found supportive resistance in various fibonacci rates during the decline.

The June 14 and June 26 tops can be counted as the 3rd and 5th waves. However, in our Euro bund analysis, we prefer to use the analysis approach with only 3 waves.

When the June 14 and June 26 tops are near price levels, note the oscillator diverge.

During the motion that ended at the bottom of July 7 (green "C"), 3.5 times of A wave was taken. Although there is not a speciality of 3.5 times coefficient, let us remember the outcome of the anticipation in the previous term / maturity contract. Repetition of such rates is a memory of price movements.

In the last wave of the C wave, the oscillator's divergence approves the July 7 bottom. The rise from this bottom will end on July 24 at 162.57 (red A).

The withdrawal starting from wave A will end on July 28 at 161.73 (red B wave).

The rise starting from B will enter the consolidation around the fibonacci rates and will end above 165.70 on September 6 (right outside your graph). Thus, the C wave that goes up to about 1.618 times of the A wave will be completed.

Strategy:

On the afternoon of July 20 taking advantage of rising prices, call bear spreads were established in the Euro bund in September term with 165.5 strike call longs, 163.5 and 164 strike call shorts. Thus, at the end of the maturity premium income was targeted.

On the same day, call bear spreads were established with call short from 126 strike and call long from 127 strike with July 24 maturity in weekly options, US note September term futures which assumed underlying asset.

On the same day again, on August 4 contract with 127.75 strike call long + 126 strike put short + September term future short, the hedging covered put strategy was established. This strategy is repeated in the following weeklys and monthlys term contracts. The aim of the strategy; likely to be released in narrow band, in 10-year US note;

a) to earn premium income with a put short and

b) to participate in a partial downward price movement with a future short.

c) Futures short hedging, are also made with the call long. If the future price increases much more than expected in the related term, it is tried to close the put short with premium income and to reopen near strike put short position. Thus, it is intended to transfer / make over the put premium profit.

On July 21 maturity contract which were hedged from 127.25 and 128 strikes call longs were hedged from 126.25 strike, calls were sold and premiums were received.

Thus, while call longs were held on weekly and monthly option contracts, during the underlying asset which released oscillator, first shorts were closed with a high premium profit and then reopened during the maturity period.

In other words, call bear spread strategies were actively managed.

Call bear spreads were set up on July 21 in US notr. Call bear spreads have been set up on weekly option contracts of Zn4 term (July 28), which accepts September futures contract as underlying asset. In the Zn4 code contract, 127 strike call was bought and 3/64 pips premium was awarded and 16/64 pips premiums were taken from 126 strike call short which has sold.

The possible maximum profit for the Zn4 term contract when is on 126 strike or below 126 strike; 16/64 - 3/64 = 13/64 pips. If the maturity ends over 127 strike; maximum possible damage is 64/64 - 13/64 = 51/64 pips.

The main argument here is; it will be profitable to open a futures short position in the near/ medium term from near 127 strike, as well as to obtain premium income. With call bear spreads made in consecutive weekly trades, the position (first options contract, next future short)cost is reduced (by adding premium).

Closing last Bund positions

On Monday, July 24, Germany and Eurozone Flash PMI data were under expectations, and as the Euro Bund crosed up on Friday level, all remaining positions were closed.

Call bear spreads's call short legs were closed with a small amount of damage. The call short legs were at 163.5 strike. Call long legs were at 165 and 165.5 strike: 15 pips short - 34 pips long = 19 pips damage and 35 pips short - 34 pips long = 1 pips gain.

The inflation slowdown in the UK, that the developed country where the first interest rate increase is expected, as the ECB and the BOJ have not changed in the past week, Trump's tax reforms each passing day becoming more difficulty; in short term it seems that the conditions to raise bond rates, have weakened. The upward revision of the Canadian Central Bank on July 12, is the only reversal of this bias. It is also possible that it is a pioneering decision for other Central Banks.

At the FOMC meeting on July 26, after a partial decline in US inflation in the last month, no significant change in the text statement appears likely. The exception to this is the addition of expressions indicating that the FED will start its normalization step in the autumn (strongly possible in September).

On July 24, at the Zn1 contract of August 4 term, 126 strike was put sold. 24/64 pips premium was received. On the same option contracts, a 3-legged strategy was established by buying call from 127.75 strike (3/64 pips premium paid) and opening 1 future short.

Put short + futures short + call long with covered put strategy was established; at the same time with the call long and future shorts, the synthetic put strategy was set up.

a) It's aimed with put short at taking a premium

b) It was aimed to benefit from the partial downward price movement with the futures short (until put short strike).

c) Put short was hedged at the same time by the futures short.

d) With the call long, futures short was hedged.

These strategies and the strategies established previously for US note will be successful in late July and early August, at the end of the terms.

On August 10, in Euro Bund contracts at September term, after rising futures prices; 165 strike calls were sold, based on the 167.5 strike call longs available. Call bear spread strategies were established.

On August 11, calls were sold from 165.5 and 166 strikes. Calls were bought from 167 strike and 167.5 strike. New call bear spread strategies were established.

On August 16, 165.5 and 166 strike calls were closed off with almost all premium profits.

On August 25, 165 strike call shorts (and remaining call longs) successfully ended as out-of-money.

Option Pain: Upcoming End Of Maturity and Price Fluctuation

In options, the time-decay is accelerated as the end of maturity approaches. In the last 1 month and under, long options (option bought) due to this time decay, will lead to loss of premiums. It is recommended that positions taken by the mid-long term option strategy be closed during this time period, that decay is accelerated. As the end of maturity approaches, it becomes easier to manipulate options because time value diminished. Unexpected price movements are common.

These sudden price fluctuations beyond external factors such as news impact, macroeconomic data impact, especially on the dates when multiple contracts (active and deep volume) end on the same day (third quarter of each month, "the triple witching" has named from the witches of Macbeth or on Friday when the weekly options which are becoming more and more common are ending). Even in the markets where price anomalies can be considered in almost every market, even in isolated markets; option is likely to occur in the last hours of the futures contracts and/or options contracts.

If the price movements of the option contracts are similar to the wave theorem towards the end of maturity over the last 10 days, the correction wave develop on counterpart to impulsive wave. If this correction wave is deep, in the last 3 days the opposite occurs, the motion in the direction of the previous impulsive wave occurred.

If the correction wave is not solid, the motion of the last 3 days may develop horizontally.

The dates we refer to are based on observations and can vary. The net observed period (pattern, form), is first exaggerated/exhausted by the market, and then changed. The pattern can also be consisting of a simple or complex time period, as well as time and price.

The new pattern will also be exhausted after a while. After a while, the old pattern reappears. This conversion is the general rule of the markets.

Let's go back to the strong action on Friday when the weekly options end; on Saturdays when the stock exchanges were active (many places were working half a day) the week was divided into two periods for evaluation: Monday - Wednesday, Wednesday - Saturday periods.

Nowadays, with the prevalence of weekly option contracts which ended on Friday, many times the price wave that started on Wednesday evening or Thursday and ended on Monday are prevailed. The weekly option effects continues until the first half of Monday despite the closing of Friday evening.

The option investor should be prepared against the possible fluctuations that will occur towards the end of the maturity (which can not be explained by the news flow and data calendar). These price movements may be in contrast to the macro (economic, financial, even political) expectation of the market or often in the form of over-buying, selling (expectation buying or selling) of this expectation.

Let's explain briefly max pain / option pain / strike price pegging, which is trying to explain the anomaly of the end of maturity (and making the profit calculation).

Max pain theory argues that, end of maturity day (except for macro news, data shock etc.), option price is ending at the level that option buyers are harmed.

Theory; institutional and major players usually write and sell options, and that these players will dominate the option (usually versus the small investor) as a result of their market dominance / manipulation abilities.

Areas / strikes concentrated on option purchase/ buying (call and put separately); followed/ observed by open interest. As the result of this theory for the expiry date of the option; the position is established at the range that the option receiver/ purchaser, will lose.

The assumptions based on max pain theory are briefly:

a) Option is a process whose trading total is '0' (zero sum).

b) Option buyers/purchasers, generally loses at the end of term.

c) Strike densities of option purchase areas can be detected.

d) Big players can manipulate the option's end of term price.

There are different calculation methods for Max pain theory, which suggest that the option will terminate the valuation outside the region where option purchases are concentrated. Some traders also add value of the option value as well as open interest.

Max pain is a new theory and it has not become prevalence in practice. Its success is controversial. Without this or that theory, the abnormal price fluctuation of options at the end of the term, can be detected even with simple observation for a while.

From this fluctuation increasing towards the end of the maturity;

a) can be avoided if option positions closed before the possible turbulence period or

b) Option sale or purchase/buying may be made only to benefit from this period of turbulence.

As the macro data and macro news effects added, it is possible to write profits in short-term with sales even purchases option strategies.

We recommend to apply only for experienced and professional traders to perform during volatile periods, which are increasing towards the end of the maturity.

APPENDIX

Z H M U MONTHS TERMS CONTRACTS: DAILY and 60 MINUTES GRAPHICS

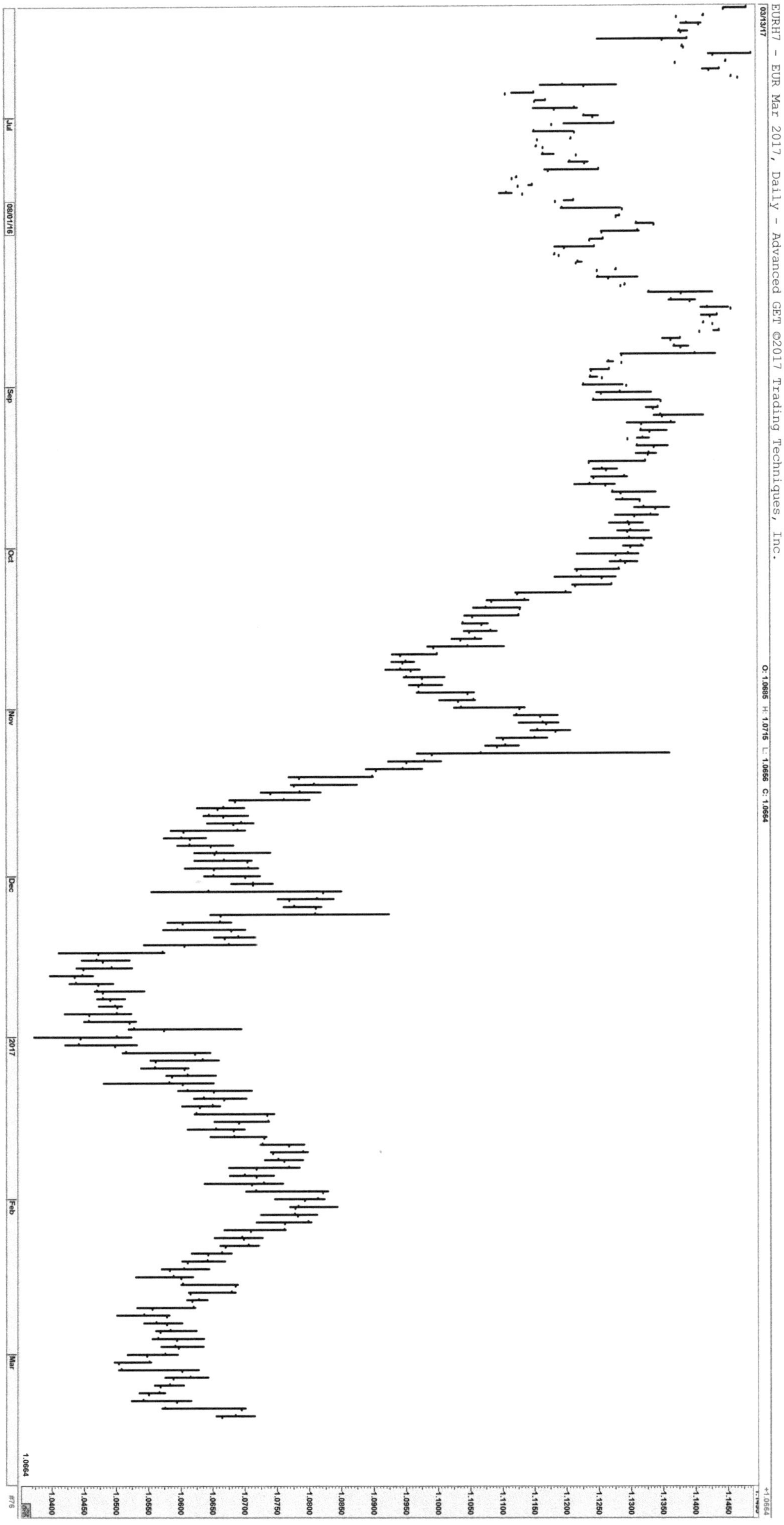
EURH7 - EUR Mar 2017, Daily - Advanced GET ©2017 Trading Techniques, Inc.
O: 1.0685 H: 1.0715 L: 1.0656 C: 1.0664

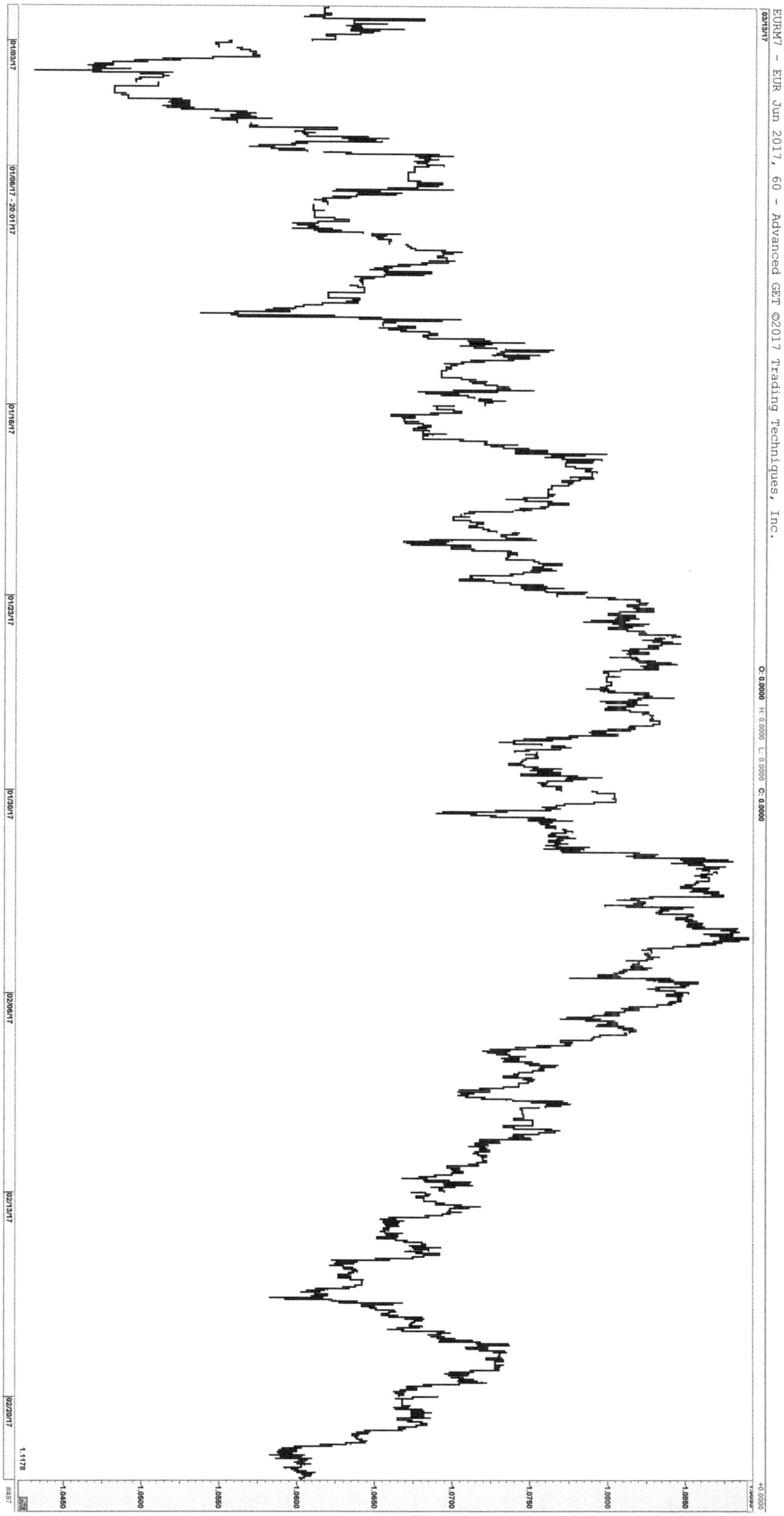
EURM7 - EUR Jun 2017, 60 - Advanced GET ©2017 Trading Techniques, Inc.
O: 0.0000 H: 0.0000 L: 0.0000 C: 0.0000
01/03/17
01/16/17
01/23/17
01/30/17
02/06/17
02/13/17
02/20/17
1.0450
1.0500
1.0550
1.0600
1.0650
1.0700
1.0750
1.0800
1.0850

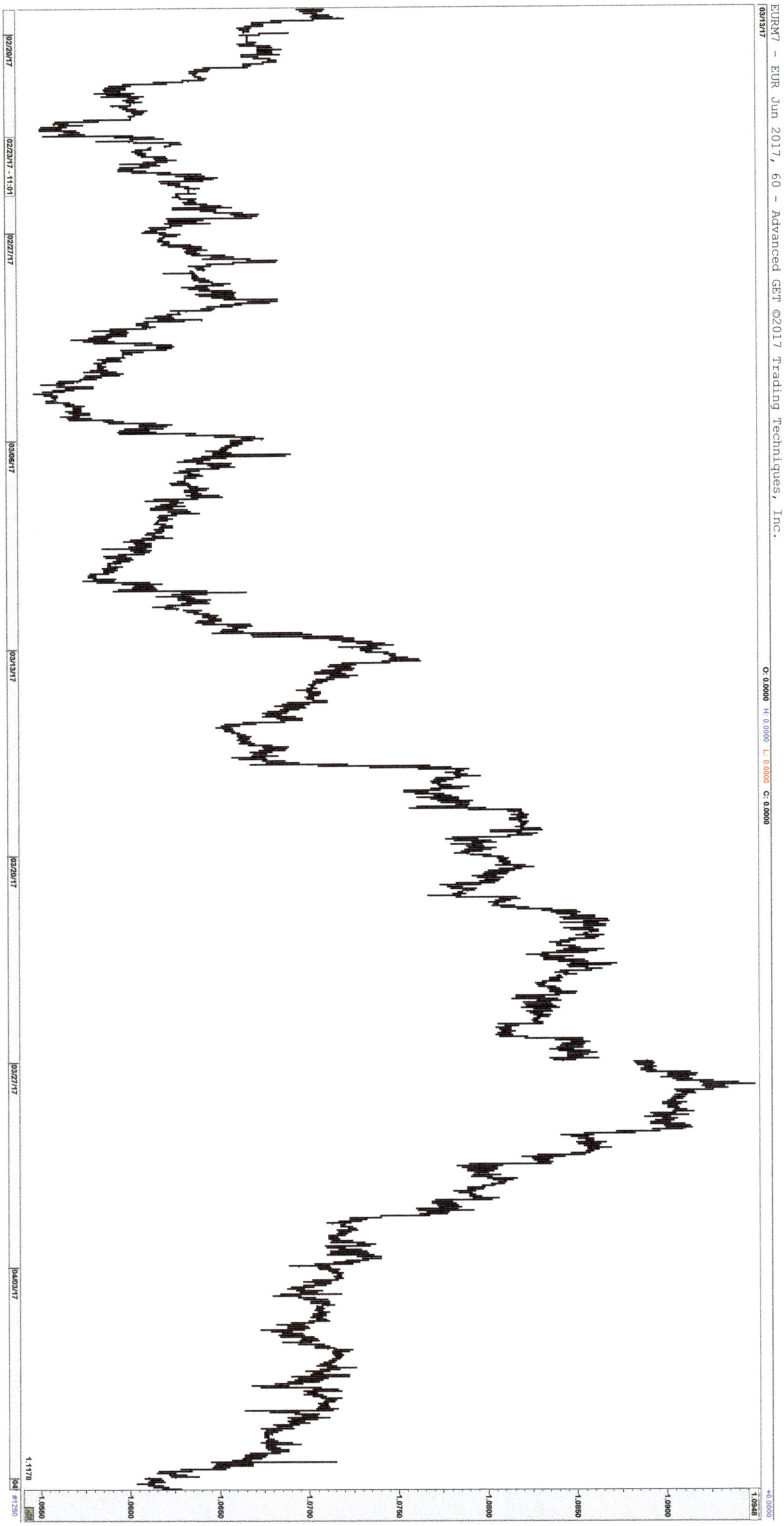
EURM7 - EUR Jun 2017, 60 - Advanced GET ©2017 Trading Techniques, Inc.
O: 0.0000 H: 0.0000 L: 0.0000 C: 0.0000
02/20/17
02/23/17 - 11:01
02/27/17
03/06/17
03/13/17
03/20/17
03/27/17
04/03/17
1.0550
1.0600
1.0650
1.0700
1.0750
1.0800
1.0850
1.0900

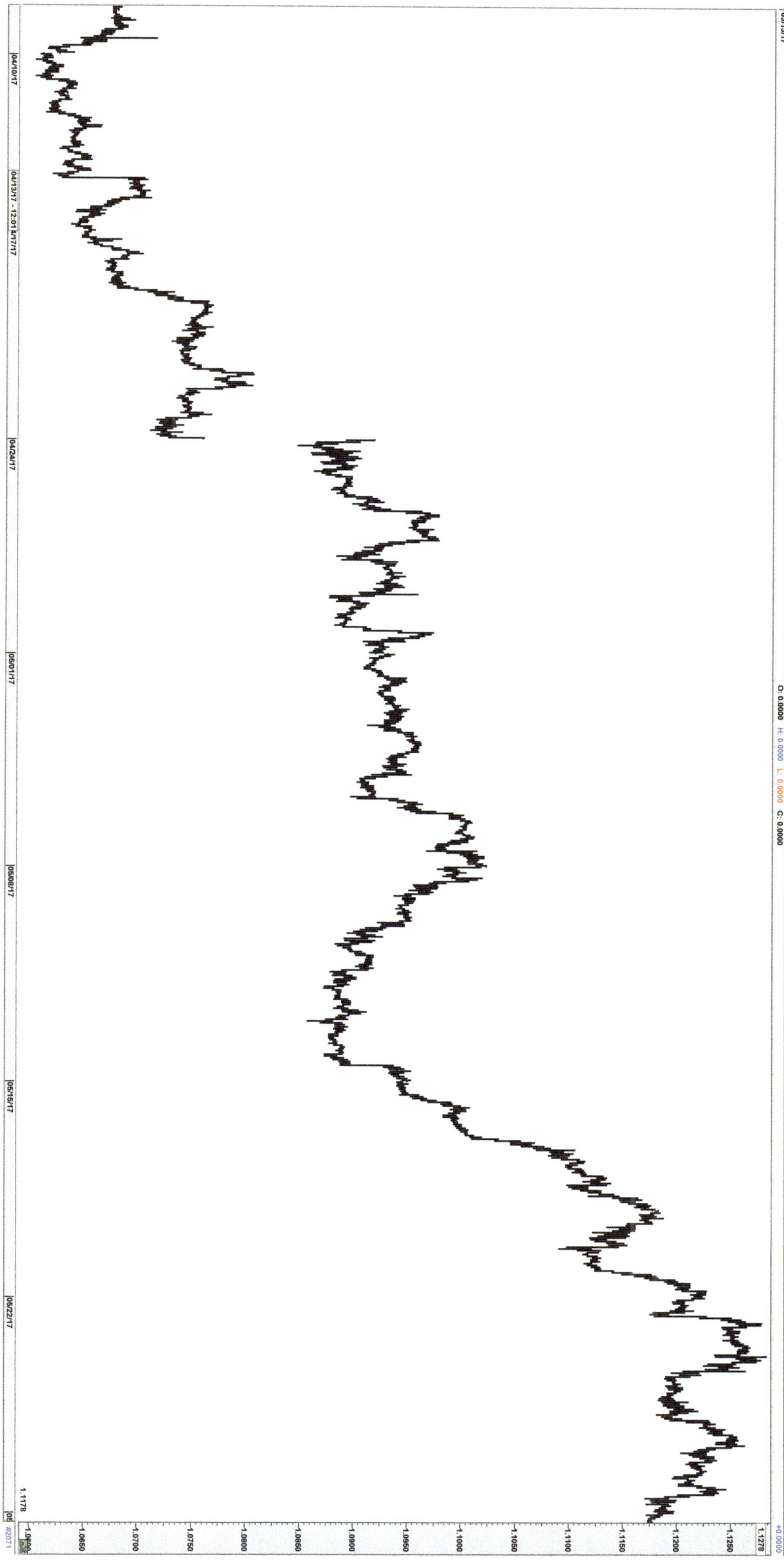
EURM7 - EUR Jun 2017, 60 - Advanced GET ©2017 Trading Techniques, Inc.
O: 0.0000 H: 0.0000 L: 0.0000 C: 0.0000

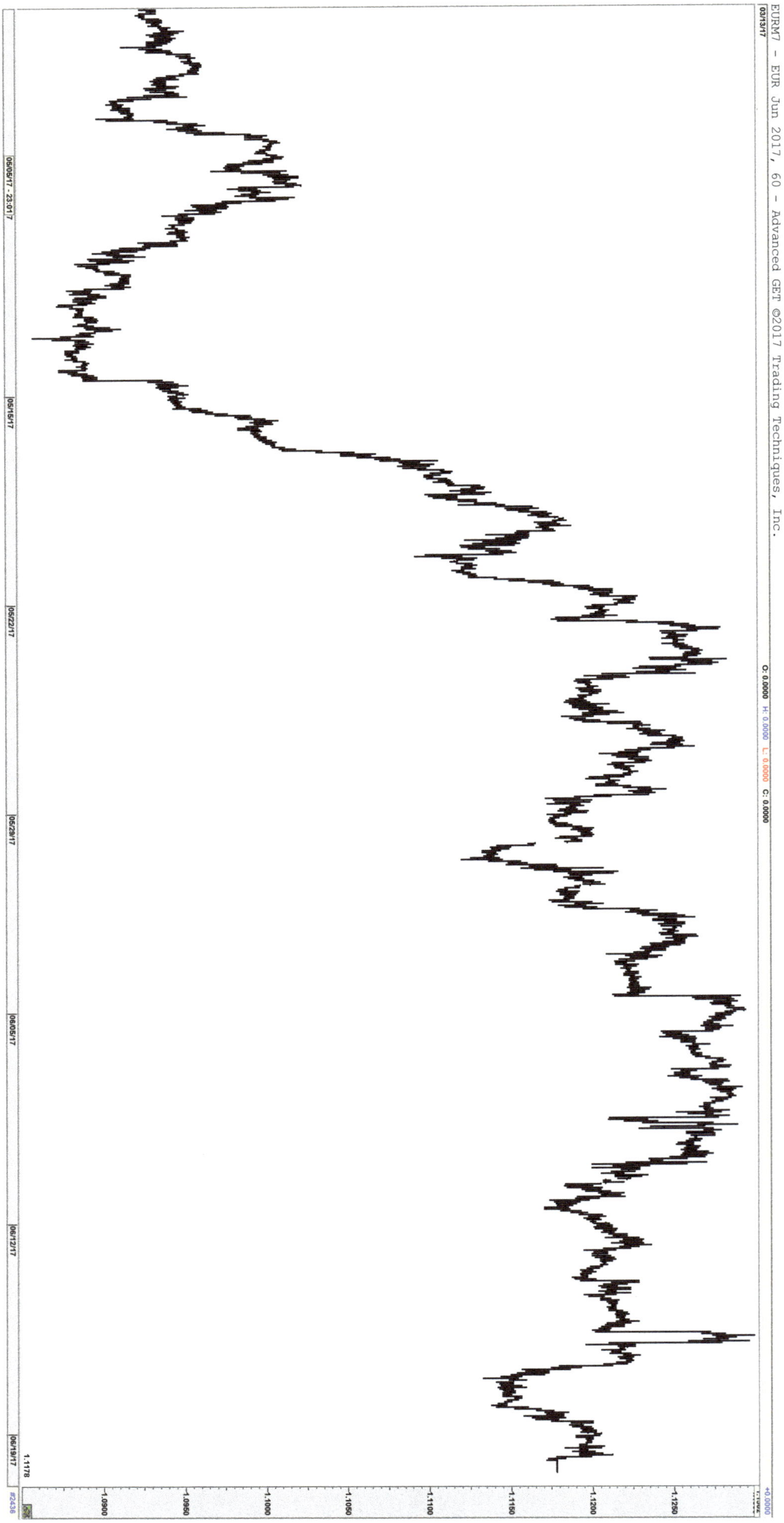
EURM7 - EUR Jun 2017, 60 - Advanced GET ©2017 Trading Techniques, Inc.
O: 0.0000 H: 0.0000 L: 0.0000 C: 0.0000
1.1178
1.0900
1.0950
1.1000
1.1050
1.1100
1.1150
1.1200
1.1250
05/15/17
05/22/17
05/29/17
06/05/17
06/12/17
06/19/17

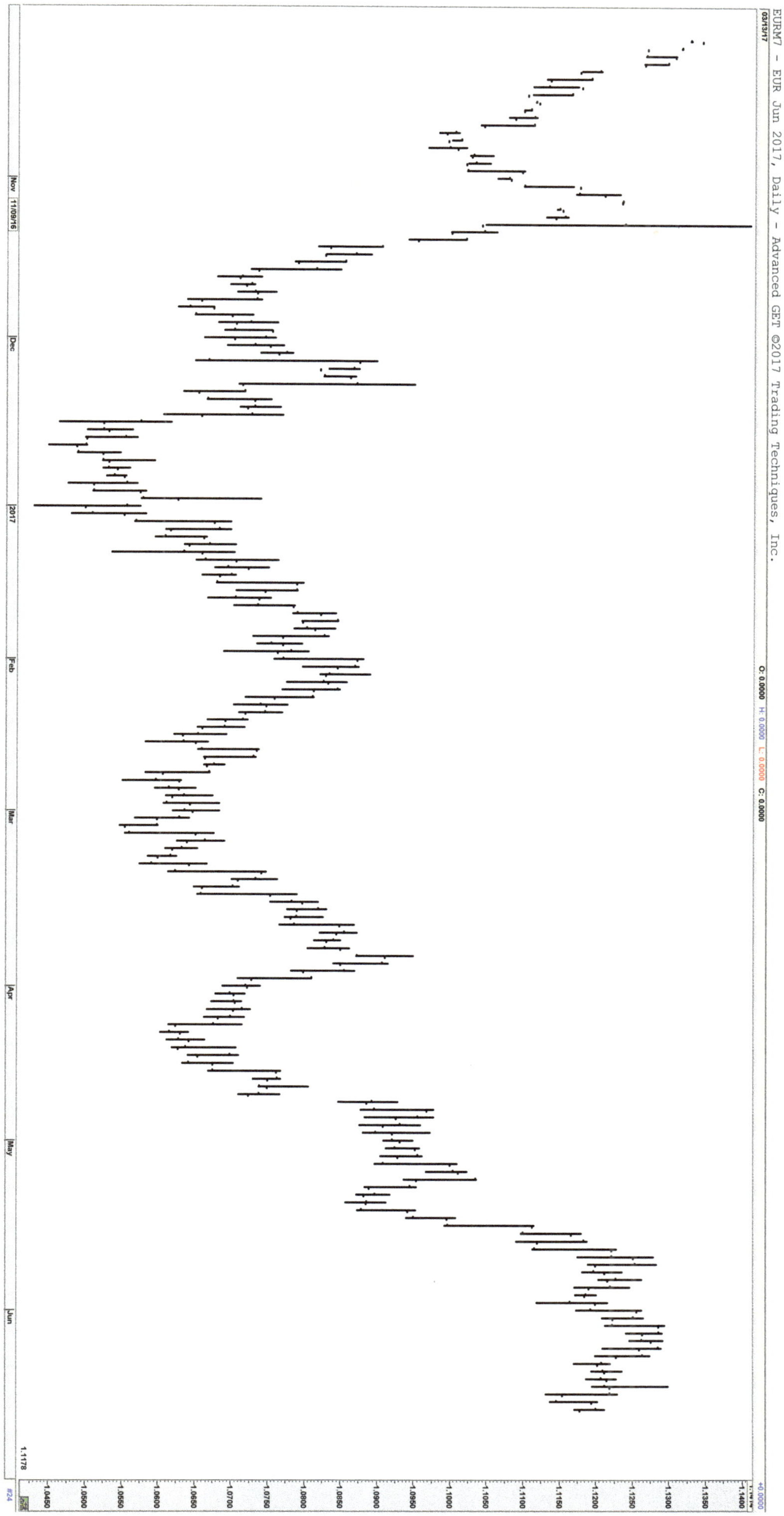
EURM7 - EUR Jun 2017, Daily - Advanced GET ©2017 Trading Techniques, Inc.
O: 0.0000 H: 0.0000 L: 0.0000 C: 0.0000
Nov 11/09/16
Dec
2017
Feb
Mar
Apr
May
Jun
1.1178

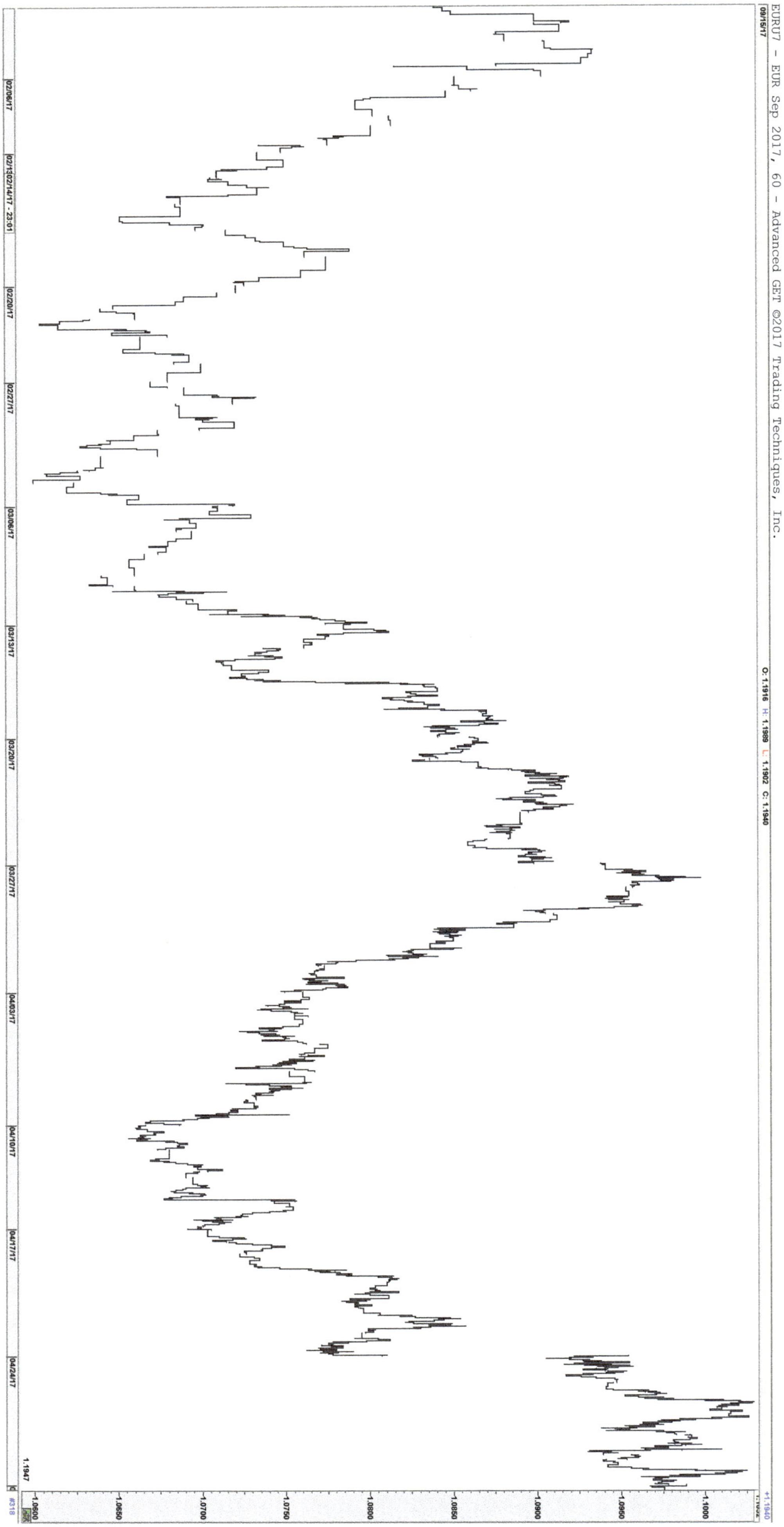
EURU7 - EUR Sep 2017, 60 - Advanced GET ©2017 Trading Techniques, Inc.
O: 1.1916 H: 1.1989 L: 1.1902 C: 1.1940
02/06/17
02/13/02/14/17 - 23:01
02/20/17
02/27/17
03/06/17
03/13/17
03/20/17
03/27/17
04/03/17
04/10/17
04/17/17
04/24/17
1.0600
1.0650
1.0700
1.0750
1.0800
1.0850
1.0900
1.0950
1.1000

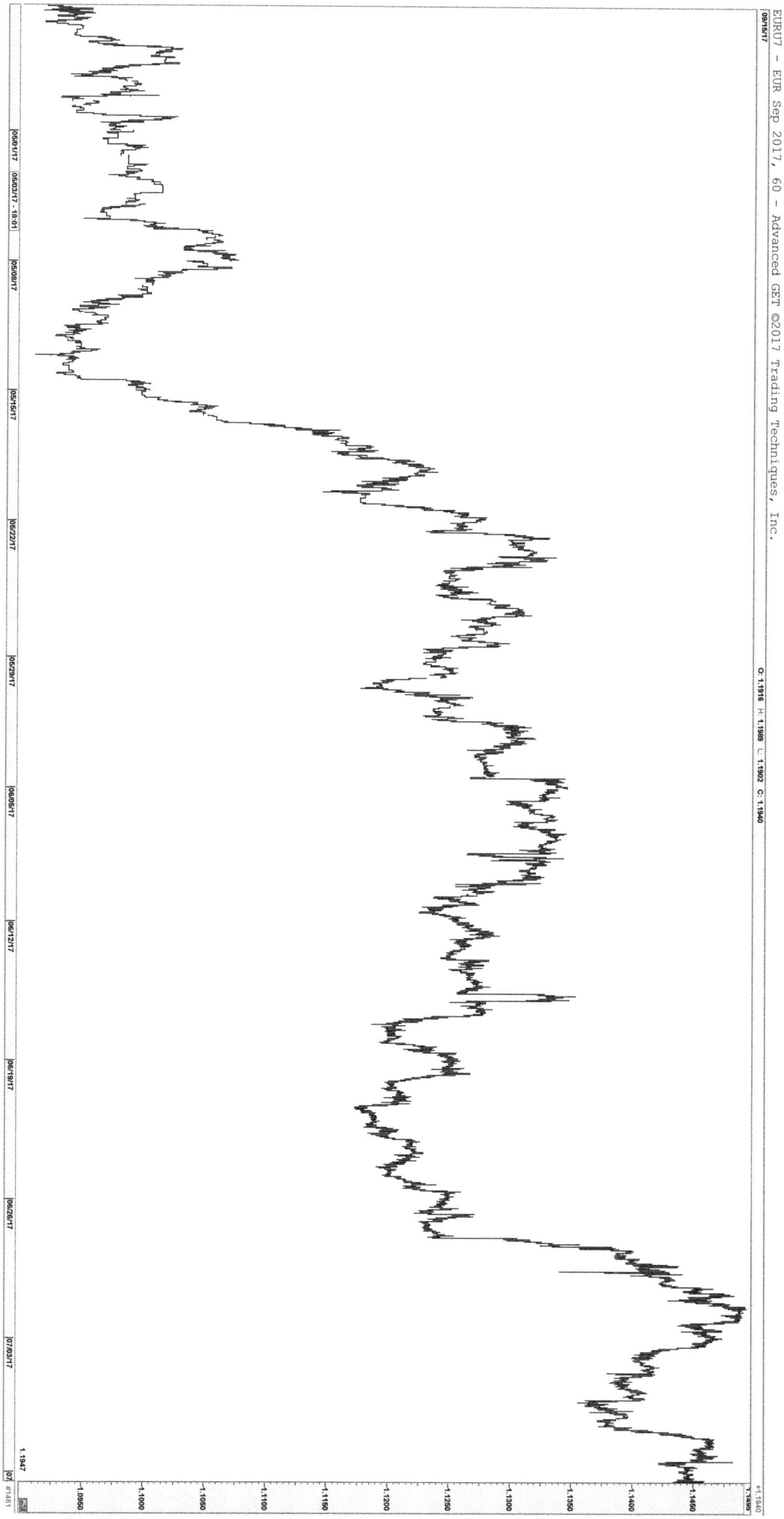
EURU7 - EUR Sep 2017, 60 - Advanced GET ©2017 Trading Techniques, Inc.
O: 1.1916 H: 1.1989 L: 1.1902 C: 1.1940
05/01/17
05/03/17 - 18:01
05/08/17
05/15/17
05/22/17
05/29/17
06/05/17
06/12/17
06/19/17
06/26/17
07/03/17
1.0950
1.1000
1.1050
1.1100
1.1150
1.1200
1.1250
1.1300
1.1350
1.1400
1.1450

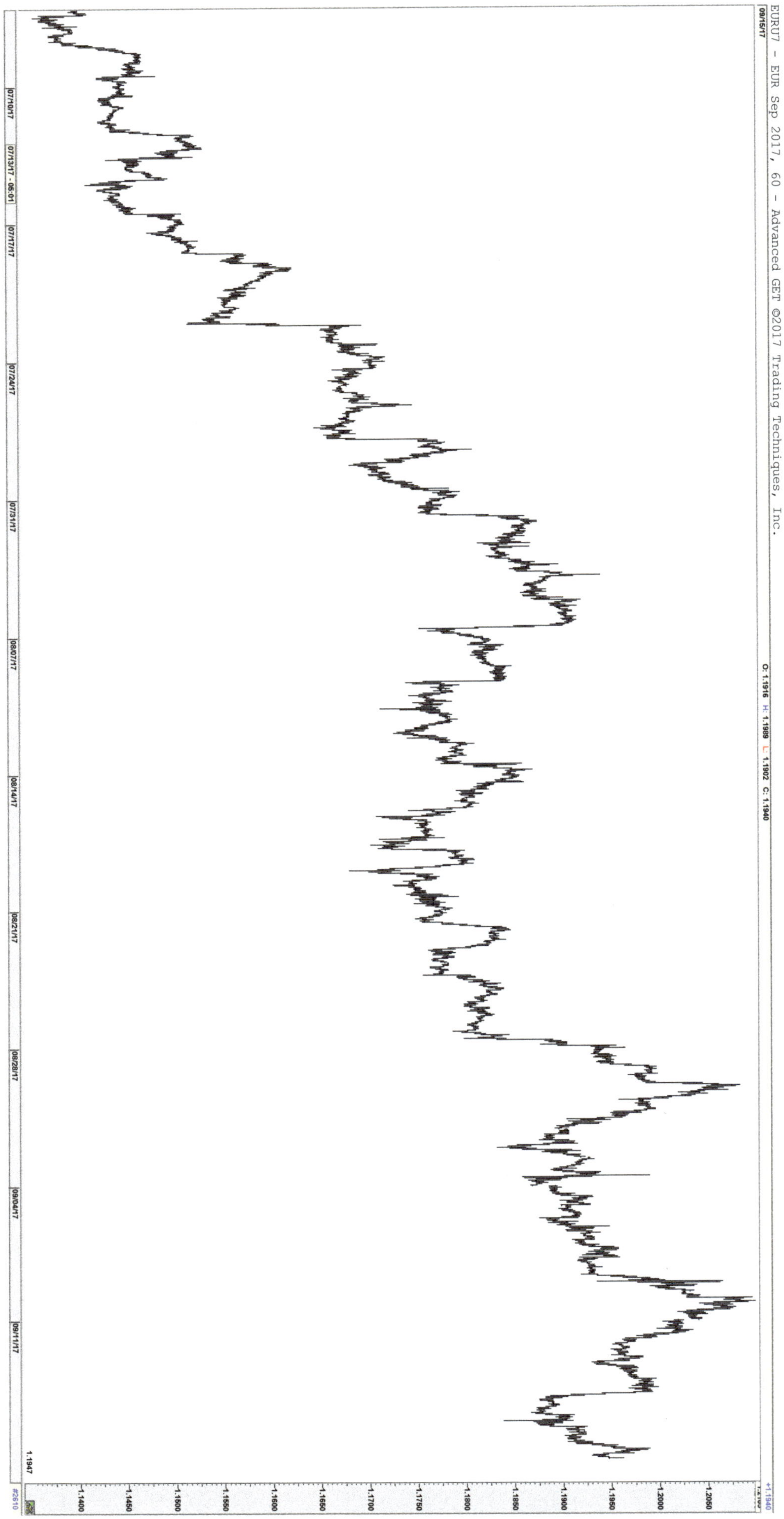
EURU7 - EUR Sep 2017, 60 - Advanced GET ©2017 Trading Techniques, Inc.
O: 1.1916 H: 1.1989 L: 1.1902 C: 1.1940
07/10/17
07/13/17 - 06:01
07/17/17
07/24/17
07/31/17
08/07/17
08/14/17
08/21/17
08/28/17
09/04/17
09/11/17
09/15/17
1.1947
1.1400
1.1450
1.1500
1.1550
1.1600
1.1650
1.1700
1.1750
1.1800
1.1850
1.1900
1.1950
1.2000
1.2050

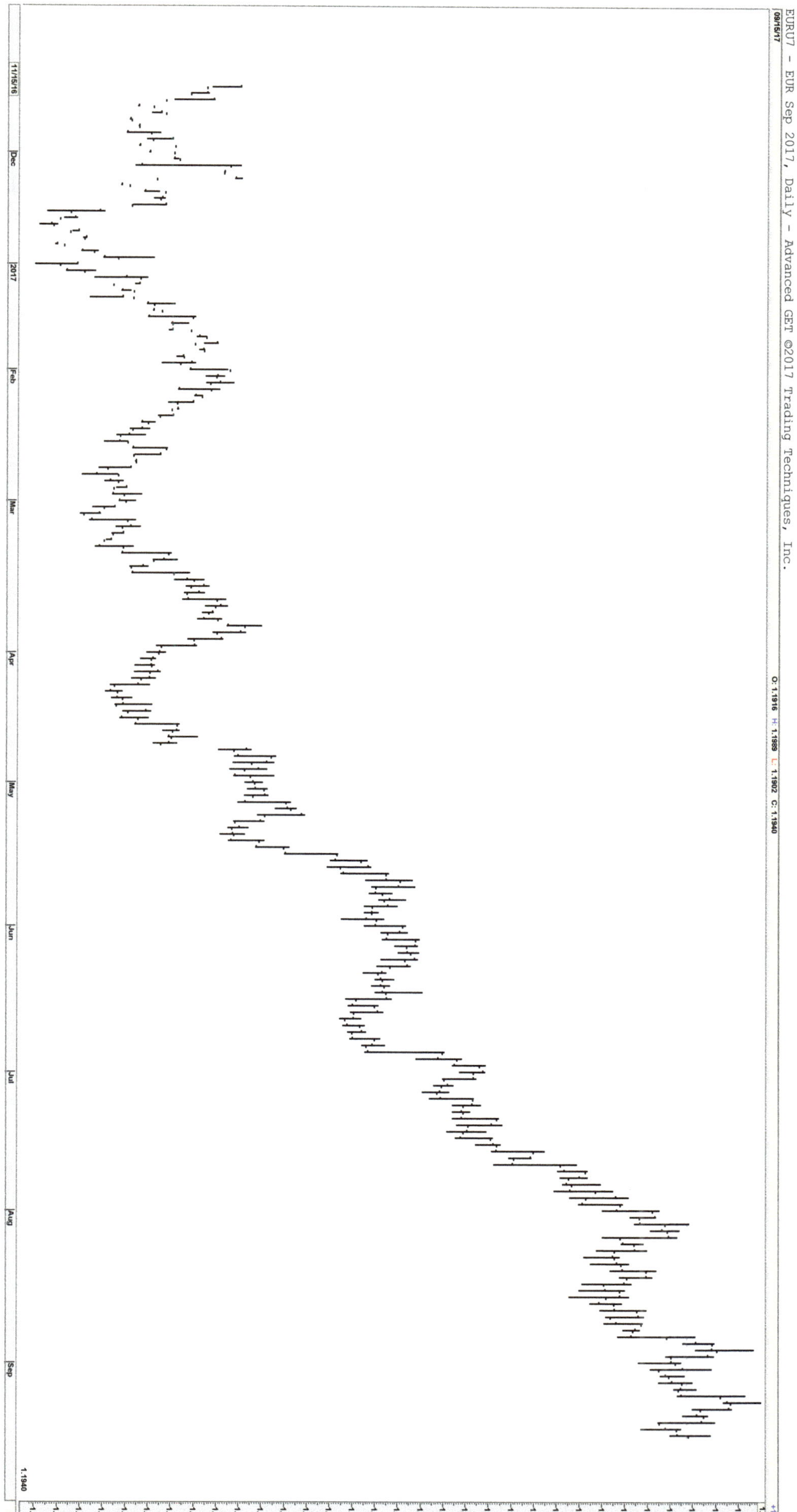
EURU7 - EUR Sep 2017, Daily - Advanced GET ©2017 Trading Techniques, Inc.
O: 1.1916 H: 1.1989 L: 1.1902 C: 1.1940

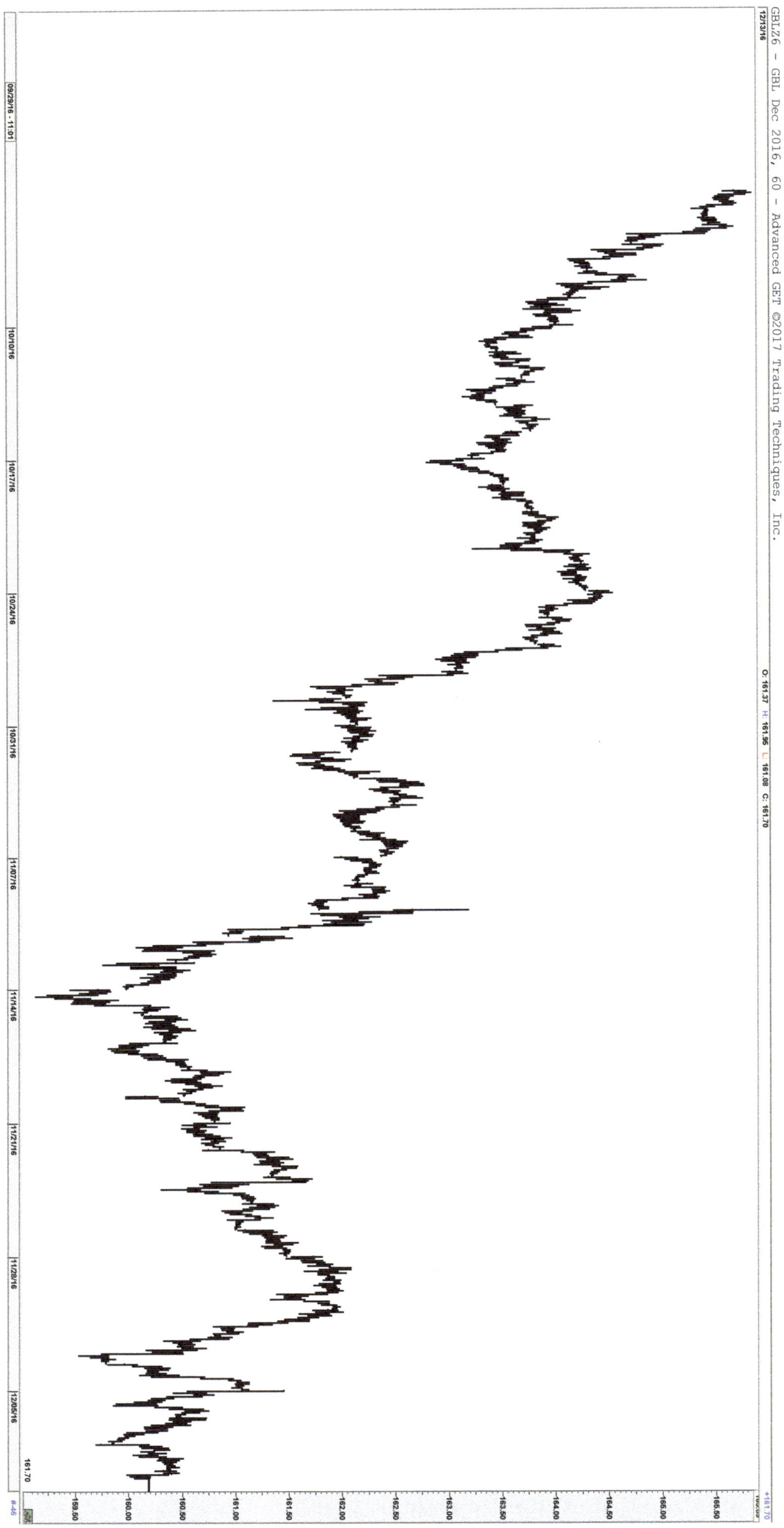
GBLZ6 - GBL Dec 2016, 60 - Advanced GET ©2017 Trading Techniques, Inc.
O: 161.37 H: 161.96 L: 161.08 C: 161.70

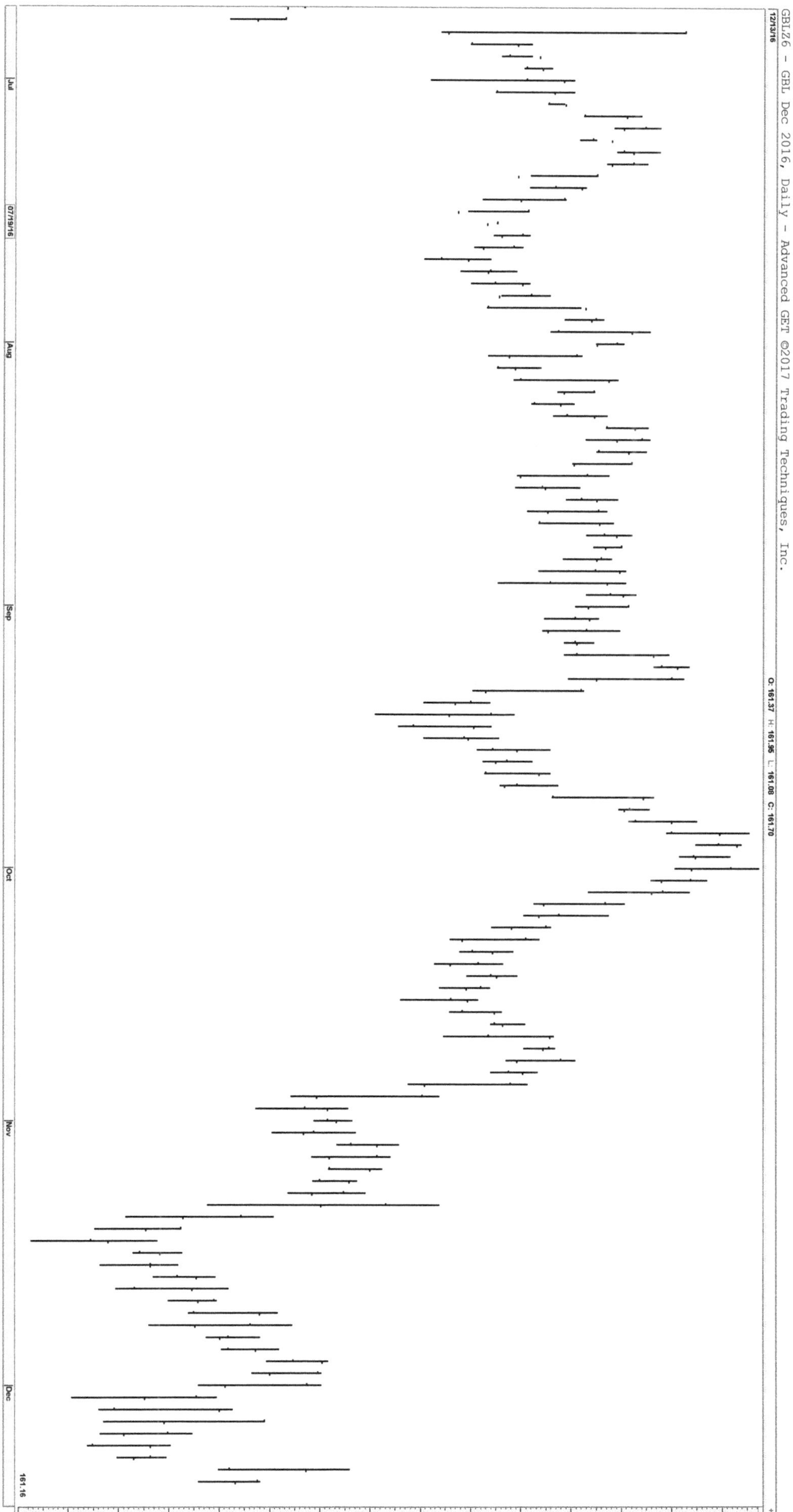
GBLZ6 - GBL Dec 2016, Daily - Advanced GET ©2017 Trading Techniques, Inc.
12/13/16
O: 161.37 H: 161.96 L: 161.08 C: 161.70
Jul
07/19/16
Aug
Sep
Oct
Nov
Dec
161.16
159.50
160.00
160.50
161.00
161.50
162.00
162.50
163.00
163.50
164.00
164.50
165.00
165.50
166.00
+161.70

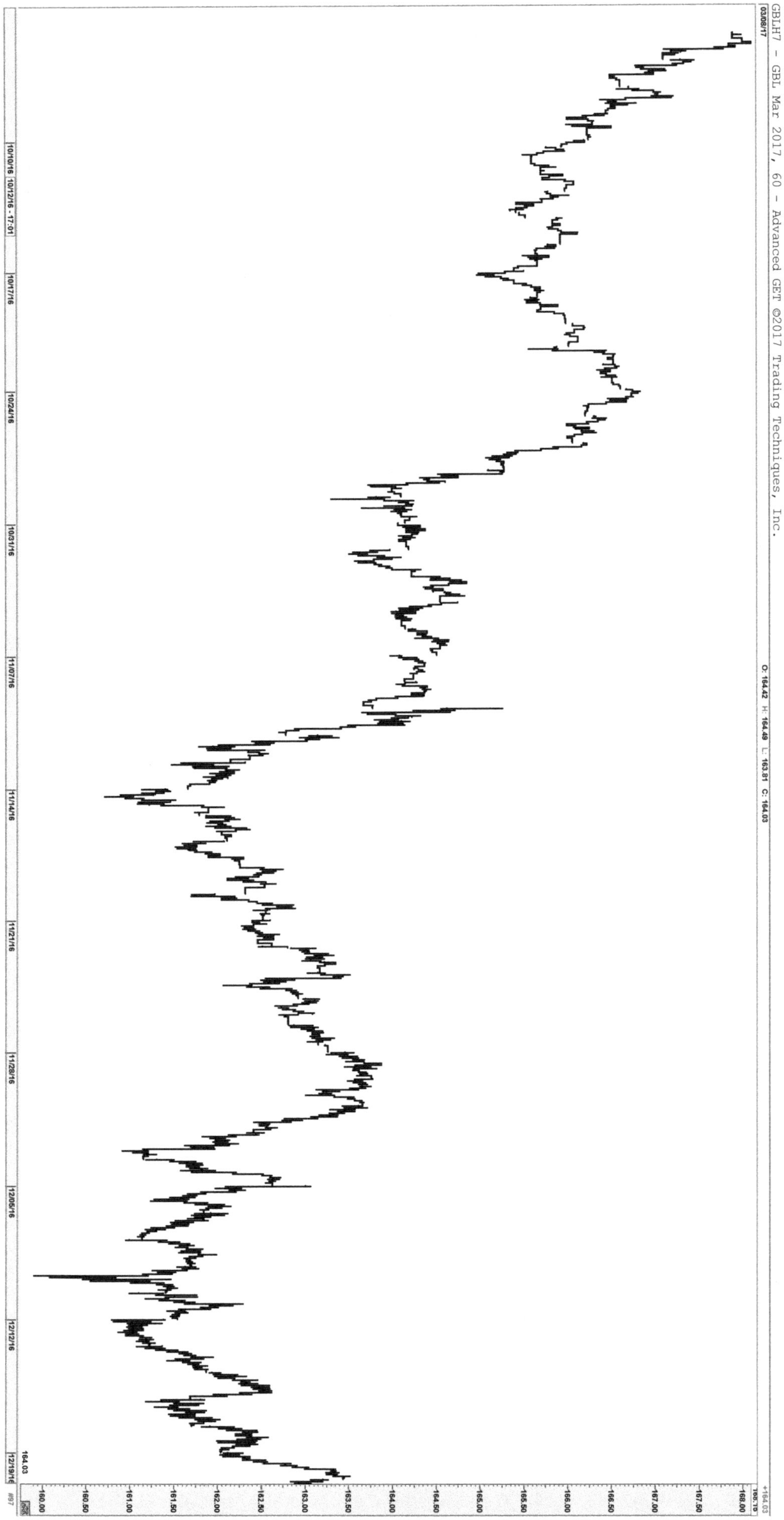
GBLH7 - GBL Mar 2017, 60 - Advanced GET ©2017 Trading Techniques, Inc.
O: 164.42 H: 164.49 L: 163.81 C: 164.03

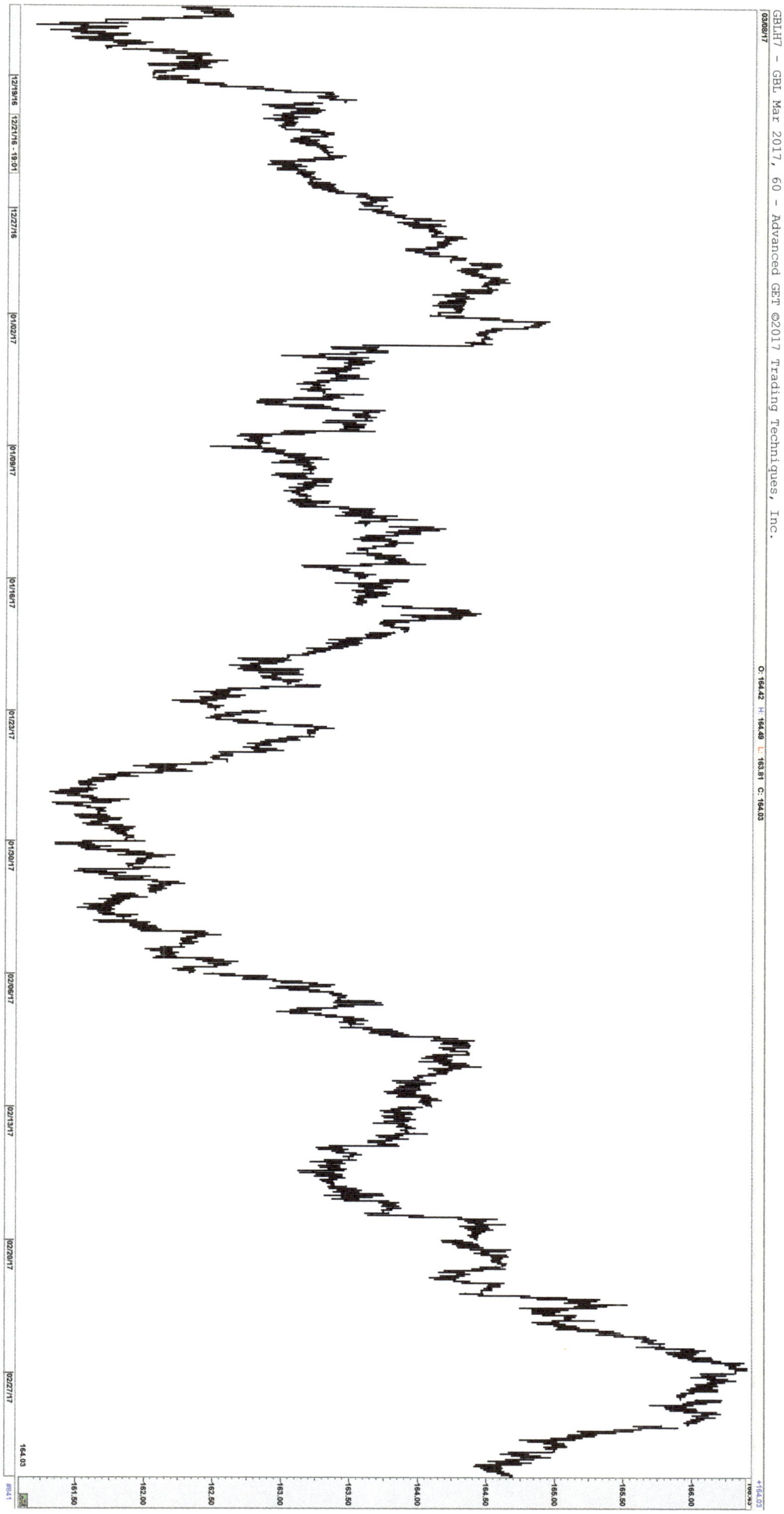
GBLH7 - GBL Mar 2017, 60 - Advanced GET ©2017 Trading Techniques, Inc.
O: 164.42 H: 164.49 L: 163.81 C: 164.03

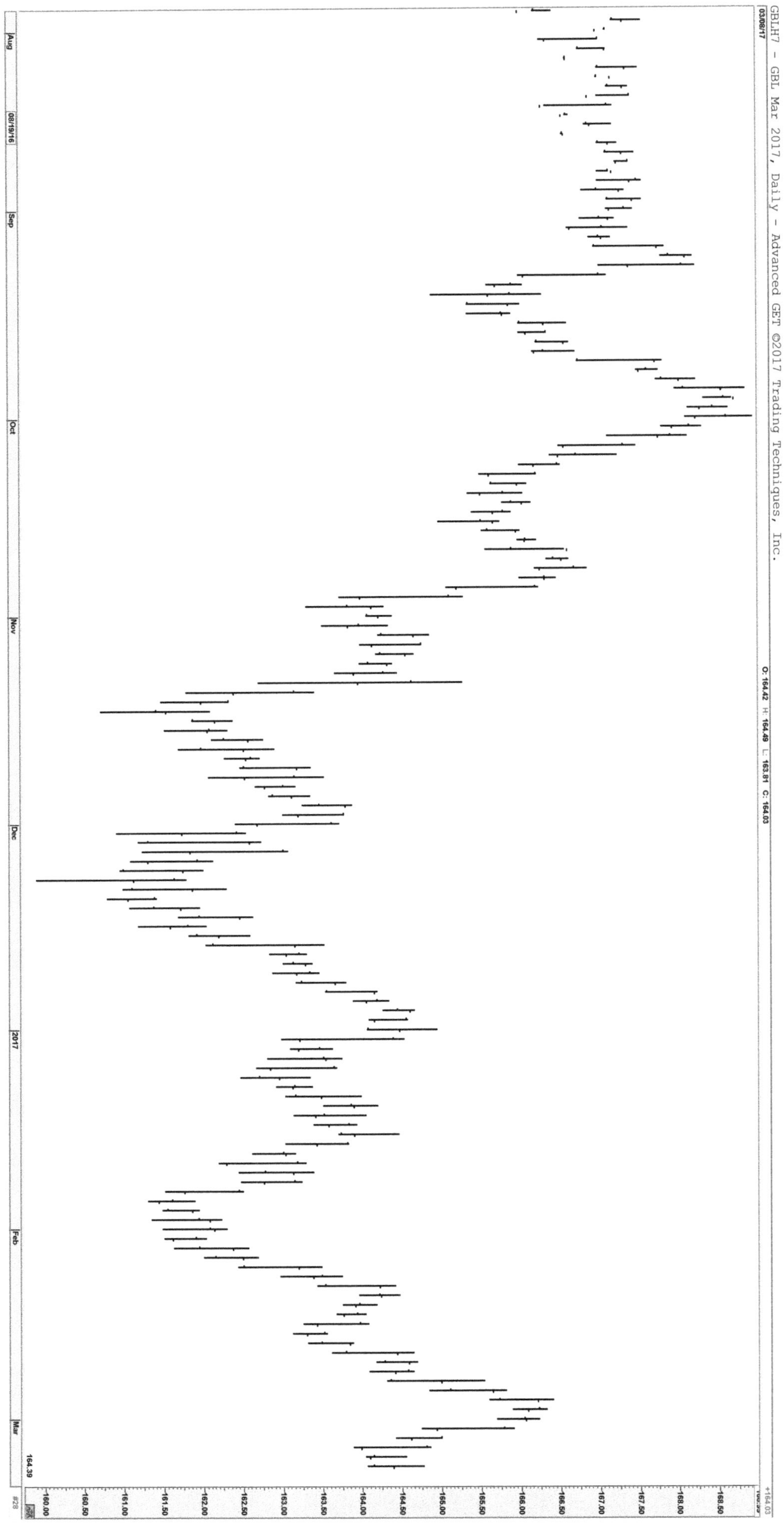
GBLH7 - GBL Mar 2017, Daily - Advanced GET ©2017 Trading Techniques, Inc.
Aug
08/19/16
Sep
Oct
Nov
Dec
2017
Feb
Mar

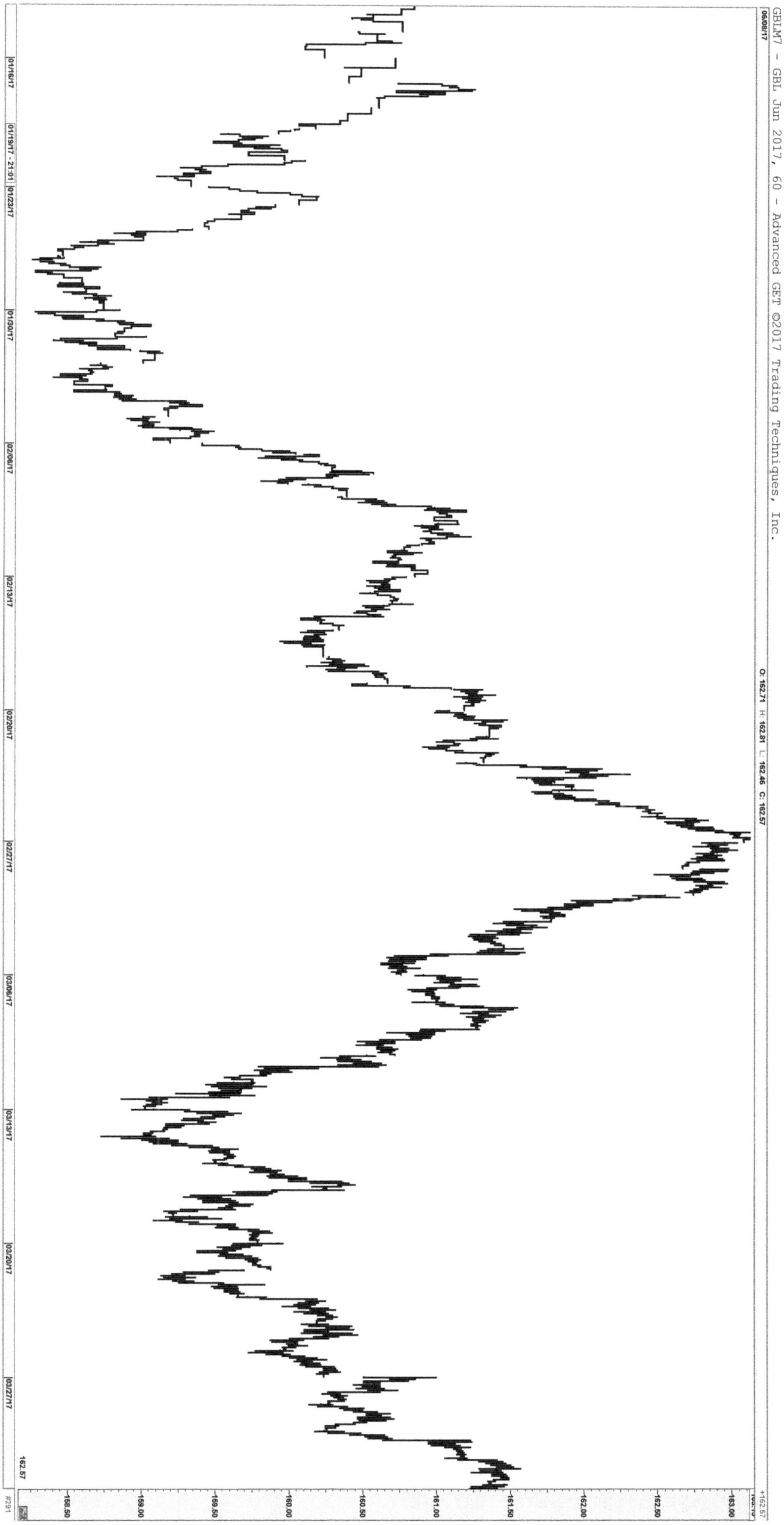
GBLM7 - GBL Jun 2017, 60 - Advanced GET ©2017 Trading Techniques, Inc.

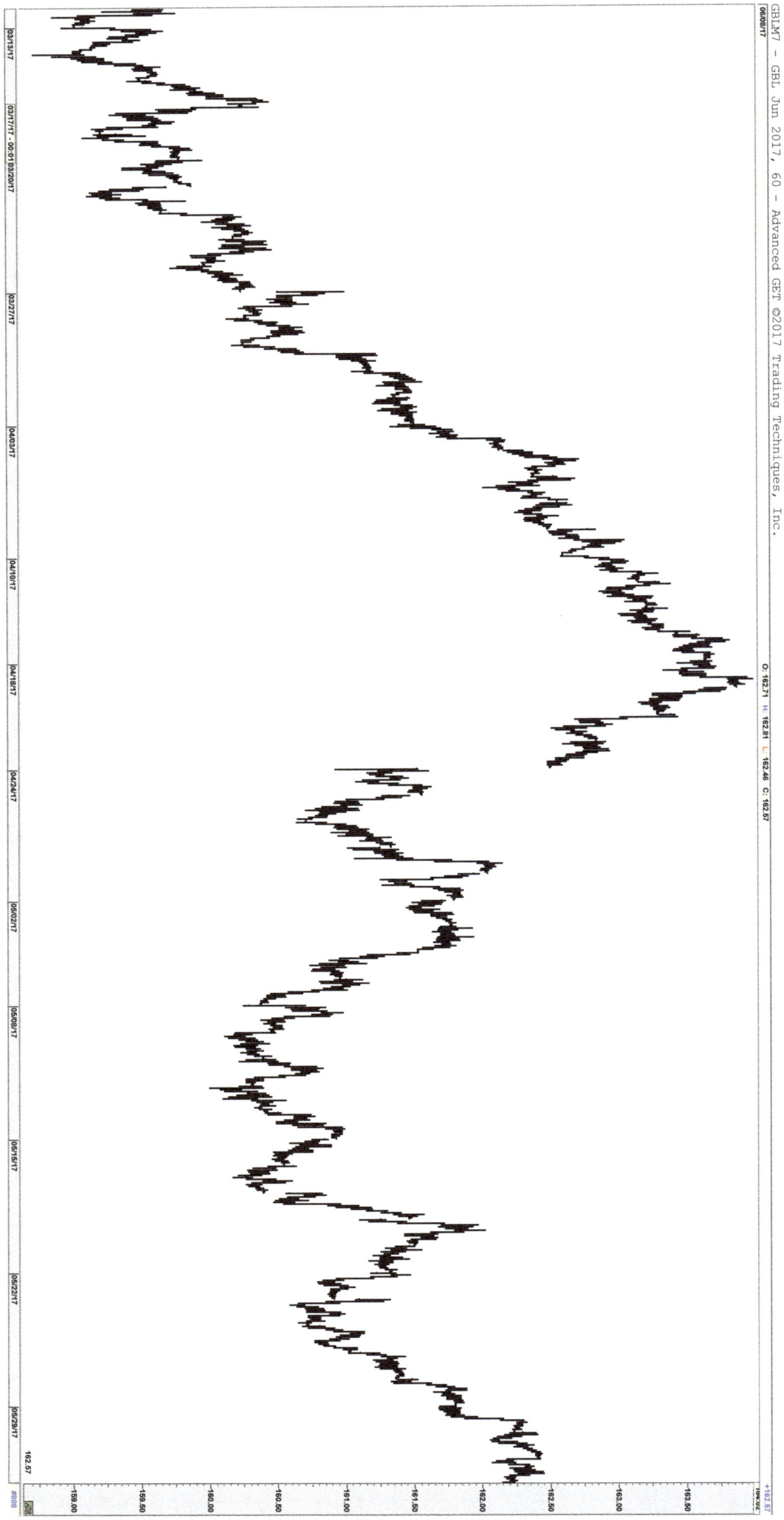
GBLM7 - GBL Jun 2017, 60 - Advanced GET ©2017 Trading Techniques, Inc.

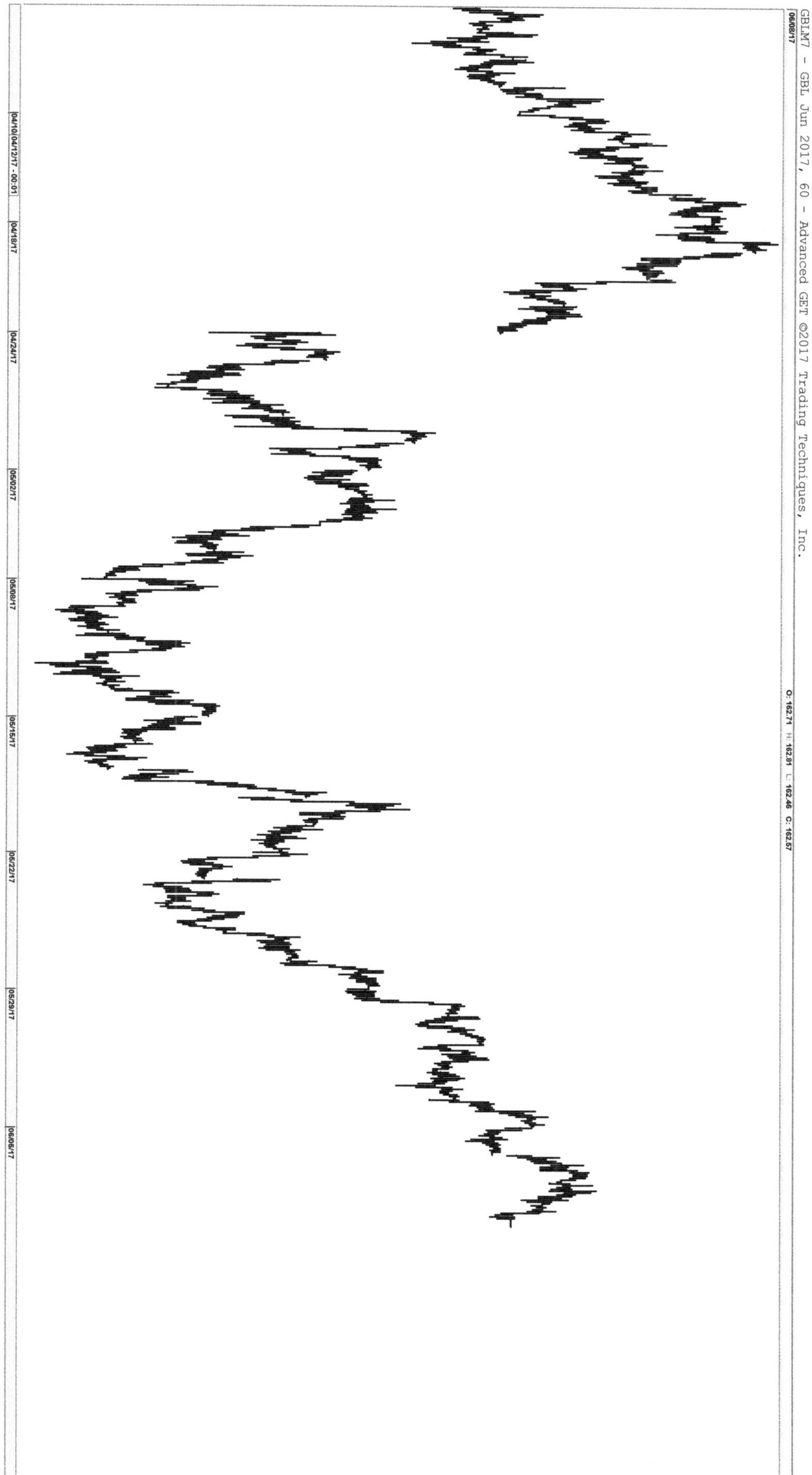
GBLM7 - GBL Jun 2017, 60 - Advanced GET ©2017 Trading Techniques, Inc.
O: 162.71 H: 162.81 L: 162.46 C: 162.57
04/10 04/12/17 - 00:01
04/18/17
04/24/17
05/02/17
05/08/17
05/15/17
05/22/17
05/29/17
06/05/17
06/08/17
160.00
160.50
161.00
161.50
162.00
162.50
163.00
163.50
162.57

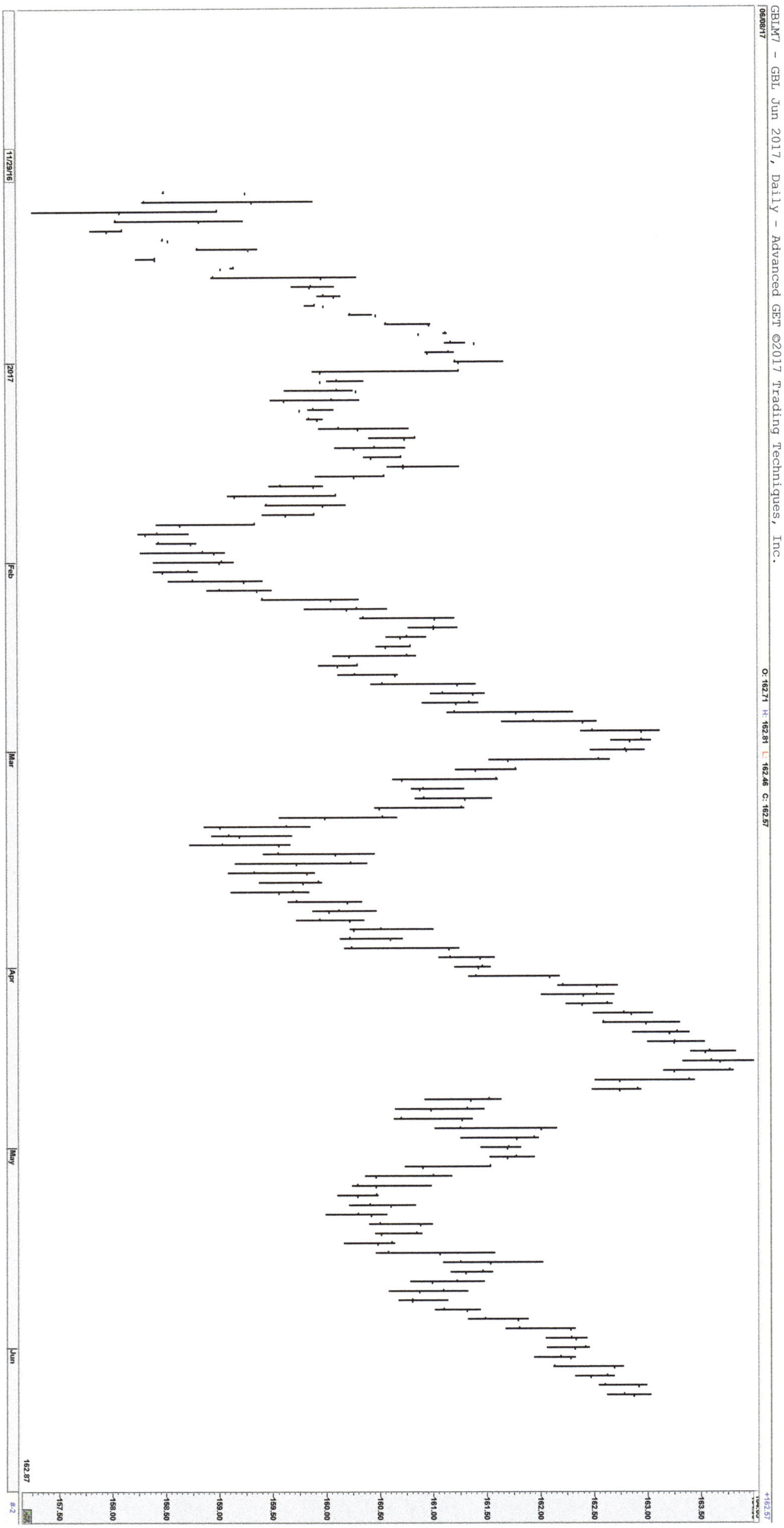
GBLM7 - GBL Jun 2017, Daily - Advanced GET ©2017 Trading Techniques, Inc.
O: 162.71 H: 162.81 L: 162.46 C: 162.57
06/08/17
11/29/16
2017
Feb
Mar
Apr
May
Jun
162.87
157.50
158.00
158.50
159.00
159.50
160.00
160.50
161.00
161.50
162.00
162.50
163.00
163.50

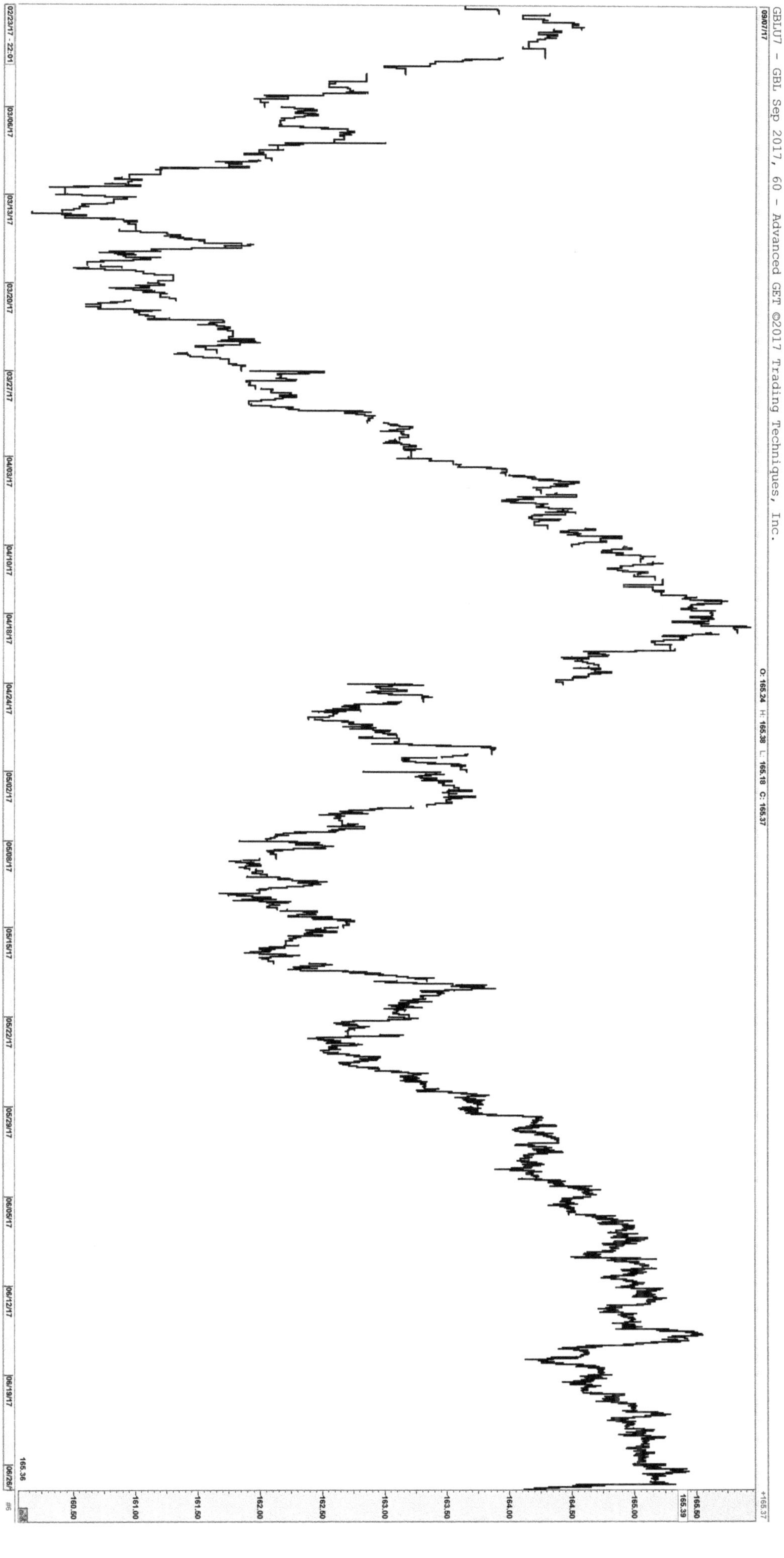
GBLU7 - GBL Sep 2017, 60 - Advanced GET ©2017 Trading Techniques, Inc.

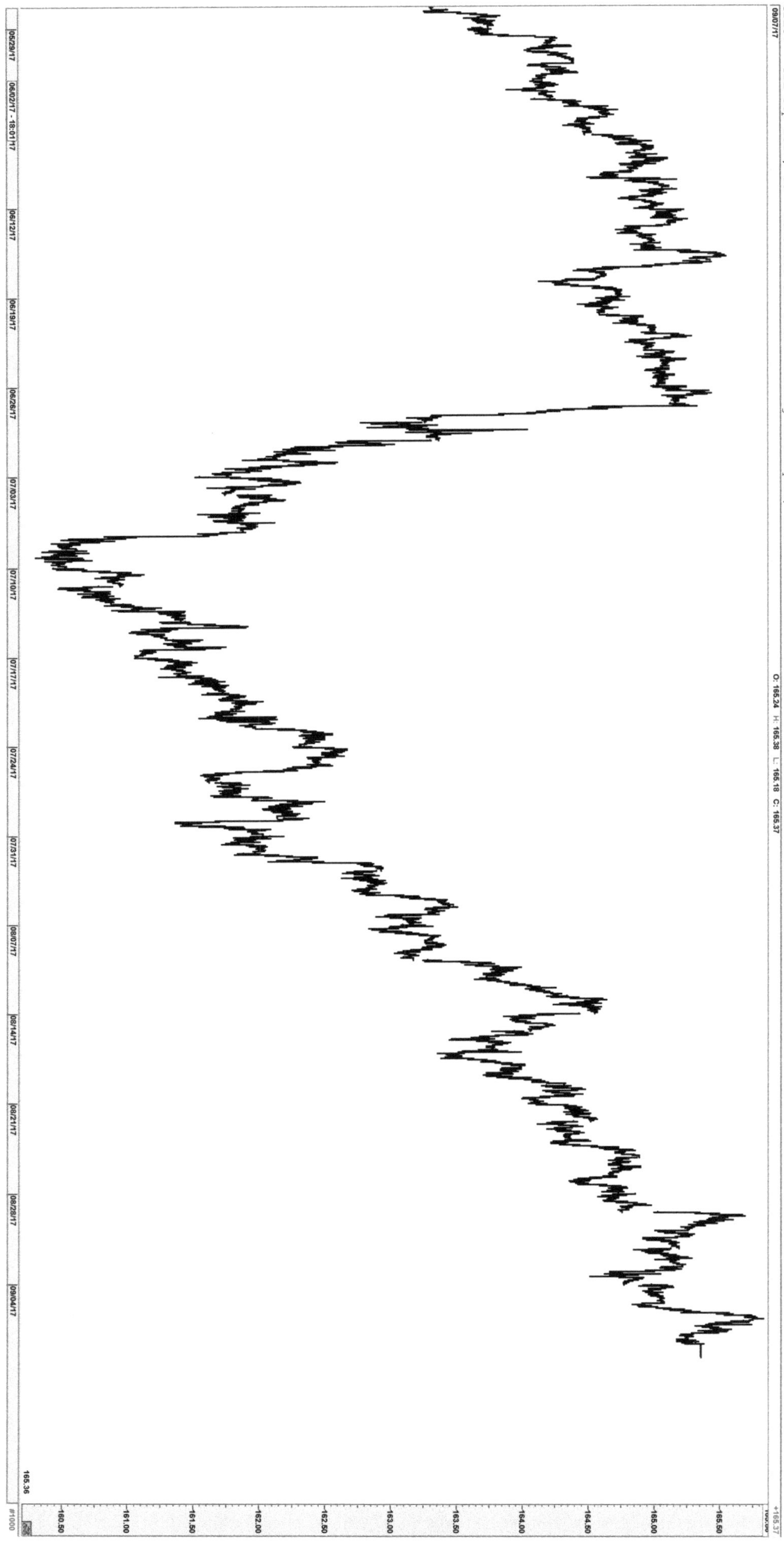
GBLU7 - GBL Sep 2017, 60 - Advanced GET ©2017 Trading Techniques, Inc.
O: 165.24 H: 165.38 L: 165.18 C: 165.37

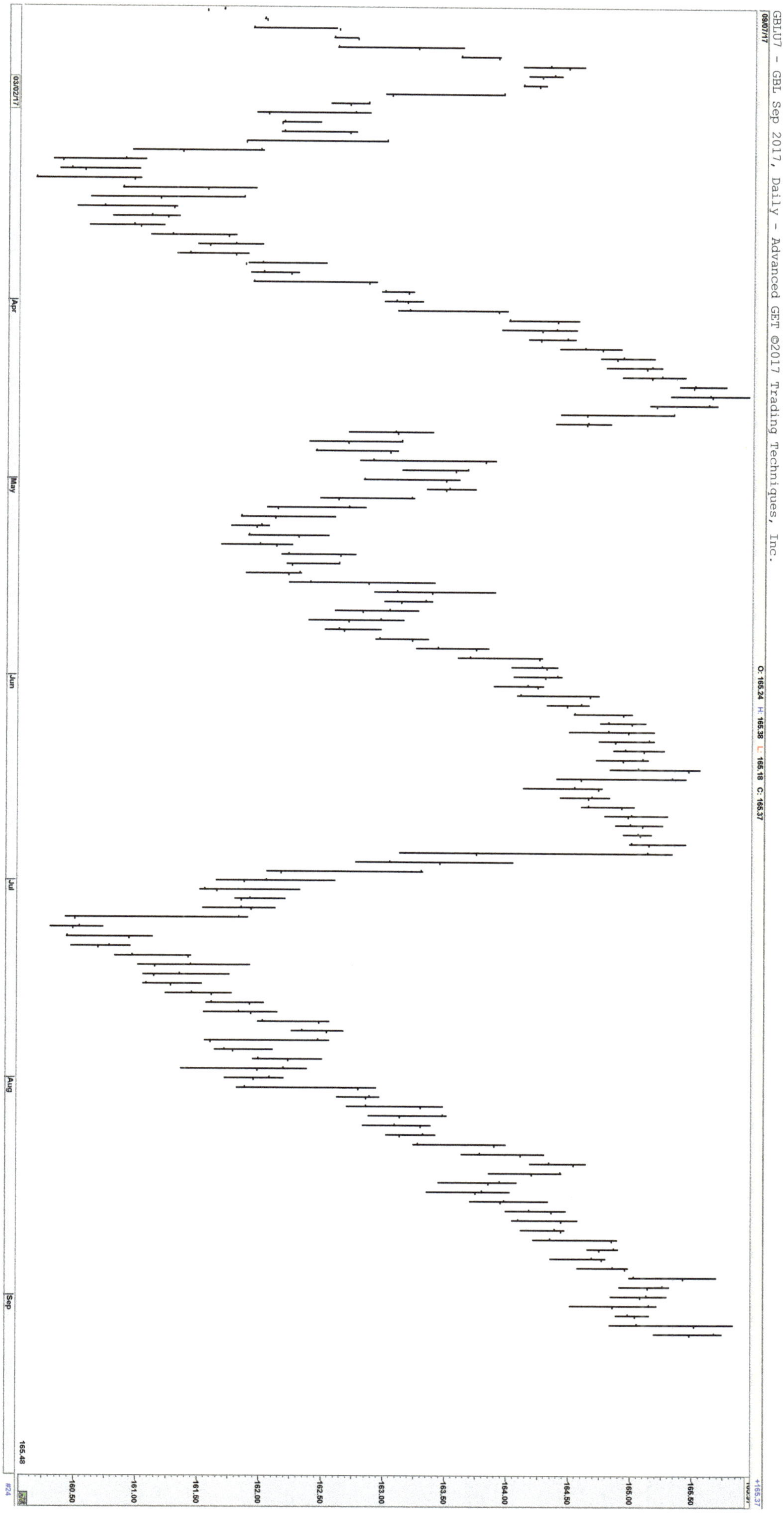
GBLU7 - GBL Sep 2017, Daily - Advanced GET ©2017 Trading Techniques, Inc.
09/07/17
O: 165.24 H: 165.38 L: 165.18 C: 165.37
03/02/17
Apr
May
Jun
Jul
Aug
Sep
165.48
160.50
161.00
161.50
162.00
162.50
163.00
163.50
164.00
164.50
165.00
165.50
165.37

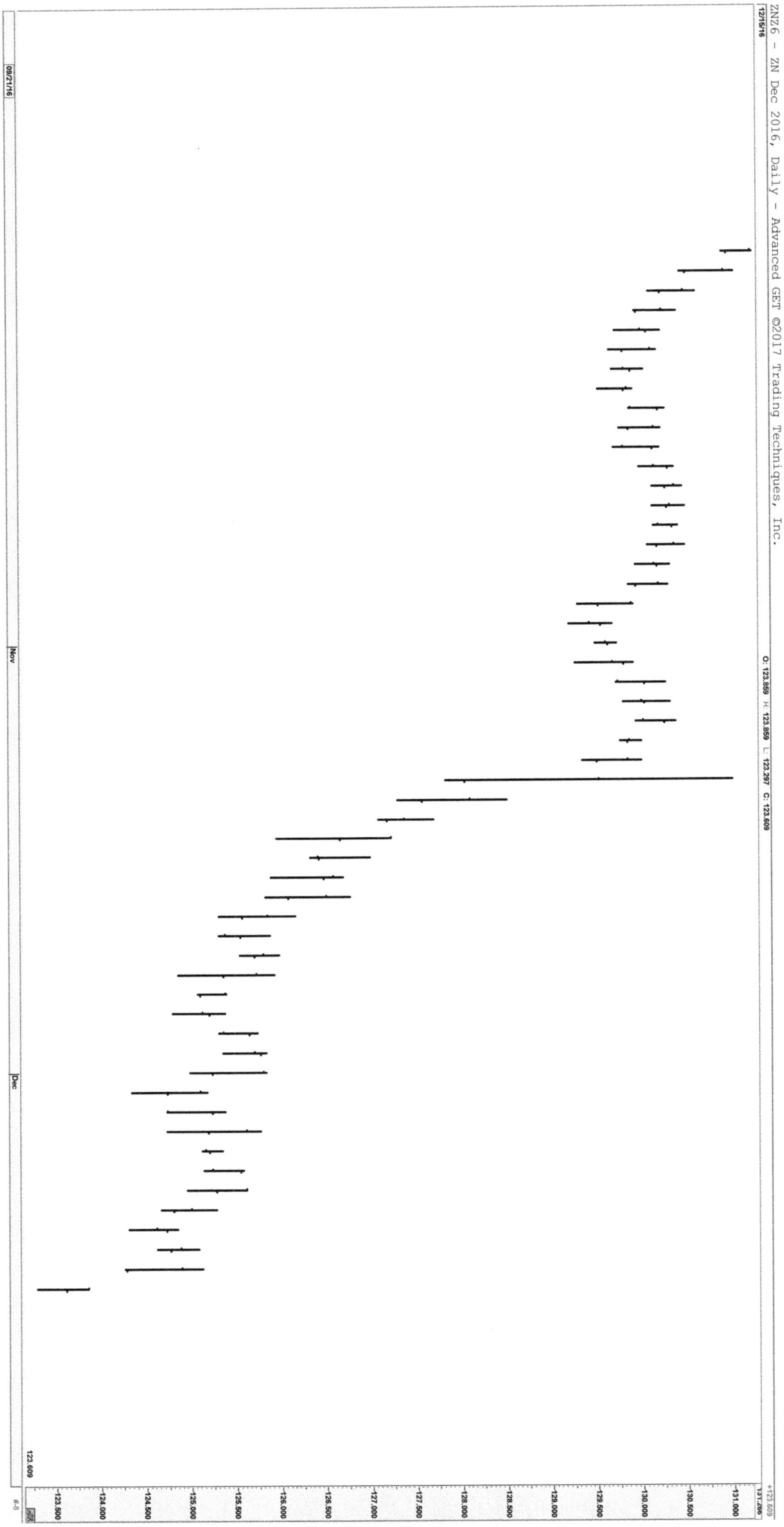
ZNZ6 - ZN Dec 2016, Daily - Advanced GET ©2017 Trading Techniques, Inc.
O: 123.859 H: 123.859 L: 123.297 C: 123.609
12/15/16
09/21/16
Nov
Dec
123.609
123.500
124.000
124.500
125.000
125.500
126.000
126.500
127.000
127.500
128.000
128.500
129.000
129.500
130.000
130.500
131.000

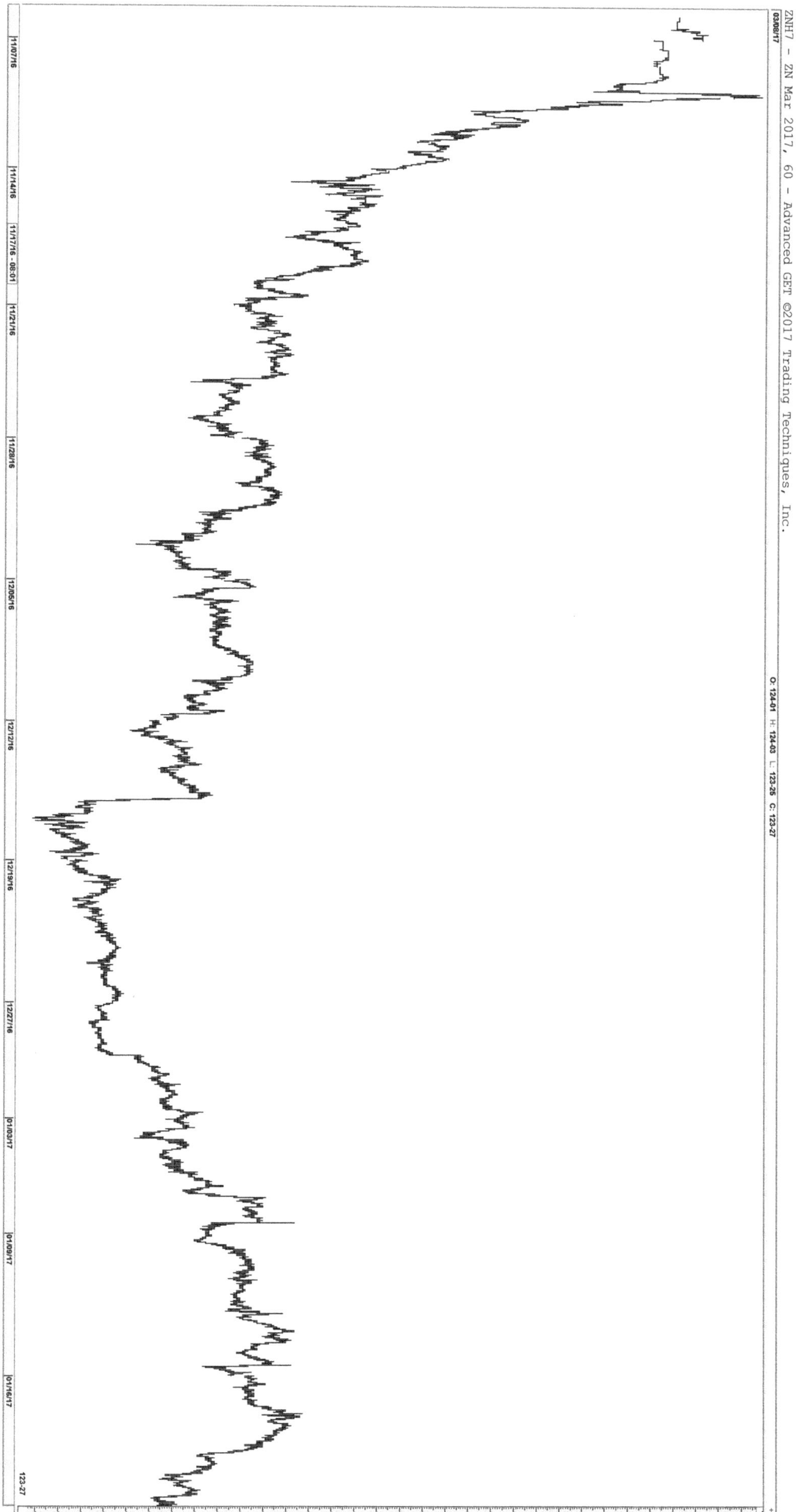
ZNH7 - ZN Mar 2017, 60 - Advanced GET ©2017 Trading Techniques, Inc.
O: 124-01 H: 124-03 L: 123-25 C: 123-27

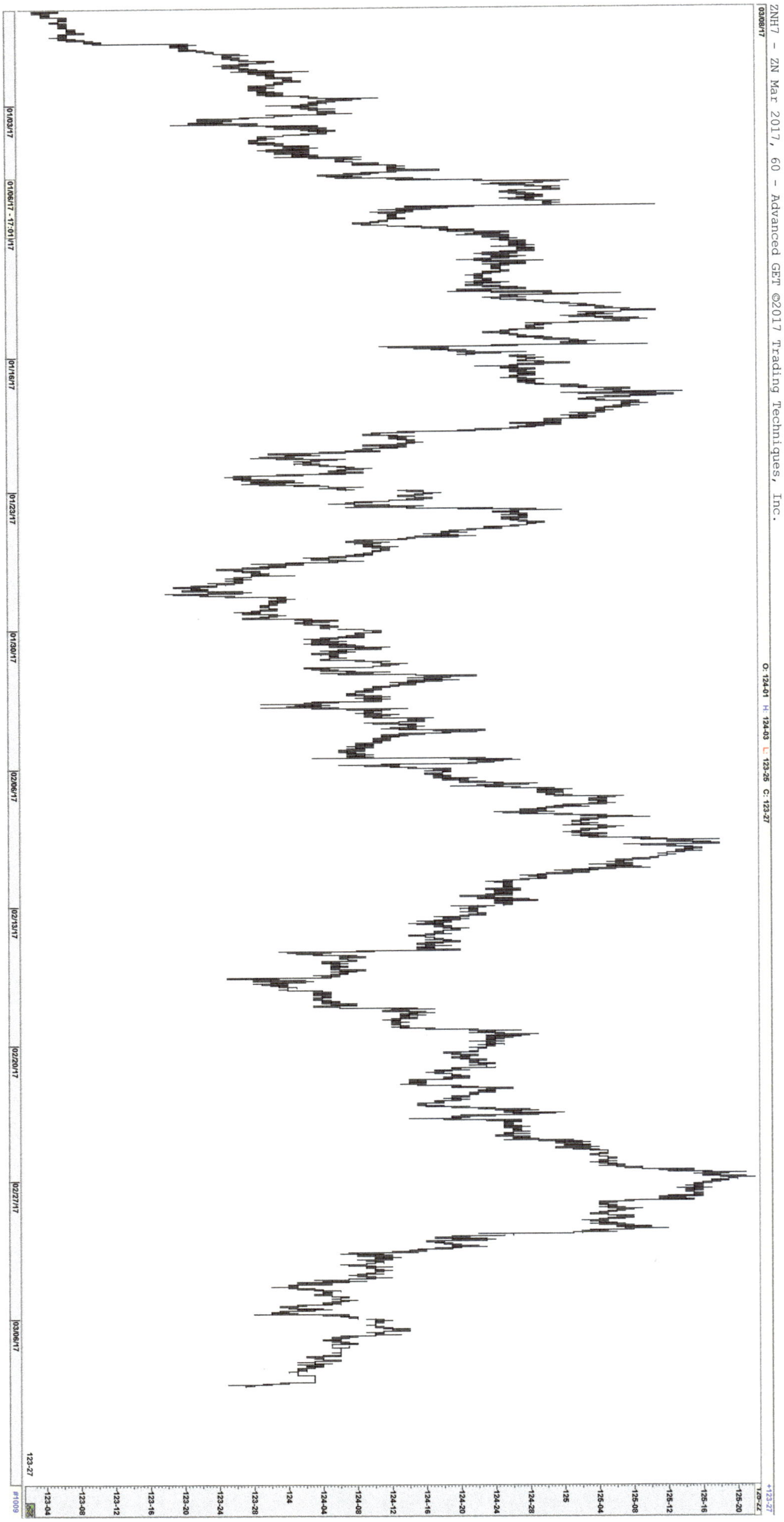
ZNH7 - ZN Mar 2017, 60 - Advanced GET ©2017 Trading Techniques, Inc.
O: 124-01 H: 124-03 L: 123-25 C: 123-27

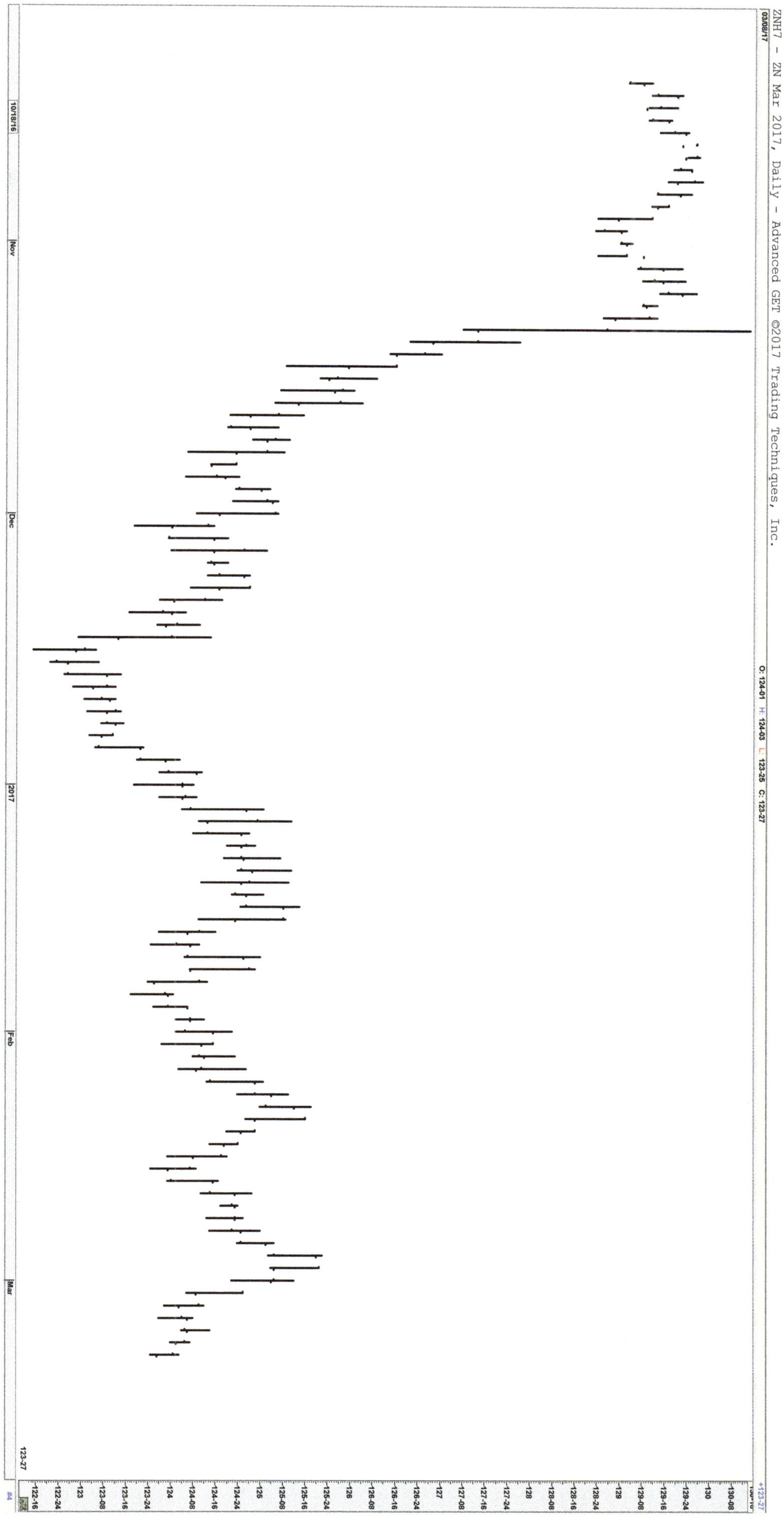
ZNH7 - ZN Mar 2017, Daily - Advanced GET ©2017 Trading Techniques, Inc.
03/08/17
O: 124-01 H: 124-03 L: 123-25 C: 123-27
10/18/16
Nov
Dec
2017
Feb
Mar
123-27

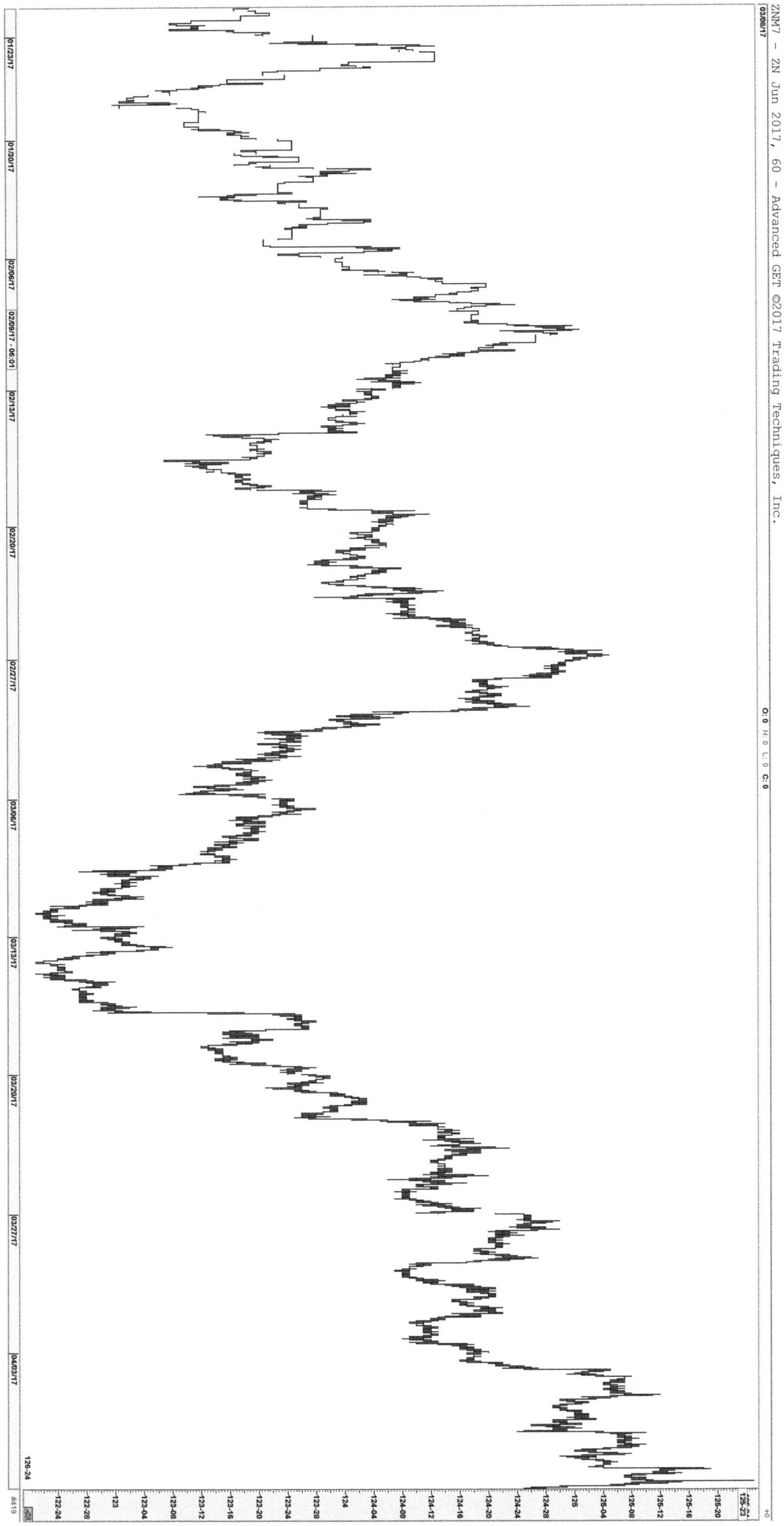
ZNM7 - ZN Jun 2017, 60 - Advanced GET ©2017 Trading Techniques, Inc.

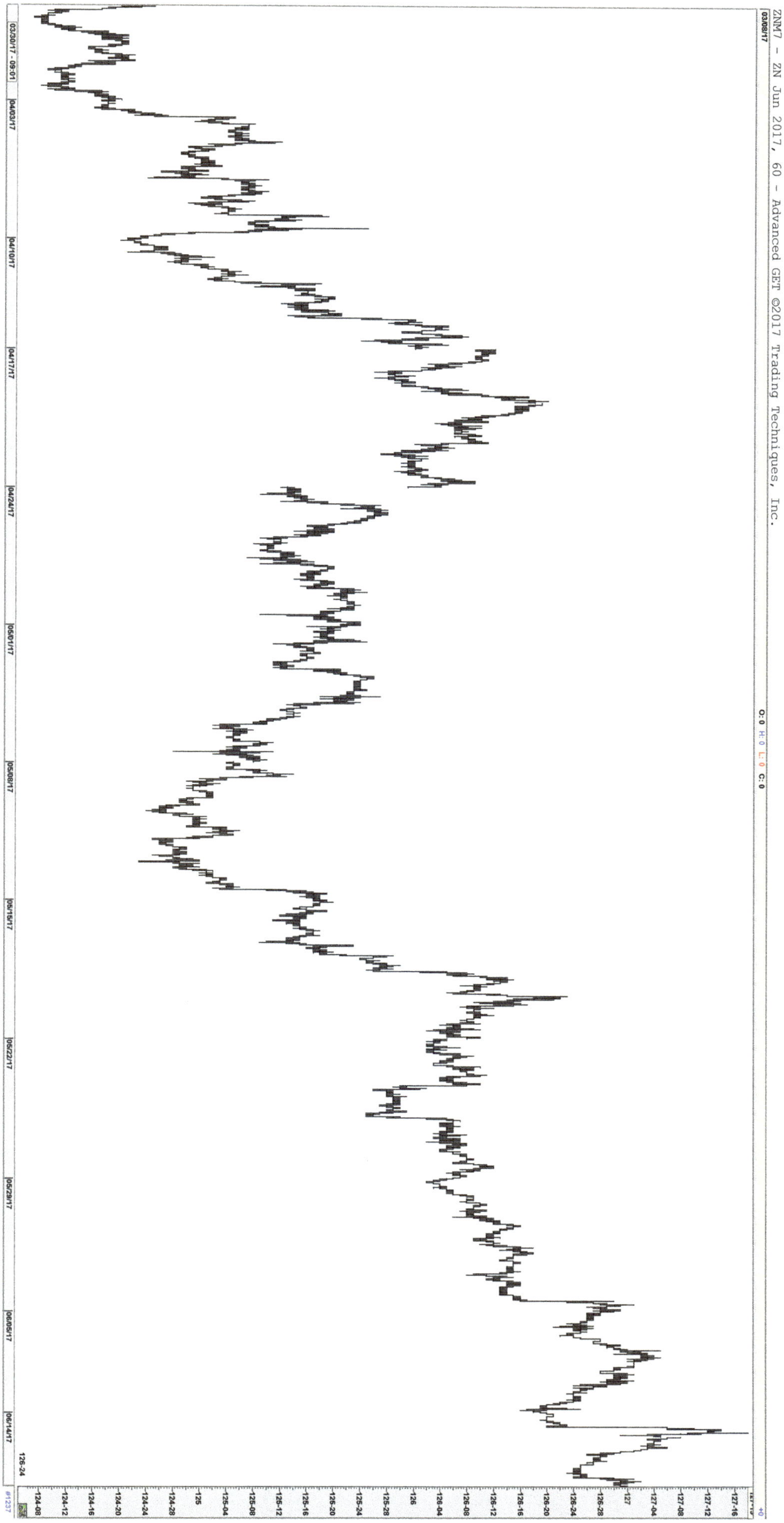
ZNM7 - ZN Jun 2017, 60 - Advanced GET ©2017 Trading Techniques, Inc.

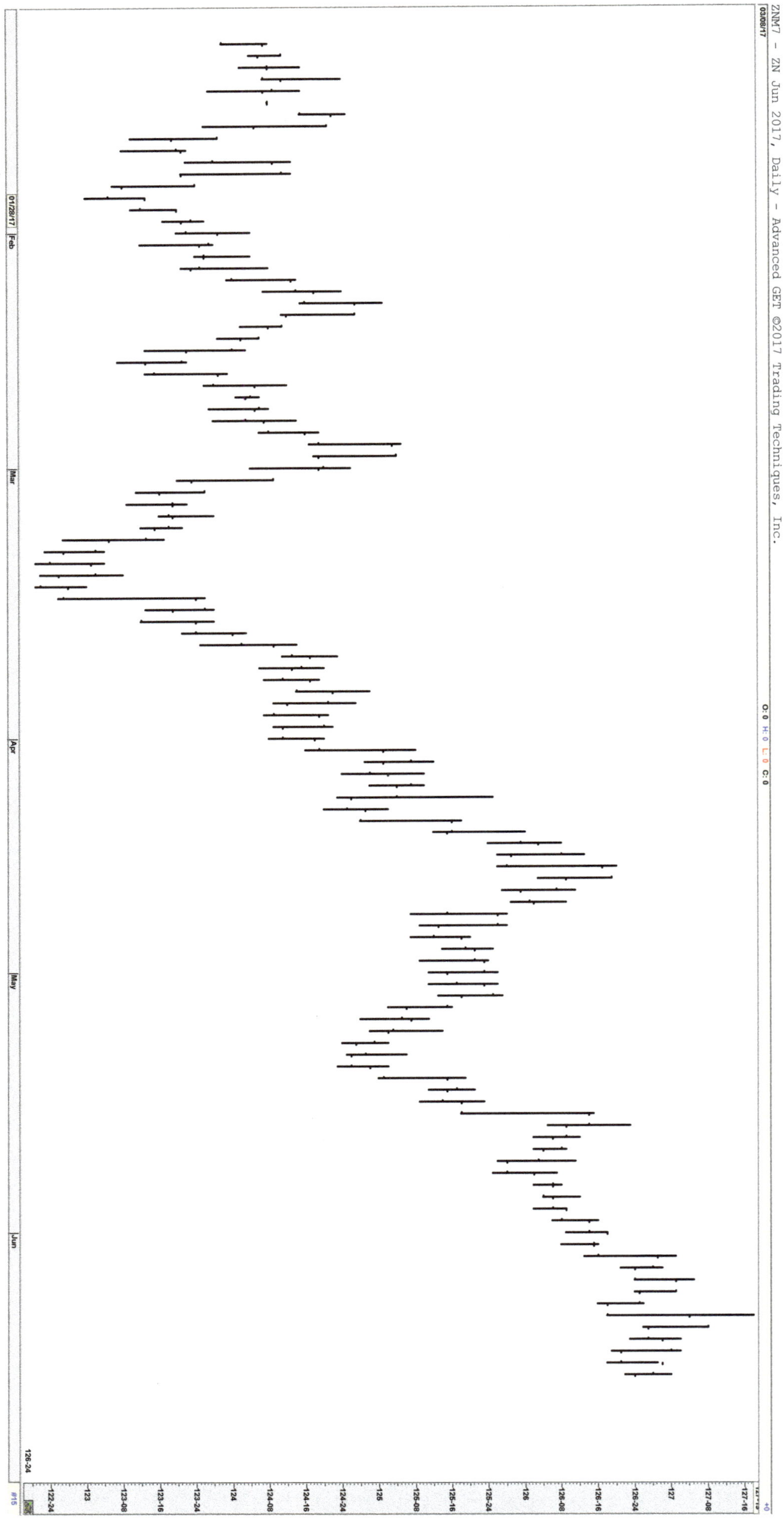
ZNM7 - ZN Jun 2017, Daily - Advanced GET ©2017 Trading Techniques, Inc.

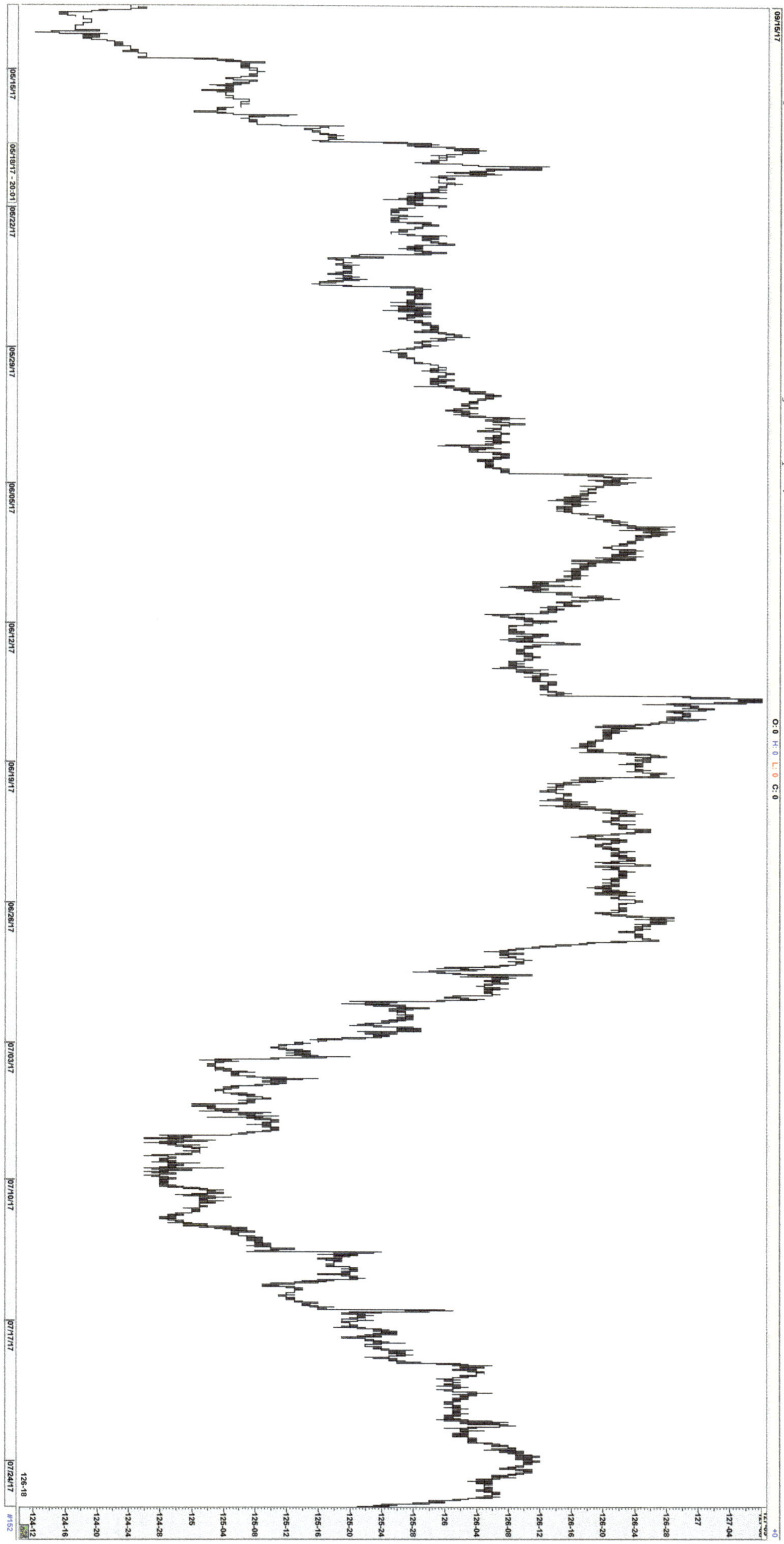
ZNU7 - ZN Sep 2017, 60 - Advanced GET ©2017 Trading Techniques, Inc.
O:0 H:0 L:0 C:0
05/15/17
05/18/17 - 20:01
05/22/17
05/29/17
06/05/17
06/12/17
06/19/17
06/26/17
07/03/17
07/10/17
07/17/17
07/24/17
126-18
124-12
124-16
124-20
124-24
124-28
125
125-04
125-08
125-12
125-16
125-20
125-24
125-28
126
126-04
126-08
126-12
126-16
126-20
126-24
126-28
127
127-04

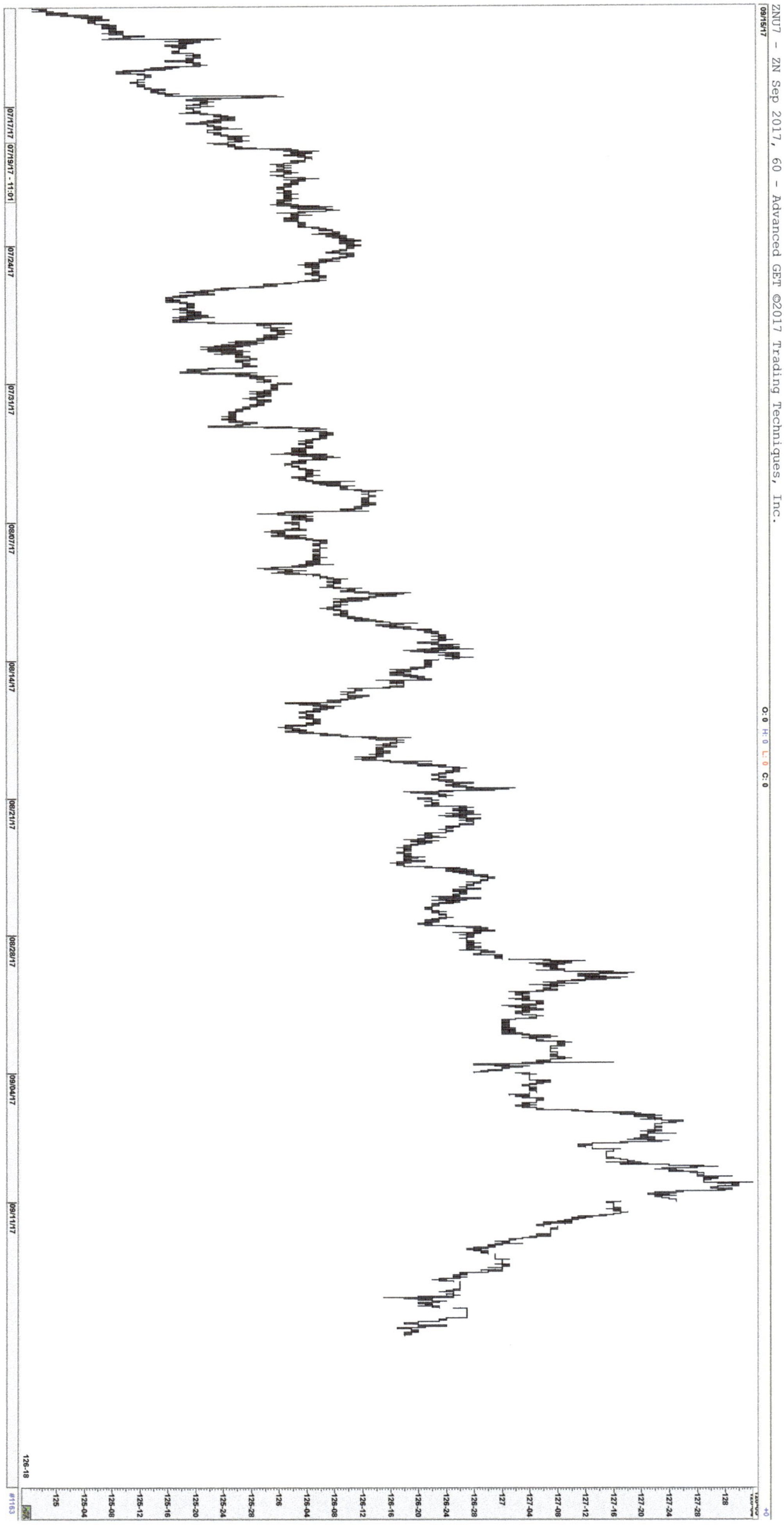
ZNU7 - ZN Sep 2017, 60 - Advanced GET ©2017 Trading Techniques, Inc.

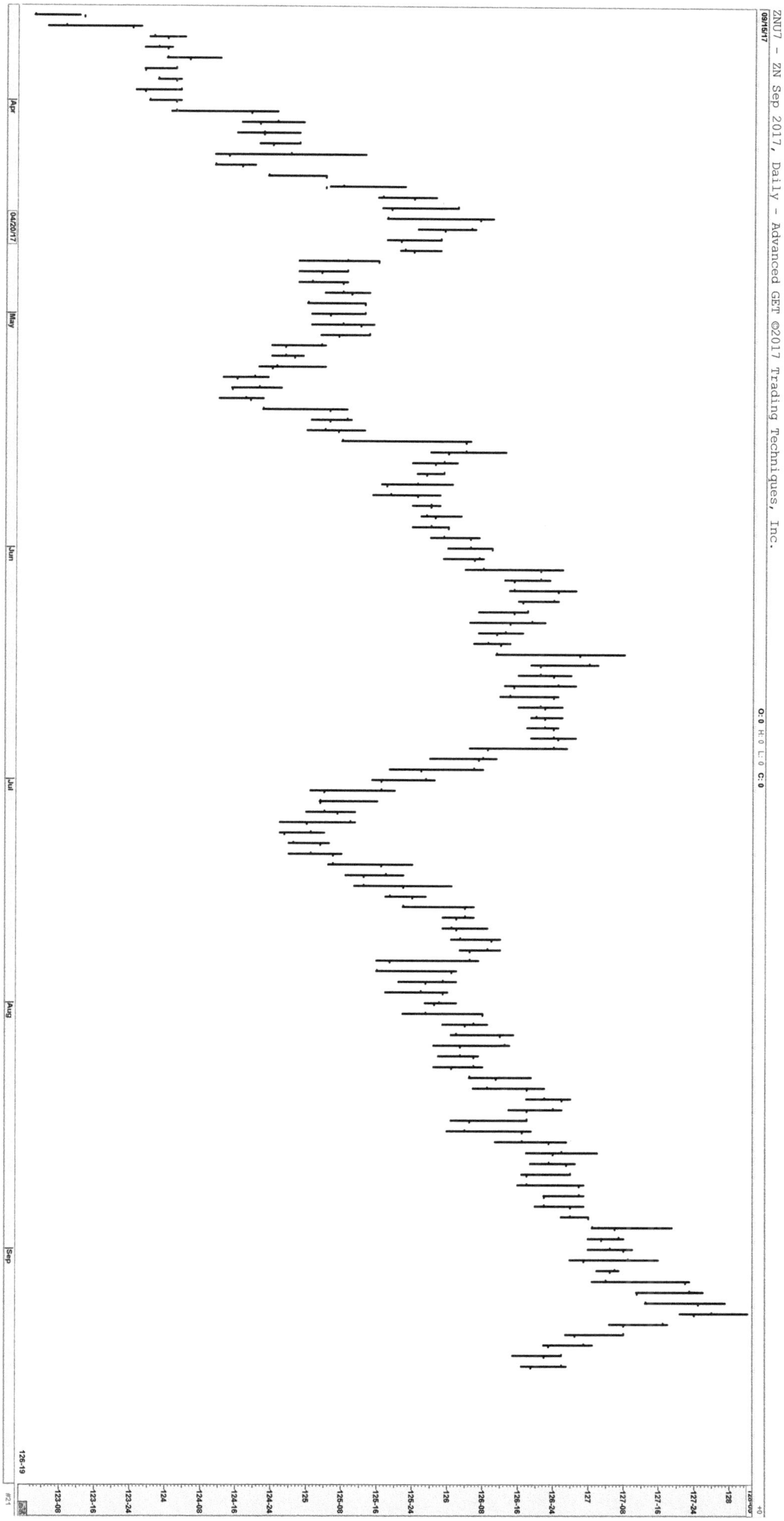
ZNU7 - ZN Sep 2017, Daily - Advanced GET ©2017 Trading Techniques, Inc.
Apr
04/20/17
May
Jun
Jul
Aug
Sep
123-08
123-16
123-24
124
124-08
124-16
124-24
125
125-08
125-16
125-24
126
126-08
126-16
126-24
127
127-08
127-16
127-24
128

DECEMBER and MARCH TERMS GERMAN CONTRACTS: DAILY and 60 MINUTES GRAPHICS

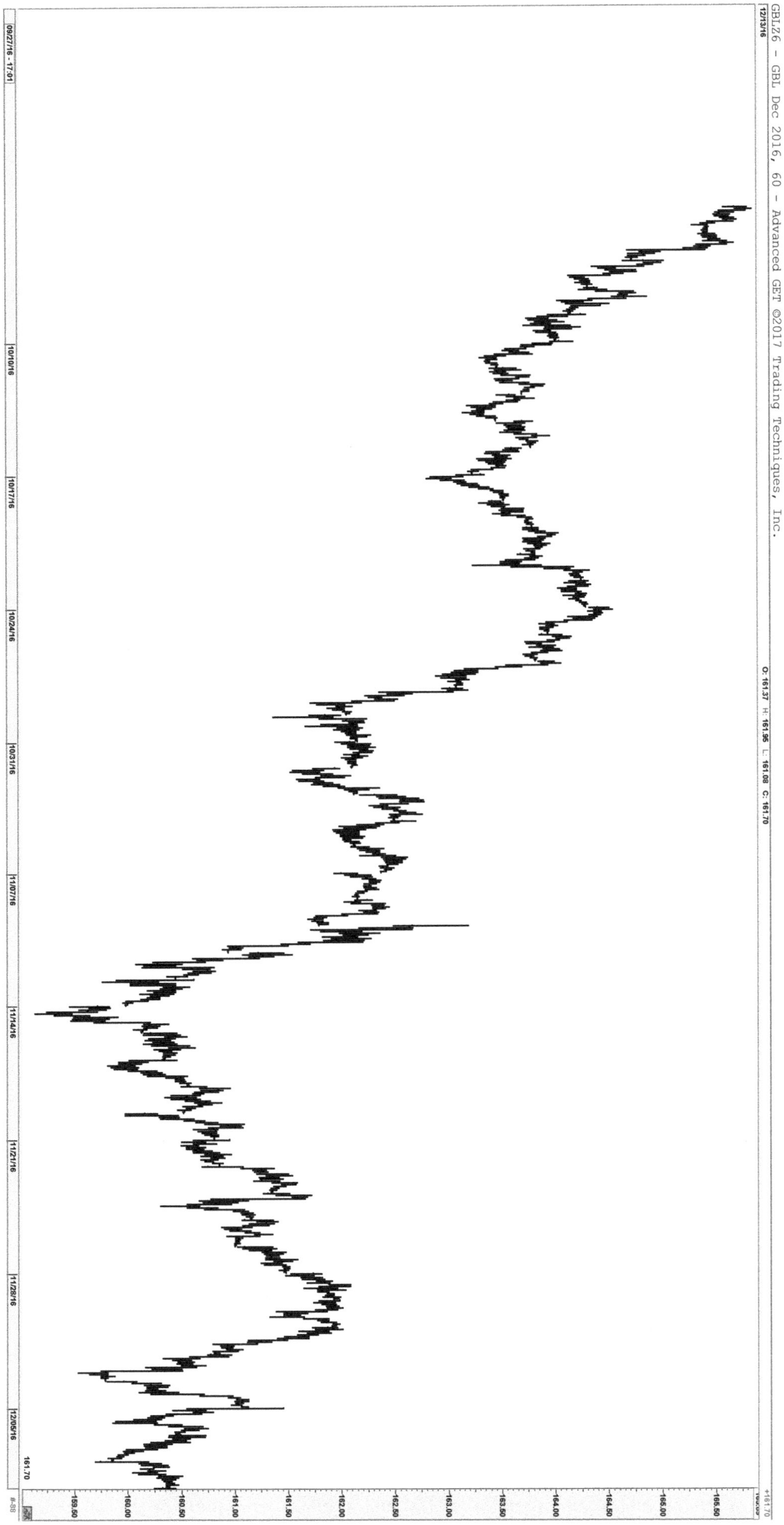
GBLZ6 - GBL Dec 2016, 60 - Advanced GET ©2017 Trading Techniques, Inc.
O: 161.37 H: 161.95 L: 161.08 C: 161.70
09/27/16 - 17:01
10/10/16
10/17/16
10/24/16
10/31/16
11/07/16
11/14/16
11/21/16
11/28/16
12/05/16
12/13/16
161.70
159.50
160.00
160.50
161.00
161.50
162.00
162.50
163.00
163.50
164.00
164.50
165.00
165.50

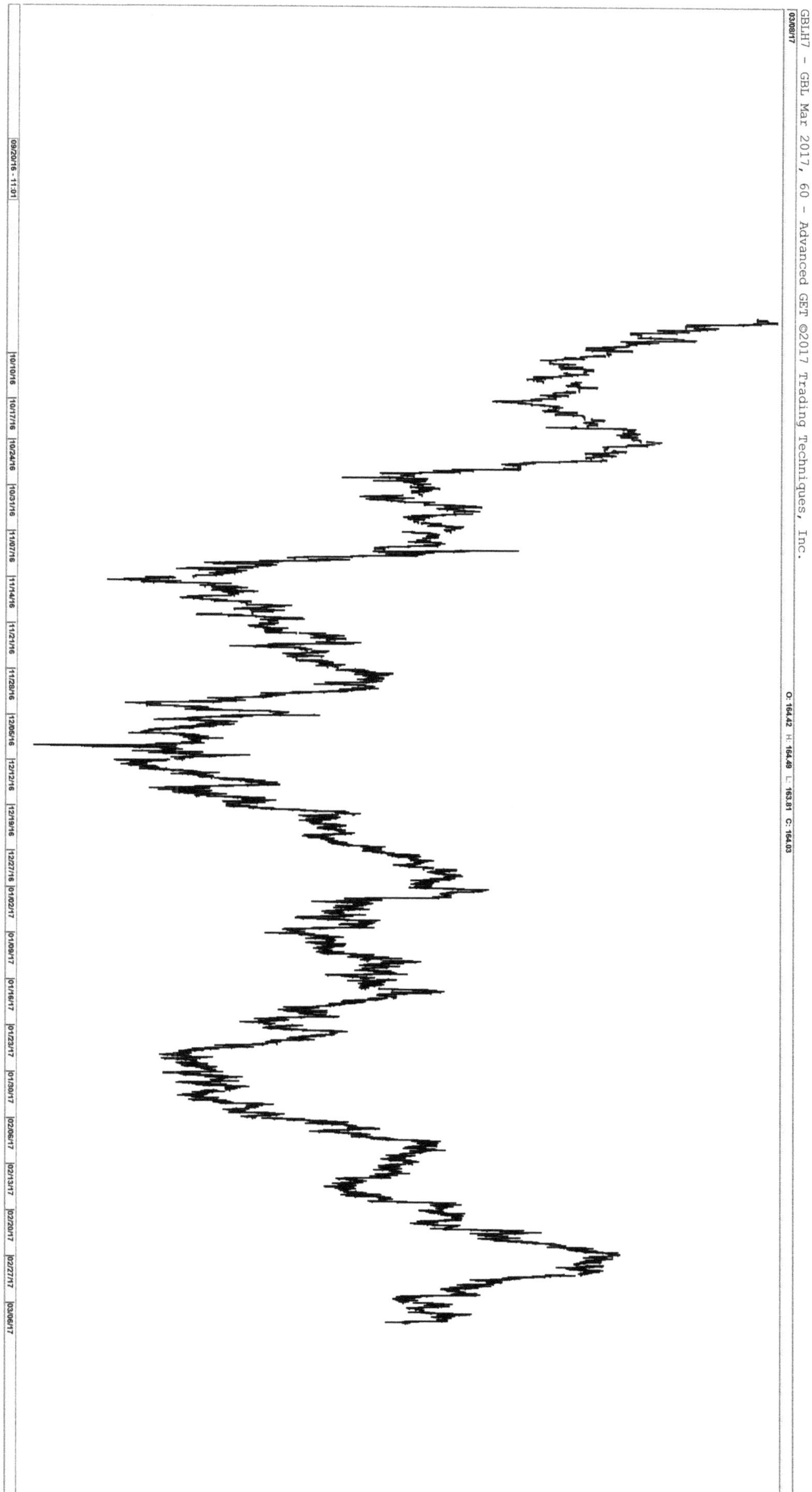
GBLH7 - GBL Mar 2017, 60 - Advanced GET ©2017 Trading Techniques, Inc.

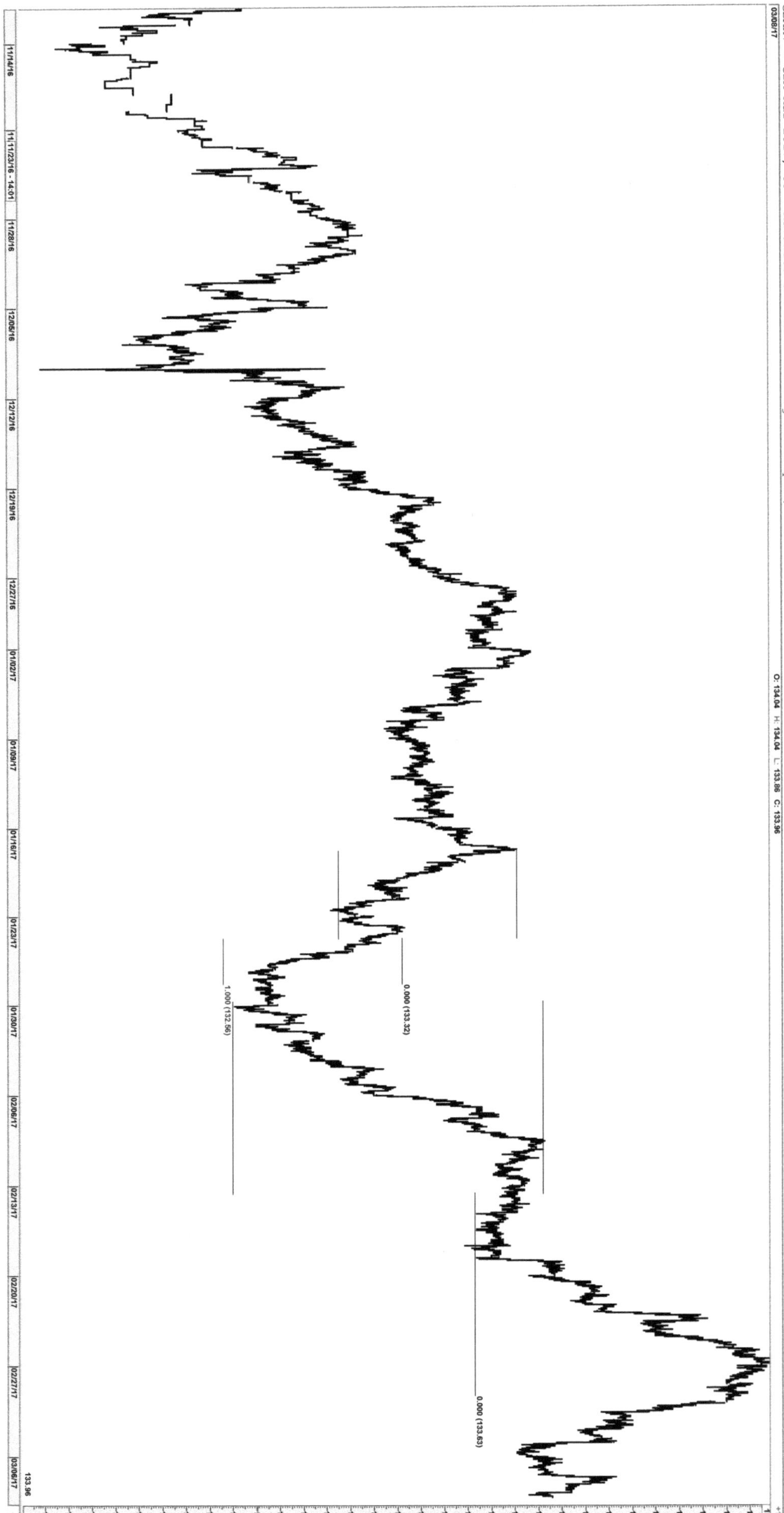
GBMH7 - GBM Mar 2017, 60 - Advanced GET ©2017 Trading Techniques, Inc.
O: 134.04 H: 134.04 L: 133.86 C: 133.96
1.000 (132.56)
0.000 (133.32)
0.000 (133.63)

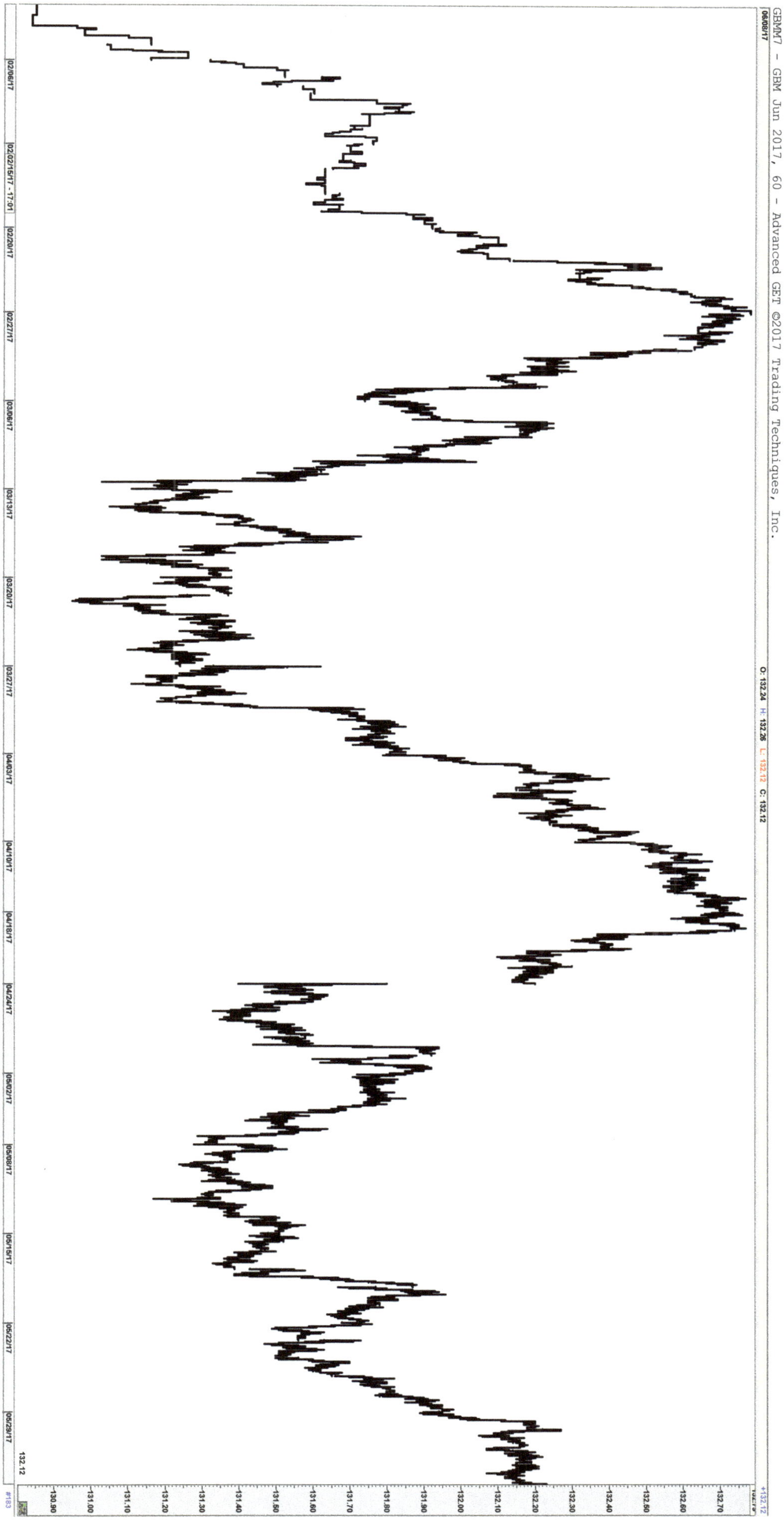
GBMM7 - GBM Jun 2017, 60 - Advanced GET ©2017 Trading Techniques, Inc.

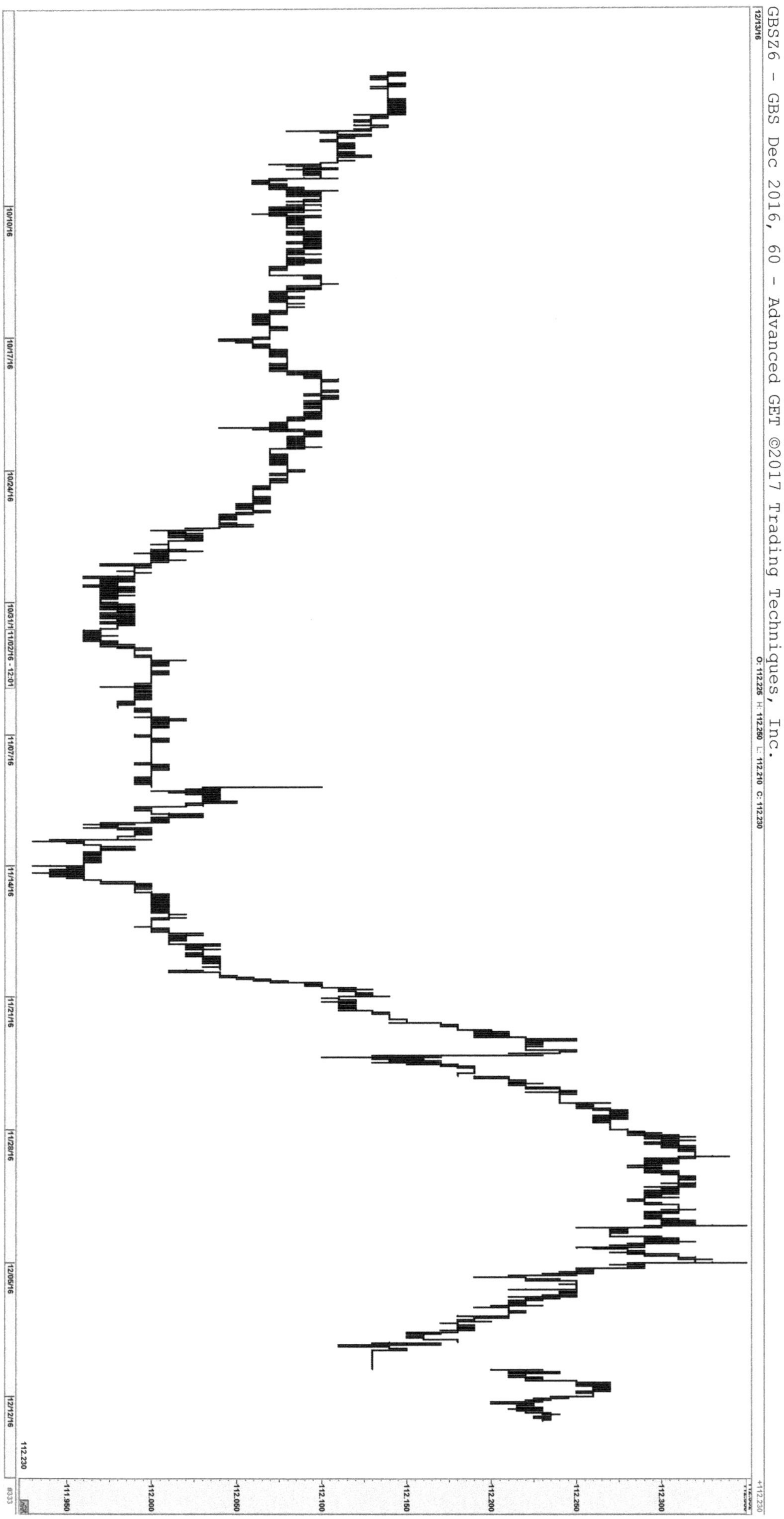
GBSZ6 - GBS Dec 2016, 60 - Advanced GET ©2017 Trading Techniques, Inc.

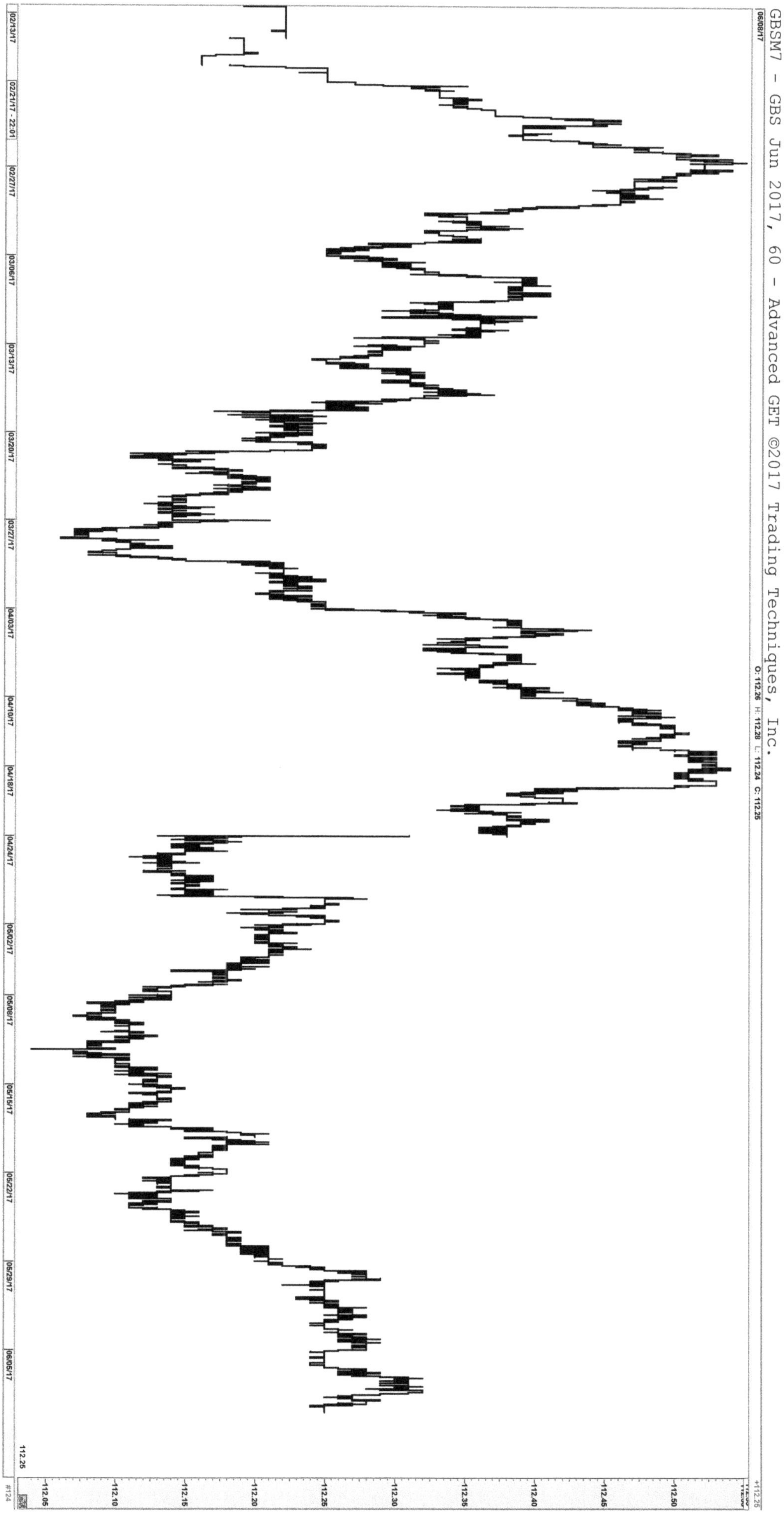
GBSM7 - GBS Jun 2017, 60 - Advanced GET ©2017 Trading Techniques, Inc.
O: 112.26 H: 112.28 L: 112.24 C: 112.25
02/13/17
02/21/17 - 22:01
02/27/17
03/06/17
03/13/17
03/20/17
03/27/17
04/03/17
04/10/17
04/18/17
04/24/17
05/02/17
05/08/17
05/15/17
05/22/17
05/29/17
06/05/17
112.05
112.10
112.15
112.20
112.25
112.30
112.35
112.40
112.45
112.50

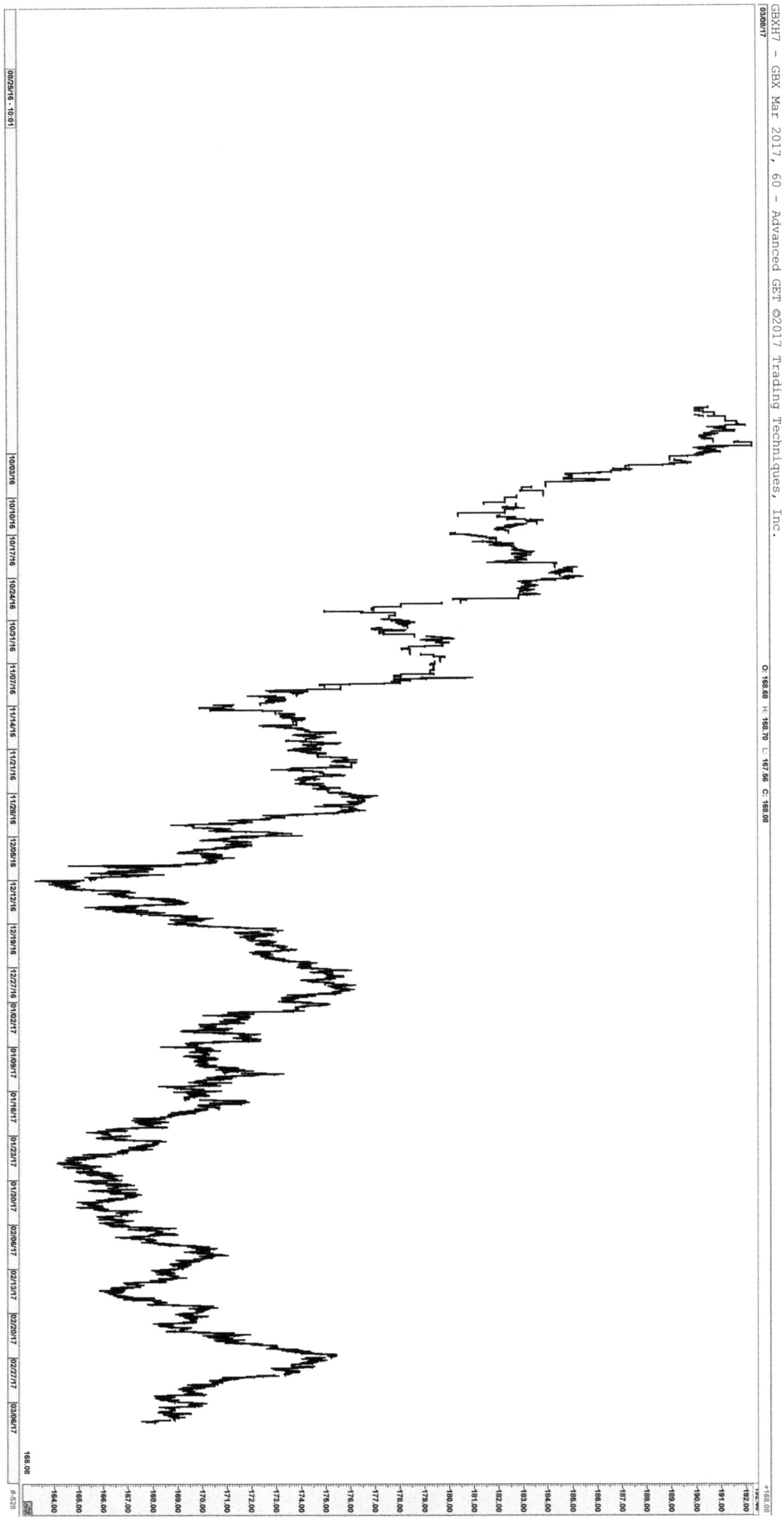
GBXH7 - GBX Mar 2017, 60 - Advanced GET ©2017 Trading Techniques, Inc.

VARIOUS GRAPHICS

10-year sovereign bond yields

10-year yield, % (both axis)

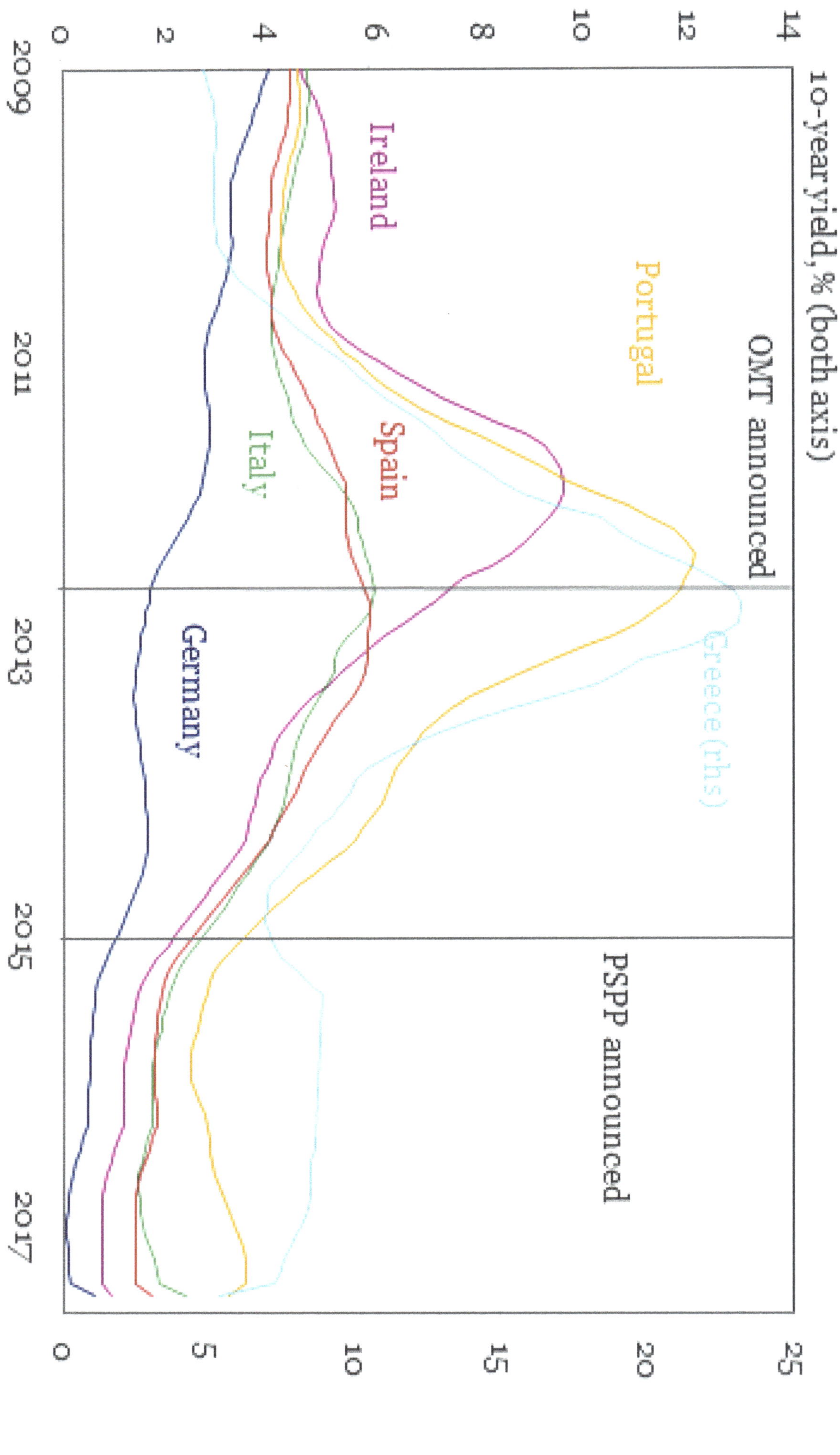

Source: Haver, IIF

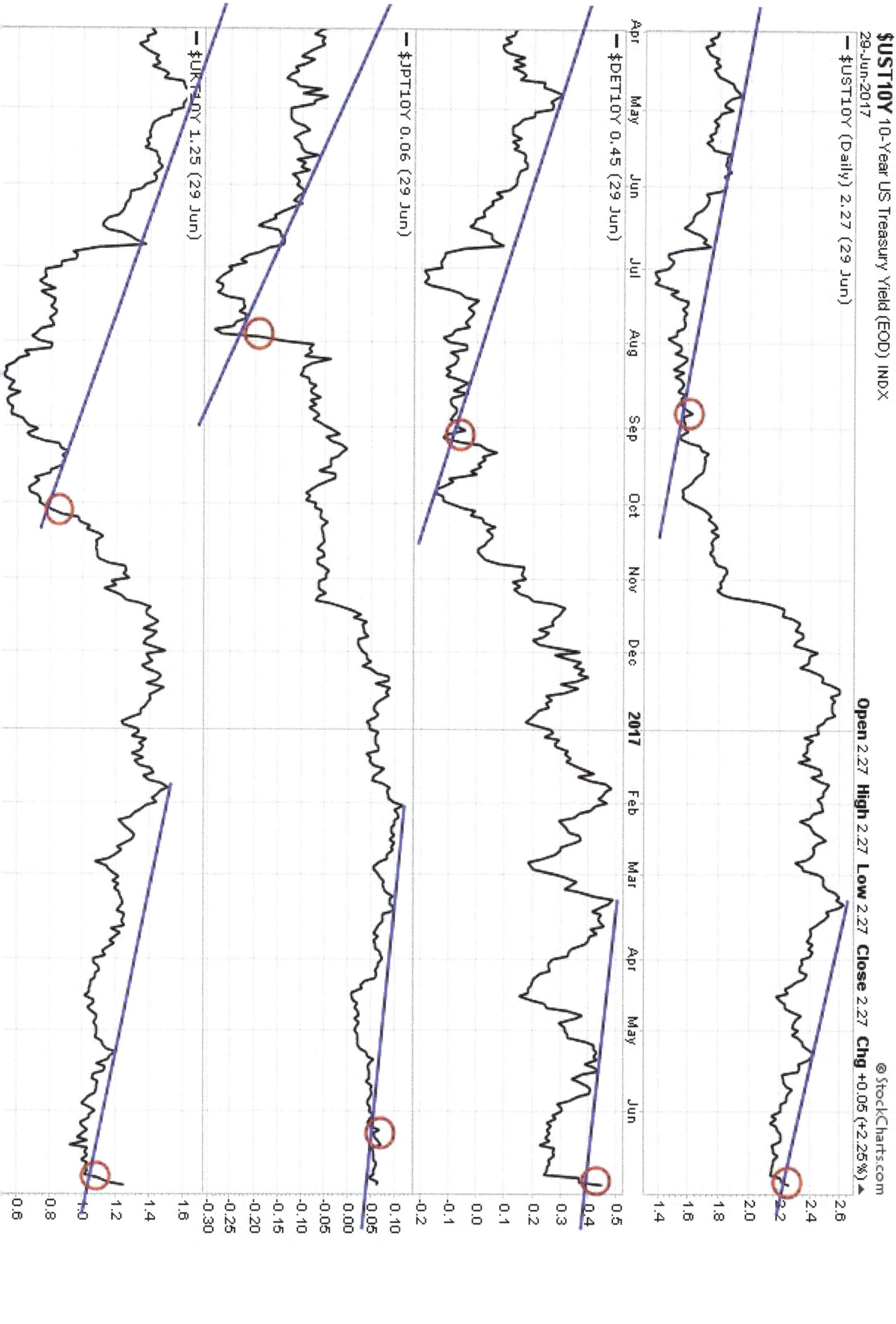

$UST10Y 10-Year US Treasury Yield (EOD) INDX
29-Jun-2017
@StockCharts.com
Open 2.27 High 2.27 Low 2.27 Close 2.27 Chg +0.05 (+2.25%)
— $UST10Y (Daily) 2.27 (29 Jun)
— $DET10Y 0.45 (29 Jun)
— $JPT10Y 0.06 (29 Jun)
— $UKT10Y 1.25 (29 Jun)
Apr
May
Jun
Jul
Aug
Sep
Oct
Nov
Dec
2017
Feb
Mar
Apr
May
Jun

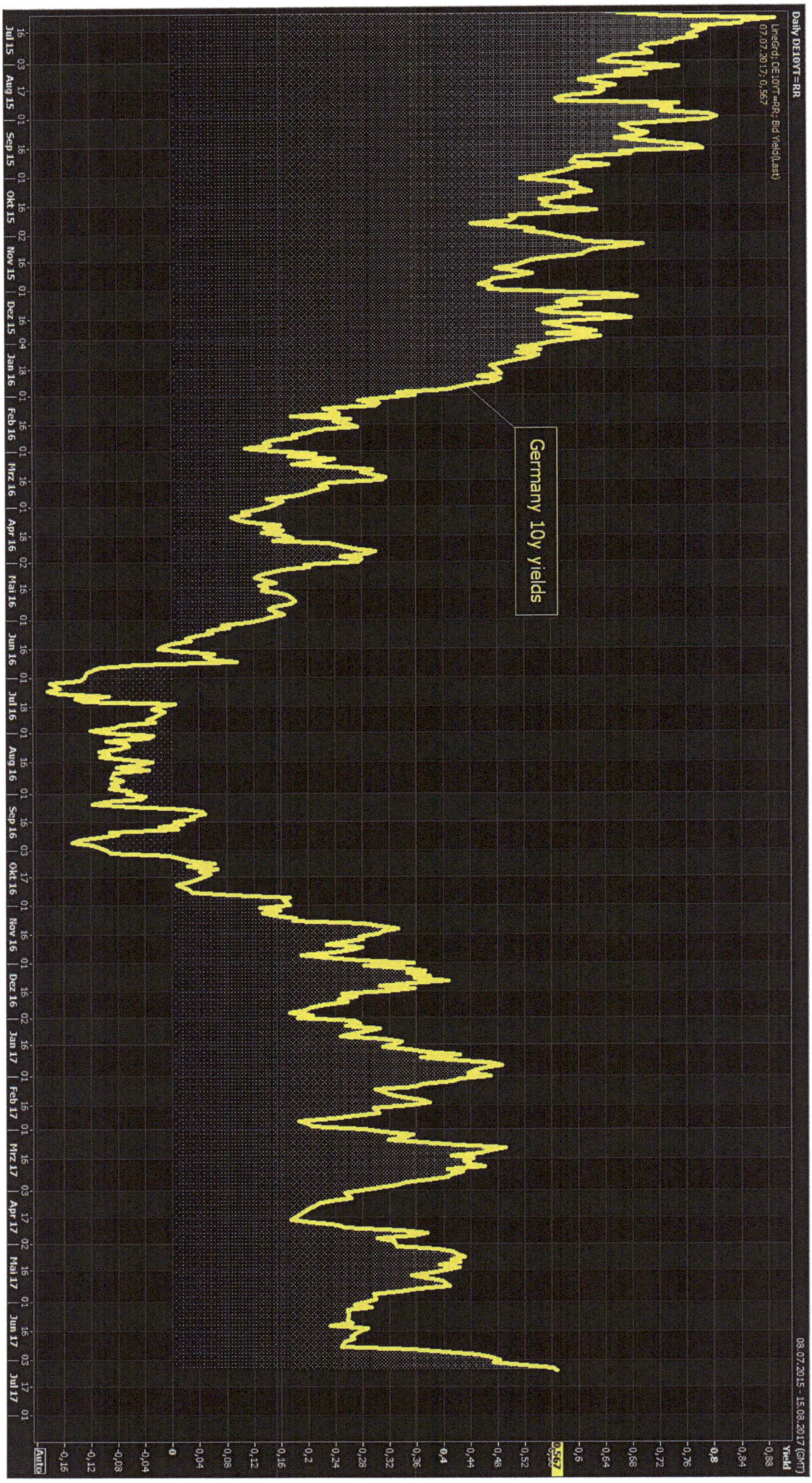
Daily DE10YT=RR
Germany 10y yields
08.07.2015 - 15.08.2017 (GMT)
Yield

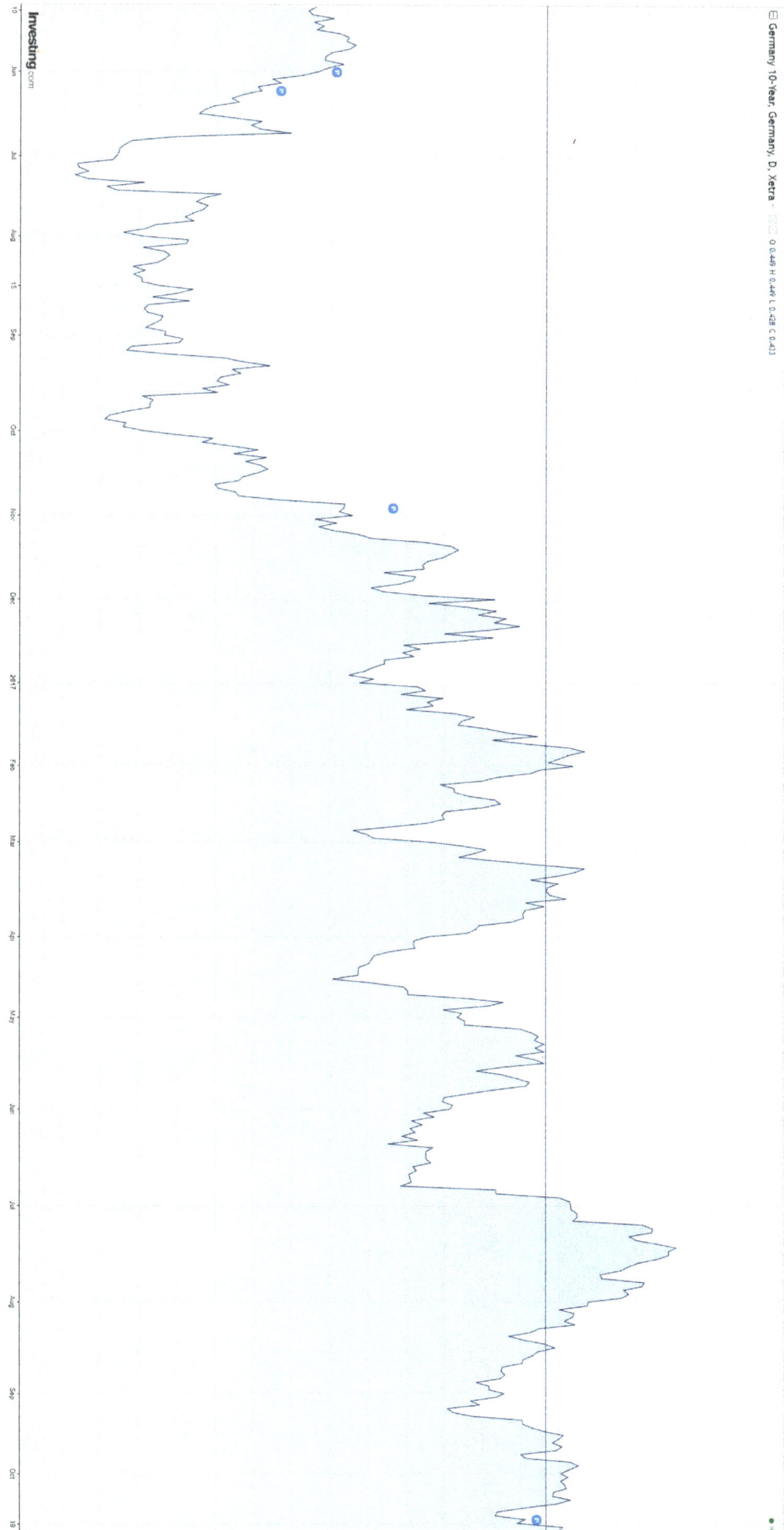
Germany 10-Year, Germany, D, Xetra
Investing.com

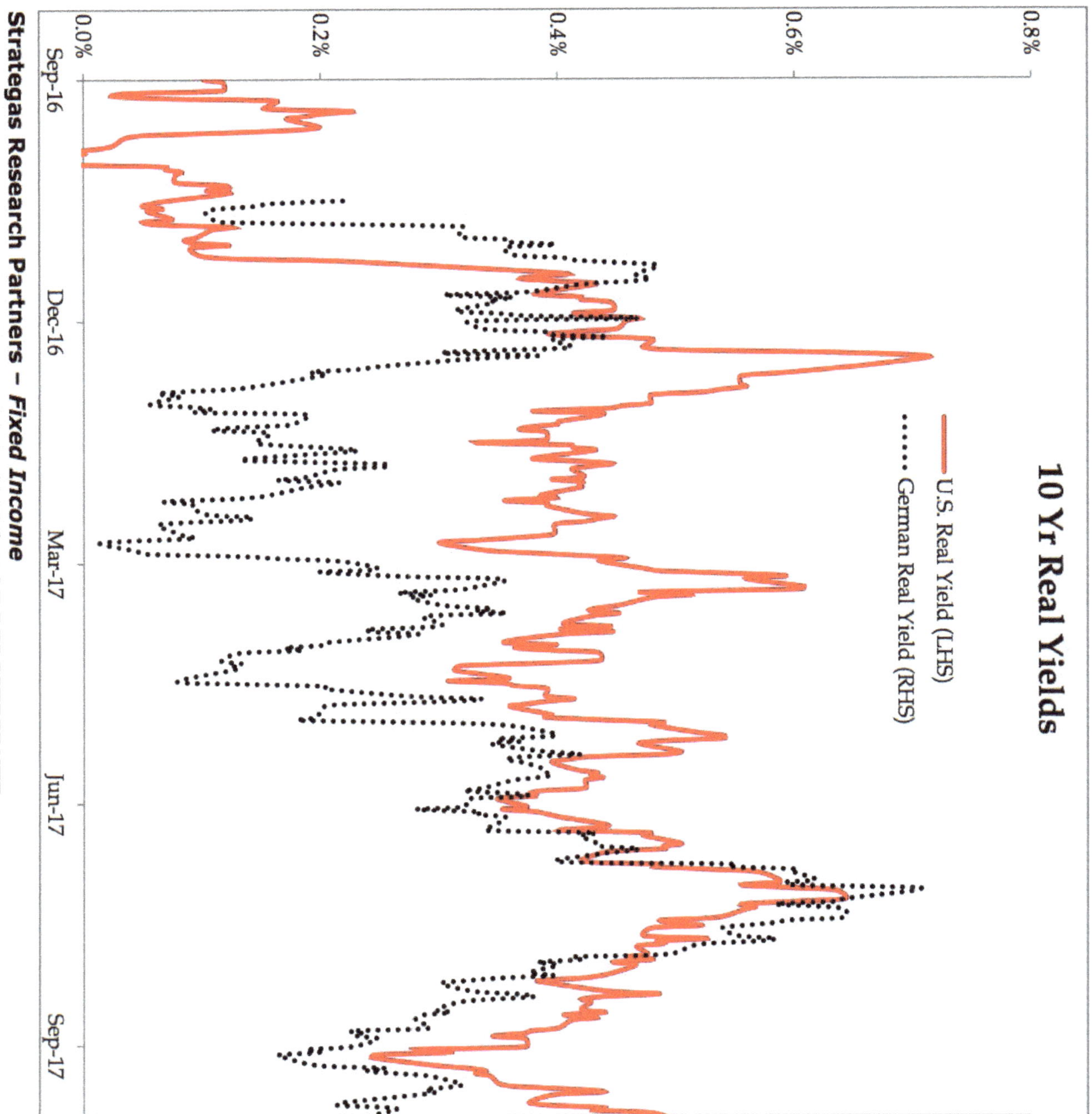
10 Yr Real Yields
U.S. Real Yield (LHS)
German Real Yield (RHS)
0.8%
0.6%
0.4%
0.2%
0.0%
-0.6%
-0.9%
-1.2%
Sep-16
Dec-16
Mar-17
Jun-17
Sep-17
Strategas Research Partners – Fixed Income
2

15. Tightening of Treasury-Bund spread consistent with EUR-USD strength

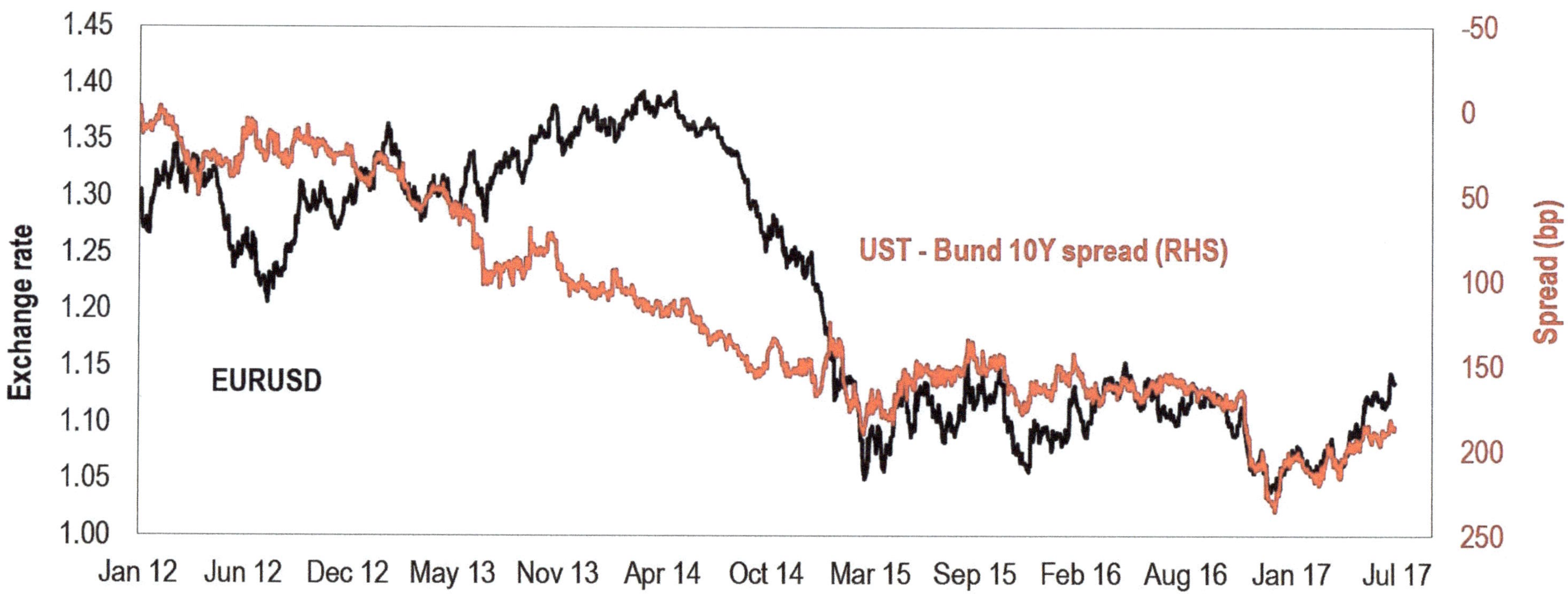

Source: HSBC, Bloomberg

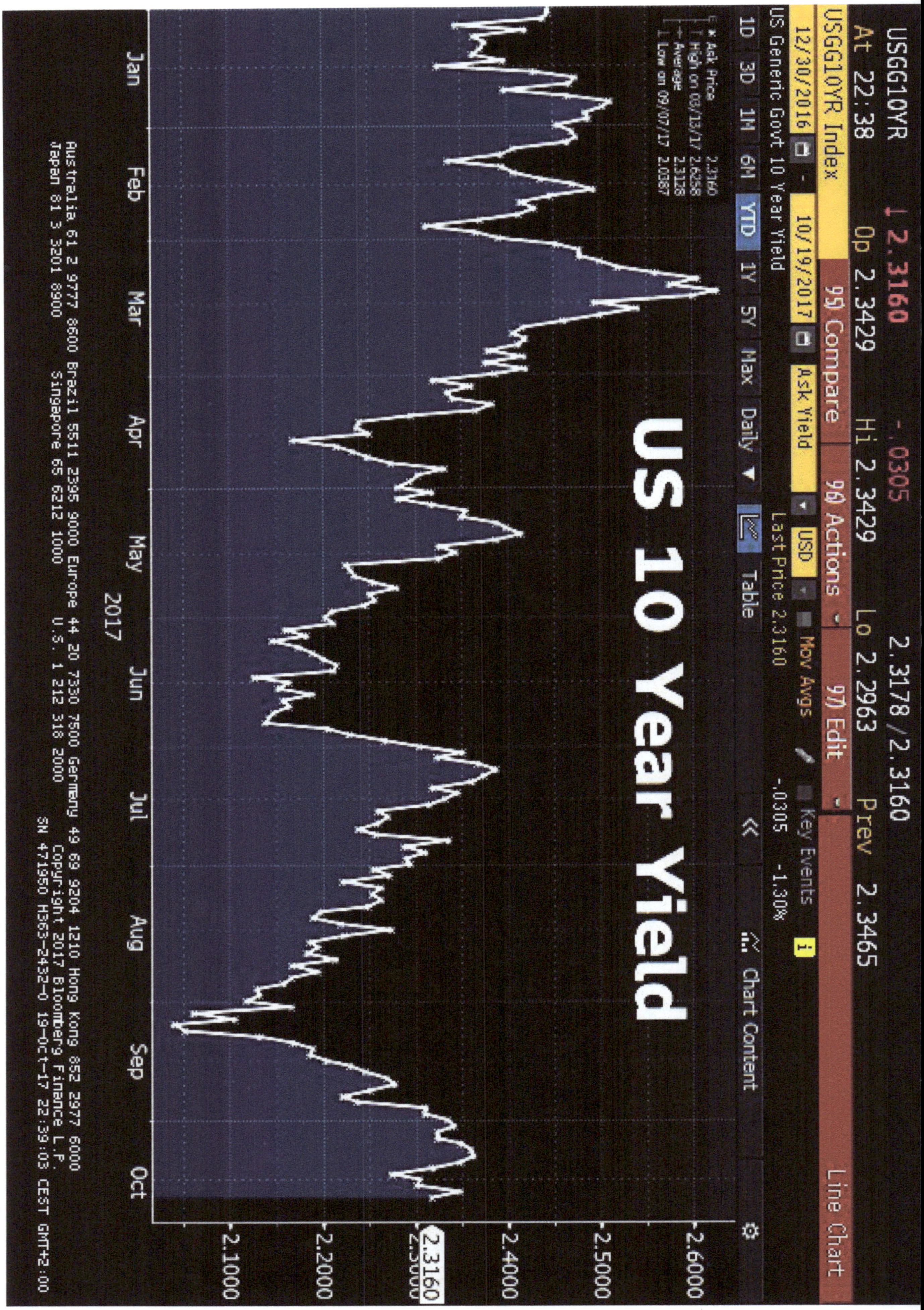
USGG10YR ↓2.3160 -.0305 2.3178/2.3160
At 22:38 Op 2.3429 Hi 2.3429 Lo 2.2963 Prev 2.3465
USGG10YR Index 95) Compare 96) Actions 97) Edit Line Chart
12/30/2016 - 10/19/2017 Ask Yield USD Mov Avgs Key Events
US Generic Govt 10 Year Yield Last Price 2.3160 -.0305 -1.30%
1D 3D 1M 6M YTD 1Y 5Y Max Daily Table Chart Content
Ask Price 2.3160
High on 03/13/17 2.6258
Average 2.3128
Low on 09/07/17 2.0387
US 10 Year Yield
2.6000
2.5000
2.4000
2.3160
2.2000
2.1000
Jan Feb Mar Apr May Jun Jul Aug Sep Oct
2017
Australia 61 2 9777 8600 Brazil 5511 2395 9000 Europe 44 20 7330 7500 Germany 49 69 9204 1210 Hong Kong 852 2977 6000
Japan 81 3 3201 8900 Singapore 65 6212 1000 U.S. 1 212 318 2000 Copyright 2017 Bloomberg Finance L.P.
SN 471950 H363-2432-0 19-Oct-17 22:39:03 CEST GMT+2:00

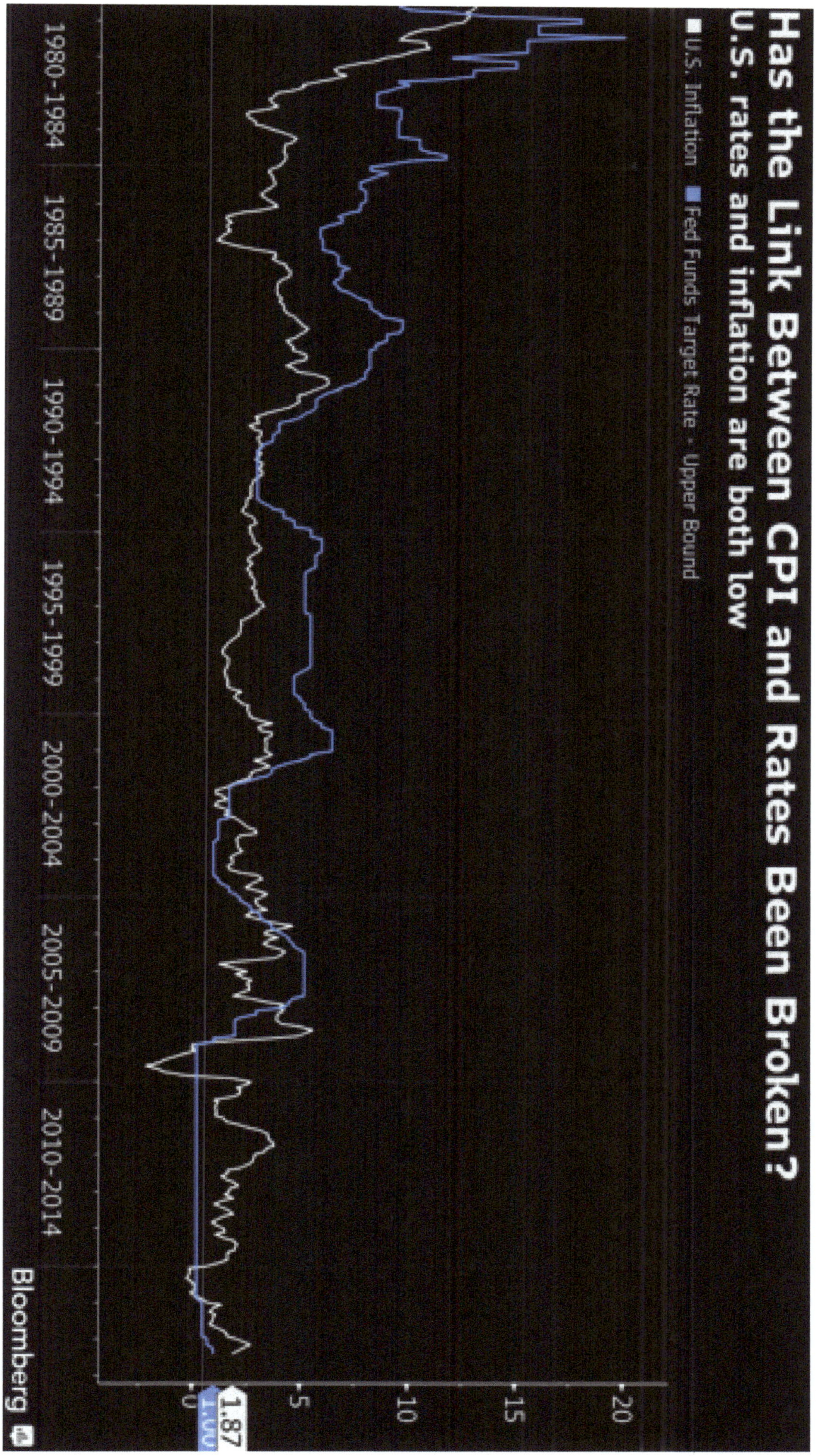
Has the Link Between CPI and Rates Been Broken?
U.S. rates and inflation are both low
U.S. Inflation
Fed Funds Target Rate - Upper Bound
20
15
10
5
1.87
1.00
0
1980-1984
1985-1989
1990-1994
1995-1999
2000-2004
2005-2009
2010-2014
Bloomberg

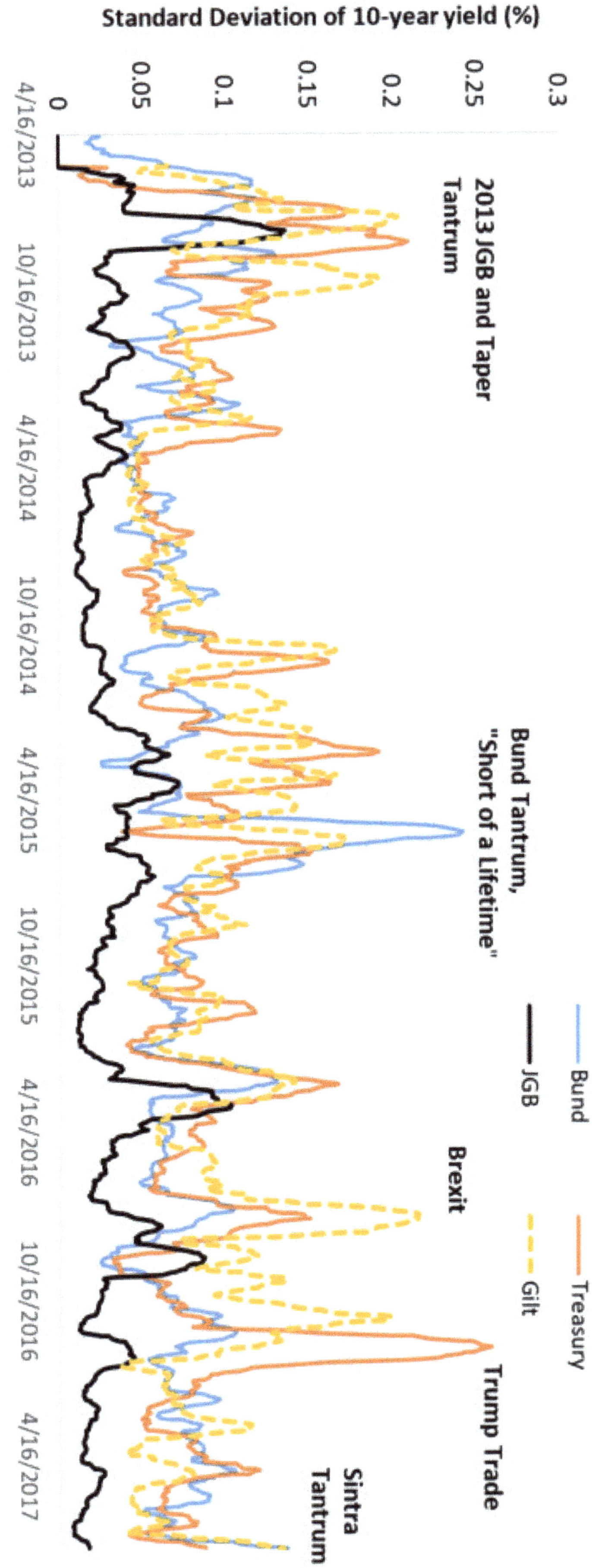

Standard Deviation of 10-year yield (%)
0.3
0.25
0.2
0.15
0.1
0.05
0
4/16/2013
10/16/2013
4/16/2014
10/16/2014
4/16/2015
10/16/2015
4/16/2016
10/16/2016
4/16/2017
2013 JGB and Taper Tantrum
Bund Tantrum, "Short of a Lifetime"
Brexit
Trump Trade
Sintra Tantrum
Bund
Treasury
JGB
Gilt

Figure 16: Eurosystem balance sheet, EUR bn, % of GDP

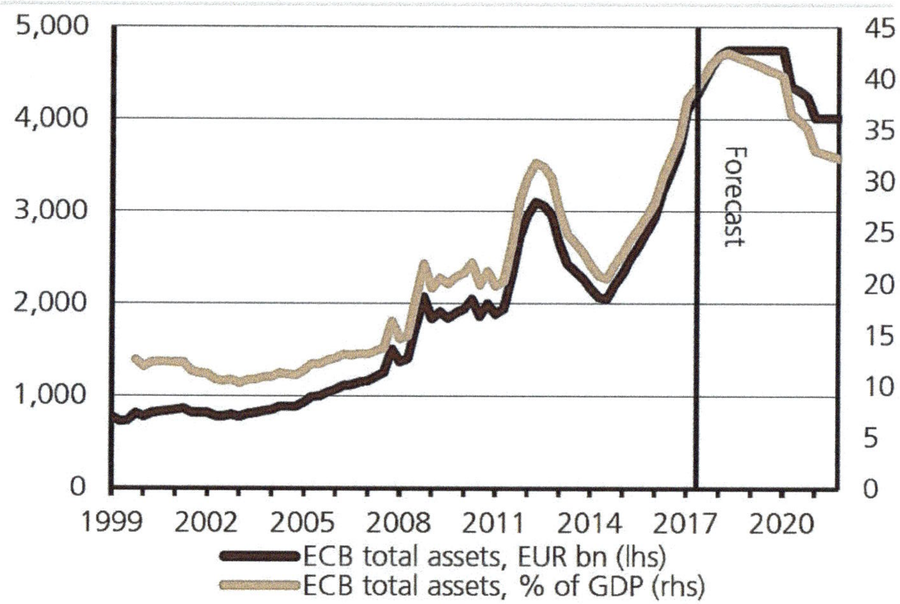

Source: Haver, ECB, UBS

Figure 17: Central bank balance sheets

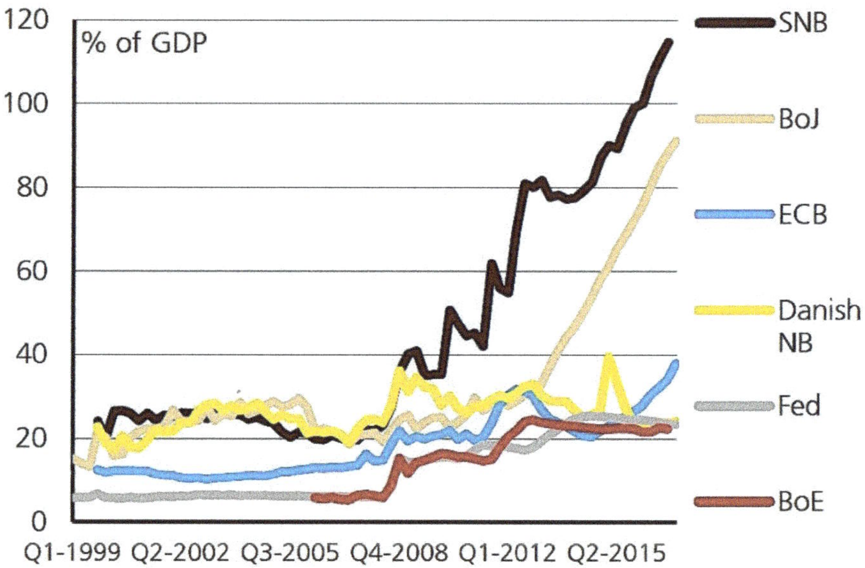

Source: Haver, ECB, UBS

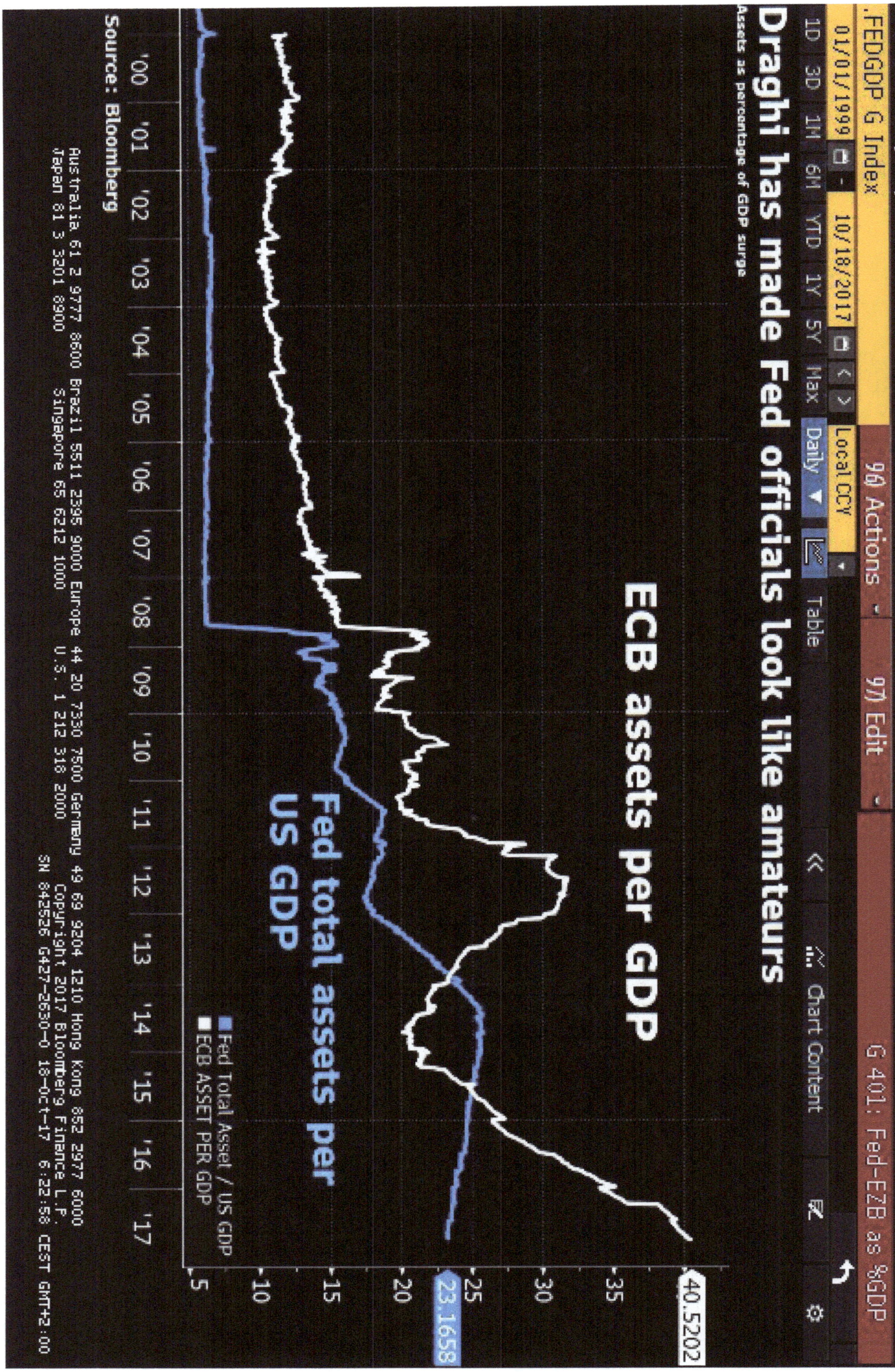

.FEDGDP G 23.1658 Description Fed Total Asset / US GDP
As of 10/18/2017 Owner BLOOMBERG L.P.
.FEDGDP G Index
96 Actions
97 Edit
G 401: Fed-EZB as %GDP
01/01/1999 - 10/18/2017
Local CCY
1D 3D 1M 6M YTD 1Y 5Y Max Daily
Table
Chart Content
Draghi has made Fed officials look like amateurs
Assets as percentage of GDP surge
ECB assets per GDP
Fed total assets per US GDP
Fed Total Asset / US GDP
ECB ASSET PER GDP
40.5202
23.1658
35
30
25
20
15
10
5
'00 '01 '02 '03 '04 '05 '06 '07 '08 '09 '10 '11 '12 '13 '14 '15 '16 '17
Source: Bloomberg
Australia 61 2 9777 8600 Brazil 5511 2395 9000 Europe 44 20 7330 7500 Germany 49 69 9204 1210 Hong Kong 852 2977 6000
Japan 81 3 3201 8900 Singapore 65 6212 1000 U.S. 1 212 318 2000 Copyright 2017 Bloomberg Finance L.P.
SN 842526 G427-2630-0 18-Oct-17 6:22:58 CEST GMT+2:00

Outstanding central government bonds by maturity

euro, bn	0-1 years	1-2	2-3	3-5	5-7	7-10	10-15	15-30	30+ years	Total	QE Eligible (1-30 years)
Germany	156	147	103	186	158	149	72	137	0	1107	951
France	118	134	166	258	187	237	167	189	46	1503	1338
Italy	194	198	187	292	272	206	171	210	6	1737	1537
Spain	77	82	98	122	81	174	70	98	5	808	726
Netherlands	39	16	30	47	39	46	21	44	0	281	243
Belgium	30	24	13	51	34	59	47	62	12	332	290
Austria	20	18	14	38	25	46	8	29	5	205	180
Ireland	6	9	25	14	14	21	9	13	16	128	105
Finland	6	5	12	16	20	15	10	7	0	90	84
Portugal	6	7	10	29	28	24	5	12	0	121	115
Total	652	640	658	1054	859	977	581	801	91	6313	5570

PSPP run-rate and projected time limits

euro, bn	Outstanding eligible paper (1-30 years) a	Projected bond issuance in 2017 b	Remaining bonds to be issued this year c	Total eligible bonds at the end of 2017 d (a + c)	33% PSPP limit rule (d x 0.33)	33% limit rule minus SMP & NCB reserve holdings e	PSPP done to date f	Estimated central gov't bonds bought g*	Bonds that could still be bought h (e - g)	PSPP run rate (latest monthly amounts) i	Assumed purchase rate of gov't bonds j*	Months of PSPP to run (h / j)	
Germany	951	160	91	1042	344	344	368	276	68	12.5	9.4	7	Germany
France	1338	200	106	1444	477	477	294	294	183	11.3	11.3	16	France
Italy	1537	270	134	1671	552	497	255	255	241	9.8	9.8	25	Italy
Spain	726	133	66	792	261	241	183	183	59	6.6	6.6	9	Spain
Netherlands	243	35	13	255	84	84	83	62	22	3.0	2.2	10	Netherlands
Belgium	290	39	17	308	102	102	51	51	50	2.0	2.0	26	Belgium
Austria	180	22	11	191	63	63	41	41	22	1.6	1.6	14	Austria
Ireland	105	13	3	108	36	26	21	21	6	0.5	0.5	11	Ireland
Finland	84	15	8	91	30	30	24	24	6	0.7	0.7	9	Finland
Portugal	115	20	11	126	42	34	27	27	7	0.5	0.5	14	Portugal

* Based on estimates that ~75% of PSPP in Germany and the Netherlands is in central gov't debt

Source: Jefferies International

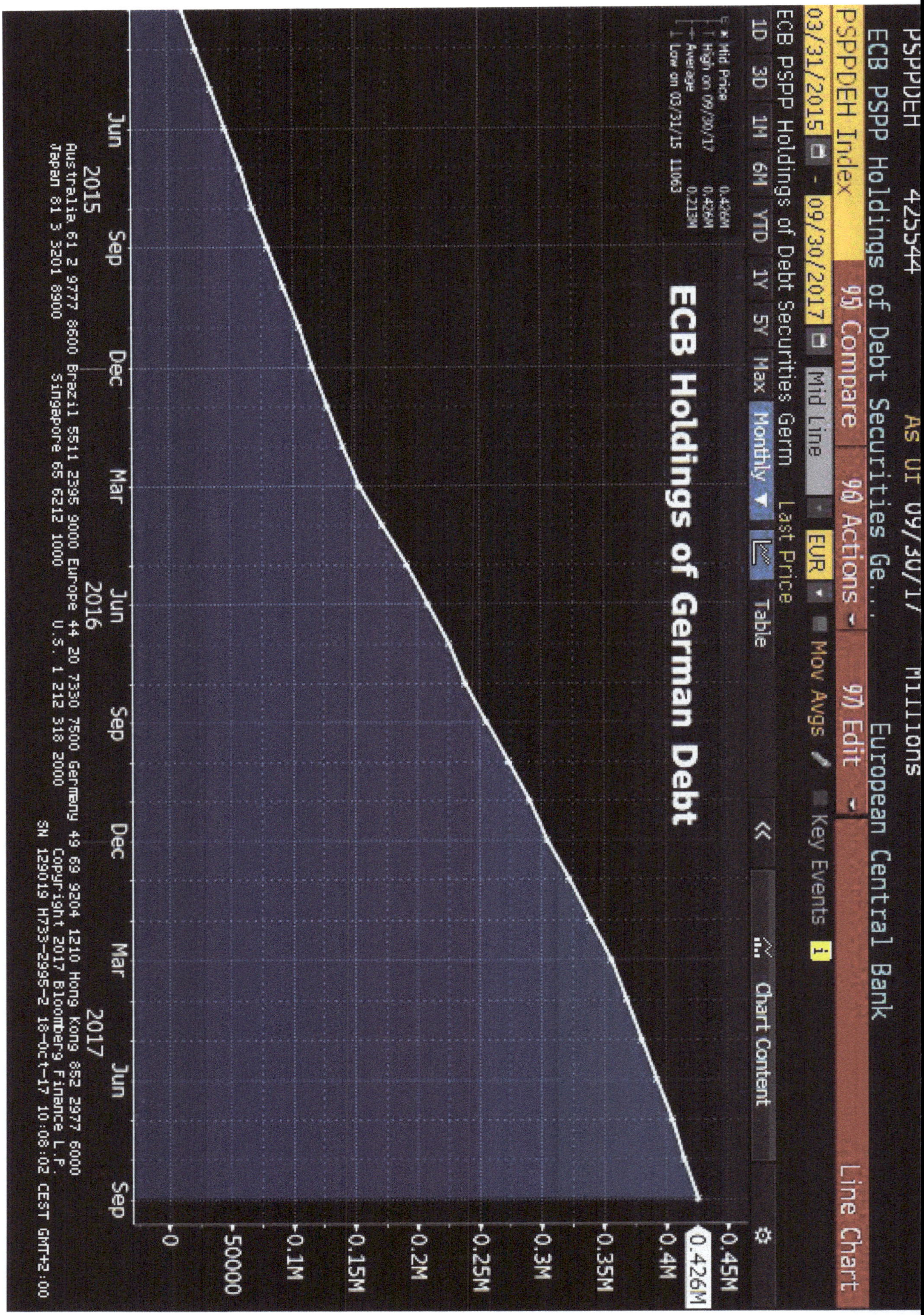
PSPPDEH 425544 As of 09/30/17 Millions
ECB PSPP Holdings of Debt Securities Ge... European Central Bank
PSPPDEH Index 95) Compare 96) Actions 97) Edit Line Chart
03/31/2015 - 09/30/2017 Mid Line EUR Mov Avgs Key Events
ECB PSPP Holdings of Debt Securities Germ Last Price
1D 3D 1M 6M YTD 1Y 5Y Max Monthly Table Chart Content
ECB Holdings of German Debt
Mid Price 0.426M
High on 09/30/17 0.426M
Average 0.213M
Low on 03/31/15 11063
Jun Sep Dec Mar Jun Sep Dec Mar Jun Sep
2015 2016 2017
0.45M 0.426M 0.4M 0.35M 0.3M 0.25M 0.2M 0.15M 0.1M 50000 0
Australia 61 2 9777 8600 Brazil 5511 2395 9000 Europe 44 20 7330 7500 Germany 49 69 9204 1210 Hong Kong 852 2977 6000
Japan 81 3 3201 8900 Singapore 65 6212 1000 U.S. 1 212 318 2000 Copyright 2017 Bloomberg Finance L.P.
SN 129019 H733-2995-2 18-Oct-17 10:08:02 CEST GMT+2:00

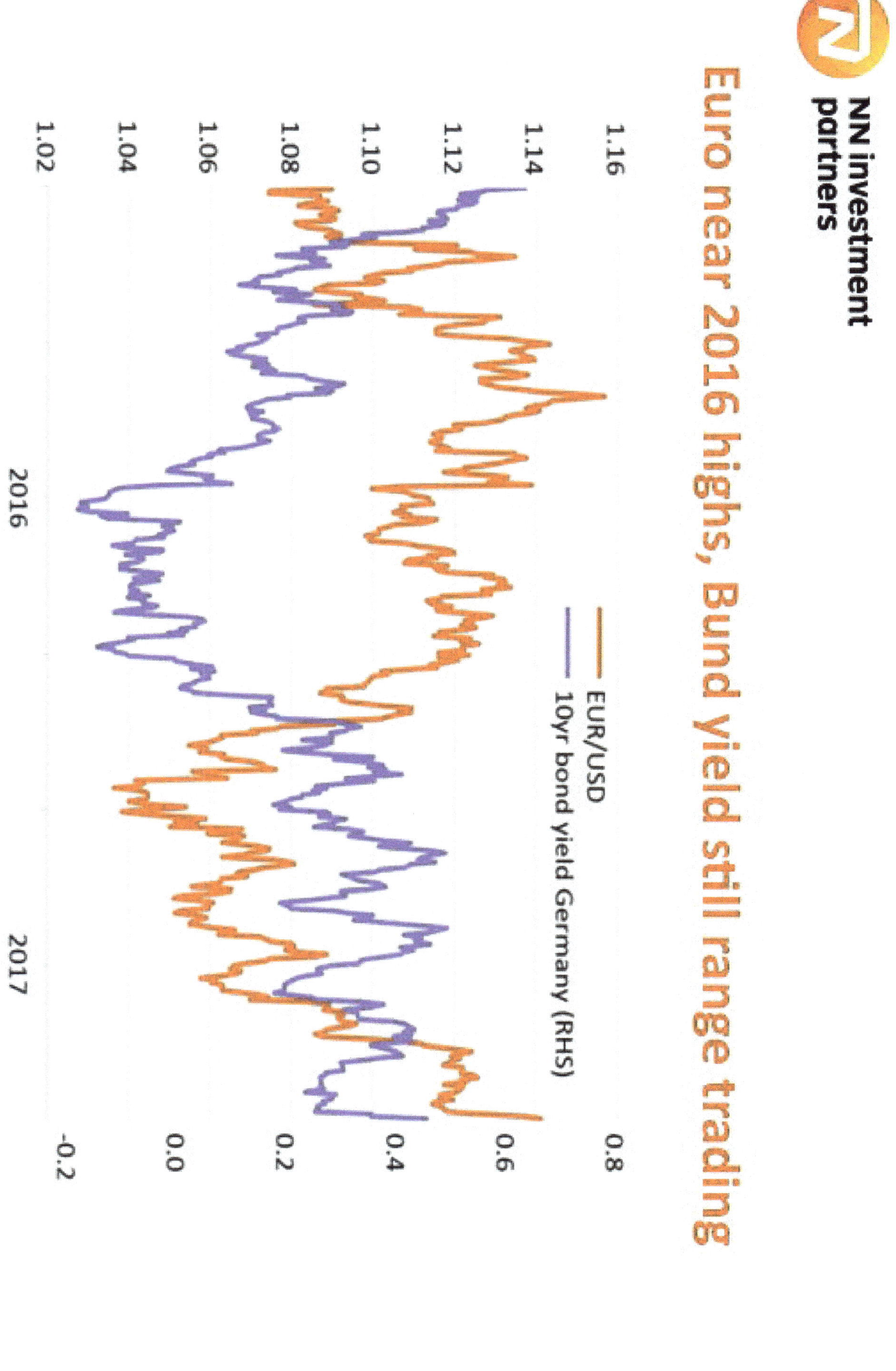
NN investment partners
Euro near 2016 highs, Bund yield still range trading
EUR/USD
10yr bond yield Germany (RHS)
1.16
1.14
1.12
1.10
1.08
1.06
1.04
1.02
0.8
0.6
0.4
0.2
0.0
-0.2
2016
2017
Source: Thomson Reuters Datastream, NN Investment Partners

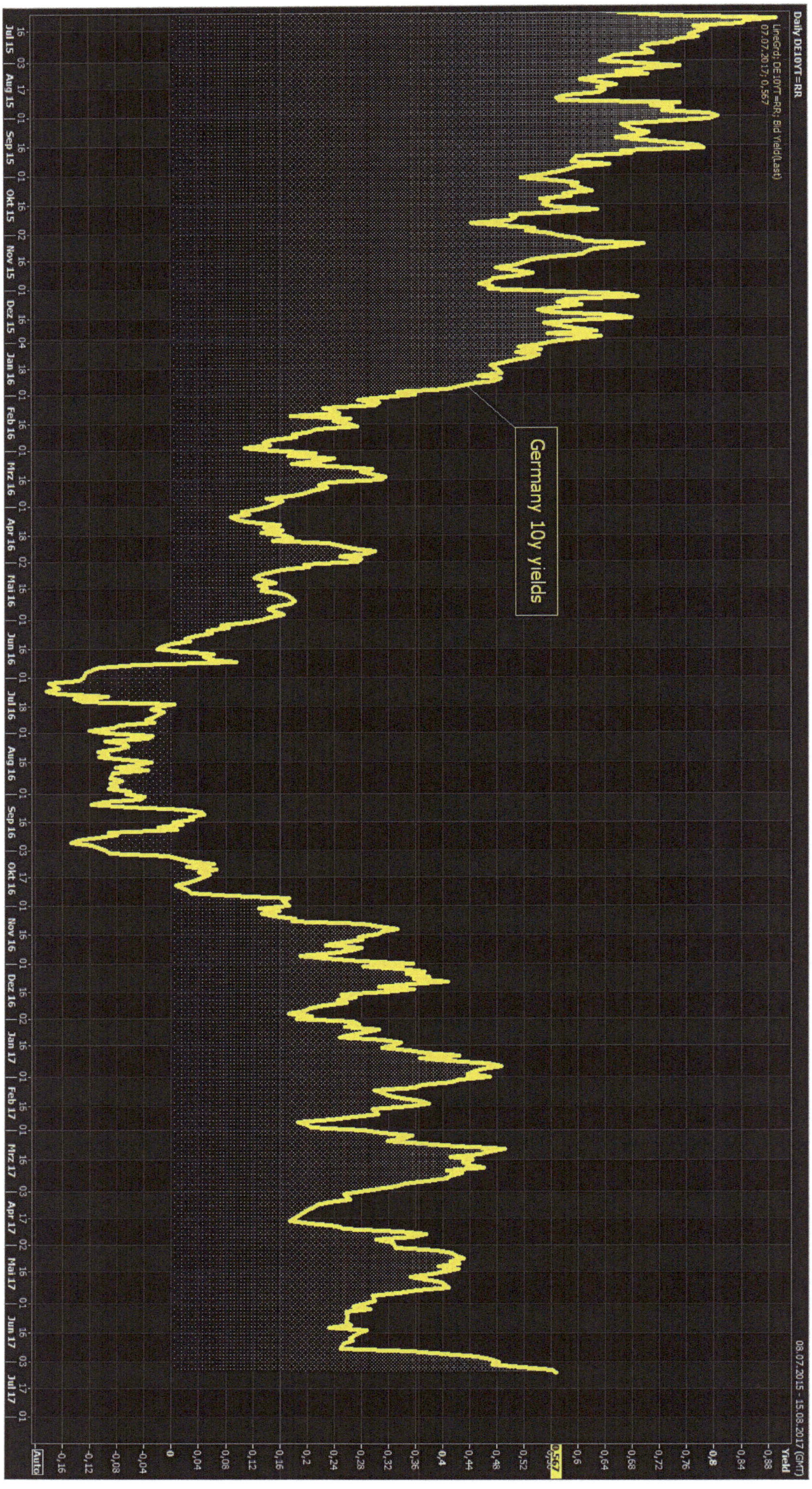
Daily DE10YT=RR
LineGrd; DE10YT=RR; Bid Yield(Last)
07.07.2017; 0,567
08.07.2015 - 15.08.2017 (GMT)
Yield
Germany 10y yields
Auto

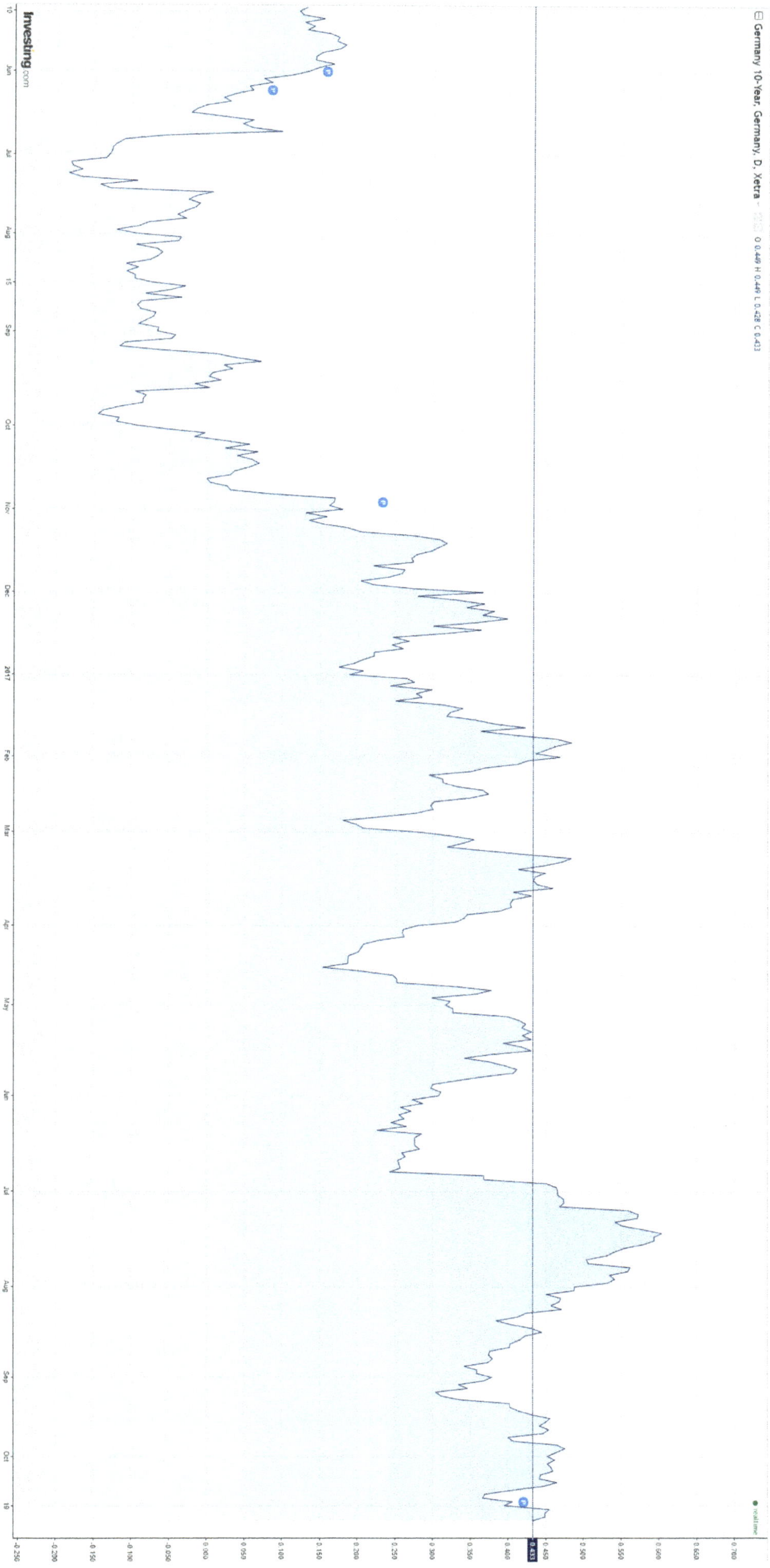
Germany 10-Year, Germany, D, Xetra
Investing.com

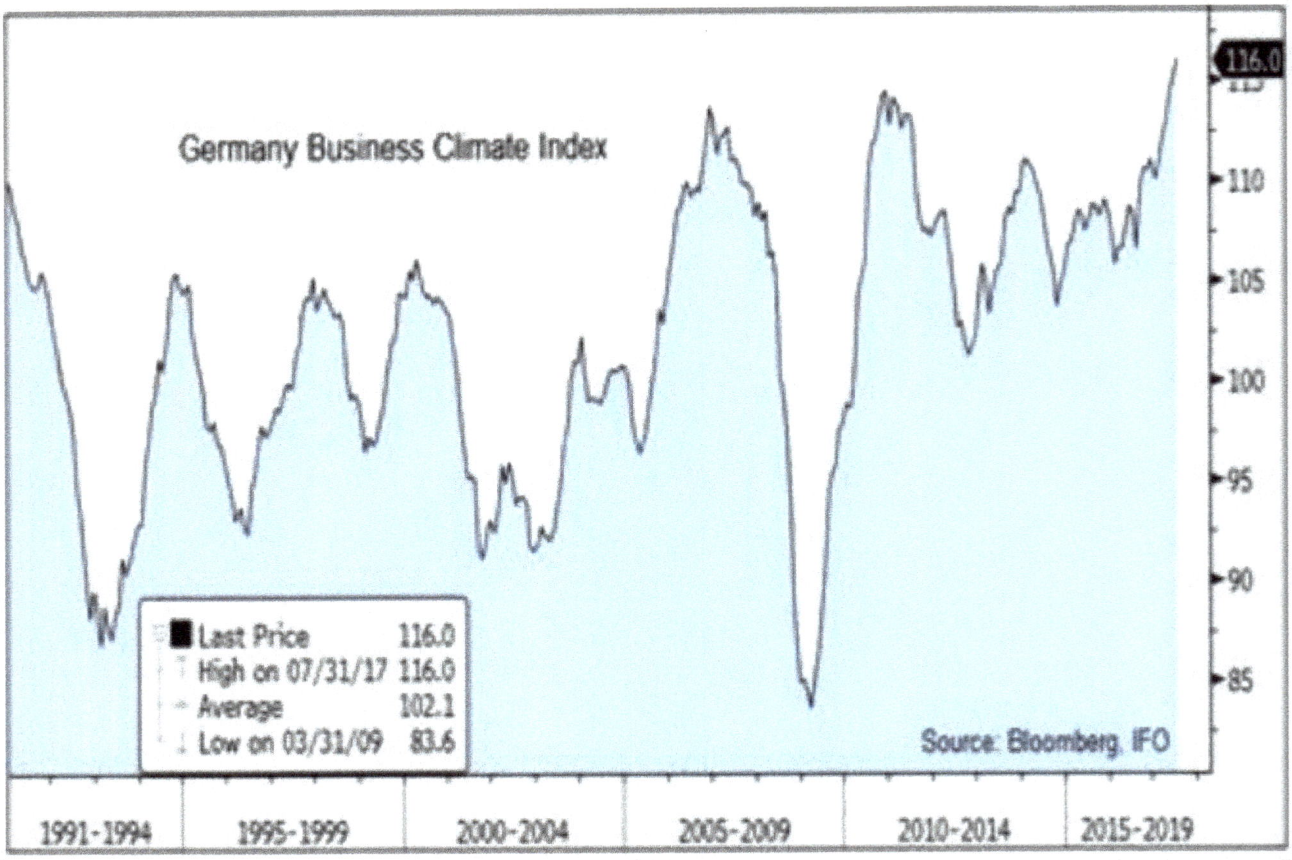
Germany Business Climate Index
116.0
110
105
100
95
90
85
Last Price 116.0
High on 07/31/17 116.0
Average 102.1
Low on 03/31/09 83.6
Source: Bloomberg, IFO
1991-1994
1995-1999
2000-2004
2005-2009
2010-2014
2015-2019

Germany IFO Index
Current Assessment
Expectations
120
110
107.3
100
90
80
Source: Bloomberg, IFO Institute
1991-1994
1995-1999
2000-2004
2005-2009
2010-2014
2015-2019

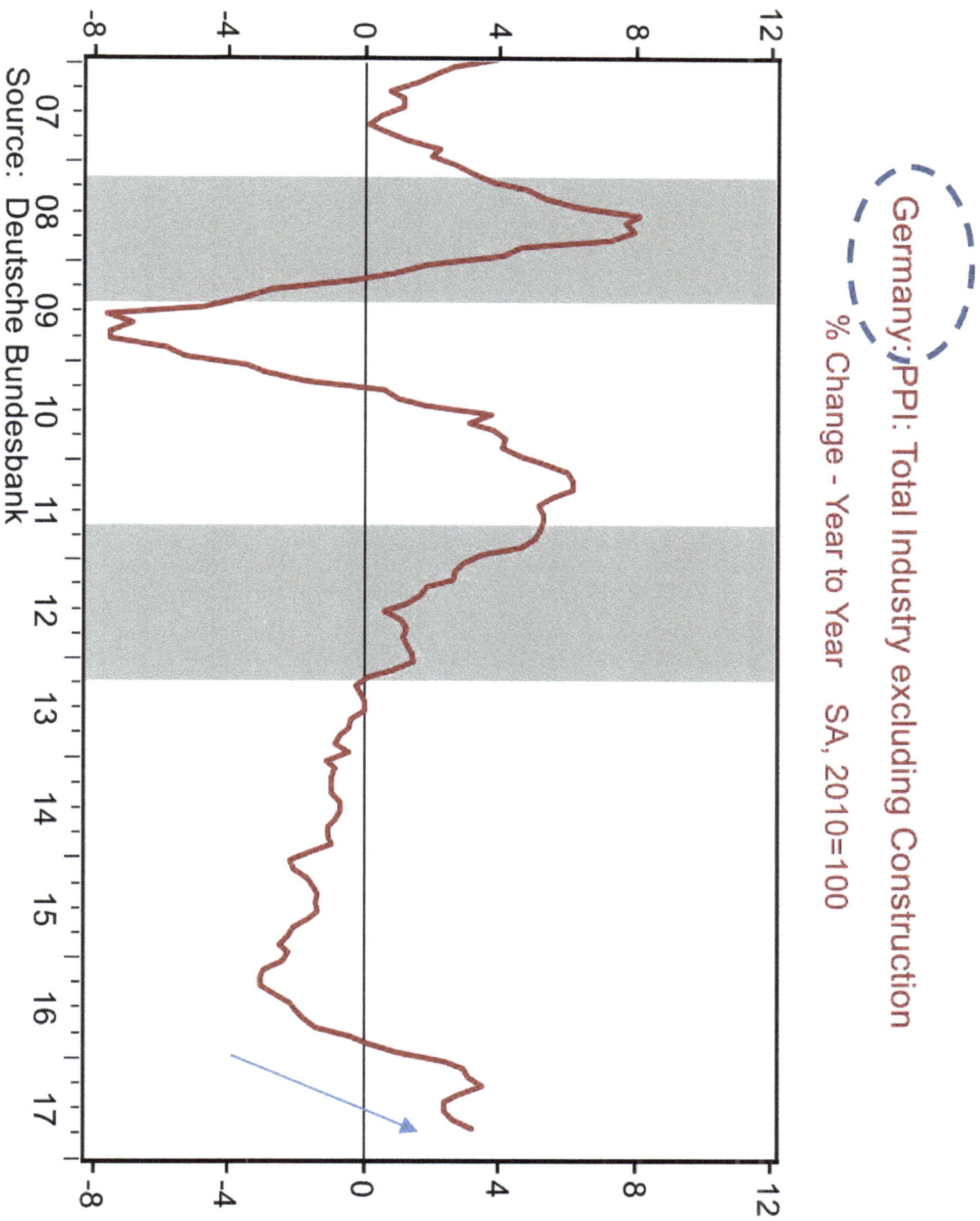

Germany: PPI: Total Industry excluding Construction
% Change - Year to Year SA, 2010=100
12
8
4
0
-4
-8
07
08
09
10
11
12
13
14
15
16
17
Source: Deutsche Bundesbank

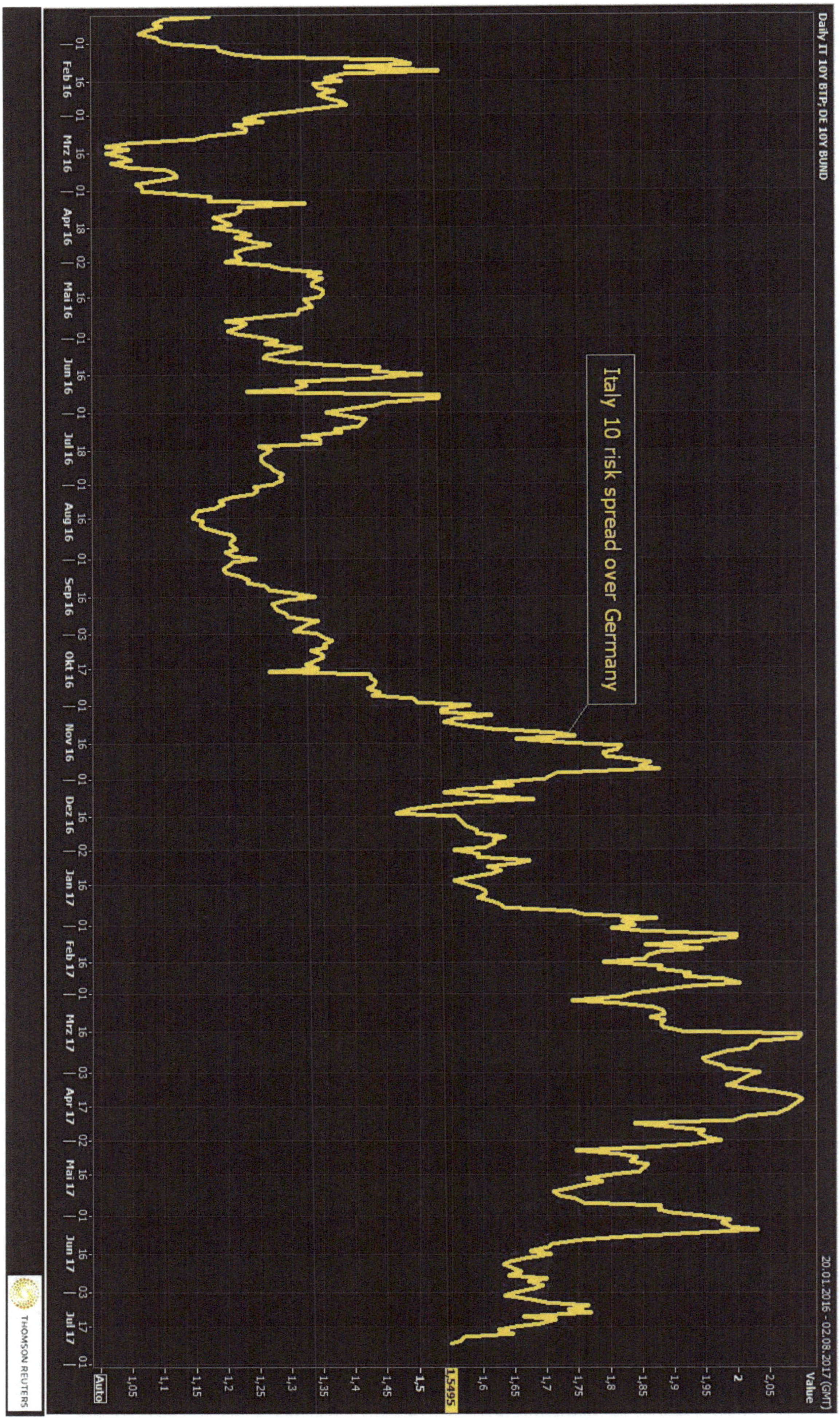
Daily IT 10Y BTP; DE 10Y BUND
20.01.2016 - 02.08.2017 (GMT)
Italy 10 risk spread over Germany
Value
THOMSON REUTERS

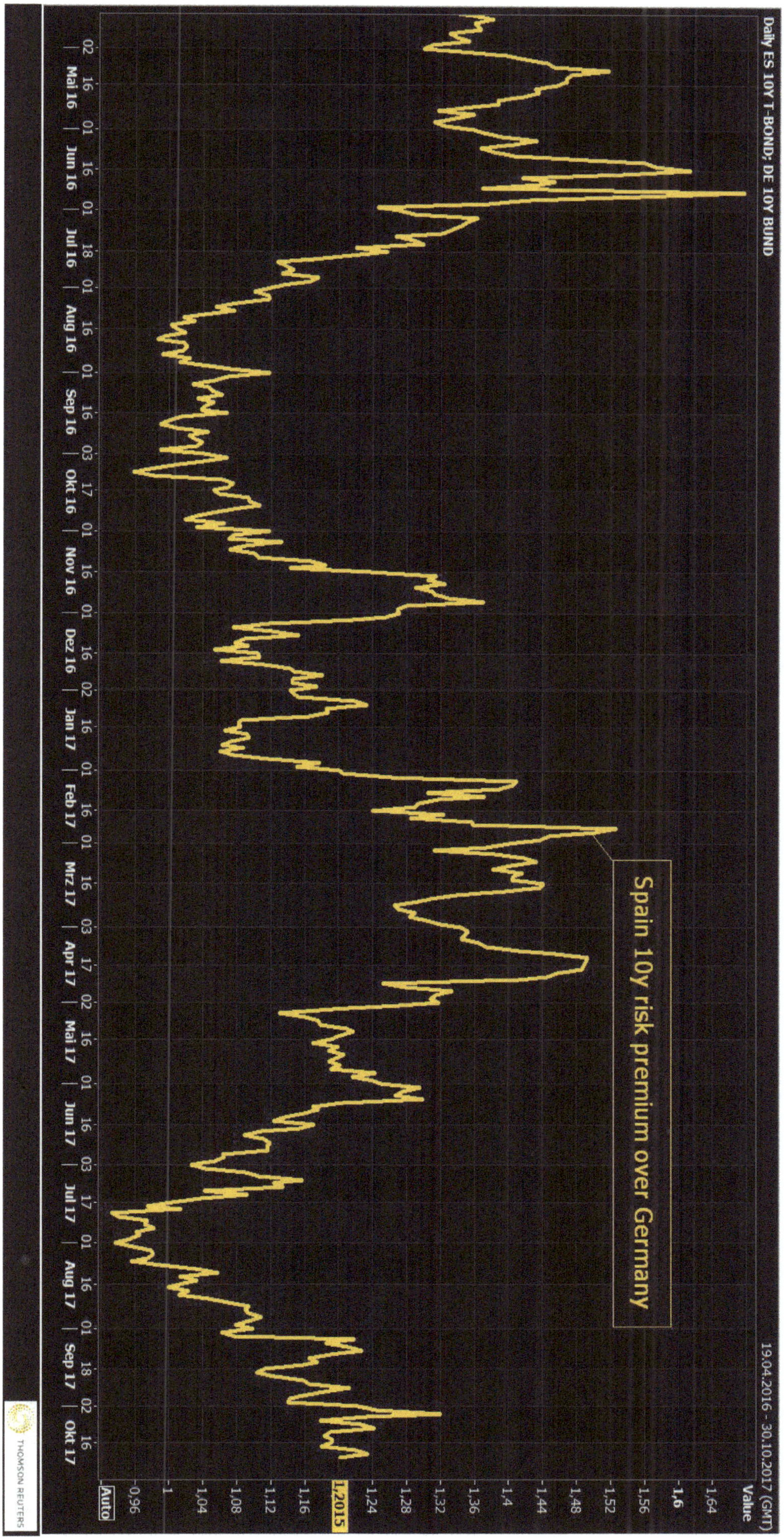
Daily ES 10Y T-BOND; DE 10Y BUND
19.04.2016 - 30.10.2017 (GMT)
Value
Spain 10y risk premium over Germany
THOMSON REUTERS

15. Tightening of Treasury-Bund spread consistent with EUR-USD strength

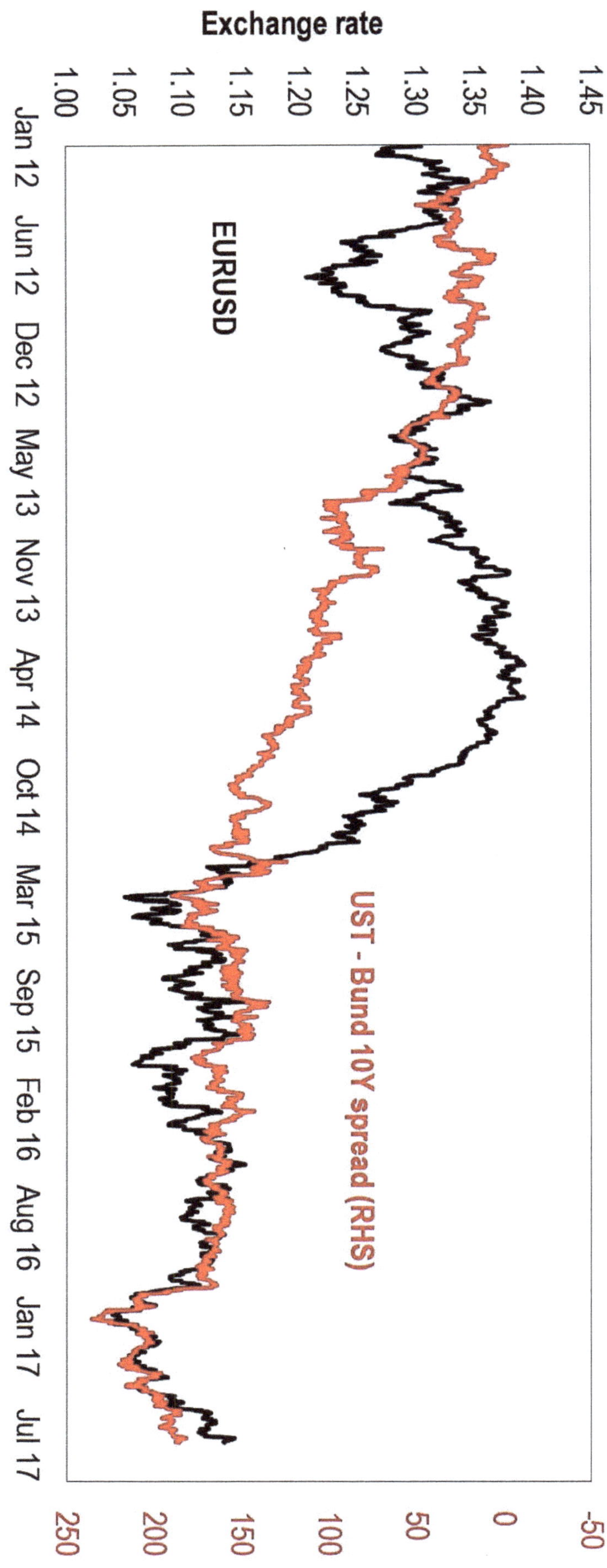

Source: HSBC, Bloomberg

US 10 Year Yield
USGG10YR
At 22:38
2.3160
-.0305
Op 2.3429
Hi 2.3429
Lo 2.2963
2.3178/2.3160
Prev 2.3465
USGG10YR Index
95) Compare
96) Actions
97) Edit
Line Chart
12/30/2016
10/19/2017
Ask Yield
USD
Mov Avgs
Key Events
US Generic Govt 10 Year Yield
Last Price 2.3160
-.0305
-1.30%
1D 3D 1M 6M YTD 1Y 5Y Max Daily
Table
Chart Content
Jan Feb Mar Apr May Jun Jul Aug Sep Oct
2017
2.6000
2.5000
2.4000
2.3160
2.2000
2.1000

OPTIONS GRAPHICS

GBL MARCH OPTIONS GRAPHICS

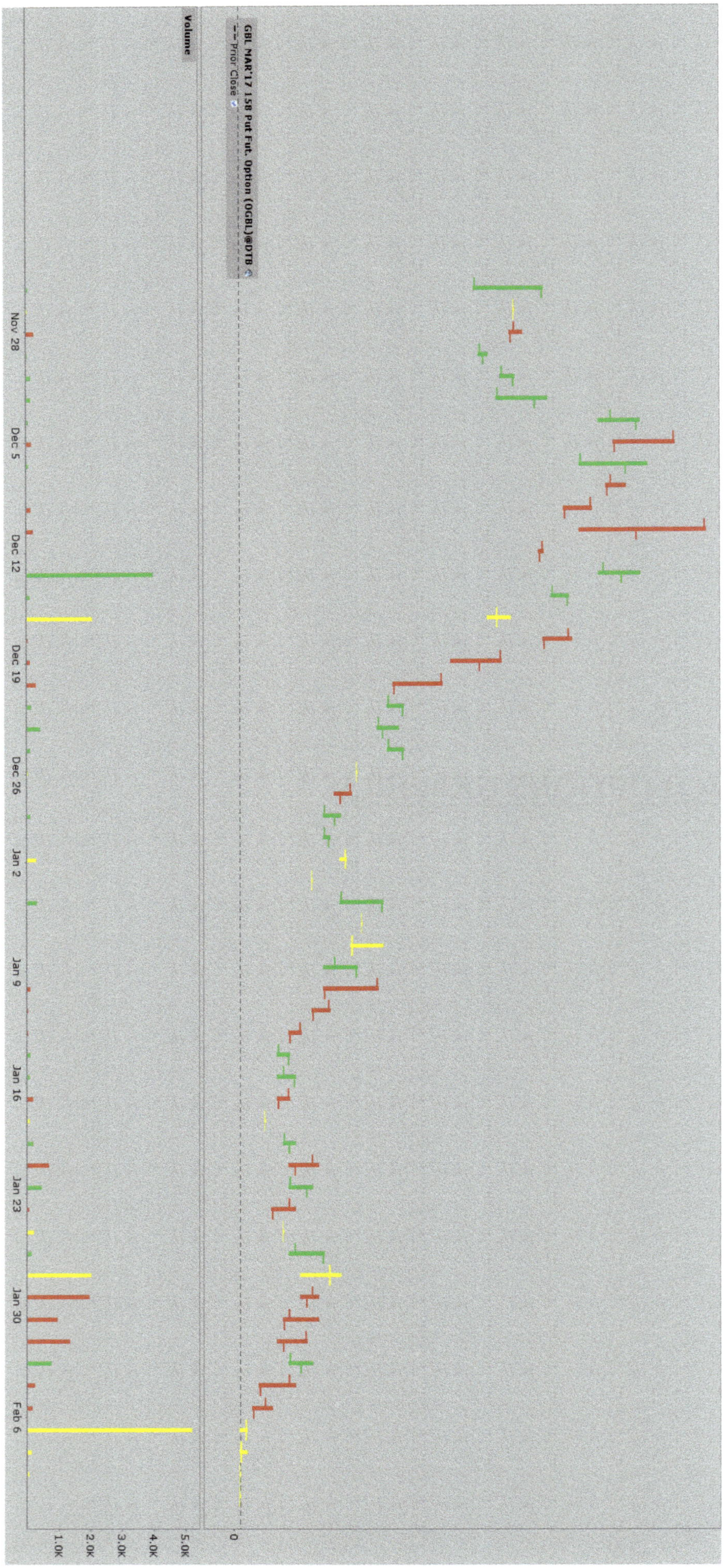
GBL MAR'17 158 Put Fut. Option (OGBL)@DTB
Prior Close
Volume
Nov 28
Dec 5
Dec 12
Dec 19
Dec 26
Jan 2
Jan 9
Jan 16
Jan 23
Jan 30
Feb 6
0
1.0K
2.0K
3.0K
4.0K
5.0K

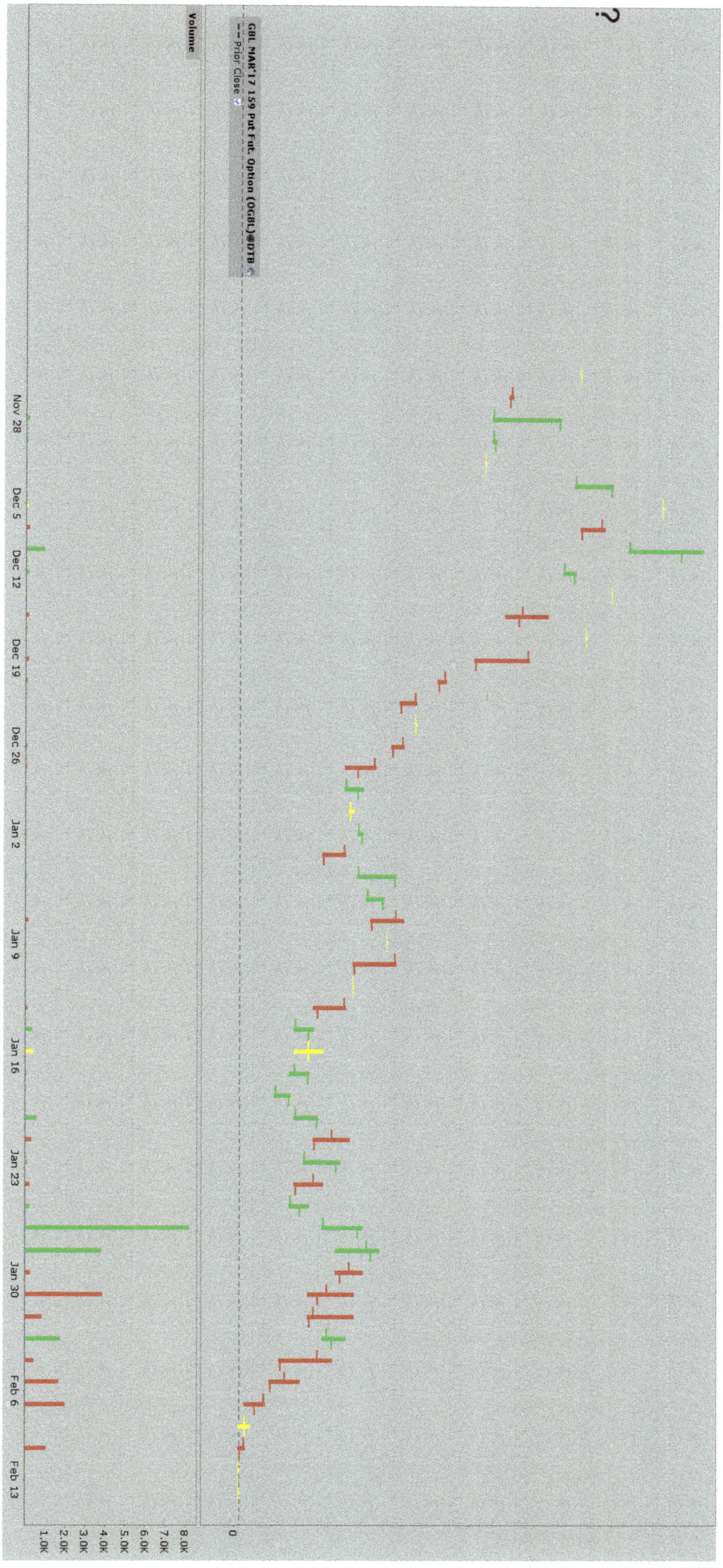
?
GBL MAR'17 1.59 Put Fut. Option (OGBL)@DTB
Prior Close
Volume
Nov 28
Dec 5
Dec 12
Dec 19
Dec 26
Jan 2
Jan 9
Jan 16
Jan 23
Jan 30
Feb 6
Feb 13
0
8.0K
7.0K
6.0K
5.0K
4.0K
3.0K
2.0K
1.0K

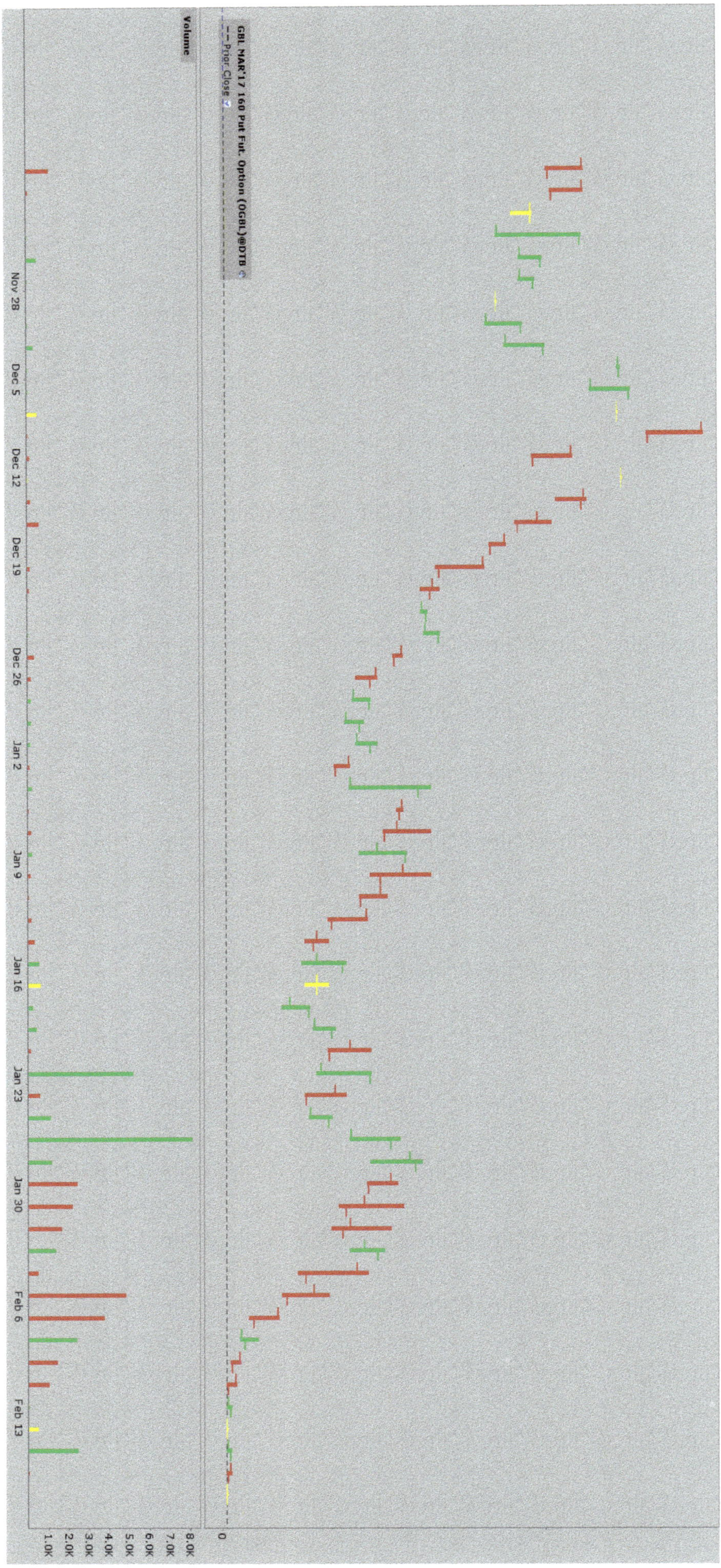
GBL MAR'17 160 Put Fut. Option (OGBL)@DTB
Prior Close
Volume
Nov 28
Dec 5
Dec 12
Dec 19
Dec 26
Jan 2
Jan 9
Jan 16
Jan 23
Jan 30
Feb 6
Feb 13
0
8.0K
7.0K
6.0K
5.0K
4.0K
3.0K
2.0K
1.0K

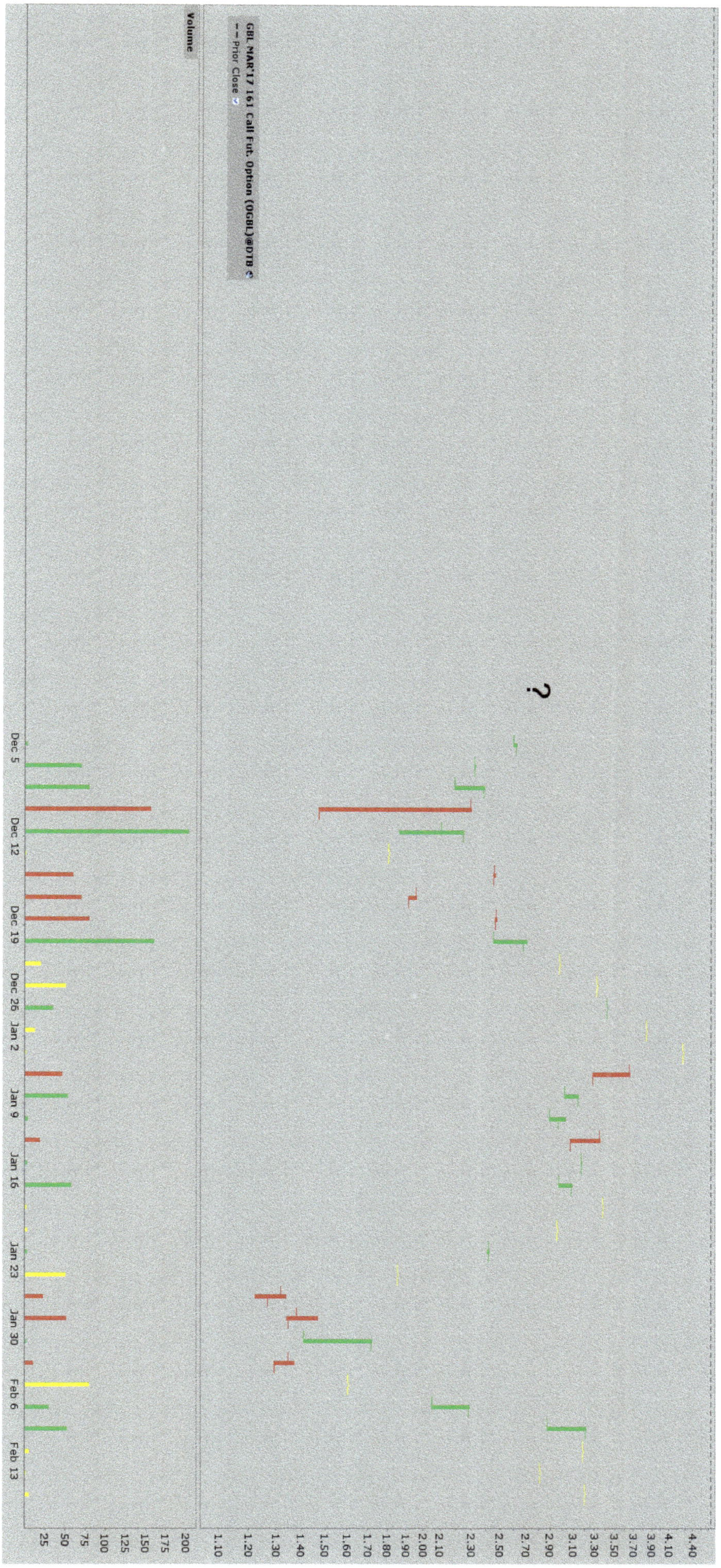
GBL MAR'17 161 Call Fut. Option (OGBL)@DTB
-- Prior Close
Volume
?
Dec 5
Dec 12
Dec 19
Dec 26
Jan 2
Jan 9
Jan 16
Jan 23
Jan 30
Feb 6
Feb 13

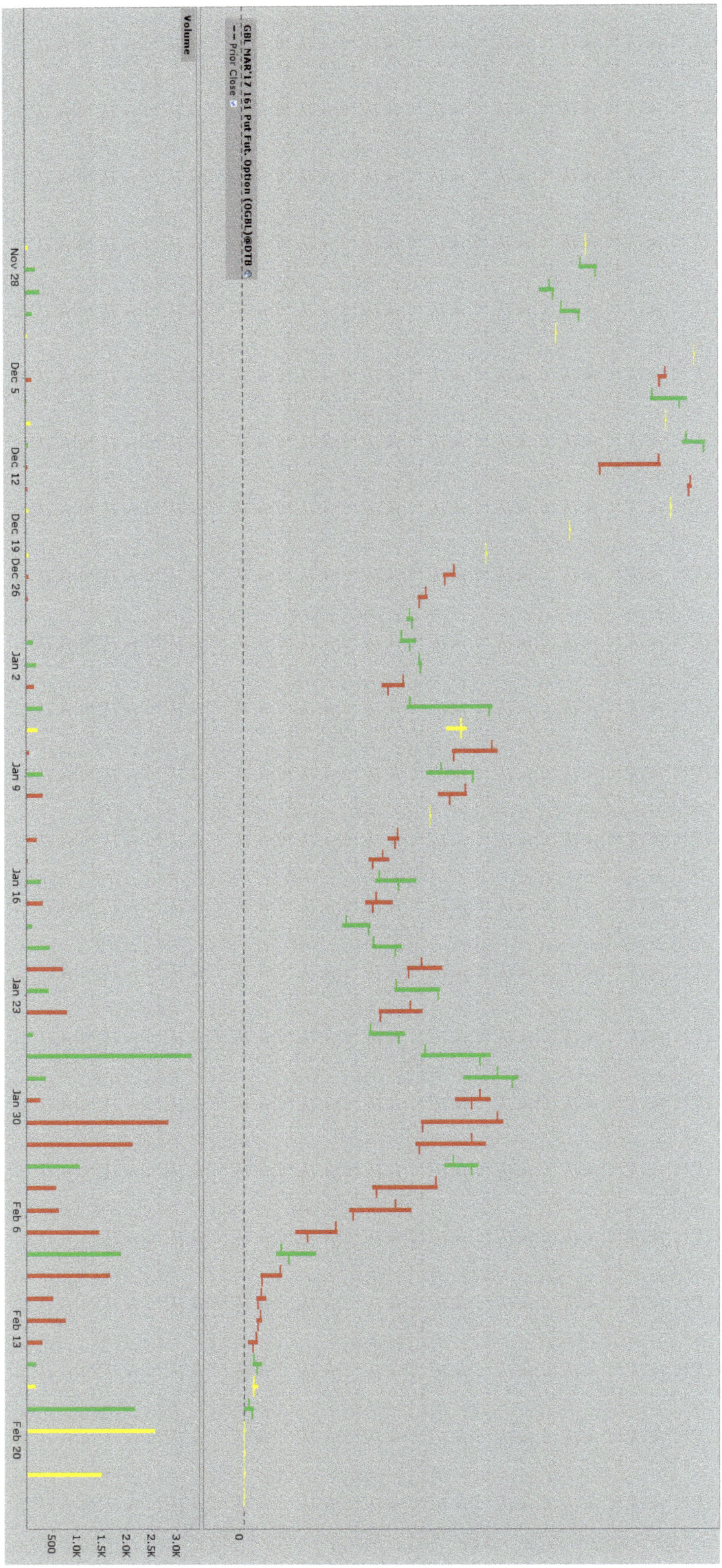
GBL MAR'17 161 Put Fut. Option (OGBL)@DTB
Prior Close
Volume
Nov 28
Dec 5
Dec 12
Dec 19
Dec 26
Jan 2
Jan 9
Jan 16
Jan 23
Jan 30
Feb 6
Feb 13
Feb 20
0
500
1.0K
1.5K
2.0K
2.5K
3.0K

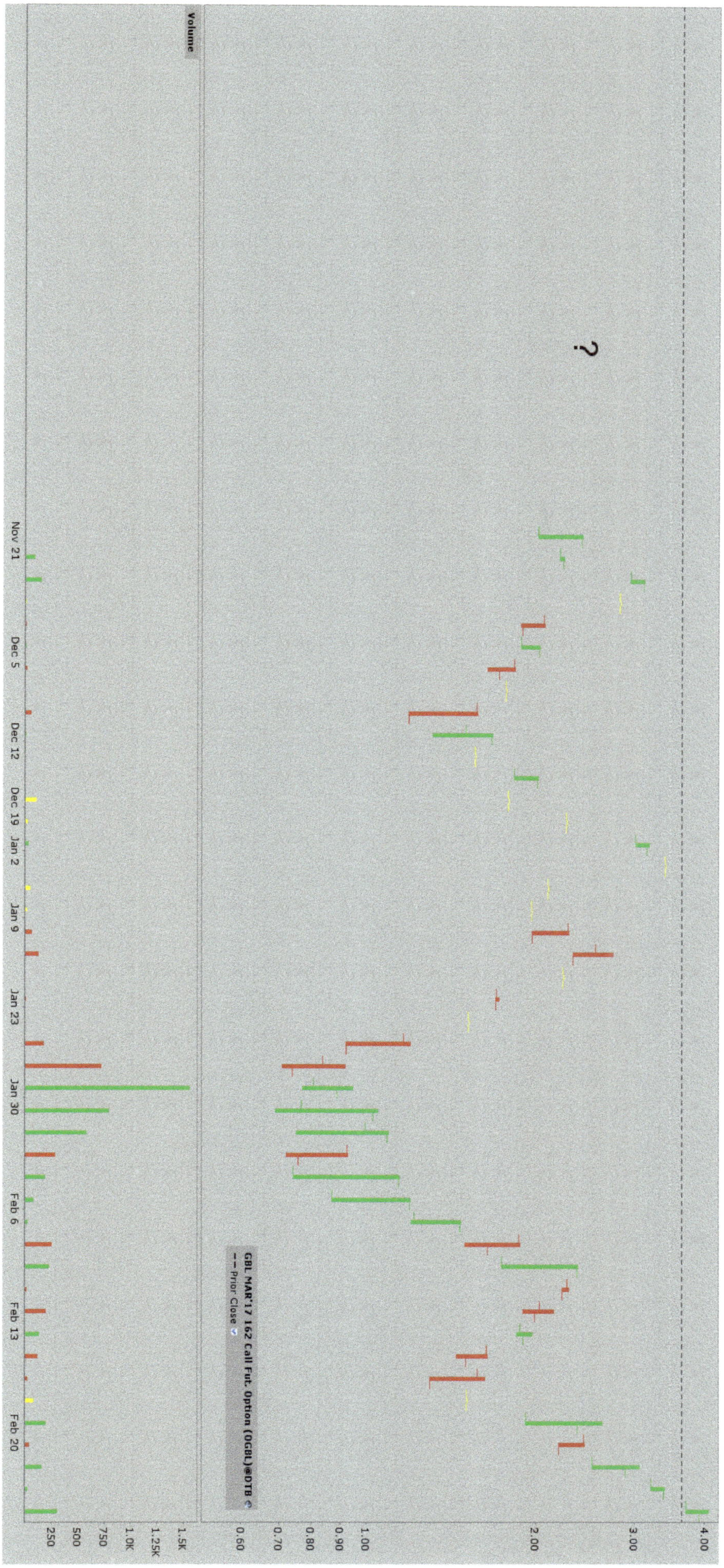

?
GBL MAR'17 162 Call Fut. Option (OGBL)@DTB
-- Prior Close
Volume
Nov 21
Dec 5
Dec 12
Dec 19
Jan 2
Jan 9
Jan 23
Jan 30
Feb 6
Feb 13
Feb 20
0.60
0.70
0.80
0.90
1.00
2.00
3.00
4.00
250
500
750
1.0K
1.25K
1.5K

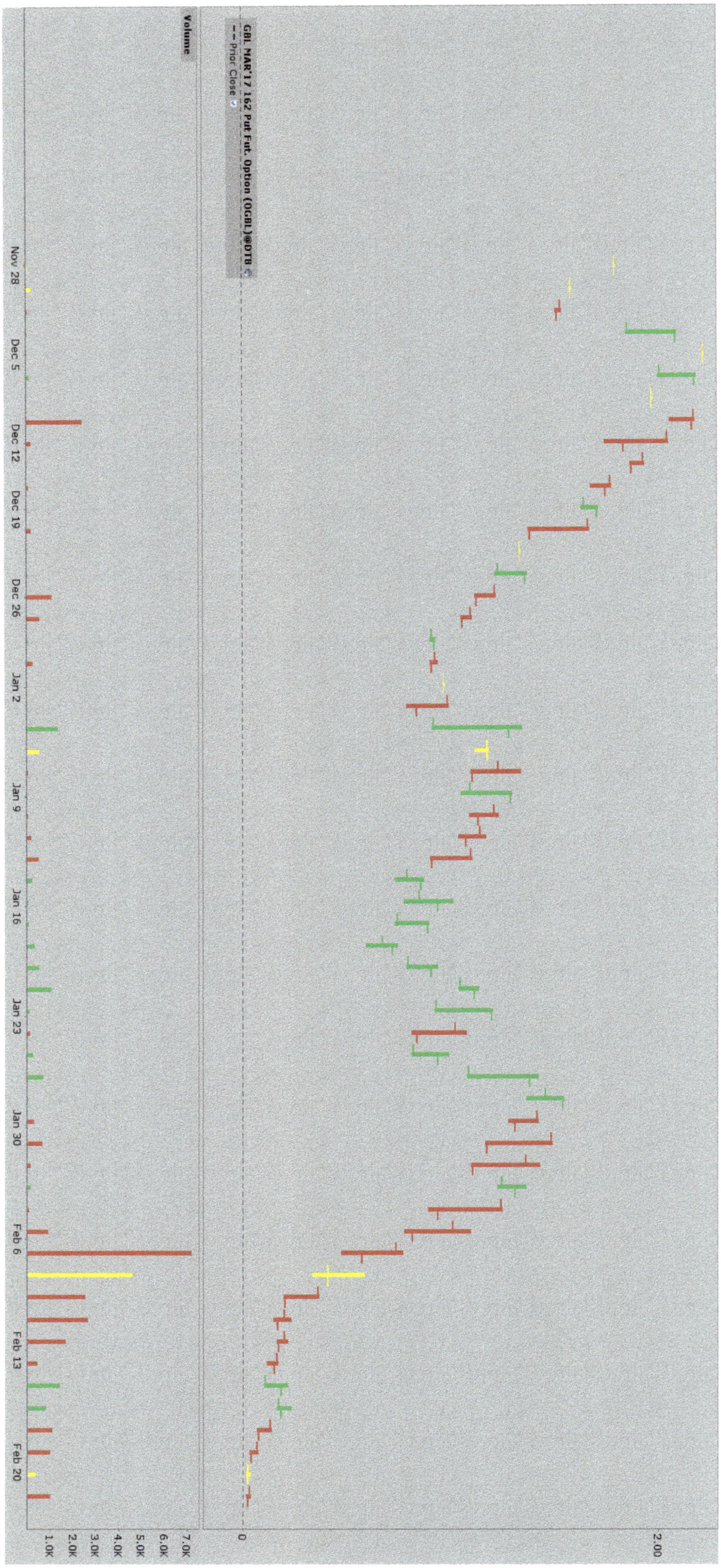
GBL MAR'17 162 Put Fut. Option (OGBL)@DTB
Prior Close
Volume
Nov 28
Dec 5
Dec 12
Dec 19
Dec 26
Jan 2
Jan 9
Jan 16
Jan 23
Jan 30
Feb 6
Feb 13
Feb 20
2.00
0
7.0K
6.0K
5.0K
4.0K
3.0K
2.0K
1.0K

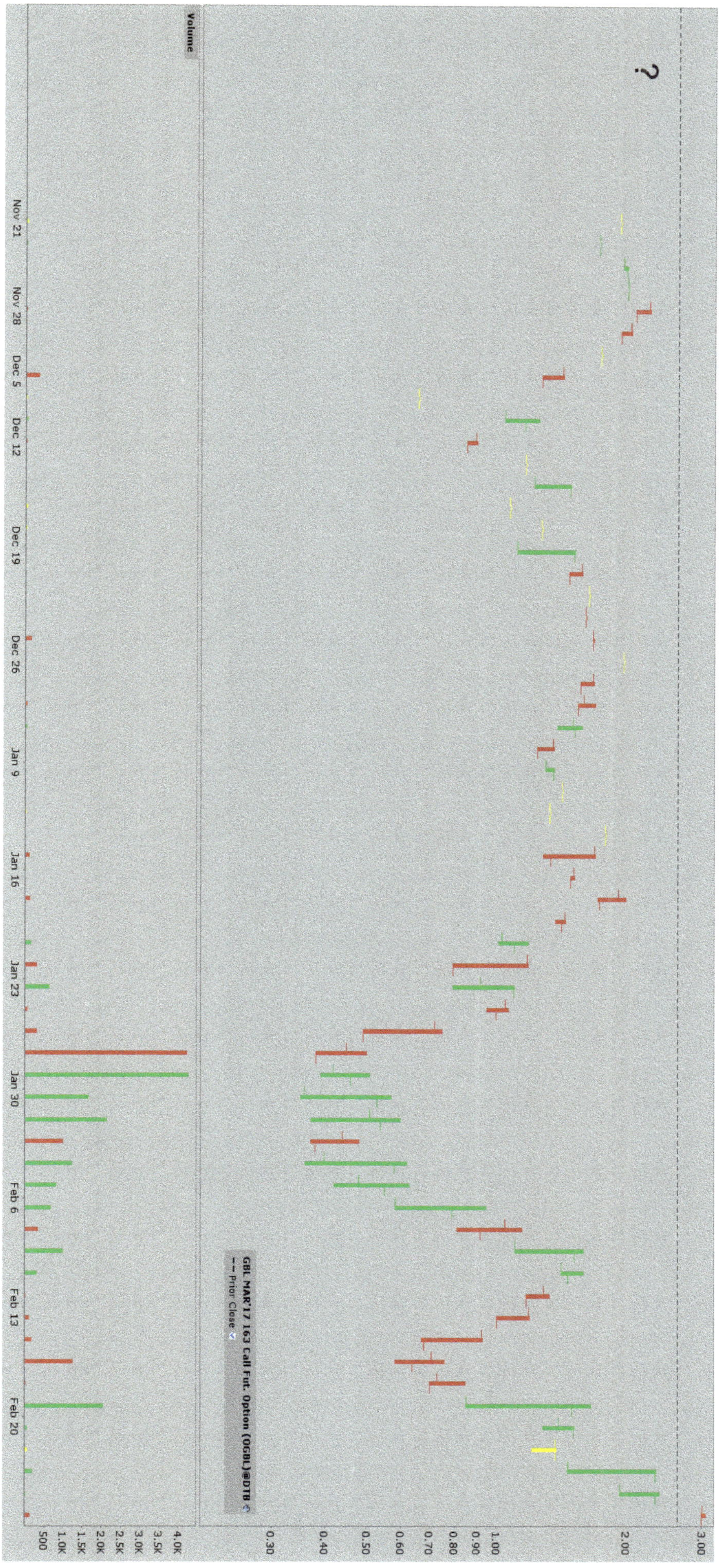
?
GBL MAR'17 163 Call Fut. Option (OGBL)@DTB
-- Prior Close
Volume
Nov 21
Nov 28
Dec 5
Dec 12
Dec 19
Dec 26
Jan 9
Jan 16
Jan 23
Jan 30
Feb 6
Feb 13
Feb 20
3.00
2.00
1.00
0.90
0.80
0.70
0.60
0.50
0.40
0.30
4.0K
3.5K
3.0K
2.5K
2.0K
1.5K
1.0K
500

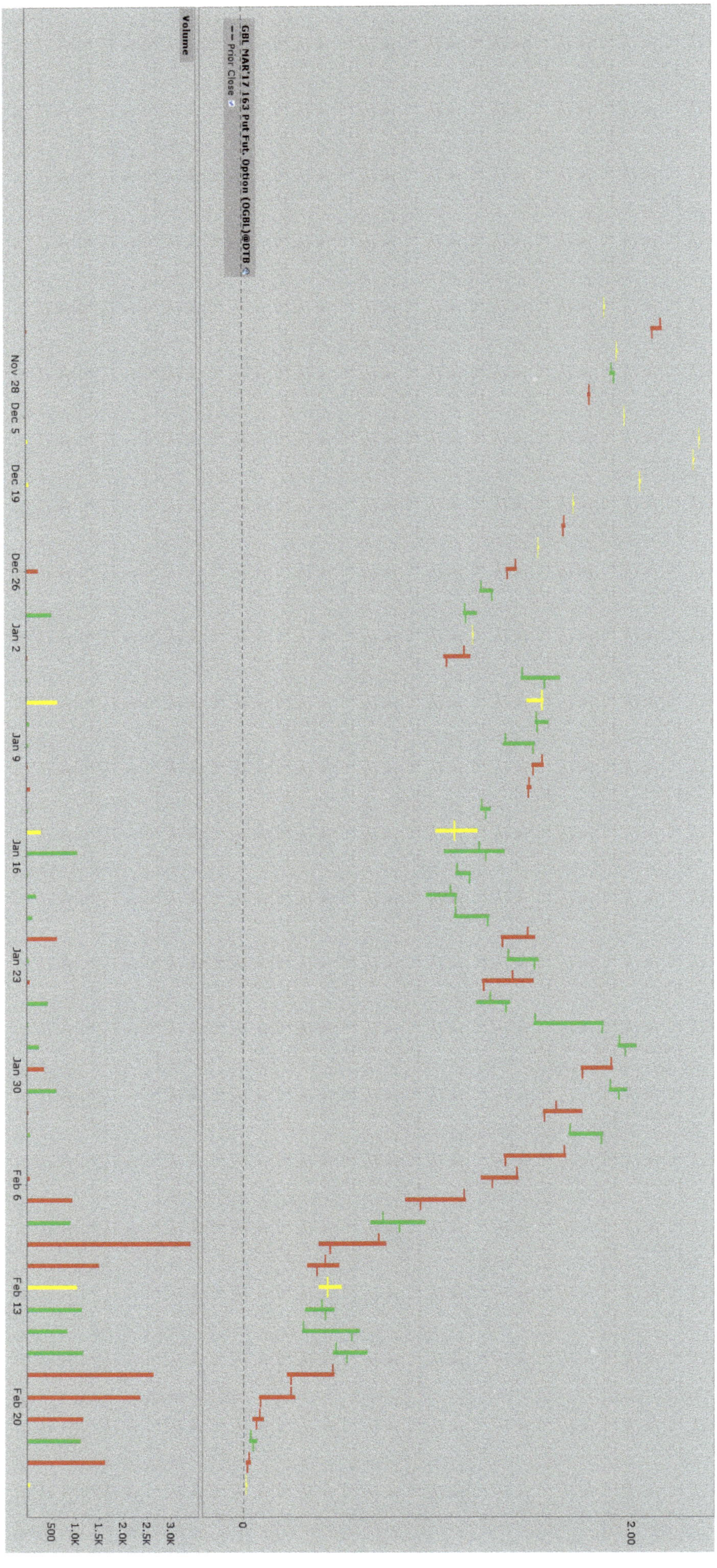
GBL MAR'17 163 Put Fut. Option (OGBL)@DTB
Prior Close
Volume
Nov 28
Dec 5
Dec 19
Dec 26
Jan 2
Jan 9
Jan 16
Jan 23
Jan 30
Feb 6
Feb 13
Feb 20
0
2.00
500
1.0K
1.5K
2.0K
2.5K
3.0K

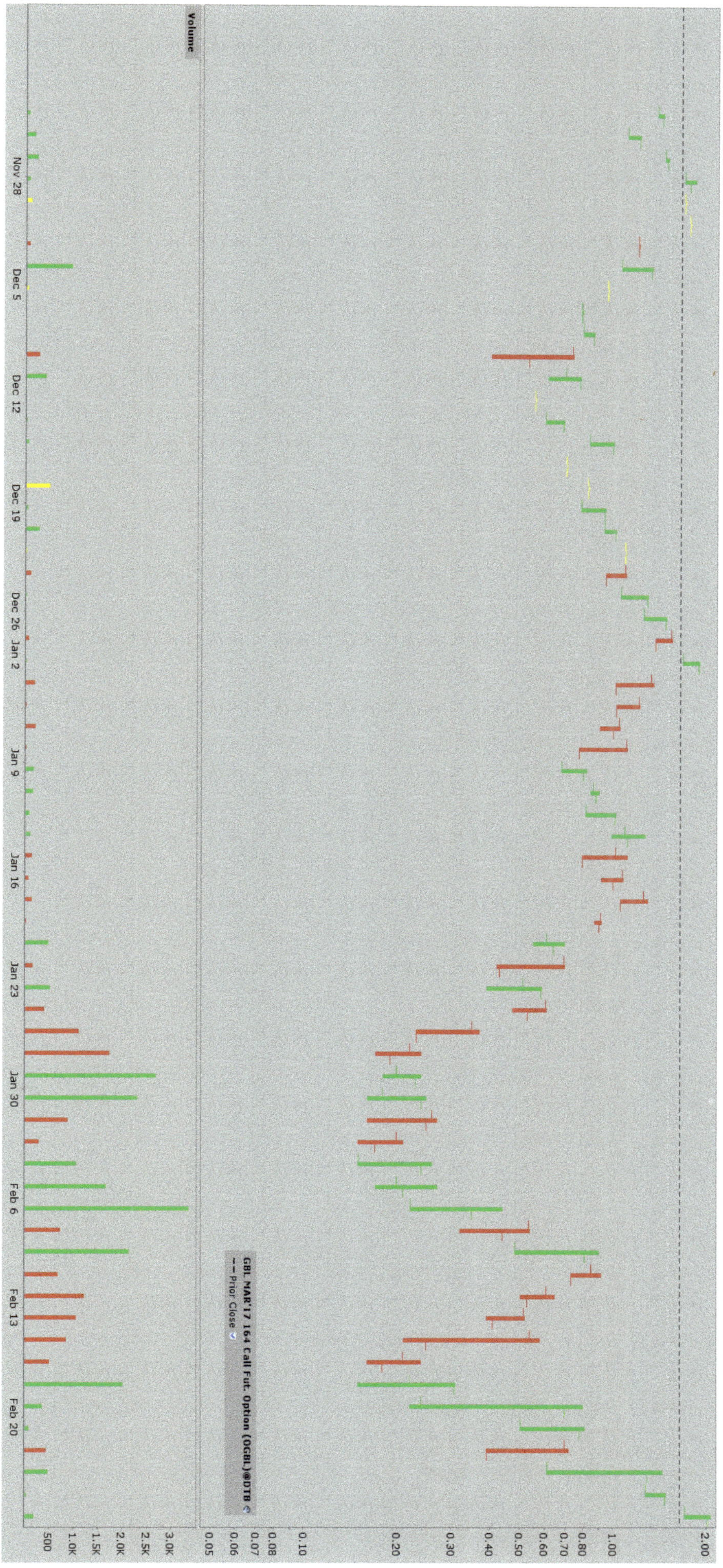
Volume
GBL MAR'17 164 Call Fut. Option (OGBL)@DTB
Prior Close
Nov 28
Dec 5
Dec 12
Dec 19
Dec 26
Jan 2
Jan 9
Jan 16
Jan 23
Jan 30
Feb 6
Feb 13
Feb 20
500
1.0K
1.5K
2.0K
2.5K
3.0K
0.05
0.06
0.07
0.08
0.10
0.20
0.30
0.40
0.50
0.60
0.70
0.80
1.00
2.00

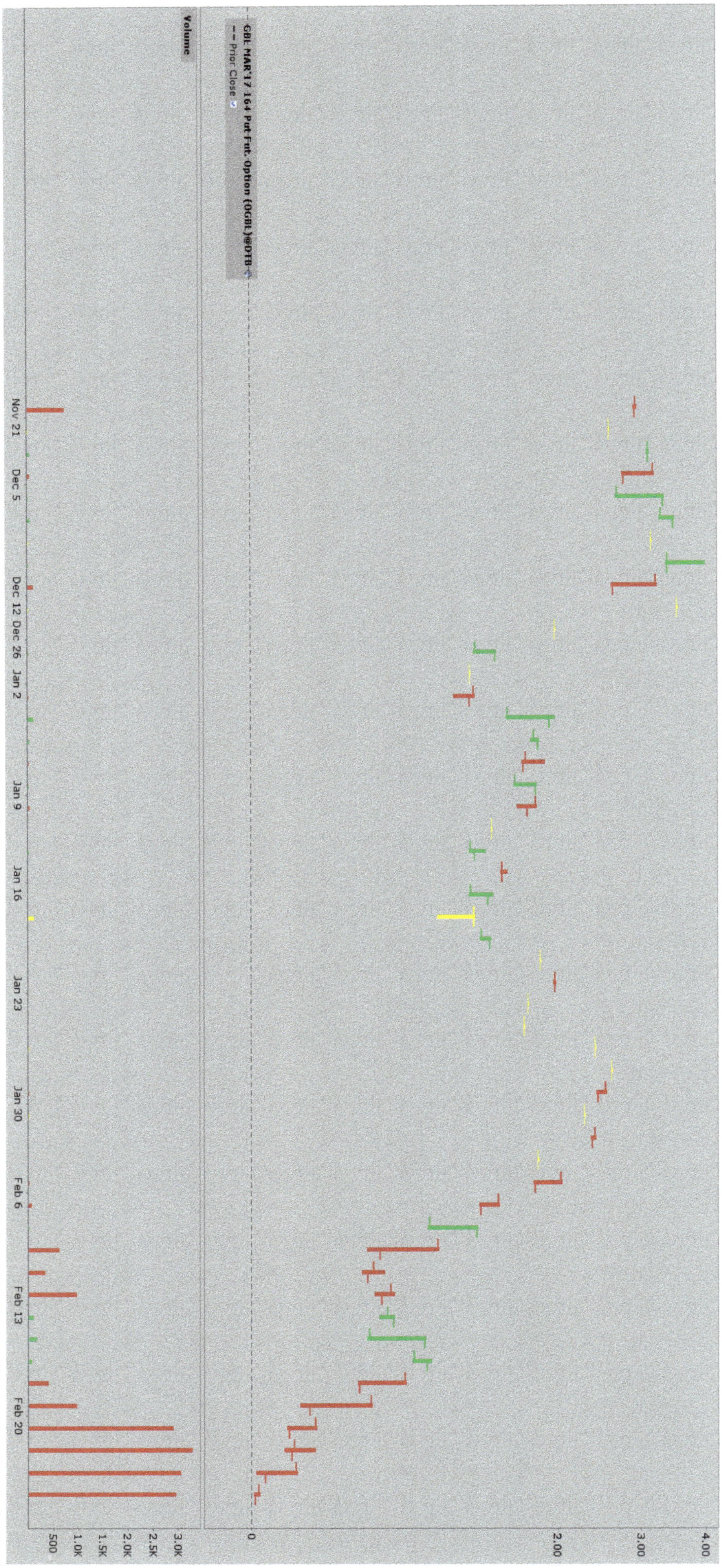
GBL MAR'17 164 Put Fut. Option (OGBL)@DTB
Prior Close
Volume
Nov 21
Dec 5
Dec 12
Dec 26
Jan 2
Jan 9
Jan 16
Jan 23
Jan 30
Feb 6
Feb 13
Feb 20
0
2.00
3.00
4.00
500
1.0K
1.5K
2.0K
2.5K
3.0K

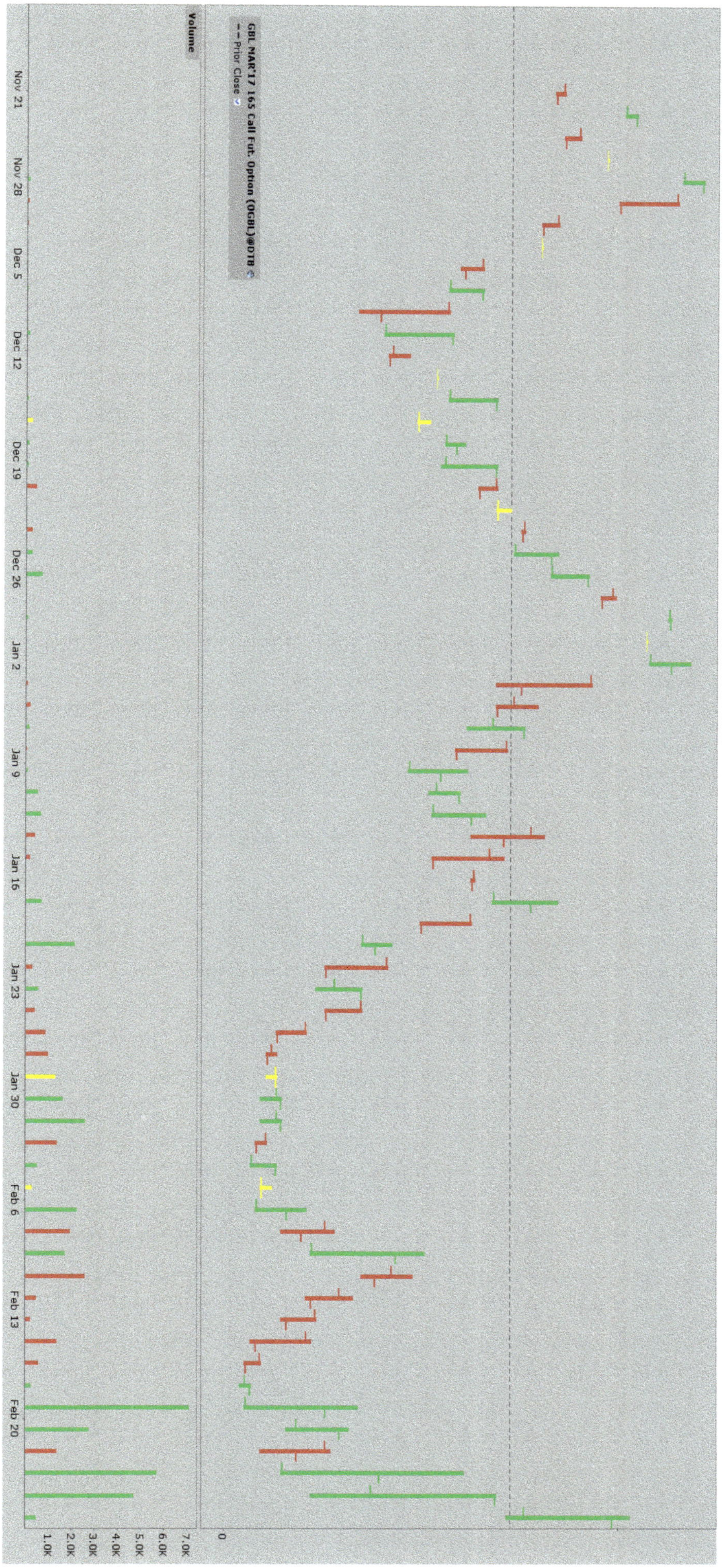
GBL MAR'17 165 Call Fut. Option (OGBL)@DTB
-- Prior Close
Volume
Nov 21
Nov 28
Dec 5
Dec 12
Dec 19
Dec 26
Jan 2
Jan 9
Jan 16
Jan 23
Jan 30
Feb 6
Feb 13
Feb 20
0
7.0K
6.0K
5.0K
4.0K
3.0K
2.0K
1.0K

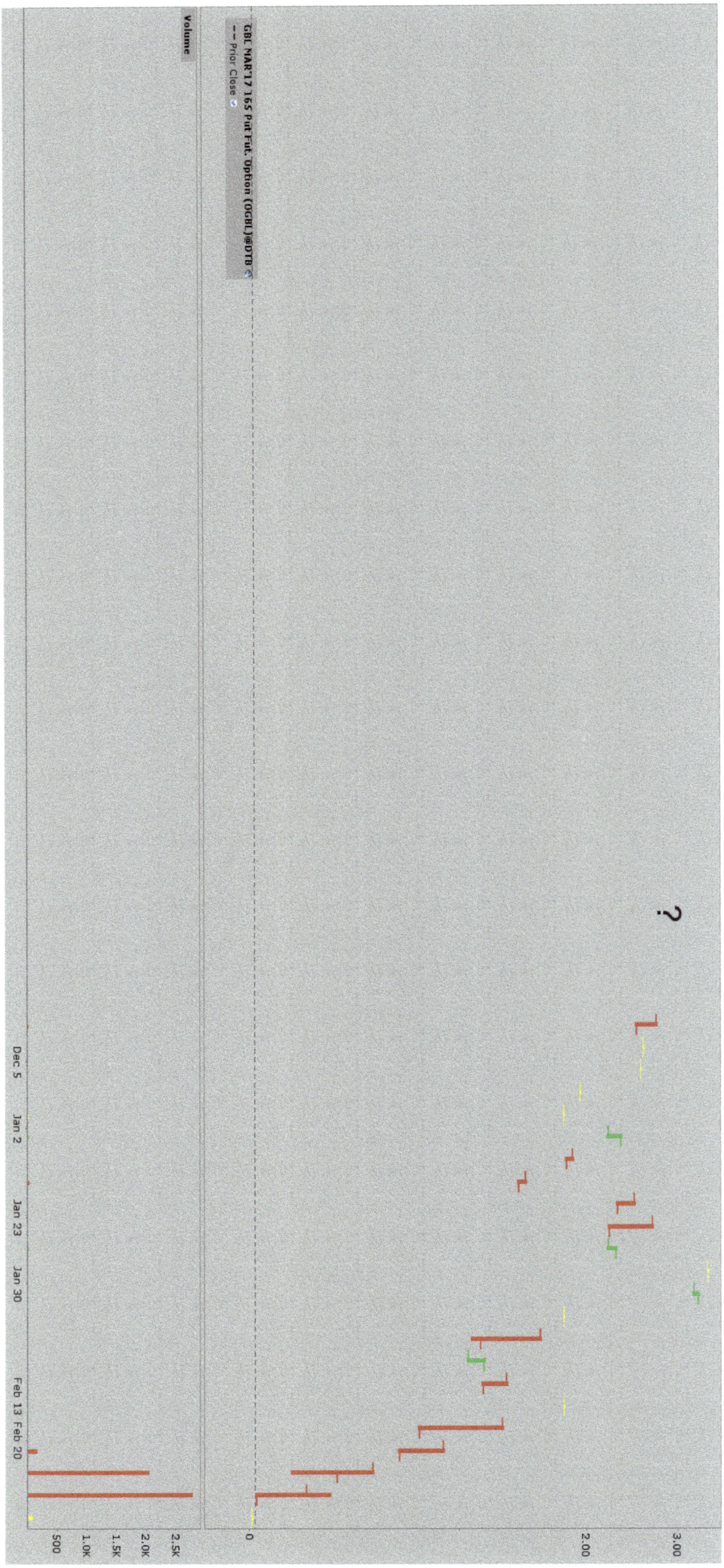
GBL MAR'17 165 Put Fut. Option (OGBL)@DTB
-- Prior Close
Volume
?
Dec 5
Jan 2
Jan 23
Jan 30
Feb 13
Feb 20
3.00
2.00
0
2.5K
2.0K
1.5K
1.0K
500

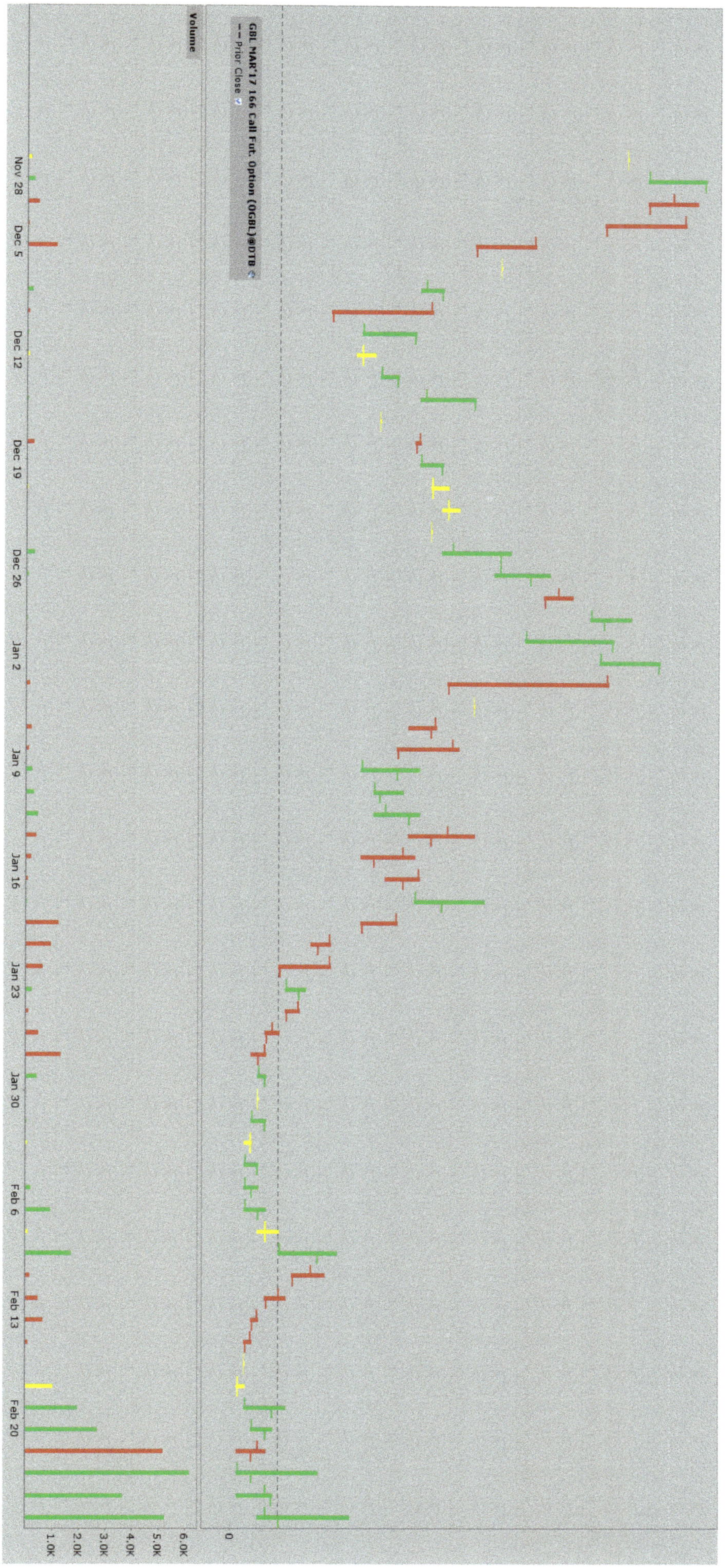
GBL MAR'17 166 Call Fut. Option (OGBL)@DTB
Prior Close
Volume
Nov 28
Dec 5
Dec 12
Dec 19
Dec 26
Jan 2
Jan 9
Jan 16
Jan 23
Jan 30
Feb 6
Feb 13
Feb 20
0
1.0K
2.0K
3.0K
4.0K
5.0K
6.0K

GBL MAR'17 166 Put Fut. Option (OGBL)@DTB
Prior Close
Volume
4.00
3.00
2.00
0
1.25K
1.0K
750
500
250
Nov 21
Nov 28
Dec 5
Dec 19
Dec 26
Jan 23
Feb 13
Feb 20

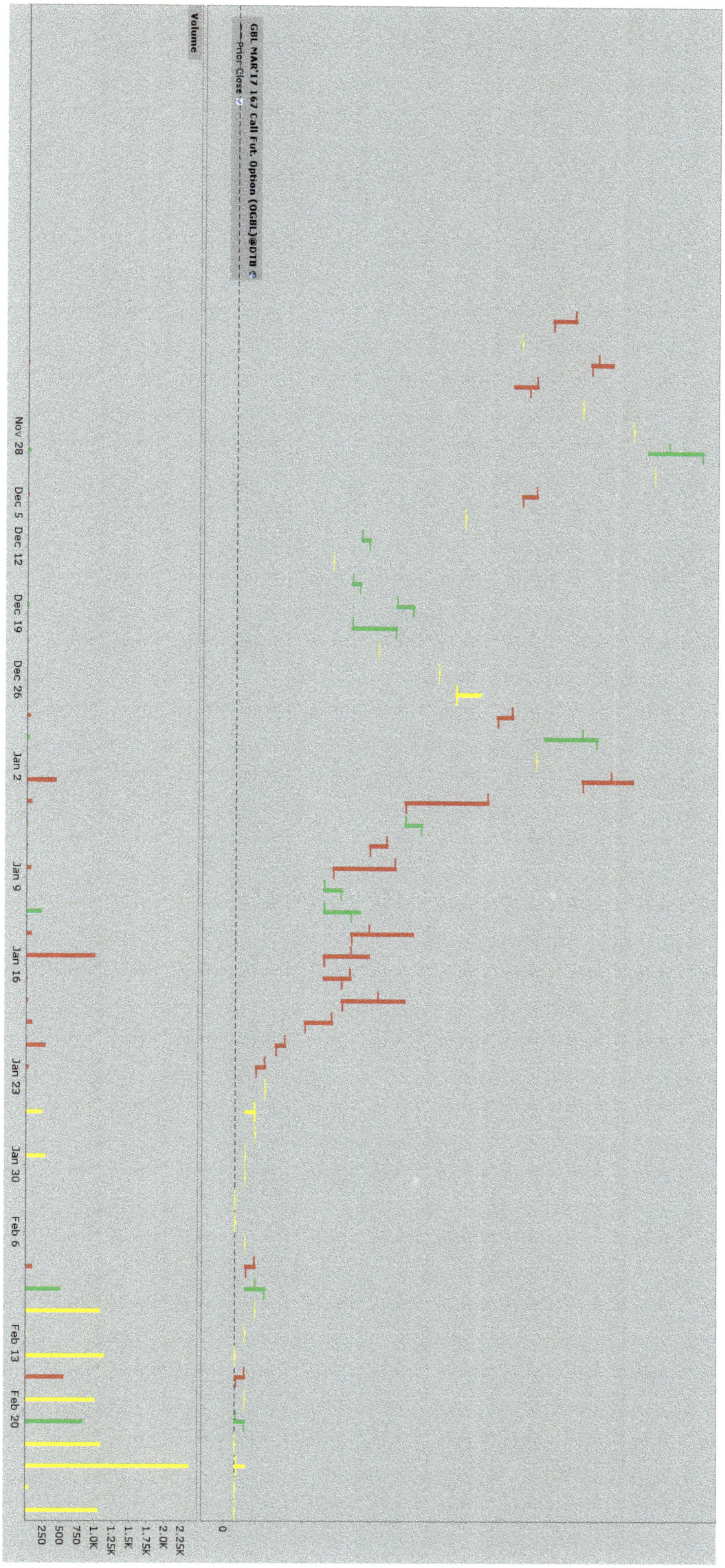
GBL MAR'17 167 Call Fut. Option (OGBL)@DTB
Prior Close
Volume
Nov 28
Dec 5
Dec 12
Dec 19
Dec 26
Jan 2
Jan 9
Jan 16
Jan 23
Jan 30
Feb 6
Feb 13
Feb 20
0
2.25K
2.0K
1.75K
1.5K
1.25K
1.0K
750
500
250

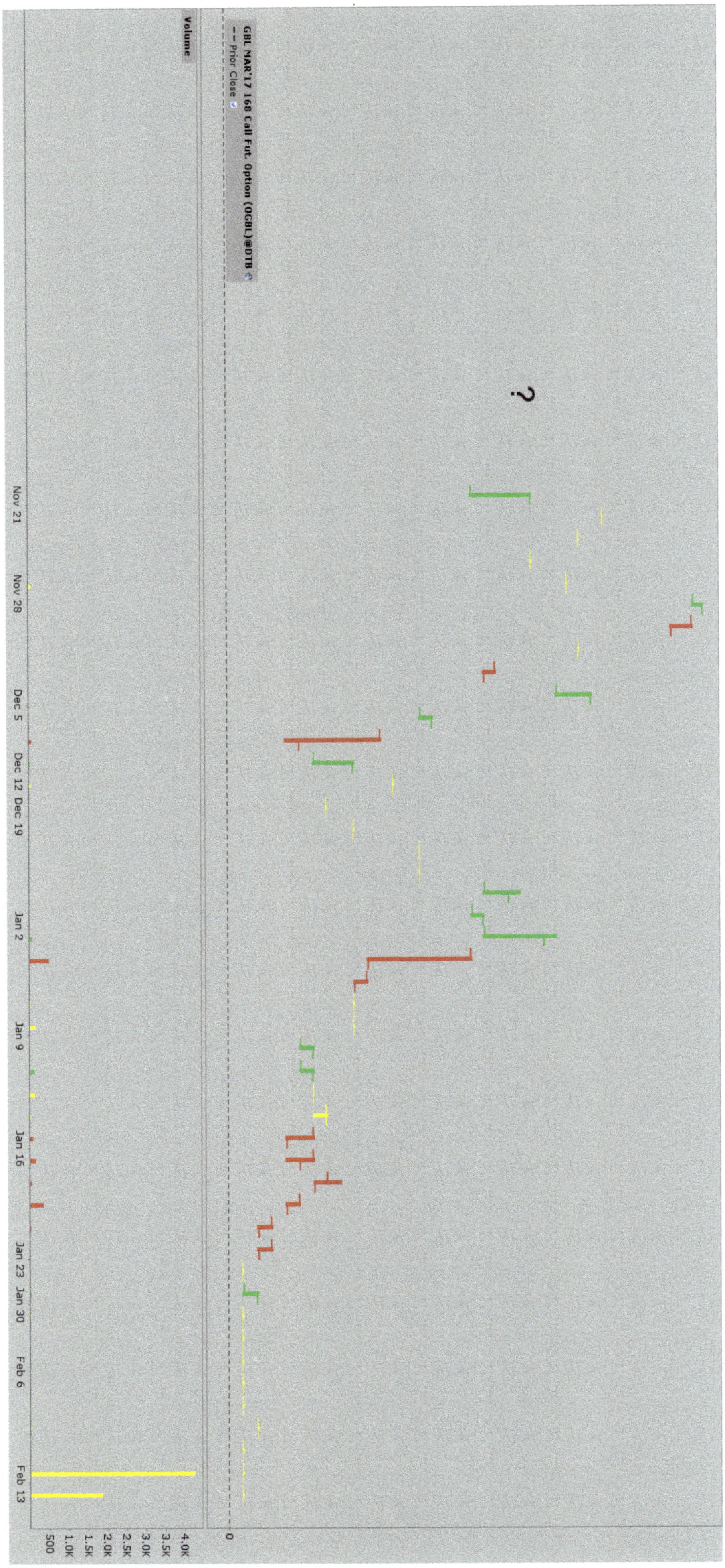
GBL MAR'17 168 Call Fut. Option (OGBL)@DTB
-- Prior Close
?
Volume
Nov 21
Nov 28
Dec 5
Dec 12
Dec 19
Jan 2
Jan 9
Jan 16
Jan 23
Jan 30
Feb 6
Feb 13
0
4.0K
3.5K
3.0K
2.5K
2.0K
1.5K
1.0K
500

4EU 28 APRIL GRAPHICS

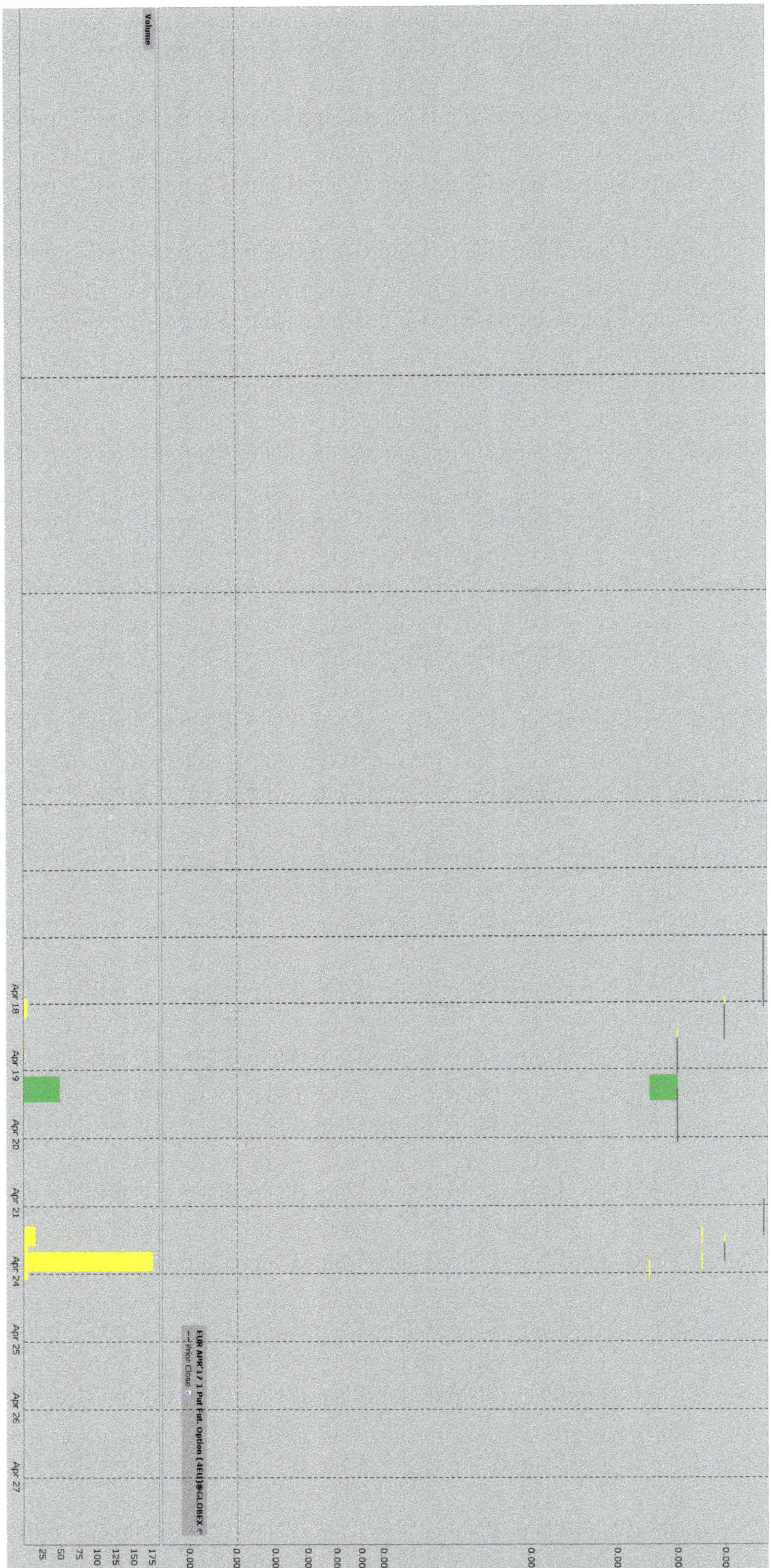
Volume
EUR APR'17 1 Put Fut. Option (4EU)@GLOBEX
Prior Close
Apr 18
Apr 19
Apr 20
Apr 21
Apr 24
Apr 25
Apr 26
Apr 27
25
50
75
100
125
150
175
0.00004
0.00005
0.00006
0.00007
0.00008
0.00009
0.00010
0.00020
0.00030
0.00040
0.00050

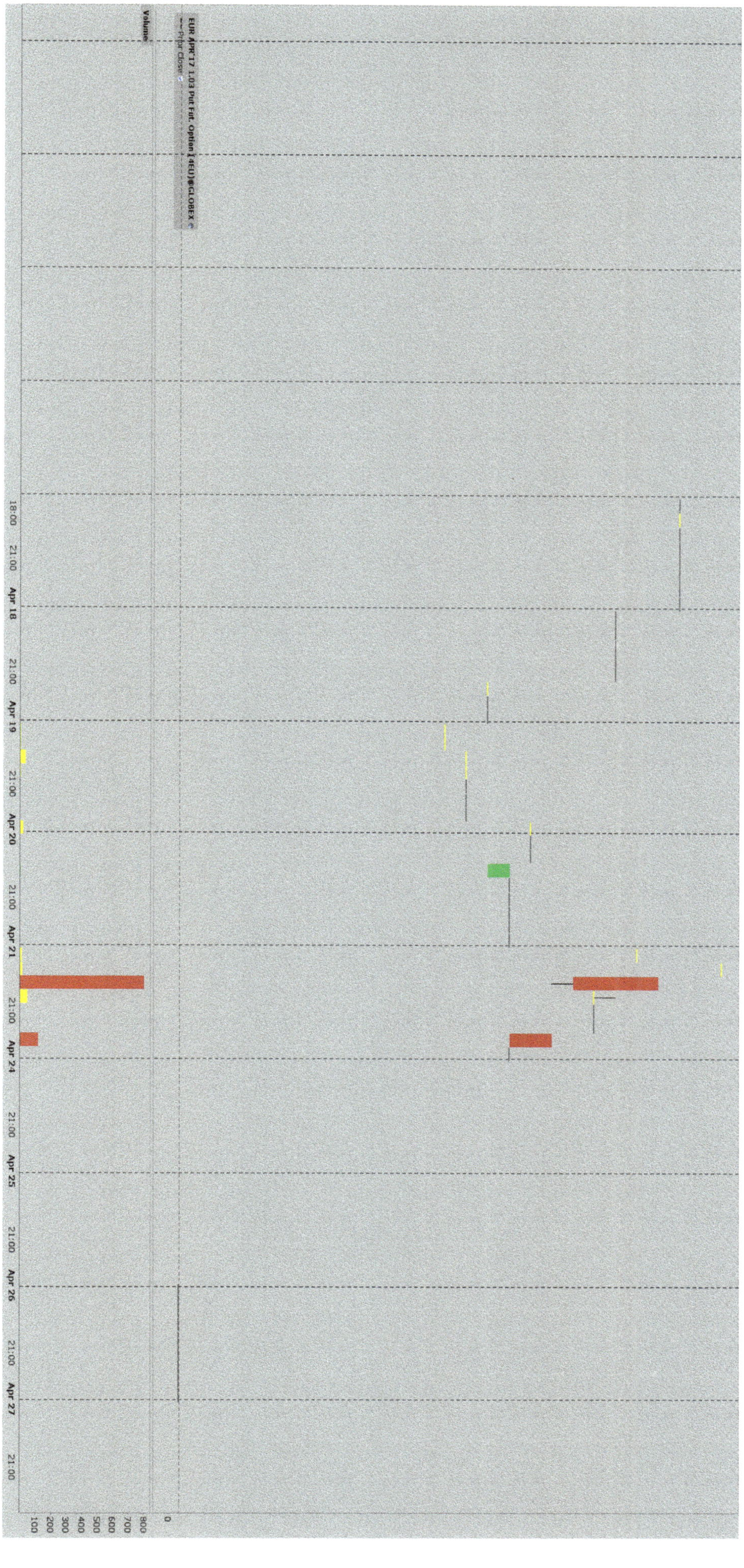

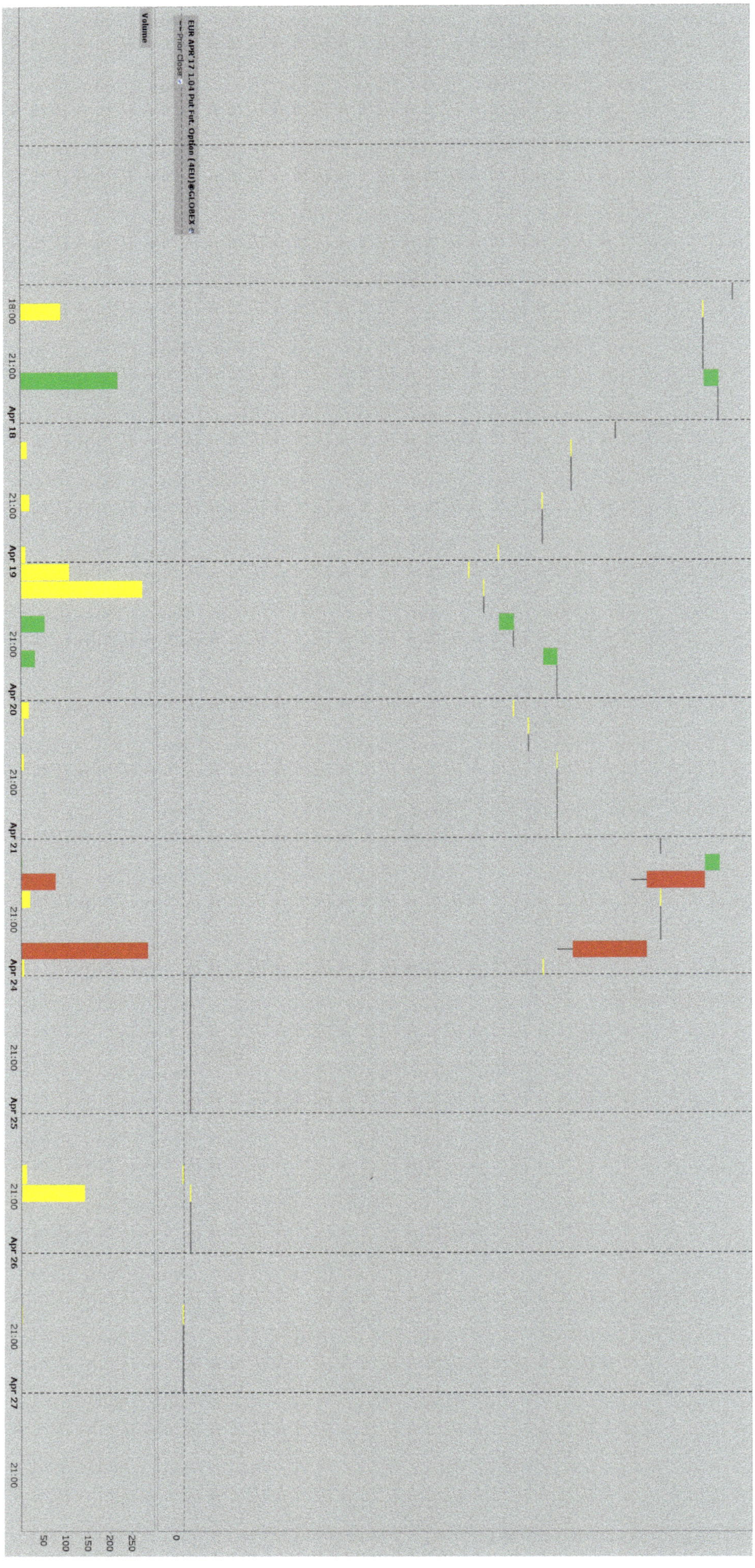
EUR APR'17 1.04 Put Fut. Option (4EU)@GLOBEX
Volume
18:00
21:00
Apr 18
Apr 19
Apr 20
Apr 21
Apr 24
Apr 25
Apr 26
Apr 27
0
50
100
150
200
250

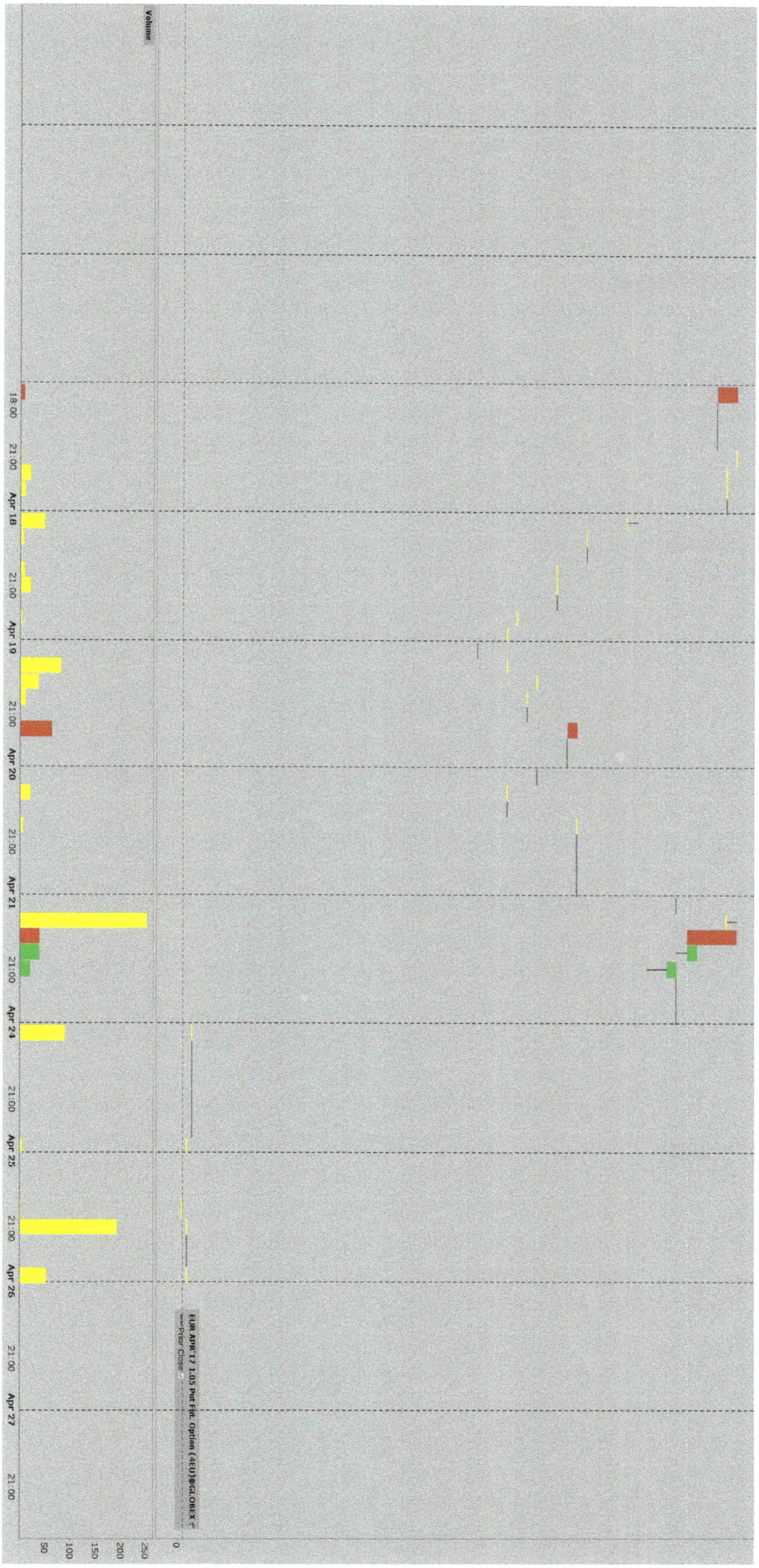
Volume
EUR APR'17 1.05 Put Fut. Option (4EU)@GLOBEX
Prior Close
18:00
21:00
Apr 18
21:00
Apr 19
21:00
Apr 20
21:00
Apr 21
21:00
Apr 24
21:00
Apr 25
21:00
Apr 26
21:00
Apr 27
21:00
0
50
100
150
200
250

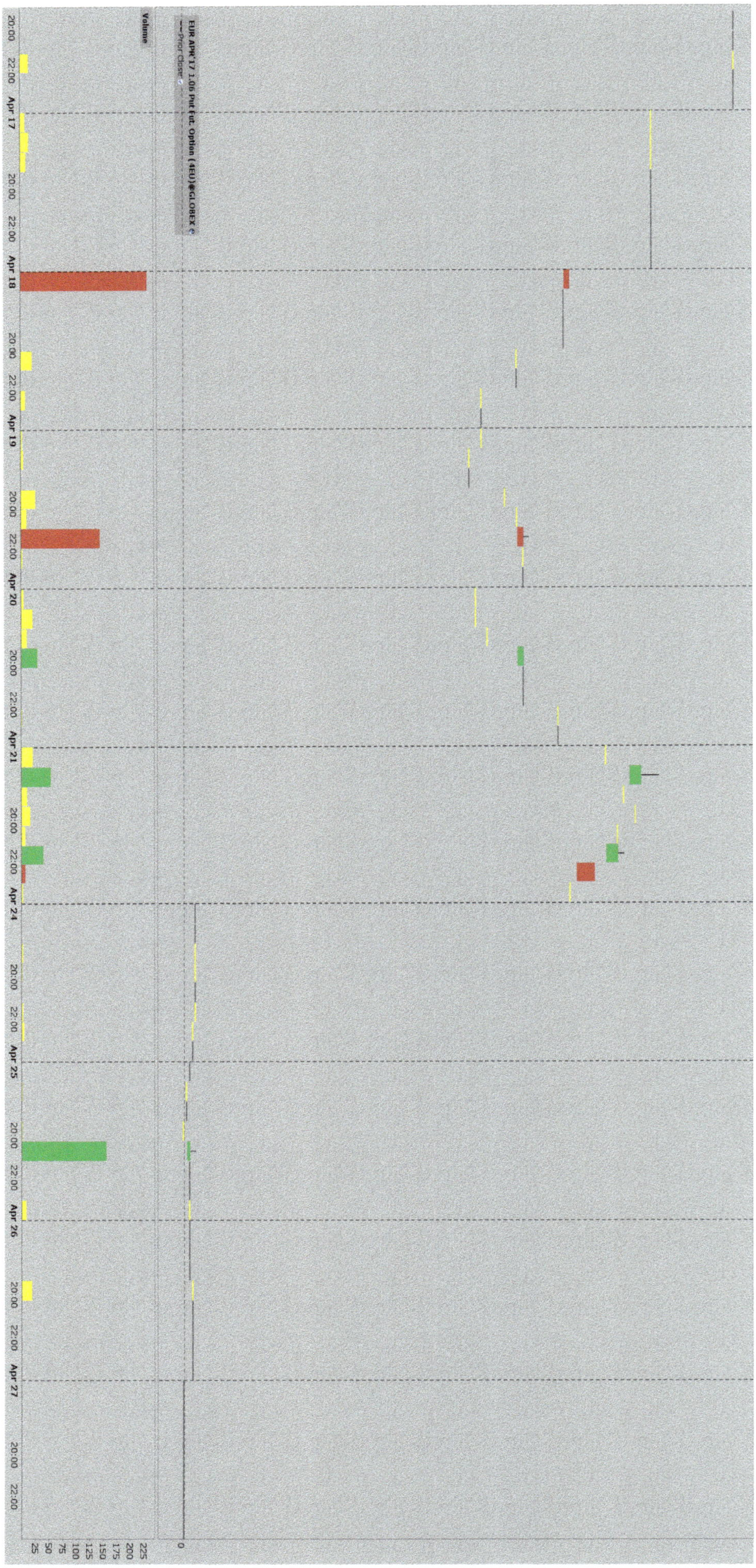
EUR APR'17 1.06 Put Fut. Option (4EUJ)@GLOBEX
Prior Close
Volume
Apr 17
Apr 18
Apr 19
Apr 20
Apr 21
Apr 24
Apr 25
Apr 26
Apr 27

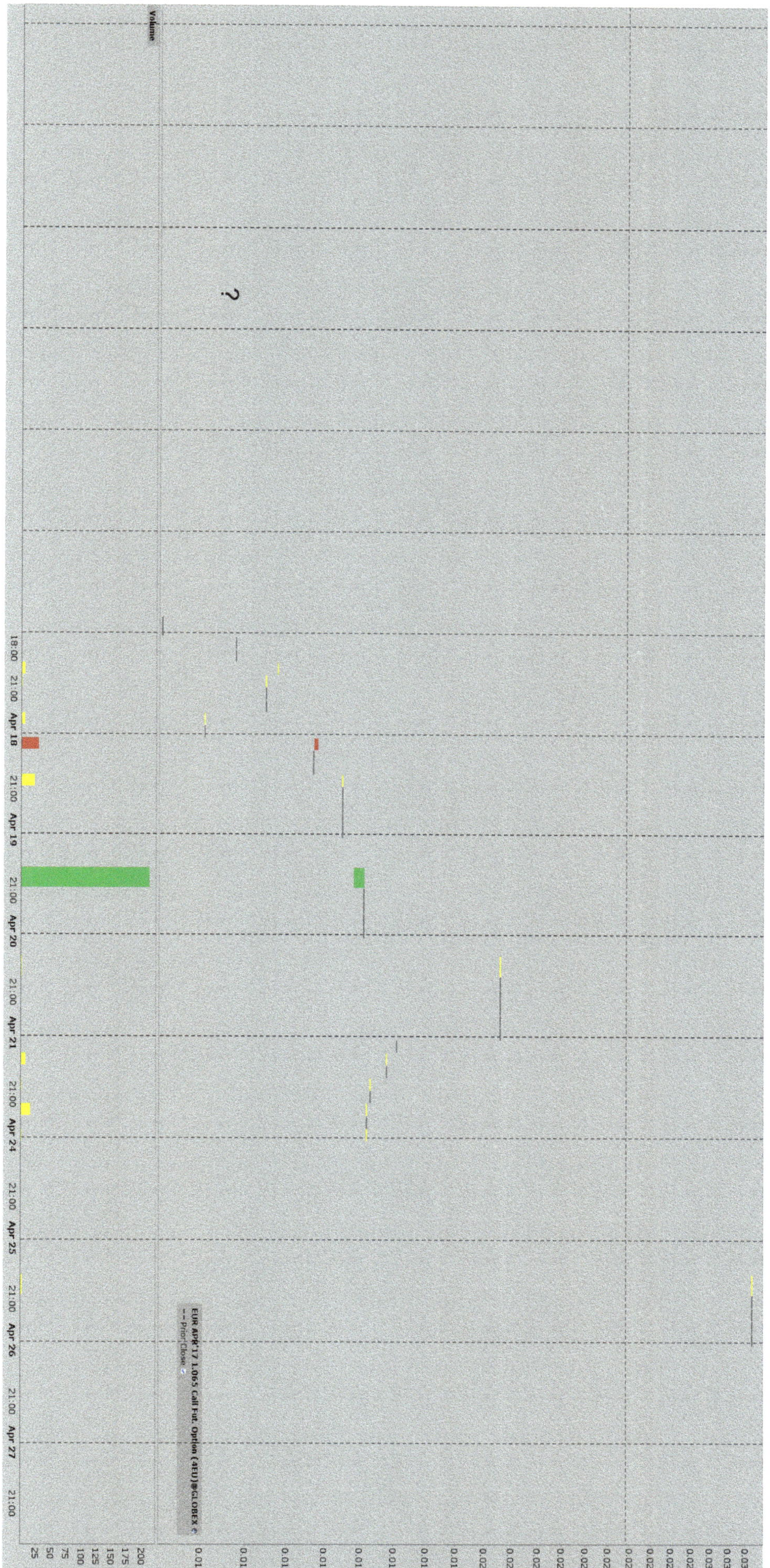
EUR APR'17 1.065 Call Fut. Option (AEU)@GLOBEX
Volume
?

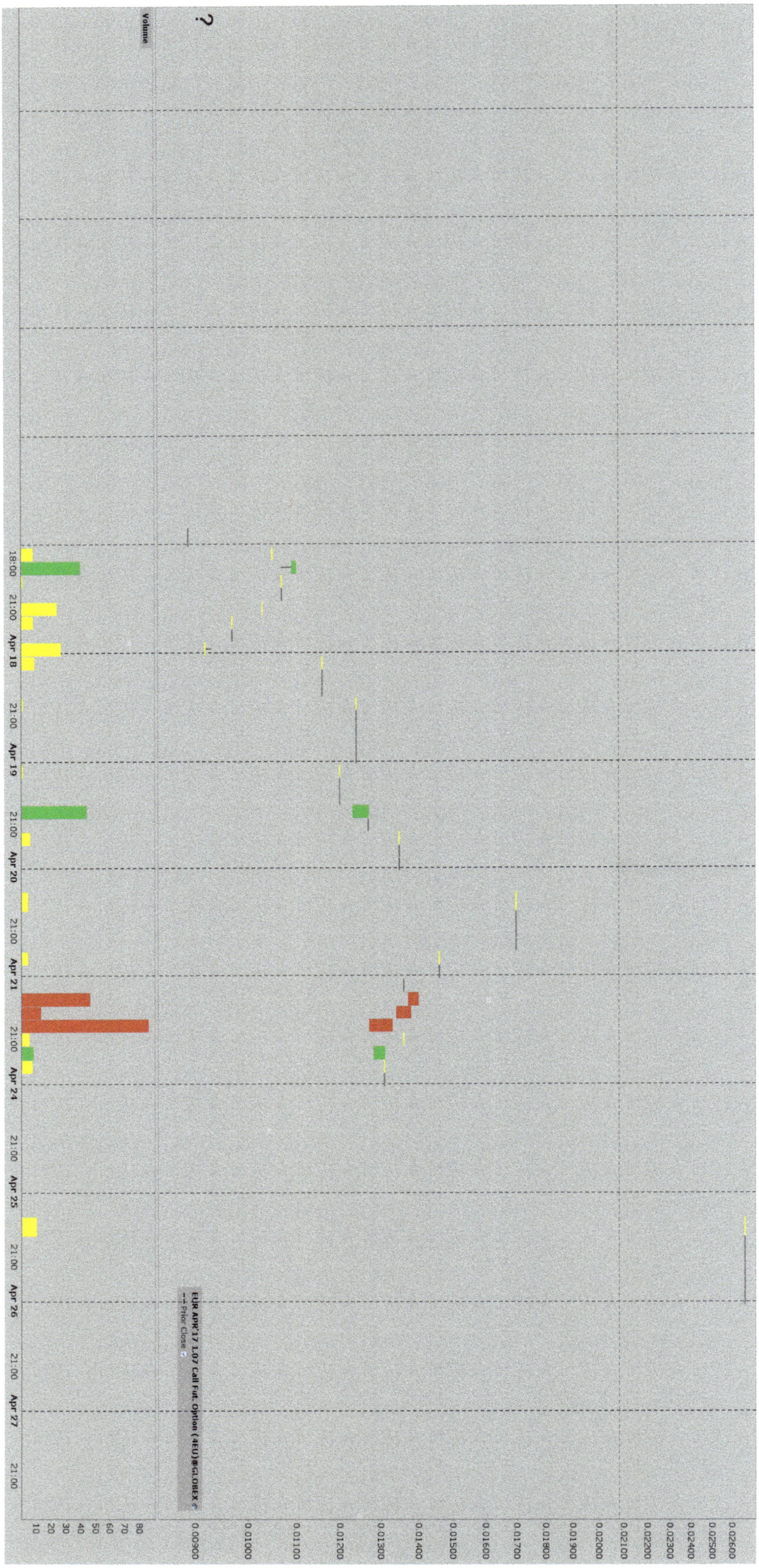
EUR APR'17 1.07 Call Fut. Option (4EU)@GLOBEX
Prior Close
Volume
?
18:00
21:00
Apr 18
21:00
Apr 19
21:00
Apr 20
21:00
Apr 21
21:00
Apr 24
21:00
Apr 25
21:00
Apr 26
21:00
Apr 27
21:00
10
20
30
40
50
60
70
80
0.00900
0.01000
0.01100
0.01200
0.01300
0.01400
0.01500
0.01600
0.01700
0.01800
0.01900
0.02000
0.02100
0.02200
0.02300
0.02400
0.02500
0.02600

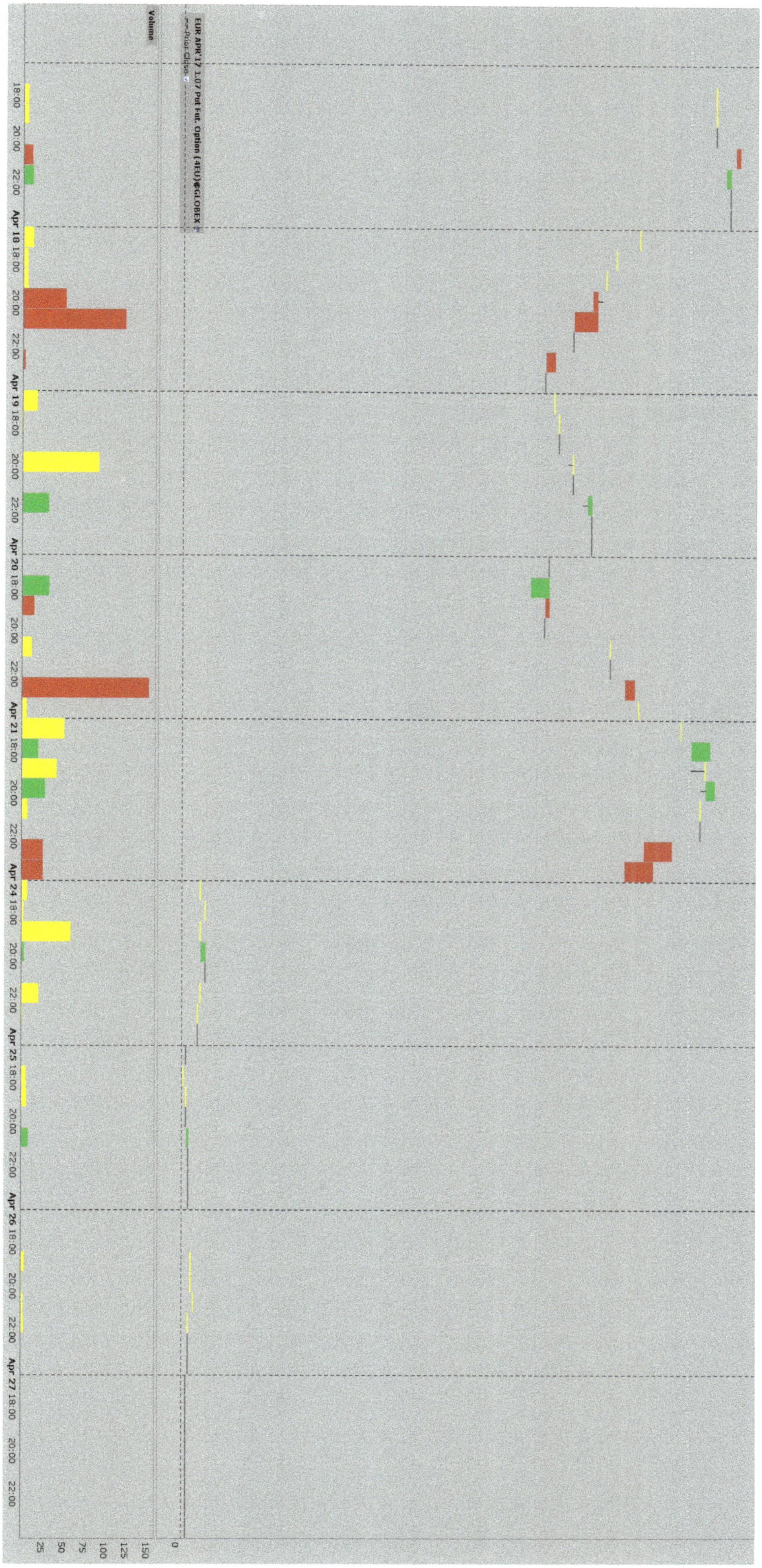
EUR APR 17 1.07 Put Fut. Option (4EU)@GLOBEX
Prior Close
Volume

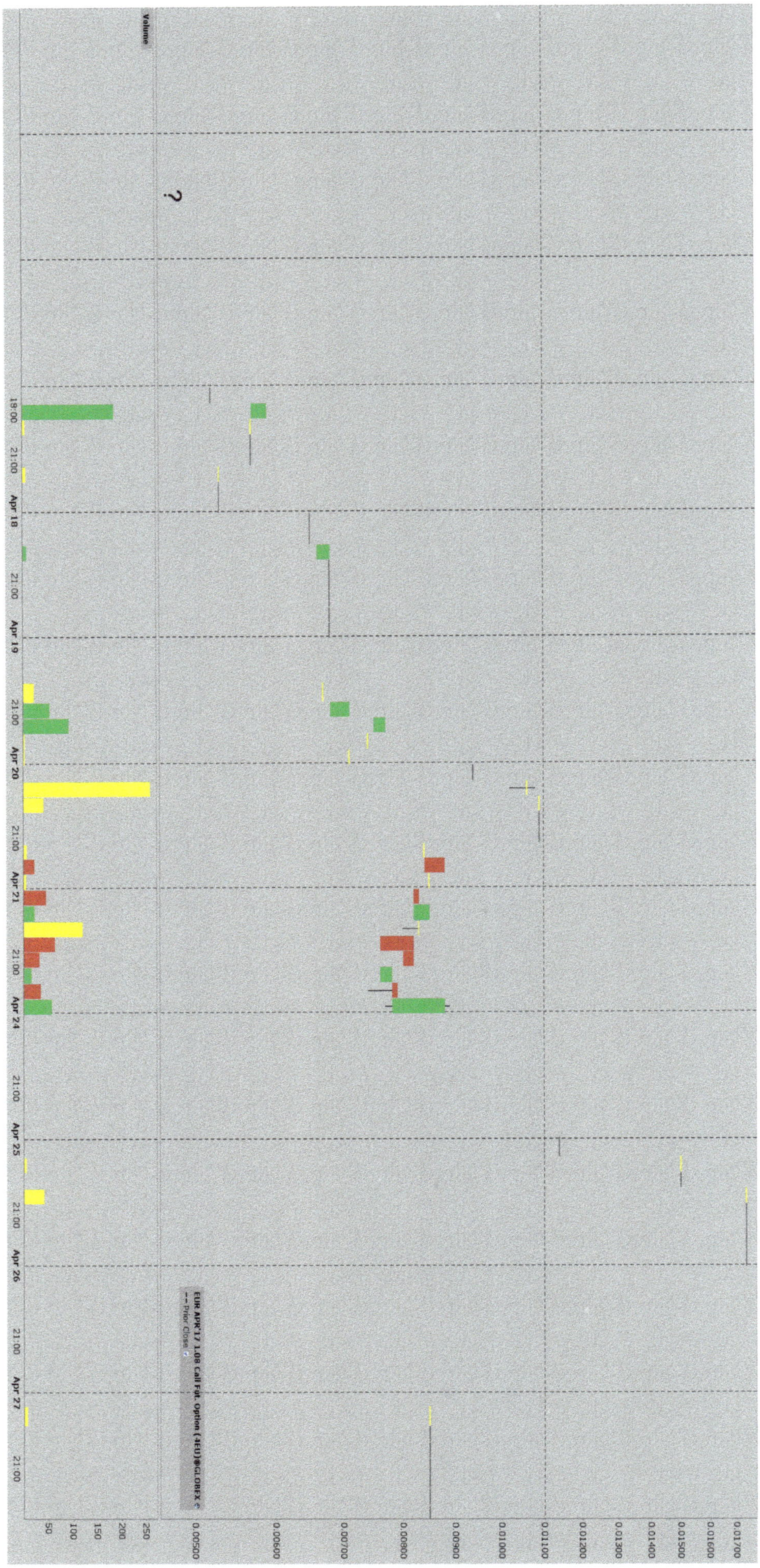

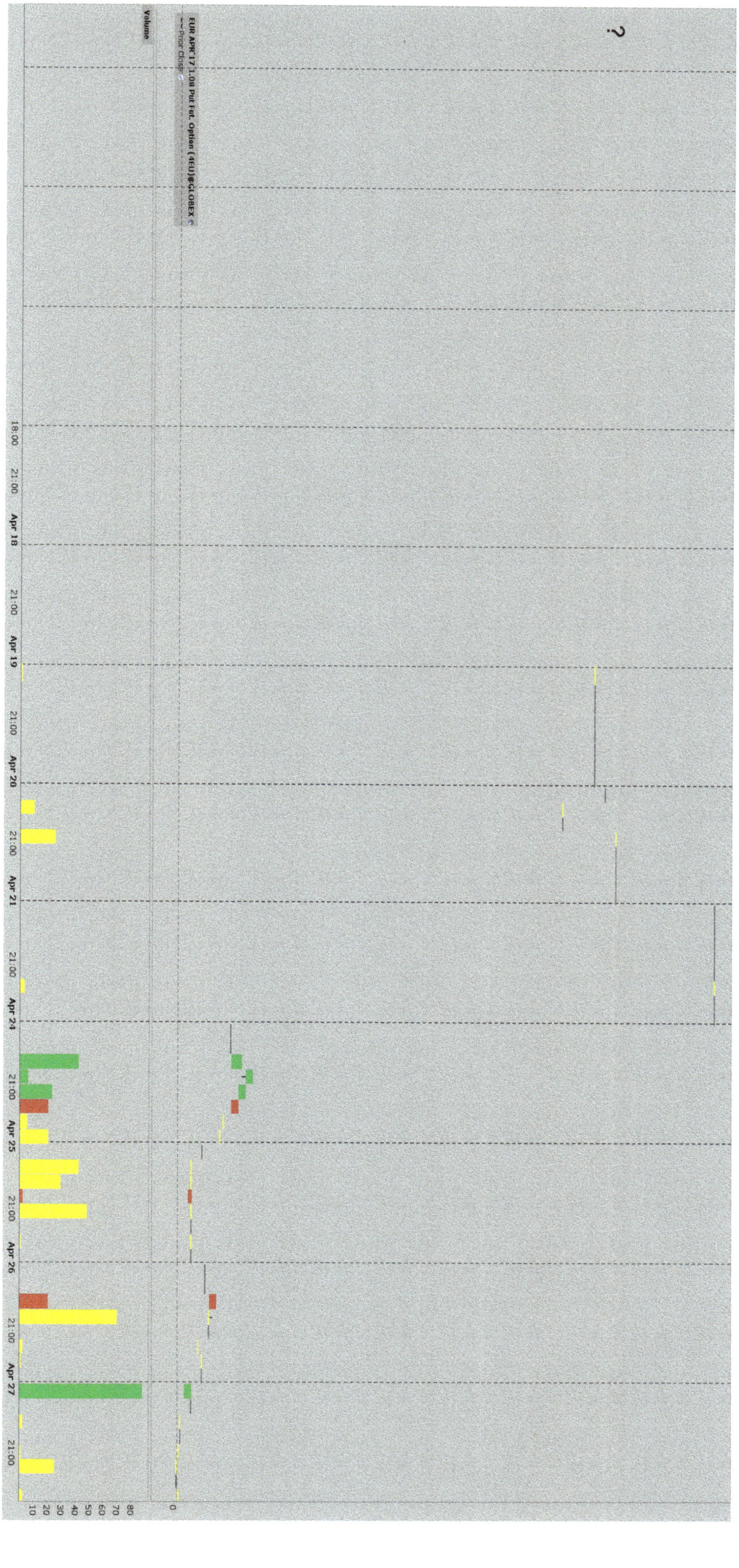
?
EUR APR'17 1.08 Put Fut. Option (4EU)@GLOBEX
Prior Close
Volume
18:00
21:00
Apr 18
21:00
Apr 19
21:00
Apr 20
21:00
Apr 21
21:00
Apr 24
21:00
Apr 25
21:00
Apr 26
21:00
Apr 27
21:00
0
80
70
60
50
40
30
20
10

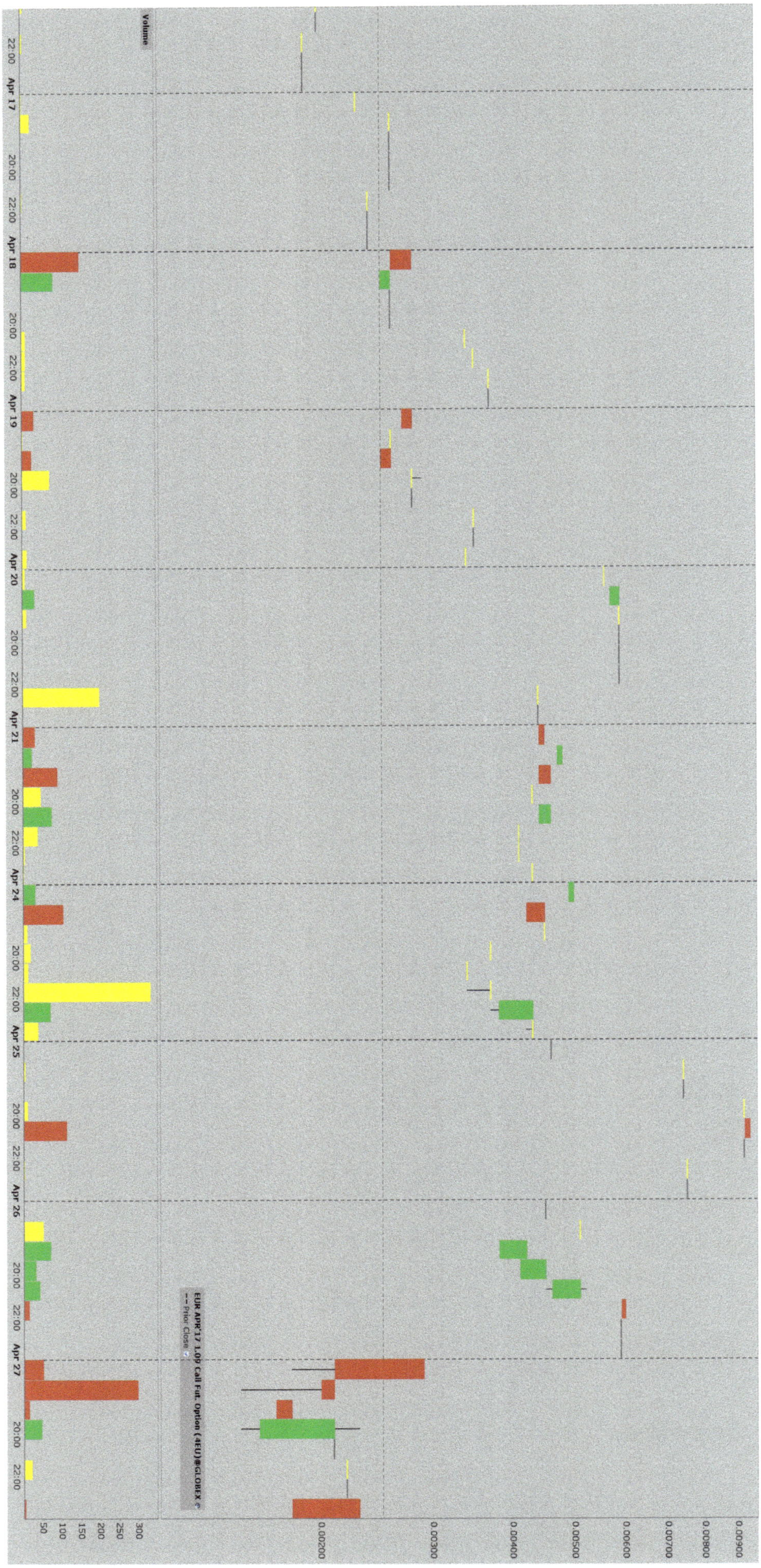
Volume
EUR APR'17 1.09 Call Fut. Option (4EU)@GLOBEX
Prior Close

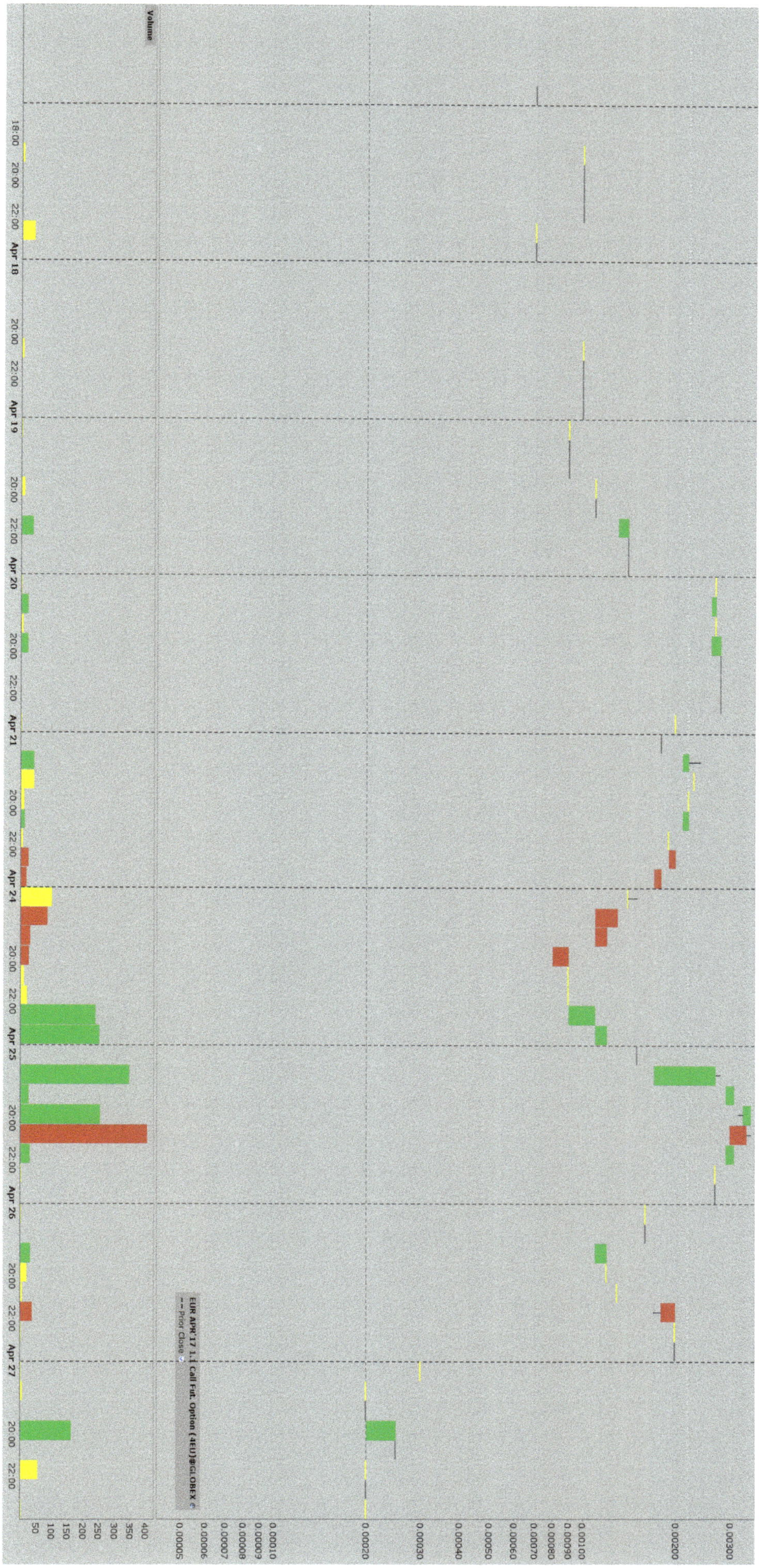

Volume
EUR APR 17 1.1 Call Fut. Option (4EU)@GLOBEX
Prior Close
18:00 20:00 22:00 Apr 18 20:00 22:00 Apr 19 20:00 22:00 Apr 20 20:00 22:00 Apr 21 20:00 22:00 Apr 24 20:00 22:00 Apr 25 20:00 22:00 Apr 26 20:00 22:00 Apr 27 20:00 22:00
50 100 150 200 250 300 350 400
0.00005 0.00006 0.00007 0.00008 0.00009 0.00010 0.00020 0.00030 0.00040 0.00050 0.00060 0.00070 0.00080 0.00090 0.00100 0.00200 0.00300

Volume
18:00
21:00
Apr 18
21:00
Apr 19
21:00
Apr 20
21:00
Apr 21
21:00
Apr 24
21:00
Apr 25
21:00
Apr 26
21:00
Apr 27
21:00

EUU 28 APRIL GRAPHICS

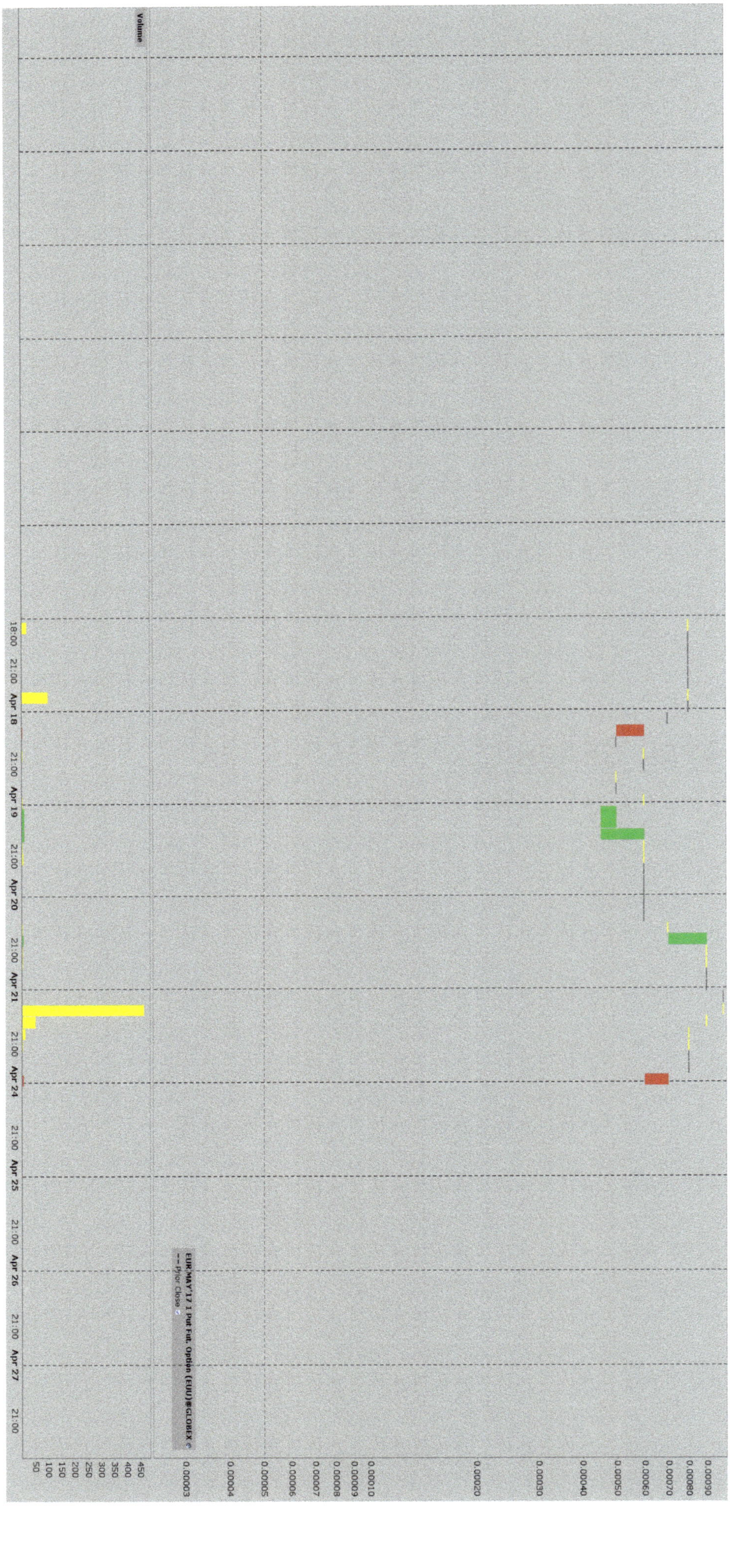
Volume
EUR MAY'17 1 Put Fut. Option (EUU)@GLOBEX
Prior Close

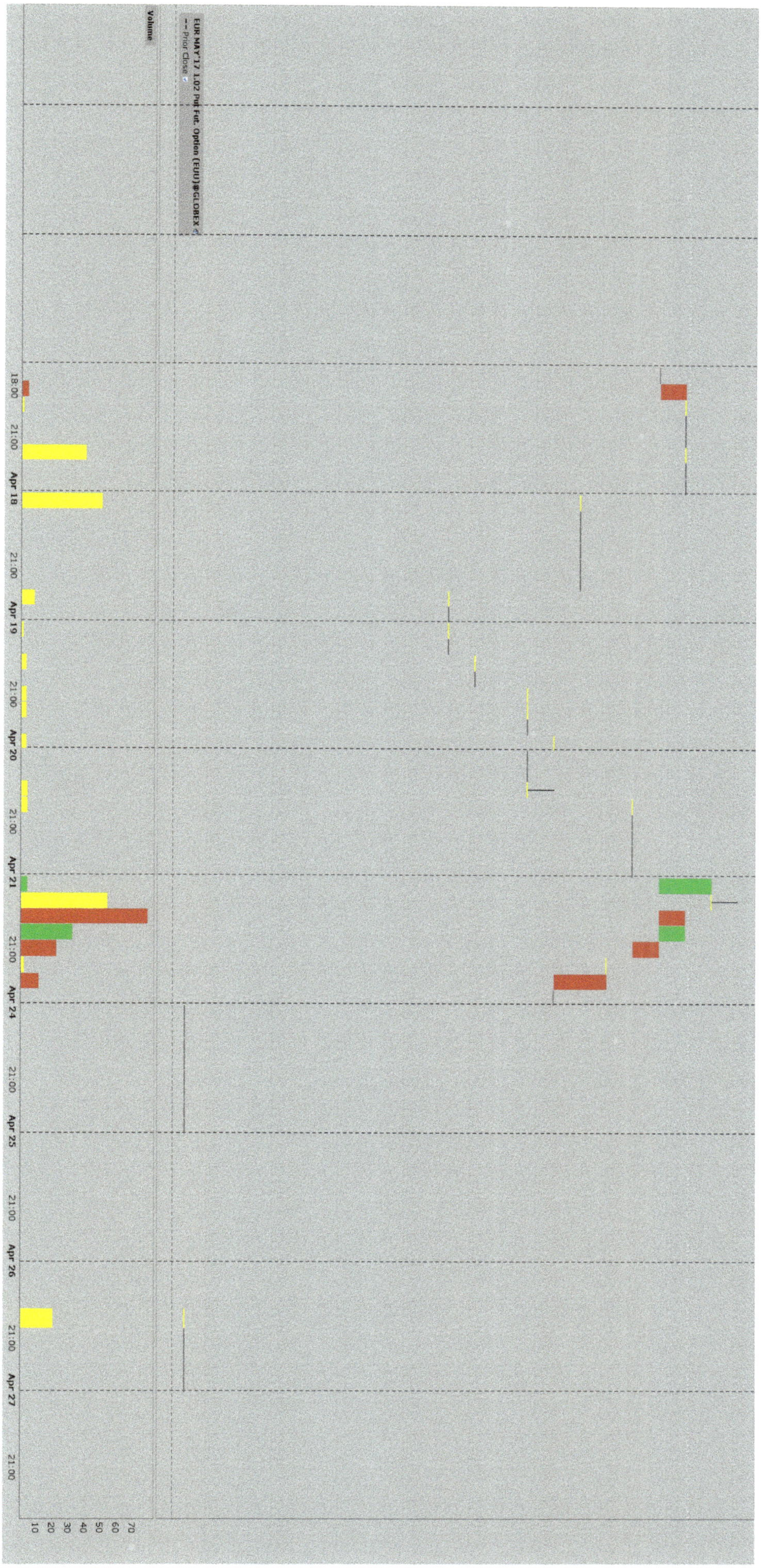
EUR MAY'17 1.02 Put Fut. Option (EUU)@GLOBEX
-- Prior Close
Volume
18:00
21:00
Apr 18
21:00
Apr 19
21:00
Apr 20
21:00
Apr 21
21:00
Apr 24
21:00
Apr 25
21:00
Apr 26
21:00
Apr 27
21:00
10
20
30
40
50
60
70

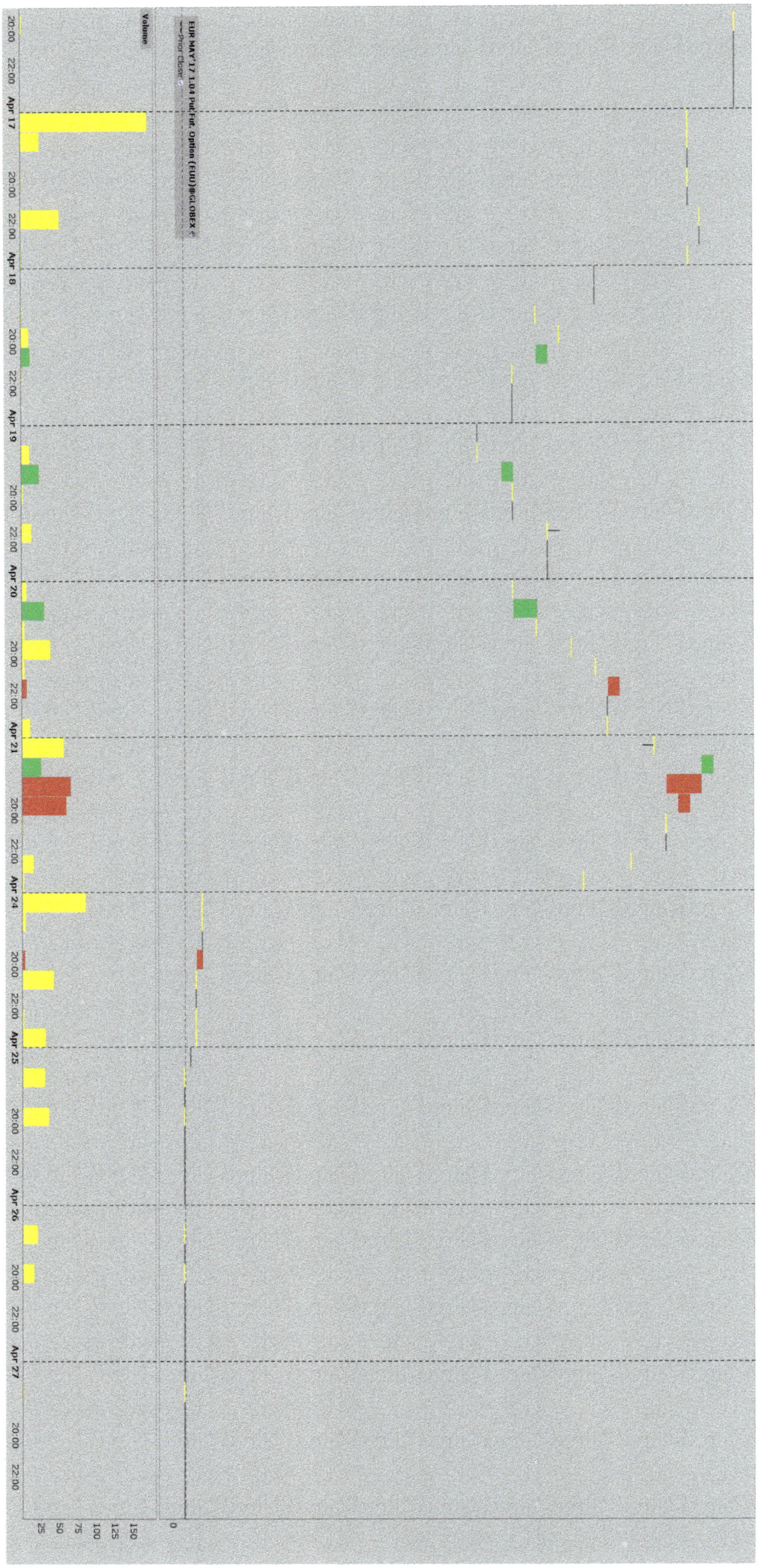
EUR MAY'17 1.04 Put Fut. Option (EUU)@GLOBEX
Prior Close
Volume
Apr 17
Apr 18
Apr 19
Apr 20
Apr 21
Apr 24
Apr 25
Apr 26
Apr 27
0
25
50
75
100
125
150

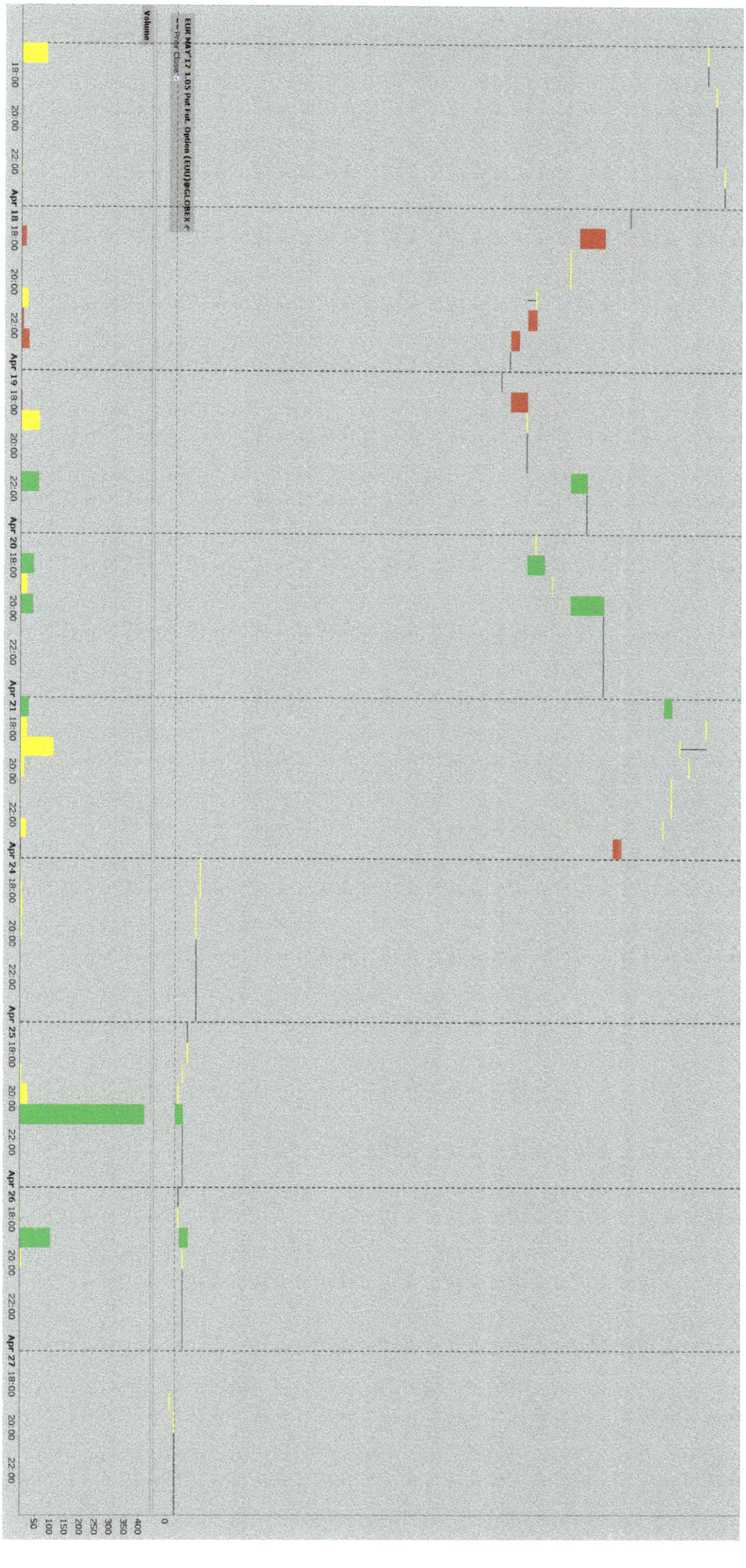
EUR MAY'17 1.05 Put Fut. Option (EU)@GLOBEX
Prior Close
Volume
18:00 20:00 22:00 Apr 18 18:00 20:00 22:00 Apr 19 18:00 20:00 22:00 Apr 20 18:00 20:00 22:00 Apr 21 18:00 20:00 22:00 Apr 24 18:00 20:00 22:00 Apr 25 18:00 20:00 22:00 Apr 26 18:00 20:00 22:00 Apr 27 18:00 20:00 22:00
0 50 100 150 200 250 300 350 400

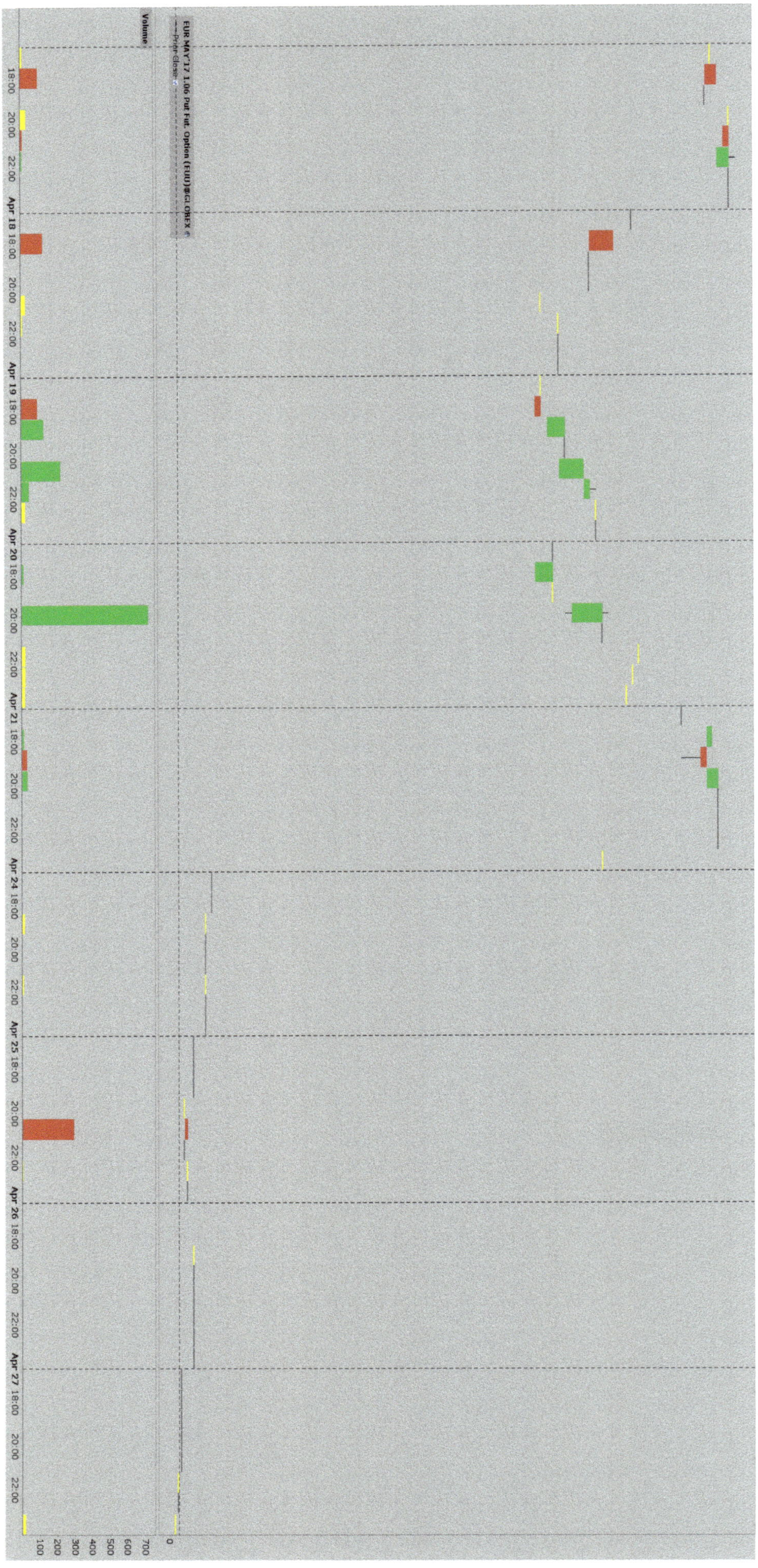

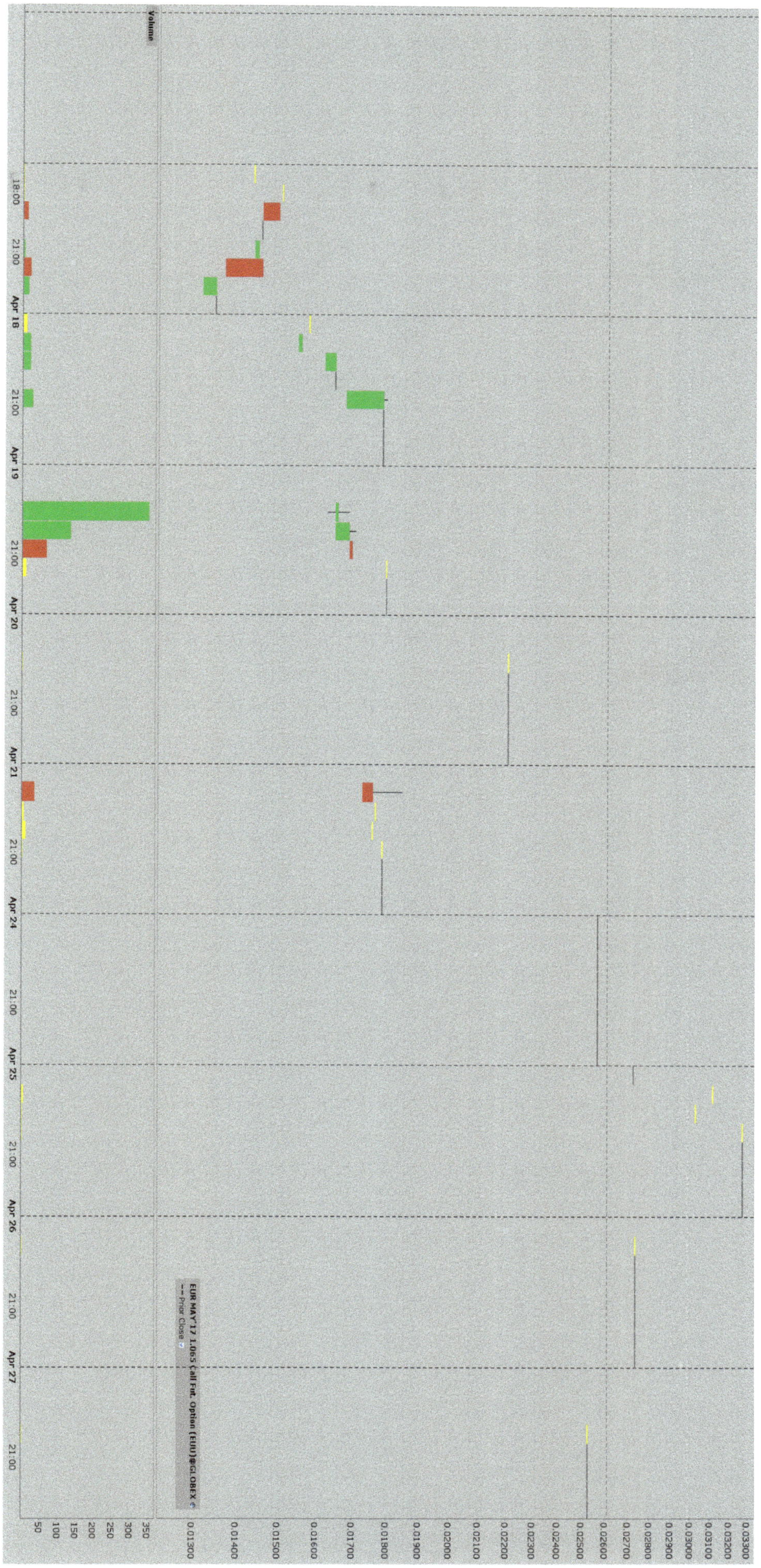
Volume
EUR MAY'17 1.065 Call Fut. Option (EUU)@GLOBEX
Prior Close
18:00
21:00
Apr 18
Apr 19
Apr 20
Apr 21
Apr 24
Apr 25
Apr 26
Apr 27
50
100
150
200
250
300
350
0.01300
0.01400
0.01500
0.01600
0.01700
0.01800
0.01900
0.02000
0.02100
0.02200
0.02300
0.02400
0.02500
0.02600
0.02700
0.02800
0.02900
0.03000
0.03100
0.03200
0.03300

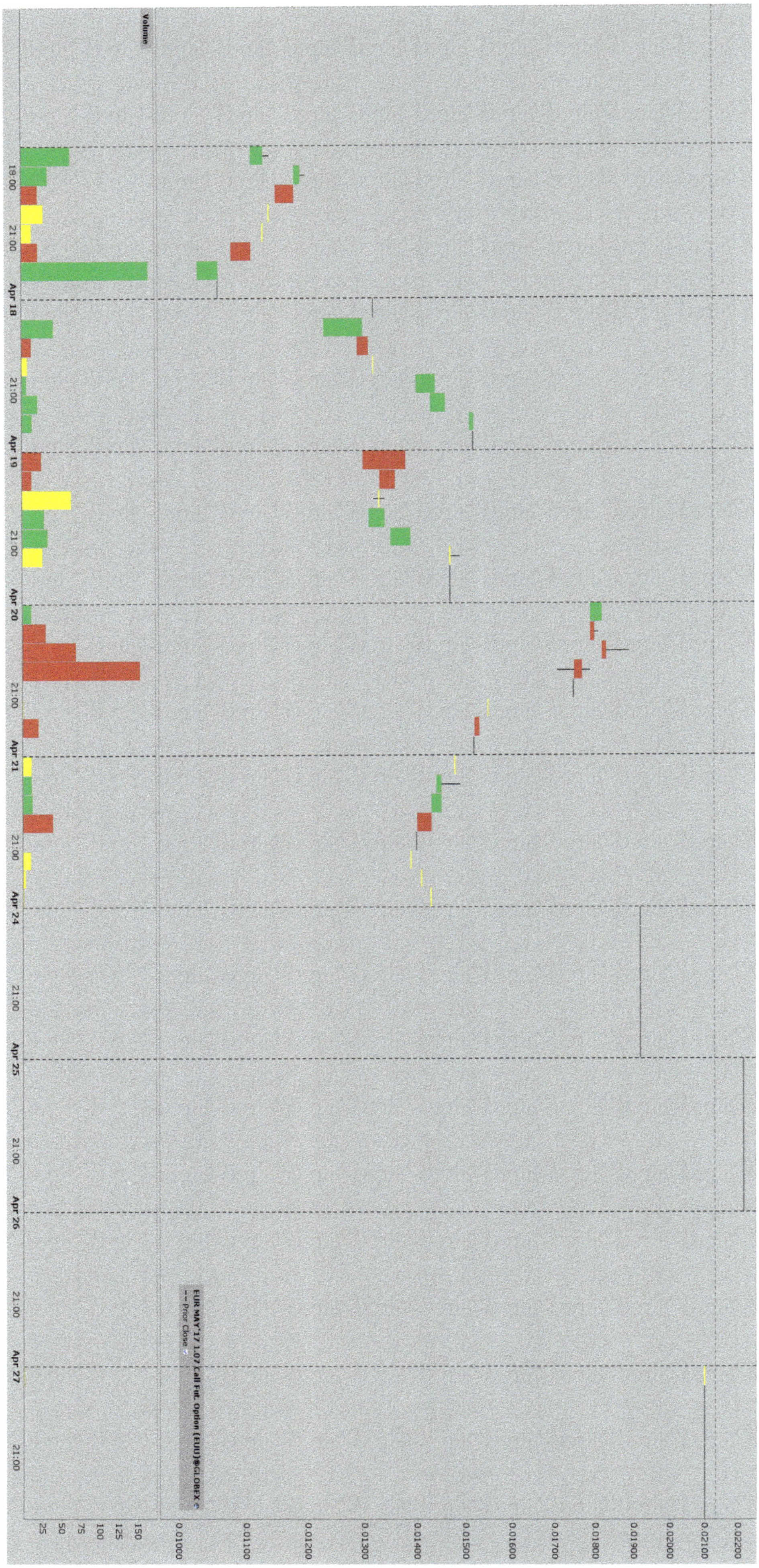
Volume
EUR MAY'17 1.07 Call Fut. Option (EUU)@GLOBEX
-- Prior Close
Apr 18
Apr 19
Apr 20
Apr 21
Apr 24
Apr 25
Apr 26
Apr 27

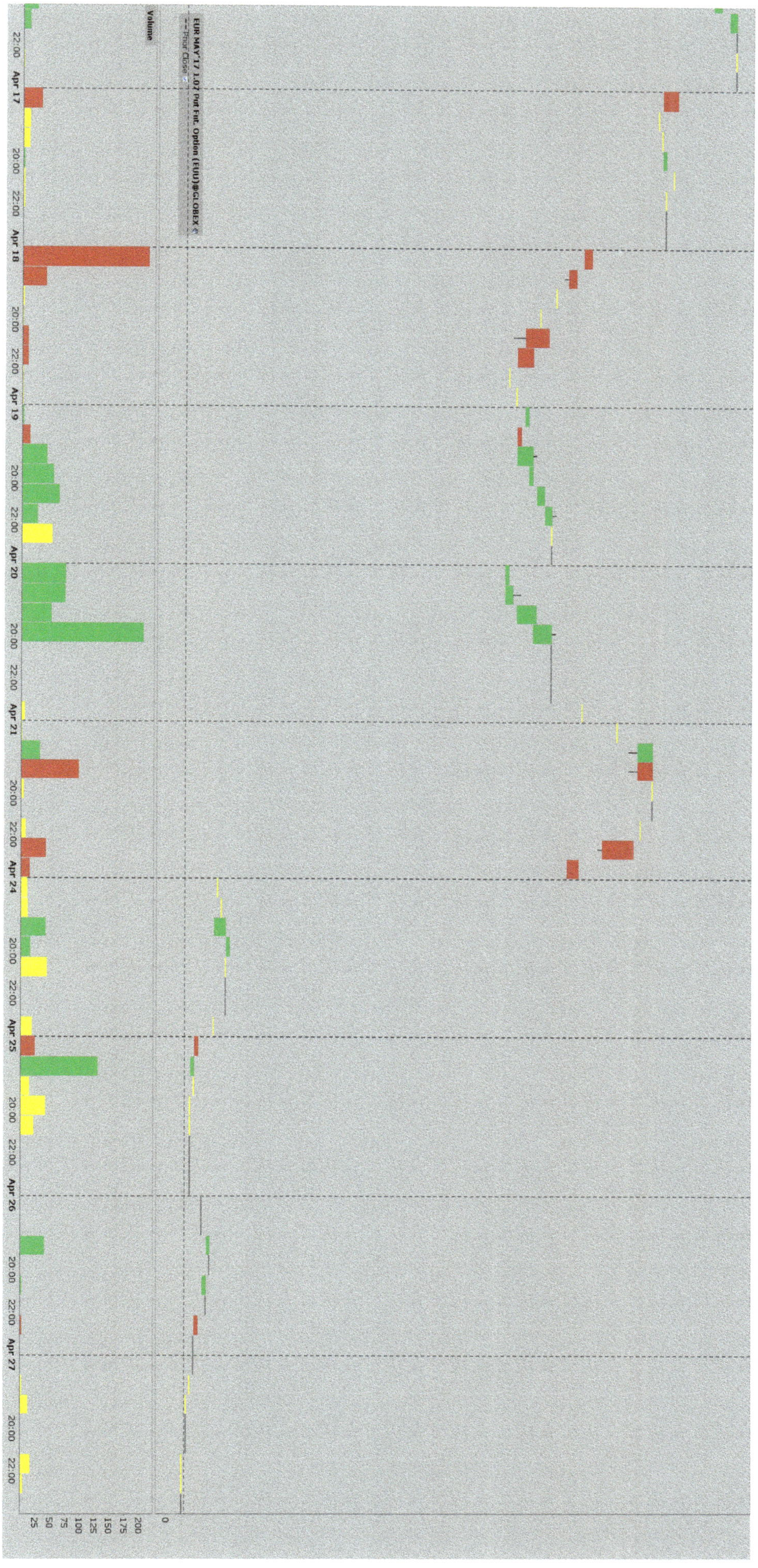
EUR MAY'17 1.07 Put Fut. Option (EUU)@GLOBEX
Prior Close
Volume
Apr 17
Apr 18
Apr 19
Apr 20
Apr 21
Apr 24
Apr 25
Apr 26
Apr 27

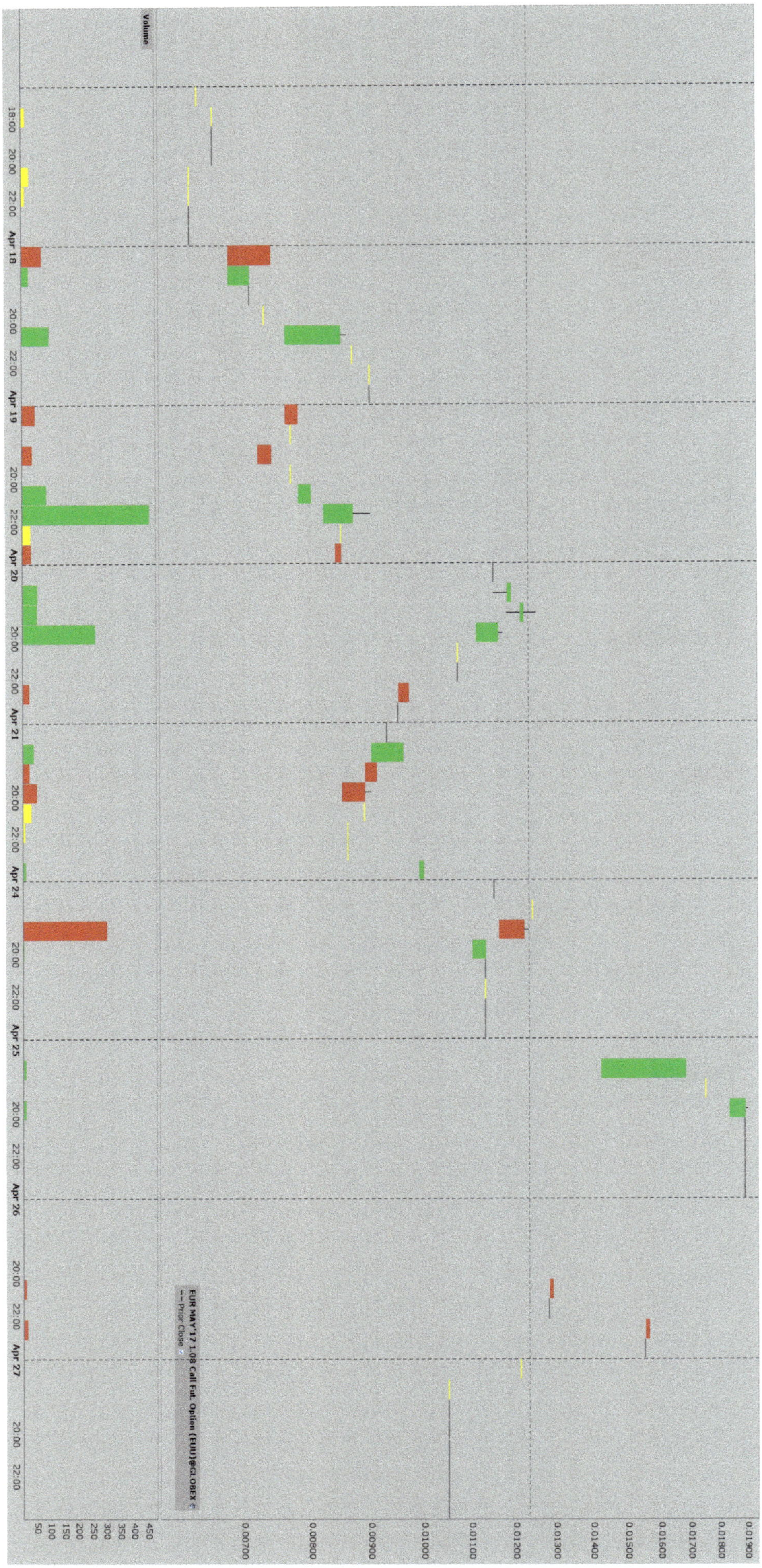
Volume
EUR MAY'17 1.08 Call Fut. Option (EUU)@GLOBEX
-- Prior Close

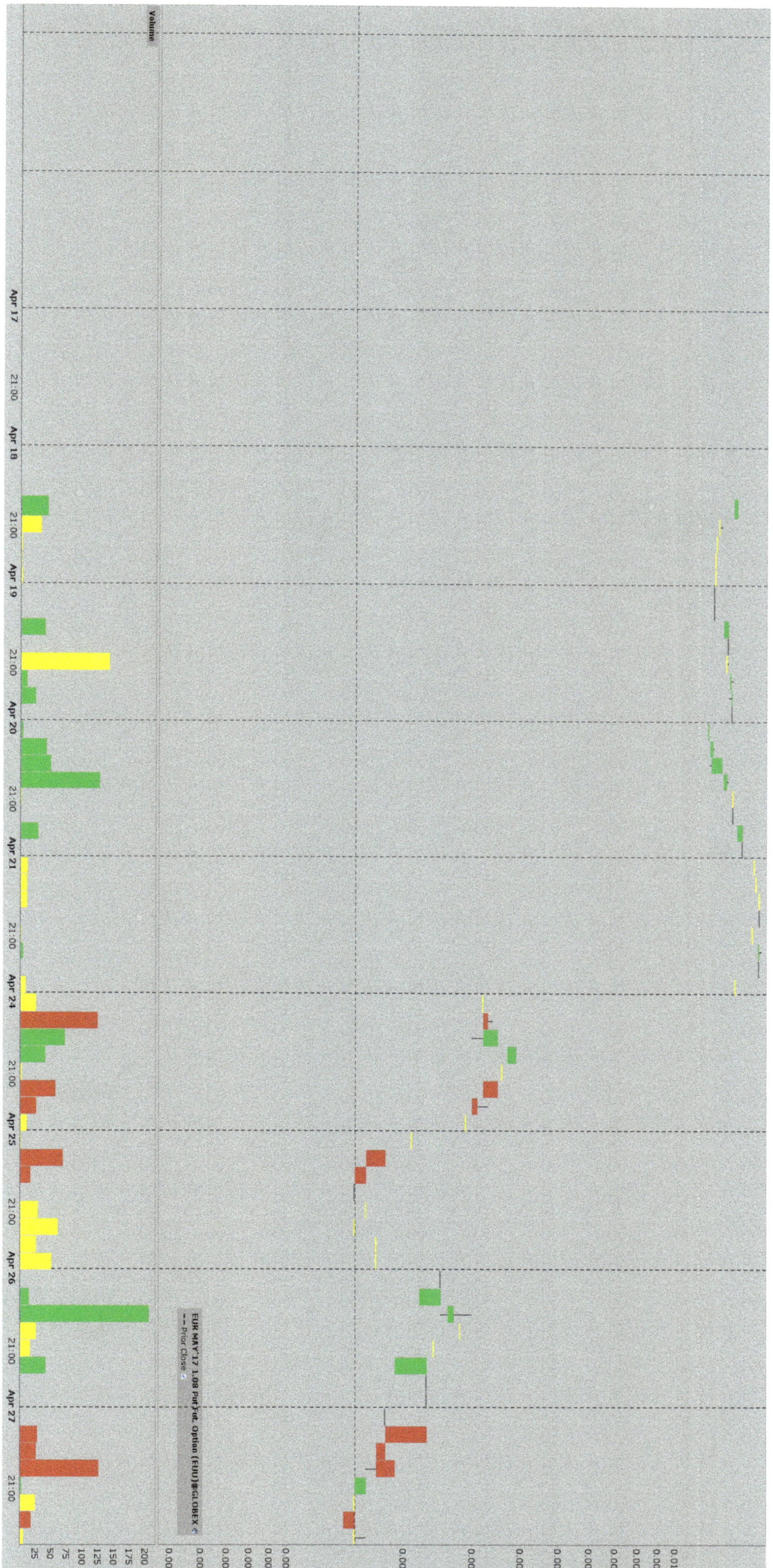

Volume
EUR MAY'17 1.08 Put Fut. Option (EU1)@GLOBEX
Prior Close
Apr 17
21:00
Apr 18
21:00
Apr 19
21:00
Apr 20
21:00
Apr 21
21:00
Apr 24
21:00
Apr 25
21:00
Apr 26
21:00
Apr 27
21:00
25
50
75
100
125
150
175
200
0.00050
0.00060
0.00070
0.00080
0.00090
0.01000
0.00200
0.00300
0.00400
0.00500
0.00600
0.00700
0.00800
0.00900
0.01000

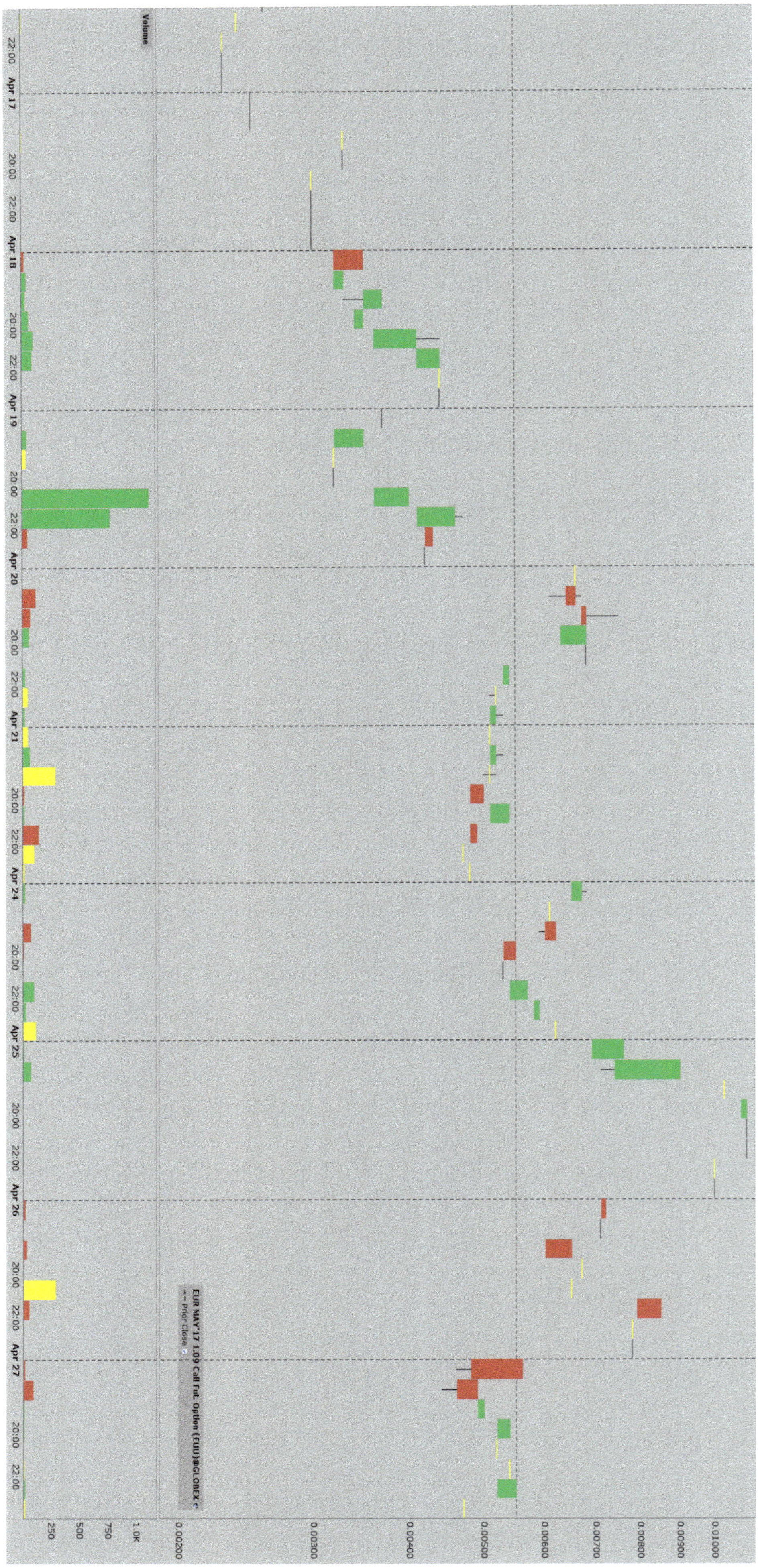
EUR MAY'17 1.09 Call Fut. Option (EUU)@GLOBEX
Prior Close
Volume
0.01000
0.00900
0.00800
0.00700
0.00600
0.00500
0.00400
0.00300
0.00200
1.0K
750
500
250
Apr 17
Apr 18
Apr 19
Apr 20
Apr 21
Apr 24
Apr 25
Apr 26
Apr 27
20:00
22:00

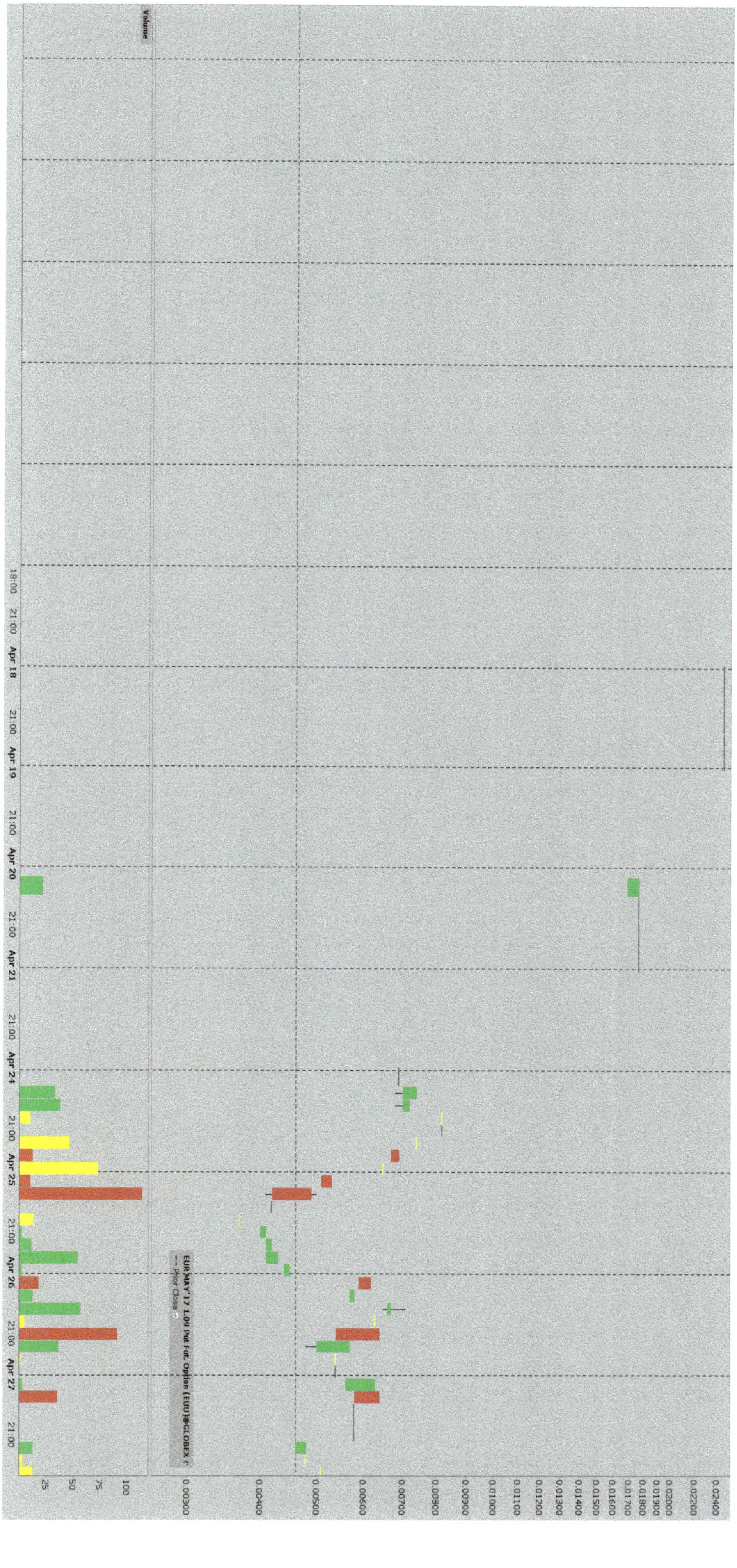
Volume
18:00
21:00
Apr 18
Apr 19
Apr 20
Apr 21
Apr 24
Apr 25
Apr 26
Apr 27
25
50
75
100
0.00300
0.00400
0.00500
0.00600
0.00700
0.00800
0.00900
0.01000
0.01100
0.01200
0.01300
0.01400
0.01500
0.01600
0.01700
0.01800
0.01900
0.02000
0.02200
0.02400

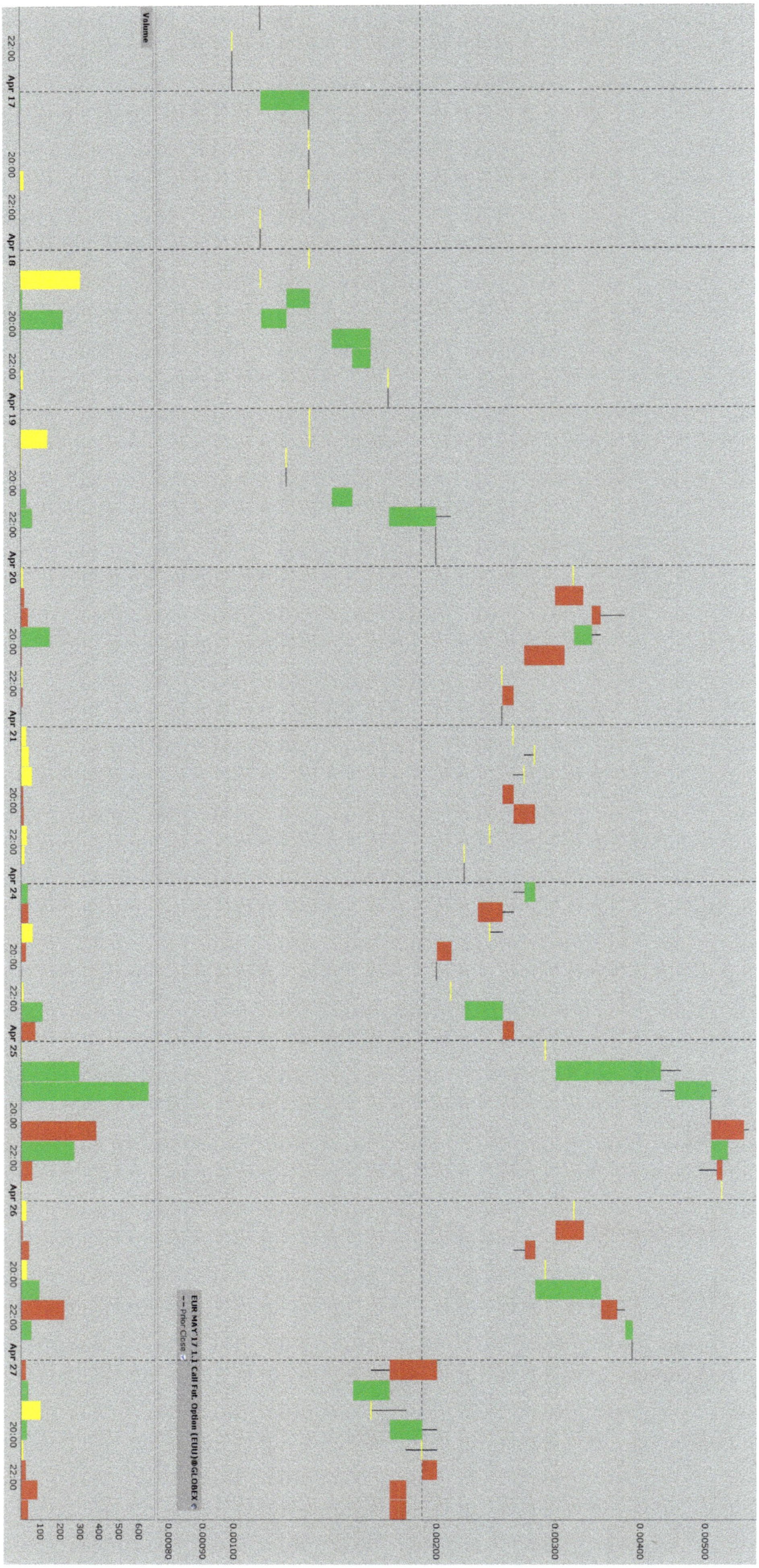
Volume
Apr 17
Apr 18
Apr 19
Apr 20
Apr 21
Apr 24
Apr 25
Apr 26
Apr 27
0.00100
0.00200
0.00300
0.00400
0.00500

28 APRIL 0GB4 GRAPHICS

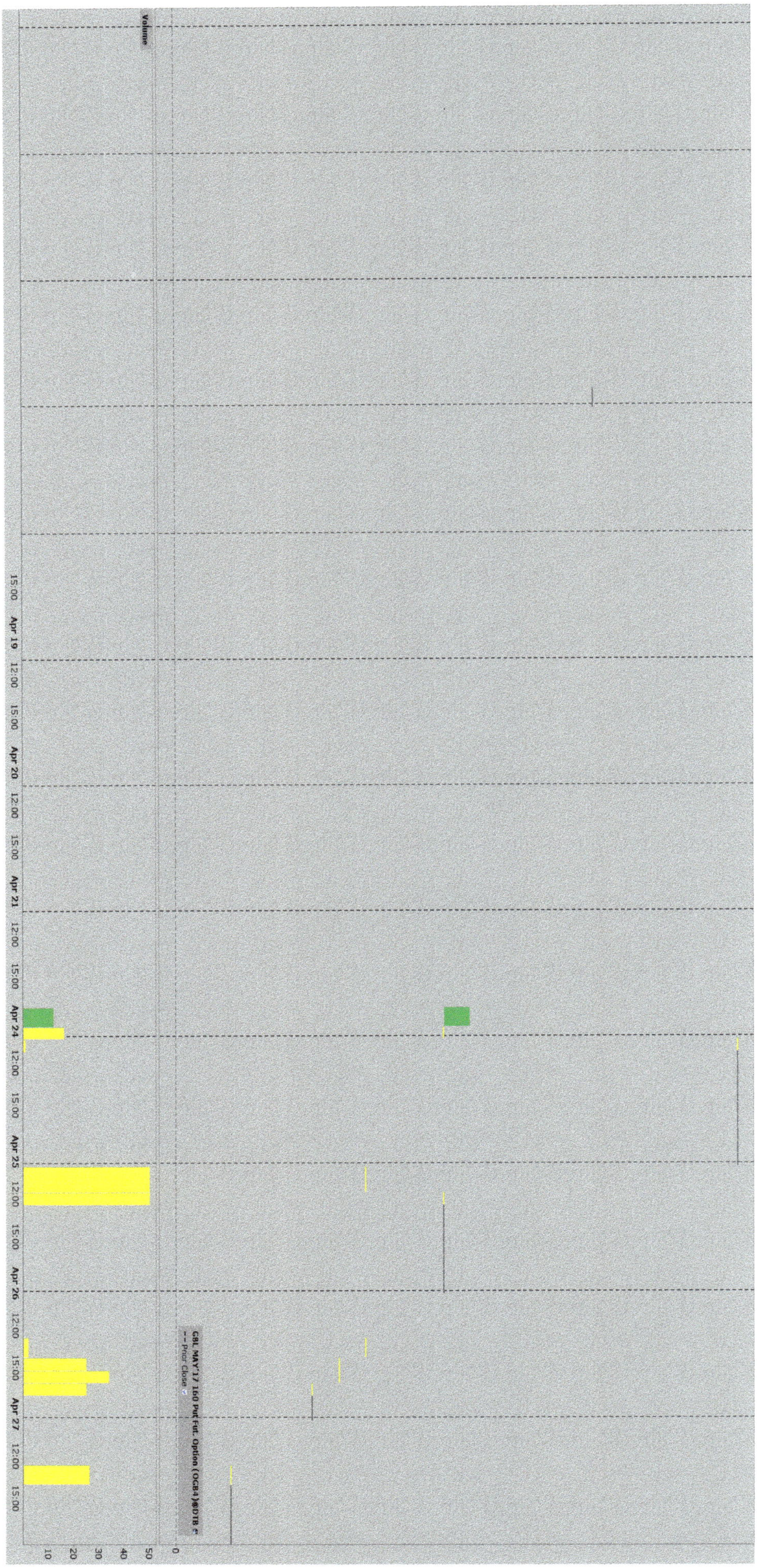
Volume
GBL MAY'17 160 Put Fut. Option (OGB4)@DTB
-- Prior Close
15:00
Apr 19
12:00
15:00
Apr 20
12:00
15:00
Apr 21
12:00
15:00
Apr 24
12:00
15:00
Apr 25
12:00
15:00
Apr 26
12:00
15:00
Apr 27
12:00
15:00
10
20
30
40
50
0

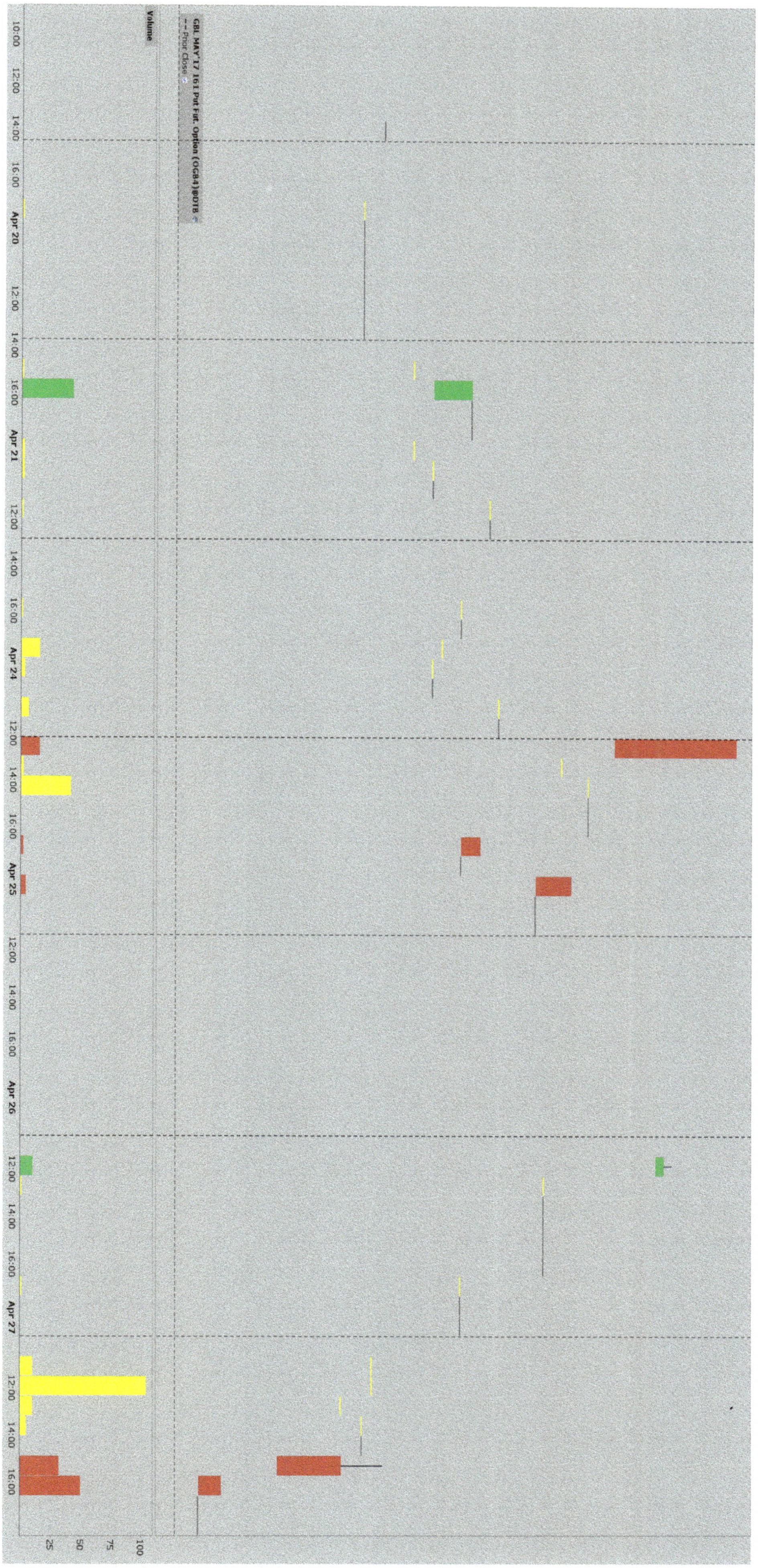
GBL MAY'17 161 Put Fut. Option (OGB4)@DTB
-- Prior Close
Volume
10:00
12:00
14:00
16:00
Apr 20
Apr 21
Apr 24
Apr 25
Apr 26
Apr 27
25
50
75
100

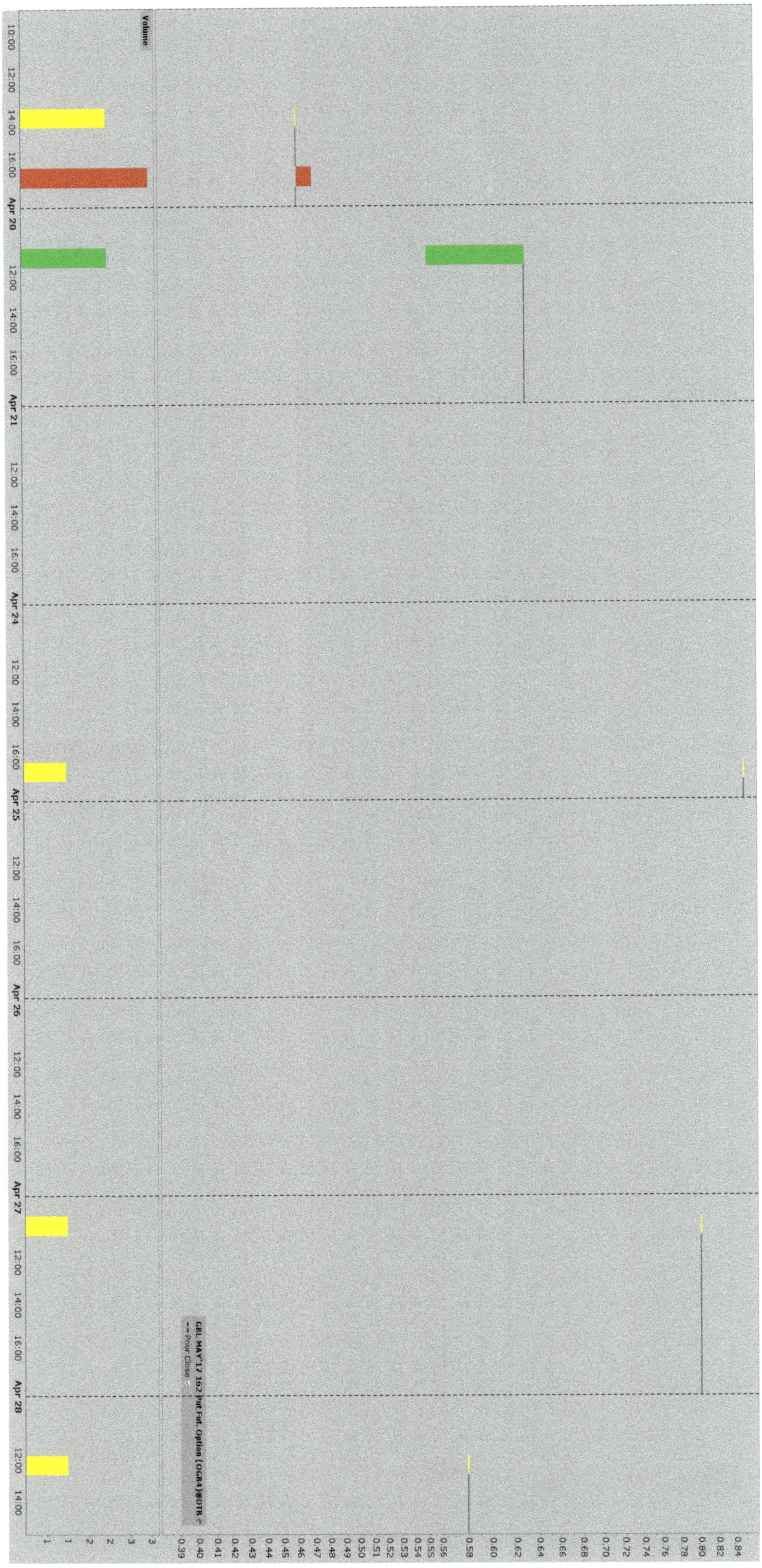

GBL MAY'17 162 Put Fut. Option (OGB4)@DTB
-- Prior Close
Volume
Apr 20
Apr 21
Apr 24
Apr 25
Apr 26
Apr 27
Apr 28

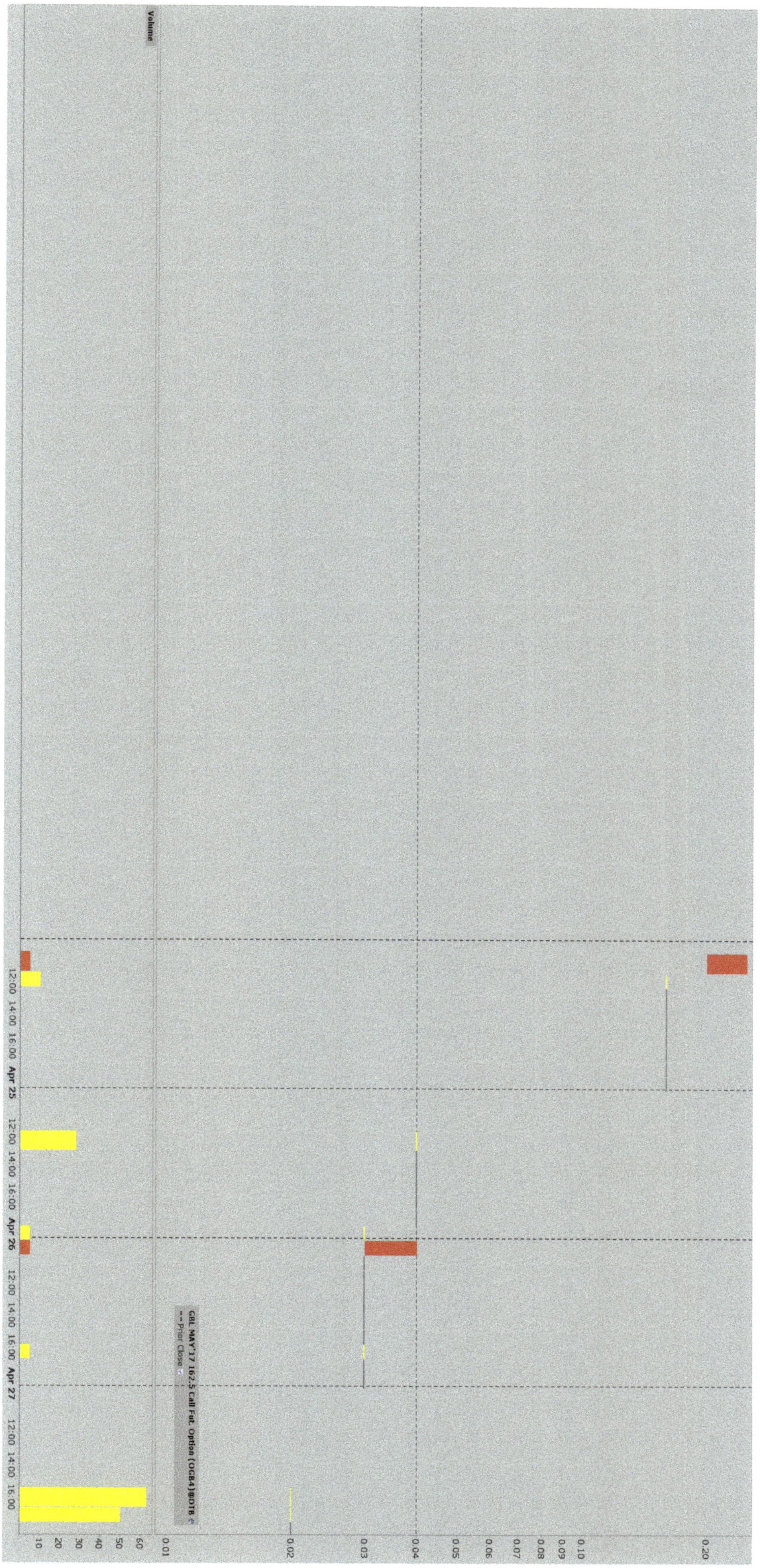
Volume
GRL MAY'17 162.5 Call Fut. Option (OGB4) @DTR
Prior Close
12:00 14:00 16:00 Apr 25 12:00 14:00 16:00 Apr 26 12:00 14:00 16:00 Apr 27 12:00 14:00 16:00
10 20 30 40 50 60
0.01 0.02 0.03 0.04 0.05 0.06 0.07 0.08 0.09 0.10 0.20

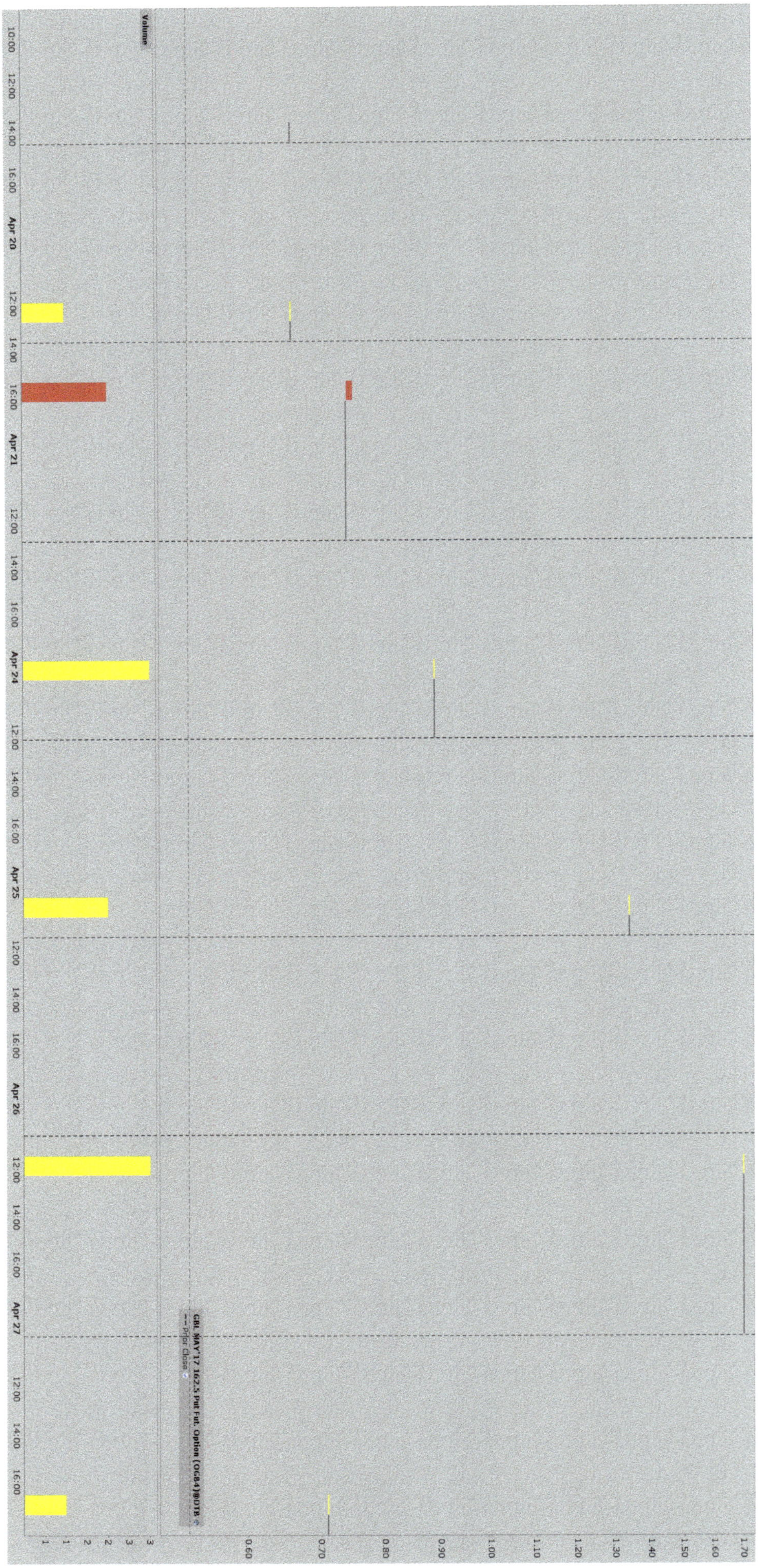

GBL MAY'17 163 Call Fut. Option (OGB4)@DTB
-- Prior Close
Volume
Apr 17
Apr 18
Apr 19
Apr 20
Apr 21
Apr 24
Apr 25

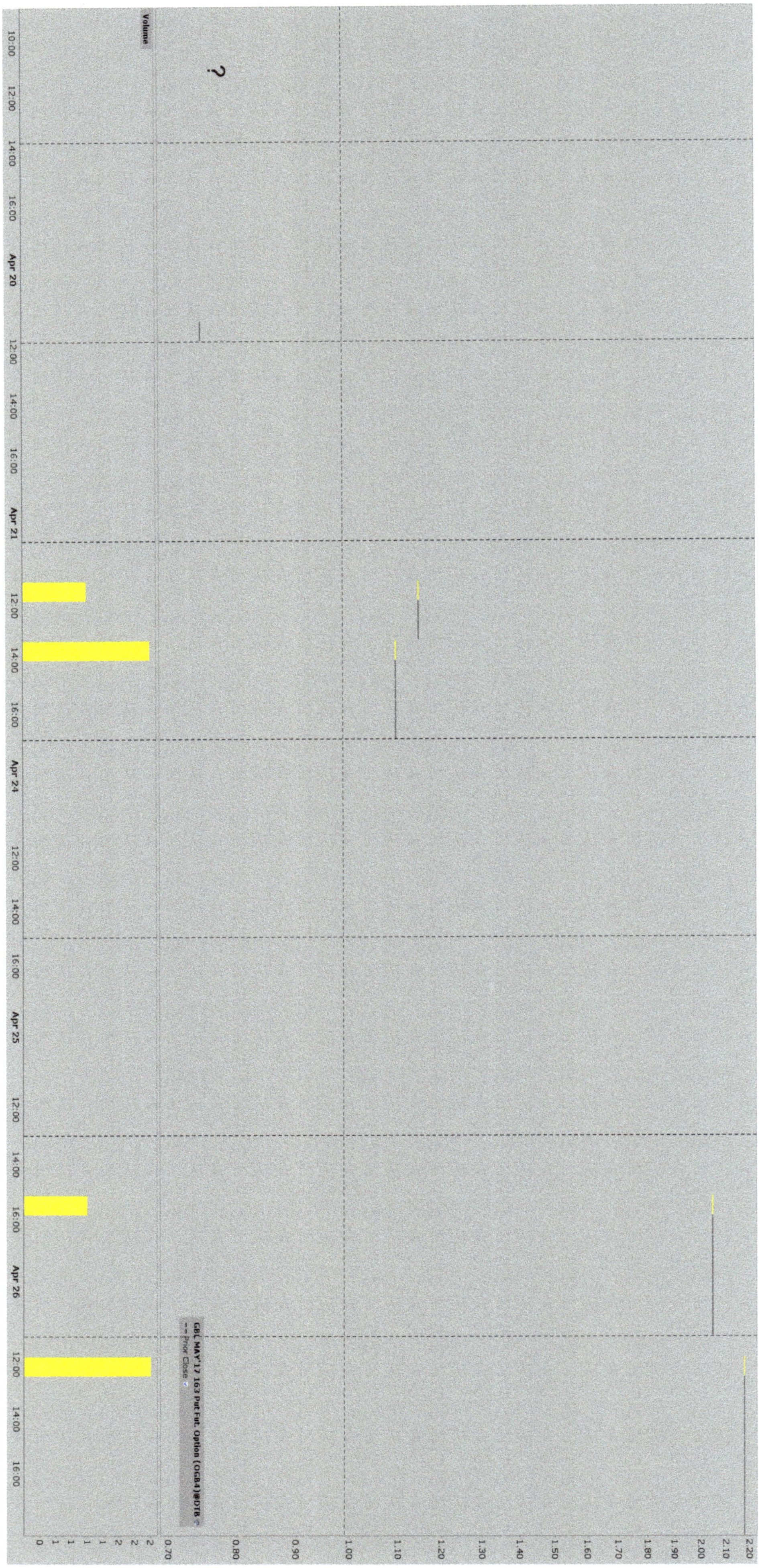
GBL MAY'17 163 Put Fut. Option (OGB4)@DTB
Prior Close
Volume
?
Apr 20
Apr 21
Apr 24
Apr 25
Apr 26
0.70
0.80
0.90
1.00
1.10
1.20
1.30
1.40
1.50
1.60
1.70
1.80
1.90
2.00
2.10
2.20

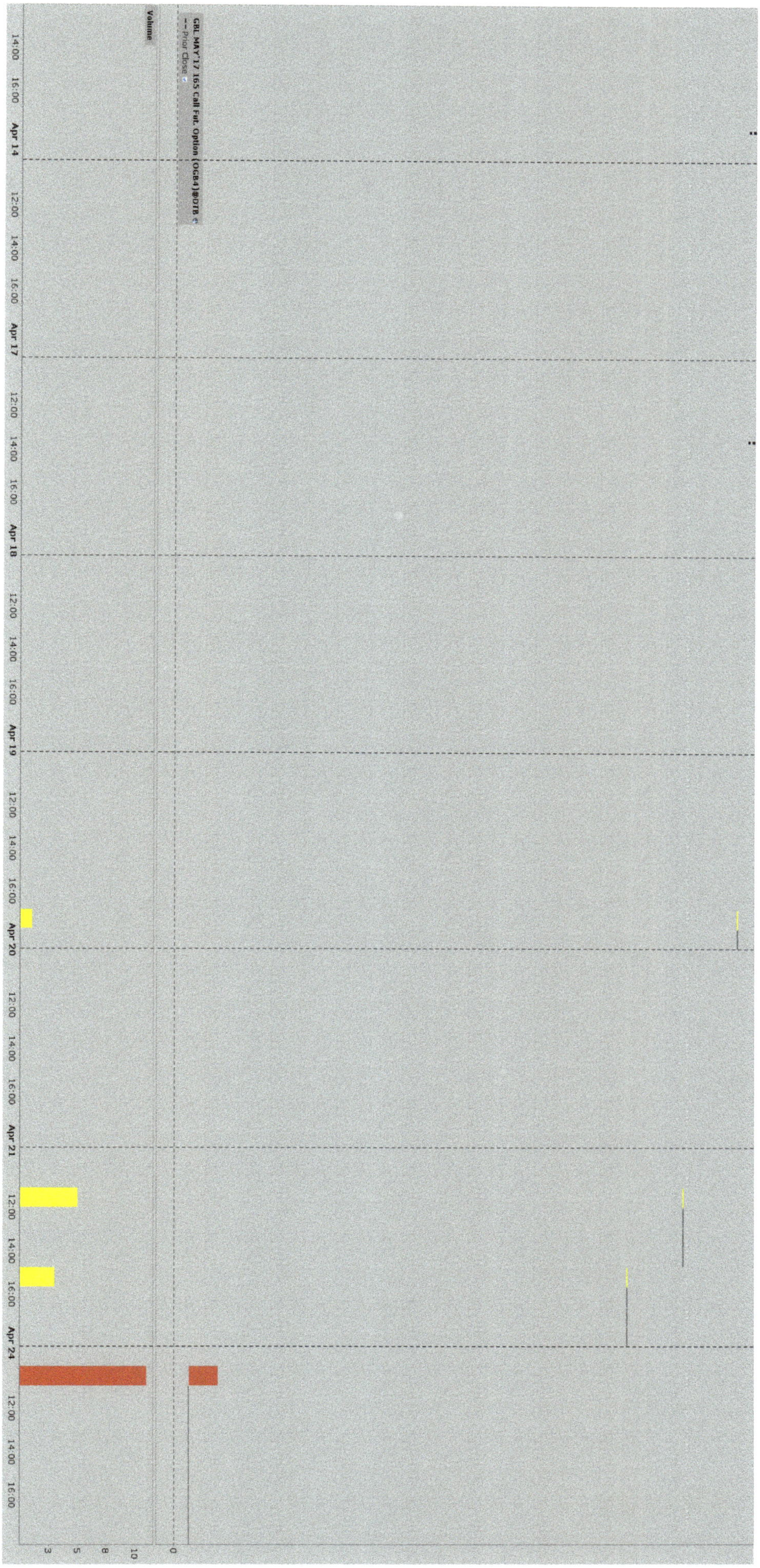
GRL MAY'17 165 Call Fut. Option [OGB4]@DTB
Prior Close
Volume
Apr 14
Apr 17
Apr 18
Apr 19
Apr 20
Apr 21
Apr 24

GBL MAY'17 166.5 Call Fut. Option (OGB4)@DTB
Prior Close
Volume
Apr 12
Apr 13
Apr 14
Apr 17
Apr 18
Apr 19
Apr 20

GBL MAY OPTIONS GRAPHICS

GBL MAY'17 159 Call Fut. Option (OGBL)@DTB
Prior Close
Wilder MA(9)
Volume
VTX (14)
VI+
VI-

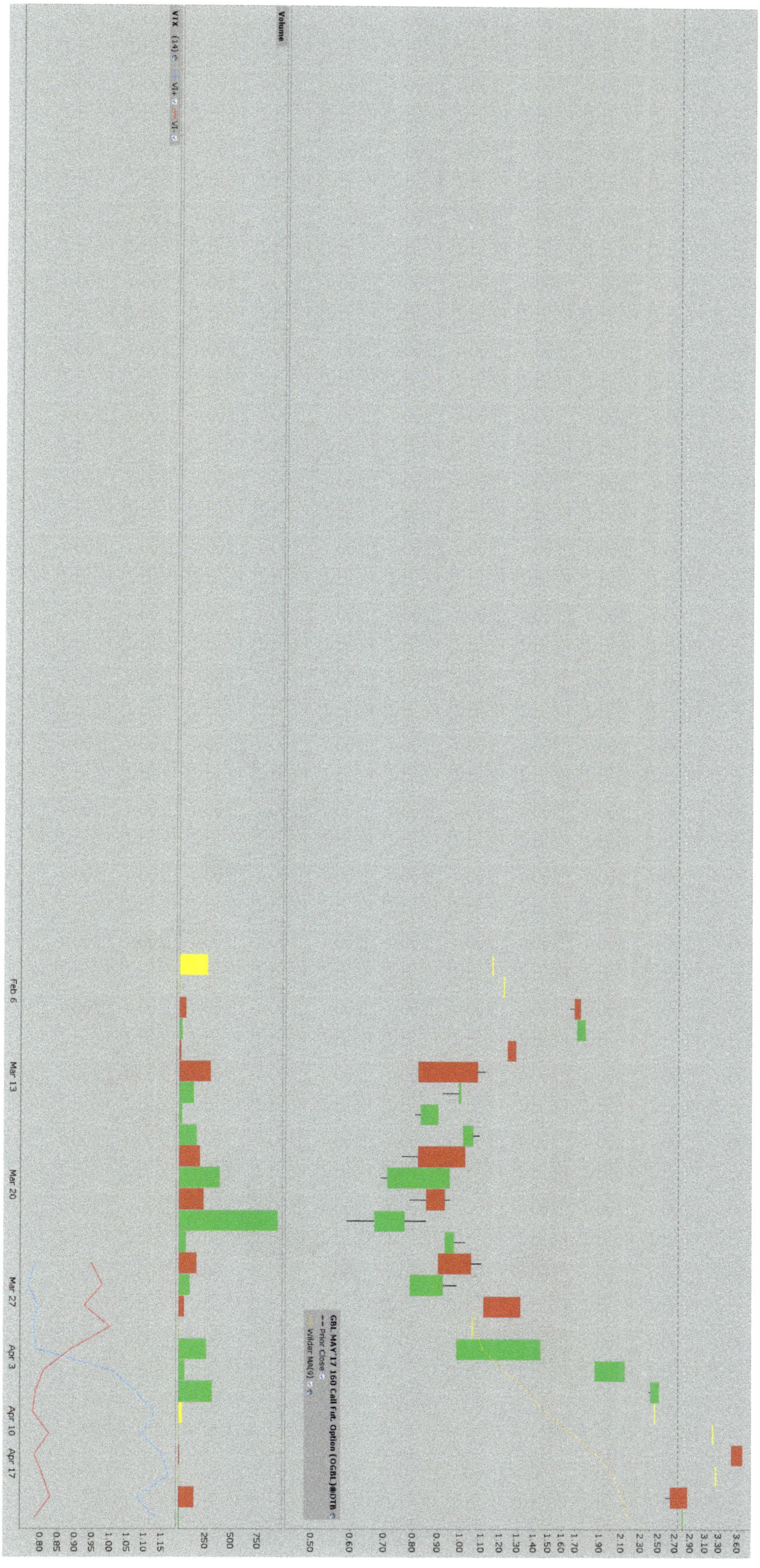
VIX (14) — VI+ — VI-
Volume
GBL MAY'17 160 Call Fut. Option (OGBL) @DTB
Prior Close
Wilder MA(9)
Feb 6
Mar 13
Mar 20
Mar 27
Apr 3
Apr 10
Apr 17
0.80
0.85
0.90
0.95
1.00
1.05
1.10
1.15
250
500
750
0.50
0.60
0.70
0.80
0.90
1.00
1.10
1.20
1.30
1.40
1.50
1.60
1.70
1.90
2.10
2.30
2.50
2.70
2.90
3.10
3.30
3.60

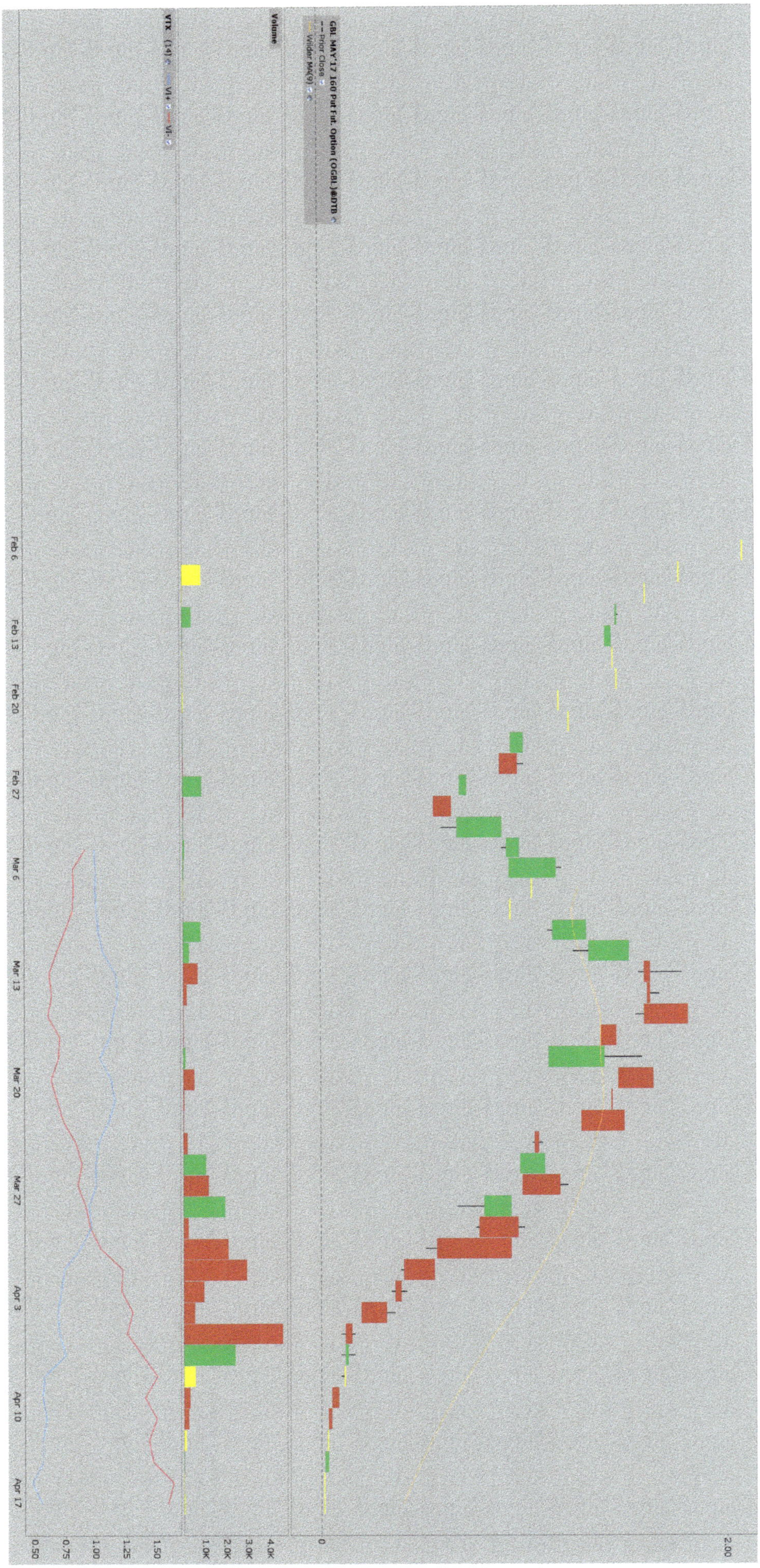
GBL MAY'17 160 Put Fut. Option (OGBL) @DTB
Prior Close
Wider MA(9)
Volume
VTX (14)
VI+
VI-
Feb 6
Feb 13
Feb 20
Feb 27
Mar 6
Mar 13
Mar 20
Mar 27
Apr 3
Apr 10
Apr 17
2.00
0
4.0K
3.0K
2.0K
1.0K
1.50
1.25
1.00
0.75
0.50

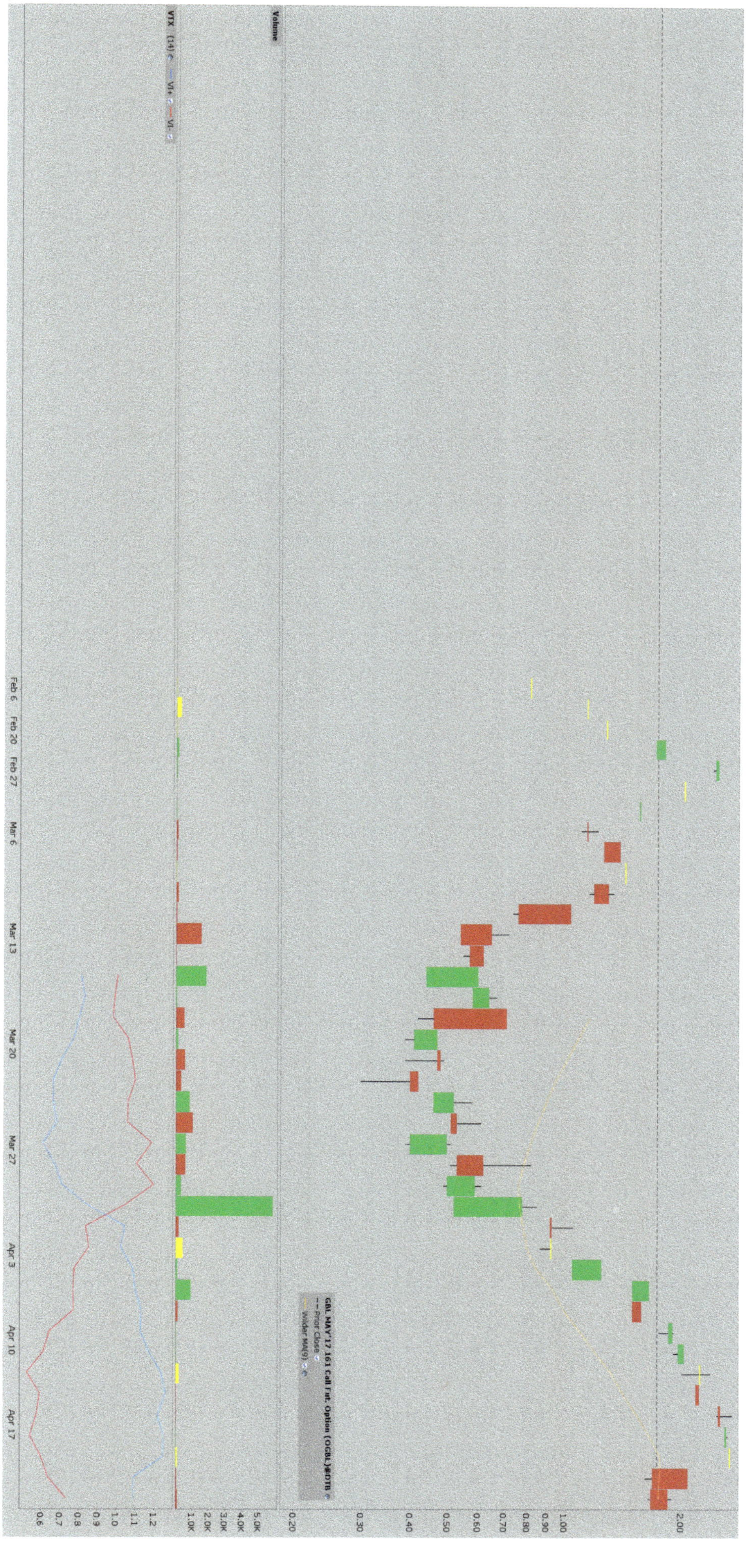
GBL MAY'17 161 Call Fut. Option (OGBL)@DTB
Prior Close
Wilder MA(9)
Volume
VTX (14)
VI+
VI-
Feb 6
Feb 20
Feb 27
Mar 6
Mar 13
Mar 20
Mar 27
Apr 3
Apr 10
Apr 17

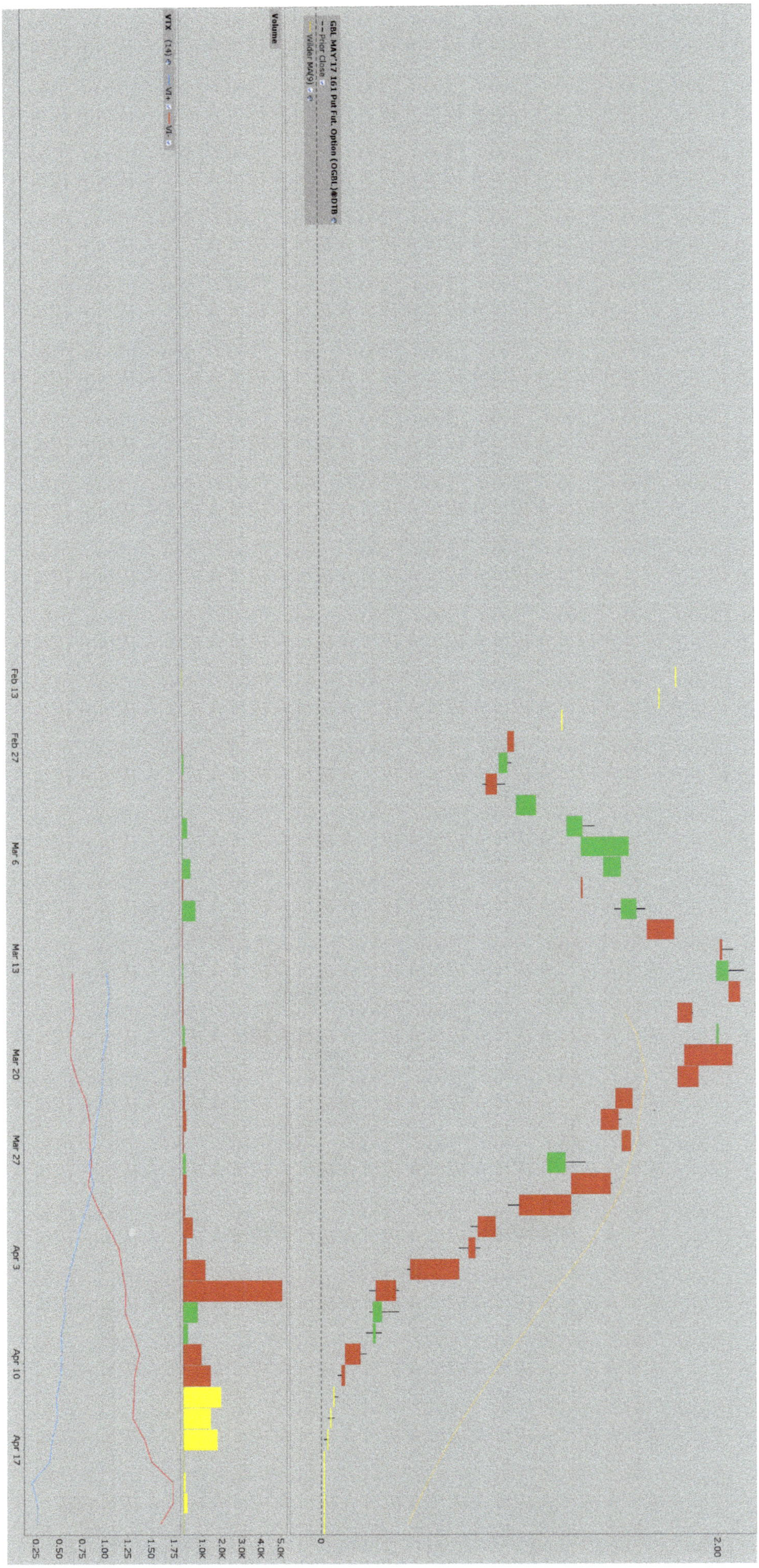
GBL MAY'17 161 Put Fut. Option (OGBL)@DTB
Prior Close
Wilder MA(9)
Volume
VTX (14)
VI+
VI-
Feb 13
Feb 27
Mar 6
Mar 13
Mar 20
Mar 27
Apr 3
Apr 10
Apr 17
2.00
0
5.0K
4.0K
3.0K
2.0K
1.0K
1.75
1.50
1.25
1.00
0.75
0.50
0.25

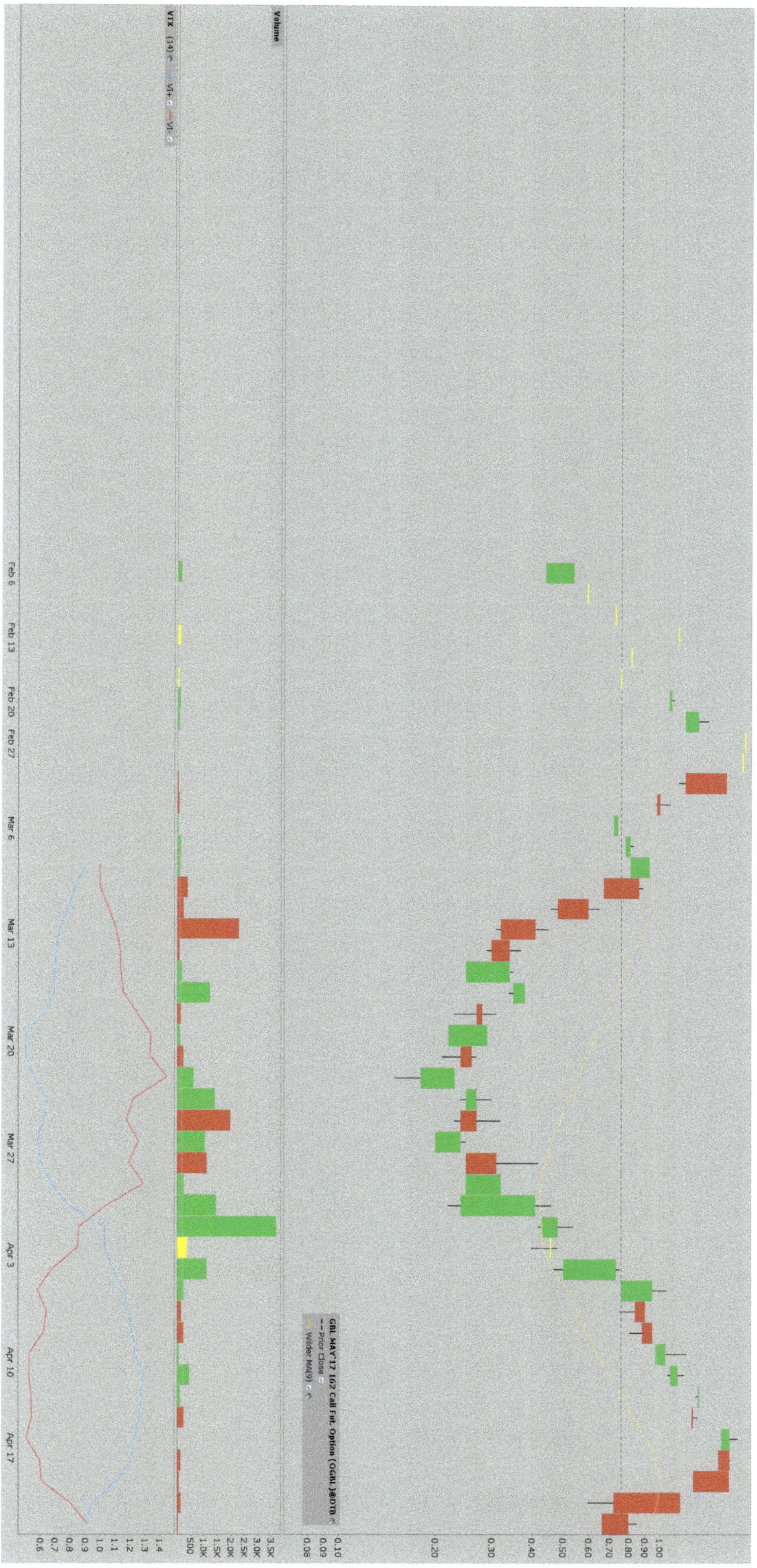

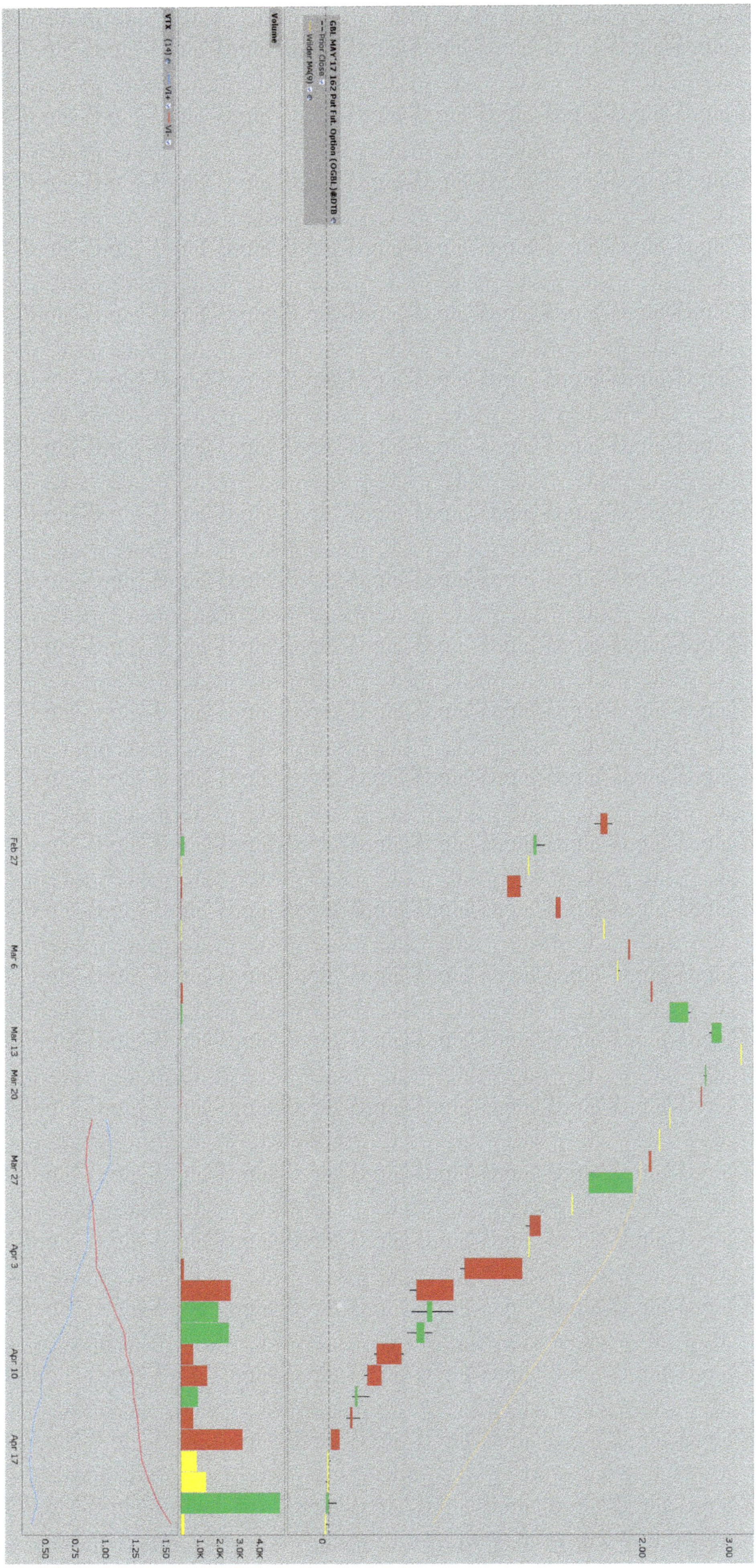
GBL MAY'17 162 Put Fut. Option (OGBL)@DTB
Prior Close
Wilder MA(9)
Volume
VTX (14)
VI+
VI-
Feb 27
Mar 6
Mar 13
Mar 20
Mar 27
Apr 3
Apr 10
Apr 17
0
2.00
3.00
1.0K
2.0K
3.0K
4.0K
0.50
0.75
1.00
1.25
1.50

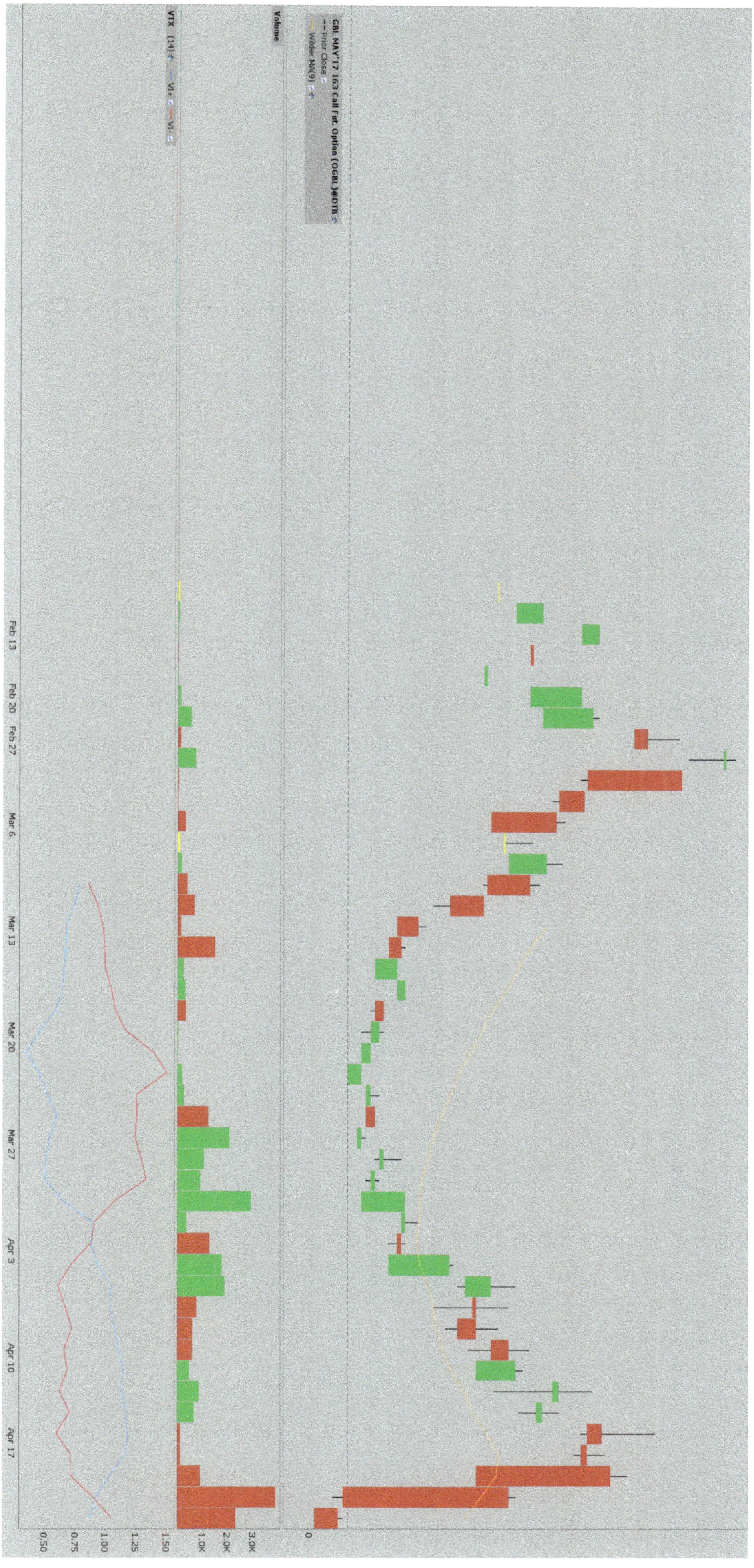
GBL MAY'17 163 Call Fut. Option (OGBL)@DTB
Prior Close
Wider MA(9)
Volume
VTX (14)
VI+
VI-
Feb 13
Feb 20
Feb 27
Mar 6
Mar 13
Mar 20
Mar 27
Apr 3
Apr 10
Apr 17
0
1.0K
2.0K
3.0K
0.50
0.75
1.00
1.25
1.50

GBL MAY'17 163 Put Fut. Option (OGBL)@DTB
Prior Close
Wilder MA(9)
Volume
VTX (14)
VI+
VI-
Mar 1
Mar 7
Mar 17
Apr 6
Apr 10
Apr 12
Apr 18
Apr 20
0
2.00
3.00
500
1.0K
1.5K
2.0K
2.5K
3.0K
3.5K
0.875
0.900
0.925
0.950
0.975

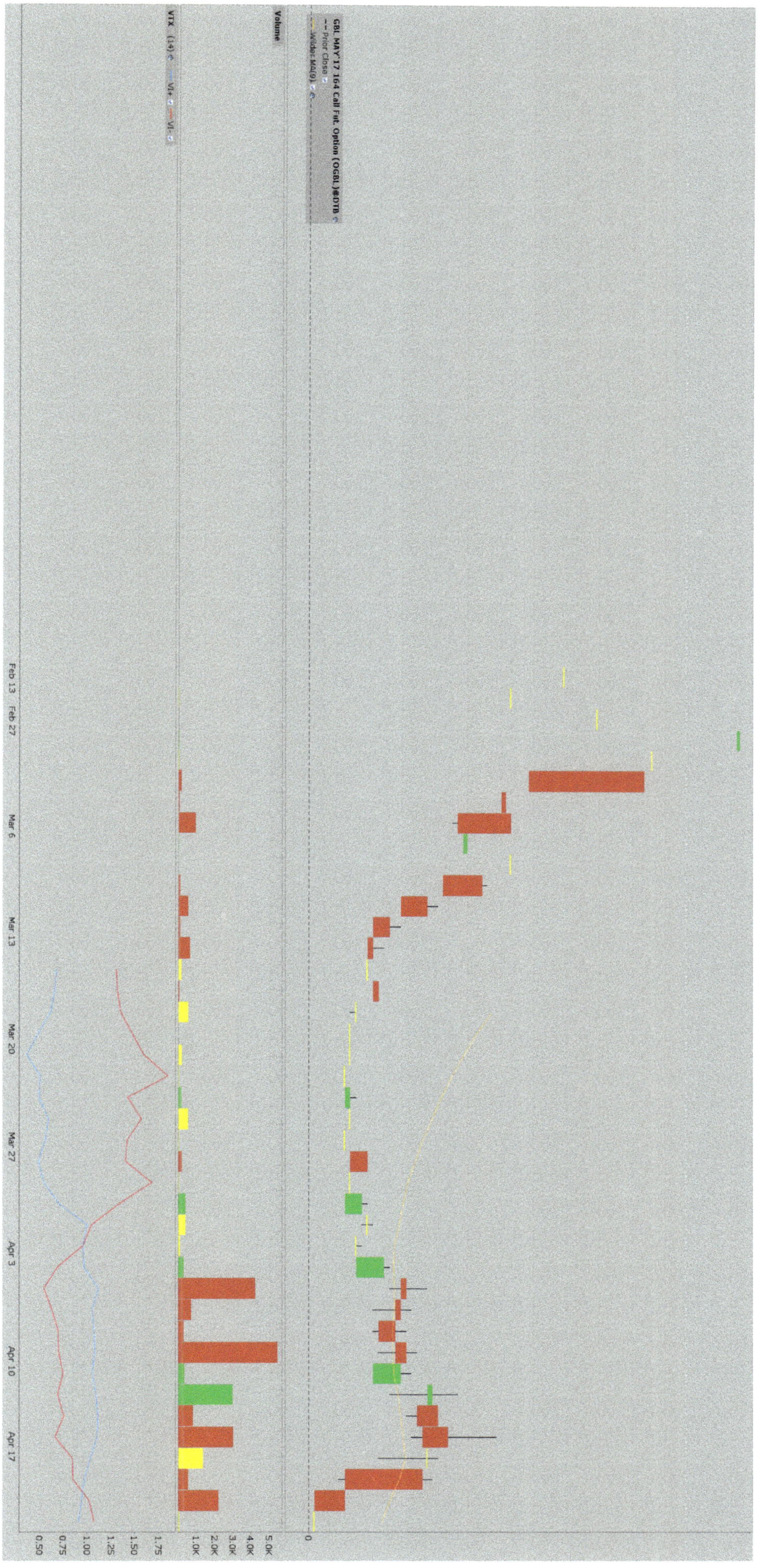
GBL MAY'17 164 Call Fut. Option (OGBL)@DTB
-- Prior Close
Volume
VTX (14)
VI+
VI-
Feb 13
Feb 27
Mar 6
Mar 13
Mar 20
Mar 27
Apr 3
Apr 10
Apr 17
0
5.0K
4.0K
3.0K
2.0K
1.0K
1.75
1.50
1.25
1.00
0.75
0.50

OGB1 2 JUNE GRAPHICS

Volume
May 23
May 24
May 25
May 26
GBL JUL17 162 Put Fut. Option [OGB1]@DTB
-- Prior Close
0
5
10
15
20
25
30
35

GBL JUL'17 162.5 Put Fut. Option (OGB1)@DTB
-- Prior Close
Volume
May 22
May 23
May 24
May 25
May 26
May 29
May 30
3
5
8
10
13
0

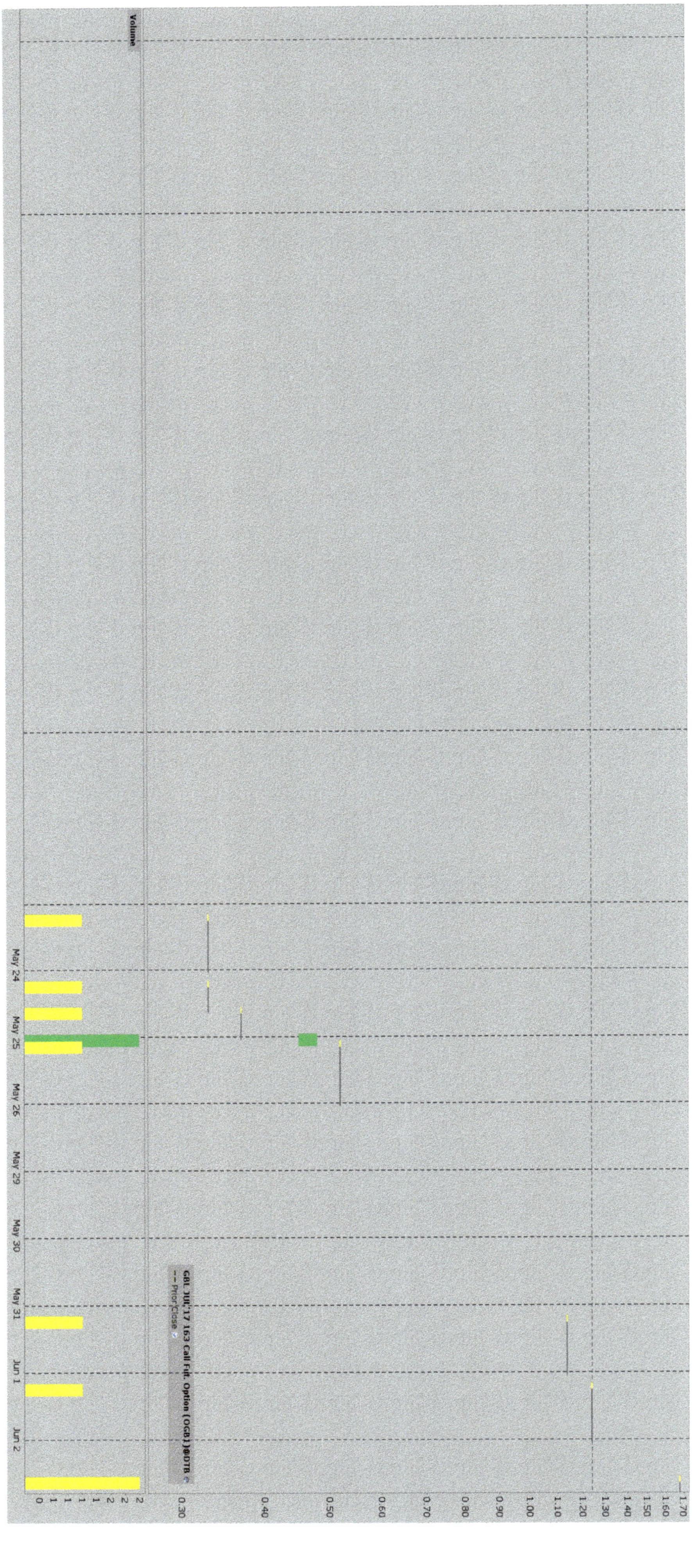
Volume
GBL JUL'17 163 Call Fut. Option (OGBJ)@DTB
-- Prior Close
May 24
May 25
May 26
May 29
May 30
May 31
Jun 1
Jun 2
0
1
1
1
1
2
2
2
0.30
0.40
0.50
0.60
0.70
0.80
0.90
1.00
1.10
1.20
1.30
1.40
1.50
1.60
1.70

Volume
May 19
May 23
May 25
May 29
May 31

Volume
GBL JUL 17 163.5 Call Fut.-Option (OGBL1)@DTB
-- Prior Close
May 16
May 17
May 18
May 19
May 22
May 23
May 24
May 25
May 26
May 29
5
10
15
20
25
0.20
0.30
0.40
0.50
0.60
0.70
0.80

Volume
GBL JUL 17 164 Call Fut. Option [OGB1]@DTB
-- Prior Close
15:00 May 19 12:00 15:00 May 22 12:00 15:00 May 23 12:00 15:00 May 24 12:00 15:00 May 25 12:00 15:00 May 26 12:00 15:00 May 29 12:00 15:00 May 30 12:00 15:00 May 31 12:00 15:00 Jun 1 12:00 15:00 Jun 2 12:00
10 20 30 40 50
0.09 0.10 0.20 0.30 0.40 0.50

Volume
GBL JUL '17 164 Put Fut. Option (OGBL)@DTB
-- Prior Close
May 31
Jun 1
Jun 2

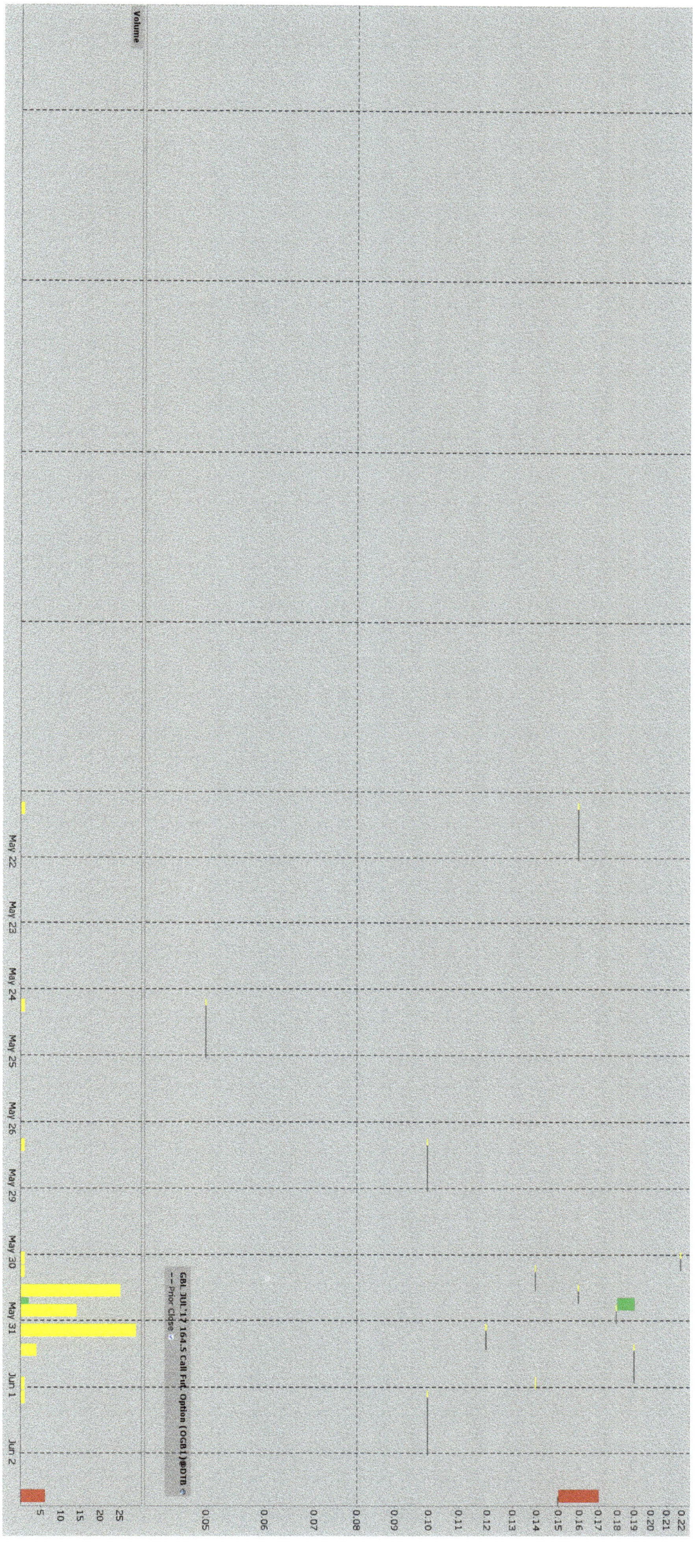
Volume
GBL JUL'17 164.5 Call Fut. Option (OGBL) @DTB
-- Prior close
May 22
May 23
May 24
May 25
May 26
May 29
May 30
May 31
Jun 1
Jun 2
5
10
15
20
25
0.05
0.06
0.07
0.08
0.09
0.10
0.11
0.12
0.13
0.14
0.15
0.16
0.17
0.18
0.19
0.20
0.21
0.22

GBL JUL 17 165 Call Fut. Option (OGBL)@DTB
-- Prior Close
Volume
May 22
May 24
May 26
May 30
0.01
0.02
0.03
0.04
0.05
0.06
0.07
0.08
0.09
0.10
1
2
3
4
5

9 JUNE OGBL2 GRAPHICS

Volume
GBL JUL'17 164 Call Fut. Option (OGB2)@DTB
-- Prior Close
May 29
May 31
Jun 2
Jun 6
Jun 8
10
20
30
40
50
60
0.30
0.40
0.50
0.60
0.70
0.80
0.90

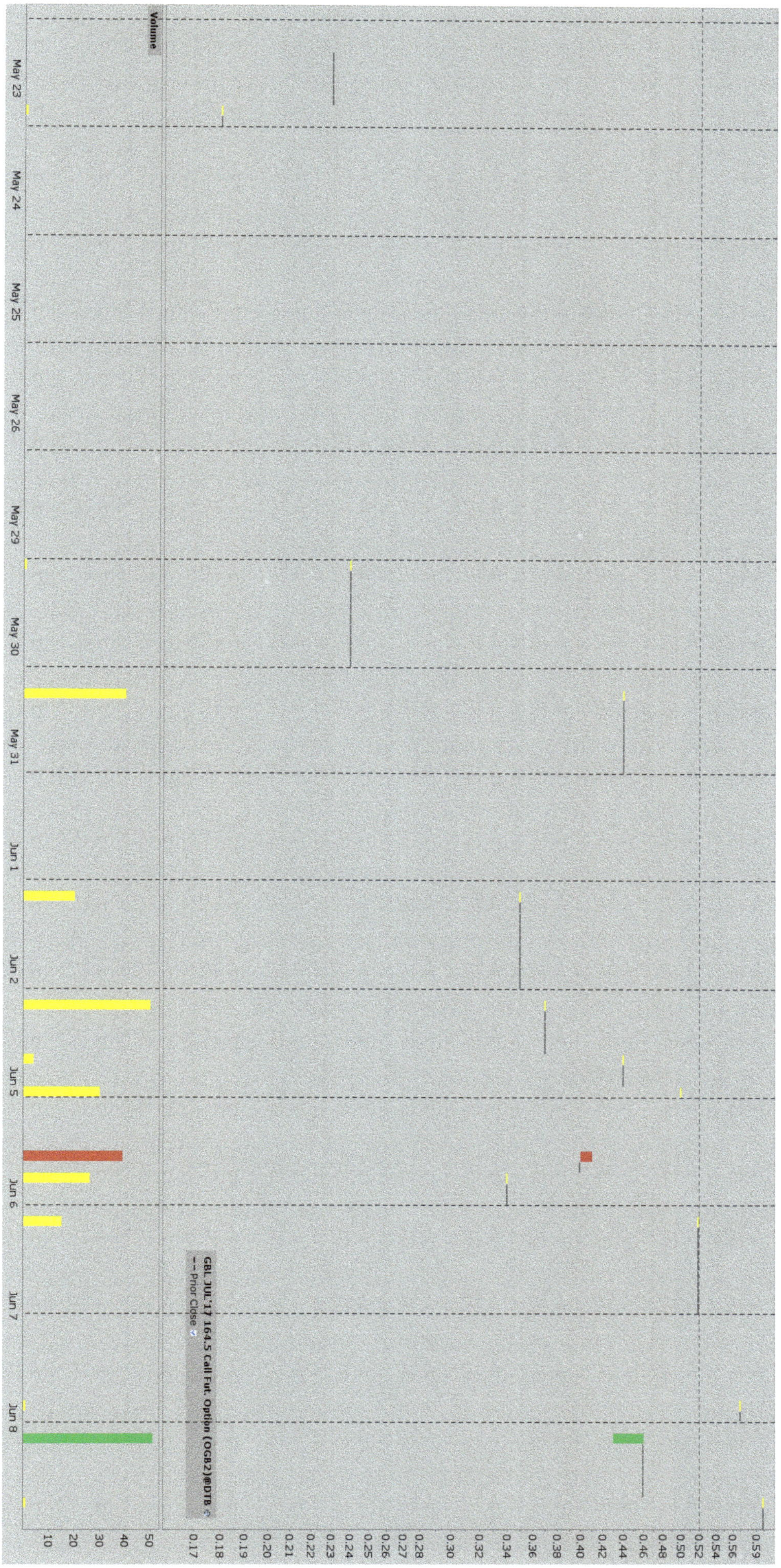
GBL JUL17 164.5 Call Fut. Option (OGB2)@DTB
-- Prior Close
Volume
May 23
May 24
May 25
May 26
May 29
May 30
May 31
Jun 1
Jun 2
Jun 5
Jun 6
Jun 7
Jun 8
10
20
30
40
50
0.17
0.18
0.19
0.20
0.21
0.22
0.23
0.24
0.25
0.26
0.27
0.28
0.30
0.32
0.34
0.36
0.38
0.40
0.42
0.44
0.46
0.48
0.50
0.52
0.54
0.56
0.59

Volume
Prior Close
Jun 5
Jun 6
Jun 7
Jun 8

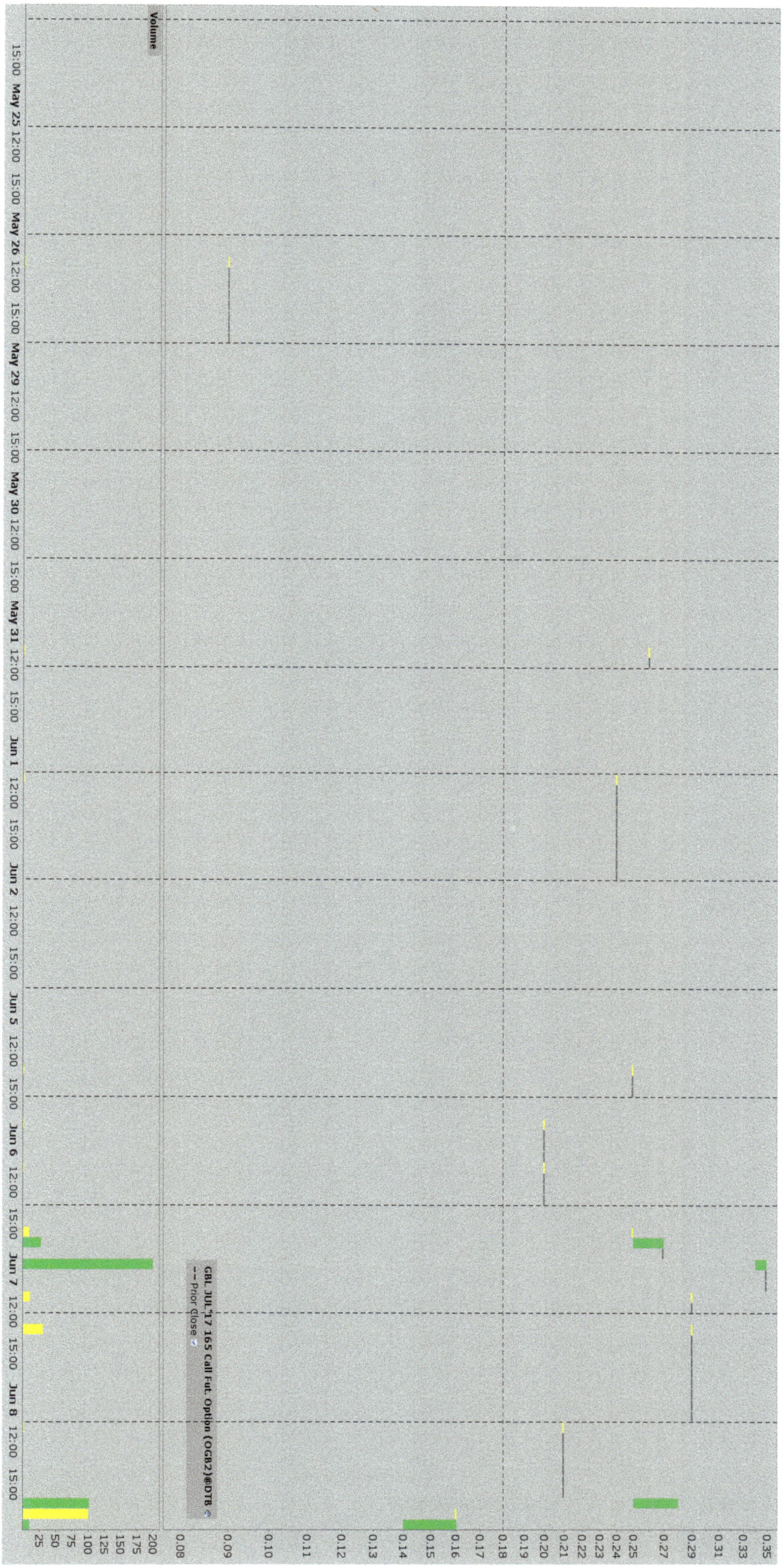
Volume
GBL JUL'17 165 Call Fut. Option (OGB2)@DTB
-- Prior close
15:00 May 25 12:00 15:00 May 26 12:00 15:00 May 29 12:00 15:00 May 30 12:00 15:00 May 31 12:00 15:00 Jun 1 12:00 15:00 Jun 2 12:00 15:00 Jun 5 12:00 15:00 Jun 6 12:00 15:00 Jun 7 12:00 15:00 Jun 8 12:00 15:00
25 50 75 100 125 150 175 200
0.08 0.09 0.10 0.11 0.12 0.13 0.14 0.15 0.16 0.17 0.18 0.19 0.20 0.21 0.22 0.23 0.24 0.25 0.27 0.29 0.31 0.33 0.35

Volume
GBL JUL'17 165 Put Fut. Option (OGBZ)@DTB
-- Prior Close
Jun 7
Jun 8
Jun 9
25
50
75
100
125
0.12
0.13
0.14
0.15
0.16
0.17
0.18
0.19
0.20
0.21
0.22
0.23
0.24
0.25
0.26
0.27
0.28
0.29
0.30
0.31
0.32
0.34
0.36
0.38

GBL JUL'17 165.5 Call Fut. Option (OGB2)@DTB
-- Prior Close
Volume
May 31
Jun 2
Jun 6
Jun 8
25
50
75
100
125
150
175
200
0.04
0.05
0.06
0.07
0.08
0.09
0.10
0.11
0.12
0.13
0.14
0.15
0.16

16 JUNE OGBL3 OPTION GRAPHICS

Volume
GBL JUL'17 164 Call Fut. Option (OGB3)@DTB
-- Prior Close

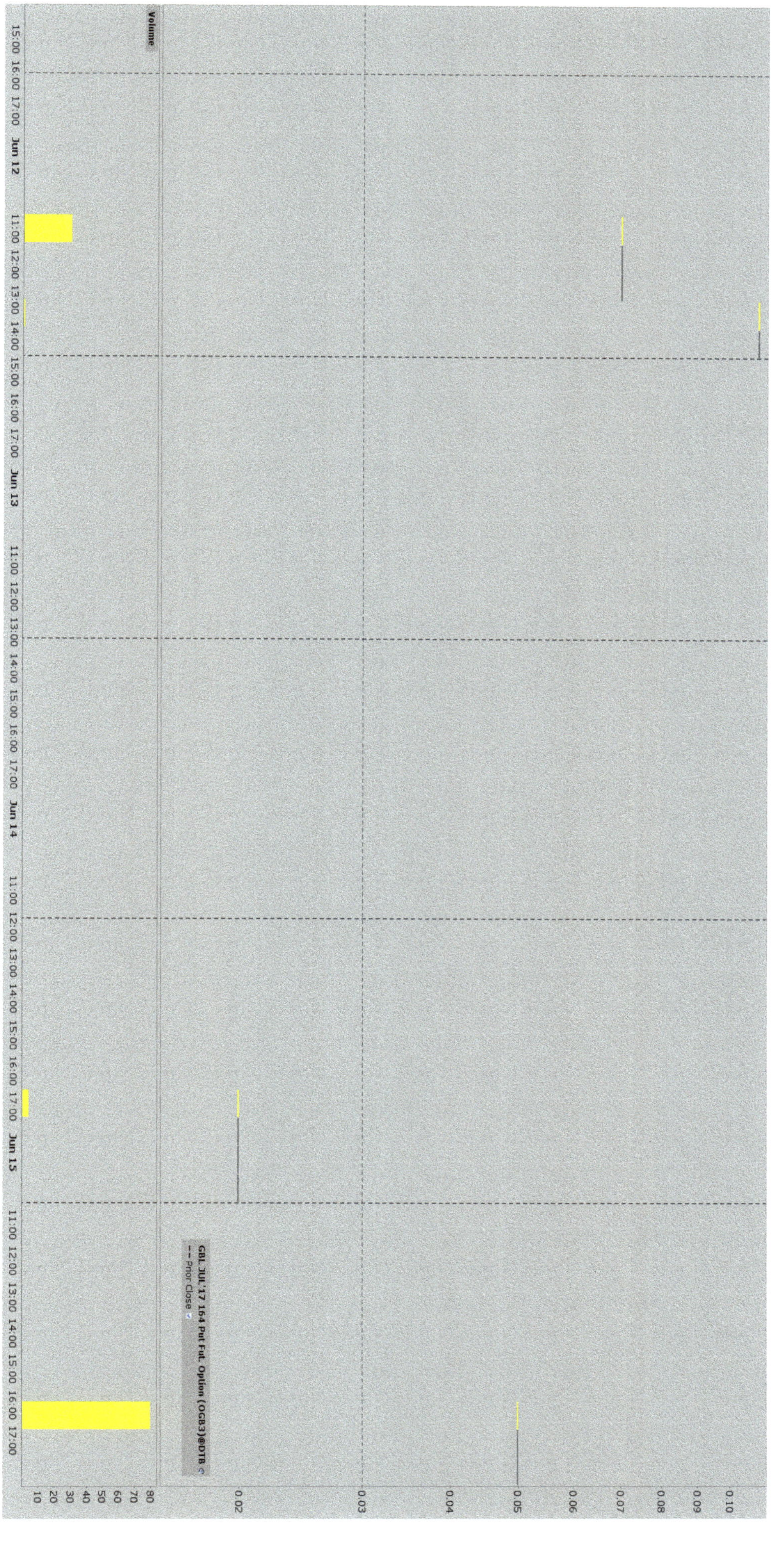
GBL JUL'17 16.4 Put Fut. Option (OGB3)@DTB
-- Prior Close
Volume
0.02
0.03
0.04
0.05
0.06
0.07
0.08
0.09
0.10
Jun 12
Jun 13
Jun 14
Jun 15

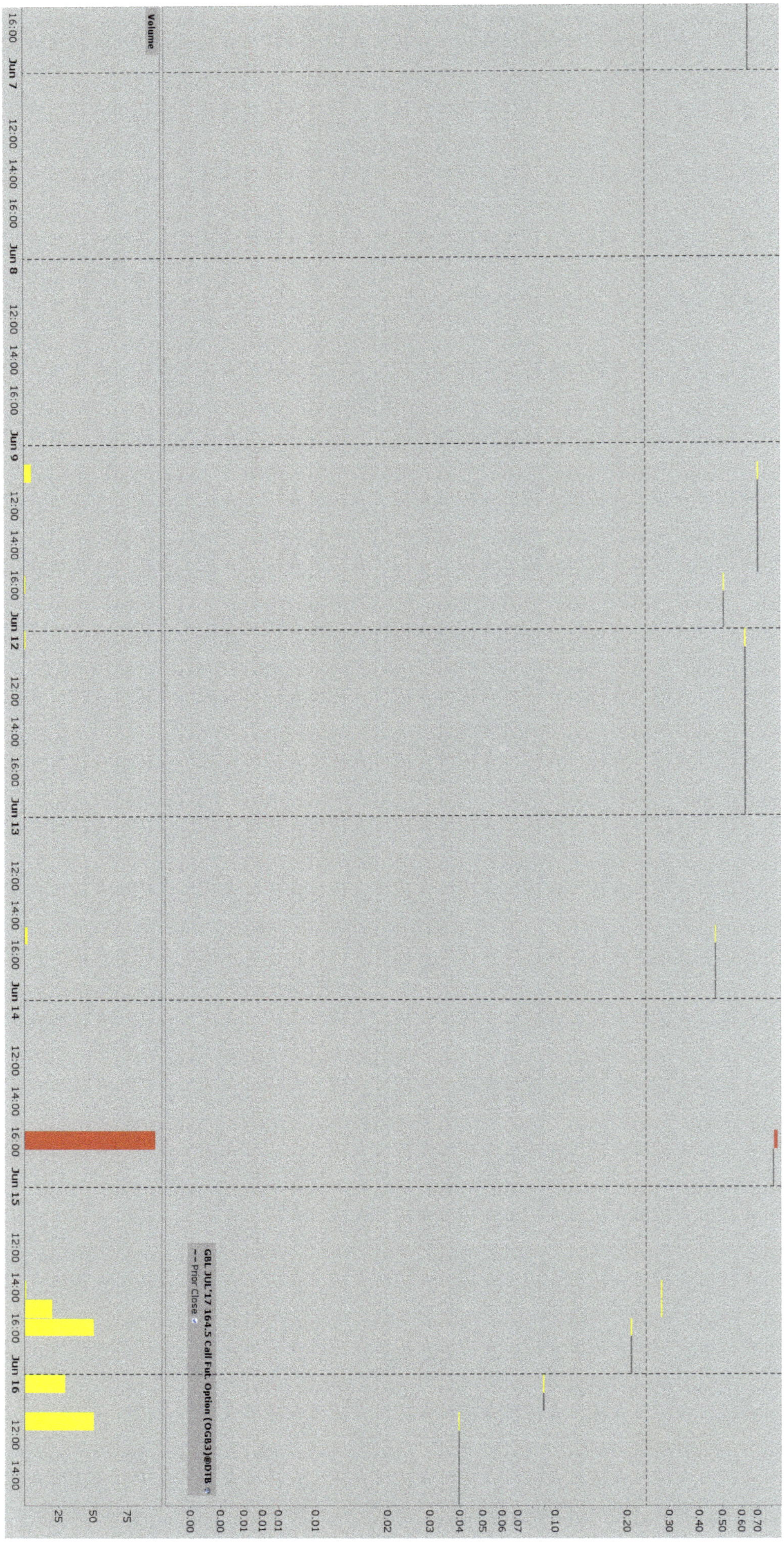
GBL JUL'17 164.5 Call Fut. Option (OGB3)@DTB
-- Prior Close
Volume

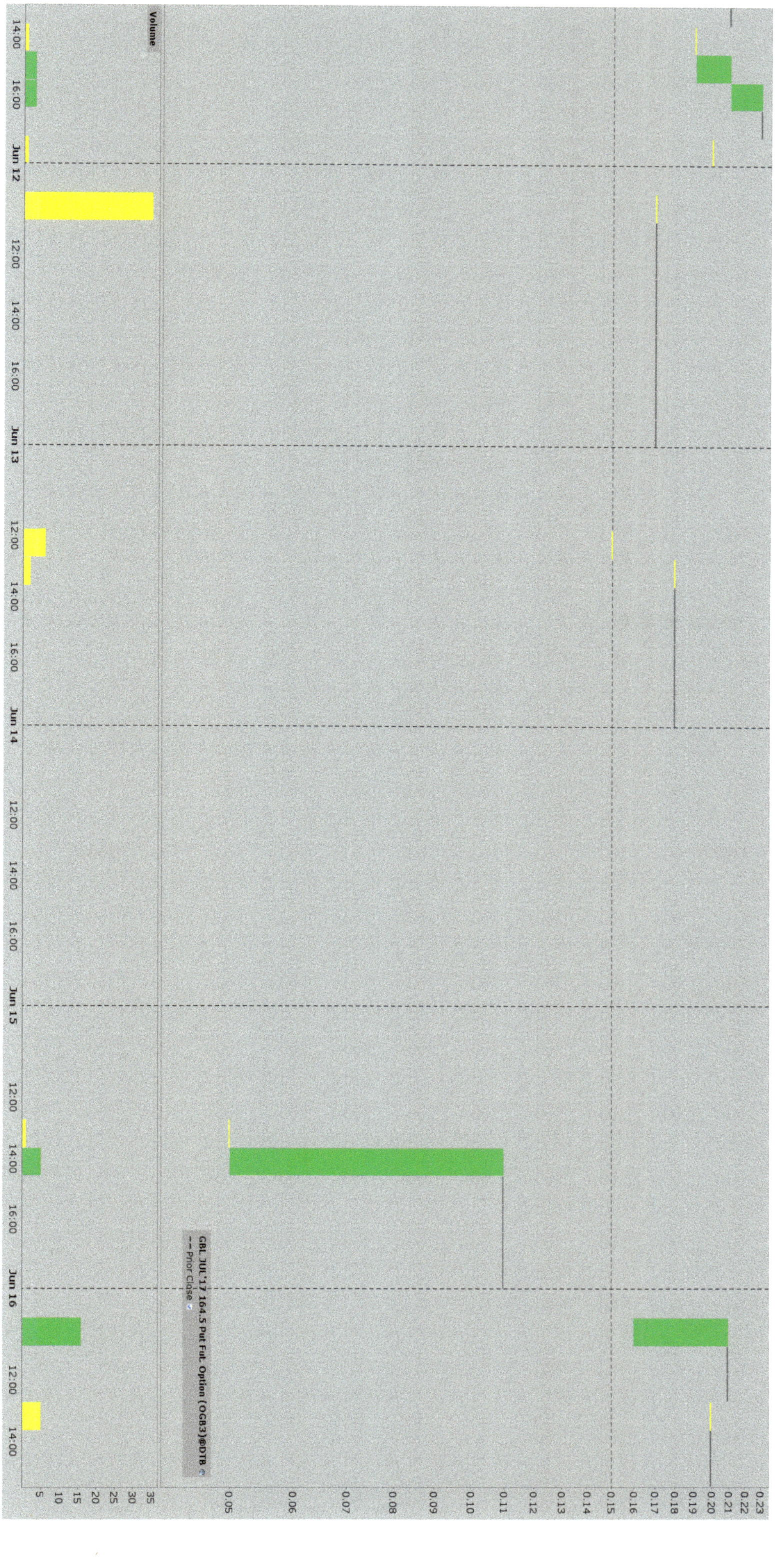

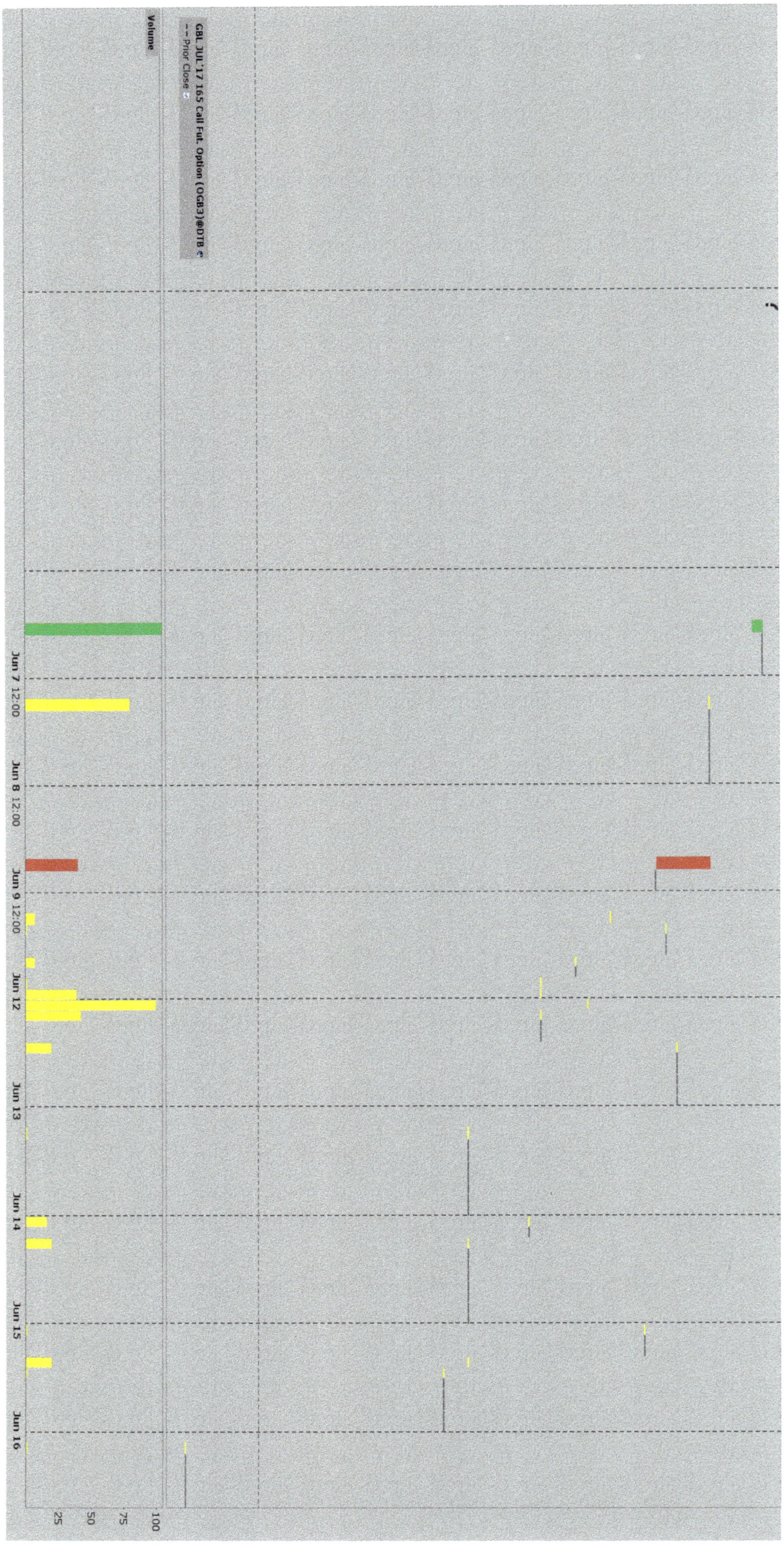
GBL JUL'17 165 Call Fut. Option (OGB3)@DTB
Prior Close
Volume
Jun 7 12:00
Jun 8 12:00
Jun 9 12:00
Jun 12
Jun 13
Jun 14
Jun 15
Jun 16
25
50
75
100

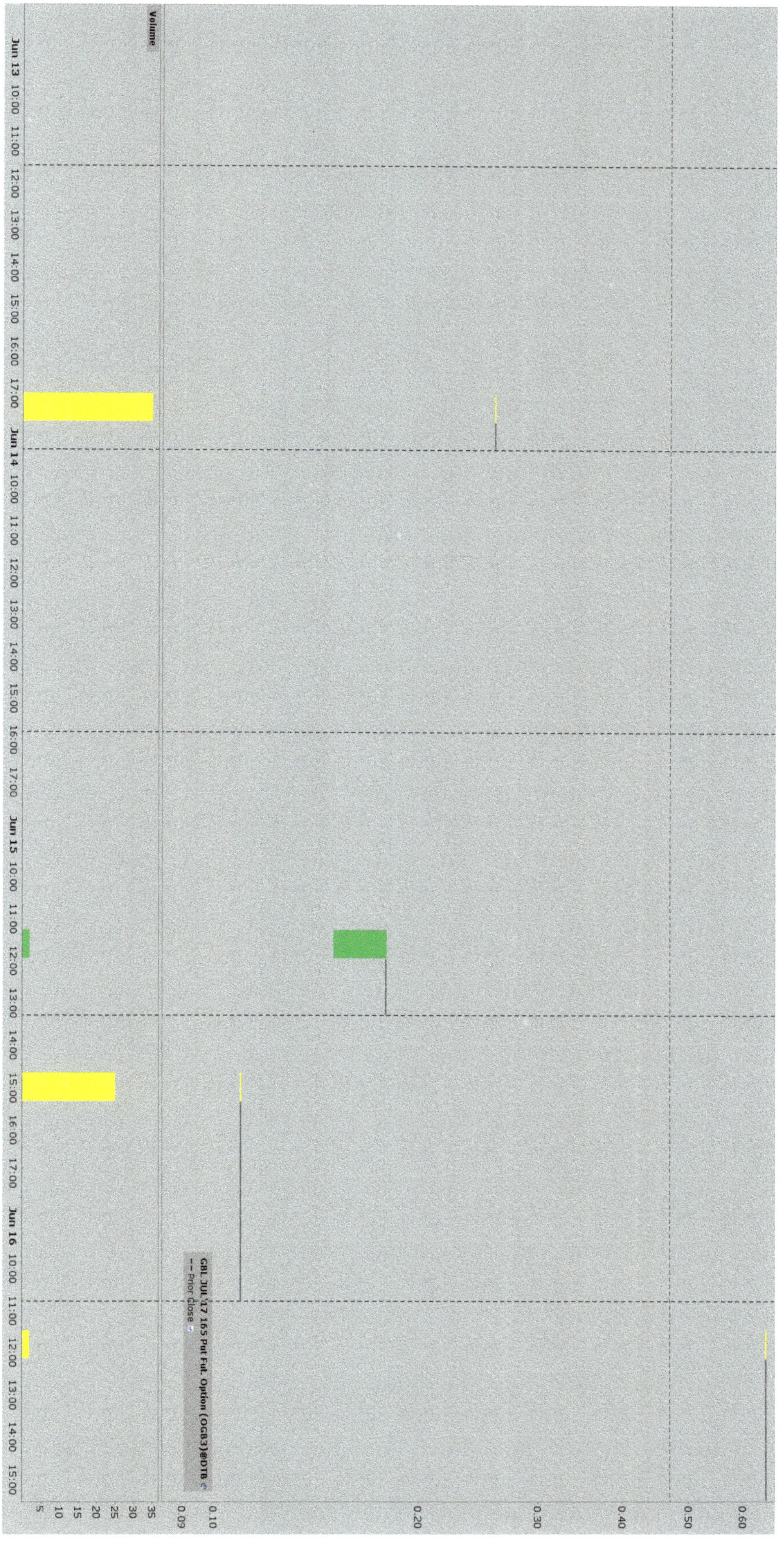
GBL JUL '17 165 Put Fut. Option (OGB3)@DTB
-- Prior Close
Volume
Jun 13
Jun 14
Jun 15
Jun 16
0.09
0.10
0.20
0.30
0.40
0.50
0.60

GBL JUL'17 165.5 Put Fut. Option (OGB3)@DTB
Prior Close
Volume
Jun 15
12:00
14:00
16:00
0.25
0.50
0.75
1.00
0.30
0.40
0.50
0.60
0.70
0.80
0.90

GBL JUL'17 165.5 Call Fut. Option (OGB3)@DTB
-- Prior Close
Volume
Jun 6
Jun 7
Jun 8
Jun 9
Jun 12
Jun 13
Jun 14
Jun 15

GBL JUL'17 166 Call Fut. Option (OGB3)@DTB
-- Prior Close
Volume
Jun 9
Jun 12
Jun 13
Jun 14
Jun 15
0
25
50
75
100

GBL JUNE OPTION GRAPHICS

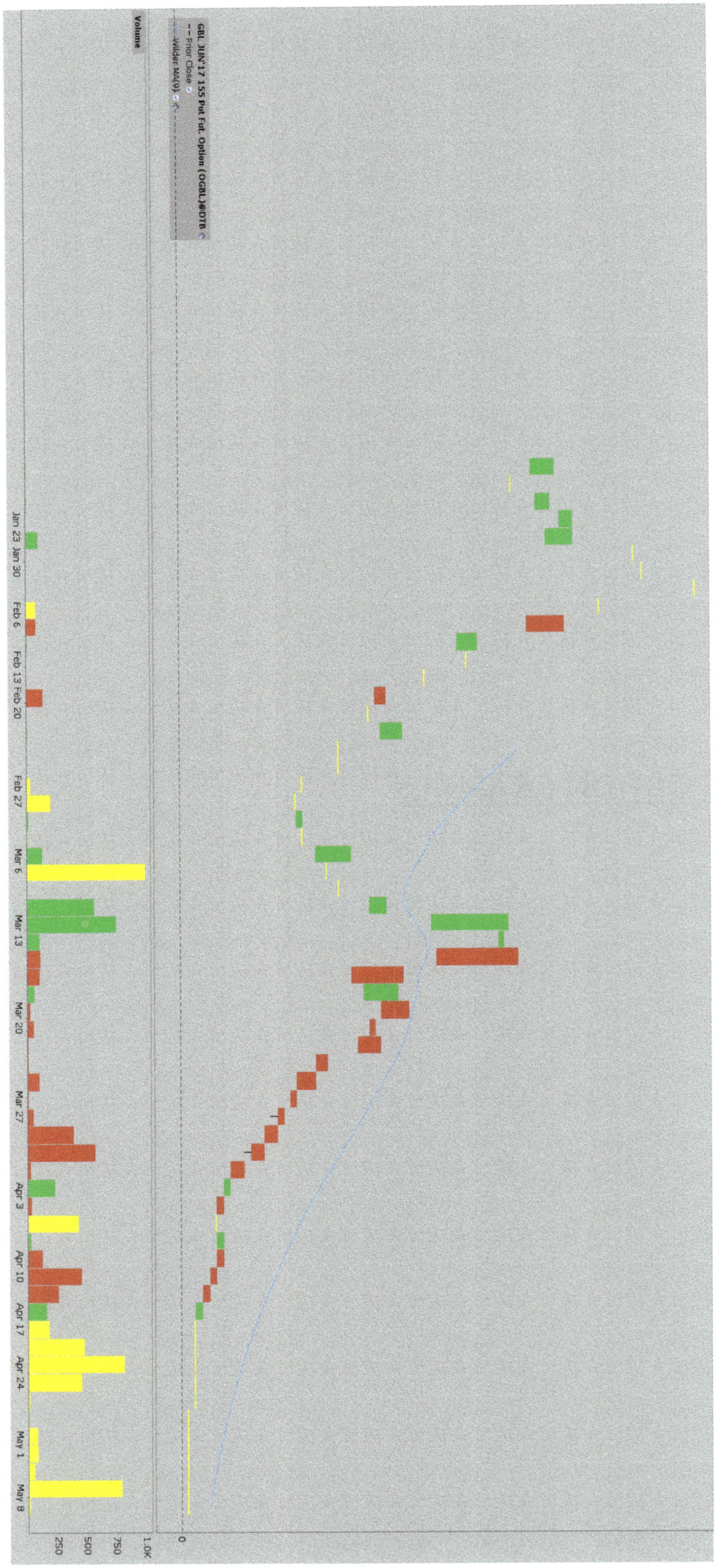
GBL JUN'17 155 Put Fut. Option (OGBL)@DTB
Prior Close
Wilder MA(9)
Volume
Jan 23
Jan 30
Feb 6
Feb 13
Feb 20
Feb 27
Mar 6
Mar 13
Mar 20
Mar 27
Apr 3
Apr 10
Apr 17
Apr 24
May 1
May 8
0
1.0K
750
500
250

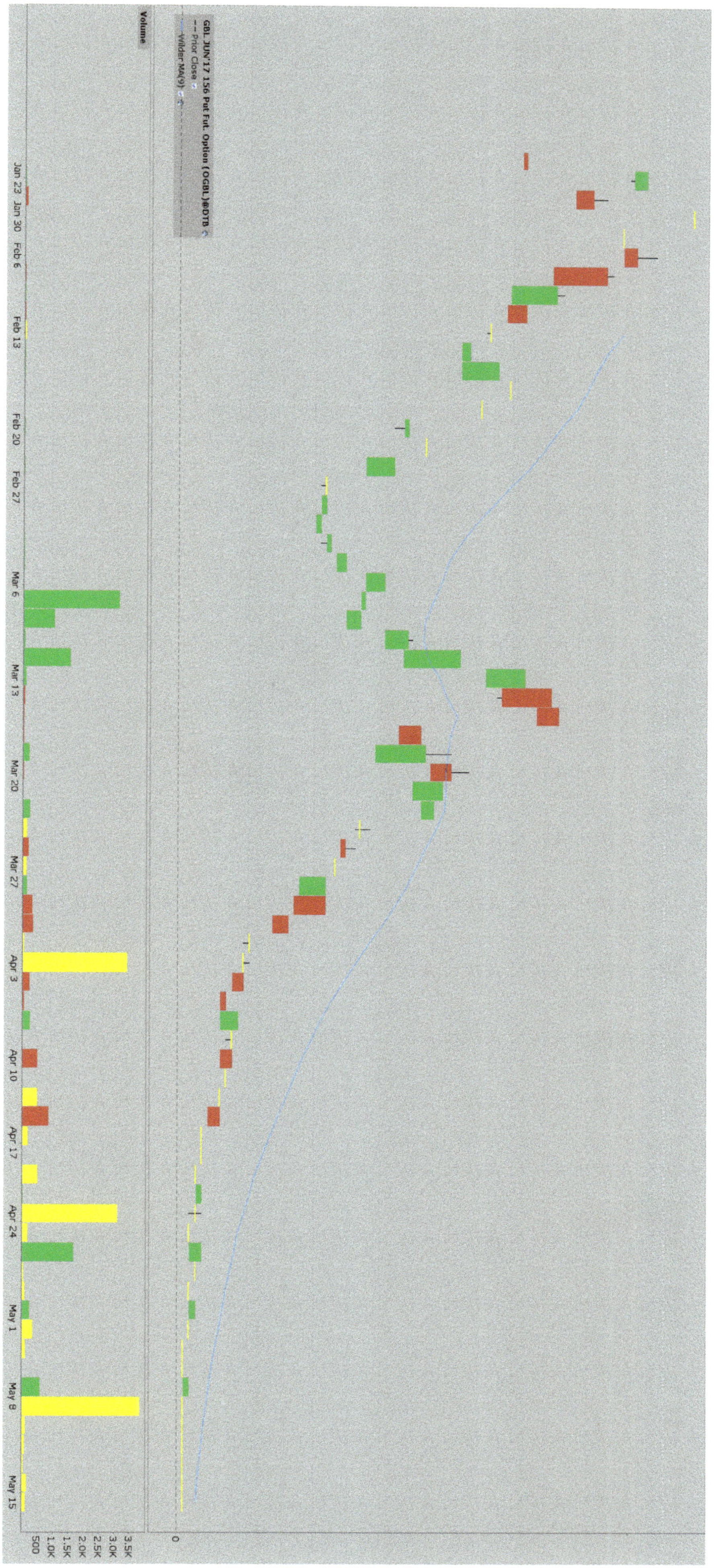
GBL JUN'17 156 Put Fut. Option (OGBL)@DTB
Prior Close
Wilder MA(9)
Volume
Jan 23
Jan 30
Feb 6
Feb 13
Feb 20
Feb 27
Mar 6
Mar 13
Mar 20
Mar 27
Apr 3
Apr 10
Apr 17
Apr 24
May 1
May 8
May 15
0
3.5K
3.0K
2.5K
2.0K
1.5K
1.0K
500

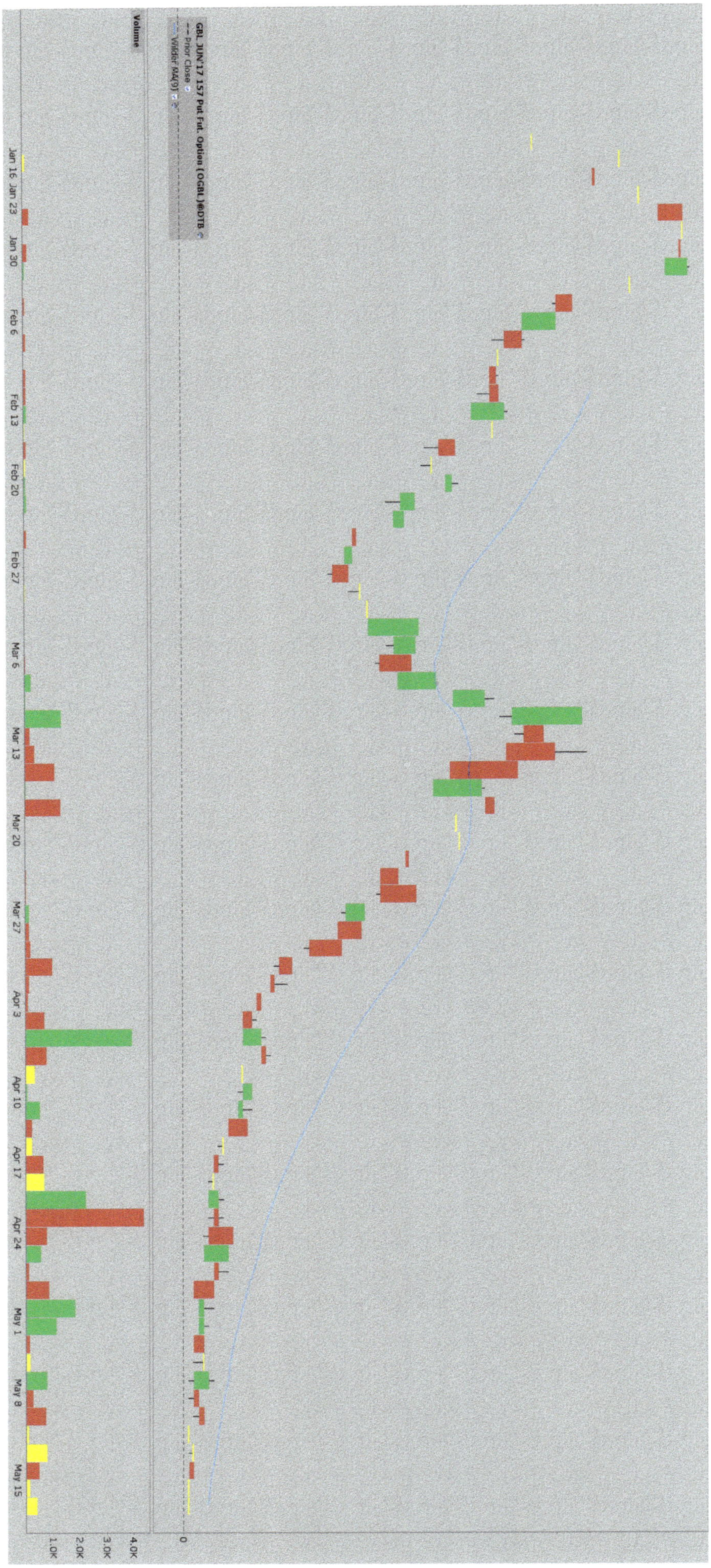
GBL JUN'17 157 Put Fut. Option (OGBL)@DTB
Prior Close
Wilder RA(9)
Volume
Jan 16
Jan 23
Jan 30
Feb 6
Feb 13
Feb 20
Feb 27
Mar 6
Mar 13
Mar 20
Mar 27
Apr 3
Apr 10
Apr 17
Apr 24
May 1
May 8
May 15
0
4.0K
3.0K
2.0K
1.0K

GBL JUN'17 158 Call Fut. Option (OGBL)@DTB
Prior Close
Wilder MA(9)
Volume
Apr '17
May '17
3
5
8
10
13
15
18
2.70
2.80
2.90
3.00
3.10
3.20
3.30
3.40
3.50
3.60
3.70
3.80
3.90

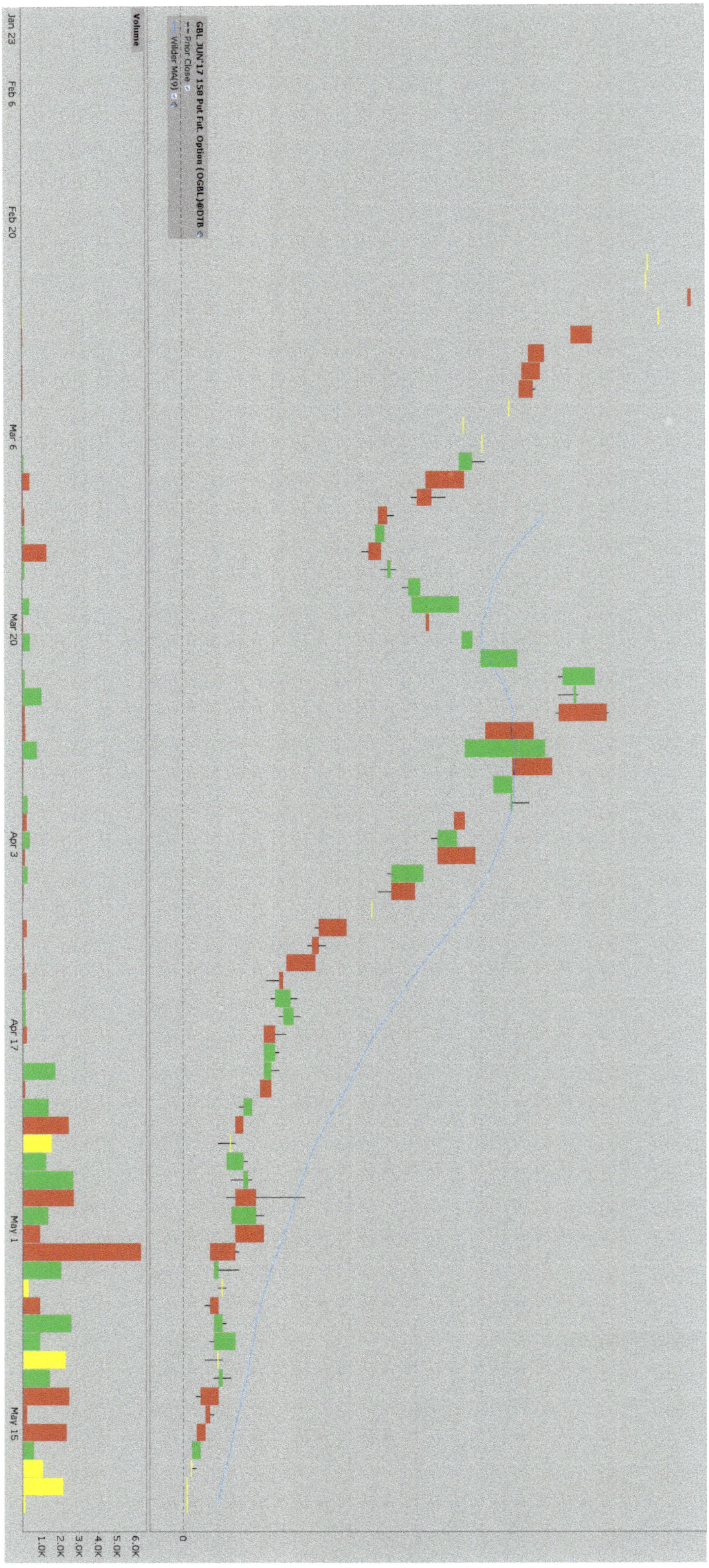
GBL JUN'17 158 Put Fut. Option (OGBL)@DTB
Prior Close
Wilder MA(9)
Volume
Jan 23
Feb 6
Feb 20
Mar 6
Mar 20
Apr 3
Apr 17
May 1
May 15
0
6.0K
5.0K
4.0K
3.0K
2.0K
1.0K

GBL JUN'17 159 Call Fut. Option (OGBL)@DTB
-- Prior Close
Wilder MA(9)
Volume
Jan 30
Feb 6
Mar 6
Mar 20
May 8

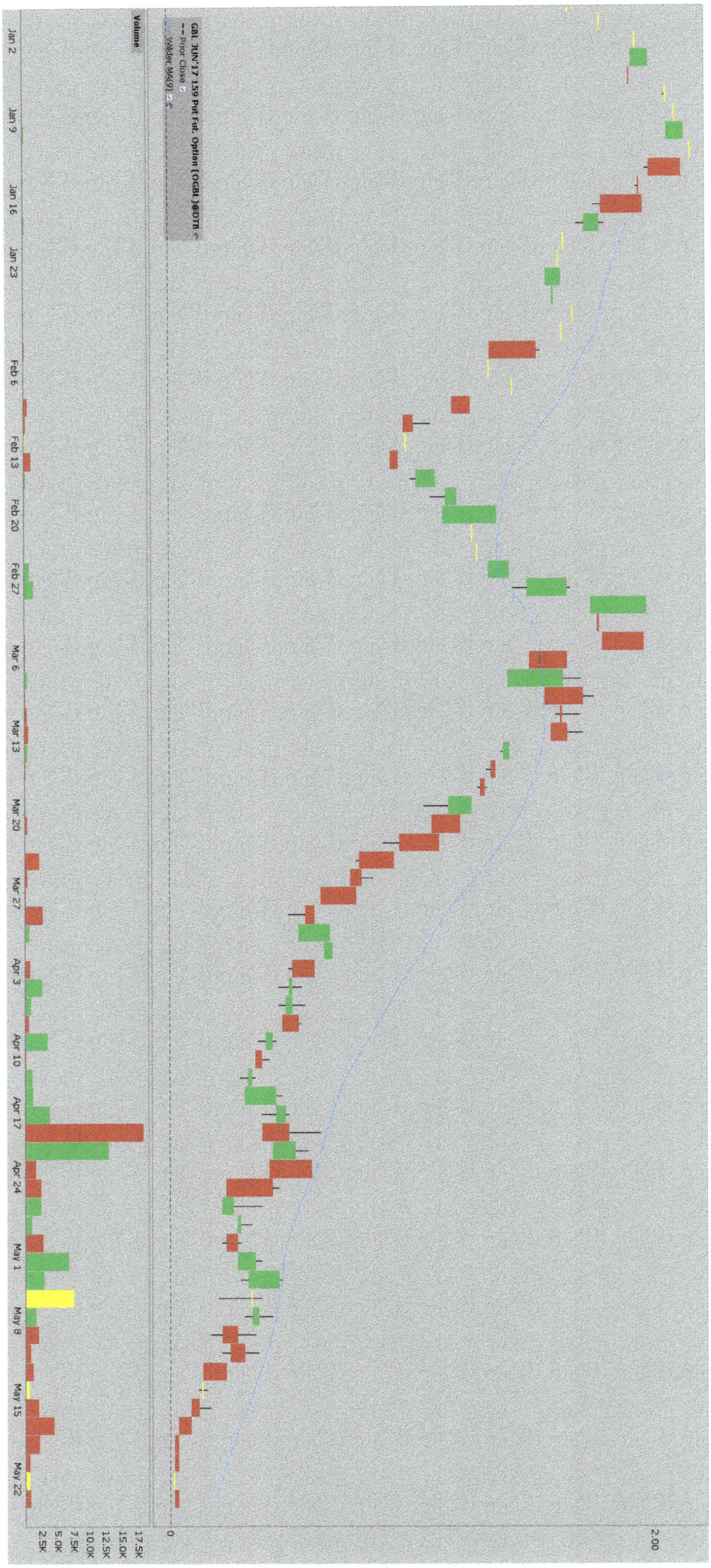
GBL JUN'17 159 Put Fut. Option (OGBL)@DTB
Prior Close
Wilder MA(9)
Volume
2.00
0
17.5K
15.0K
12.5K
10.0K
7.5K
5.0K
2.5K
Jan 2
Jan 9
Jan 16
Jan 23
Feb 6
Feb 13
Feb 20
Feb 27
Mar 6
Mar 13
Mar 20
Mar 27
Apr 3
Apr 10
Apr 17
Apr 24
May 1
May 8
May 15
May 22

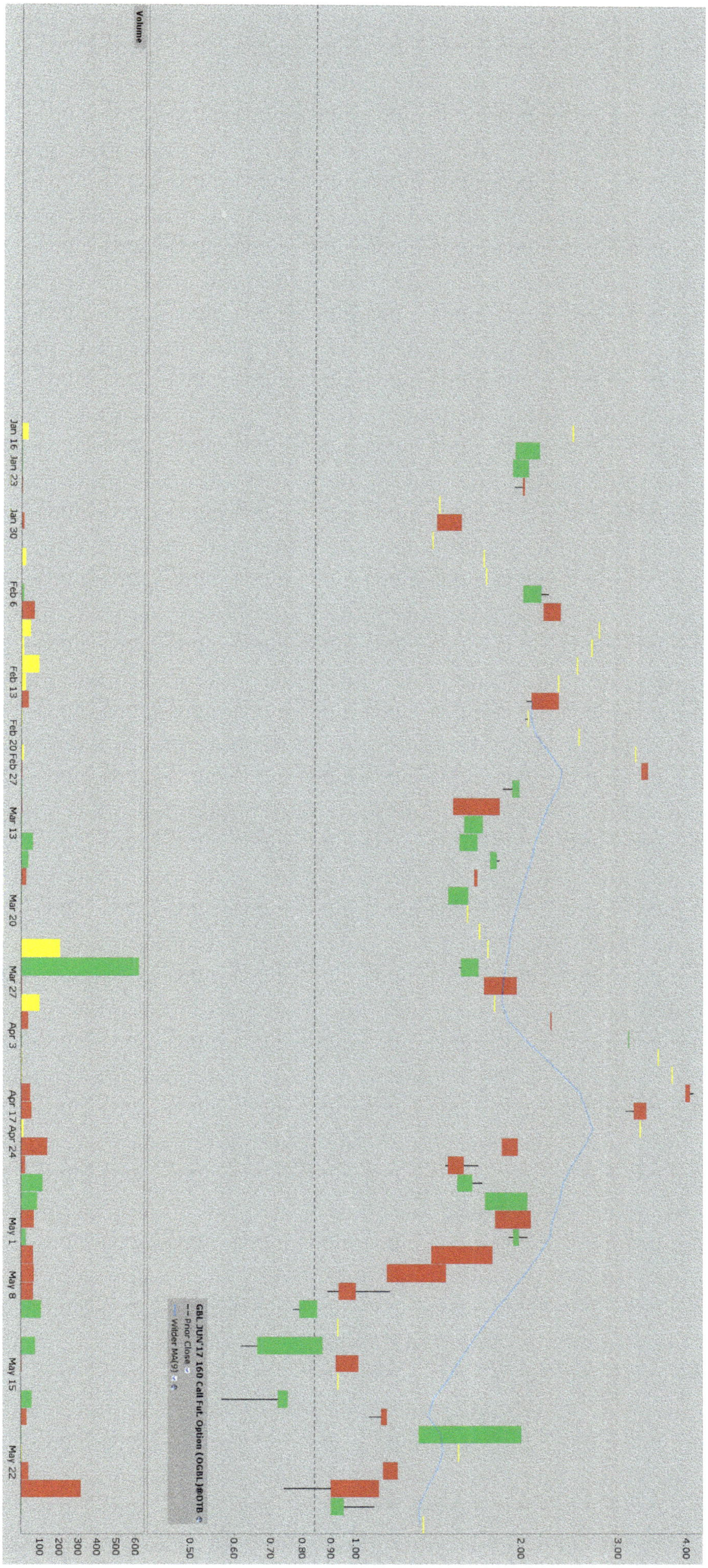
GBL JUN'17 160 Call Fut. Option (OGBL)@DTB
Prior Close
Wilder MA(9)
Volume
Jan 16
Jan 23
Jan 30
Feb 6
Feb 13
Feb 20
Feb 27
Mar 13
Mar 20
Mar 27
Apr 3
Apr 17
Apr 24
May 1
May 8
May 15
May 22
100
200
300
400
500
600
0.50
0.60
0.70
0.80
0.90
1.00
2.00
3.00
4.00

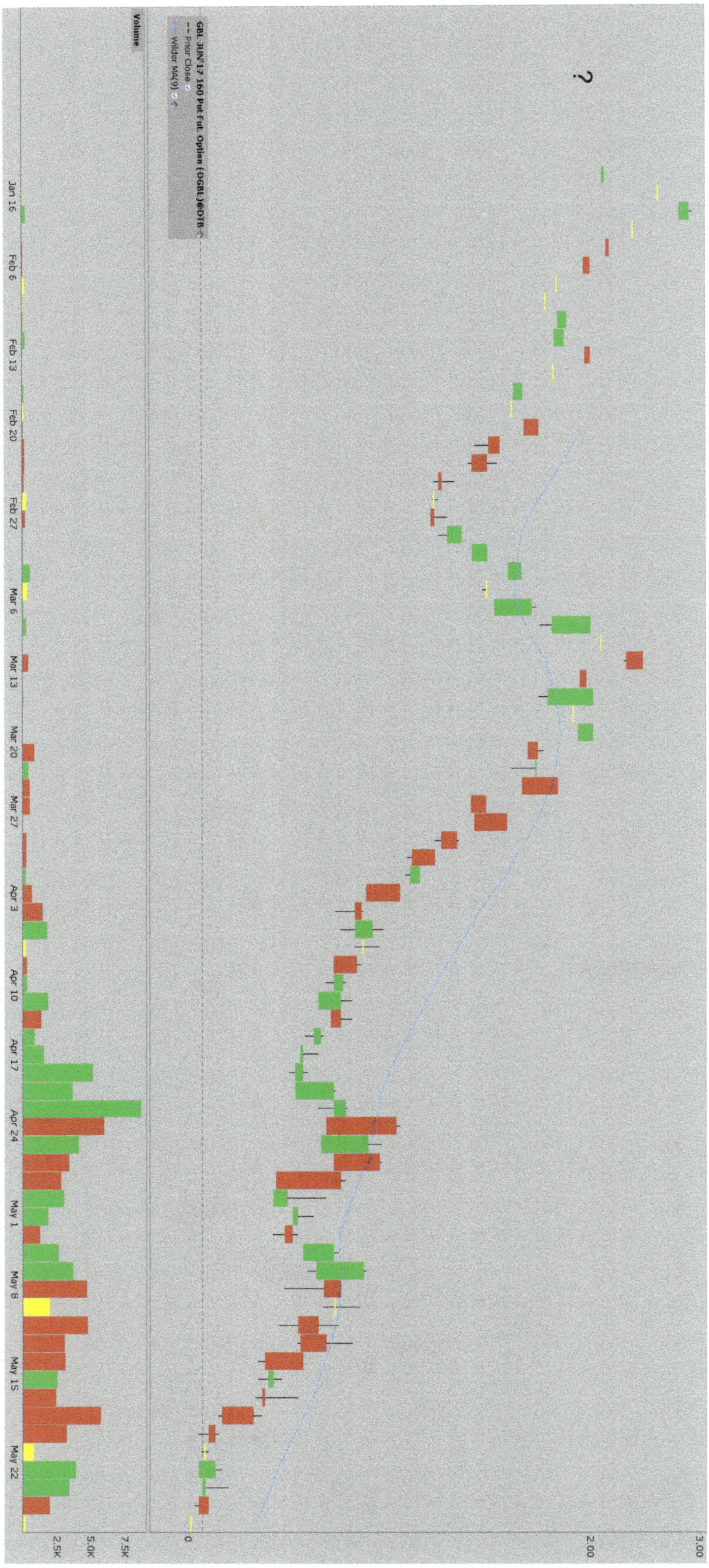
?
GBL JUN'17 160 Put Fut. Option (OGBL)@DTB
Prior Close
Wilder MA(9)
Volume
Jan 16
Feb 6
Feb 13
Feb 20
Feb 27
Mar 6
Mar 13
Mar 20
Mar 27
Apr 3
Apr 10
Apr 17
Apr 24
May 1
May 8
May 15
May 22
0
2.00
3.00
2.5K
5.0K
7.5K

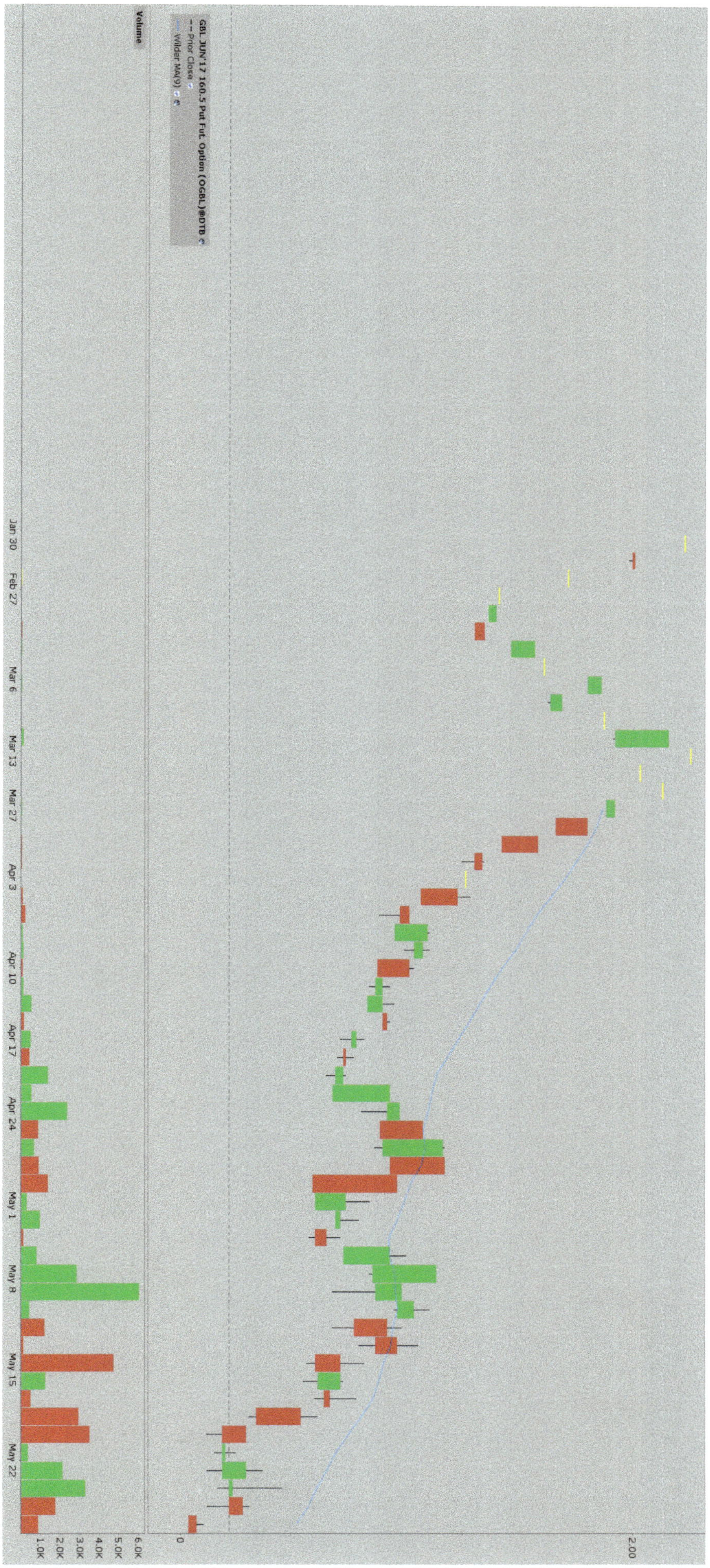
GBL JUN'17 160.5 Put Fut. Option (OGBL)@DTB
Prior Close
Wilder MA(9)
Volume
Jan 30
Feb 27
Mar 6
Mar 13
Mar 27
Apr 3
Apr 10
Apr 17
Apr 24
May 1
May 8
May 15
May 22
0
2.00
1.0K
2.0K
3.0K
4.0K
5.0K
6.0K

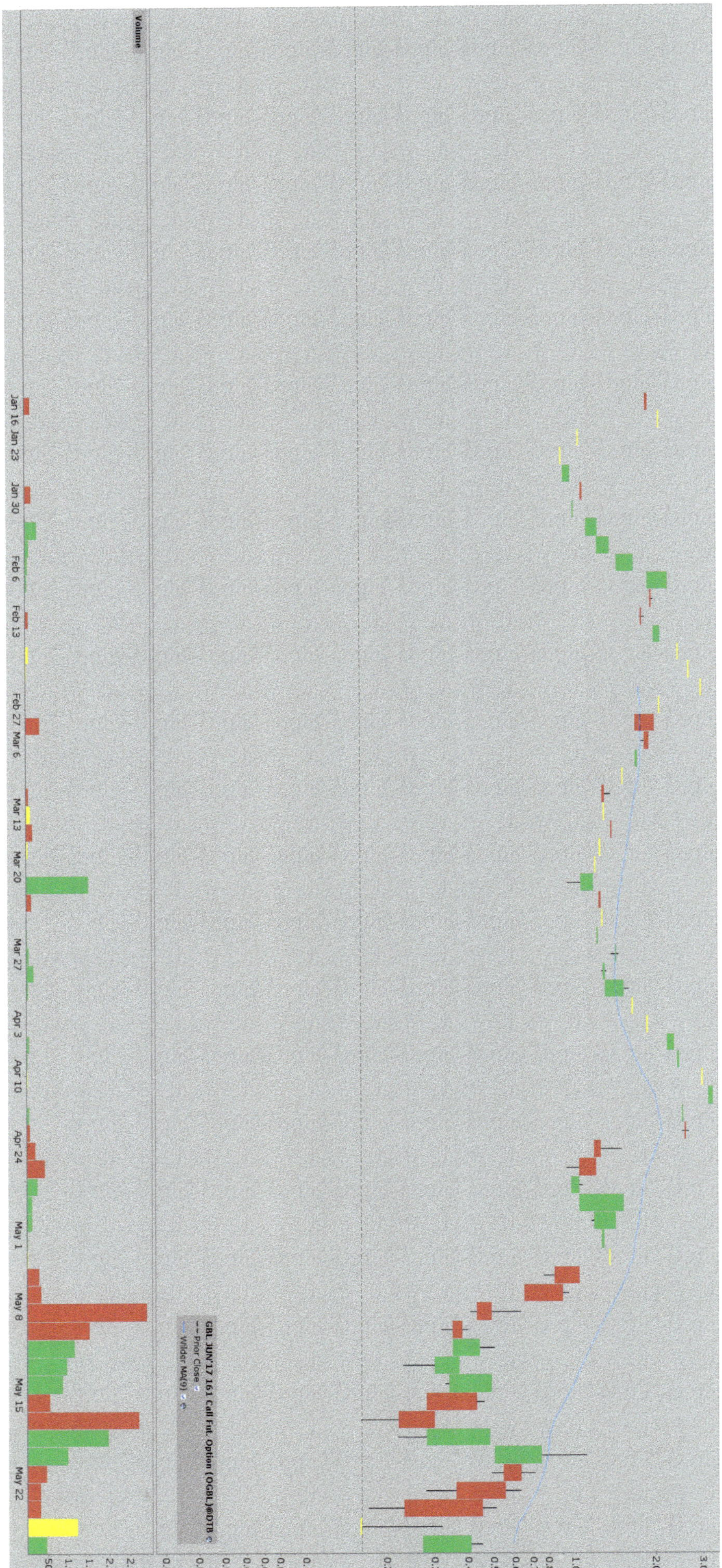
GBL JUN'17 161 Call Fut. Option (OGBL)@DTB
Prior Close
Wilder MA(9)
Volume

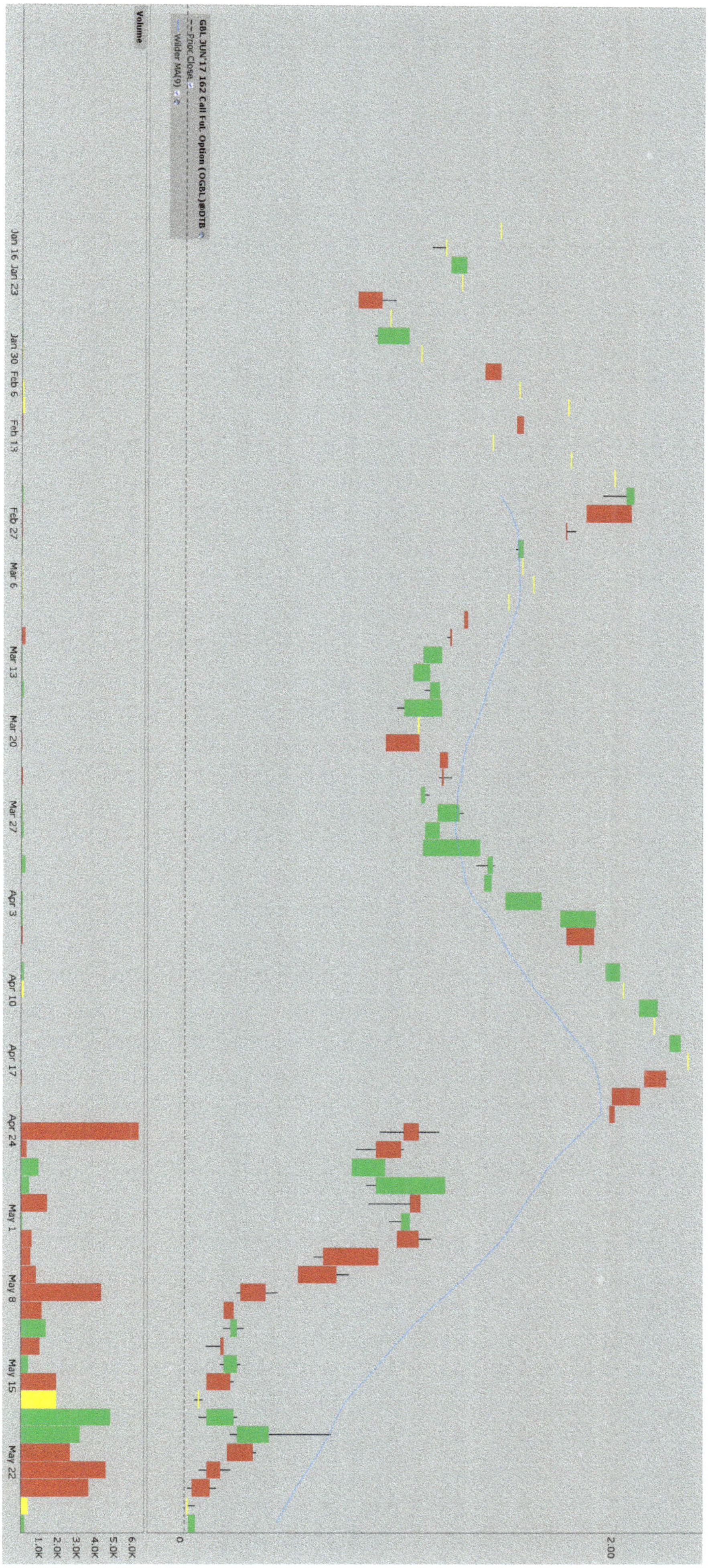
GBL JUN'17 162 Call Fut. Option (OGBL)@DTB
Prior Close
Wilder MA(9)
Volume
Jan 16 Jan 23
Jan 30 Feb 6
Feb 13
Feb 27
Mar 6
Mar 13
Mar 20
Mar 27
Apr 3
Apr 10
Apr 17
Apr 24
May 1
May 8
May 15
May 22
0
2.00
1.0K
2.0K
3.0K
4.0K
5.0K
6.0K

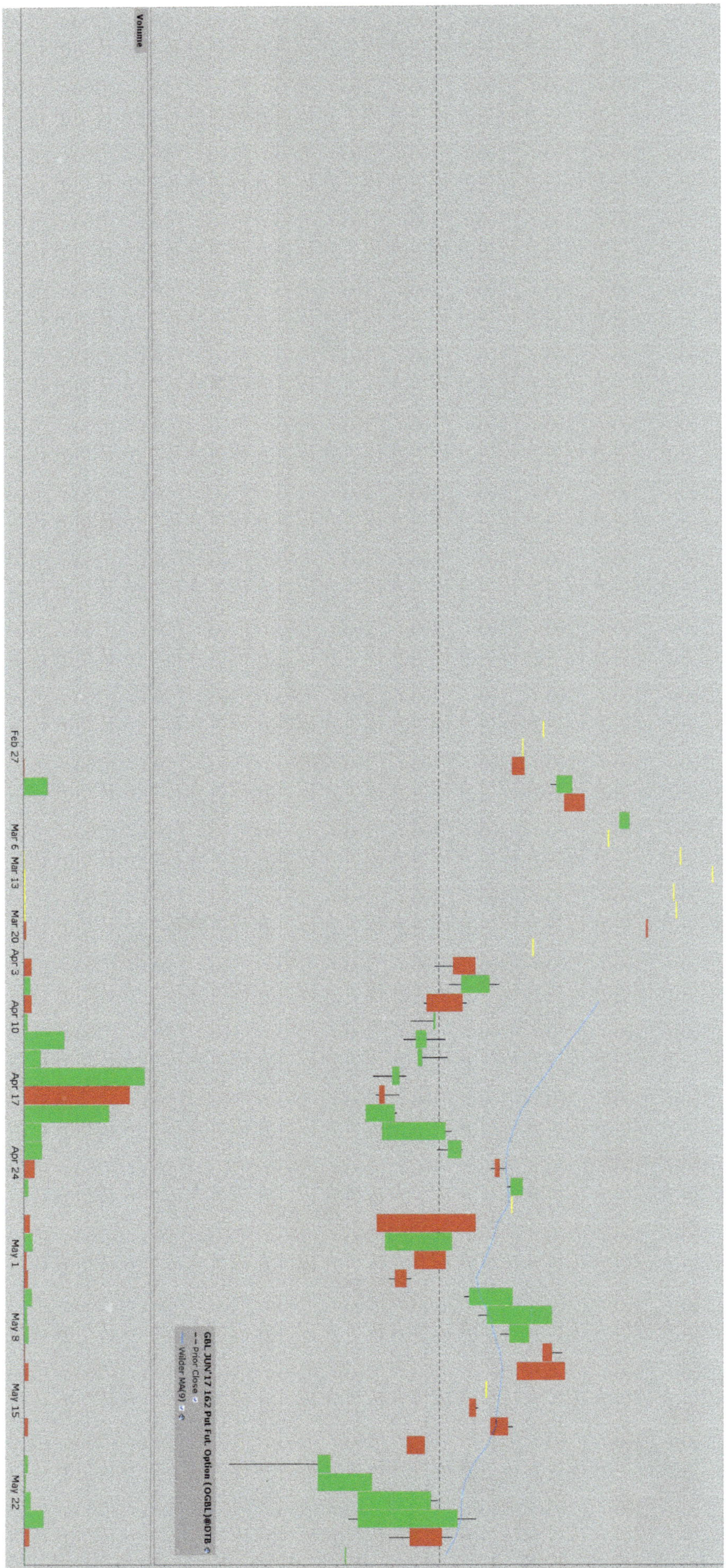
GBL JUN'17 162 Put Fut. Option (OGBL)@DTB
Prior Close
Wilder MA(9)
Volume
Feb 27
Mar 6
Mar 13
Mar 20
Apr 3
Apr 10
Apr 17
Apr 24
May 1
May 8
May 15
May 22
1.0K
2.0K
3.0K
4.0K
5.0K
0.40
0.50
0.60
0.70
0.80
0.90
1.00
1.10
1.20
1.30
1.40
1.50
1.60
1.70
1.90
2.10
2.30
2.50
2.70
2.90
3.10
3.30
3.50

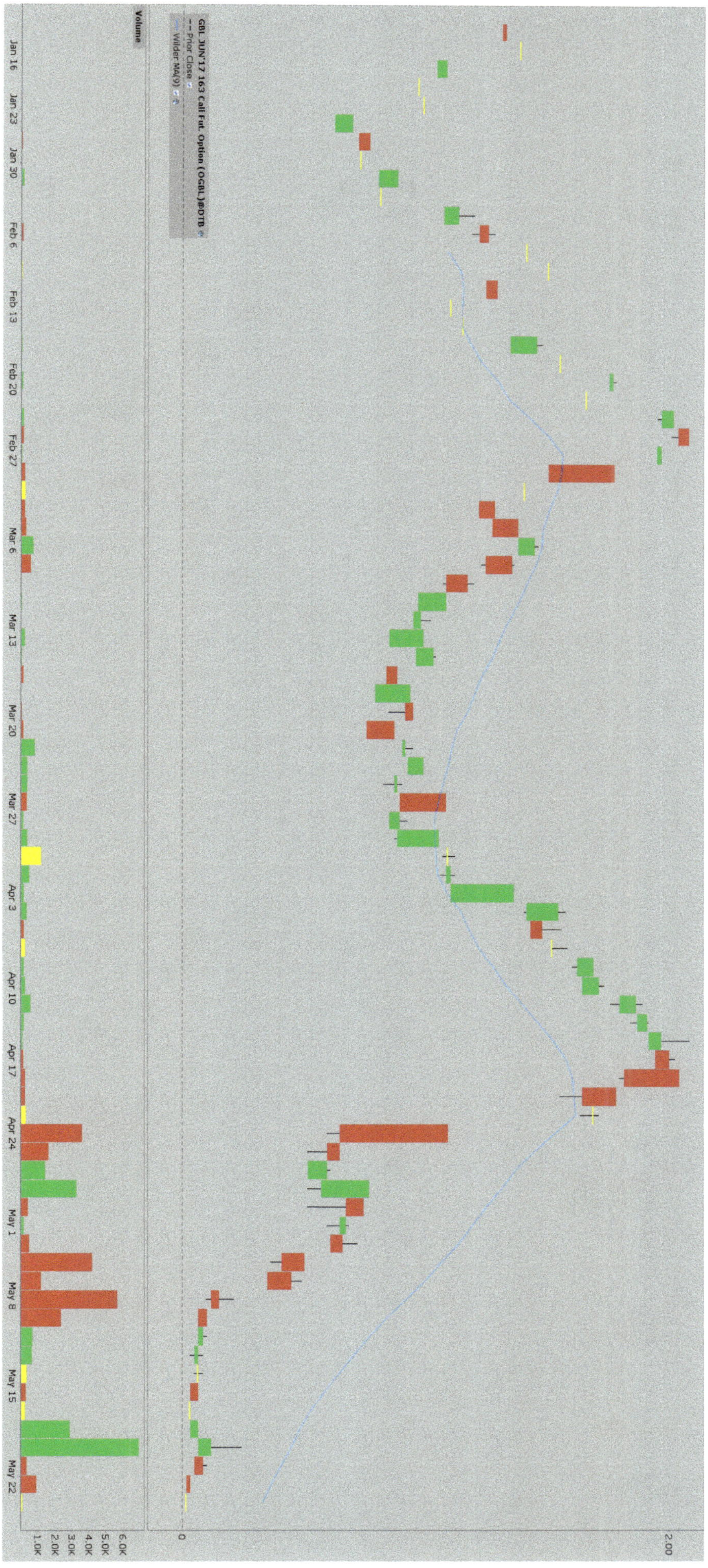
GBL JUN'17 163 Call Fut. Option (OGBL)@DTB
-- Prior Close
Wilder MA(9)
Volume
Jan 16
Jan 23
Jan 30
Feb 6
Feb 13
Feb 20
Feb 27
Mar 6
Mar 13
Mar 20
Mar 27
Apr 3
Apr 10
Apr 17
Apr 24
May 1
May 8
May 15
May 22
2.00
0
6.0K
5.0K
4.0K
3.0K
2.0K
1.0K

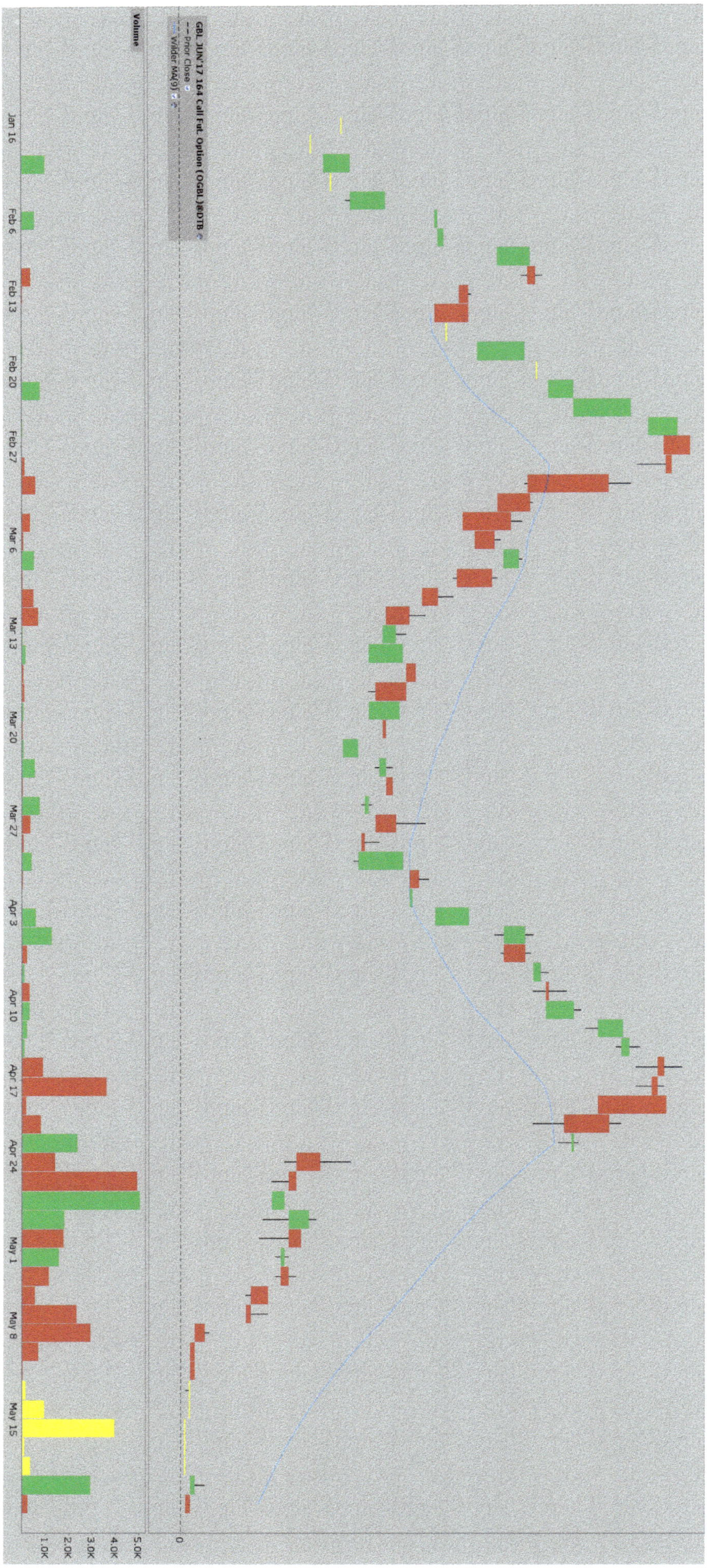
GBL JUN'17 164 Call Fut. Option (OGBL)@DTB
Prior Close
Wilder MA(9)
Volume
Jan 16
Feb 6
Feb 13
Feb 20
Feb 27
Mar 6
Mar 13
Mar 20
Mar 27
Apr 3
Apr 10
Apr 17
Apr 24
May 1
May 8
May 15
0
5.0K
4.0K
3.0K
2.0K
1.0K

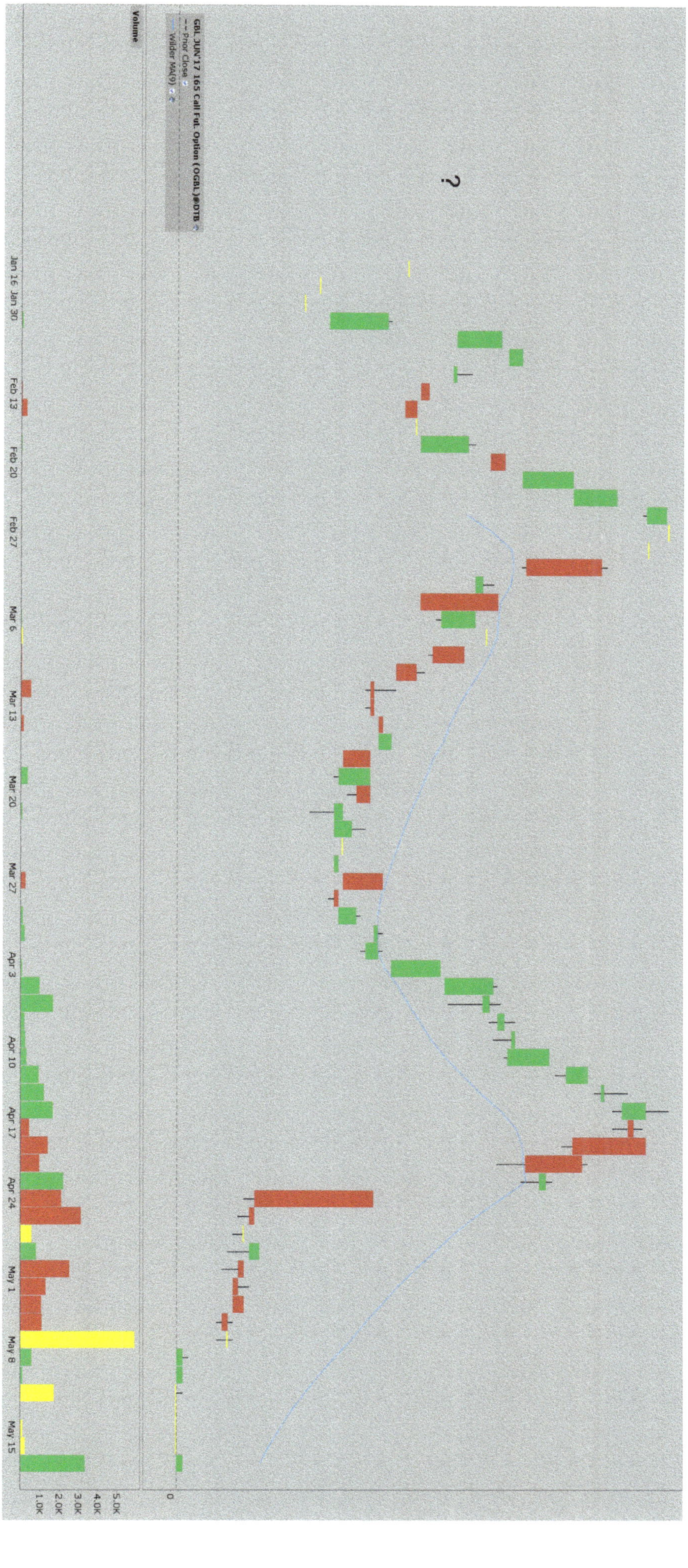
GBL JUN'17 165 Call Fut. Option (OGBL)@DTB
Prior Close
Wilder MA(9)
?
Volume
Jan 16
Jan 30
Feb 13
Feb 20
Feb 27
Mar 6
Mar 13
Mar 20
Mar 27
Apr 3
Apr 10
Apr 17
Apr 24
May 1
May 8
May 15
0
1.0K
2.0K
3.0K
4.0K
5.0K

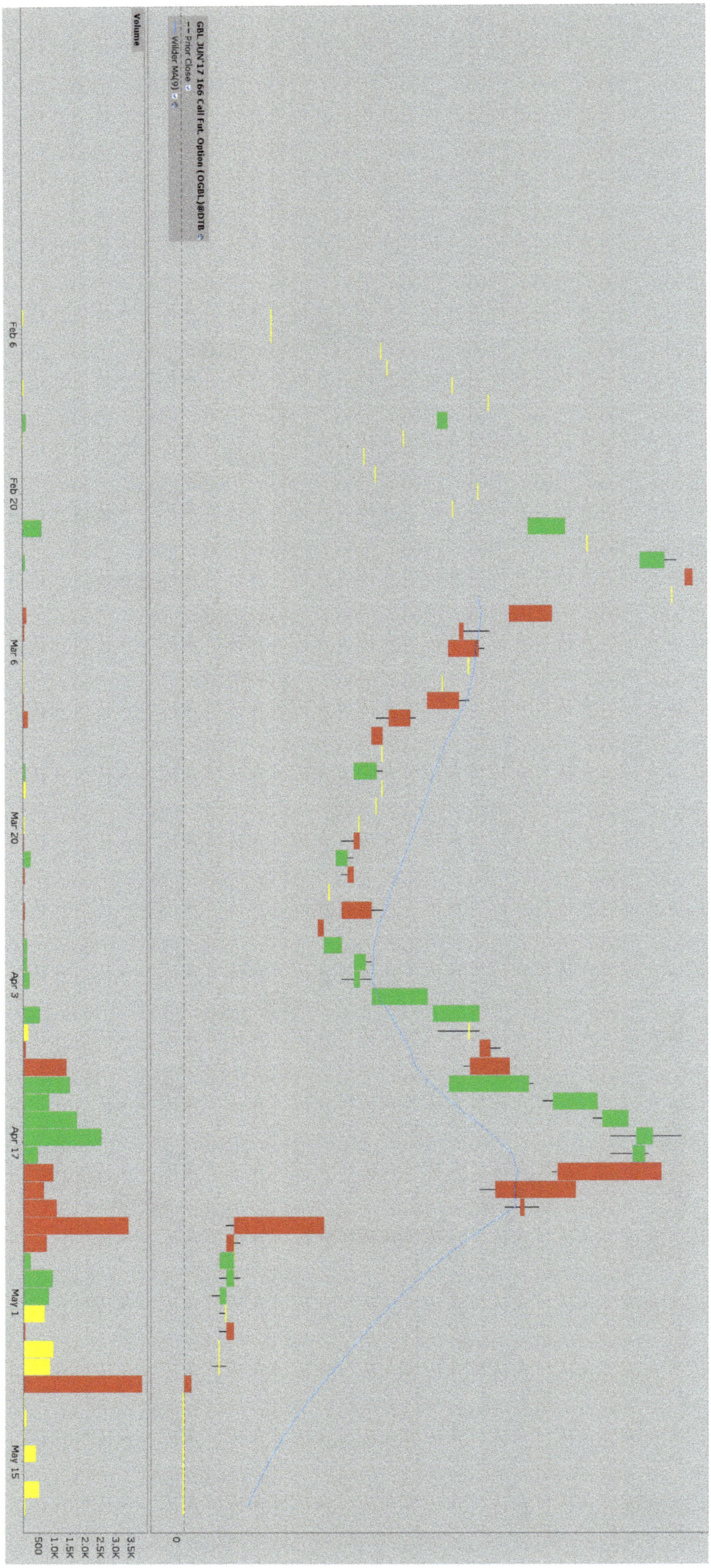
GBL JUN'17 166 Call Fut. Option (OGBL)@DTB
-- Prior Close
Wilder MA(9)
Volume
Feb 6
Feb 20
Mar 6
Mar 20
Apr 3
Apr 17
May 1
May 15
0
3.5K
3.0K
2.5K
2.0K
1.5K
1.0K
500

OGBL5 30 JUNE GRAPHICS

GBL JUL'17 163 Call Fut. Option (OGBL)@DTB
Prior Close
Volume

Volume
Jun 26
12:00
Jun 27
12:00
Jun 28
12:00
Jun 29
12:00
GBL JUL'17 163 Put Fut. Option (OGBS)@DTB
Prior Close
25
50
75
100
125
150
175
200
0.07
0.08
0.09
0.10
0.20
0.30
0.40
0.50
0.60
0.70
0.80

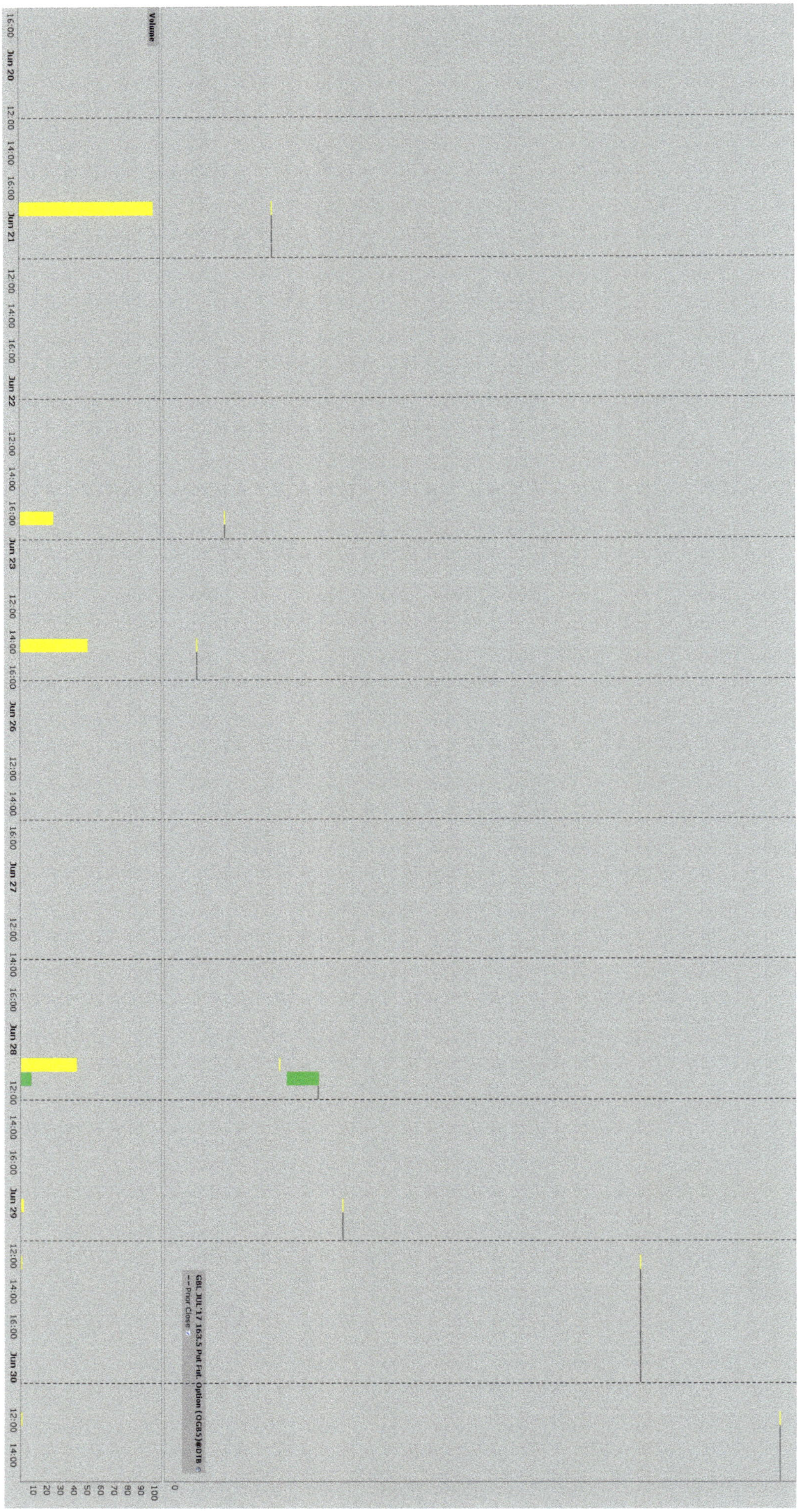
GBL JUL'17 163.5 Put Fut. Option (OGBS)@DTB
-- Prior Close
Volume
Jun 20
Jun 21
Jun 22
Jun 23
Jun 26
Jun 27
Jun 28
Jun 29
Jun 30

Volume
Prior Close
Jun 19
Jun 20
Jun 21
Jun 22
Jun 23
Jun 26
Jun 27
Jun 28
Jun 29
Jun 30
5
10
15
20
25
30
35
40
0

Volume
GBL JUL17 164.5 Call Fut. Option (OGBS)@DTB
Prior Close
12:00
Jun 20
Jun 21
Jun 22
Jun 23
Jun 26
Jun 27
Jun 28
16:00
50
100
150
200
250
300

Volume
12:00
Jun 20
Jun 21
Jun 22
Jun 23
Jun 26
Jun 27
Jun 28
Jun 29
Jun 30
25
50
75
100

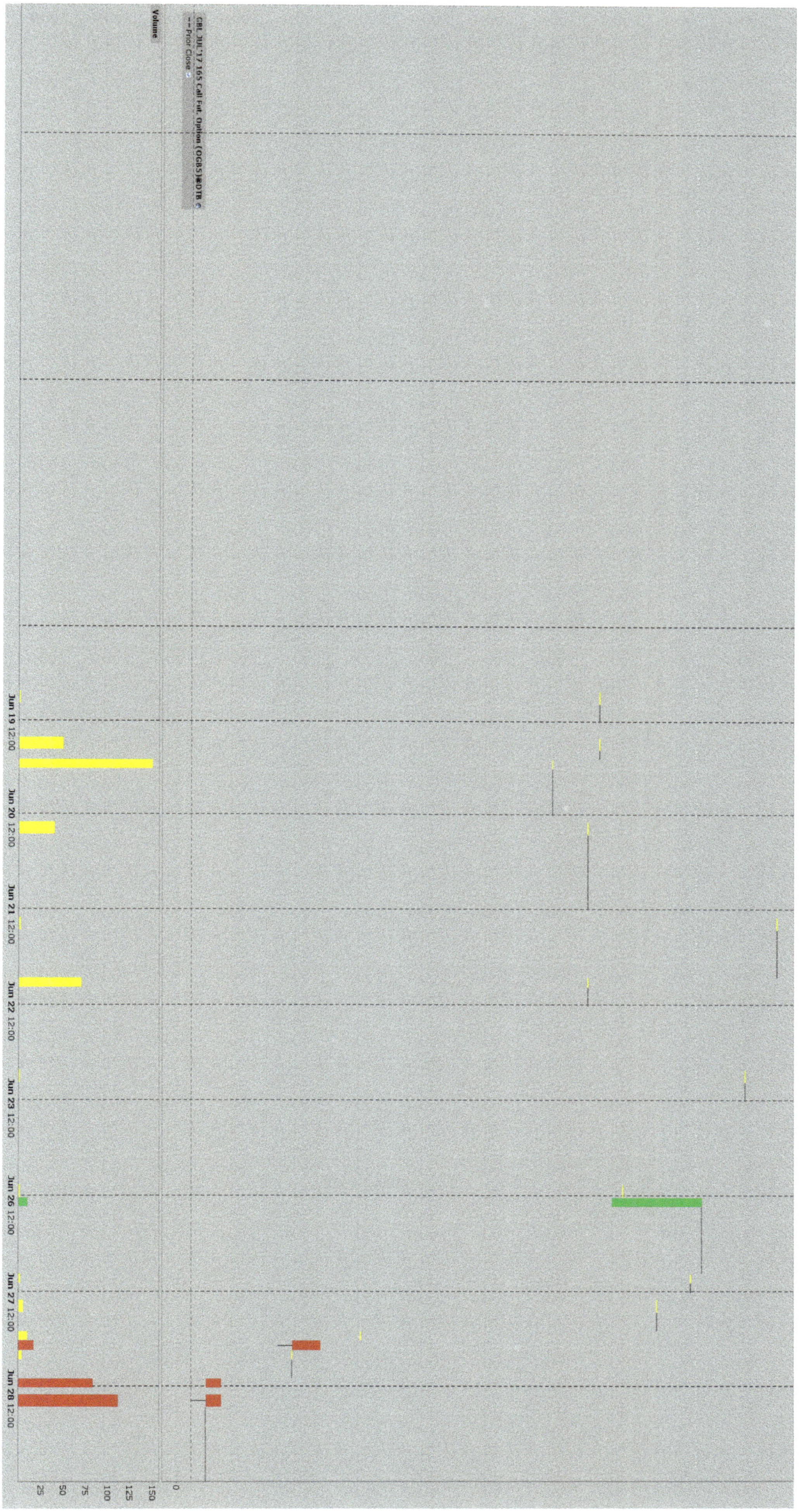

Volume
Jun 19 12:00
Jun 20 12:00
Jun 21 12:00
Jun 22 12:00
Jun 23 12:00
Jun 26 12:00
Jun 27 12:00
Jun 28 12:00
25
50
75
100
125
150
0

Volume
Jun 21
Jun 22
Jun 23
Jun 26
Jun 27
Jun 28
Jun 29
Jun 30
10
20
30
40
50
60
70
80
90
100
0.07
0.08
0.09
0.10
0.20
0.30
0.40
0.50
0.60
0.70
0.80
0.90
1.00
2.00

Volume
GBL JUL 17 166 Call Fut. Option (OGBS)@DTB
Prior Close
Jun 14
Jun 16
Jun 20
Jun 22
Jun 26

OGBL JULY GRAPHICS

Volume
GBL AUG'17 159 Call Fut. Option (OGBL)@DTB
-- Prior Close
Jul 10
10
20
30
40
50
60
70
1.60
1.70
1.80
1.90
2.00
2.10
2.20
2.30
2.40
2.50
2.60
2.70
2.80
2.90
3.00
3.10
3.20
3.30
3.40
3.50
3.60
3.70
3.80
3.90
4.00
4.10
4.20
4.30
4.40
4.50

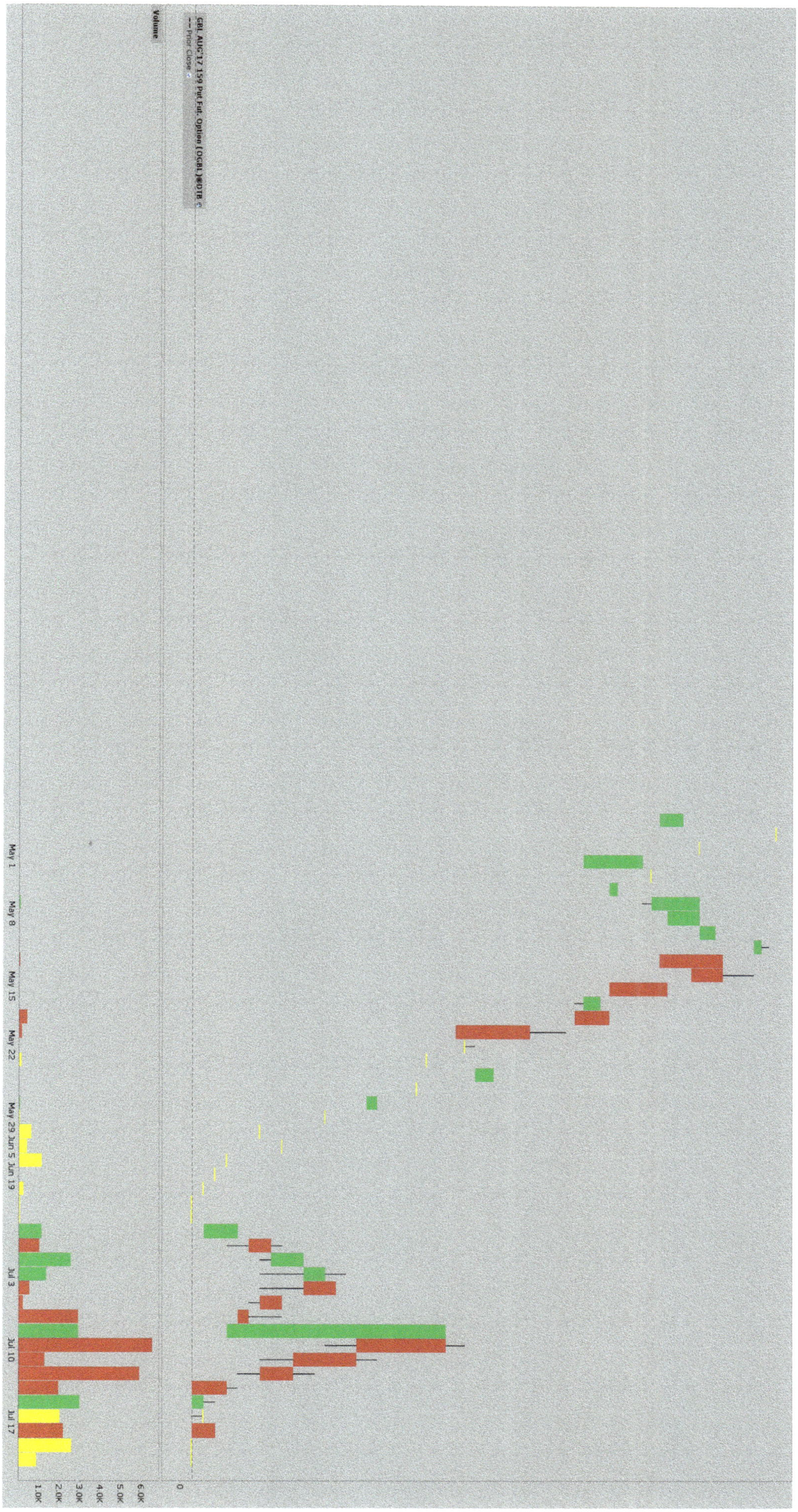
GBL AUG'17 159 Put Fut. Option (OGBL) @DTB
-- Prior Close
Volume
May 1
May 8
May 15
May 22
May 29
Jun 5
Jun 19
Jul 3
Jul 10
Jul 17
0
1.0K
2.0K
3.0K
4.0K
5.0K
6.0K

Volume
GBL AUG'17 100 Call Fut. Option (OGBL) @DTB
-- Prior Close
May 15
Jun 5
Jun 26
Jul 3
Jul 10
Jul 17
50
100
150
200
250
300
350
400
450
0.80
0.90
1.00
2.00
3.00
4.00
5.00

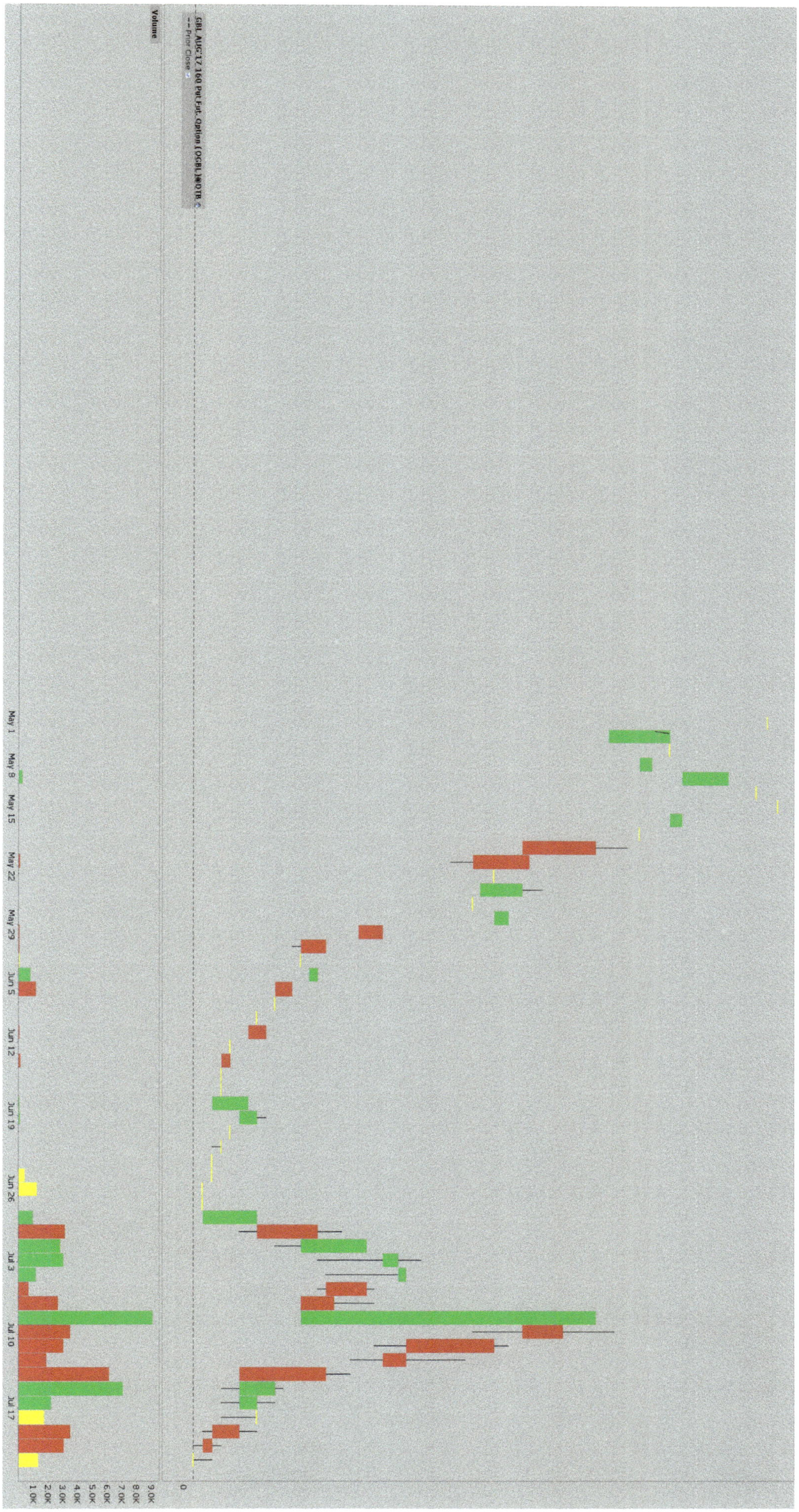
GBL AUG'17 160 Put Fut. Option (OGBL)@DTB
-- Prior Close
Volume
May 1
May 8
May 15
May 22
May 29
Jun 5
Jun 12
Jun 19
Jun 26
Jul 3
Jul 10
Jul 17
0
1.0K
2.0K
3.0K
4.0K
5.0K
6.0K
7.0K
8.0K
9.0K

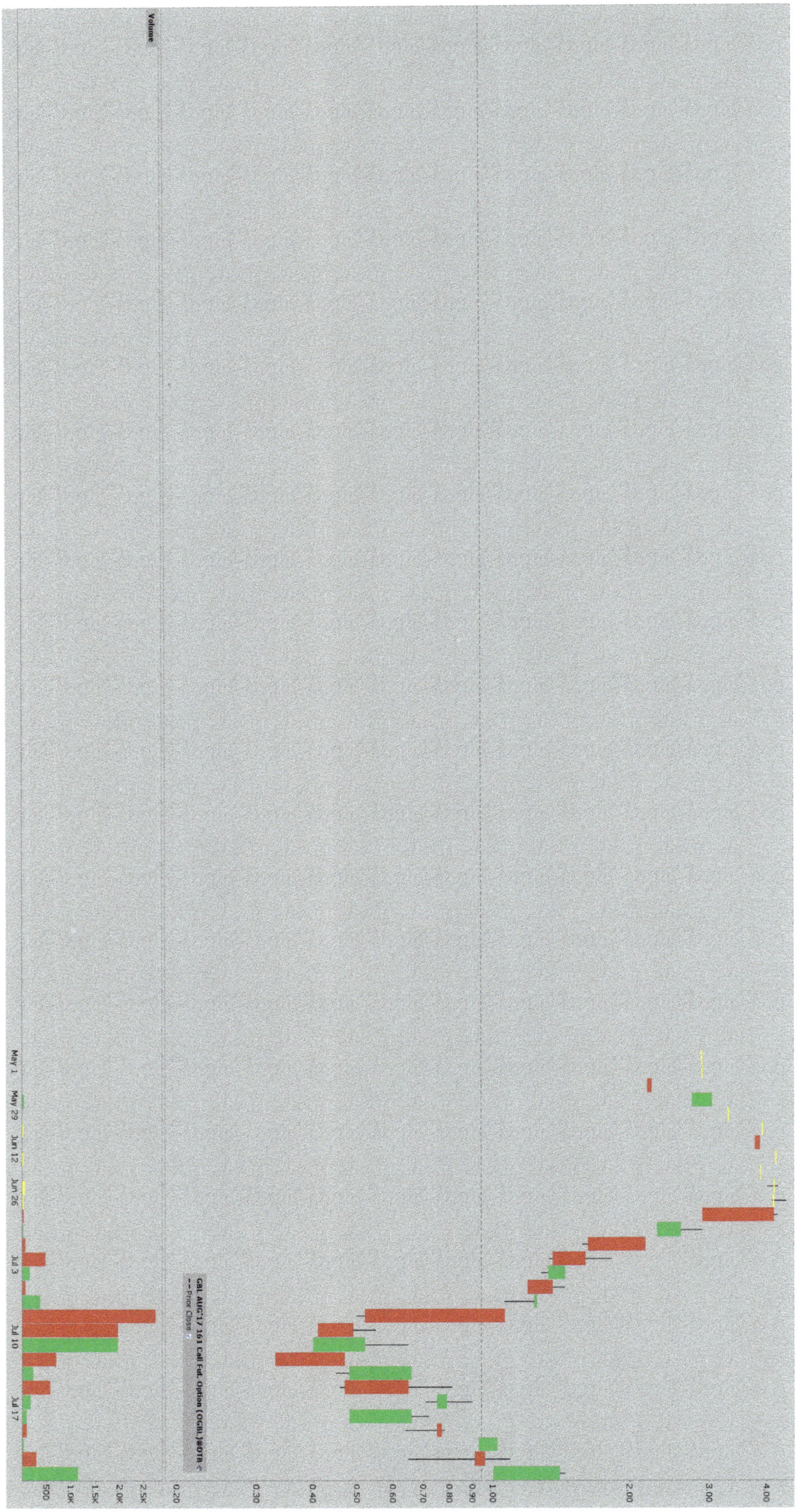
Volume
GBL AUG'17 161 Call Fut. Option (OGBL)@DTB

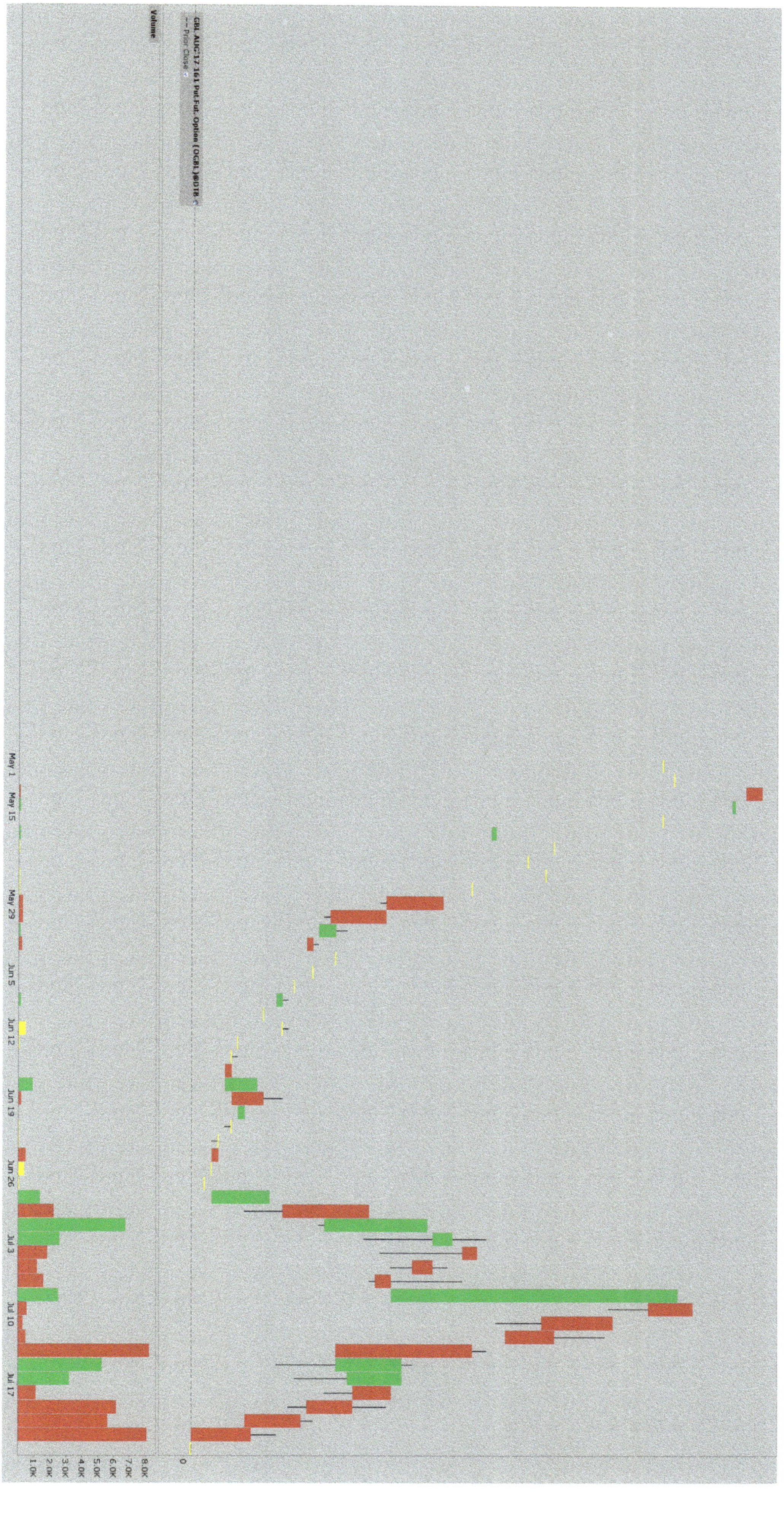
GBL AUG'17 161 Put Fut.-Option (OGBL)@DTB
-- Prior Close
Volume
May 1
May 15
May 29
Jun 5
Jun 12
Jun 19
Jun 26
Jul 3
Jul 10
Jul 17
0
1.0K
2.0K
3.0K
4.0K
5.0K
6.0K
7.0K
8.0K

GBL AUG'17 162 Call Fut. Option (OGBL)@DTB
-- Prior Close
Volume
May 8
Jun 5
Jun 26
Jul 3
Jul 10
Jul 17
2.5K
5.0K
7.5K
10.0K
12.5K
0
2.00
3.00

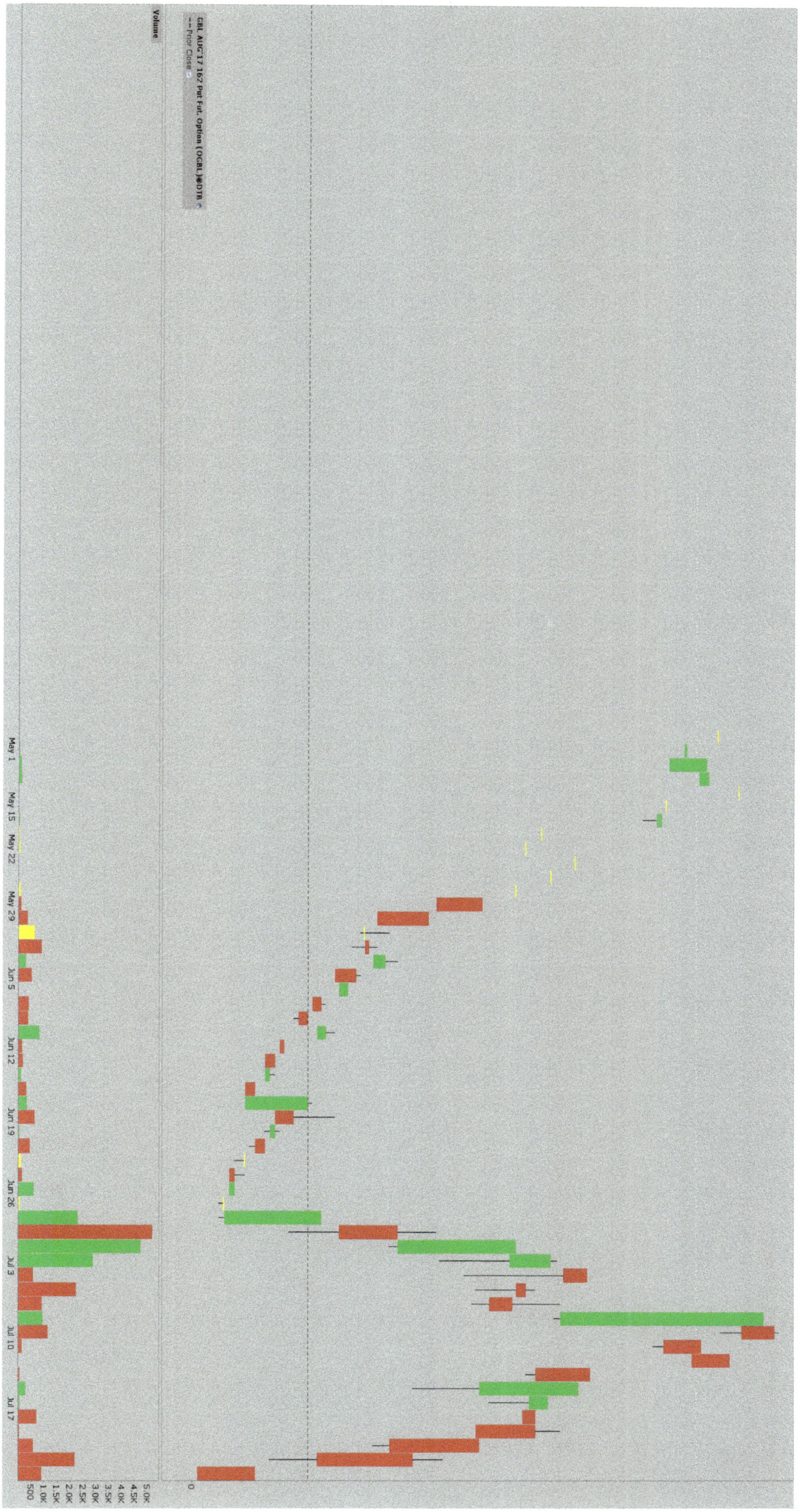
GBL AUG'17 167 Put Fut. Option (OGBL)@DTB
-- Prior Close
Volume
May 1
May 15
May 22
May 29
Jun 5
Jun 12
Jun 19
Jun 26
Jul 3
Jul 10
Jul 17
0
5.0K
4.5K
4.0K
3.5K
3.0K
2.5K
2.0K
1.5K
1.0K
500

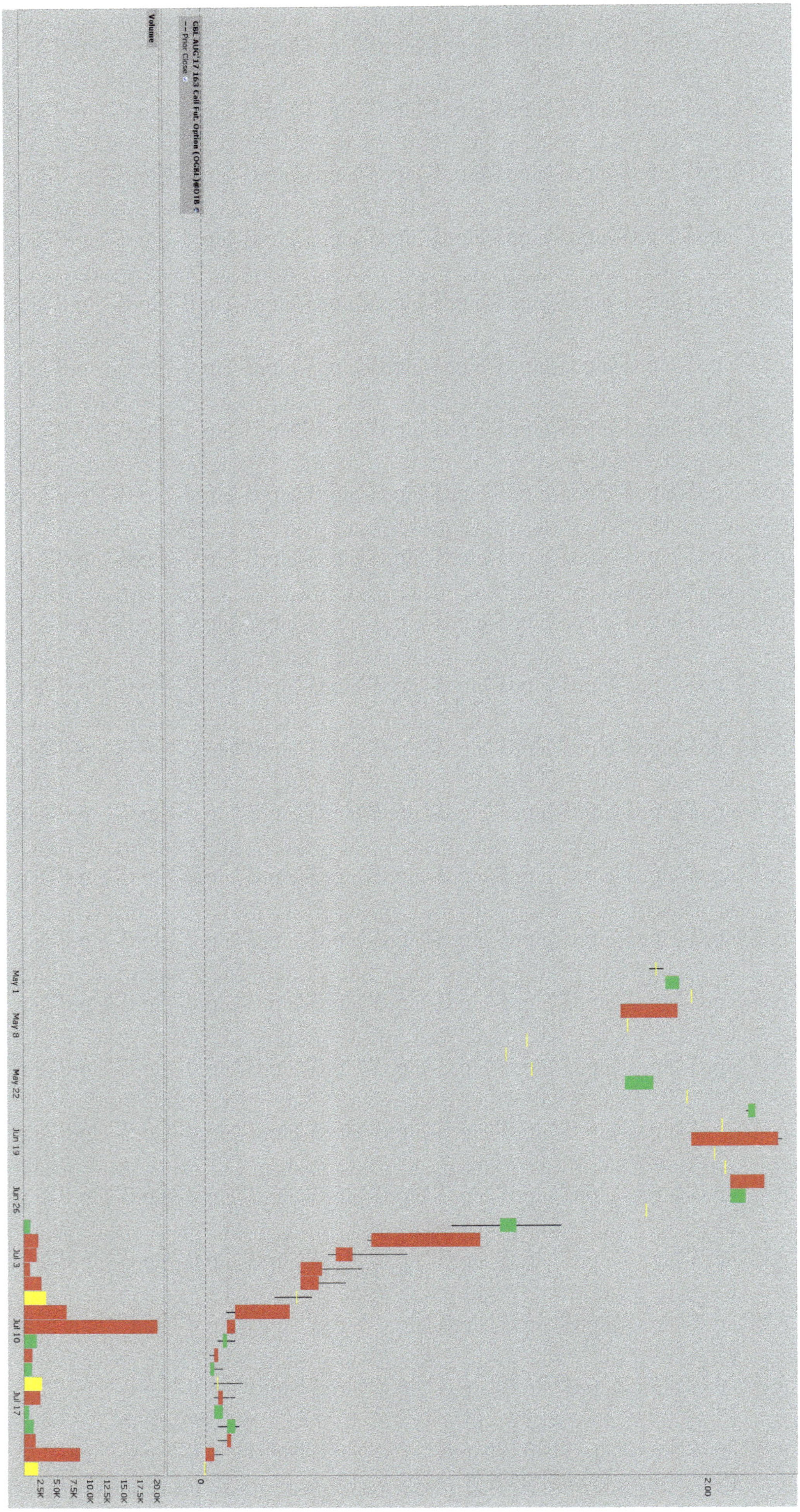
GBL AUG'17 163 Call Fut. Option (OGBL) @DTB
-- Prior Close
Volume
May 1
May 8
May 22
Jun 19
Jun 26
Jul 3
Jul 10
Jul 17
0
2.00
2.5K
5.0K
7.5K
10.0K
12.5K
15.0K
17.5K
20.0K

Volume
GBL AUG'17 163 Put Fut. Option (OGBL)@DTB
-- Prior Close
May 1
May 8
May 15
May 29
Jun 5
Jun 12
Jun 19
Jun 26
Jul 3
Jul 10
Jul 17
1.0K
2.0K
3.0K
4.0K
5.0K
0.01
0.02
0.03
0.04
0.05
0.06
0.07
0.08
0.10
0.20
0.30
0.40
0.50
0.60
0.70
0.80
1.00
2.00

GBL AUG'17 164 Call Fut. Option (OGBL)@DTB
-- Prior Close
Volume
May 8
May 22
Jun 5
Jun 12
Jun 19
Jun 26
Jul 3
Jul 10
Jul 17
0
500
1.0K
1.5K
2.0K
2.5K
3.0K
3.5K
4.0K
4.5K
5.0K

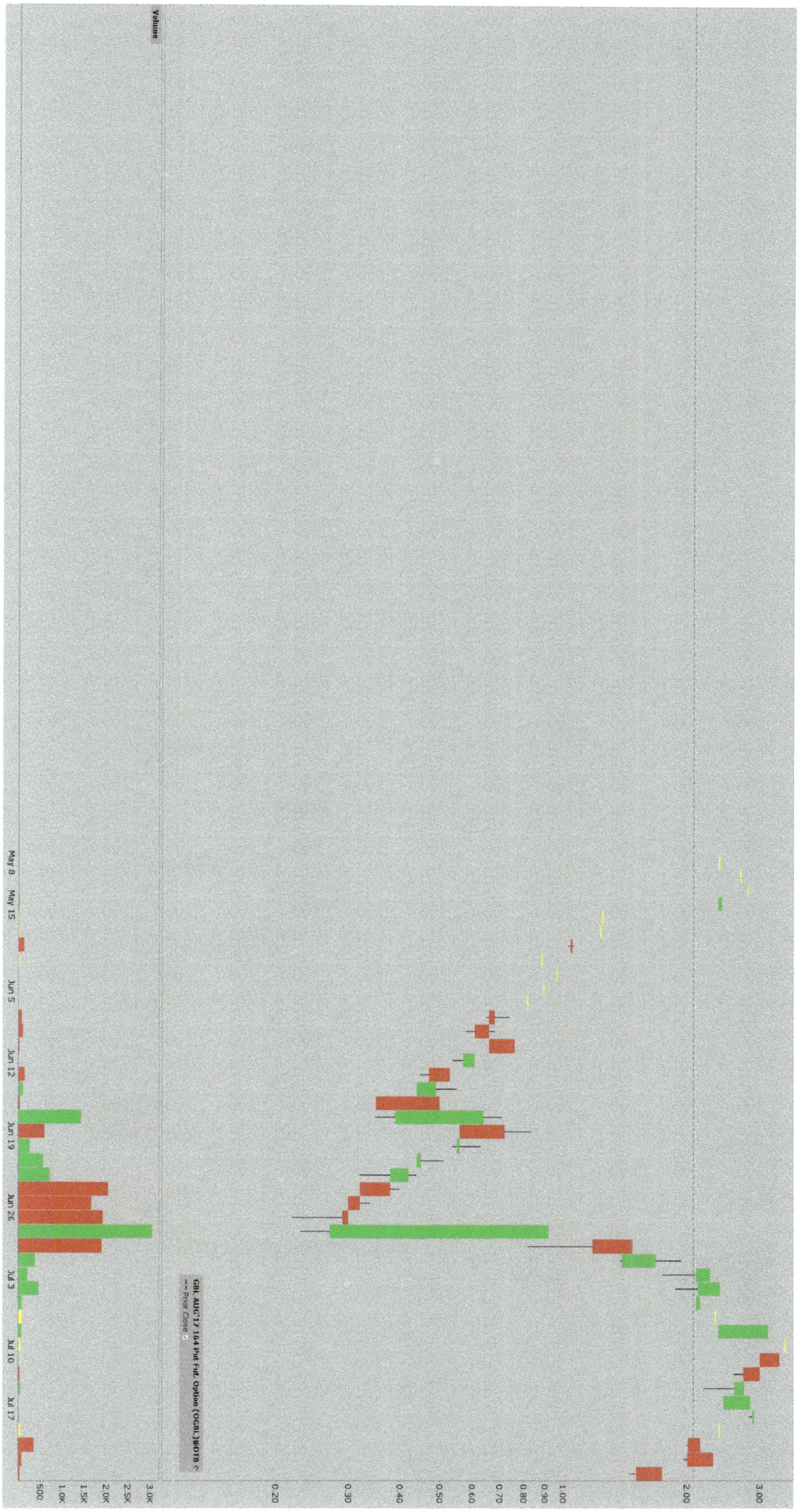
Volume
GBL AUG'17 164 Put Fut. Option (OGBL)@DTB
-- Prior Close
May 8
May 15
Jun 5
Jun 12
Jun 19
Jun 26
Jul 3
Jul 10
Jul 17
500
1.0K
1.5K
2.0K
2.5K
3.0K
0.20
0.30
0.40
0.50
0.60
0.70
0.80
0.90
1.00
2.00
3.00

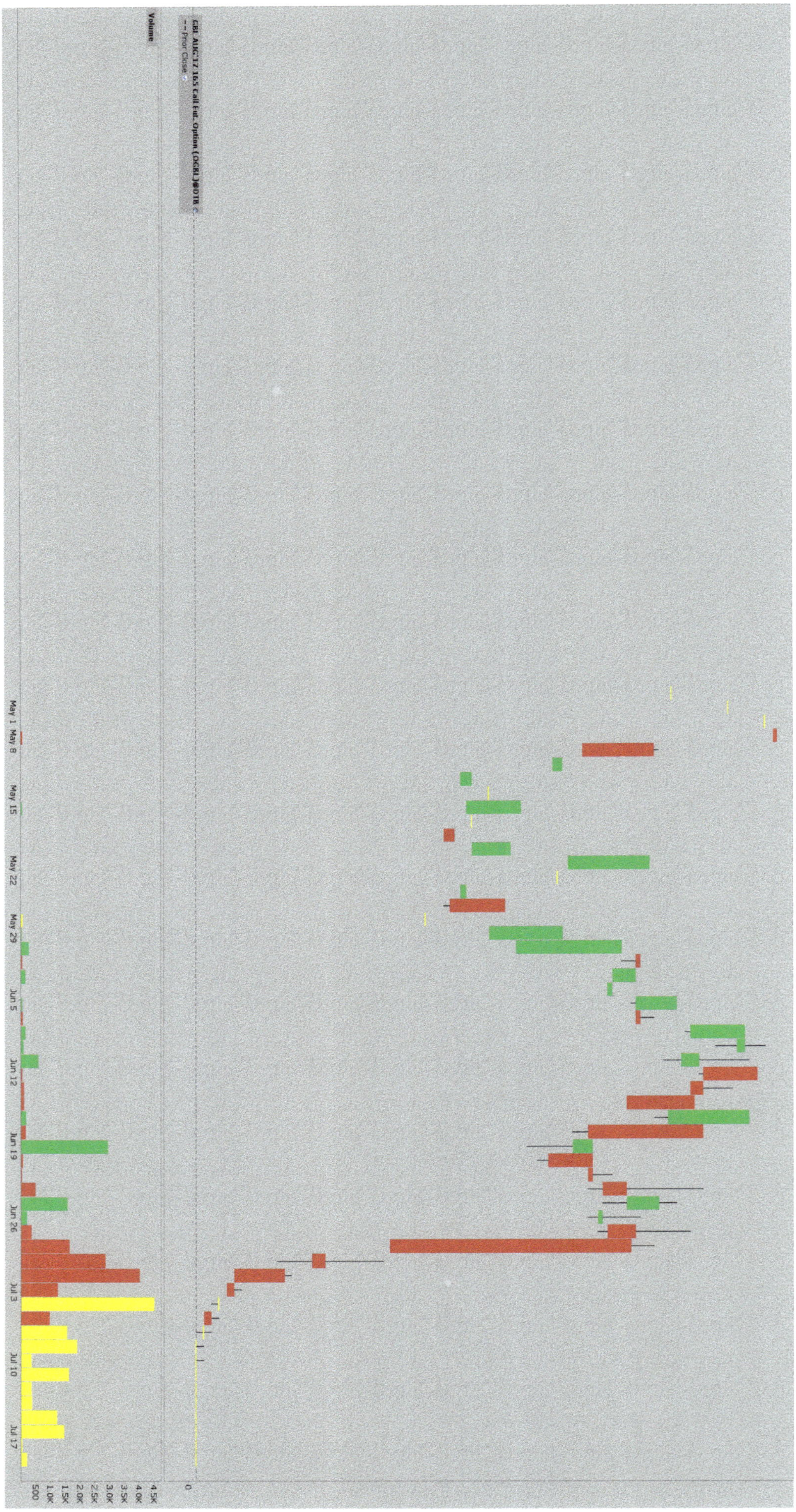
Volume
GBL AUG'17 165 Call Fut. Option (OGBL)@DTB
-- Prior Close
May 1
May 8
May 15
May 22
May 29
Jun 5
Jun 12
Jun 19
Jun 26
Jul 3
Jul 10
Jul 17
500
1.0K
1.5K
2.0K
2.5K
3.0K
3.5K
4.0K
4.5K
0

Volume
GBL AUG'17 165 Put Fut. Option (OGBL) @DTB
-- Prior Close
Jun 5
Jun 12
Jun 19
Jun 26
Jul 3
Jul 10
Jul 17
500
1.0K
1.5K
2.0K
2.5K
3.0K
3.5K
0.40
0.50
0.60
0.70
0.80
0.90
1.00
2.00
3.00
4.00

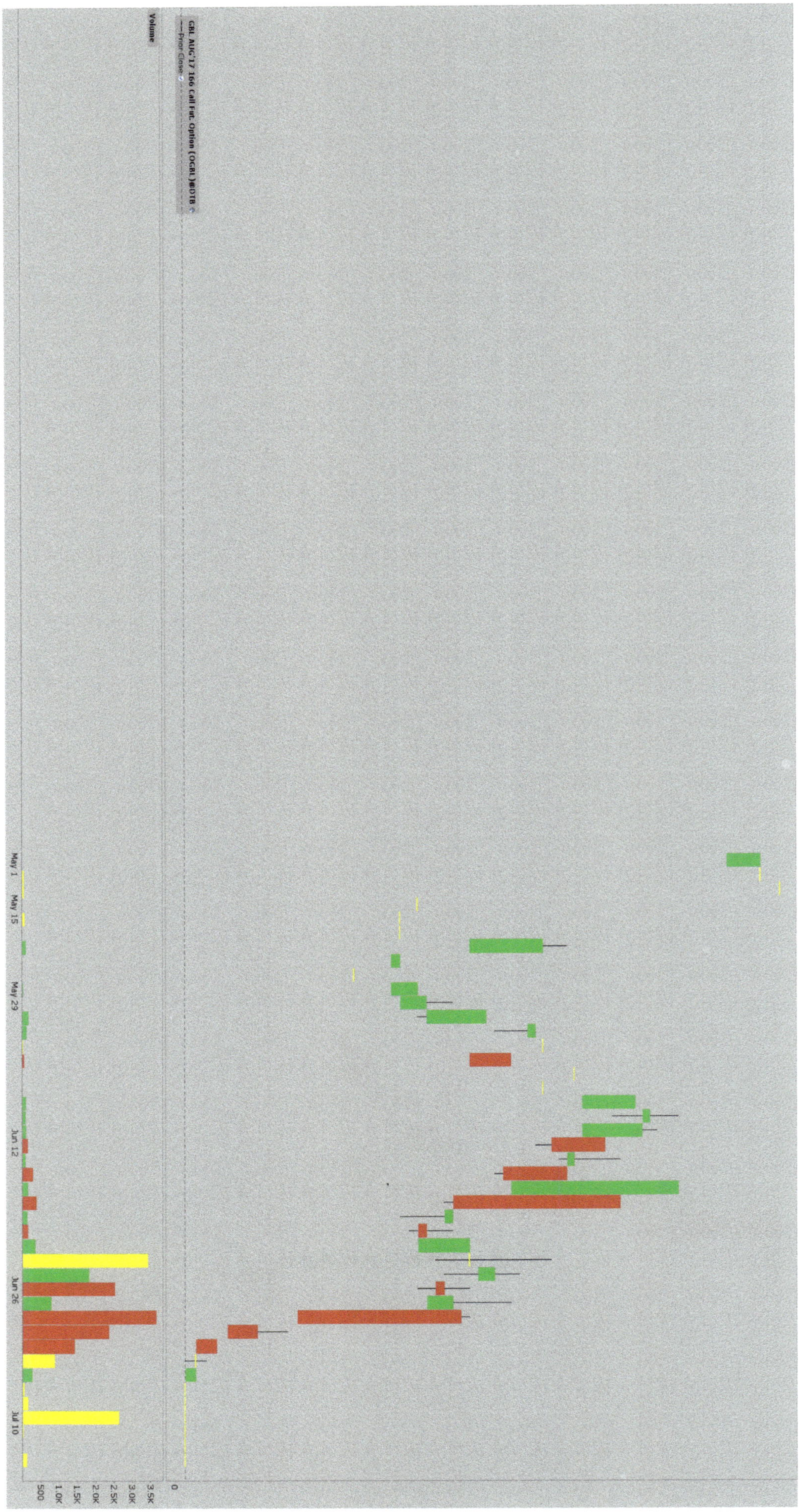
GBL AUG'17 166 Call Fut. Option (OGBL)@DTB
Prior Close
Volume
May 1
May 15
May 29
Jun 12
Jun 26
Jul 10
0
500
1.0K
1.5K
2.0K
2.5K
3.0K
3.5K

GBL AUG'17 167 Call Fut. Option (OGBL)@DTB
-- Prior Close
Volume
Jun '17
Jul '17
0.00
0.00
0.01
0.01
0.01
0.01
0.01
0.02
0.03
0.04
0.05
0.06
0.07
0.08
0.09
0.10
0.20
500
1.0K
1.5K
2.0K
2.5K
3.0K
3.5K
4.0K
4.5K

Volume
May 29
Jun 12
Jun 26
Jul 10

GBL SEPTEMBER GRAPHICS

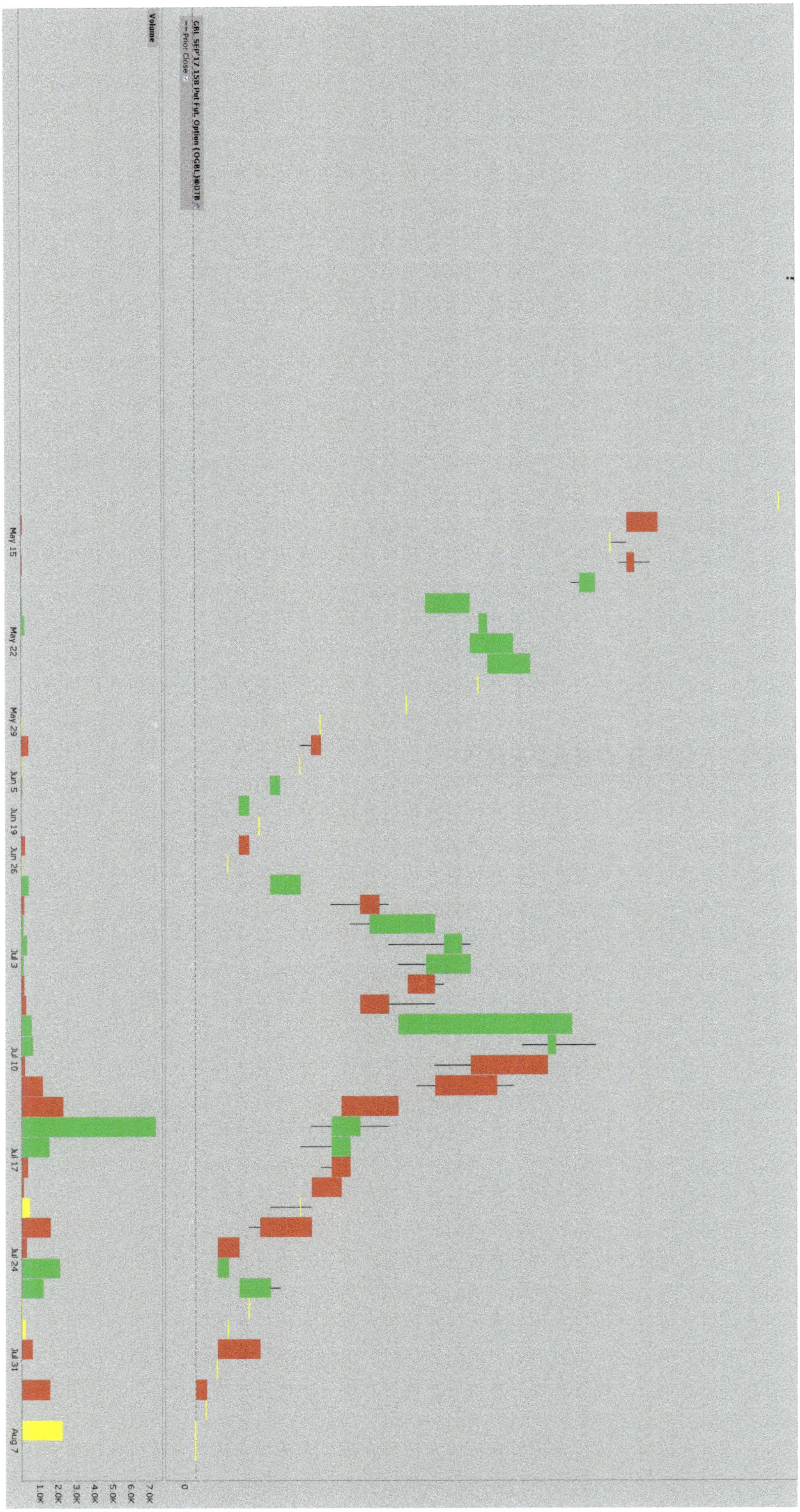
Volume
Prior Close
May 15
May 22
May 29
Jun 5
Jun 19
Jun 26
Jul 3
Jul 10
Jul 17
Jul 24
Jul 31
Aug 7
7.0K
6.0K
5.0K
4.0K
3.0K
2.0K
1.0K
0

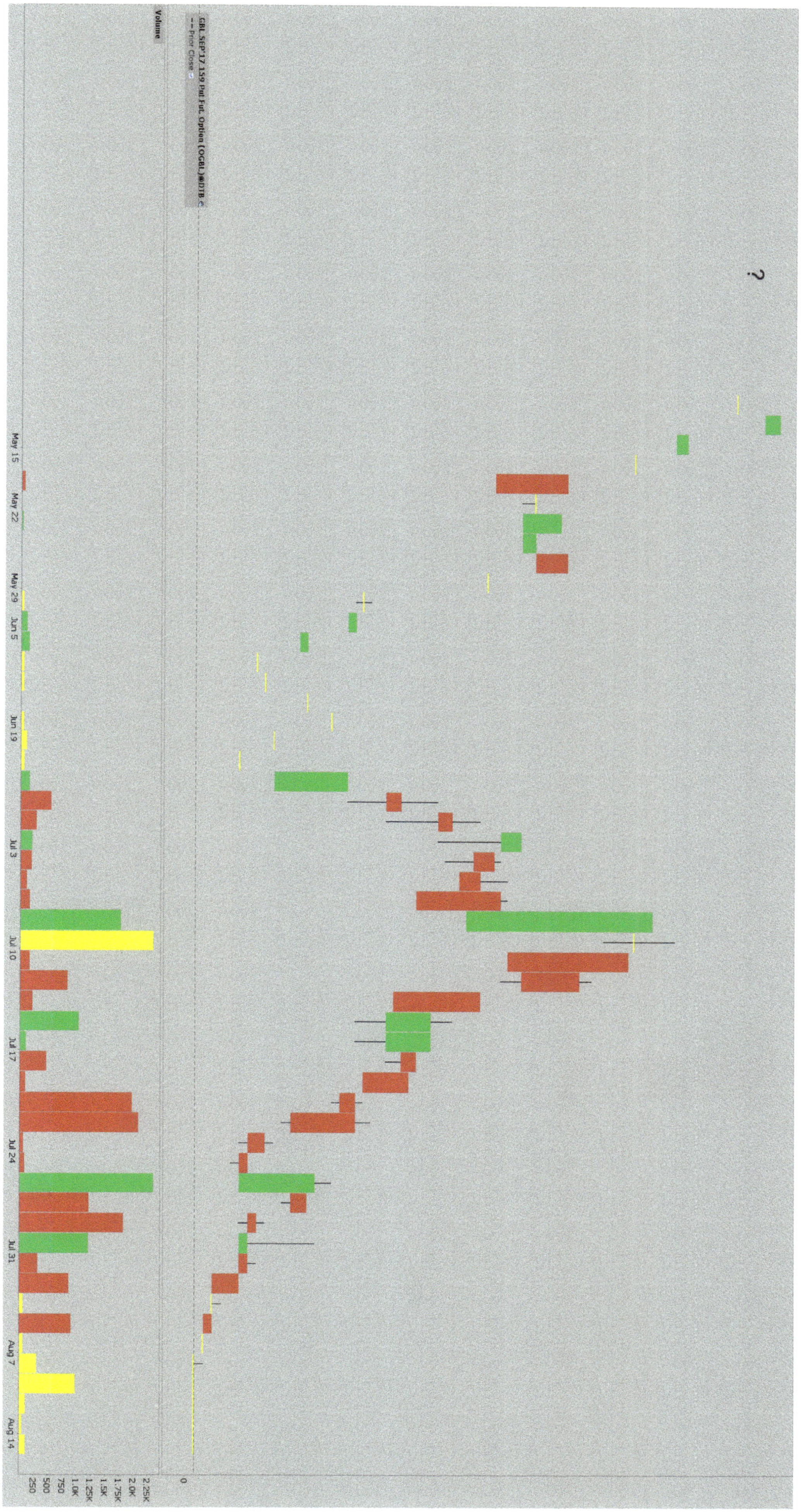
GBL SEP'17 159 Put Fut. Option [OGBL]@DTB
-- Prior Close
Volume
?
May 15
May 22
May 29
Jun 5
Jun 19
Jul 3
Jul 10
Jul 17
Jul 24
Jul 31
Aug 7
Aug 14
0
2.25K
2.0K
1.75K
1.5K
1.25K
1.0K
750
500
250

Volume
GBL SEP'17 160 Call Fut. Option (OGBL)@DTB
-- Prior Close
Jul 5
Jul 6
Jul 7
Jul 10
Jul 18
Jul 21
Jul 25
Jul 26
Aug 4
Aug 18
Aug 23
Aug 25

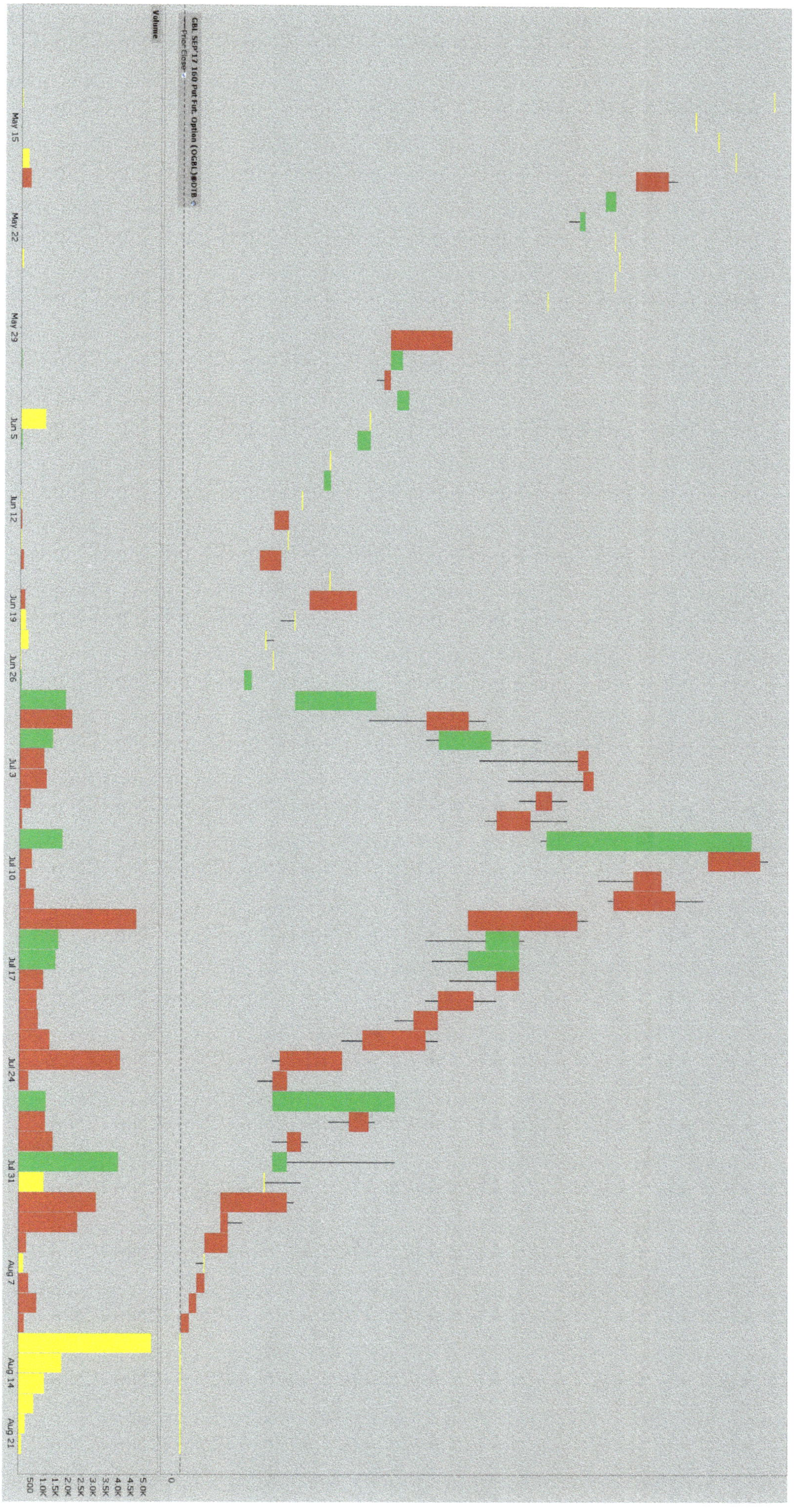
GBL SEP'17 160 Put Fut. Option (OGBL)@DTB
Prior Close
Volume
May 15
May 22
May 29
Jun 5
Jun 12
Jun 19
Jun 26
Jul 3
Jul 10
Jul 17
Jul 24
Jul 31
Aug 7
Aug 14
Aug 21
0
5.0K
4.5K
4.0K
3.5K
3.0K
2.5K
2.0K
1.5K
1.0K
500

GBL SEP'17 161 Call Fut. Option (OGBL)@DTB
Volume

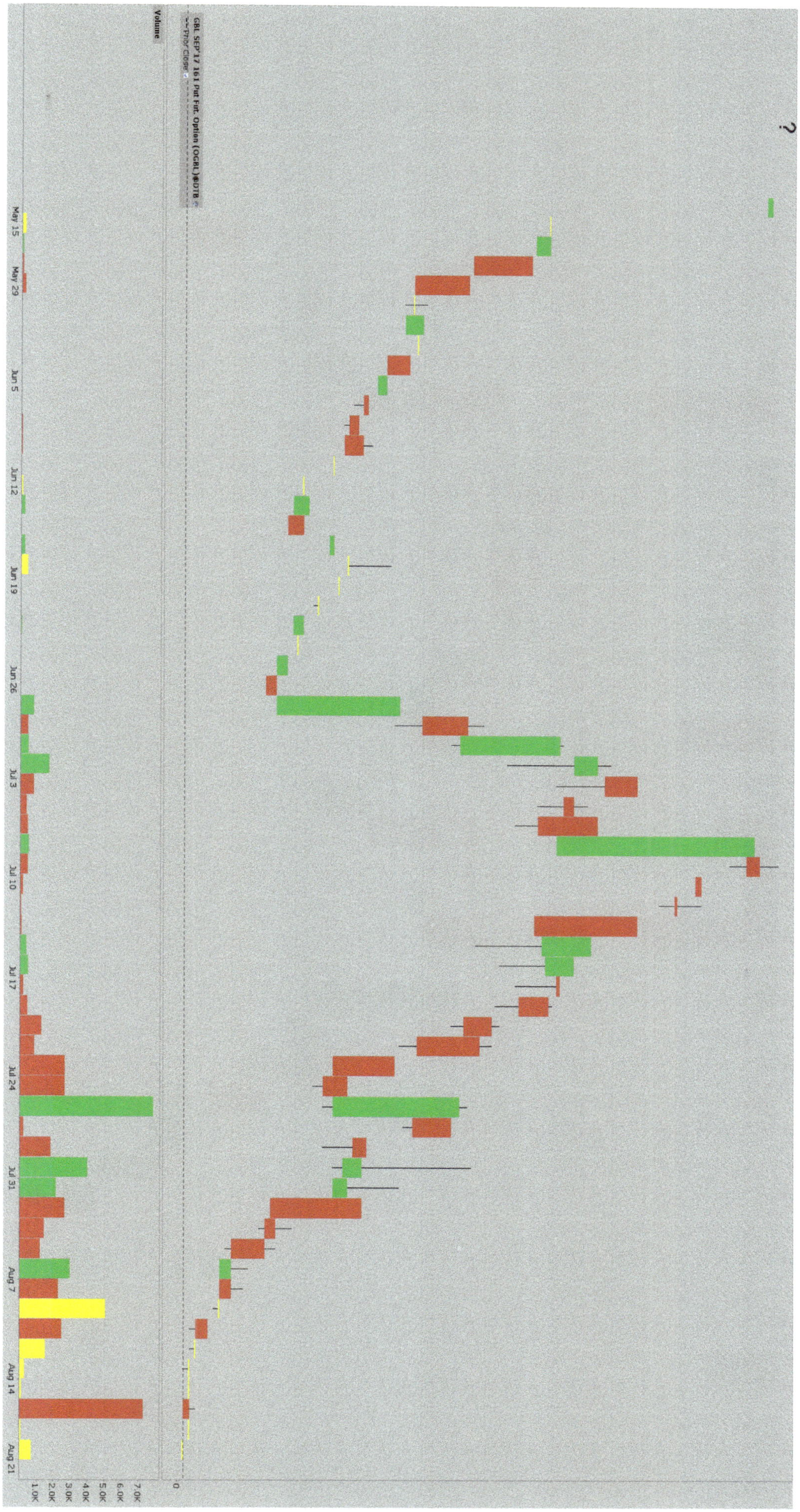
?
GBL SEP 17 161 Put Fut. Option (OGBL)@DTB
Volume
May 15
May 29
Jun 5
Jun 12
Jun 19
Jun 26
Jul 3
Jul 10
Jul 17
Jul 24
Jul 31
Aug 7
Aug 14
Aug 21
0
1.0K
2.0K
3.0K
4.0K
5.0K
6.0K
7.0K

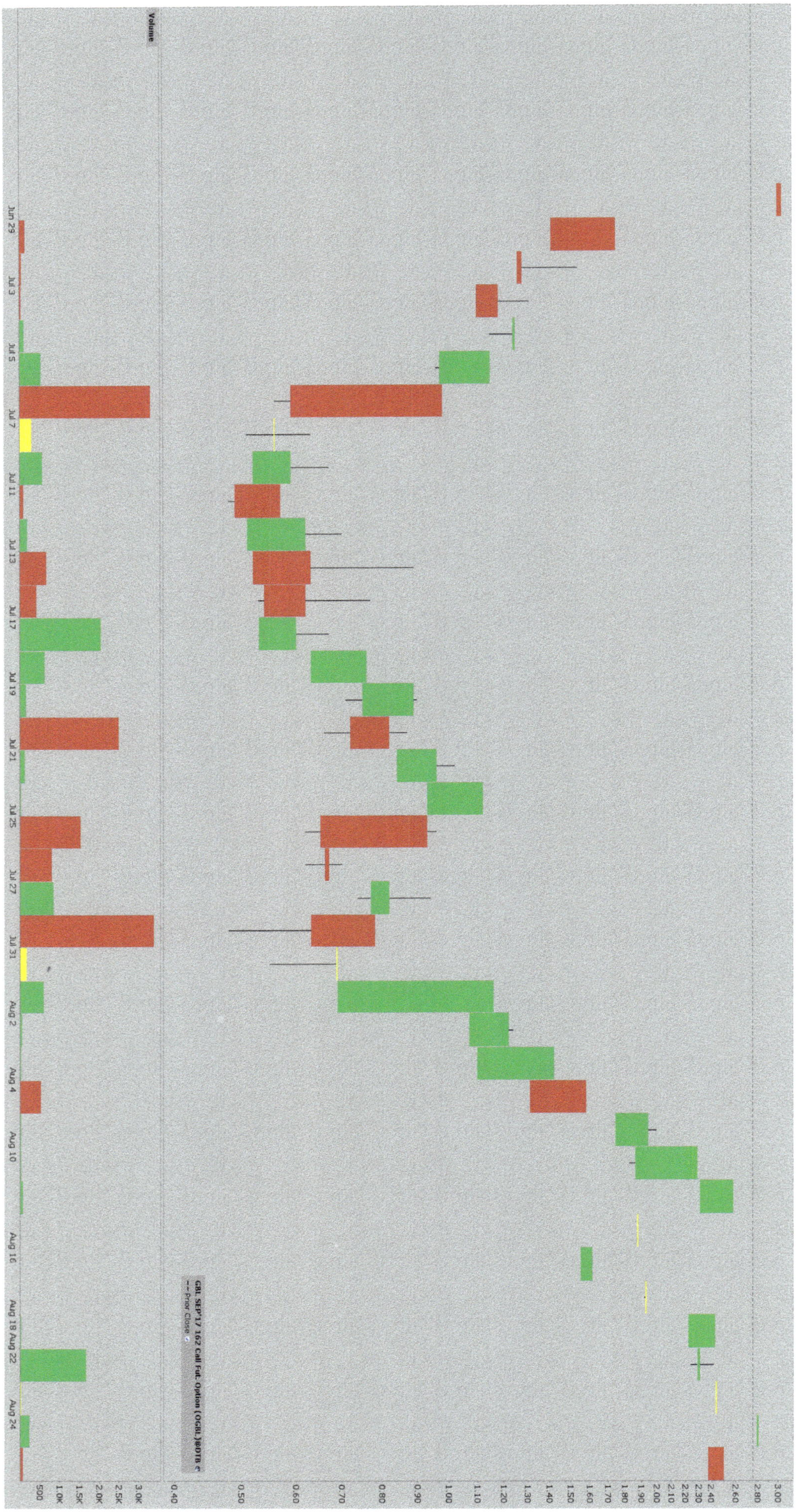
Volume
GBL SEP17 162 Call Fut. Option (OGBL)@DTB
-- Prior Close

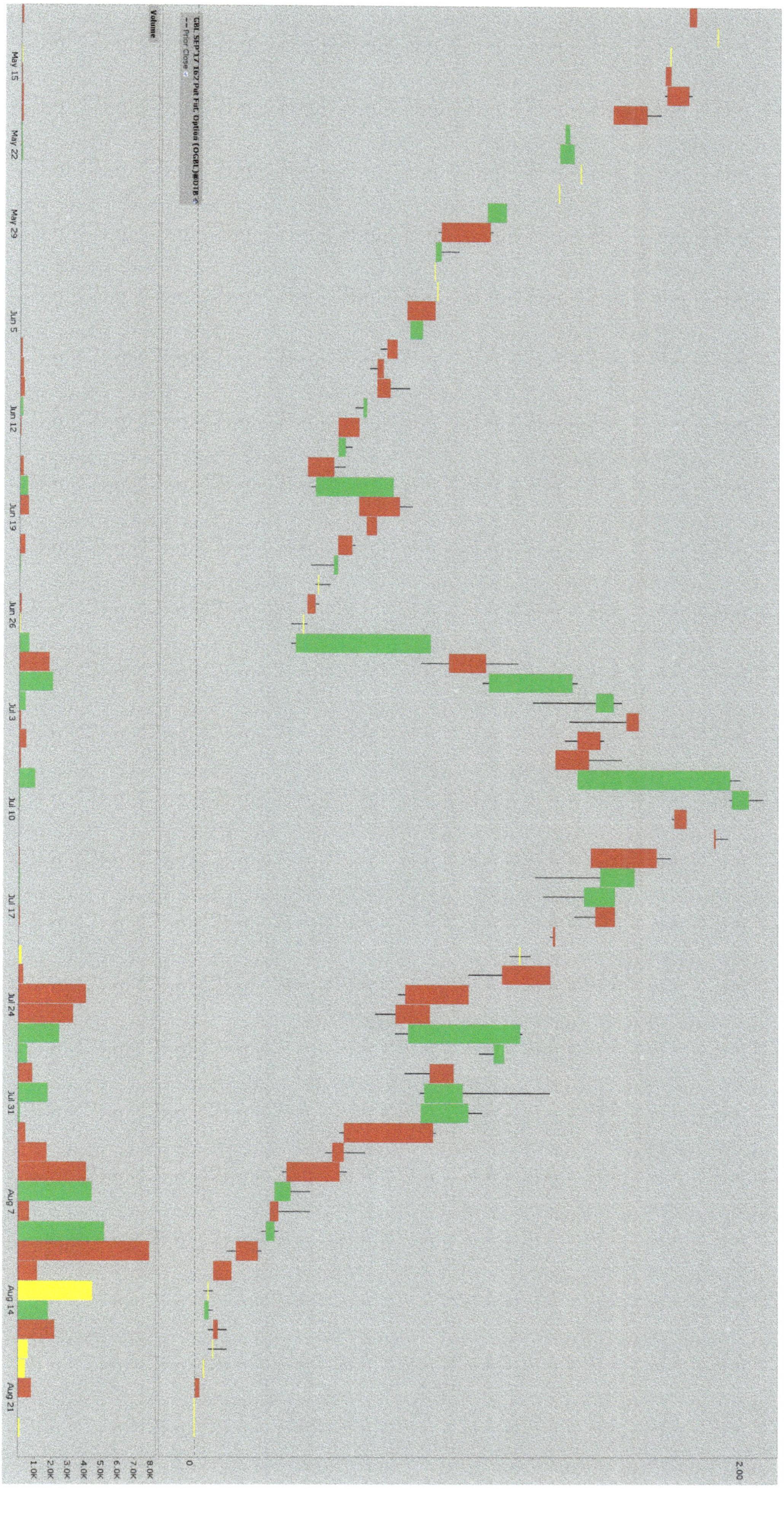
Volume
Prior Close
May 15
May 22
May 29
Jun 5
Jun 12
Jun 19
Jun 26
Jul 3
Jul 10
Jul 17
Jul 24
Jul 31
Aug 7
Aug 14
Aug 21
1.0K
2.0K
3.0K
4.0K
5.0K
6.0K
7.0K
8.0K
0
2.00

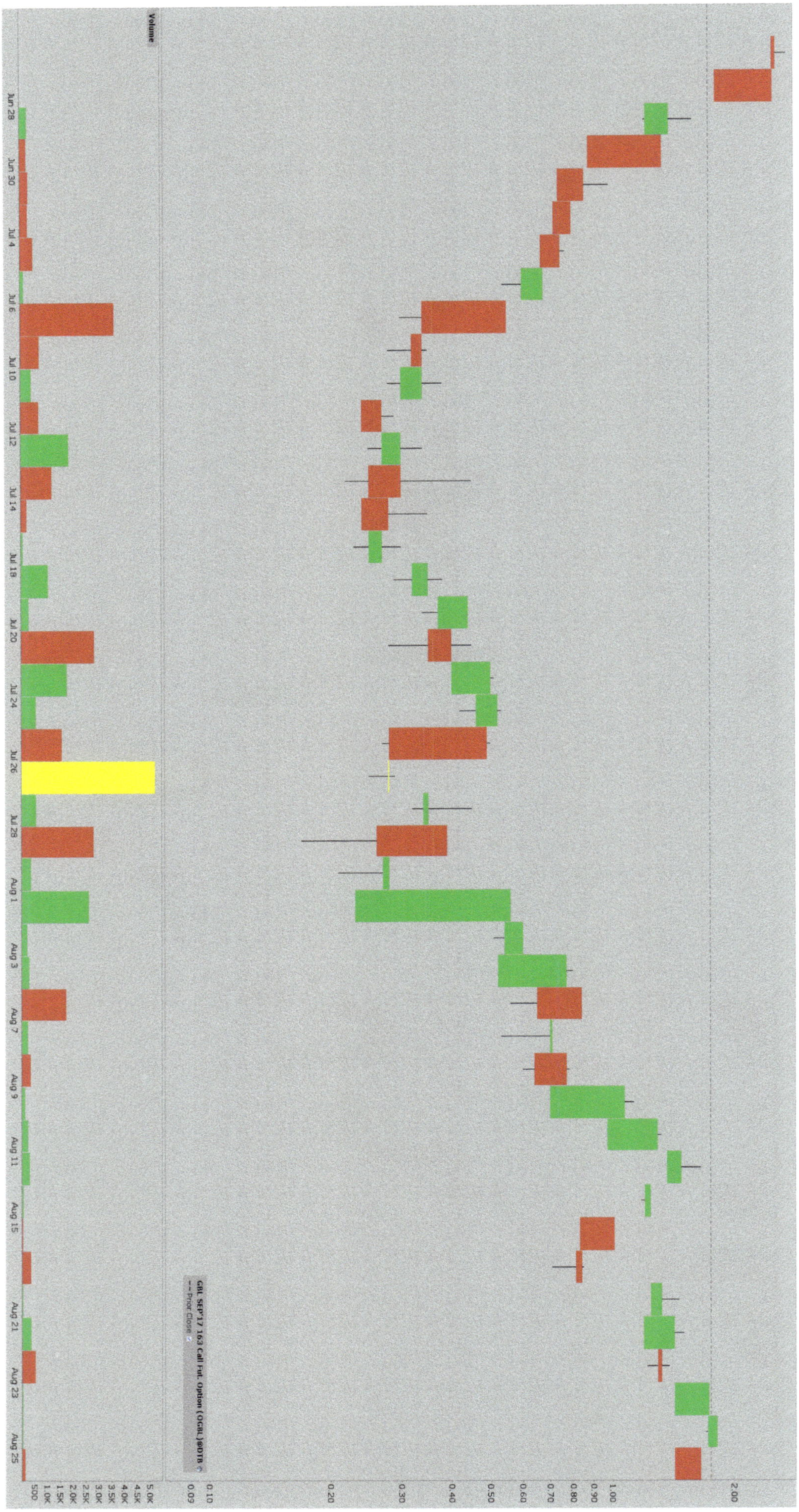

Volume
GBL SEP'17 163 Call Fut. Option (OGBL)@DTB
Prior Close

GBL SEP'17 163 Put Fut. Option (OGBL)@DTB
-- Prior Close
Volume
Jul 10
Jul 17
Jul 24
Jul 31
Aug 7
Aug 14
Aug 21
?
?
?
0
2.00
3.00
2.5K
5.0K
7.5K
10.0K
12.5K
15.0K

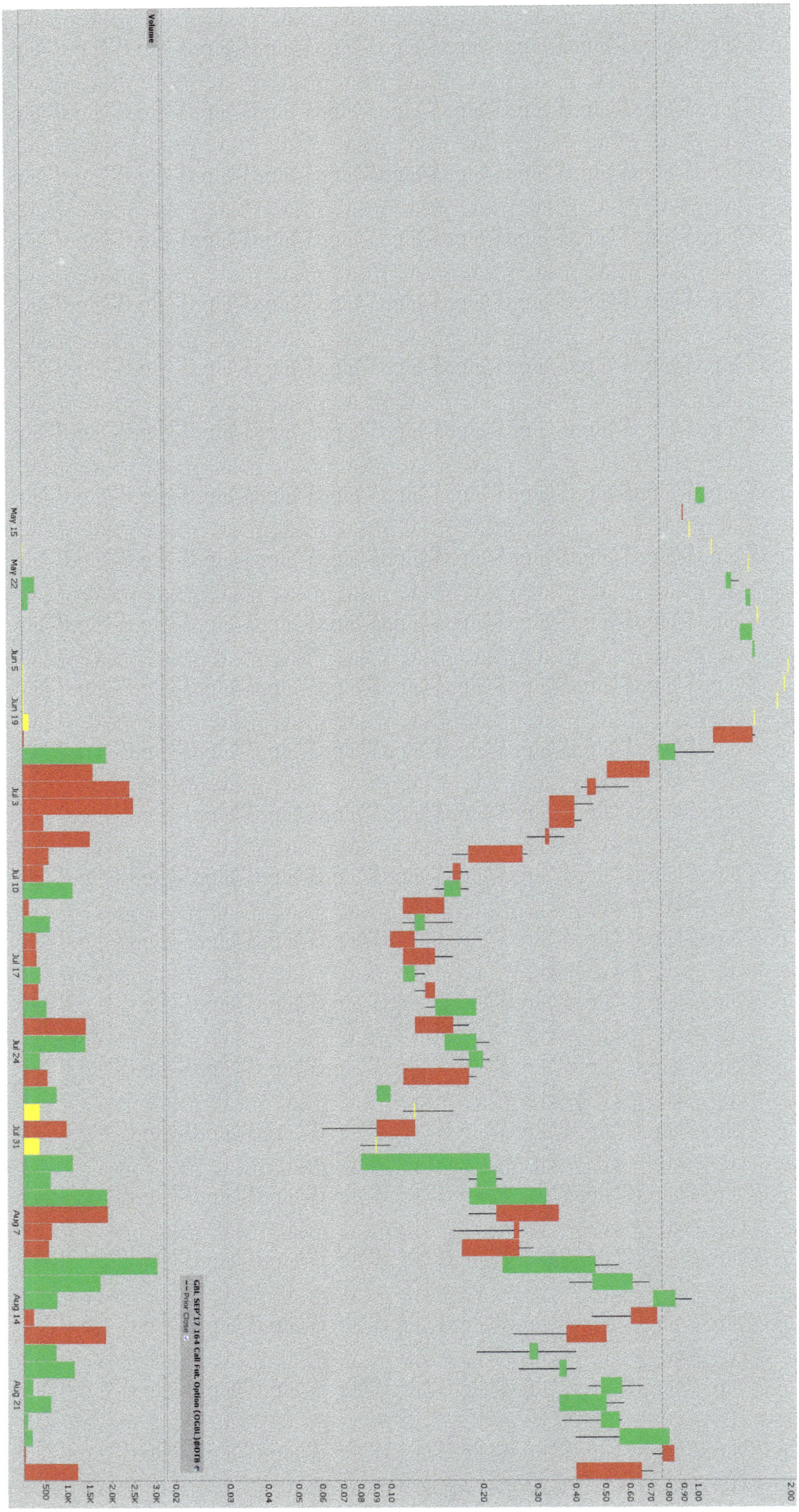
Volume
May 15
May 22
Jun 5
Jun 19
Jul 3
Jul 10
Jul 17
Jul 24
Jul 31
Aug 7
Aug 14
Aug 21

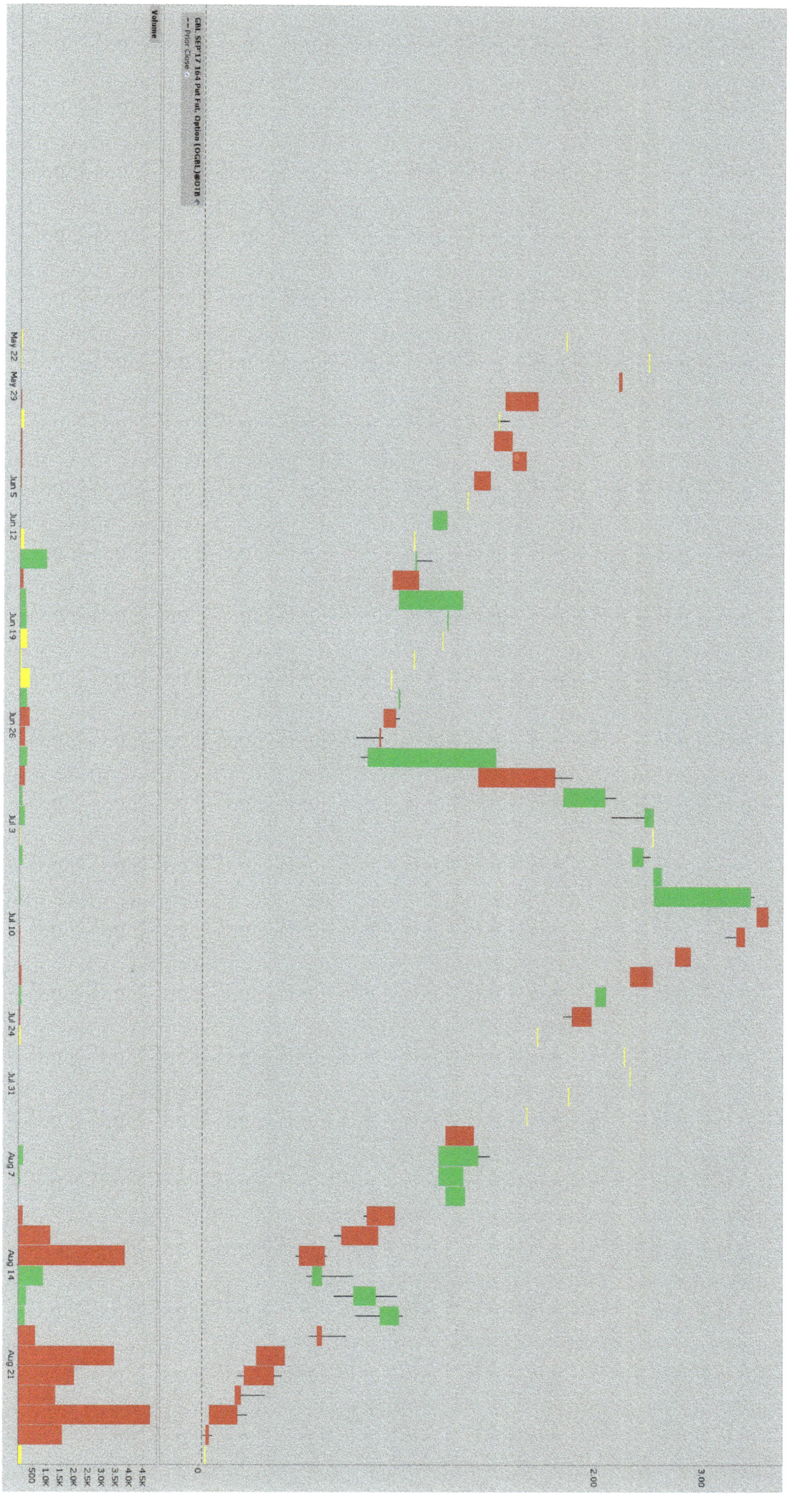
GBL SEP'17 164 Put Fut. Option (OGBL)@DTB
-- Prior Close
Volume
May 22
May 29
Jun 5
Jun 12
Jun 19
Jun 26
Jul 3
Jul 10
Jul 24
Jul 31
Aug 7
Aug 14
Aug 21
0
2.00
3.00
500
1.0K
1.5K
2.0K
2.5K
3.0K
3.5K
4.0K
4.5K

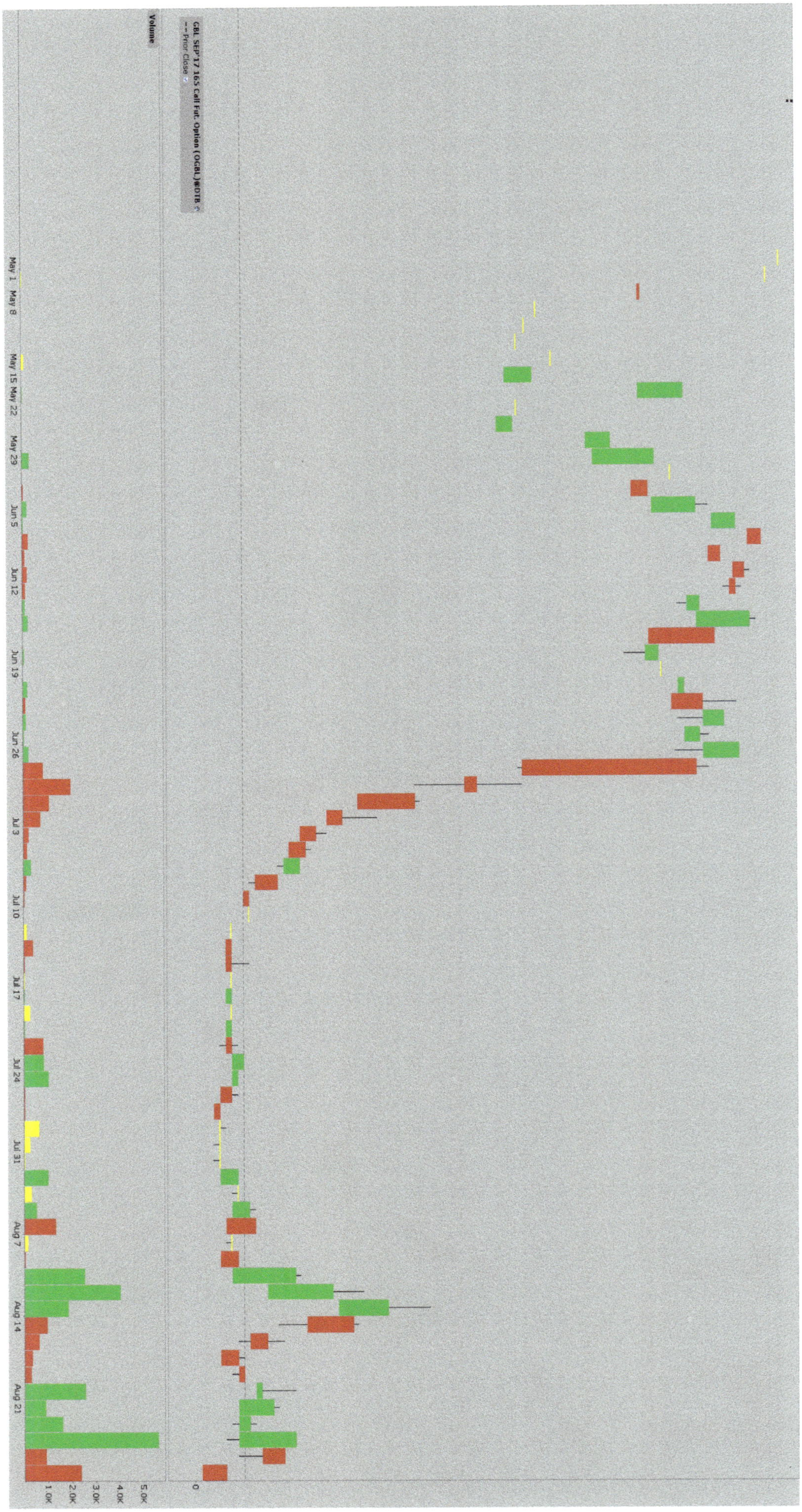
GBL SEP'17 16.5 Call Fut. Option (OGBL)@DTB
-- Prior Close
Volume
May 1
May 8
May 15
May 22
May 29
Jun 5
Jun 12
Jun 19
Jun 26
Jul 3
Jul 10
Jul 17
Jul 24
Jul 31
Aug 7
Aug 14
Aug 21
0
1.0K
2.0K
3.0K
4.0K
5.0K

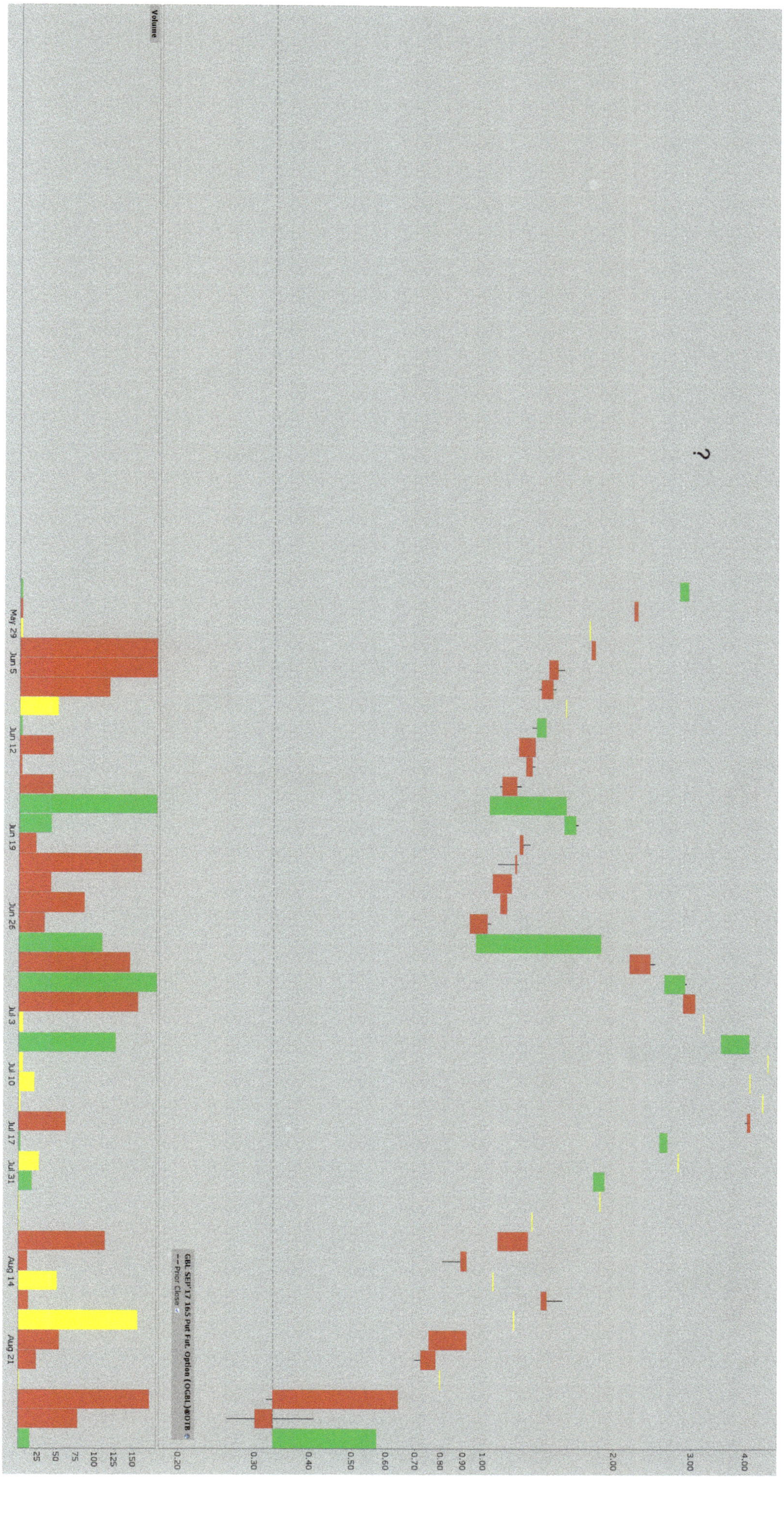
Volume
GBL SEP'17 165 Put Fut. Option (OGBL) @DTB
Prior Close
?
May 29
Jun 5
Jun 12
Jun 19
Jun 26
Jul 3
Jul 10
Jul 17
Jul 31
Aug 14
Aug 21
25
50
75
100
125
150
0.20
0.30
0.40
0.50
0.60
0.70
0.80
0.90
1.00
2.00
3.00
4.00

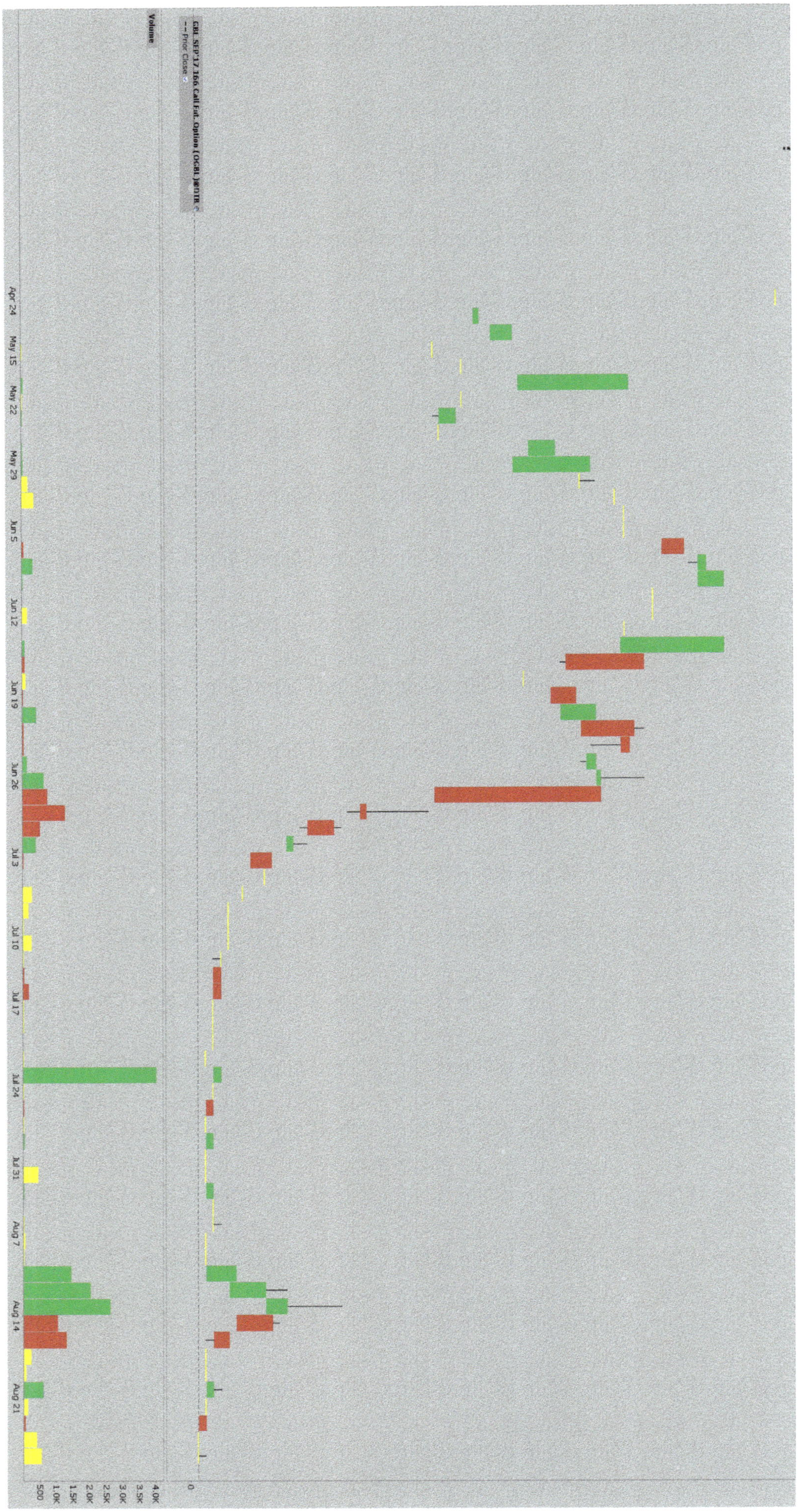
GBL SEP'17 166 Call Fut. Option (OGBL)@DTR
-- Prior Close
Volume
Apr 24
May 15
May 22
May 29
Jun 5
Jun 12
Jun 19
Jun 26
Jul 3
Jul 10
Jul 17
Jul 24
Jul 31
Aug 7
Aug 14
Aug 21
0
4.0K
3.5K
3.0K
2.5K
2.0K
1.5K
1.0K
500

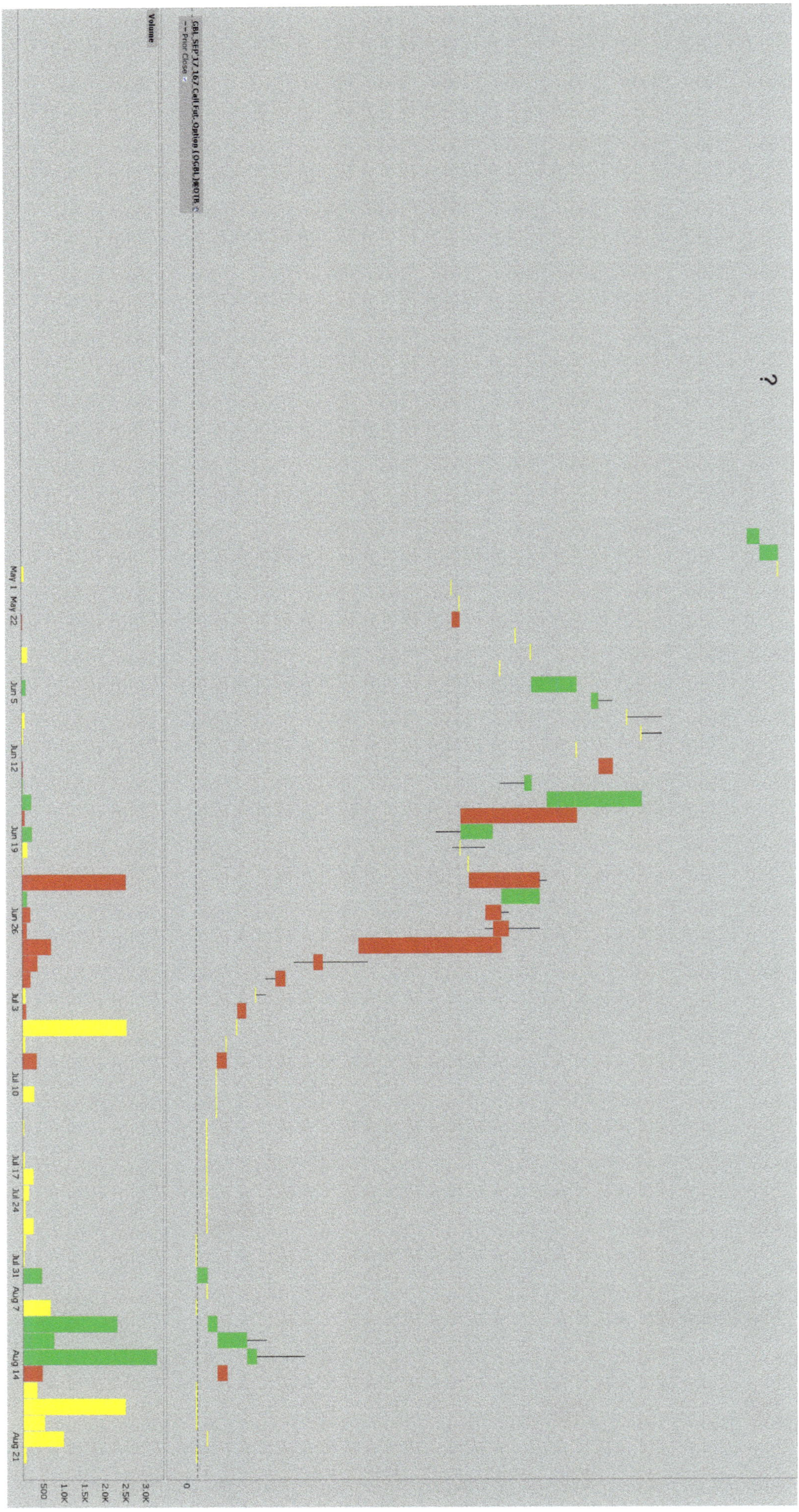
Volume
Prior Close
?
May 1
May 22
Jun 5
Jun 12
Jun 19
Jun 26
Jul 3
Jul 10
Jul 17
Jul 24
Jul 31
Aug 7
Aug 14
Aug 21
0
3.0K
2.5K
2.0K
1.5K
1.0K
500

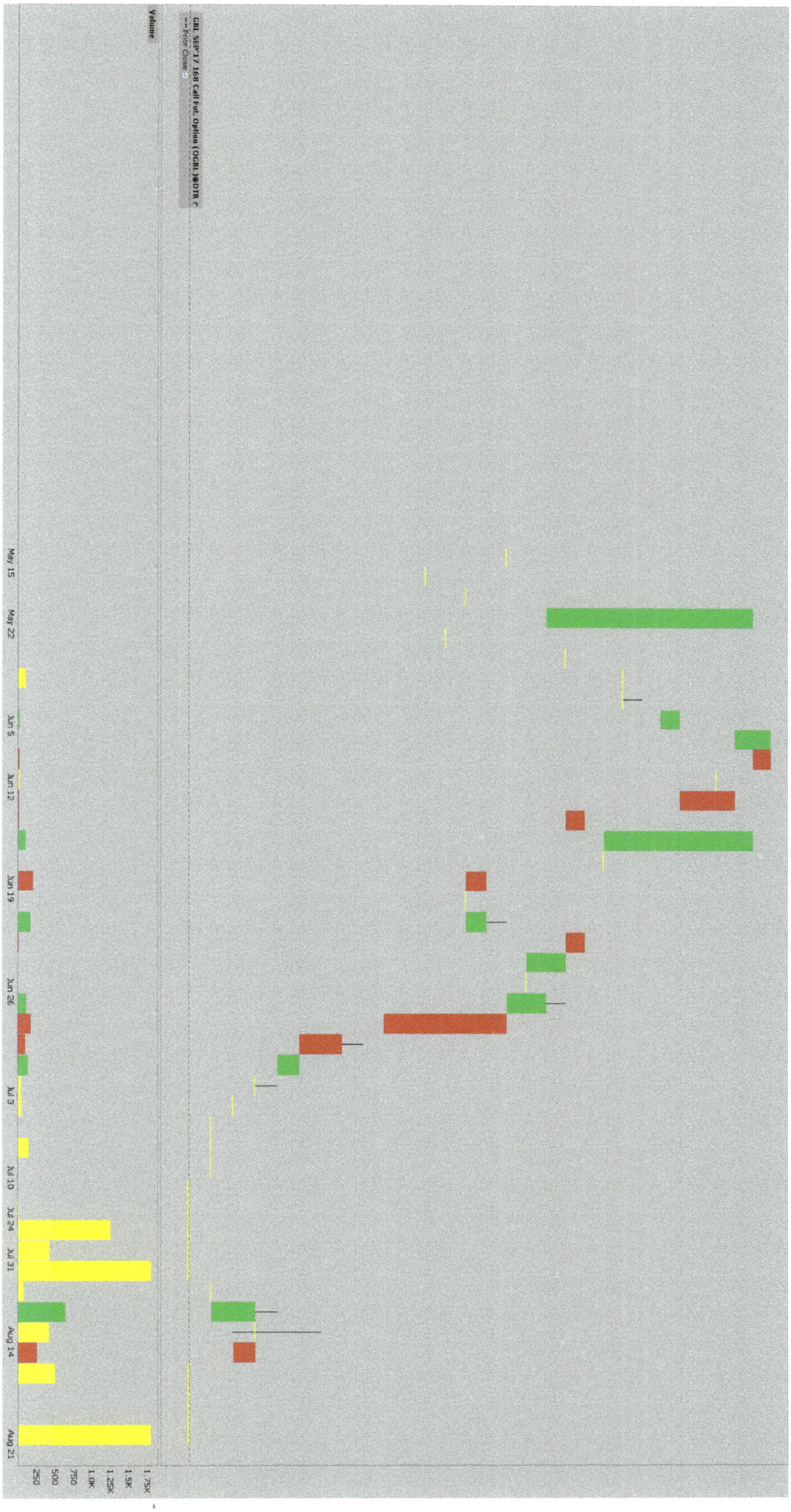
Volume
Prior Close
May 15
May 22
Jun 5
Jun 12
Jun 19
Jun 26
Jul 3
Jul 10
Jul 24
Jul 31
Aug 14
Aug 21
250
500
750
1.0K
1.25K
1.5K
1.75K

ZN SEPTEMBER GRAPHICS

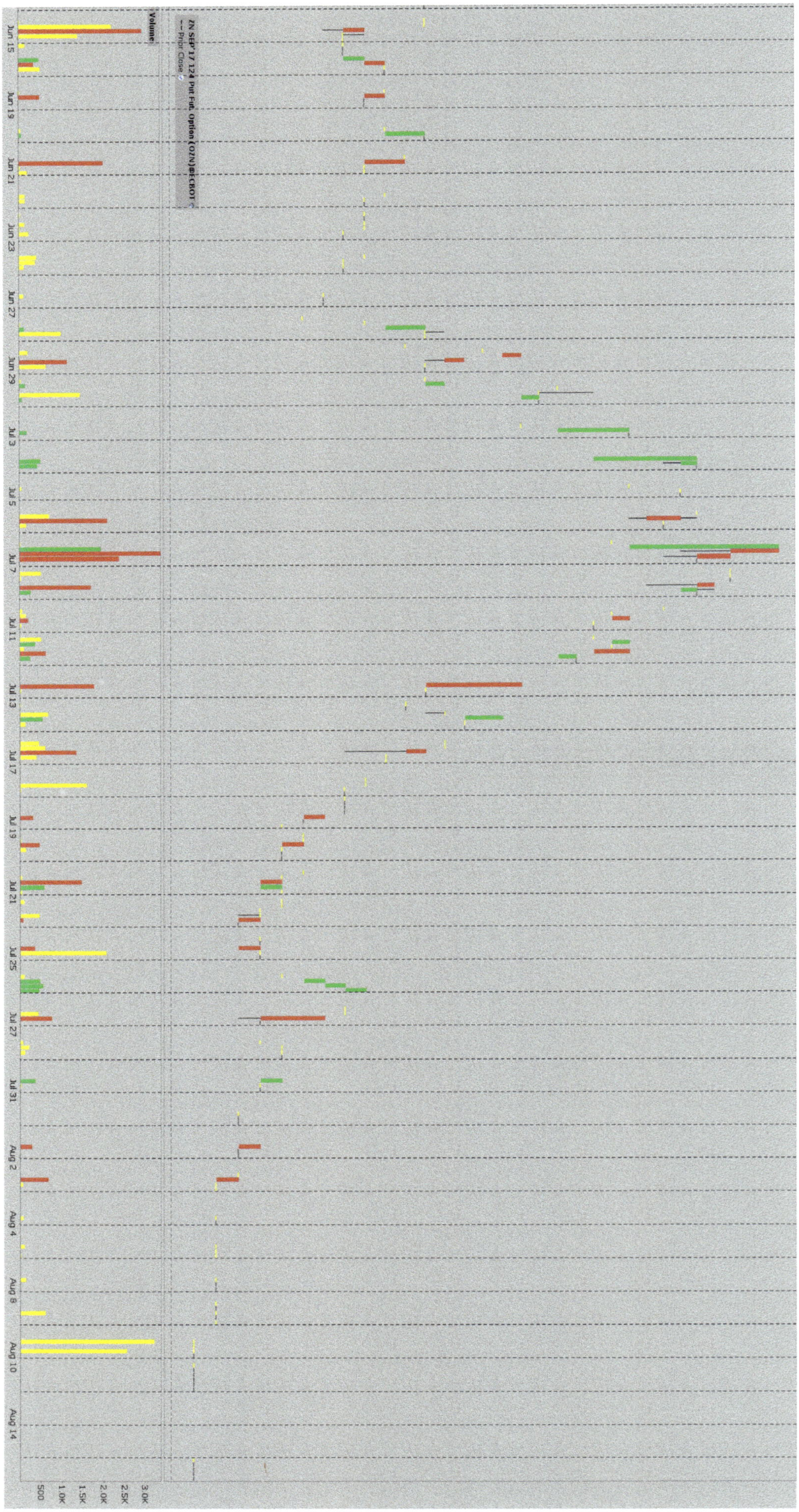
Volume
ZN SEP'17 124 Put Fut. Option (OZN)@ECBOT
-- Prior Close
Jun 15
Jun 19
Jun 21
Jun 23
Jun 27
Jun 29
Jul 3
Jul 5
Jul 7
Jul 11
Jul 13
Jul 17
Jul 19
Jul 21
Jul 25
Jul 27
Jul 31
Aug 2
Aug 4
Aug 8
Aug 10
Aug 14
500
1.0K
1.5K
2.0K
2.5K
3.0K

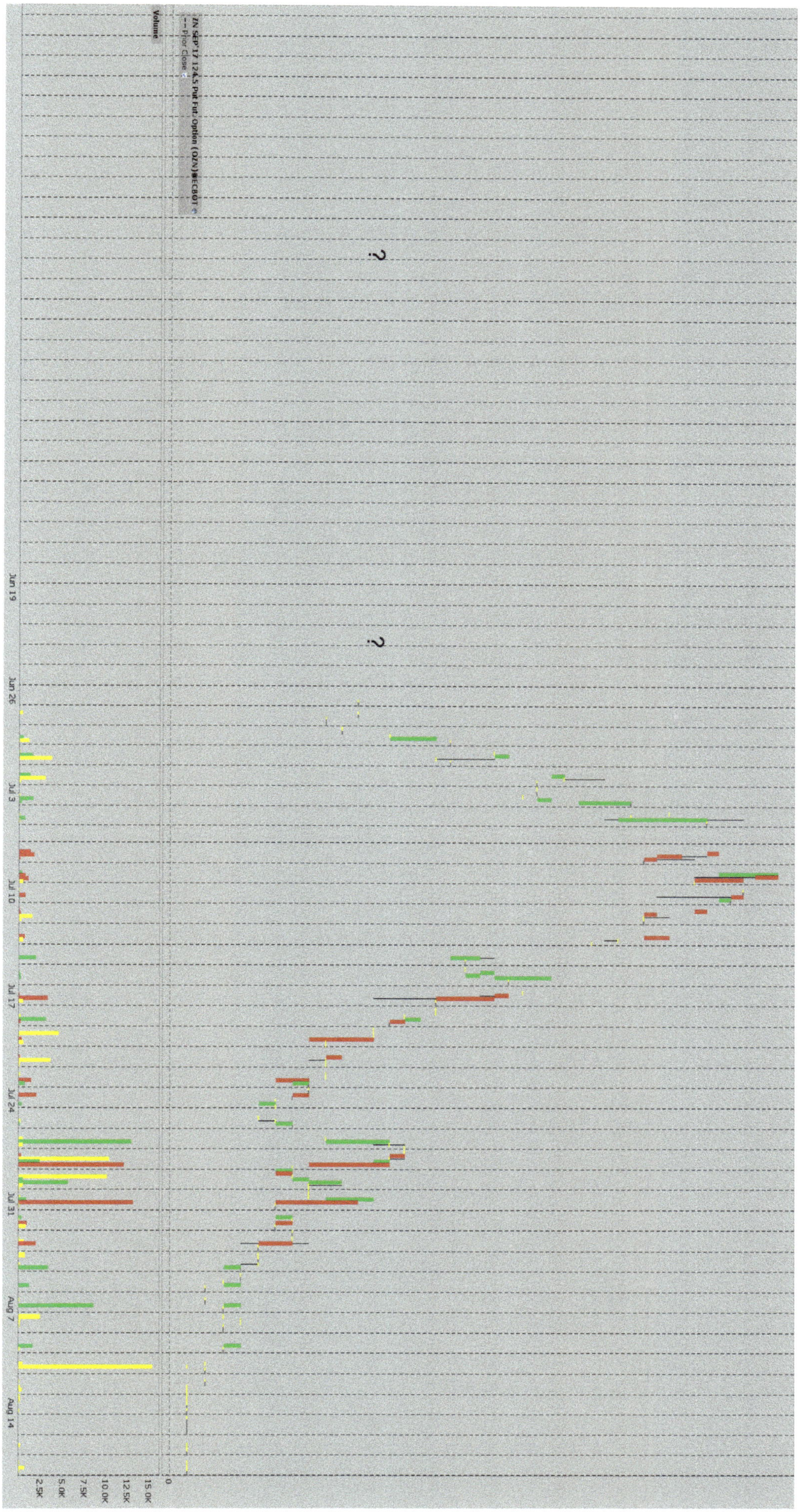
Volume
Jun 19
Jun 26
Jul 3
Jul 10
Jul 17
Jul 24
Jul 31
Aug 7
Aug 14
0
2.5K
5.0K
7.5K
10.0K
12.5K
15.0K
?
?

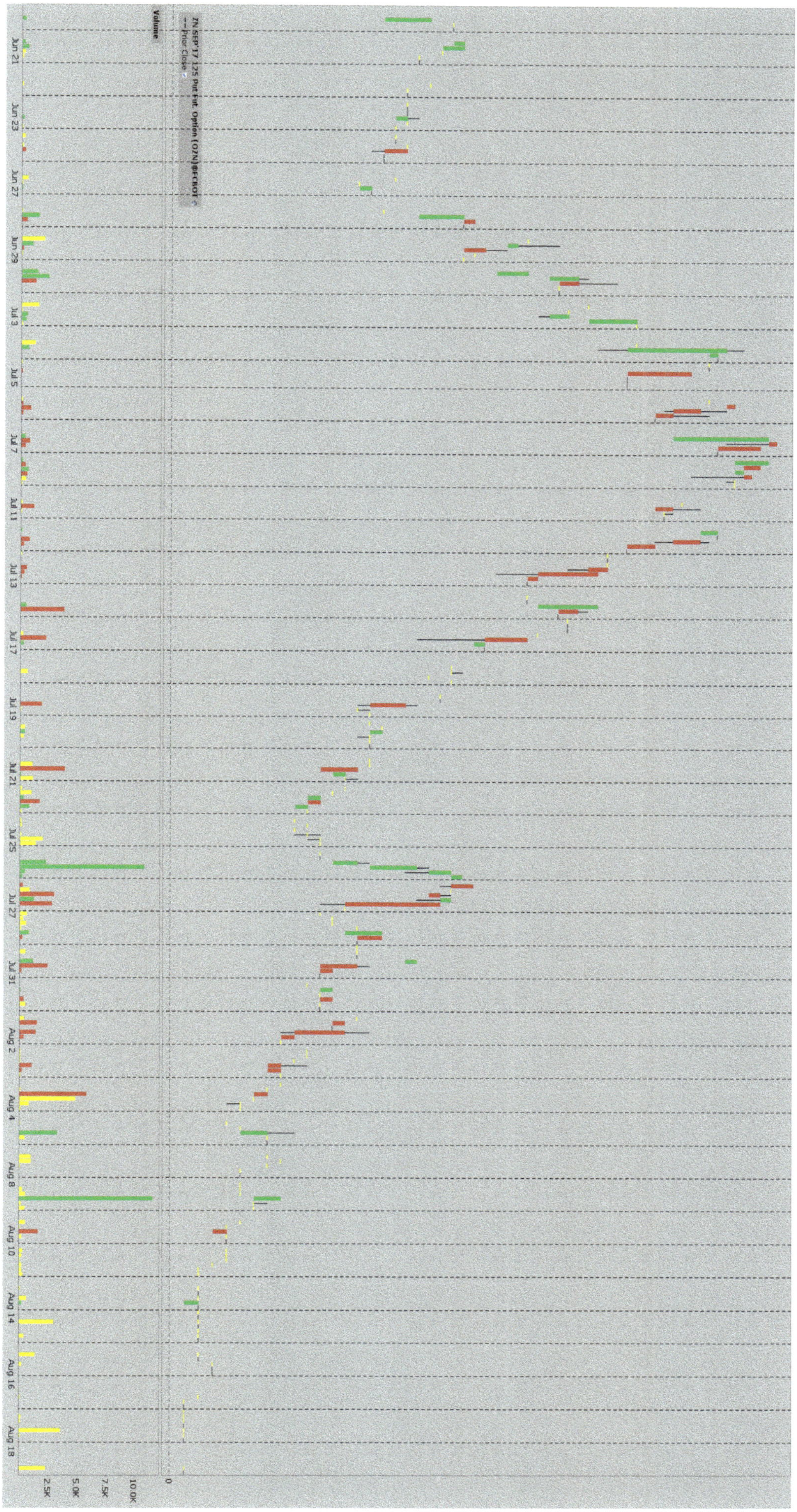

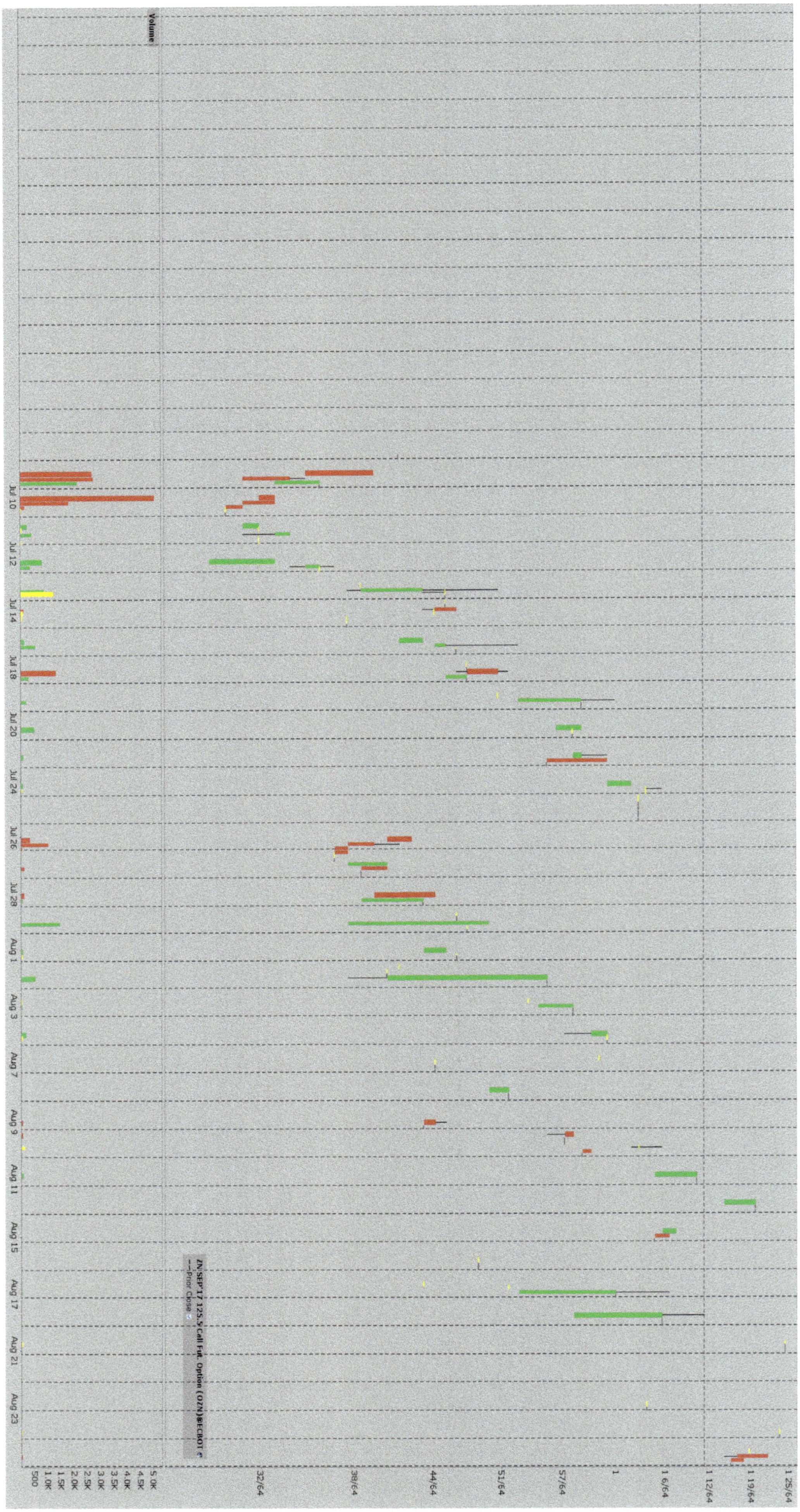
Volume
Jul 10
Jul 12
Jul 14
Jul 18
Jul 20
Jul 24
Jul 26
Jul 28
Aug 1
Aug 3
Aug 7
Aug 9
Aug 11
Aug 15
Aug 17
Aug 21
Aug 23
500
1.0K
1.5K
2.0K
2.5K
3.0K
3.5K
4.0K
4.5K
5.0K
32/64
38/64
44/64
51/64
57/64
1
1 6/64
1 12/64
1 19/64
1 25/64

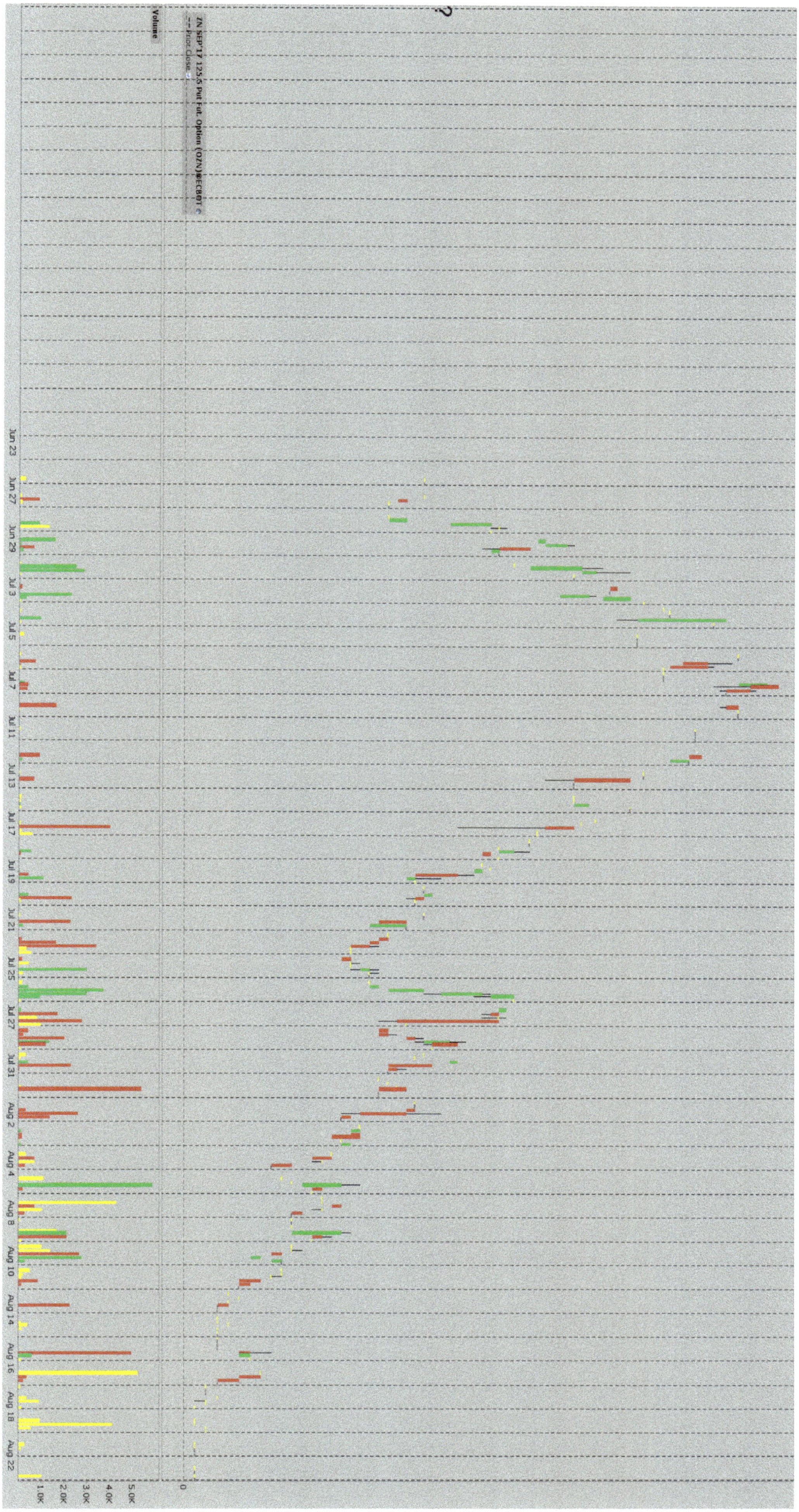
Volume
Jun 23
Jun 27
Jun 29
Jul 3
Jul 5
Jul 7
Jul 11
Jul 13
Jul 17
Jul 19
Jul 21
Jul 25
Jul 27
Jul 31
Aug 2
Aug 4
Aug 8
Aug 10
Aug 14
Aug 16
Aug 18
Aug 22
1.0K
2.0K
3.0K
4.0K
5.0K
0

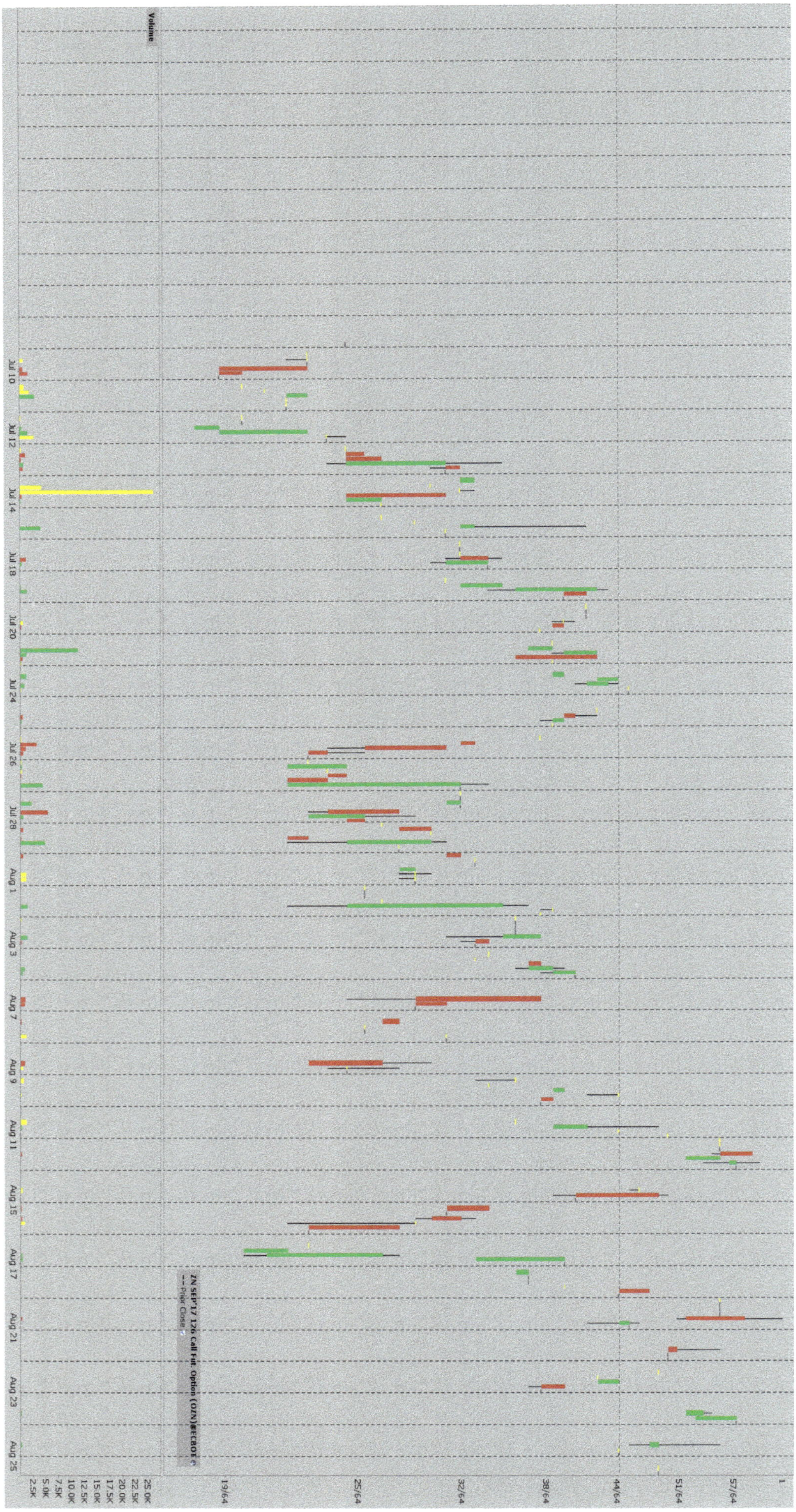
Volume
Jul 10
Jul 12
Jul 14
Jul 18
Jul 20
Jul 24
Jul 26
Jul 28
Aug 1
Aug 3
Aug 7
Aug 9
Aug 11
Aug 15
Aug 17
Aug 21
Aug 23
Aug 25
2.5K
5.0K
7.5K
10.0K
12.5K
15.0K
17.5K
20.0K
22.5K
25.0K
19/64
25/64
32/64
38/64
44/64
51/64
57/64

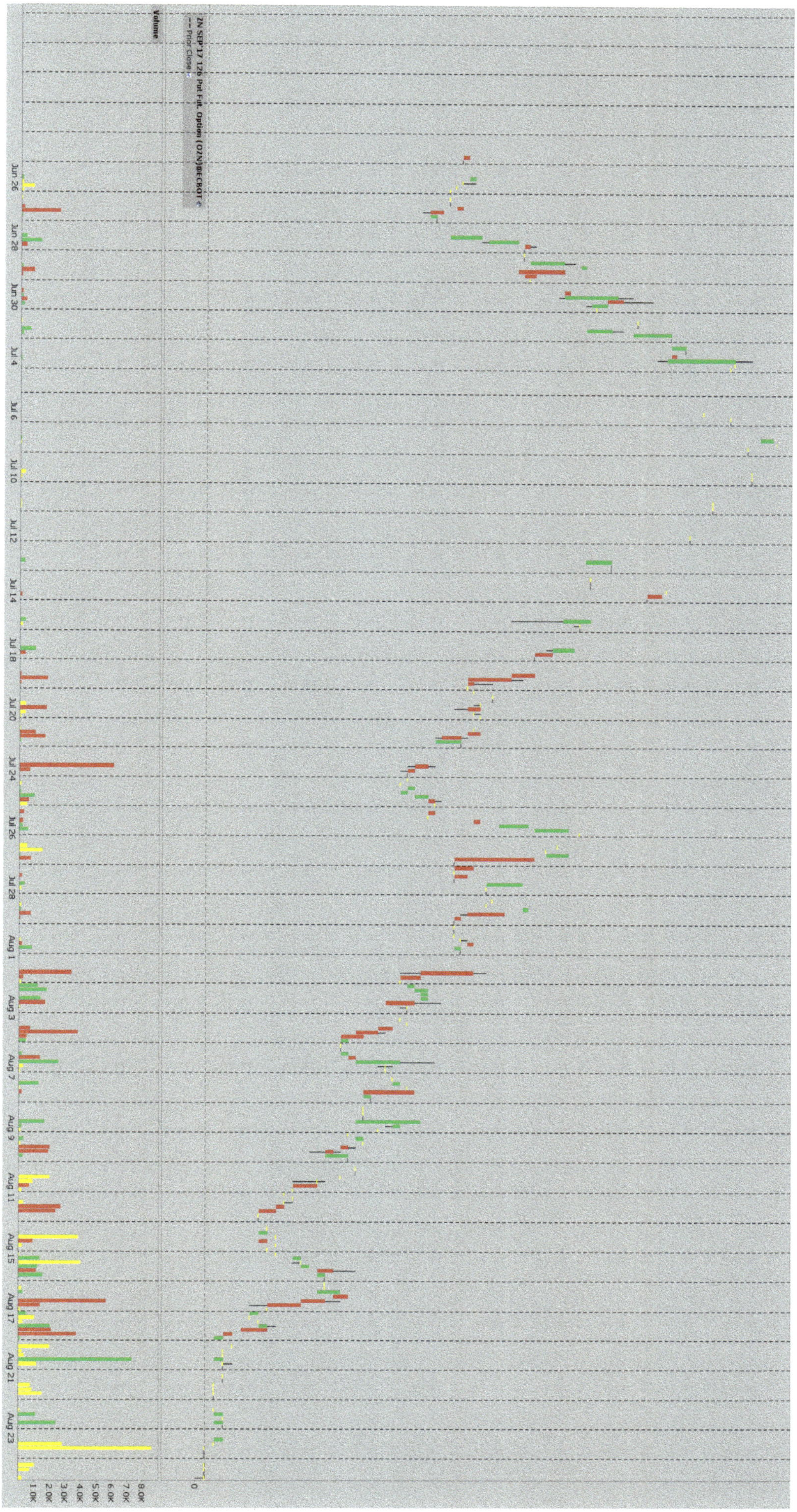
Volume
Jun 26
Jun 28
Jun 30
Jul 4
Jul 6
Jul 10
Jul 12
Jul 14
Jul 18
Jul 20
Jul 24
Jul 26
Jul 28
Aug 1
Aug 3
Aug 7
Aug 9
Aug 11
Aug 15
Aug 17
Aug 21
Aug 23
0
1.0K
2.0K
3.0K
4.0K
5.0K
6.0K
7.0K
8.0K

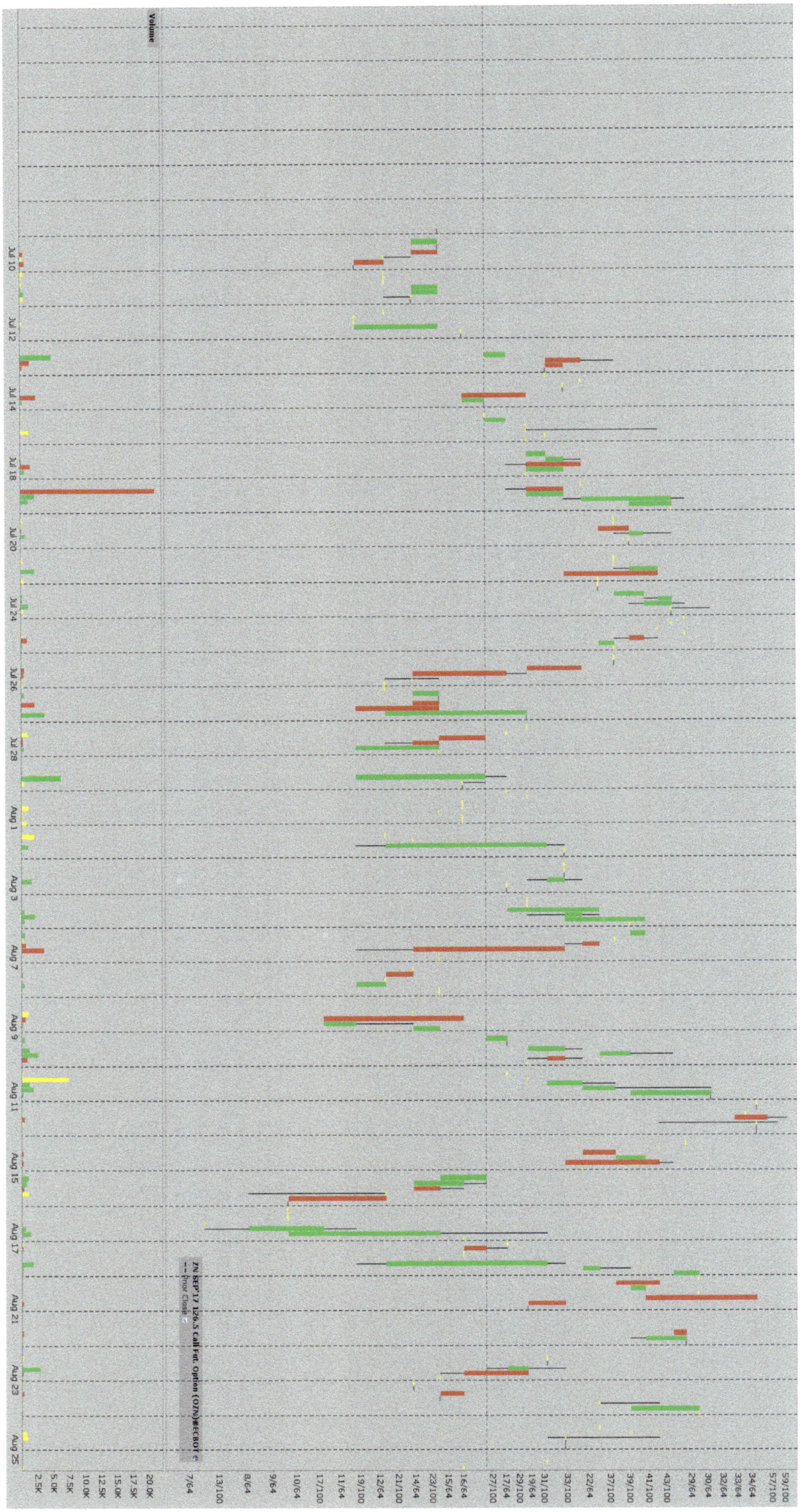
Volume
ZN SEP'17 126.5 Call Fut. Option (OZN)@CBOT
-- Prior Close

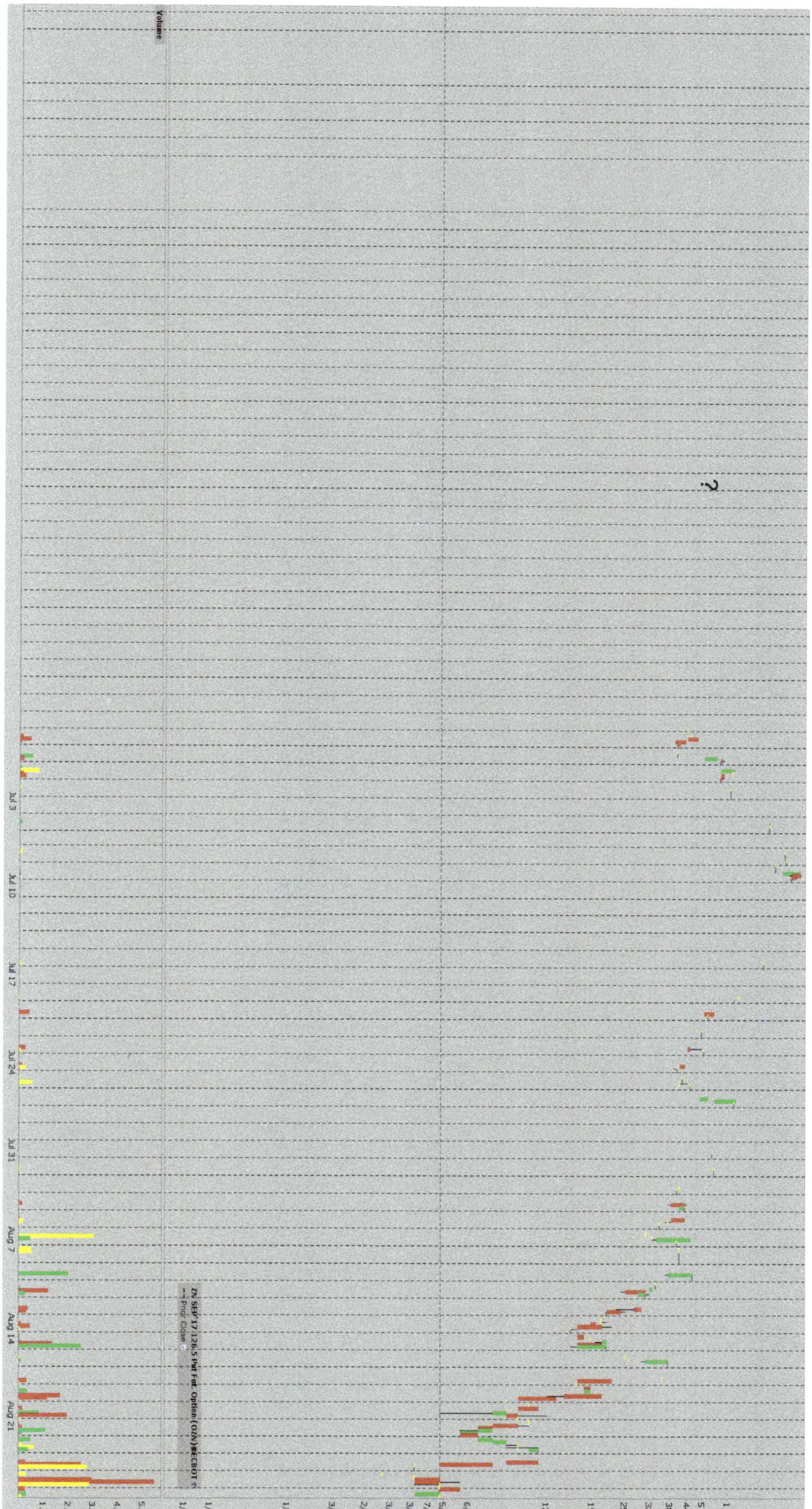
ZN SEP 17 126.5 Put Fut. Option (OZN) @CBOT
Prior Close
Volume
Jul 3
Jul 10
Jul 17
Jul 24
Jul 31
Aug 7
Aug 14
Aug 21
1.0K
2.0K
3.0K
4.0K
5.0K
1/125
1/100
1/64
3/100
2/64
3/64
3/64
7/100
5/64
6/64
12/64
19/64
25/64
32/64
38/64
44/64
51/64
1

Volume
Jul 10
Jul 12
Jul 14
Jul 18
Jul 20
Jul 24
Jul 26
Jul 28
Aug 1
Aug 3
Aug 7
Aug 9
Aug 11
Aug 15
Aug 17
Aug 21
Aug 23
Aug 25
2.5K
5.0K
7.5K
10.0K
ZN SEP'17 127 Call Fut. Option (OZN)@ECBOT
Prior Close
1/64
3/100
2/64
3/64
7/100
5/64
9/100
6/64
12/64
19/64

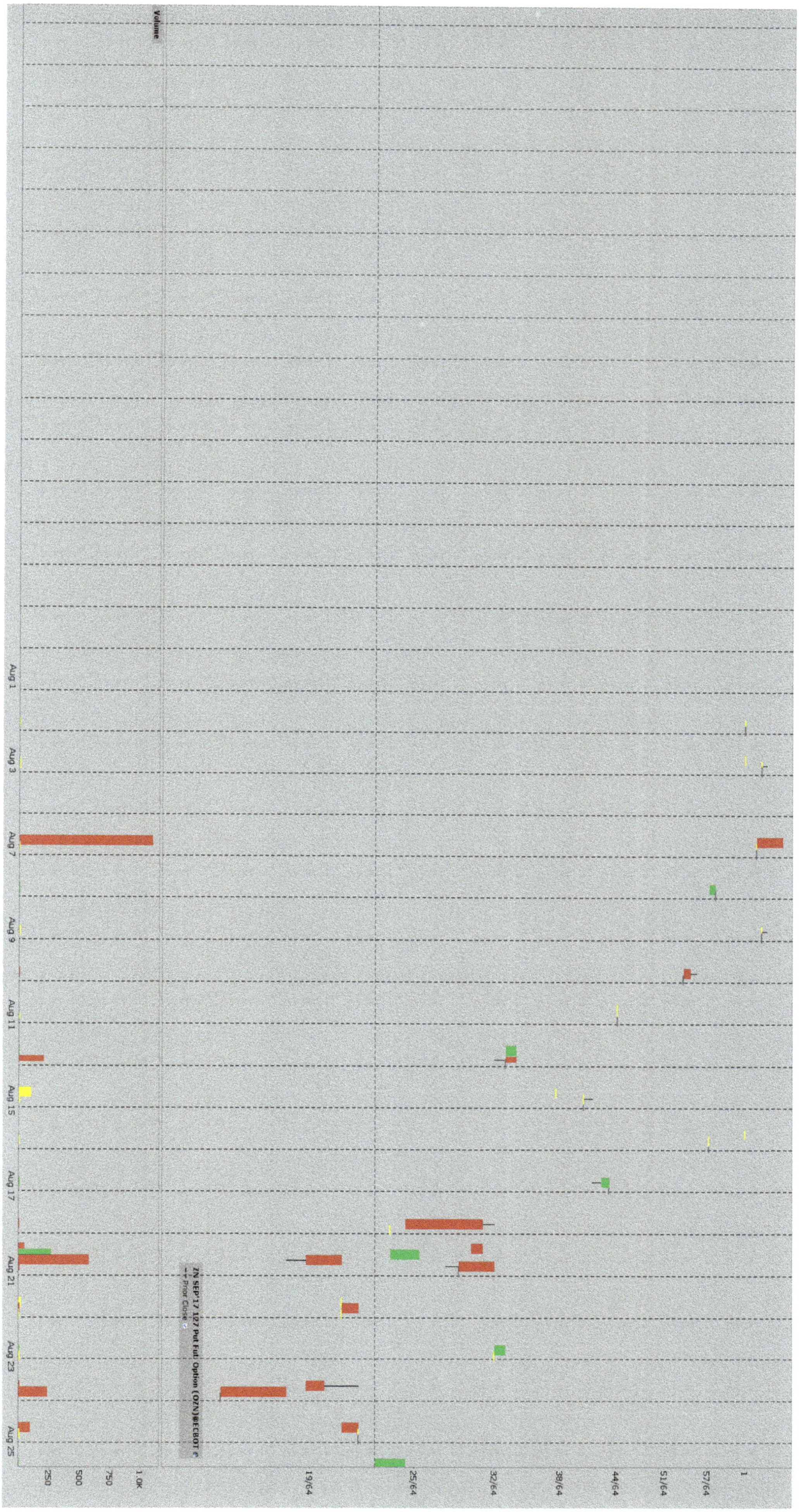
Volume
Aug 1
Aug 3
Aug 7
Aug 9
Aug 11
Aug 15
Aug 17
Aug 21
Aug 23
Aug 25
250
500
750
1.0K
19/64
25/64
32/64
38/64
44/64
51/64
57/64
1

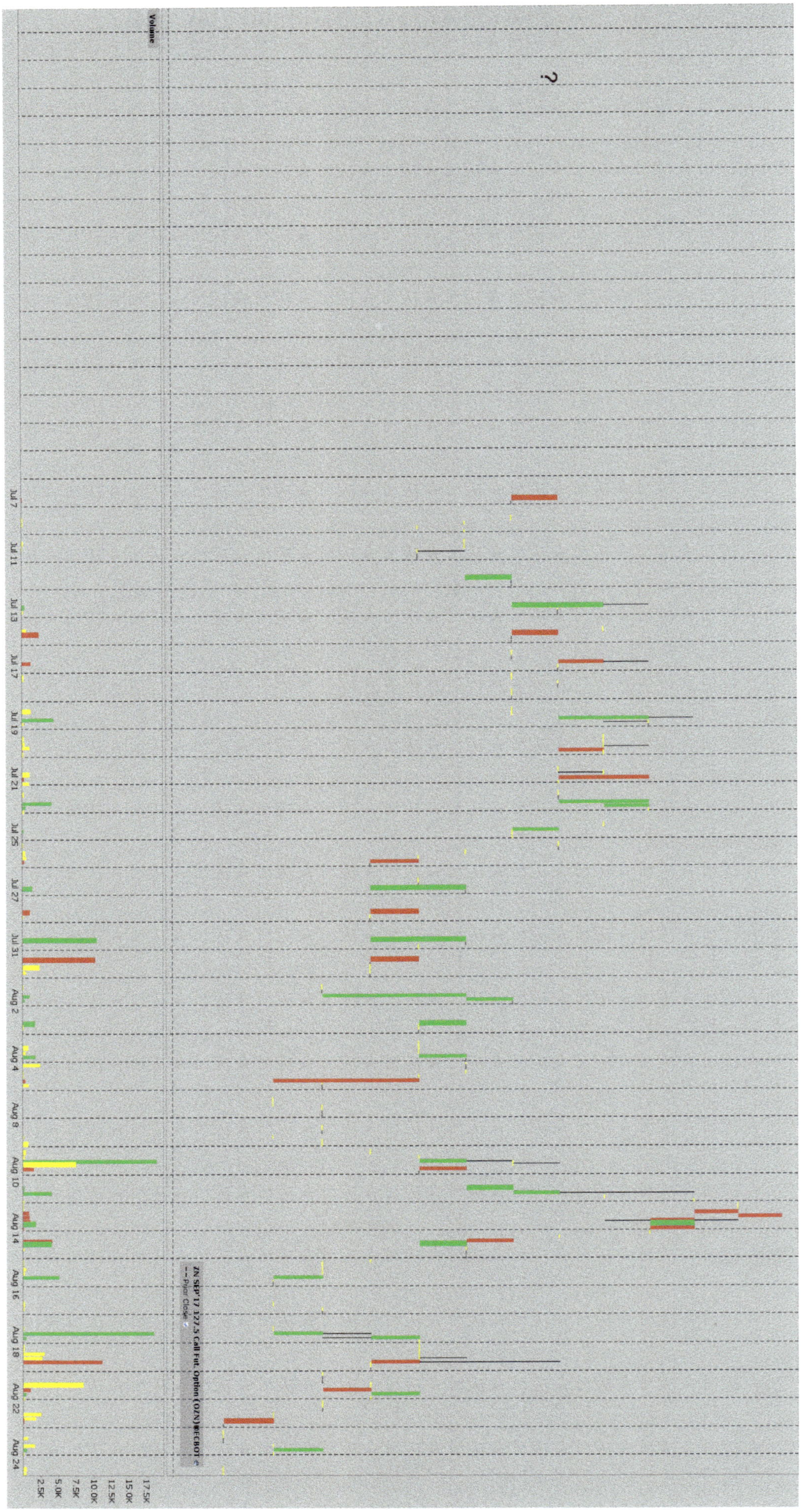
Volume
?
ZN SEP'17 127.5 Call Fut. Option (OZN)@ECBOT
-- Prior Close
Jul 7
Jul 11
Jul 13
Jul 17
Jul 19
Jul 21
Jul 25
Jul 27
Jul 31
Aug 2
Aug 4
Aug 8
Aug 10
Aug 14
Aug 16
Aug 18
Aug 22
Aug 24
2.5K
5.0K
7.5K
10.0K
12.5K
15.0K
17.5K

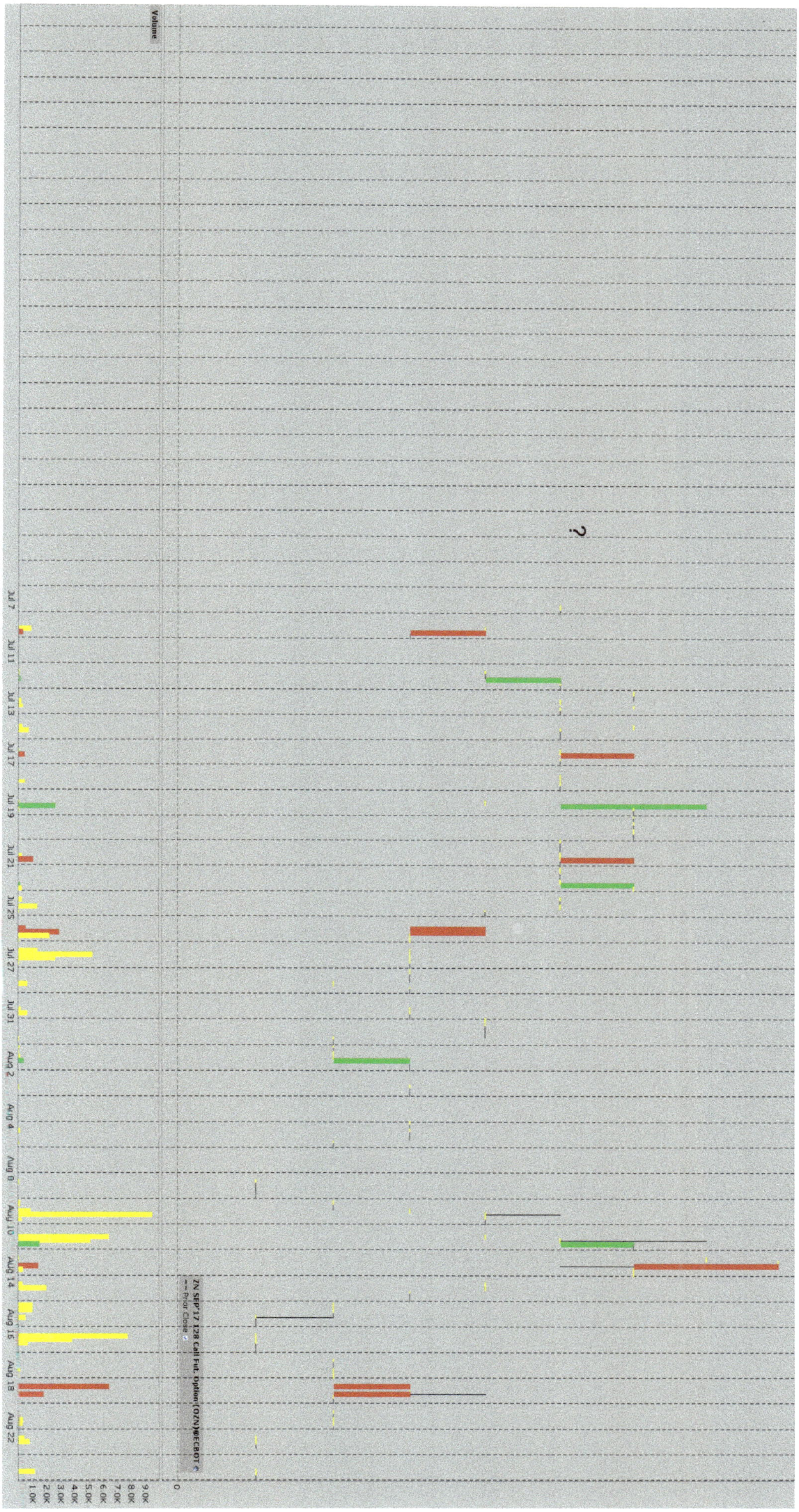
Volume
ZN SEP 17 128 Call Fut. Option (OZN)@ECBOT
Prior Close

www.ingramcontent.com/pod-product-compliance
Lightning Source LLC
Chambersburg PA
CBHW041512210926
51847CB00012B/125